A Custom Edition for The Community College of Baltimore County

ECONOMICS
Principles & Tools

Arthur O'Sullivan and Steven M. Sheffrin

Taken from
Economics: Principles & Tools, Fourth Edition
by Arthur O'Sullivan and Steven M. Sheffrin

Cover: *Twist 1*, by Barry Cronin

Taken from:

Economics: Principles & Tools, Fourth Edition
by Arthur O'Sullivan and Steven M. Sheffrin
Copyright © 2006, 2003, 2001 by Pearson Education, Inc.
Published by Prentice-Hall, Inc.
Upper Saddle River, New Jersey 07458

This special edition published in cooperation with Pearson Custom Publishing.

Printed in the United States of America

10 9 8 7 6 5 4 3 2 1

ISBN 0-536-96526-9

2005160349

MT

Please visit our web site at *www.pearsoncustom.com*

PEARSON CUSTOM PUBLISHING
75 Arlington Street, Suite 300, Boston, MA 02116
A Pearson Education Company

Brief Contents

Preface

When we set out to write an economics text, we were driven by the vision of the sleeping student. A few years prior to writing this book, one of the authors was in the middle of a fascinating lecture on monopoly pricing when he heard snoring. It wasn't the first time a student had fallen asleep in one of his classes, but this was the loudest snoring he had ever heard—it sounded like a sputtering chain saw. The instructor turned to "Bill," who was sitting next to the sleeping student, and asked, "Could you wake him up?" Bill looked at the sleeping student and then gazed theatrically around the room at the other students. He finally looked back at the instructor and said, "Well, professor, I think you should wake him up. After all, you put him to sleep." That experience changed the way we taught economics. It highlighted for us a basic truth—for many students, economics isn't exactly exciting. We took this as a challenge—to get first-time economics students to see the relevance of economics to their lives, their careers, and their futures.

In order to get students to see the relevance of economics, we knew that we had to engage them. With the first three editions of the book, we helped professors to do that by emphasizing an active learning approach. We engaged students by teaching them how to do something—economic analysis. We kept the book brief, lively, and to the point and used the five key principles of economics as an organizing theme. The result was that our first three editions were a success in classrooms across the country, and we strove in this edition to do even better.

Teaching Philosophy

We began with the idea that an introductory economics course should be taught as if it were the last economics class a student would ever take. Because this is true for most students, we have just one opportunity to teach them how to use economics. The best way to teach economics is to focus on a few key concepts and ideas and apply them repeatedly in different circumstances.

We start the book with the five key principles of economics and then apply them throughout the book. This approach gives students the big picture—the framework of economic reasoning. We make the key concepts unforgettable by using them repeatedly, illustrating them with intriguing examples, and giving students many opportunities to practice what they've learned.

Our book is designed to be accessible to students. We have kept the writing lean, the examples lively and topical, and the visuals exciting.

Principles and Tools

In keeping with the themes of relevance and student accessibility, we have once again organized our text around the five key principles of economics. Throughout the text, every point of theory is connected to the five key principles and is indicated by the key symbol (see margin).

1. **The Principle of Opportunity Cost.** The opportunity cost of something is what you sacrifice to get it.
2. **The Marginal Principle.** Pick the level of an activity at which the marginal benefit equals the marginal cost.
3. **The Principle of Diminishing Returns.** If we increase one input while holding the other inputs fixed, output will increase, but at a decreasing rate.
4. **The Principle of Voluntary Exchange.** A voluntary exchange between two people makes both people better off.
5. **The Real–Nominal Principle.** What matters to people is the real value of money or income—its purchasing power—not the face value of money or income.

We use these principles to explain the logic underpinning the most important tools of economics. By using these five principles repeatedly, we reveal the logic of economic reasoning and demystify the tools of economics. Students see the big picture and also learn how to use the tools of economics properly.

"What I Do, I Understand"—Confucius

Our book is based on active learning, a teaching approach based on the idea that students learn best by doing. Our book engages students by letting them do activities as they read. We implement active learning with the following features:

▶ **Economic Puzzle** exercises provide a few clues and then ask the student to solve the economic puzzle.
▶ **Using the Tools** questions at the end of each chapter give students opportunities to do their own economic analysis.
▶ **Economic Experiments** actively involve the student in role-playing as consumers, producers, and policymakers. All these activities are designed to be fun for students and easy for professors, who decide when and how to use them.
▶ **Test Your Understanding** questions help students determine whether they understand the preceding material before continuing. These are straightforward questions that ask students to review and synthesize what they have read. Complete answers appear at the end of each chapter.
▶ **Chapter-Opening Stories** open each chapter and provide motivation for the chapter's subject matter. Each chapter starts with a list of **practical questions** that are answered in the chapter.
▶ **Lively Examples** are integrated throughout the text and help bring economic concepts to life. We have hundreds of fresh, new examples in this edition.
▶ **A Closer Look** boxes are featured throughout the text and provide brief, interesting examples of the tools and concepts discussed in the text.

Part of active learning is feedback on exercises completed by the student. At the end of each chapter, we list the answers to the Test Your Understanding exercises and the chapter-opening questions. At the end of the book, we list the answers to odd-numbered end-of-chapter exercises. At the request of instructors who used the third edition, we have removed the answers to the Using the Tools exercises and instead provide them in the Instructor's Manual. This approach allows instructors to assign these exercises as homework.

Book Organization

Micro Organization

A course in microeconomics starts with the first four chapters of the book, which provide a foundation for more detailed study of individual decision-making and markets. Part 2 provides a closer look at supply and demand, including elasticity, market efficiency, and consumer choice. Part 3 discusses the circumstances under which markets break down, including imperfect information, public goods, and environmental degradation. In Part 4 we start with a discussion of production and costs, setting the stage for an examination of alternative market structures, including the extremes of perfect competition and monopoly, as well as the middle ground of monopolistic competition and oligopoly. The last chapter in Part 4 discusses antitrust policy and deregulation. The final part explores the labor market and the distribution of income.

Macro Organization

Throughout most of the 1990s, the U.S. economy performed very well—low inflation, low unemployment, and rapid economic growth. This robust performance led to increasing interest on the part of economists trying to understand the processes of economic growth. Our theories of economic growth address the fundamental question of how long-term living standards are determined and why some countries prosper while others do not. This is the essence of economic growth. As Nobel laureate Robert E. Lucas, Jr., once wrote: "Once you start thinking about growth, it is hard to think of anything else."

Yet the great economic expansion of the 1990s came to an end in 2001, as the economy started to contract. Difficult economic times remind us that macroeconomics is also concerned with understanding the causes and consequences of economic fluctuations. Why do economies experience recessions and depressions, and what steps can be taken to stabilize the economy and ease the devastation people suffer form them? This has been a constant theme of macroeconomics throughout its entire history.

A key dilemma confronting economics professors has always been how much time to devote to classical topics such a growth and production, versus economic fluctuations and business cycles. Our book is designed to let professors choose. It works like this: To pursue a classical approach, professors should initially concentrate on the first four chapters, followed by the first four chapters in the macroeconomics section. To focus on economic fluctuations, start with Chapters 1 through 4, cover the first two chapters in macroeconomics, and then turn to the chapter on aggregate demand and supply.

In this edition, we made several important changes in the macro organization to facilitate instruction. The most important is the instructors can now cover all aspects of macroeconomics—monetary and fiscal policy, for example—just using aggregate demand-and-supply analysis. For those instructors who still like to use the traditional Keynesian income-expenditure model, we provide a self-contained chapter, which also can serve as a foundation for aggregate demand. We also added a new chapter on fiscal policy following our discussion of aggregate demand and supply.

Key Changes

We knew that our text's brevity and student accessibility were key strengths, and we worked to enhance and preserve them in the fourth edition. We also found that professors and students truly appreciated our concerted effort to use economic principles to explain current and topical events. For the fourth edition, we made a systematic attempt to refine this feature of the book. We made a special effort to enhance our chapter-opening stories, Closer Look boxes, and Economic Puzzles (formerly known as the Economic Detective exercises). The result is a text that applies economic reasoning to current economic issues and debates.

We restructured the introductory chapters to focus more on the key ideas of economics. The first chapter uses three current policy issues—traffic congestion, poverty in Africa, and Japan's prolonged recession—to explain the economic way of thinking. Chapter 3 is devoted entirely to exchange and trade. We discuss the fundamental rationale for exchange and introduce some of the institutions developed in modern societies to facilitate trade.

There are some other important changes in the book. We moved the chapters on market failure forward in the book to immediately follow the discussion of supply and demand and market efficiency. The first of these chapters deals with imperfect information, an exciting new area in economics that garnered a Nobel Prize for economists George Akerlof, Michael Spence, and Joseph Stiglitz in 2001. In the chapter on environmental policy, we use a recent study of sulfur dioxide emissions to discuss the appropriate level of pollution and evaluate alternative policy options to achieve that level. We wrote a new chapter on consumer choice, using modern consumer theory rather than the outdated and awkward theory of utility. In the chapter on strategic behavior, we added a discussion of advertising strategy.

We also made some important changes in the macroeconomic chapters. Following the suggestions of our reviewers, we restructured the chapters and refined out models so that an instructor can cover all the material in macroeconomics just using an aggregate demand-and-supply framework. For those instructors still wishing to use the traditional Keynesian income-expenditure model, we now have a separate self-contained chapter that covers this topic. Now our book can easily be used by instructors who employ a wide range of pedagogical approaches. We also added a new chapter covering all aspects of fiscal policy.

We incorporated new material on emerging policy issues and developed fresh applications of basic economic concepts. For example, in the microeconomics area, we added new sections on the distribution of income, strategic advertising, health insurance, sulfur dioxide pollution, traffic congestion, and music piracy. Among the fresh applications are cartoon imports from China, EverQuest (the online role-playing game), marketable permits for greenhouse gases, soda vending machines that charge more on hot days, price fixing by vitamin sellers, and evidence for racial discrimination in hiring.

In macroeconomics, we also added additional material on the stock market, the concept of present value, and placed greater emphasis on the role of expectations in both monetary policy and unemployment and inflation dynamics. Through our applications, we explored the causes of the 2001 recession, the effectiveness of tax rebates in stimulating the economy, the relationships between growth and inequality and novel ways of measuring fiscal imbalances, as well as the role that increases in the value of homeowners' equity can stimulate consumption spending.

The Active Learning Package

A fully-integrated teaching and learning package is necessary for today's classroom. A total package of supplements is available for this edition with an emphasis on making the classroom an "active" one.

Print Supplements

Test Banks

Our team of instructors have thoroughly checked, modified, and enhanced the near 5,000 questions available in the two test banks that accompany this textbook. All new questions comprise 25% percent of each test bank. To ensure the highest level of quality, a team of checkers carefully examined the content for accuracy, consistency with the text, a balance of difficulty level and question type, and overall functionality for the purpose of testing student knowledge of the material.

Each test bank offers multiple-choice, true/false, and short-answer questions. The questions are referenced by topic and are presented in sequential order. Each question is keyed by degree of difficulty as *easy, moderate,* or *difficult.* Easy questions involve straightforward recall of information in the text. Moderate questions require some analysis on the student's part. Difficult questions usually entail more complex analysis and may require the student to go one step further than the material presented in the text. Questions are also classified as *fact, definition, conceptual,* and *analytical.* A question labeled Fact tests student's knowledge of factual information presented in the text. A Definition question asks the student to define an economic concept. Conceptual questions test a student's understanding of a concept. Analytical questions require the student to apply an analytical procedure to answer the question.

The test banks include tables and series of questions asking students to solve for numerical values, such as profit or equilibrium output. They also contain numerous questions based on graphs. The test banks include examples of all of the graphs that students have seen in the textbook. The questions ask the students to interpret the information that is presented in the graph. There are also many questions in the test banks that do not refer to a graph, but which require students to sketch out a graph on their own to be able to answer the question.

Testbank #1 (prepared by Sang Lee of Southeastern Louisiana University) Each testbank for *Microeconomics: Principles and Tools* and *Macroeconomics: Principles and Tools* offers approximately 3,000 multiple-choice, true/false, short-answer, and graphing questions. Many new, more applied questions have been added.

Testbank #2 (prepared by Nora Underwood of University of Central Florida) Each of these testbanks for *Microeconomics: Principles and Tools* and *Macroeconomics: Principles and Tools* contains over 2,000 multiple-choice, true/false, and short-answer questions.

Instructor's Manuals

The Instructor's Manuals, revised by Daniel Condon of Dominican University, for *Microeconomics: Principles and Tools* and *Macroeconomics: Principles and Tools,* both follow the textbook's organization, incorporating useful exercises, extra questions, and Internet links. The manuals also provide detailed outlines (suitable for use as lecture notes) and solutions to all questions in the textbook. The Instructor's Manuals are also designed to help the instructor incorporate applicable elements of the supplement package.

Each Instructor's Manual contains by chapter: a summary, objectives, extended examples and class exercises, solutions to all of the problems in the text, and an outline incorporating key terminology, teaching tips, and topics for class discussion.

The Instructor's Manuals are also available for download from the Instructor's Resource Center.

Study Guides

Both Study Guides for *Macroeconomics: Principles and Tools* and *Microeconomics: Principles and Tools,* created by Janice Boucher Breuer of University of South Carolina, emphasize the practical application of theory. Each Study Guide is a practicum designed to promote comprehension of economic principles and develop each student's ability to apply them to different problems.

Integrated throughout each Study Guide are Performance-Enhancing Tips (PETs), which are designed to help students understand economics by applying the principles and promoting analytical thinking.

Two practice exams, featuring both multiple-choice and essay questions, are included at the end of each chapter. Both exams require students to apply one or more economic principles to arrive at each correct answer. Full solutions to the multiple-choice questions are included, not only listing each correct answer but also explaining in detail why one answer is correct and the others are not. Detailed answers to the essay questions are also provided.

The Study Guide contains by chapter: an overview of the corresponding chapter in the textbook, a checklist to provide a quick review of material covered in the textbook and lectures, a list of key terms and their definitions, practice exams, and the detailed answer keys. Each chapter is centered on the checklist and provides a summary, PETs, and questions specifically related to the topics covered.

MICRO AND MACRO Color Transparencies

All figures and tables from the Micro and Macro texts are reproduced as full-page, four-color acetates.

Technology Supplements

Companion Website: http://www.prenhall.com/osullivan

The Website contains Internet exercises, activities, and resources related specifically to the fourth edition of *Economics: Principles and Tools*

For Students

Link to **EconUpdates** site, where you will find updated **In the News** articles and **Internet Exercises**. Nearly every chapter of the textbook will be updated with economics-based articles from current news publications as well as Web-destination exercises that will direct students to an appropriate Website to gather data and analyze a specific economic problem.

The **Online Study Guide** offers students another opportunity to sharpen their problem-solving skills and to assess their understanding of the text material. The

Online Study Guide grades each question submitted by the student, provides immediate feedback for correct and incorrect answers, and allows students to e-mail results to up to four e-mail addresses.

Printable version of the **PowerPoint Lecture Presentation**.

For Instructors

Syllabus Manager, which allows instructors to create a syllabus that they may publish for their students to access. Instructors may add exams or assignments of their own, edit any of the student resources available on the companion Website, post discussion topics, and more.

Instructors may find **downloadable resources** from the link for the Instructor's Resource Center described below.

Instructor's Resource Center

This password-protected site is accessible from **www.prenhall.com/osullivan** and hosts all of the resources listed next. Instructors may click on the *Help downloading Instructor Resources* link for easy-to-follow instructions on getting access or may contact their sales representative for further information.

Classroom Response Systems (CRS)

CRS is an exciting new wireless polling technology that makes large and small classrooms even more interactive because it enables instructors to pose questions to their students, record results, and display those results instantly. Students can easily answer questions using compact remote control style transmitters. Prentice Hall has partnerships with leading classroom response systems providers, and can show you everything you need to know about setting up and using a CRS system. We'll provide the classroom hardware, text-specific PowerPoint slides, software and support, and show you how your students can benefit.

Instructor's Manual

Solutions to questions included on the student side of the EconUpdates site

The PowerPoint Lecture Presentation: This lecture presentation tool offers the following features and benefits:

▶ Follows the exact layout of the textbook, by title and subtitle and provides an identical reproduction of textbook graphics, content sequence, and color consistency.
▶ Includes all the graphs, tables, and equations in the textbook.
▶ Displays figures in step-by-step, automated mode, using a single click per slide.
▶ Makes efficient use of space and crisp graphics designed to look the best in the space available.
▶ Contains end-of-chapter key terms with hyperlinks to relevant slides.
▶ The package will allow for instructors to make full-color, professional-looking presentations.
▶ A separate set of slides for students to easily print out for the purpose of note taking is also available.

TestGen-EQ software: The printed test banks are designed for use with the TestGen-EQ test-generating software. This computerized package allows instructors to custom-design, save, and generate classroom tests. The test program permits instructors to edit, add, or delete questions from the test banks; edit existing graphics and create new graphics; analyze test results; and organize a database of tests and student results. This new software allows for greater flexibility and ease of use. It provides many options for organizing and displaying tests, along with a search-and-sort feature. The software as well as the four test banks are available for download here.

Instructor's Resource Center on CD-ROM

All of the resources mentioned under the Instructor Resource Center are also available on this CD-ROM. With this new, **highly accessible menu**, faculty can easily customize presentations or build their own online courses. By simply clicking on a chapter or searching for a keyword, they can access an interactive library of resources. Faculty can pick and choose from the various supplements and export them to their hard drive.

OneKey

Available by using one of the access codes shrink-wrapped with the book, OneKey is Prentice Hall's exclusive new resource for instructors and students. OneKey gives you access to the best online teaching and learning tools—all available 24 hours a day, 7 days a week. OneKey means all your resources are in one place for maximum convenience, simplicity, and success. **Instructors** have access online, in the course management system of their choosing, to all available course supplements. Instructors can create and assign tests, quizzes, or graded homework assignments. OneKey saves instructors time by grading all questions and tracking results in the online course grade book. **Students** have access to interactive exercises, quizzes, useful links, and much more. The following resources are available:

▶ **Active Graphs.** Two levels of interactive graphs help students to understand economic concepts. Active Graphs Level One support key graphs in the text. These JAVA applications invite students to change the value of variables and curves and see the effects in the movement of the graph. Active Graphs Level Two include exercises that ask students to modify graphs based on an economic scenario and questions. Students receive an instant response detailing how they should have changed the graph.

▶ **Egraph and Graphing Questions.** This electronic tool allows students to create precise, colorful graphs using Flash technology. Students can e-mail these graphs to their professor or print and save them. To apply this technology, we have included *Graphing Questions* that require students to analyze information gathered on the Web and then create graphs using the Graphing Tool. Complete answers, with graphs, are included.

▶ **EconUpdates.**

▶ **Practice Quizzes.**

▶ **PowerPoint Lecture Presentation.**

▶ **Learning Objectives.**

▶ **Chapter Summaries.**

▶ **Research Navigator.** Your OneKey course gives you direct access to Prentice Hall's powerful online research tool, Research Navigator™. Research Navigator is an online academic research service that helps students learn and master the skills needed to write effective papers and complete research assignments. Research Navigator includes three databases of credible and reliable source material.

▶ **EBSCO's ContentSelect™** Academic Journal database gives you instant access to thousands of academic journals and periodicals. You can search these online journals by keyword, topic, or multiple topics. It also guides students step-by-step through the writing of a research paper.

▶ The *New York Times* **Search-by-Subject**™ Archive allows you to search by subject and by keyword

▶ **Link Library** It is a collection of links to Websites, organized by academic subject and key terms. The links are monitored and updated each week.

▶ *OneKey for CourseCompass* allows instructors to communicate with students, distribute course material, and access student progress online. For access to this material, see http://www.prenhall.com/coursecompass.

▶ *OneKey for WebCT* provides content and enhanced features to help instructors create a complete online course. See http://www.prenhall.com/webct for more information.

▶ *OneKey for Blackboard* allows instructors to create online courses using the Blackboard tools, which include design, communications, testing, and course management tools. See **http://www.prenhall.com/blackboard** for more information.

Subscriptions

Analyzing current events is an important skill for economic students to develop. To sharpen this skill and further support the book's theme of exploration and application, Prentice Hall offers you and your students three news subscription offers:

The Wall Street Journal Print and Interactive Editions Subscription

Prentice Hall has formed a strategic alliance with the *Wall Street Journal*, the most respected and trusted daily source for information on business and economics. For a small additional charge, Prentice Hall offers your students a 10- or 15-week subscription to the *Wall Street Journal* print edition and the *Wall Street Journal* interactive edition. Upon adoption of a special package containing the book and the subscription booklet, professors will receive a free one-year subscription of the print and interactive versions as well as weekly subject-specific *Wall Street Journal* educators' lesson plans.

The Financial Times

We are pleased to announce a special partnership with *The Financial Times*. For a small additional charge, Prentice Hall offers your students a 15-week subscription to *The Financial Times*. Upon adoption of a special package containing the book and the subscription booklet, professors will receive a free one-year subscription. Please contact your Prentice Hall representative for details and ordering information.

Economist.com

Through a special arrangement with Economist.com, Prentice Hall offers your students a 12-week subscription to Economist.com for a small additional charge. Upon adoption of a special package containing the book and the subscription booklet, professors will receive a free six-month subscription. Please contact your Prentice Hall representative for further details and ordering information.

A World of Thanks

A long road exists between the initial vision of an innovative principles text and the final product. Along our journey we participated in a structured process to reach our goal.

We wish to acknowledge the assistance of the many people who participated in this process. First we want to thank the participants who took part in the focus groups for the first and second editions; they helped us see the manuscript from a fresh perspective:

Carlos Aquilar, El Paso Community College
Jim Bradley, University of South Carolina
Thomas Collum, Northeastern Illinois University
David Craig, Westark College
Jeff Holt, Tulsa Junior College
Thomas Jeitschko, Texas A & M University
Gary Langer, Roosevelt University
Mark McCleod, Virginia Polytechnic Institute and State University
Tom McKinnon, University of Arkansas
Amy Meyers, Parkland Community College
Hassan Mohammadi, Illinois State University
John Morgan, College of Charleston

Norm Paul, San Jancinto Community College
Nampeang Pingkaratwat, Chicago State University
Scanlan Romer, Delta Community College
Barbara Ross-Pfeiffer, Kapiolani Community College
Virginia Shingleton, Valparaiso University
Zahra Saderion, Houston Community College
Jim Swofford, University of South Alabama
Linda Wilson, University of Texas–Arlington
Janet West, University of Nebraska–Omaha
Michael Youngblood, Rock Valley Community College

A special acknowledgment goes to the instructors who were willing to class-test drafts in different stages of development. They provided us with instant feedback on parts that worked and parts that needed changes:

Sheryl Ball, Virginia Polytechnic Institute and State University
John Constantine, University of California, Davis
James Hartley, Mt. Holyoke College
John Farrell, Oregon State University
Kailash Khandke, Furman College

Peter Lindert, University of California, Davis
Louis Makowski, University of California, Davis
Stephen Perez, California State University, Sacramento
Barbara Ross-Pfeiffer, Kapiolani Community College

Many people read all or parts of the manuscript at various stages. For their helpful criticisms, we thank:

Christine Amsler, Michigan State University
Karijit K. Arora, Le Moyne College
Alex Azarchs, Pace University
Kevin A. Baird, Montgomery County Community College
Donald Balch, University of South Carolina
Collette Barr, Santa Barbara Community College
Mahamudu Bawumia, Baylor University
Charles Scott Benson, Jr., Idaho State University
Jay Bhattacharya, Okaloosa-Walton Community College
John Payne Bigelow, Louisiana State University
Scott Bloom, North Dakota State University
Janice Boucher Breuer, University of South Carolina
Kathleen K. Bromley, Monroe Community College
Cindy Cannon, North Harris College
Katie Canty, Cape Fear Community College
David L. Coberly, Southwest Texas State University
John L. Conant, Indiana State University
Ana-Maria Conley, DeVry Institute of Technology
Ed Coulson, Penn State University
Lee Craig, North Carolina State University

Peggy Crane, San Diego State University
Albert B. Culver, California State University, Chico
Norman Cure, Macomb Community College
Irma de Alonso, Florida International University
Sel Dibooglu, Southern Illinois University
Martine Duchatelet, Barry University
Mousumi Duttaray, Indiana University
Ghazi Duwaji, University of Texas, Arlington
David Eaton, Murray State University
Duane Eberhardt, Missouri Southern State College
Carl Enomoto, New Mexico State University
David Figlio, University of Oregon
Dan Georgianna, University of Massachusetts–Dartmouth
Linda Ghent, East Illinois University
Hossein Gholami, Fayetteville Tech Community College
Susan Glanz, St. John's University
Randy R. Grant, Linfield College
Paul C. Harris, Jr., Camden County College
James E. Hartley, Mount Holyoke College
Rowland Harvey, DeVry Institute of Technology
John Henry, California State University, Sacramento

Robert Herman, Nassau Community College

Charles W. Haase, San Francisco State University

Charlotte Denise Hixson, Midlands Technical College

Jeff Holt, Tulsa Community College

Brad Hoppes, Southwest Missouri State University

Calvin Hoy, County College of Morris

Jonathan O. Ikoba, Scott Community College

John A. Jascot, Capital Community Technical College

Thomas Jeitschko, Texas A & M University

George Jensen, California State University, Los Angeles

Taghi T. Kermani, Youngstown State University

Rose Kilburn, Modesto Junior College

Philip King, San Francisco State University

Steven F. Koch, Georgia Southern University

James T. Kyle, Indiana Sate University

Gary Langer, Roosevelt University

Susan Linz, Michigan State University

Marianne Lowery, Erie Community College

Melanie Marks, Longwood College

Jessica McCraw, University of Texas, Arlington

Bret McMurran, Chaffey College

Thomas J. Meeks, Virginia State University

Jeannette Mitchell, Rochester Institute of Technology

Rahmat Mozayan, Heald College

William Neilson, Texas A & M University

Alex Obiya, San Diego City College

Paul Okello, University of Texas, Arlington

Charles M. Oldham, Jr., Fayetteville Technical Community College

Jack W. Osman, San Francisco State University

Carl Parker, Fort Hays State University

Randall Parker, East Carolina University

Stephen Perez, California State University, Sacramento

Stan Peters, Southeast Community College

Chirinjev Peterson, Greenville Technical College

Nampeang Pingkarawat, Chicago State University

L. Wayne Plumly, Jr., Valdosta State University

Fatma Abdel-Raouf, Cleveland State University

Dan Rickman, Oklahoma State University

John Robertson, University of Kentucky

Barbara Ross-Pfeiffer, Kapiolani Community College

George Schatz, Maine Maritime Academy

Kurt Schwabe, Ohio University

Mark Siegler, Williams College

Terri Sexton, California State University, Sacramento

Dennis Shannon, Belleville Area College

Virginia Shingleton, Valparaiso University

Garvin Smith, Daytona Beach Community College

Noel Smith, Palm Beach Community College

Xiaochuan Song, San Diego Mesa College

Ed Sorensen, San Francisco State University

Abdulwahab Sraiheen, Kutztown University

Rodney Swanson, University of California-Los Angeles

James Swofford, University of South Alabama

Evan Tanner, Thunderbird, The American Graduate School of International Management

Robert Tansky, St. Clair County Community College

Denise Turnage, Midlands Technical College

Tracy M. Turner, Kansas State University

Fred Tyler, Fordham University

James R. VanBeek, Blinn College

Daniel Villegas, Cal Polytechnic State University

Chester Waters, Durham Technical Community College, Shaw University

Irvin Weintraub, Towson State University

Donald Wells, University of Arizona

James Wheeler, North Carolina State University

Gilbert Wolfe, Middlesex Community College

Virginia York, Gulf Coast Community College

Our greatest appreciation goes out to Carlos Aguilar and his economics students from El Paso Community College, who gave us their feedback and evaluations with comparable textbooks. The students provided us with positive feedback and constructive criticism that helped us prepare the third edition:

Erik Acona

Erica Avila

Jaime Bermudez

Israel Castillo

Maribell Castillo

Sarah Davis

Rebekah Dennis

Michele Donohoe

Emmanuel Eck

Patrick Espinoza

Edward Estrada

Kim Gardner

Aleisa Garza

Daniel Heitz

Laura Herebia

Hilda Howard

Melanie Johnson

Brenda Jordan

Eugene Jordan

Vanessa Lara

Harmony Lopez

Stacey Lucas

Maria Lynch

Sindy McElvany

Roger Mitchell

Benny Ontiveros

Louie Ortega

Karen Seitz

Ana Smith

Beverly Stephens

Adrian Terrazas

Chris Wright

For the fourth edition, we enlisted a large group of reviewers; their comments and suggestions helped us improve the coverage and presentation of the book.

Rashid Al-Hmoud, Texas Technical University

Jay Bhattacharya, Oklahoma Walton Community College

Charles Benson, Jr., Idaho State University

Edward Bierhanzl, Florida A&M University

Calvin Blackwell, College of Charlestown

Matthew Brown, Santa Clara University

Bruce Brunton, James Madison University

Tom Carroll, Central Oregon Community College

Peggy Crane, Southwestern College

John Farrell, Oregon State University

Harry Ellis, University of North Texas

David Gillette, Truman State University

Lowell Glenn, Utah Valley State College

John Graham, Rutgers University

Miren Ivankovic, Southern Wesleyan University

Paul Johnson, University of Alaska, Anchorage

Janis Kea, West Valley College

Youn Kim, Monash University

Sang Lee, Southeastern Louisiana University

Anthony Lima, California State University, Hayward

Marty Ludlum, Oklahoma City Community College

Martin Markovich, Florida A & M University

Pete Mavrokordatos, Tarrant County College/University of Phoenix

Thomas McCaleb, Florida State University

Stephen Miller, University of Nevada, Las Vegas

Ted Muzio, St. John's University, Jamaica, NY

Jon J Nadenichek, California State University, Northridge

Tahany Naggar, West Chester University

Michael Nelson, Texas A & M University

Stan Peters, Southeast Community College

James Ragan, Kansas State University

Taghi Ramin, William Patterson University

Joseph Santos, South Dakota State University

Richard Stahl, Louisiana State University

Tesa Stegner, Idaho State University

Lawrence Stelmach, Delaware Valley College

Rodney Swanson, University of California, Los Angeles

James Swofford, University of South Alabama

Greg Trandel, University of Georgia

Chad Turner, Clemson University

Brock Williams, Metropolitan Community College

Virginia York, Gulf Coast Community College

We would also like to acknowledge the team of dedicated authors that contributed to the various ancillaries that accompany this book: Janice Boucher Breuer of University of South Carolina, Diego Mendez-Carbajo of Illinois Wesleyan University, Daniel Condon of Dominican University, Tori H. Knight of Carson-Newman College, Sang Lee of Southeastern Louisiana University, Cathleen Leue of University of Oregon, William Mosher of Clark University, Fernando Quijano of Dickinson State University, Robin D. Turner of Rowan Cabarrus Community College and Nora Underwood of University of Central Florida.

We also owe a special thanks to Stephen J. Perez of California State University, Sacramento. He acted as the supplement coordinator and advisor. He provided valuable advice, guidance, and in-depth feedback on the entire supplement package.

From the start, Prentice Hall provided us with first-class support and advice. Over the first four editions, many people contributed to the project, including Leah Jewell, Rod Banister, P. J. Boardman, Marie McHale, Gladys Soto, Lisa Amato, Victoria Anderson, Cynthia Regan, Kathleen McLellan, Sharon Koch, David Theisen, Steve Deitmer, and Christopher Bath. We want to single out two people for special mention. Our development editor, Amy Ray, did an outstanding job identifying parts of the book that could be improved for the fourth edition, and had many suggestions on how to improve it. Finally, we are indebted to David Alexander, executive editor at Prentice Hall, who guided the project from start to finish.

Last but not least, we must thank our families, who have seen us disappear, sometimes physically and other times mentally, to spend hours wrapped up in our own world of principles of economics. A project of this magnitude is very absorbing, and our families have been particularly supportive in this endeavor.

Arthur O'Sullivan
Steven Sheffrin

Features List

Part

1

Introduction and Key Principles

Introduction: What Is Economics?

conomics is the science of choice, exploring the choices made by individual people and organizations. In the last few centuries, these choices have led to substantial gains in the standard of living around the globe. The typical American household today has roughly seven times the income and purchasing power of a household 100 years ago. Our prosperity is the result of choices made by all sorts of people, including inventors, workers, entrepreneurs, and the people who saved money and loaned it to others to invest in machines and other tools of production. One reason we have prospered is greater efficiency: We have discovered better ways to use our resources—raw materials, time, energy—to produce the goods and services we value.

Although prosperity and efficiency are widespread, they are not universal. In some parts of the world, many people live in poverty. For example, in sub-Saharan Africa, 290 million people—almost half the population—live on less than $1 per day. And in all nations of the world, there are still inefficiencies, with valuable resources being wasted. For example, each year the typical urban commuter in the United States wastes more than 60 hours and $150 in gasoline while trapped in rush hour traffic.

Economics provides a framework to diagnose all sorts of problems faced by society and then evaluate various proposals to solve them. Economics can help us develop strategies to replace poverty with prosperity, to replace waste with efficiency. In this chapter, we explain what economics is and how it can be used to think about practical problems.

What Is Economics?

Economics studies the choices that can be made when there is scarcity. **Scarcity** is a situation in which resources—the things we use to produce goods and services—are limited in quantity and can be used in different ways. Because our resources are limited, or finite, we must sacrifice one thing for another. Here are some examples of scarcity:

▶ Like everyone else, you have a limited amount of time. If you take a part-time job, each hour on the job means one less hour for study or play.
▶ A city has a limited amount of land, so if the city uses an acre for a park, it has one less acre for housing, retailers, or industry.
▶ You have limited income this year, so every dollar you spend on music means one less dollar spent on other products, or one less dollar saved.

We make our choices in a variety of ways. Sometimes we make our decisions as individuals, and other times we participate in collective decision-making, allowing the government and other organizations to choose for us. Many of our choices happen within markets, where we buy and sell things. For example, most of us participate in the labor market, exchanging our time for money, and we all participate in consumer markets. On the other hand, we make other choices outside markets—from our personal decisions about everyday life to our political choices about matters that concern society as a whole. What unites all these decisions is the notion of scarcity: We can't have it all; there are trade-offs.

Economists are always reminding us that there is scarcity—that there are trade-offs in everything we do. Suppose that in a conversation with an economist, you share your enthusiasm about an upcoming launch of the space shuttle. The economist is likely to remind you that the resources used for the shuttle could be used instead for an unmanned mission to Mars. By introducing the notion of scarcity into your conversation, the economist is simply reminding you that there are trade-offs, that one thing (a shuttle mission) is sacrificed for another (a Mars mission). Talking about alternatives is the first step in a process that can help us make better choices about how to use our resources. For example, we could compare the scientific benefits of a shuttle mission to the benefits of a Mars mission, and choose the mission with the largest benefit.

The resources used for the Space Shuttle could be used instead to launch a mission to Mars. This is an example of the tradeoffs our society faces.

Positive Versus Normative Analysis

It's important to note that economics doesn't tell us what to choose—shuttle mission or Mars mission—but simply helps us understand the trade-offs. President Harry Truman once remarked,

> All my economists say, "On the one hand, . . . ; On the other hand, . . . " Give me a one-handed economist!

An economist might say, "On the one hand, we could use a shuttle mission to do more experiments in the gravity-free environment in earth orbit; on the other hand, we could use a Mars mission to explore the possibility of life on other planets." In using both hands, the economist is not being evasive, but simply doing economics, discussing the alternative uses of our resources. The ultimate decision about how to use our resources—shuttle mission or Mars exploration—is the responsibility of citizens or their elected officials.

Positive economics

Analysis that answers the questions, "What is?" or "What will be?"

Most modern economic analysis is based on positive analysis. **Positive economics** predicts the consequences of alternative actions, answering the questions "What is?" or "What *will be*?" Here are some questions answered by positive economics:

▶ If the minimum wage increases, how many workers will lose their jobs?
▶ If two office-supply firms merge, will the price of office supplies increase?
▶ If income taxes are cut, what fraction of the tax cut will be spent on consumer goods?
▶ If a nation restricts shoe imports, who benefits, and who bears the cost?

A second type of economic reasoning is normative in nature. **Normative economics** answers the question "What *ought to be*?" Here are some normative questions:

▶ Should the government increase the minimum wage?
▶ Should the government provide $1 billion in foreign aid to an African country?
▶ Should the government subsidize a college education?
▶ Should the government cut taxes to stimulate the economy?
▶ Should a nation reduce the size of its government?

Normative questions lie at the heart of policy debates. Economists contribute to policy debates by doing positive analysis about the consequences of alternative actions. For example, an economist could predict the effects of a minimum wage on the number of people employed, the income of families with minimum-wage workers, and consumer prices. Armed with the conclusions of the economist's positive analysis, citizens and policymakers could then make a normative decision about whether to increase the minimum wage. Similarly, an economist could study the projects that could be funded with $1 billion in foreign aid, predicting the effects of each project on the per capita income in an African country. Armed with this positive analysis, policymakers could then decide which projects to support.

It's important to note that economists don't always reach the same conclusions in their positive analyses. The disagreements often concern the magnitude of a particular effect. For example, most economists agree that an increase in the minimum wage will decrease employment, but there is disagreement about just how many people will lose their jobs. Similarly, economists agree that spending $1 billion to improve education in Africa will increase productivity and income, but there may be disagreement about just how much income will increase. There are ongoing efforts by economists to quantify these sorts of economic phenomena, but many factual questions remain unanswered. For a discussion of some of the points of agreement and disagreement among economists, read "A Closer Look: When Do Economists Agree?"

Decisions in a Modern Economy: The Invisible Hand?

Economic decisions are made at every level in society. Individuals decide what products to buy, what occupations to pursue, and how much money to save. Firms decide what products to produce and how to produce them. Governments decide what projects and programs to complete and how to pay for them. The choices made by individuals, firms, and governments answer three questions.

1 What products do we produce? There are trade-offs: If a hospital uses its resources to perform more heart transplants, it has fewer resources to care for premature infants.
2 How do we produce the products? There are alternative means of production: Power companies can produce electricity with coal, natural gas, or wind power; professors can teach in large lecture halls or small classrooms.
3 Who consumes the products? We must decide how the products of society are distributed among people. If some people earn more money than others, should they consume more goods? How much money should be taken from the rich and given to the poor?

Normative economics
Analysis that answers the question "What ought to be?"

A CLOSER LOOK   When Do Economists Agree?

Although economists often disagree about policy matters, there is widespread agreement about many of today's most important issues. A recent survey asked economists to indicate whether they agreed or disagreed with a number of propositions.[1] Here are some of the statements for which there was widespread agreement, with the percentages of economists who agreed shown in parentheses.

1. The U.S. trade deficit is *not* primarily due to trade barriers erected by other nations (95%).
2. The best way to control pollution is to tax polluters—or to issue a limited number of pollution permits and allow firms to buy and sell the permits (93%).
3. Import restrictions and import taxes usually reduce the general welfare of society (93%).
4. The federal government can use its tax and spending policies to stimulate a sluggish economy and encourage investment (84%).
5. A large federal budget deficit has an adverse effect on the economy (80%).
6. Minimum wages increase unemployment among young and unskilled workers (74%).
7. Antitrust laws should be enforced vigorously to reduce monopoly power from its current level (71%).

On other issues, economists have not reached a consensus. For example, economists disagree about whether an economy would naturally correct the problem of widespread unemployment without intervention by the government. They also disagree about whether cutting taxes on investment income will promote economic growth and general prosperity. On the issue of why men earn more than women, some economists believe the wage gap is caused largely by differences in productivity and career choices, whereas others believe that sex discrimination plays an important role in the wage gap. The fact that economists disagree on these issues reflects our imperfect knowledge about various facets of the economy. There is still much work to be done to improve our knowledge and design policies to eliminate waste and promote prosperity.

As we'll see later in the book, most of these decisions are made in markets, with prices playing a key role in determining what products we produce, how we produce them, and who gets the products. In Chapter 3, we'll examine the role of markets in modern economies, exploring the virtues as well as the shortcomings of markets.

Economic Analysis and Modern Problems

Economic analysis provides important insights into real-world problems. To explain how economic analysis can be used in problem solving, we provide three examples, each of which will be explained here and in more detail later in the book.

Example 1: Traffic Congestion

Consider first the problem of traffic congestion. According to the Texas Transportation Institute, the typical U.S. commuter wastes about 62 hours per year because of traffic congestion.[2] In some cities, the time wasted by the typical commuter is much higher:

136 hours in Los Angeles, 92 hours in San Francisco, and 75 hours in Houston. In addition to time lost, we also waste $9 billion worth of gasoline and diesel fuel each year.

To an economist, the diagnosis of the congestion problem is straightforward. When you drive onto a busy highway during rush hour, your car takes up space and decreases the distance between the vehicles on the highway. The normal reaction to a shorter distance between moving cars is to slow down. So when you enter the highway, you are essentially forcing other commuters to spend more time on the highway. If each of your 900 fellow commuters spends just two extra seconds on the highway, you have increased the total travel time of the group by 30 minutes. But since you don't lose the 30 minutes all yourself, it's likely that you ignore this effect when deciding whether or not to enter. Similarly, your fellow commuters ignore the cost they impose on you and others when they enter the highway. Since no single commuter pays the full cost, too many people use the highway, and everyone wastes time.

One possible solution to the congestion problem is to force people to pay for using the road, just as they pay for gasoline and tires. A congestion tax of $8 per trip could be imposed on rush hour commuters. We could use a debit card system to collect the tax: Every time a car passes a checkpoint, a transponder would charge the commuter's card. Traffic volume during rush hours would then decrease as travelers (a) shift their travel to off-peak times, (b) switch to ride sharing and mass transit, and (c) shift their travel to other routes. The job for the economist is to compute the appropriate congestion tax and predict the consequences of imposing the tax.

Example 2: Poverty in Africa

Consider next the issue of poverty in Africa. In the last two decades of the twentieth century, the world economy grew rapidly, and the average per capita income (income per person) increased by about 35%. By contrast, the economies of poverty-stricken sub-Saharan Africa shrank, and per capita income decreased by about 6%. Economists have found that as a nation's economy grows, its poorest households share in the general prosperity.[3] Therefore, one way to reduce poverty in sub-Saharan Africa would be to increase economic growth. Economic growth occurs when a country expands its production facilities (machinery and factories), improves its public infrastructure (highways and water systems), widens educational opportunities, and adopts new technology.

The recent experience of sub-Saharan Africa is somewhat puzzling because in the last few decades, the region has expanded educational opportunities and received large amounts of foreign aid. Some recent work by economists on the sources of growth suggests that institutions such as the legal system and the regulatory environment play key roles in economic growth.[4] In sub-Saharan Africa, a simple legal dispute about a small debt takes about 30 months to resolve, compared to five months in the United States. In Mozambique, it takes 174 days to complete the procedures required to set up a business, compared to just two days in Canada.[5] In many cases, institutions impede rather than encourage the sort of investment and risk taking that causes economic growth and reduces poverty. As a consequence, economists and policymakers are exploring ways to reform the region's institutions. They are also challenged with choosing among development projects that will generate the biggest economic boost per dollar spent—that is, the biggest bang per buck.

Example 3: Japan's Economic Problems

Consider next the economic problems experienced by Japan in the last decade. Following World War II, Japan grew rapidly, with per capita income increasing by about 4% per year between 1950 and 1992. But in 1992, the economy came to a screeching halt. For the next 10 years, per capita income, or income per person, either decreased or increased slightly. In 1995, the prices of all sorts of goods—including consumer goods and housing—actually started to decrease, and the downward slide continued for years. In an economy with declining prices, consumers expect lower prices tomorrow, so they are reluctant to buy things today. Business managers are reluctant to borrow money to invest in production facilities because if prices for their products drop, they might not have enough money to repay the loans.

The challenge for economists was to develop a set of policies to get the Japanese economy moving again. Economists responded by designing policies to stimulate spending by consumers and businesses and to make needed changes to their financial system. The Japanese political system was slow to adopt these difficult reforms, but recent political developments in Japan have increased the likelihood that the necessary reforms will be made in the future.

TEST Your Understanding

1. List the three basic questions asked about an economy.
2. Why is economics labeled the "dismal science?"
3. Explain the difference between positive and normative analysis.

The Economic Way of Thinking

How do economists think about problems and decision-making? The economic way of thinking is best summarized by British economist John Maynard Keynes (1883–1946), who is responsible for a branch of economics bearing his name:

> The theory of economics does not furnish a body of settled conclusions immediately applicable to policy. It is a method rather than a doctrine, an apparatus of the mind, a technique of thinking which helps its possessor draw correct conclusions.

Let's look at the three elements of the economic way of thinking.

1. Use Assumptions to Simplify
Economists use assumptions to make things simpler and focus attention on what really matters. If you use a road map to plan a car trip from Seattle to San Francisco, you make two unrealistic assumptions to simplify your planning:

▶ The earth is flat: The flat road map doesn't show the curvature of the earth.
▶ The roads are flat: The standard road map doesn't show hills and valleys.

Instead of a map, you could use a globe that shows all the topographical features between Seattle and San Francisco, but you don't need those details to plan your trip. A map, with its unrealistic assumptions, will suffice because the curvature of the earth and the topography of the highways are irrelevant to your trip. Although your analysis of your road trip is based on two unrealistic assumptions, that does not mean your analysis is invalid. Similarly, if economic analysis is based on unrealistic assumptions, that doesn't mean the analysis is faulty.

What if you decide to travel by bike instead of by automobile? Now the assumption of flat roads really matters, unless of course you are eager to pedal up and down mountains. If you use a standard map and thus assume there are no mountains between the two cities, you may inadvertently pick a mountainous route instead of a flat one. In this case, the simplifying assumption makes a difference. The lesson is that we must think carefully about whether a simplifying assumption is truly harmless.

2. Isolate Variables—*Ceteris Paribus*

Economic analysis often involves variables and how they affect one another. A **variable** is a measure of something that can take on different values. Economists are interested in exploring relationships between two variables; for example, the relationship between the price of apples and the quantity of apples purchased. Of course, the quantity of apples purchased depends on many other variables, including the consumer's income. To explore the relationship between the quantity and price of apples, we must assume that the consumer's income—and anything else that influences apple purchases—doesn't change.

Alfred Marshall (1842–1924), was a British economist who refined the economic model of supply and demand and provided a label for this process.[6] He picked one variable that affected apple purchases (price) and threw the other variable (income) into what he called the "pound" (in Marshall's time, the "pound," was an enclosure for holding stray cattle; nowadays, a pound is for stray dogs). The "other" variables waited in the pound

Variable
A measure of something that can take on different values.

To study a single variable, Alfred Marshall threw the other variables into a "pound" where they waited until he examined the influence of the first variable. This notion of isolating variables is called *ceteris paribus*.

while Marshall examined the influence of the first variable. Marshall labeled the pound ***ceteris paribus***, the Latin expression meaning that other variables are held fixed:

> . . . the existence of other tendencies is not denied, but their disturbing effect is neglected for a time. The more the issue is narrowed, the more exactly can it be handled.

Ceteris paribus
The Latin expression meaning other variables being held fixed.

This book contains many statements about the relationship between two variables. For example, the quantity of computers produced by a firm depends on the price of computers, the wage of computer workers, and the cost of microchips. When we say, "An increase in the price of computers increases the quantity of computers produced," we are implicitly assuming that the other two variables—the wage and the cost of microchips—do not change. Sometimes, we will make this assumption explicit by adding "*ceteris paribus.*"

3. Think at the Margin

Economists often consider how a small change in one variable affects another variable and what impact that has on people's decision-making. In other words, if circumstances change ever so slightly, how will people respond? A small, one-unit change in value is called a **marginal change**. The key feature is that the first variable changes by only one unit. For example, you might ask, If I study just one more hour, by how much will my exam score increase? Economists call this process "thinking at the margin." Thinking at the margin is sort of like thinking on the edge. You will encounter marginal thinking throughout this book. Here are some other marginal questions:

Marginal change
A small, one-unit change in value.

- ▶ If I stay in school and earn another degree, by how much will my lifetime earnings increase?
- ▶ If a car dealer hires one more sales associate, how many more cars will the dealer sell?
- ▶ If national income increases by $1 billion, by how much will spending on consumer goods increase?

As we'll see in the next chapter, economists use the answer to a marginal question as a first step in deciding whether to do more or less of something.

Rational People Respond to Incentives

A key assumption of most economic analysis is that people act rationally, meaning that they act in their own self-interest. British philosopher Adam Smith (1723–1790), who is also considered the founder of economics, wrote that he discovered within mankind:[7]

> a desire of bettering our condition, a desire which, though generally calm and dispassionate, comes with us from the womb, and never leaves us until we go to the grave.

Smith didn't say that people are motivated exclusively by self-interest, but instead that self-interest is more powerful than kindness or altruism. In this book, we will assume that people act in their own self-interest.

Rational people respond to incentives. When the payoff, or benefit, from doing something changes, people change their behavior to get the benefit. For an example of incentives and corresponding behavior, read "A Closer Look: Even Kids Respond to Incentives ."

Application: Thinking About Congestion

To illustrate the three elements of the economic way of thinking, let's consider again how an economist would approach the problem of traffic congestion. Recall that each driver on the highway slows down other drivers but ignores these costs when deciding whether or not to use the highway. If the government imposes a congestion tax to alleviate congestion during rush hour, the question for the economist is: How high should the tax be?

To determine the appropriate congestion tax, we, as economists, would use the three elements of the economic way of thinking.

▶ Make Assumptions. To simply the problem, we would assume that every car has the same effect on the travel time of other cars. Of course, this is unrealistic because people drive cars of different sizes in different ways. But the alternative— looking at the effects of each car on travel speeds—would needlessly complicate the analysis.

▶ Isolate Variables (*Ceteris Paribus*). To focus attention on the effects of a congestion tax on the number of cars using the highway, we would make the *ceteris paribus* assumption that everything else that affects travel behavior—the price of gasoline, bus fares, and consumer income—remains fixed.

▶ Think at the Margin. To think at the margin, we would estimate the effects of adding one more car to the highway. The marginal question is: If we add one more car to the highway, by how much does the total travel time for commuters increase?

Before London imposed an $8, rush-hour congestion tax, the city experienced some of the worst congestion in Europe.

Once we answer this question, we could determine the cost imposed by the marginal driver. If the marginal driver forces each of the 900 commuters to spend two extra seconds on the highway, total travel time increases by 30 minutes. If the value of time is $16 per hour, the appropriate congestion tax would be $8.

If the idea of charging people for using roads seems odd and dismal, consider the city of London, which for decades had experienced the worst congestion in Europe. In February of 2003, the city imposed an $8 tax per day for driving in the city between 7:00 A.M. and 6:30 P.M. The tax reduced traffic volume and cut travel times for cars and buses in half. This application of economics decreased the time and fuel wasted in traffic. Given the success of London's congestion tax, other cities are exploring similar policies.

TEST Your Understanding

4. **List the three elements of the economic way of thinking.**
5. **Suppose your grade on an economics exam is affected by the number of lectures you attend. What is the relevant marginal question?**

Preview of Coming Attractions: Microeconomics

Microeconomics
The study of the choices made by households, firms, and government and of how these choices affect the markets for goods and services.

There are two types of economic analysis: microeconomics and macroeconomics. **Microeconomics** is the study of the choices made by households, firms, and government and of how these choices affect the markets for goods and services. Let's look at three ways we can use microeconomic analysis.

A CLOSER LOOK   Even Kids Respond to Incentives

To illustrate the notion that people are rational and respond to incentives, consider an experiment conducted by researchers at St. Luke's Roosevelt Hospital in New York City.[8] The researchers addressed the following question: If a child must pedal a stationary bicycle to run a television set, will he watch less TV?

The researchers randomly assigned obese children, age 8 to 12, to two types of TVs. The first had a stationary bicycle in front of the TV, but the TV operated independently of the bicycle: No pedaling was required to operate the TV. In contrast, the second type of TV worked only if the child pedaled a bike facing the TV. The kids in the control group (no pedaling required) watched an average of 21 hours of TV per week, whereas the kids in the treatment group (pedaling required) watched just two hours per week. In other words, kids respond to incentives, watching less TV when the cost of watching is higher.

To Understand Markets and Predict Changes

One reason for studying microeconomics is to better understand how markets work. Once you know how markets operate, you can use economic analysis to predict how various events affect product prices and quantities. In this book, we answer dozens of practical questions about markets and how they operate. Let's look at one practical question that can be answered with some simple economic analysis.

How would a tax on beer affect the number of highway deaths among young adults? Research has shown that the number of highway fatalities among young adults is roughly proportional to the total beer consumed by that group. A tax on beer would make the product more expensive, and young adults, like other beer drinkers, would therefore consume less of it. Consequently, a tax that decreases beer consumption by 10% will decrease highway deaths among young adults by about 10% too.

To Make Personal and Managerial Decisions

On the personal level, we use economic analysis to decide how to spend our time, what career to pursue, and how to spend and save the money we earn. As workers, we use economic analysis to decide how to produce goods and services, how much to produce, and how much to charge for them. Let's use some economic analysis to look at a practical question confronting someone considering starting a business.

If the existing music stores in your city are profitable, and you have enough money to start your own music store, should you do it? If you enter this market, the competition among the stores for consumers will heat up, leading to lower prices for CDs. In addition, your costs may be higher than the costs of the stores that are already established. It would be sensible to enter the market only if you expect a small drop in price and a small difference in cost. Of course, there is the risk that the existing stores may try to protect their market shares by cutting prices and increasing their advertising. Indeed, entering what appears to be a lucrative market may turn out to be a financial disaster.

To Evaluate Public Policies

Although modern societies use markets to make most of the decisions concerning production and consumption, the government has several important roles in a market-based society. We can use economic analysis to determine how well the government performs its roles in the market economy. We can also explore the trade-offs associated with various public policies. Let's look at a practical question about public policy.

Like other innovations, prescription drugs are protected by patents, giving the developer the exclusive right to sell the drug for a fixed period of time. Once the patent expires, generic versions of a drug are marketed, causing prices to drop. Should drug patents be shorter? There are some trade-offs associated with shortening the patent. The good news is that a shorter patent means that generic versions of the drug will be available sooner, so prices will be lower. The bad news is that a shorter patent means the payoff from developing new drugs will be smaller, so drug companies won't develop as many new drugs. The question is whether the benefit of shorter patents (lower prices) exceeds the cost (fewer drugs developed).

Preview of Coming Attractions: Macroeconomics

Macroeconomics

The study of the nation's economy as a whole.

Macroeconomics is the study of the nation's economy as a whole. In macroeconomics we learn about important topics that are regularly discussed in newspapers and on television, including unemployment, inflation, the budget deficit, and the trade deficit. Macroeconomics explains why economies grow and change and why economic growth is sometimes interrupted. Let's look at three ways we can use macroeconomics:

To Understand Why Economies Grow

As we discussed earlier in the chapter, the world economy has been growing in recent decades, with per capita income increasing by about 1.5% per year. Increases in income translate into a higher standard of living for consumers—better cars, houses, and clothing, and more options for food, entertainment, and travel. People in a growing economy can consume more of all goods and services because the economy has more of the resources needed to produce these products. Macroeconomics explains why some of these resources increase over time and how an increase in these resources translates into a higher standard of living. Let's look at a practical question about economic growth:

Why do some countries grow much faster than others? In recent decades, the economic growth rate was 2.1% per year in the United States, compared to 2.4% in Mexico and 2.8% in France. But in some countries, the economy actually shrunk, and per capita income dropped. Among the countries with declining income were Romania, Sierra Leone, Haiti, and Zambia. In the fastest-growing countries, citizens save a large fraction of the money they earn. Firms can then borrow the funds saved to purchase machinery and equipment that make their workers more productive. The fastest-growing countries also have well-educated workforces, allowing firms to quickly adopt new technologies that increase worker productivity.

To Understand Economic Fluctuations

All economies, including ones that experience a general trend of growth, are subject to economic fluctuations, including periods when the economy shrinks. During an economic downturn, some of the economy's resources are idle. Many workers are unemployed, and many factories and stores are closed. By contrast, sometimes the economy grows too rapidly, causing inflation. Macroeconomics helps us understand why these fluctuations occur—why the economy sometimes cools and sometimes overheats—and what we can do to moderate the fluctuations. Let's look at a practical question about economic fluctuations.

Should Congress and the president do something to reduce the unemployment rate? If unemployment is very high, they may want to reduce it. However, it is important not to reduce the unemployment rate too much because, as we'll see later in the book, a low unemployment rate will cause inflation. Moreover, unemployment can't be reduced overnight. Therefore, it is sensible to take action only if we believe that inaction will cause persistent unemployment.

To Make Informed Business Decisions

A third reason for studying macroeconomics is to make informed business decisions. A manager who intends to borrow money for a new factory or store could use knowledge of macroeconomics to predict the effects of current public policies on interest rates and then decide whether to borrow the money now or later. Similarly, a manager must keep an eye on the inflation rate to help decide how much to charge for the firm's products and how much to pay workers. A manager who studies macroeconomics will be better equipped to understand the complexities of unemployment, interest rates, and inflation and how they affect the firm.

A CLOSER LOOK

"Dismal" Depends On Your Point of View

You may have heard economics called "the dismal science." Economic historian David Levy recently discovered that the label comes from the British essayist Thomas Carlyle,[9] who in 1849 wrote that economics was "dismal, dreary, and desolate" because it found "the secret of the universe in supply and demand." Just like economists today, economists in the nineteenth century argued that markets empower common people to make their own choices. In contrast, Carlyle believed that most people were incapable of making good choices for themselves and should rely on the advice of religious and civic leaders. Given Carlyle's discomfort with individual choice, it's not surprising that he was hostile to markets (supply and demand).

So what did Carlyle find so "dismal" about individual choice and markets? Carlyle wrote his essay "Occasional Discourse on the Negro Question" 16 years after the emancipation of black slaves in the West Indies. Emancipation extended market choices to former slaves, allowing them to voluntarily participate in markets and decide for themselves what to produce. They could continue to produce the export products they had produced as slaves—cinnamon, pepper, and other spices for British consumers—or they could instead produce food for themselves. They chose food over spices, much to the dismay of Carlyle. In Carlyle's mind, economics was dismal because the application of its fundamental ideas—individual choice and markets—didn't result in an outcome he preferred—cheap spices for British consumers.

SUMMARY

This chapter explains what economics is and why it is useful. Economics is about making choices when the options are limited. We can use economic analysis to understand the consequences of our choices, as individuals, organizations, and society as a whole. Here are the main points of the chapter.

1 Positive analysis answers the questions "What *is*?" or "What *will be*?"
2 Normative analysis answers the question "What *ought to be*?"

3 To think like an economist, we (a) use assumptions to simplify, (b) use the notion of *ceteris paribus* to focus on the relationship between two variables, and (c) think in marginal terms.
4 Rational people respond to incentives.
5 We use microeconomics to understand how markets work, make personal and managerial decisions, and evaluate the merits of public policies.
6 We use macroeconomics to understand why an economy grows, understand economic fluctuations, and make informed business decisions.

KEY TERMS

ceteris paribus, 10
economics, 3
macroeconomics, 14

marginal change, 10
microeconomics, 12
normative economics, 5

positive economics, 4
scarcity, 3
variable, 9

PROBLEMS AND DISCUSSION QUESTIONS

1 President Truman had a sign on his desk that read, "The Buck Stops Here." Is the philosophy behind this sign consistent with his complaint about two-handed economists?
2 "If I study one more hour for my economics exam, I expect my grade to increase by 3 points." List the variables that are assumed to be fixed in the statement.

3 It's your first day on your job in the advertising department of a baseball team. Your boss wants to know whether it is sensible to run one more television advertisement for an upcoming game. List the relevant marginal questions.

MODEL ANSWERS

Answers: Test Your Understanding

1 What products do we produce? How do we produce the products? Who consumes the products?
2 Economists discuss scarcity, alternatives, and trade-offs.
3 Positive analysis answers the questions "What *is*?" or "What *will be*?" Normative analysis answers the question "What *ought to be*?"

4 To think like an economist, we (a) use assumptions to simplify, (b) use the notion of *ceteris paribus* to focus on the relationship between two variables, and (c) think in marginal terms.
5 "If I attend one more lecture, by how much will my exam grade increase?"

NOTES

1. Dan Fuller, and Doris Geide-Stevenson, "Consensus Among Economists: Revisited," *Journal of Economic Education*, Fall 2003, pp. 369–387.
2. Texas Transportation Institute, *2002 Urban Mobility Study* (*http://mobility.tamu.edu/ums/*).
3. William Easterly, *The Elusive Quest for Growth* (Cambridge MA: MIT Press, 2001), Chapter 1.
4. William Easterly, *The Elusive Quest for Growth* (Cambridge MA: MIT Press, 2001).
5. World Bank, *World Development Report 2000/2001: Attacking Poverty* (New York: Oxford University Press, 2000).
6. Alfred Marshall, *Principles of Economics*, 9th ed., edited by C.W. Guillebaud (London: Macmillan, 1961 [first published in 1920]), p. 366.
7. Adam Smith, *An Inquiry into the Nature and Causes of the Wealth of Nations* (First published in 1776; New York, Random House, 1973), Book 2, Chapter 3.
8. Myles Faith et al., "Effects of Contingent Television on Physical Activity and Television Viewing in Obese Children," *Pediatrics* vol. 107, May 2001, pp. 1043–1048; *USA Today*, April 19, 1999, p. 1.
9. David Levy, *How the Dismal Science Got Its Name: Classical Economics and the Ur-Test of Racial Politics* (Ann Arbor, MI: University of Michigan Press, 2001); Thomas Carlyle, "Occasional Discourse on the Negro Question," *Fraser's Magazine for Town and Country*, 40 (1849), p. 672; Thomas Carlyle, *Past and Present*, edited by Richard D. Altick (Boston, MA: Houghton Mifflin, 1965), p. 211.

APPENDIX

Using Graphs and Formulas

In this appendix, we review the mechanics of graphing. You'll recognize most of the simple graphs and formulas in this appendix because they were covered in your high school mathematics. We'll review them here to prepare you to use them as you begin your own economic analysis.

Using Graphs to Show Relationships

A graph is a visual representation of the relationship between two variables. As we saw earlier in Chapter 1, a variable is a measure of something that can take on different values. For example, suppose that you have a part-time job and you are interested in the relationship between the number of hours you work and your weekly income. The relevant variables are the hours you work per week and your weekly income.

We can use a table of numbers such as Table 1A.1 to show the relationship between time worked and income. Let's assume that your weekly allowance from your parents is $40 and your part-time job pays $8 per hour. If you work 10 hours per week, for

TABLE 1A.1				
Hours worked per week	0	10	22	30
Income per week	$40	$120	$216	$280

Relationship Between Work Time and Income

example, your weekly income is $120 ($40 from your parents and $80 from your job). The more you work, the higher your weekly income: If you work 22 hours, your weekly income is $216; if you work 30 hours, it is $280.

Drawing a Graph

A graph makes it easier to see the relationship between time worked and income. To draw a graph, we perform seven simple steps:

1. Draw a horizontal line to represent the first variable. In Figure 1A.1, we measure time worked along the horizontal axis (also known as the *x* axis). As we move to the right along the horizontal axis, the number of hours worked increases, from zero to 30 hours.
2. Draw a vertical line intersecting the first line to represent the second variable. In Figure 1A.1, we measure income along the vertical axis (also known as the *y* axis). As we move up along the vertical axis, income increases from zero to $280.
3. Pick a combination of time worked and income from the table of numbers. From the second column, for instance, time worked is 10 hours and income is $120.
4. Find the point on the horizontal axis with that number of hours worked—10 hours worked—and draw a dashed line vertically straight up from that point.
5. Find the point on the vertical axis with the income corresponding to those hours worked ($120) and draw a dashed line horizontally straight to the right from that point.
6. The intersection of the dashed lines shows the combination of those hours worked and the income for working those hours. Point *b* shows the combination of 10 hours worked and $120 income.
7. Repeat steps 3 through 6 for different combinations of work time and income from the table of numbers. Once you have a series of points on the graph (*b*, *c*, and *d*), you can connect them to draw a curve that shows the relationship between hours worked and income.

Positive relationship
A relationship in which an increase in the value of one variable increases the value of another variable.

Negative relationship
A relationship in which an increase in the value of one variable decreases the value of another variable.

There is a **positive relationship** between two variables if an increase in the value of one variable increases the value of the other variable. An increase in the time you work increases your income, so there is a positive relationship between the two variables. As you increase the time you work, you move upward along the curve shown in Figure 1A.1 to higher income levels.

There is a **negative relationship** between two variables if an increase in the value of one variable decreases the value of the other variable. For example, there is a negative relationship between the amount of time you work and your performance in

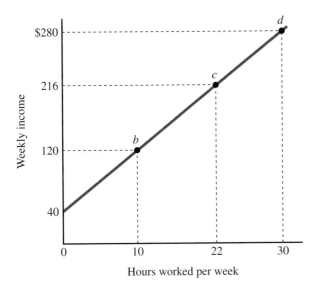

FIGURE 1A.1

Relationship Between Hours Worked and Total Income

There is a positive relationship between the amount of work time and income. The slope of the curve is $8: Each additional hour of work increases income by $8.

school. Some people refer to a positive relationship as a *direct* relationship and to a negative relationship as an *inverse* relationship.

Computing the Slope

How sensitive is one variable to changes in the other variable? We can use the slope of the curve to measure this sensitivity. The **slope of a curve** is the change in the variable on the vertical axis resulting from a one-unit increase in the variable on the horizontal axis. Once we pick two points on a curve, we can compute the slope as follows:

Slope of a curve
The change in the variable on the vertical axis resulting from a one-unit increase in the variable on the horizontal axis.

$$\text{slope} = \frac{\text{vertical difference between two points}}{\text{horizontal difference between two points}}$$

To compute the slope of a curve, we take four steps:

1 Pick two points on the curve: For example, points *b* and *c* in Figure 1A.1.
2 Compute the vertical distance between the two points (also known as the rise). For points *b* and *c*, the vertical distance between the points is $96 ($216 − $120).
3 Compute the horizontal distance between the same two points (also known as the run). For points *b* and *c*, the horizontal distance between the points is 12 hours (22 hours − 10 hours).
4 Divide the vertical distance by the horizontal distance to get the slope. The slope between points *b* and *c* is $8 per hour:

$$\text{slope} = \frac{\text{vertical difference}}{\text{horizontal difference}} = \frac{96}{12} = 8$$

In this case, a 12-hour increase in time worked increases income by $96, so the increase in income per hour of work is $8, which makes sense because this is the hourly wage.

Because the curve is a straight line, the slope is the same at all points along the curve. You can check this yourself by using the values between points *c* and *d* to calculate the slope.

Moving Along the Curve Versus Shifting the Curve

Up to this point, we've explored the effect of changes in variables that cause movement along a given curve. In Figure 1A.1, we see the relationship between a student's hours of work (on the horizontal axis) and her income (on the vertical axis). The student's income also depends on her allowance and her wage; so we can make two observations about the curve in Figure 1A.1:

1 To draw this curve, we must specify the weekly allowance ($40) and the hourly wage ($8).

2 The curve shows that an increase in time worked increases the student's income, *ceteris paribus.* In this case, we are assuming that her allowance and her wage are fixed.

A change in the student's weekly allowance will shift the curve showing the relationship between time worked and income. In Figure 1A.2, when the allowance increases from $40 to $70, the curve shifts upward by $30. For a given time worked, the student's income increases by $30. Now the income associated with 10 hours of work and the higher allowance is $150 (point *z*), compared to $120 with 10 hours of work and the original allowance (point *b*). In general, an increase in the allowance shifts the curve upward and leftward: For a given amount of time worked, the student will have more income (an upward shift as a result of the increased allowance). To reach a given amount of income, the student needs fewer hours of work (a leftward shift).

FIGURE 1A.2

Shifting the Curve
To draw a curve showing the relationship between hours worked and total income, we assume that the weekly allowance ($40) and the wage ($8) are fixed. An increase in the weekly allowance form $40 to $70 shifts the curve upward by $30: For each quantity of work hours, income is $30 higher.

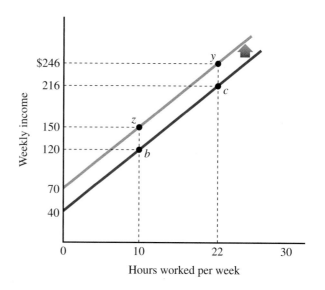

This book uses dozens of two-dimensional curves, each of which shows the relationship between only two variables. That is all a single curve can show. A common error is to forget that a single curve tells only part of the story. In Figure 1A.2, we needed two curves to show what happened when we looked at three variables (work time, allowance, and income). Here are some simple rules that will help us avoid this error:

▶ A change in one of the variables shown on the graph causes movement along the curve. In Figure 1A.2, an increase in work time causes movement along the curve from point *b* to point *c*.
▶ A change in one of the variables that is not shown on the graph (one of the variables held fixed in drawing the curve) shifts the entire curve. In Figure 1A.2, an increase in the allowance causes the entire curve to shift upward.

Negative and Nonlinear Relationships

We can use a graph to show a negative relationship between two variables. Consider a consumer who has a monthly budget of $300 to spend on CDs (at a price of $20 per CD) and cassette tapes (at a price of $10 per tape). Table 1A.2 shows the relationship between the number of CDs purchased and the number of tapes purchased. If the consumer buys 5 CDs in a certain month, he will spend a total of $100 on CDs, leaving $200 to spend on tapes. With the $200, he can buy 20 tapes at a price of $10 per tape. As the number of CDs increases, the number of tapes decreases, from 20 tapes and 5 CDs, to 10 tapes and 10 CDs, to zero tapes and 15 CDs.

Using the seven-step process outlined earlier, we can use the numbers in Table 1A.2 to draw a curve showing this negative relationship. In Figure 1A.3, the curve is negatively sloped: The more the consumer spends on CDs, the fewer tapes he can buy. We can use points *e* and *f* to compute the slope of the curve. The slope is −2 tapes per CD: A five-unit increase in CDs (the horizontal difference, or the run) decreases the number of tapes by 10 (the vertical difference, or the rise):

$$\text{slope} = \frac{\text{vertical difference}}{\text{horizontal difference}} = \frac{-10}{5} = -2$$

The curve is a straight line with a constant slope of −2 tapes per CD.

We can use a graph to show a nonlinear relationship between two variables. Panel A of Figure 1A.4 shows the relationship between study time and the exam grade that results from study time. Although the exam grade increases as study time increases, the grade increases at a decreasing rate; that means the increase in grade is smaller and

Number of CDs purchased	0	5	10	15
Number of tapes purchased	30	20	10	0

TABLE 1A.2

Relationship Between CDs and Tapes

...

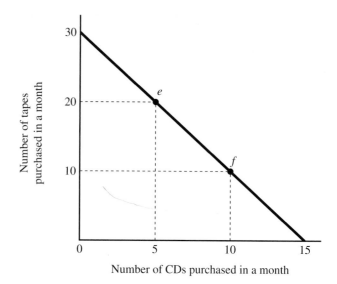

FIGURE 1A.3

A Negative Relationship Between CD Purchases and Tape Purchases

There is a negative relationship between the number of CDs purchased and the number of cassette tapes purchased. Because the price of CDs is $20 and the price of tapes is $10, the slope of the curve is –2 tapes per CD: Each additional CD decreases the number of tapes by 2.

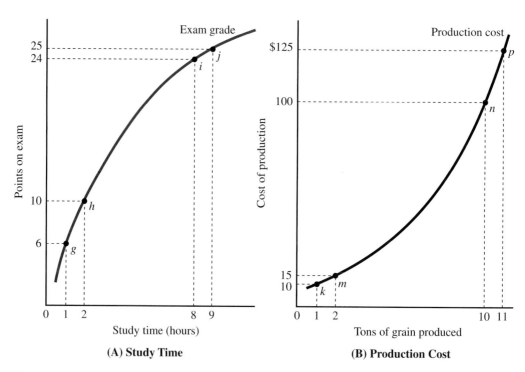

(A) Study Time

(B) Production Cost

FIGURE 1A.4 Nonlinear Relationships

(A) Study time There is a positive and nonlinear relationship between study time and the grade on an exam. As study time increases, the exam grade increases at a decreasing rate. For example, the second hour of study increases the grade by 4 points (from 6 points to 10 points), but the ninth hour of study increases the grade by only 1 point (from 24 points to 25 points).

(B) Production cost There is a positive and nonlinear relationship between the quantity of grain produced and total production cost. As the quantity increases, total cost increases at an increasing rate. For example, to increase production from 1 ton to 2 tons, production cost increases by $5 (from $10 to $15), but to increase production from 10 to 11 tons, total cost increases by $25 (from $100 to $125).

smaller for each additional hour of study. For example, the second hour of study increases the grade by 4 points (from 6 points to 10 points), but the ninth hour of study increases the grade by only 1 point (from 24 points to 25 points). This is a non-linear relationship: The slope of the curve changes as we move along the curve. In Figure 1A.4, the slope decreases as we move to the right along the curve: The slope is 4 between points g and h but only 1 between points i and j.

Another possibility for a nonlinear curve is that the slope increases (the curve becomes steeper) as we move to the right along the curve. This is shown in Panel B of Figure 1A.4. The slope of the curve increases as the amount of grain increases, meaning that total production cost increases at an increasing rate. If the producer increases production from 2 tons to 3 tons, the total cost increases by $5 (from $10 to $15). On the upper portion of the curve, if the producer increases production from 10 to 11 tons, the total cost increases by $25 (from $100 to $125).

Using Formulas to Compute Values

Economists often use formulas to compute the values of the relevant variables. Here is a brief review of the mechanics of formulas.

Computing Percentage Changes

In many cases, the formulas that economists use involve percentage changes. In this book, we use the simple approach to computing percentage changes: We divide the change in the variable by the initial value of the variable and then multiply by 100. For example, if the price of pizzas increases from $20 to $22, the percentage change is 10%: The change ($2) divided by the initial value ($20) is 0.10; multiplying this number by 100 generates a percentage change of 10%:

$$\text{percentage change} = \frac{\text{absolute change}}{\text{initial value}} = \frac{2}{20} = 0.10 = 10\%$$

Going in the other direction, if the price decreases from $20 to $19, the percentage change is −5%: The change (−$1) divided by the initial value ($20) is −0.05, or −5%. The alternative to the simple approach is the midpoint approach, under which the percentage change equals the absolute change in the variable divided by the average value or the midpoint of the variable. For example, if the price of pizza increases from $20 to $22, the computed percentage change under the midpoint approach would be 9.52381%:

$$\text{percentage change} = \frac{\text{absolute change}}{\text{average value}} = \frac{2}{(20 + 22)/2}$$

$$= \frac{2}{21} = 0.0952381 = 9.52381\%$$

If the change in the variable is relatively small, the extra precision associated with the midpoint approach is usually not worth the extra effort. The simple approach allows us to spend less time doing tedious arithmetic and more time doing economic analysis. In this book, we use the simple approach to compute percentage changes: If the price increases from $20 to $22, the price has increased by 10%.

If we know a percentage change, we can translate it into an absolute change. For example, if a price has increased by 10% and the initial price is $20, then we add 10% of the initial price ($2 is 10% of $20) to the initial price ($20), for a new price of $22. If the price decreases by 5%, we subtract 5% of the initial price ($1 is 5% of $20) from the initial price ($20) for a new price of $19.

Using Formulas to Compute Missing Values

It will often be useful to compute the value of the numerator or the denominator of a formula. To do so, we use simple algebra to rearrange the formula to put the missing variable on the left side of the equation. For example, consider the relationship between time worked and income. The formula for the slope is

$$\text{slope} = \frac{\text{difference in income}}{\text{difference in work time}}$$

If we're interested in how much more income you'll earn from more work hours, we rearrange the formula by multiplying both sides of the equation by the difference in work time:

$$\text{slope} \times \text{difference in work} = \text{difference in income}$$

Then swapping sides, we get

$$\text{difference in income} = \text{slope} \times \text{difference in work time}$$

For example, if the slope is $8 and you work seven extra hours, your increase in income will be $56, computed as $8 per hour times seven hours.

We can use the same process to compute the difference in work time required to achieve a target change in income. In this case, we multiply both sides of the slope formula by the difference in work time and then divide both sides by the slope. The result is

$$\text{difference in work time} = \frac{\text{difference in income}}{\text{slope}}$$

For example, to achieve a target of $56 more income, you need to work seven hours, computed as $56/$8 per hour.

KEY TERMS

PROBLEMS AND DISCUSSION QUESTIONS

1 Suppose you belong to a tennis club that has a monthly fee of $100 and a charge of $5 per hour for court time to play tennis.
  a. Use a curve to show the relationship between the monthly bill from the club and the hours of tennis played.
  b. What is the slope of the curve?
  c. If you increase your monthly tennis time by three hours, by how much will your monthly bill increase?

2 Suppose that to make pizza, Terry uses three ingredients: tomato sauce, dough, and cheese. Terry initially uses 100 gallons of tomato sauce per day, and the cost of the other ingredients (dough, cheese) is $500 per day.
  a. Draw a curve to show the relationship between the price of tomato sauce and the daily cost of producing pizza (for prices between $1 and $5).
  b. To draw the curve, what variables are assumed to be fixed?
  c. What sort of changes would cause movement upward along the curve?
  d. What is the slope of the curve?
  e. What sort of changes would cause the entire curve to shift upward?

3 Compute the percentage changes for the following changes:

Initial Value	New Value	Percentage Change
10	11	_____
100	98	_____
50	53	_____

4 The price of jeans decreases by 15%. If the original price was $20, what is the new price?

5 Suppose the slope of a curve showing the relationship between the number of burglaries per month (on the vertical axis) and the number of police officers (on the horizontal axis) is −0.5 burglaries per police officer. Use the slope formula to compute the change in the number of burglaries resulting from hiring eight additional police officers.

6 Complete the statement: A change in one of the variables shown on a graph causes movement _____ a curve, while a change in one of the variables that is not shown on the graph _____ the curve.

The Key Principles of Economics

our student film society is looking for an auditorium to use for an all-day Hitchcock film program and is willing to pay up to $200 for one. Your college has a new auditorium that would be perfect for your event. However, according to the campus facility manager, "The daily rent on the auditorium is $450, an amount that includes $300 to help pay for the cost of building the auditorium, $50 to help pay for insurance, and $100 to cover the extra costs of electricity and janitorial services for a one-day event."

How should you respond to the facility manager? As we'll see, if you could persuade the manager to use the marginal principle—one of the five key principles of economics—you should be able to get the facility for an amount between $100 and $200.

I n this chapter, we introduce five key principles that provide a foundation for economic analysis. A principle is a self-evident truth that most people readily understand and accept. For example, most people readily accept the principle of gravity. As you read through the book, you will see the five key principles of economics again and again as you do your own economic analysis. Here are some practical questions we answer in this chapter using those principles:

1 What do military goods such as bombs and warships really cost in terms of what we sacrifice to pay for them?

2 When is it sensible to tighten the emissions standards on cars in order to reduce pollution? Does it ever make sense to loosen emissions standards?

3 After a market transaction is completed, both people—buyer and seller—usually say, "Thank you." Are they just being polite, or is there a reason to be thankful?

4 If a firm doubles its workforce, is the company's total output likely to double too?

5 If you graduate with $20,000 in student loans, which type of an economy would make it easier for you to repay them: one with steady prices, one with rising prices (inflation), or one with falling prices (deflation)?

The Principle of Opportunity Cost

Opportunity cost
What you sacrifice to get something.

The principle of **opportunity cost** incorporates the notion of scarcity: No matter what we do, there is always a trade-off. We must trade off one thing for another because resources are limited and can be used in different ways. By acquiring something, we use up resources that could have been used to acquire something else. The notion of opportunity cost allows us to measure this trade-off.

 Principle OF OPPORTUNITY COST
The opportunity cost of something is what you sacrifice to get it.

Most decisions involve several alternatives. For example, if you spend an hour studying for an economics exam, you have one less hour to pursue other activities. To determine the opportunity cost of something, we look at what you consider the best of these "other" activities. For example, suppose the alternatives to studying economics are studying for a history exam and working in a job that pays $10 per hour. If you consider studying for history a better use of your time than working, then the opportunity cost of studying economics is what you sacrifice by not studying history. We ignore the work option because that is not the best alternative use of your time.

How can we measure the opportunity cost of an hour spent studying for an economics exam? Suppose an hour of studying history—instead of economics—would increase your grade on a history exam by four points. In this case the opportunity cost of an hour studying economics is four points lost on the history exam. On the other hand, if the best alternative to studying economics were working, then the opportunity cost would be the $10 your could earn in your job.

The principle of opportunity cost can also be applied to decisions about how to spend money on a fixed budget. For example, suppose that you have a fixed budget to spend on music. You can either buy your music at a local music store for $15 per CD or you can buy your music online for $1 per song. The opportunity cost of one CD is 15 one-dollar online songs. A hospital with a fixed salary budget can increase the number of doctors only at the expense of nurses or physician's assistants. If a doctor costs five times as much as a nurse, the opportunity cost of a doctor is five nurses.

In some cases, a product that appears to be free actually has a cost. That's why economists are fond of saying, "There's no such thing as a free lunch." Suppose someone offers to buy you lunch if you agree to listen to a sales pitch for a time-share condominium. Although you don't pay any money for the lunch, there is an opportunity cost because you could spend that time in another way. The lunch isn't free because you sacrifice an hour of your time to get it.

Opportunity Cost and the Production Possibilities Curve

Factors of production
The inputs used to produce goods and services.

Just as individual people face limits, so do entire economies. The production possibilities curve shown in Figure 2.1 illustrates the principle of opportunity cost for an entire economy. The ability of an economy to produce goods and services is determined by its **factors of production**, including labor, land, and capital (machines and buildings). Figure 2.1 shows a production possibilities graph for an economy that produces products on farms (wheat, barley, beef) and factory products (cars, computers, boats, steel, lamps,

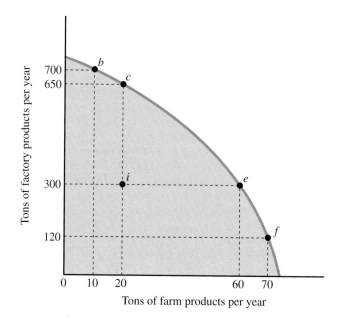

desks). The horizontal axis shows the quantity of farm products produced by the economy, and the vertical axis shows the quantity of factory products produced. The shaded area shows all the possible combinations of the two goods that can be produced. At point *b* for example, the economy can produce 700 tons of factory products and 10 tons of farm products. By contrast, at point *i*, the economy can produce 300 tons of factory goods and 20 tons of farm products. The set of points on the border between the shaded and unshaded area is called the **production possibilities curve** (or *production possibilities frontier*) because it separates the combinations that are attainable (the shaded area within the curve and the curve itself) from the combinations that are not attainable (the unshaded area outside the curve). The points on the curve show the combinations that are possible if the economy's resources are fully employed or "maxed" out.

The production possibilities curve illustrates the notion of opportunity cost. If an economy is fully utilizing its resources, it can produce more of one product only if it produces less of another product. So, to produce more farm goods, we must take resources away from factories. As we move resources out of factory production, the quantity of factory goods will decrease. For example, if we move from point *b* to point *c* along the production possibilities curve in Figure 2.1, we sacrifice 50 tons of factory goods (700 tons − 650 tons) to get 10 more tons of farm goods (20 tons − 10 tons). Further down the curve, if we move from point *e* to point *f*, we sacrifice 180 tons of factory goods to get the same 10-ton increase in farm goods.

Why is the production possibilities curve bowed outwards, with the opportunity cost farm goods increasing as we move down the curve? The reason is that resources are not perfectly adaptable for the production of both goods. Some resources are more suitable for factory production, whereas others are more suitable for farming. Starting at point *b*, the economy uses its most fertile land to produce farm goods. A 10-ton increase in farm goods reduces the quantity of factory goods by only 50 tons because plenty of fertile land is available for conversion to farming. As the economy moves downward along the production possibilities curve, farmers will be forced to use land that is progressively less fertile, so to increase farm output by 10 tons, more and more resources must be diverted from factory production. In the move from point *e* to point *f*, the land converted to farming is so poor that increasing farm output by 10 tons decreases factory output by 180 tons.

The production possibilities curve shows the production options for a given set of resources. As shown in Figure 2.2, an increase in the amount of resources available to the economy shifts the production possibilities outward. For example, if we start at point *d* and the economy's resources increase, we can produce more factory goods (point *g*), more farm goods (point *h*), or more of both goods (points between *g* and *h*). The curve will also shift outward as a result of technological innovations that allow us to produce more output with a given quantity of resources.

Production possibilities curve

A curve that shows the possible combinations of products that an economy can produce, given that its productive resources are fully employed and efficiently used.

Using the Principle: Military Spending, Collectibles

We can also use the principle of opportunity cost to explore the cost of military spending. In 1992, Malaysia bought two warships. For the price of the warships, the country instead could have provided safe drinking water for five million citizens who lacked it.[1] In other words, the opportunity cost of the warships was safe drinking water for five million

FIGURE 2.2

**Shifting the Production
Possibilities Curve**

An increase in the quantity
of resources in an economy
shifts the production
possibilities curve outward.
Starting from point *d*, a
nation could produce more
agricultural goods (point *h*),
more manufacturing goods
(point *g*), or more of both
goods (points between *g*
and *h*).

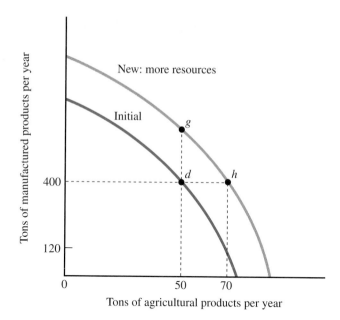

people. Likewise, in the United States, the opportunity cost of warships could be spent on housing programs for the homeless, or vice versa. For another interesting illustration of the trade-offs opportunity costs present, read "A Closer Look: Swords vs. Ecotels?"

What is the cost of buying a collectible good such as a baseball card, an antique Barbie doll, a Beanie Baby, or a work of art? Suppose you buy an antique Barbie doll for $1,000, intending to resell it for more money a year later. If the price doesn't change and you resell it for $1,000, does that mean that owning the doll for a year didn't cost you anything? Applying the principle of opportunity cost, you could have invested the $1,000 in a bank account earning 5% interest, so the cost of having the Barbie doll is the $50 you could have earned in a bank account during the year.

Using the Principle: The Cost of College

What is the opportunity cost of a college degree? Consider a student who spends a total of $40,000 for tuition and books. Instead of going to college, the student could have spent this money on a wide variety of goods, including housing, stereo equipment, and world

For Malaysia, the opportunity cost of a single battleship is safe drinking water for 2.5 million people.

travel. Part of the opportunity cost of college is the $40,000 worth of other goods the student sacrifices to pay for tuition and books. Also, instead of going to college, the student could have worked as a bank clerk for $20,000 per year and earned $80,000 over four years. That makes the total opportunity cost of this student's college degree $120,000:

Opportunity cost of money spent on tuition and books	$ 40,000
Opportunity cost of college time (four years at $20,000 per year)	80,000
Economic cost or total opportunity cost	$120,000

We haven't included the costs of food or housing in our computations of opportunity cost. That's because a student must eat and live somewhere even if he or she doesn't go to college. But if housing and food are more expensive in college, then we would include the extra costs of housing and food in our calculations.

There are other things to consider in a person's decision to attend college. As we'll see later, a college degree can increase a person's earning power, so there are benefits from a college degree. In addition, there is the thrill of learning and the pleasure of meeting new people. To make an informed decision about whether to attend college, we must compare the benefits to the opportunity costs.

A CLOSER LOOK

Swords vs. Ecotels?

The prophet Isaiah predicted, "They will beat their swords into plowshares, and their spears into pruning hooks." This quote illustrates the opportunity cost of military equipment: The opportunity cost of a sword is a plowshare; the opportunity cost of a spear is a pruning hook.

All over Central America, old military facilities are being transformed to give ecotourists a close look at the region's flora and fauna. In the middle of Panama's rain forest, a radar tower used earlier by the U.S. military has been transformed into a seven-room ecolodge, giving tourists from around the world the opportunity to watch king vultures soar above the forest and view howler monkeys swing from the trees.[2] *Audubon* magazine selected the tower, now called Canopy Tower, as one of the world's nine "ultimate outposts" for bird lovers.

On the Atlantic side of Panama, the infamous School of the Americas—where the U.S. military once educated Latin America military dictators in the arts of war—has been con-

The conversion of old military facilities into wildlife viewing sites like the Canopy Tower in Panama illustrates the notion of opportunity cost.

verted into a 310-room hotel. Its concrete amphitheater that once hosted military briefings is now being used as a vantage point for tourists viewing monkeys and tropical birds.

The Marginal Principle

The marginal principle provides a simple decision-making rule that helps individuals and organizations make decisions. Economists think in marginal terms, considering how a one-unit change in one variable affects the value of another variable and people's decisions. When we say *marginal*, we're looking at the effect of only a small, or incremental, change.

The marginal principle is based on a comparison of the marginal benefits and marginal costs of a particular activity. The **marginal benefit** of some activity is the extra benefit resulting from a small increase in the activity; for example, the extra revenue generated by keeping a barbershop open for one more hour. Similarly, the **marginal cost** is the additional cost resulting from a small increase in the activity; for example, the additional expense incurred by keeping the barbershop open for one more hour. Applying the marginal principle to the barber's problem, the barber should stay open for one more hour if the extra revenue from the additional hour is at least as large as the extra cost. In other words, people have an incentive to perform an activity if it provides them a marginal benefit over and above their marginal cost. When deciding whether to engage in an activity or how much to do, people should follow the marginal principle.

Marginal benefit
The extra benefit resulting from a small increase in some activity.

Marginal cost
The additional cost resulting from a small increase in some activity.

MARGINAL *Principle*

Increase the level of an activity if its marginal benefit exceeds its marginal cost; reduce the level of an activity if its marginal cost exceeds its marginal benefit. If possible, pick the level at which the activity's marginal benefit equals its marginal cost.

Thinking at the margin enables us to fine-tune our decisions. We can use the marginal principle to determine whether a one-unit increase in a variable would make us better off. Just as a barber could decide whether to keep the shop open for one more hour, you could decide whether to study one more hour for a psychology midterm. When we reach the level where the marginal benefit equals the marginal cost, the fine-tuning is done.

Example: How Many Movie Sequels?

To illustrate the marginal principle, let's consider movie sequels. When a movie is successful, its producer naturally thinks about doing another movie, continuing the story line with the same set of characters. If the first sequel is successful too, the producer thinks about producing a second sequel, then a third, and so on. We can use the marginal principle to explore the decision of how many movies to produce.

Table 2.1 shows the marginal benefits and marginal costs for movies. On the benefit side, a movie sequel typically generates about 30% less revenue than the original

TABLE 2.1

Marginal Benefits and Marginal Costs of Movie Sequels

Number of Movies	Marginal Benefit	Marginal Cost
1	$300 million	$125 million
2	$210 million	$150 million
3	$135 million	$175 million

movie, and revenue continues to drop for additional movies. In the second column of Table 2.1, the first movie generates $300 million in revenue (point *b*), the second generates $210 million, and the third generates $135 million. This is shown in Figure 2.3 as a negatively sloped marginal-benefit curve. In the United States, the typical movie costs about $50 million to produce and about $75 million to promote.[3] In the third column of Table 2.1, the cost of the first movie (the original) is $125 million. The marginal cost increases with the number of movies because film stars typically demand higher salaries to appear in sequels. For example, Angelina Jolie was paid more for *Tomb Raider 2* than for *Tomb Raider*, and the actors in *Charlie's Angels 2* received raises too. In Table 2.1, the marginal cost increases to $150 million for the second movie and to $175 for the third. This is shown in Figure 2.3 as a positively sloped marginal-cost curve.

In this example, the first two movies are profitable, but the third is not. For the original movie, the marginal benefit ($300 million) exceeds the marginal cost ($125 million), generating a profit of $175 million. Although the second movie has a higher cost and a lower benefit, it is profitable because the marginal benefit still exceeds the marginal cost, so the profit on the second movie is $60 million ($210 million – $150 million). In contrast, the marginal cost of the third movie of $175 million exceeds its marginal benefit of only $135 million, so the third movie is a losing proposition. In this example, the movie producer should stop after the second movie.

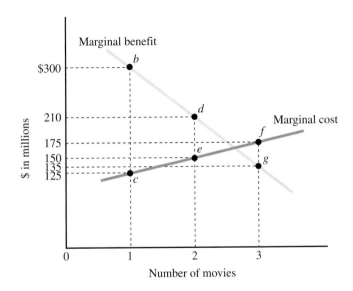

FIGURE 2.3

The Marginal Principle and Movie Sequels
The marginal benefit of movies in a series decreases because revenue falls off with each additional movie, whereas the marginal cost increases because actors demand higher salaries. The marginal benefit exceeds the marginal cost for the first two movies, so it is sensible to produce two, but not three, movies.

Although this example shows that only two movies are profitable, other outcomes are possible. If the revenue for the third movie were larger, making the marginal benefit greater than the marginal cost, it would be sensible to produce the third movie. Similarly, if the marginal cost of the third movie were lower—if the actors didn't demand such high salaries—the third movie could be profitable. Indeed, there are many examples of movies with multiple sequels. Conversely, there are many examples of profitable movies that didn't result in any sequels. In these cases, the expected drop off in revenues and the run-up in costs for the second movie were large enough to make a sequel unprofitable.

Using the Marginal Principle: Renting College Facilities, Emissions Standards

Recall the chapter opener about renting a college auditorium to your student film society. Suppose the society offers to pay $150 for using the auditorium? Should the college accept the offer? The college could use the marginal principle to make the decision.

To decide whether to accept the group's offer, the college should determine the marginal cost of renting out the auditorium. The marginal cost equals the extra costs the college incurs by allowing the student group to use an otherwise vacant auditorium. In our example, the extra cost is $100 for additional electricity and janitorial services. It would be sensible for the college to rent the auditorium because the marginal benefit ($150 offered by the student group) exceeds the marginal cost ($100). In fact, the college should be willing to rent the facility for any amount greater than $100. If the students and the college's facility manager split the difference between the $200 the students are willing to pay and the $100 marginal cost, they would agree on a price of $150, leaving both parties better off by $50.

Most colleges do not use this sort of logic. Instead, they use complex formulas to compute the perceived cost of renting out a facility. In most cases, the perceived cost includes some costs that are unaffected by renting out the facility for the day. In our example, the facility manager included $300 worth of construction costs and $50 worth of insurance, for a total cost of $450 instead of just $100. Because many colleges include costs that aren't affected by the use of a facility, they overestimate the actual cost of renting out their facilities, missing opportunities to serve student groups and make some money at the same time.

We can use the marginal principle to analyze emissions standards for automobiles. The U.S. government specifies how much carbon monoxide a new car is allowed to emit per mile. The marginal question is: "Should the standard be stricter, with fewer units of carbon monoxide allowed?" On the benefit side, a stricter standard reduces health care costs resulting from pollution: If the air is cleaner, people with respiratory ailments will make fewer visits to doctors and hospitals, have lower medication costs, and lose fewer work days. On the cost side, a stricter standard requires more expensive control equipment on cars and may also reduce fuel efficiency. Using the marginal principle, the government should make the emissions standard stricter as long as the marginal benefit (savings in health care costs and work time lost) exceeds the marginal cost (the cost of additional equipment and extra fuel used).

Marginal Airlines Lives Up to Its Name

Marginal Airlines runs 10 flights per day at a total cost of $40,000, or an average of $4,000 per flight. On the tenth flight, there are only 20 passengers on the 40-seat aircraft. Each passenger pays $150, so the revenue from the tenth flight is only $3,000. Although the tenth flight doesn't seem to generate enough revenue to cover its costs, the company continues to run the flight. The managers of the airline are neither stupid nor irrational. Solve this puzzle: Why does the airline continue to run the flight?

The key to solving the puzzle is in the airline's name: Marginal Airlines bases its decision about running the tenth flight on the marginal benefit and marginal cost of the flight. The marginal benefit is the $3,000 in revenue from passengers. Although the average cost is $4,000 per flight, what matters is the *marginal* cost of the tenth flight. If the marginal cost of the tenth flight is only $2,000, the marginal benefit exceeds the marginal cost, and the airline can make $1,000 (equal to $3,000 − $2,000) by running the flight.

This example is based on the actual experience of Continental Airlines, which in the 1960s used the marginal principle to increase its profits.[4] At the time, the average cost of a flight was about $4,000, half of which involved fixed costs such as airport fees and the cost of running the reservation system. The other half of the average cost involved costs that varied with the number of flights, including the cost of a flight crew, jet fuel, and that wonderful airline food. These other costs added up to $2,000 per flight. In other words, the marginal cost of a flight was only $2,000, so running a flight that generated $3,000 in revenue was sensible. Using the marginal principle, Continental ran flights with up to half the seats empty, making money in the process. ∎

TEST Your Understanding

1. True or false: The cost of a master's degree in engineering equals tuition plus the cost of books.
2. Explain the logic behind the economist's quip, "There is no such thing as a free lunch."
3. If a bus company adds a third daily bus between two cities, the company's total costs will increase from $500 to $600 per day and its total revenue will increase by $150 per day. Should the company add the third bus?
4. If a company decides to replace a double-bladed razor with a triple-bladed razor, what does this mean about how much consumers are willing to pay for razors?

The Principle of Voluntary Exchange

The principle of voluntary exchange is based on the notion that people act in their own self-interest.

Principle OF VOLUNTARY EXCHANGE

A voluntary exchange between two people makes both people better off.

Self-interested people won't exchange one thing for another unless the trade makes them better off. Here are some examples.

▶ If you voluntarily exchange money for a college education, you must expect you'll be better off with a college education. The college voluntarily provides a college education in exchange for your money, so the college must be better off too.
▶ If you have a job, you voluntarily exchange your time for money, and your employer exchanges money for your labor services. Both you and your employer are better off as a result.

Exchange and Markets

Adam Smith stressed the importance of voluntary exchange as a distinctly human trait.[5] He noticed

> a propensity in human nature . . . to truck, barter, and exchange one thing for another. . . . It is common to all men, and to be found in no other . . . animals. . . . Nobody ever saw a dog make a fair and deliberate exchange of one bone for another with another dog.

Market

An arrangement that allows people to exchange things.

A **market** is an arrangement that allows people to exchange things. If participation in a market is voluntary, both buyer and seller must be better off as a result of a transaction. The next time you see a market transaction, listen to what people say after money changes hands. If both people say "Thank you," that's the principle of voluntary exchange in action: the double thank-you reveals that both people are better off.

The next chapter of the book explains the rationale for voluntary exchange. The alternative to exchange is self-sufficiency: Each of us could produce everything for ourselves. As we'll see in the next chapter, it is more sensible to specialize, doing what we do best and then buy products from other people, who in turn are doing what they do best. For example, if you are good with numbers but an awful carpenter, you could specialize in accounting and buy furniture from Woody, who could specialize in furniture and pay someone to do his bookkeeping. In general, exchange allows us to take advantage of differences in people's talents and skills.

The exchange principle tells us that both buyer and seller are made better off by an exchange. But under what circumstances can we infer that a market exchange makes society as a whole better off? If the exchange doesn't affect anyone else, then clearly the two market participants are better off and society as a whole is better off too. If, however, another person—a third party—is affected by the transaction, we can't be sure that the transaction makes society as a whole better off. Later in the book, we will explore what happens when a third party is either helped or harmed by a transaction. If these third parties are integrated into the exchange process as voluntary participants, the exchange principle will be relevant: A set of voluntary transactions will make all the participants better off.

The Principle of Diminishing Returns

Xena has a small copy shop, with one copying machine and one worker. When the backlog of orders piled up, she decided to hire a second worker, expecting that doubling her workforce would double the output of her copy shop from 500 pages per hour to 1,000. She was surprised when output increased to only 800 pages per hour. If she had known about the principle of diminishing returns, she would not have been surprised.

 Principle OF DIMINISHING RETURNS

Suppose output is produced with two or more inputs and we increase one input while holding the other input or inputs fixed. Beyond some point—called the point of diminishing returns—output will increase at a decreasing rate.

Xena added a worker (one input) while holding the number of copying machines (the other input) fixed. Because the two workers shared a single copying machine, each worker spent some time waiting for the machine to be available. As a result, adding the second worker increased the number of copies, but did not double the output. With a single worker and a single copy machine, Xena has reached the point of diminishing returns: That is, as she increases the number of workers, output increases, but at a decreasing rate. The first worker increases output by 500 pages (from 0 to 500), but the second worker increases output by only 300 pages (from 500 to 800).

This principle of diminishing returns is relevant when we try to produce more output in an existing production facility (a factory, a store, an office, or a farm) by increasing the number of workers sharing the facility. When we add a worker to the facility, each worker becomes less productive because he or she works with a smaller piece of the facility: There are more workers to share the machinery, equipment, and factory space. As we pack more and more workers into the factory, total output increases, but at a decreasing rate.

It's important to emphasize that diminishing returns occurs because one of the inputs to the production process is fixed. When a firm can vary all of its inputs, including the size of the production facility, the principle of diminishing returns is not relevant. For example, if a firm doubled all of its inputs, building a second factory and hiring a second workforce, we would expect the total output of the firm to at least double. The principle of diminishing returns does not apply when a firm is flexible in choosing all its inputs.

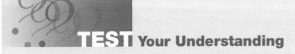 **TEST Your Understanding**

5. True or false: When two people involved in a market exchange say "Thank you" afterwards, they are merely being polite.

(continued)

6. When a table producer hired its tenth worker, the output of its factory increased by five tables per month. Would you expect the same increase in output for the twentieth worker and the thirtieth worker?

7. True or false: According to the principle of diminishing returns, an additional worker decreases total output.

The Real–Nominal Principle

One of the key ideas in economics is that people are interested not just in the amount of money they have but also in how much their money will buy.

REAL–NOMINAL *Principle*

What matters to people is the real value of money or income— its purchasing power—not the "face" value of money or income.

To illustrate this principle, suppose you work in your college bookstore to earn extra money for movies and newspapers. If your take-home pay is $10 per hour, is this a high wage or a low wage? The answer depends on the prices of the goods you buy. If a movie costs $4 and a newspaper costs $1, with one hour of work you could afford to see two movies and buy two papers. The wage may seem high enough for you. But if a movie costs $8 and a newspaper costs $2, an hour of work would buy only one movie and one paper, and the same $10 wage doesn't seem so high. This is the real–nominal principle in action: What matters is not how many dollars you earn, but what those dollars will purchase.

The real–nominal principle can explain how people choose the amount of money to carry around with them. Suppose you typically withdraw $40 per week from an ATM to cover your normal expenses. If the prices of all the goods you purchase during the week double, you would have to withdraw $80 per week to make the same purchases. The amount of money people carry around depends on the prices of the goods and services they buy.

Economists use special terms to express the ideas behind the real–nominal principle:

Nominal value

The face value of an amount of money.

Real value

The value of an amount of money in terms of what it can buy.

▶ The **nominal value** of an amount of money is simply its face value. For example, the nominal wage paid by the bookstore is $10 per hour.

▶ The **real value** of an amount of money is measured in terms of the quantity of goods the money can buy. For example, the real value of your bookstore wage would fall as the prices of movies and newspapers increase, even though your nominal wage stayed the same.

Economic Experiment

Producing Fold-its

Here is a simple economic experiment that takes about 15 minutes to run. The instructor places a stapler and a stack of paper on a table. Students produce "fold-its" by folding a page of paper in thirds and stapling both ends of the folded page. One student is assigned to inspect each fold-it to be sure that it is produced correctly. The experiment starts with a single student, or worker, who has one minute to produce as many fold-its as possible. After the instructor records the number of fold-its produced, the process is repeated with two students, three students, four students, and so on. The question is, "How does the number of fold-its change as the number of workers increases?" ●

Using the Principle: Government Programs, Statistics, and Repaying College Loans

Government officials use the real–nominal principle when they design public programs. For example, Social Security payments are increased each year to ensure that the checks received by the elderly and other recipients will purchase the same amount of goods and services, even if prices have increased.

The government also uses this principle when it publishes statistics about the economy. For example, when the government issues reports about changes in "real wages" in the economy over time, these statistics take into account the prices of the goods purchased by workers. Therefore, the real wage is stated in terms of its buying power, rather than its face value or nominal value.

For another application of the principle, recall the chapter-opening question about repaying college loans. Suppose you finish college this year with $20,000 in student loans payable in 10 years and start a job that pays $40,000 in the first year. If all prices in the economy are stable—including the price of labor (yours, too)—the real cost of repaying your loans is the half-year of work you must do to earn the $20,000. However, if prices and wages increase over the 10-year period, doubling your nominal wage to $80,000, it will take you only a quarter of a year to earn the $20,000. A general increase in prices lowers the real cost of your loan. If on the other hand, prices and wages decrease, dropping your annual salary to $20,000, it will take you a full year to earn the money to repay the loan. In other words, a general decrease in prices increases the real cost of your loan.

 **TEST** Your Understanding

8. Average hourly earnings in the United States increased between 1970 and 1993, but real hourly earnings fell. How could this occur? *(continued)*

9. Suppose your wage doubles and so do the prices of all consumer goods. Are you better off, worse off, or just as well off?

10. Suppose your savings account pays 4% per year: Each $100 in the bank grows to $104 over a one-year period. If prices increase by 3% per year, how much do you really gain by keeping $100 in the bank for a year?

USING THE TOOLS

We've explained the five key principles of economics, which provide the foundation of economic analysis. Here are some opportunities to use the principles to do your own economic analysis.

1. The Cost of an Army

Your job is to estimate the economic cost of maintaining an army for one year. There are 50 soldiers, who are picked at random from the population and forced to serve. Each soldier is paid $1,000 per year. The cost of supplies and equipment is $10,000 per year, and the military occupies a base that could be rented to the private sector for $30,000 per year. According to an economist, "The economic cost of the army is $1,040,000." Explain the logic behind the economist's calculation.

2. How Many Police Officers?

As the mayor of a city where the only crime is burglary, you must decide how many police officers to hire. The cost of each police officer (for salary, benefits, and general support) is $40,000 per year. Each burglary involves the loss of $5,000 worth of possessions. The first officer hired will reduce crime by 40 burglaries, and each additional officer will reduce crime by half as much as the previous one. How many officers should the city hire? Illustrate your answer with a completely labeled graph.

3. Tiger Woods as Weed Whacker

The swinging skills that make Tiger Woods one of the world's best golfers also make him a skillful weed whacker. If he can knock down weeds faster than the best gardener in town, should he take care of his own weeds? Explain.

4. Cost of Living in Different Cities

Suppose you are currently living and working in Cleveland, Ohio, earning a salary of $60,000 per year. Your boss has decided to transfer you to a California city where the housing is 50% more expensive. If your annual housing cost is $10,000 in Cleveland, how much higher must your salary be in California to generate the same real income?

SUMMARY

This chapter covers five key principles of economics, the simple, self-evident truths that most people readily accept. If you understand these principles, you are ready to read the rest of the book, which will show you how to do your own economic analysis. In fact, if you've done the exercises in this chapter, you're already doing economic analysis.

1 Principle of opportunity cost. The opportunity cost of something is what you sacrifice to get it.

2 Marginal principle. Increase the level of an activity if its marginal benefit exceeds its marginal cost; reduce the level if its marginal cost exceeds its marginal benefit. If possible, pick the level at which the marginal benefit equals the marginal cost.

3 Principle of voluntary exchange: A voluntary exchange between two people makes both people better off.

4 Principle of diminishing returns. Suppose that output is produced with two or more inputs and that we increase one input while holding the other inputs fixed. Beyond some point—called the *point of diminishing returns*—output will increase at a decreasing rate.

5 Real–nominal principle. What matters to people is the real value of money or income—its purchasing power—not the face value of money or income.

KEY TERMS

factors of production, 28
marginal benefit, 32
marginal cost, 32

market, 36
nominal value, 38
opportunity cost, 27

production possibilities curve, 29
real value, 38

PROBLEMS AND DISCUSSION QUESTIONS

1 Consider the following statements about costs. Are they correct? If not, provide a correct statement about the relevant cost.
   a. One year ago, I loaned $100 to a friend, and she just paid me back the whole $100. The loan didn't cost me anything.
   b. Our sawmill bought five truckloads of logs a year ago for $20,000. Today, we'll use the logs to make picnic tables. The cost of using the logs is $20,000.
   c. Our new football stadium was built on land that a wealthy alum donated to our university. The university didn't have to buy the land, so the cost of the stadium equals the $50 million construction cost.

2 Opie is currently renting a house for $800 per month, with utilities included in the rent. He just inherited an identical house from his grandmother. The market value of the inherited house is $200,000 (not expected to change) and the monthly costs for maintenance, insurance, and utilities add up to $100. If Opie moves into the inherited house, by how much will his monthly housing cost increase or decrease? If you don't have enough information to answer the ques-

tion, make up some numbers for the missing information and answer with your assumed numbers.

3 Jack left a job that paid $50,000 per year to start his own business in a building he owns. Similar buildings rent for $10,000 per year. Over the course of the year, Jack paid his part-time employees $75,000 and paid $150,000 for supplies. What is the economic cost of Jack's business?

4 You are about to buy a personal computer and must decide how much random-access memory (RAM) to have in the computer. Suppose each 128-megabyte block of RAM costs $40. For example, a computer with two blocks of memory (256 MB) costs $40 more than a computer with one block (128 MB). The marginal benefit of memory is $320 for the first block and decreases by half for each additional block, to $160 for the second block, $80 for the third block, and so on. How many blocks of memory should you get in your computer? Illustrate your answer with a graph.

5 Consider a city that must decide how many mobile cardiac arrest units (specially equipped ambulances designed to treat people immediately after a heart attack) to deploy. Explain how you

could use the marginal principle to help make the decision.

6 You are the manager of a firm that makes computers. If you had to decide how much output to produce in the next week, would you use the principle of diminishing returns? If you had to decide how much output to produce 10 years from now, would you use the principle of diminishing returns?

7 Your coffee shop has a single espresso machine. As the firm adds more and more workers, would you expect output (espressos per hour) to increase at a constant rate? Why or why not?

8 Explain this statement: In the last 10 years, the salaries of baseball players have increased in both real and nominal terms.

MODEL ANSWERS

Chapter-Opening Questions

1 To get a warship, we must sacrifice something else, such as safe drinking water for 2.5 million Malaysians.

2 According to the marginal principle, the standard should be made stricter if the marginal benefit (the savings in health care costs from a cleaner environment) exceeds the marginal cost (the cost of additional equipment and extra fuel).

3 According to the exchange principle, a voluntary exchange between two people makes both people better off.

4 If the firm experiences diminishing returns, output will increase but will not double.

5 A world with rising prices is best for a debtor because it causes higher wages. That means it will take less time to earn the $20,000 you owe. For example, if prices double, your wage will double too, so it will take you half as much time to earn money to pay back the loan.

Answers: Test Your Understanding

1 False. This statement ignores the opportunity cost of time spent in school.

2 One of the costs of a lunch is the time spent eating it. Even if someone else pays for your lunch, it is not truly free.

3 The marginal benefit is $150, and the marginal cost is only $100 (equal to $600 − $500), so it would be sensible to add the third bus.

4 The marginal benefit (the extra revenue from selling three-bladed razors) must be greater than the marginal cost (the extra cost associated with producing razors with three blades instead of two).

5 False. Both people involved in a voluntary transaction are better off, so each thank-you could be sincere.

6 No. If the factory experiences diminishing returns, the marginal product of the tenth worker will exceed that of the twentieth worker, which exceeds that of the thirtieth worker.

7 False. The principle says that output increases but at a decreasing rate. Its does not say that hiring another worker decreases output, although this is a possibility with a very crowded factory.

8 The price of consumer goods increased faster than wages.

9 Your real wage hasn't changed, so you are just as well off.

10 A set of goods that cost you $100 will cost you $103 today, so you must use $3 of your $4 interest earnings to cover the higher costs, leaving you with only $1 in actual interest earnings.

NOTES

1. United Nations Development Program, *Human Development Report 1994* (New York: Oxford University Press, 1994).
2. Jose de Cordoba, "Panama Has Plans for U.S. War Stuff: Turn It Into Hotels," *Wall Street Journal*, January 11, 2000, p. A1.
3. Colin Kennedy, "Lord of the Screens," *Economist: The World in 2003*, p. 29 (London, 2003).
4. "Airline Takes the Marginal Bone," *Business Week*, April 20, 1963, pp. 111–114.
5. Adam Smith, *An Inquiry into the Nature and Causes of the Wealth of Nations* (First published in 1776; New York: Random House, 1973), Book 1, Chapter 2.

Exchange and Markets

The Barbie doll, the most profitable doll in history, is sold in 140 countries around the world at a rate of two dolls per second. Annual sales are $1.7 billion.[1] Most people think the Barbie doll symbolizes American culture, but the truth is, Barbie is really an international product. The dolls are designed in the United States, but most of the production occurs elsewhere. Saudi Arabia provides the oil used in Taiwanese factories to produce the vinyl plastic pellets that become Barbie's body. Japan supplies Barbie's nylon hair, and China provides her cotton clothes. The machinery used in Barbie factories in China, Indonesia, and Malaysia comes from Japan, Europe, and the United States. The United States provides the molds used to form the dolls and the pigments and oils used to paint them. Barbie dolls come in a box labeled "Made in China," but only about $0.33 of the $10 retail price goes to the factories in China that assemble the dolls. The rest goes to input suppliers around the world and to Mattel, which collects a $1 profit on each Barbie sold.

In Chapter 1, we saw that a society makes three types of economic decisions: what products to produce, how to produce them, and who gets them. In modern economies, most of these decisions are made in markets. Most of us participate in the labor market and are paid for jobs in which we produce goods and services for others. All of us participate in consumer markets, spending our incomes on food, clothing, housing, and other products. In this chapter, we first explain why markets exist, and then we explore the virtues and the shortcomings of markets. We also examine the role of government in a market-based economy.

The material in this chapter will help you understand the reasons for exchange and markets. Here are some of the practical questions we answer:

1 Why aren't people self-sufficient, producing everything they need for themselves?
2 Why have the economies of the former Soviet Union and China moved away from central planning, relying to a greater extent on market dynamics?
3 Why are profits an important part of a market economy?
4 How does EverQuest, the online multiplayer adventure game, illustrate the benefits of exchange and markets?

Comparative Advantage and Exchange

Markets exist to facilitate exchange between people. The alternative to exchange is to be self-sufficient, with each of us producing everything we need for ourselves. Rather than going it alone, most of us specialize by producing one or two products for others and exchanging the money we earn for the products we want to consume.

Specialization and the Gains from Trade

We can explain how people can benefit by specialization and trade with a simple example of two people and two products: Paintings and pizza. As shown in the first row in Table 3.1, Abe can produce either 2 paintings or 6 pizzas per day, while Bea can produce either a painting or a pizza per day. We can use one of the key principles to explore the rationale for specialization.

Principle OF OPPORTUNITY COST

The opportunity cost of something is what you sacrifice to get it.

TABLE 3.1

TABLE 3.1
Productivity and
Opportunity Costs

	Abe		Bea	
	Paintings	Pizzas	Paintings	Pizzas
Output per day	2	6	1	1
Opportunity cost	3 pizzas	1/3 painting	1 pizza	1 painting

Abe's opportunity cost of a painting is 3 pizzas—that's how many pizzas he could produce in the time it takes him to produce 1 painting. Similarly, Abe's opportunity cost of a pizza is 1/3 of a painting, the number of paintings he could produce in the time it takes him to produce 1 pizza. For Bea, the opportunity cost of a painting is 1 pizza and the opportunity cost of a pizza is 1 painting.

To demonstrate the benefits of exchange, let's imagine that both people are initially self-sufficient, with each producing enough of both goods to satisfy their own desires. Suppose there are 6 workdays per week. As shown in the first row of Table 3.2, Abe initially devotes 2 days per week to painting (producing 4 paintings) and 4 days per week to pizzas (producing 24 pizzas). He then consumes everything he produces. In a week, Bea produces and consumes 1 painting and 5 pizzas. As shown in the last two columns of the table, the total output for the two people is 5 paintings and 29 pizzas.

Specialization will increase total output. It is sensible for each person to specialize in the good for which he or she has a lower opportunity cost. We say that a person has a **comparative advantage** in producing a particular product if he or she has a lower opportunity cost than another person.

Comparative advantage
The ability of one person or nation to produce a good at a lower opportunity cost than another person or nation.

TABLE 3.2 Specialization, Exchange, and Gains from Trade

	Abe		Bea		Total	
	Paintings per Week	Pizzas per Week	Paintings per Week	Pizzas per Week	Paintings per Week	Pizzas per Week
Abe and Bea are self-sufficient.	4	24	1	5	5	29
Abe and Bea specialize.	0	36	6	0	6	36
After specializing, Abe and Bea exchange 2 pizzas per painting.	0 + 5 = **5** (Abe gets 5 paintings)	36 − 10 = **26** (Abe gives up 10 pizzas)	6 − 5 = **1** (Bea gives up 5 paintings)	0 + 10= **10** (Bea gets 10 pizzas)	6	36
Gain from specialization and exchange.	1	2	0	5	1	7

- Abe has a comparative advantage producing pizzas because his opportunity cost of pizzas is 1/3 painting, compared to 1 painting per pizza for Bea.
- Bea has a comparative advantage in painting because her opportunity cost of paintings is 1 pizza, compared to 3 pizzas per painting for Abe.

As shown in the second row of Table 3.2, when the two people specialize, Abe produces 36 pizzas and Bea produces 6 paintings. The total output of both goods increases: The number of paintings increases by 1 (from 5 to 6), and the number of pizzas increases by 7 (from 29 to 36). Specialization increases the output of both goods because both people are focusing on what they do best.

If specialization is followed by exchange, both people can be made better off. Suppose Abe and Bea agree to exchange 2 pizzas per painting. Abe could give up 10 pizzas to get 5 paintings. As shown in the third row of Table 3.2, that leaves him with 5 paintings and 26 pizzas, so compared to the self-sufficient outcome, he has more of both goods—one more painting and two more pizzas. If Bea gives up 5 paintings to get 10 pizzas, that leaves her with 1 painting and 10 pizzas, which is better than her self-sufficient outcome of 1 painting and 5 pizzas. Specialization and exchange make both people better off, illustrating one of the key principles of economics:

Principle OF VOLUNTARY EXCHANGE

A voluntary exchange between two people makes both people better off.

Production and Consumption Possibilities

Figure 3.1 provides a graphical representation of the numbers in Table 3.2. Let's start with the effects of specialization. The figure shows the production possibilities curves for the two people. In contrast with the possibilities curves drawn in Chapter 2, these curves are linear, reflecting the assumption that opportunity costs don't change as a person devotes more and more time to a particular product. In other words, there is a constant trade-off between the two activities. The self-sufficiency points are a_1 for Abe (4 paintings and 24 pizzas) and b_1 for Bea (1 painting and 5 pizzas). With specialization, each person produces only one of the products and thus moves to a point on either the horizontal or vertical axis.

- Abe produces only pizzas, so he moves to point a_2 on the vertical axis.
- Bea produces only paintings, so she moves to point b_2 on the horizontal axis.

The next step is to show the effects of exchange. In Figure 3.1, the **consumption possibilities curve** shows the possible combinations of the two goods when Abe and Bea specialize and exchange two pizzas per painting, For Abe, one option is to stay at point a_2, consuming all the pizzas he produces. Another option is to exchange 10 pizzas for 5 paintings, moving him to point a_3. Compared to the self-sufficient outcome (point a_1), he consumes more of both goods, so he is better off. Bea can move from her

Consumption possibilities curve

A curve showing the combinations of two goods that can be consumed when a nation specializes in the production of one good and trades with another nation.

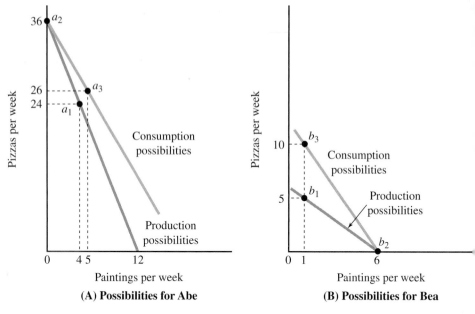

FIGURE 3.1 **Gains from Specialization and Exchange**

(A) Abe starts at the self-sufficient point a_1. Specialization moves him to point a_2, and exchange moves him down the consumption possibilities to point a_3. Compared to the self-sufficient point, he gets more of both goods.

(B) Bea starts at the self-sufficient point b_1. Specialization moves her to point b_2, and exchange moves her up the consumption possibilities curve to point b_3. Compared to the self-sufficient point, she gets more pizzas and the same number of paintings.

specialized point (b_2) to point b_3, exchanging 5 paintings for 10 pizzas. Compared to the self-sufficient outcome (point b_1), she consumes the same number of paintings and 5 more pizzas, so she is better off too.

Comparative Advantage Versus Absolute Advantage

We've seen that it is beneficial for each person to specialize in the product for which he or she has a comparative advantage, that is, a lower opportunity cost. You may have noticed that Abe is more productive than Bea in producing both goods. Economists say that Abe has an **absolute advantage** in producing both goods. Despite his absolute advantage, Abe gains from specialization and trade because he has a comparative advantage in pizza. Abe is twice as productive as Bea in producing paintings, but *six* times as productive in producing pizza. By relying on Bea to produce paintings, Abe frees up time to spend producing pizza, the good for which he has the largest productivity advantage over Bea. The lesson is that specialization and exchange result from comparative advantage, not absolute advantage.

Absolute advantage

The ability of one person or nation to produce a good at a lower absolute cost than another person or nation.

The Division of Labor and Exchange

So far, we've seen that specialization and trade exploit differences in people's innate productivities. Adam Smith noted that specialization actually increased productivity through the division of labor. He used the example of the pin factory to illustrate how the division of labor increased output:[2]

A workman . . . could scarce, perhaps with his utmost industry, make one pin a day, and certainly could not make twenty. But the way in which this business is now carried on . . . one man draws out the wire, another straightens it, a third cuts it, a fourth points it, a fifth grinds the top for receiving the head; to make the head requires two or three distinct operations. . . . The . . . making of a pin is, in this manner, divided into about eighteen distinct operations. . . . I have seen a small manufactory of this kind where ten men . . . make among them . . . upward of fourty eight thousand pins in a day.

Smith listed three reasons for productivity to increase with specialization, with each worker performing a single production task.

1 Repetition. The more times a worker performs a particular task, the more proficient the worker becomes at that task.

2 Continuity. A specialized worker doesn't spend time switching from one task to another. This is especially important if switching tasks requires a change in tools or location.

3 Innovation. A specialized worker gains insights into a particular task that leads to better production methods. Smith believed that workers were innovators:[3]

> A great part of the machines made use of in those manufactures in which labour is most subdivided, were originally the inventions of common workmen, who, being each of them employed in some simple operation, naturally turned their thoughts toward finding out easier and readier methods of performing *it*.

To summarize, specialization and exchange result from differences in productivity. Differences in productivity result from differences in innate skills and the benefits associated with the division of labor. Adam Smith wrote that "every man thus lives by exchanging, or becomes in some measure a merchant, and the society itself grows to be what is properly a commercial society."[4]

Comparative Advantage and International Trade

The lessons of comparative advantage and specialization apply to trade between nations. Each nation could be self-sufficient, producing all the goods it consumes, or it could instead specialize in products for which it has a comparative advantage. Even if one nation is more productive than a second nation in producing all goods, trade will be beneficial if the first nation has a bigger productivity advantage in one product—that is, if one nation has a comparative advantage in some product. For an example of comparative advantage giving rise to trade, read "A Closer Look: Buzz Lightyear of China."

National governments often intervene in international trade by erecting barriers to trade. One motivation for a trade barrier is to protect domestic industries from foreign competition. To illustrate the rationale for protectionist policies, let's extend our example of Abe and Bea to the international scale. Suppose Abeland is populated by people identical to Abe, while Bealand is full of people like Bea. Both nations are initially self-sufficient, with half the people in Abeland producing paintings and the other half producing pizzas. Similarly, the population in Bealand is split equally between painting and pizza making. Suppose that each occupation requires four years of schooling.

If both nations allowed international trade, Abeland would specialize in pizza and Bealand would specialize in painting. As in the earlier example with two individuals, specialization will increase total output of both products, generating net gains from trade. If you were a painter in Bealand, you would certainly be better off because your painting job would be secure and you would get more pizzas per painting. Instead of exchanging (within Bealand) one pizza per painting, you could get two pizzas per painting. But what about the former pizza makers, who would lose their jobs and be forced to switch to painting? If the two jobs required identical skills, the transition would be relatively easy. But because the two jobs require different skills (and education), former pizza workers will bear a cost from free trade. Similarly, there is a cost associated with switching painters in Abeland to pizza making.

The government can respond to this problem in two ways. One option is to cover the costs of switching occupations by paying the educational expenses of workers who must retrain for new careers. For example, the government could pay the educational expenses for former painters switching to pizza production. A second option is to erect barriers to trade such as an import tax or quota (a limit on the volume of goods imported). These trade barriers impose a cost on consumers, who miss the opportunity to pay lower prices for imported goods. For example, restrictions in the United States on textile imports protect 126,000 jobs at an annual cost of $10 billion, or $82,000 for each protected job.

Many people are skeptical about the idea that international trade can make everyone better off. President Abraham Lincoln expressed his discomfort with importing goods:[5]

> I know if I buy a coat in America, I have a coat and America has the money—If I buy a coat in England, I have the coat and England has the money.

What Lincoln didn't understand is that when he buys a coat in England, he sends dollars to England, and the dollars don't just sit there, but eventually are sent back to the United States to buy goods produced by American workers. In the words of economist Todd Buchholz, the author of *New Ideas from Dead Economists*:[6]

> Money may not make the world go round, but money certainly goes around the world. To stop it prevents goods from traveling from where they are produced most inexpensively to where they are desired most deeply.

TEST Your Understanding

1. In an hour, Abby can produce two financial statements or answer eight phone calls. What is the opportunity cost of a financial statement? What is the opportunity cost of a phone call?
2. Suppose Abby has an officemate, Slokum, who in an hour can either produce a financial statement or answer a phone call. How should the two tasks be allocated between the two workers?
3. Wally, the manager of a car wash, is more productive at washing cars than any of the potential workers he could hire. Should he wash all the cars himself?

A CLOSER LOOK

Buzz Lightyear of China

Buzz Lightyear is a distinctly American cartoon character, but the 30,000 frames of *Buzz Lightyear of the Star Command* were actually drawn in China by the artists of Shenzhen Jade Animation Company.[7] The company employs 300 artists and produces cartoon frames for studios in the United States, Canada, France, and Japan. With a monthly salary of $845, veteran cartoon artists in China cost a fraction of their American counterparts. The Chinese have a comparative advantage in producing cartoon frames.

Markets

In a **market economy**, people exchange things, trading what they have for what they want. Most people specialize in one productive activity—that is, they have one occupation and use their incomes to buy most of the goods they consume. In addition to consumer markets, many of us also participate in the market for financial capital, lending money for interest income (earned on savings accounts, bonds, or stocks) or borrowing money and paying interest. Friedrich Hayek, a famous economist from the twentieth century, suggested that if the market system hadn't arisen naturally, it would have been proclaimed the greatest invention in human history.

Although it appears markets arose naturally, a number of social inventions have made them work better.

► Contracts specify the terms of exchange, facilitating exchange between strangers.

Market economy
An economy in which people exchange things, trading what they have for what they want.

▶ Insurance reduces the risk associated with commercial ventures, making new ventures more viable for entrepreneurs.

▶ Patents increase the profitability of inventions, encouraging people to develop new products and production processes.

▶ Accounting rules provide reliable information about commercial enterprises, encouraging other people to invest their time and money in them.

Virtues of Markets

Centrally planned economy

An economy in which a government bureaucracy decides how much of each good to produce, how to produce the goods, and who gets them.

To assess the virtues of the market system, imagine the alternative—a **centrally planned economy** in which a planning authority decides what products to produce, how to produce them, and who gets them. To make these decisions, a planner must first collect a huge amount of widely dispersed information about consumption desires (what products each individual wants), production techniques (what resources are required to produce each product), and the availability of productive resources (labor, raw materials, and machines). Then the planner must decide how to allocate the productive resources among the alternative products. Finally, the planner must divide the output among the economy's citizens. Clearly, the planner has a formidable task.

Under a market system, the people with dispersed information about consumers' desires, production technology, and resources make the decisions. Their decisions are guided by prices. To illustrate, suppose you buy a wool coat. The dozens of people who contributed to the production of the coat—including the farmers who manage the sheep, the workers who transform raw wool into cloth and the cloth into a coat, the truckers who transport the inputs and the actual coat, and the merchant who sold the coat—didn't know you wanted a coat. The farmer knew that the price of wool was high enough to justify raising and shearing sheep. The workers knew that wages were high enough to make their efforts worthwhile. The merchant knew that the price of the coat was high enough to make it worthwhile to acquire the coat in anticipation of selling it. In a market system, prices provide individuals the information they need to make decisions.

Prices provide signals about the relative scarcity of a product and help an economy respond to scarcity. For example, suppose wool becomes more scarce, either because a new use for wool is discovered or an old source of wool disappears. The greater scarcity will increase the price of wool, and consumers and producers will respond in ways that diminish scarcity. The higher price encourages fabric producers to use the available wool more efficiently and encourages farmers to produce more of it. The higher price also encourages consumers to switch to alternative fabrics. These two responses help the economy accommodate an increase in scarcity. Consumers and producers don't need to know why wool is more scarce for these mechanisms to kick in—only that the price is higher.

The decisions made in markets result from the interactions of millions of people, each motivated by their own interests. Adam Smith used the metaphor of the "invisible hand" to explain that people acting in self-interest may actually promote the interest of society as a whole:[8]

> It is not from the benevolence of the butcher, the brewer, or the baker that we expect our dinner, but from their regard to their own interest. **We address ourselves, not to their**

humanity but to their self-love, and never talk to them of our own necessities but of their advantages. . . . [Man is] led by an invisible hand to promote an end which was no part of this intention. . . . By pursuing his own interest he frequently promotes that of the society more effectually than when he really intends to promote it. . . . Nobody but a beggar chooses to depend chiefly upon the benevolence of his fellow citizens.

The market system works by getting each person, motivated by self-interest, to produce products for other people.

Entrepreneurs play a key role in a market economy. Prices and profits provide signals to entrepreneurs about what to produce. If a product suddenly becomes popular, competition among consumers will increase its price and increase the profits earned by producers. Entrepreneurs will enter the market and increase production to meet the higher demand, converting resources that had been used to produce other products. As entrepreneurs enter the market, they compete for customers, driving the price back down to the level that generates just enough profit for them to remain in business. In contrast, if a product becomes less popular, the process is reversed. Producers will cut prices in order to sell the product to the smaller number of customers who want it. Entrepreneurs will leave the unprofitable market, finding other products to produce, and the price will eventually rise back to the level where profits are high enough for the remaining producers to justify staying in business.

One way to see the advantages of a market system is to see what happened in economies that were once centrally planned.[9] In the former Soviet Union, state-run auto repair shops, plagued by shortages of parts, were replaced by repair shops run by entrepreneurs with a profit incentive. In China, farmers moved away from the inefficient communal system and started selling their produce themselves.

Adam Smith, the founder of economics, stressed that markets guide people with an "invisible hand," promoting the general interest.

Prisoners of war used cigarettes to facilitate exchange of food, clothing, and laundry services.

Example: Exchange in a Prisoner of War Camp

To illustrate the pervasiveness of exchange, consider the emergence of markets in prisoner of war (POW) camps in World War II, as documented by economist Roy Radner. During World War II, the Red Cross gave each Allied prisoner a weekly parcel, with the same mix of products—tinned milk, jam, butter, biscuits, corned beef, chocolate, sugar, and cigarettes. In addition, many prisoners received private parcels from family and friends. The prisoners used barter to exchange one good for another, and cigarettes emerged as the medium of exchange.[10] Prisoners wandered through the camp calling out their offers of goods. For example, "cheese for seven" meant that the prisoner was willing to sell a cheese ration for seven cigarettes. In addition to food, the prisoners bought and sold clothing (80 cigarettes per shirt) laundry services (2 cigarettes per garment), and hot cups of coffee (2 cigarettes per cup).

The prices of products reflected their scarcity. The tea-drinking British prisoners, who were confined to their compound, demanded little coffee. Consequently, packets of coffee beans sold for just a few cigarettes in that compound. Enterprising British prisoners subsequently bribed prison guards to permit them to travel to the French compound, where they could sell the cheap coffee for dozens of cigarettes. Similarly, the demand for beef among Sikhs was low. One prisoner who knew the Sikh language bought beef at a low price in the Sikh compound and sold it at a higher price in other compounds. Eventually, other people entered the Sikh beef trade, and beef prices across compounds became roughly equal. For another example of a market appearing unexpectedly, read "A Closer Look: EverQuest and Fantasy Exchanges."

Shortcomings of Markets

Although markets often operate efficiently, sometimes they do not. This phenomenon is known as "market failure," which is what happens when markets fail to produce the most efficient outcomes on their own. One example of market failure is pollution. For

A CLOSER LOOK

EverQuest and Fantasy Exchanges

As another illustration of the power of exchange, consider the virtual world of online games. EverQuest is a role-playing game that allows thousands of people to interact online, moving their characters through a landscape of survival challenges. Each player constructs a character—called an "avatar"—by choosing some initial traits for it. The player then navigates the avatar through the game's challenges, where it acquires skills and accumulates assets, including clothing, weapons, armor, and even magic spells. The currency in EverQuest is a "platinum piece" (PP). Avatars can earn PP by performing various tasks and use PP to buy and sell assets.

The curious part about EverQuest is that players use real-life auction sites, including eBay and Yahoo!Auction, to buy things normally purchased in the game with PP.[11] Byron, who wants a piece of armor for his avatar (say, a Rubicite girdle), can use eBay to buy one for $50 from Selma. The two players then enter the online game, and Selma's avatar transfers the armor to Byron's avatar. It is even possible to buy another player's avatar, with all of its skills and assets. Given the time required to acquire various objects like Rubicite girdles in the game versus the prices paid for them on eBay, the implicit wage earned by the typical online player auctioning them off is $3.42 per hour: That's how much the player could earn by first taking the time to acquire the assets in the game and then selling them in the "real world."

markets to work efficiently, the people making the decisions about production and consumption must bear the full costs and reap the full benefits related to their decisions. When they don't, market failure occurs. The role of government is to correct this problem. Market failure can also occur when buyers and sellers have imperfect information about the quality of goods and services they are exchanging. Later in the book, we'll explore several cases of market failure and what government can do to help.

TEST Your Understanding

4. List the social inventions that support markets.
5. Why would a POW who didn't smoke trade some of his rations for cigarettes?
6. How could you earn money playing the online adventure game EverQuest?

The Role of Government in a Market Economy

What is the role of government in a market-based economy? As mentioned earlier in the chapter, the government deals with the problems associated with market failure. In addition, the government enforces property rights, protecting property and possessions from theft. The protection of private property encourages production and exchange because people are assured that they can keep the fruits of their efforts. The government has two additional roles to play:

▶ Establishing rules for exchange in markets and using its police power to enforce the rules

▶ Reducing economic uncertainty and providing for people who are unlucky—because of job losses, poor health, bad luck, or other circumstances

Government Enforces the Rules of Exchange

The market system is based on exchanges between strangers, who may have trouble trusting each other. These exchanges are covered by implicit and explicit contracts that establish the terms of trade. For example, real-estate transactions are sealed with contracts that specify who pays what, and when. To facilitate exchange, the government helps to enforce contracts by maintaining a legal system that punishes people who violate contracts. This allows people to trade with the confidence that the terms of the contract will be met.

In the case of consumer goods, the implicit contract is that the product is safe to use. The government enforces this implicit contract through product liability or tort law. If a consumer is harmed by using a particular product, the consumer can file a lawsuit and seek compensation for the harm done. For example, some consumers who are injured in defective automobiles are awarded settlements to cover the cost of medical care, lost work time, and pain and suffering.

Another role in the realm of exchange is the dissemination of information on consumer products. Producers are required by the government to provide information to consumers about the features of their products, including warnings about potentially harmful uses of the product.

To ensure that innovators benefit from their inventions, the U.S. government enforces patent laws. The costs associated with inventing new products and production processes—research and development costs—can be substantial. A patent grants an inventor the exclusive right to sell the product for a specified time (currently 20 years), increasing the payoff from innovation and encouraging people to invest resources in the development of new products and processes. Later in the book, we'll take a closer look at patents and innovation.

As noted earlier in the chapter, one of the virtues of a market system is that competition among producers tends to keep prices low. Another set of government policies is designed to foster competition between firms. As we'll see later in the book, antitrust policy can be used to (a) break up a monopoly, (b) prevent firms from colluding to fix prices, and (c) prevent two competing firms from merging into a single firm. There are some markets in which a single firm—a monopolist—is inevitable. Governments regulate these firms, controlling the price of the products they produce.

Government Can Reduce Economic Uncertainty

A market economy provides plenty of opportunities to people, but there are risks. Your level of success in a market economy—how much income you earn and how much wealth you accumulate—will depend on your innate intelligence as well as your efforts. But there is also an element of luck: Your fate is affected by where you were born, what occupation you choose, and your genetic makeup and health. There are also chance events such as natural disasters and human accidents that can affect your prosperity. Finally, some people lose their jobs when the national economy is in a slump.

Given the uncertainty of the market economics, most governments have a "social safety net" that provides for citizens who fare poorly in markets. The safety net includes programs that redistribute income from rich to poor and other programs of support. The idea behind having a social safety net is to guarantee a minimum income to people who suffer from job losses, poor health, or bad luck.

Of course, there are private responses to economic uncertainty. For example, we can buy insurance to cover losses from fire and theft, to cover our medical expenses, and to provide death benefits to our survivors in the event of an accident or disaster. Private insurance works because only a fraction of the people who buy insurance file claims and receive reimbursements from insurance companies. In other words, the payments, or premiums, of many are used to pay the claims of a few. Private insurance works when enough low-risk people purchase insurance to cover the costs of reimbursing the high-risk people.

Some types of insurance are unavailable in the private insurance market. As a result, the government steps in to fill the void. For example, unemployment insurance (UI) is a government program that provides 26 weeks of compensation for people who lose their jobs. It is financed by contributions from employers. Because UI is mandatory, all employers, including those facing low risks and high risks of unemployment, contribute to the system, thereby keeping the cost of the insurance down.

USING THE TOOLS

1. Prices in a POW Camp

Recall the discussion of markets in the POW camps. Suppose the price of bread is initially 40 cigarettes. Predict the effects of the following events on the price of bread; will the price of bread increase, decrease, or remain unchanged?
a. Prisoners' cigarette rations double while their food rations remain the same.
b. All rations—for cigarettes as well as food—are cut in half.
c. Air raids near the camp increase prisoners' anxiety, increasing cigarette consumption as a coping mechanism.

2. Arbitrage: Exploiting Price Differences

Late in World War II, a German guard exchanged bread and chocolate at the rate of one loaf for one chocolate bar. Inside the Allied POW camp, the price of chocolate was 15 cigarettes per bar, and the price of bread was 40 cigarettes per loaf. Arbitrage refers to the process of buying and selling products in different places to exploit differences in prices.
a. Design an arbitrage scheme for a prisoner in the POW camp. For each exchange with the German guard, what is the prisoner's profit?
b. Predict the effects of arbitrage on the prices of bread and chocolate within the POW camp.

3. Comparative Advantage and the Gains from Trade

Robin and Terry are stranded on a deserted island and consume two products, coconuts and fish. In a day, Robin can catch two fish or gather eight coconuts, and Terry can catch one fish or gather one coconut.
a. Use these numbers to prepare a table like Table 3.1. Which person has a comparative advantage in fishing? Which person has a comparative advantage in gathering coconuts?
b. Suppose that each person is initially self-sufficient. In a six-day week, Robin produces and consumes 32 coconuts and four fish, and Terry produces and consumes four coconuts and two fish. Show that specialization and exchange (at a rate of three coconuts per fish) allows Robin to consume more coconuts and the same number of fish and allows Terry to consume more coconuts and the same number of fish. Use a graph like Figure 3.1 and a table like Table 3.2 to illustrate your answer.

SUMMARY

This chapter explored specialization and exchange and the virtues and shortcomings of markets. We also discussed the role of government in a market economy. Here are the main points of the chapter:

1 It is sensible for a person to produce the product for which he or she has a comparative advantage, that is, a lower opportunity cost than another person.
2 Specialization increases productivity through the division of labor, a result of the benefits of repetition, continuity, and innovation.

3 A system of international specialization and trade is sensible because nations have different opportunity costs of producing goods, giving rise to comparative advantages.
4 Under a market system, self-interested people, guided by prices, make the decisions about what products to produce, how to produce them, and who gets them.
5 Government roles in a market economy include establishing the rules for exchange, reducing economic uncertainty, and responding to market failures.

KEY TERMS

absolute advantage, 48

centrally planned economy, 52

comparative advantage, 46

consumption possibilities curve, 47

market economy, 51

PROBLEMS AND DISCUSSION QUESTIONS

1 Recall the example of Abe and Bea shown in Table 3.1. Suppose a technological innovation increases painting productivity of both people: Abe can now produce three paintings per day, while Bea can now produce two paintings per day. Their productivity for pizza has not changed. Suppose they agree to trade one painting for each pizza. Will both people gain from specialization and trade?

2 Consider two financial planners, Phil and Frances. In an hour Phil can either produce one financial statement or answer 10 phone calls, while Frances can either produce three financial statements or answer 12 phone calls. Does either person have an absolute advantage in producing both products? Should the two planners be self-sufficient (each producing statements and answering phones), or should they specialize?

3 Professor Lucy is a better teacher than Professor Buster for both an undergraduate course (U) and a graduate course (G). Teaching performance is measured by the average score on students' standardized tests:

	Professor Lucy	Professor Buster
Average Score in Undergraduate Course	48	24
Average Score in Graduate Course	60	20

a. If each professor teaches one course and the objective is to maximize the sum of the test scores, which course should each professor teach?
b. Is your answer to (a) consistent with Lucy teaching the course for which she has the largest productivity advantage over Buster?

4 Use the notion of comparative advantage to explain why two countries, one of which is less efficient in producing all products, will still find it advantageous to trade.

MODEL ANSWERS

Chapter-Opening Questions

1 Markets exist because most people are not self-sufficient but instead specialize in producing one or two products and then buy other products from other people.

2 Under a market system, self-interested people, guided by the prices of products and resources, make better decisions.

3 Profits provide incentives for entrepreneurs to enter markets and produce goods that consumers are willing to pay for.

4 EverQuest players use online auction sites like eBay to purchase assets (armor, weapons, spells) for their characters in the game, which are then transferred from one character to another within the game.

Test Your Understanding

1 The opportunity cost of a financial statement is four phone calls, and the opportunity cost of a phone call is one-fourth of a financial statement.

2 Abby has the lower opportunity cost for phone calls (one-fourth of a financial statement), and Slokum has the lower opportunity cost for financial statements (one phone call). Abby should answer the phone, and Slokum should prepare the financial statements.

3 No. If he has a comparative advantage at managerial tasks such as doing the books or marketing, he should hire some workers to wash the cars, allowing him to specialize in the tasks for which he has a comparative advantage.

4 Contracts, insurance, patents, and accounting rules.

5 Cigarettes served as a medium of exchange.

6 Acquire assets in the game and sell them on eBay.

NOTES

1. Rone Tempest, "Barbie and the World Economy," *Los Angeles Times*, September 22, 1996, p. A1. ***http://www.surferess.com/ CEO/html/jill_barad.html***

2. Adam Smith, *An Inquiry into the Nature and Causes of The Wealth of Nations* (First published in 1776; New York: Random House, 1973), Book 1, Chapter 1.

3. Adam Smith, *An Inquiry into the Nature and Causes of The Wealth of Nations* (First published in 1776; New York: Random House, 1973), Book 1, Chapter 1.

4. Adam Smith, *An Inquiry into the Nature and Causes of The Wealth of Nations* (First published in 1776; New York: Random House, 1973), Book 1, Chapter 4.

5. Todd G. Buchholz, *New Ideas from Dead Economists* (New York: Penguin, 1999), p. 75.

6. Todd G. Buchholz, *New Ideas from Dead Economists* (New York: Penguin, 1999), p. 76.

7. Associated Press Online, "China Targets Cartoons," October 4, 2000.

8. Adam Smith, *An Inquiry into the Nature and Causes of The Wealth of Nations* (First published in 1776; New York: Random House, 1973), Book 4, Chapter 2.

9. Steven Greenhouse, *"The Global March to Free Markets,"* *New York Times*, July 19, 1987, Sec. 3, p. 1.

10. R.A. Radford, "The Economic Organization of a P.O.W. Camp," *Economica*, November, 1945.

11. Robert Shapiro, *Fantasy Economics* (slate.msn.com, February 4, 2003); Edward Castronova, "Virtual Worlds: A First-Hand Account of Market and Society on the Cyberian Frontier," CESifo Working Paper No. 618, December 2001.

Supply, Demand, and Market Equilibrium

etween 2000 and 2002, the price of va
beans quadrupled, from $50 to $200 p
kilo. Was this good news for vanilla
growers in Madagascar, the world's
leading producer? The soaring price was
actually bad news for the growers. The pric
hike was caused by tropical storms that reduc
harvests, so the growers sold a smaller quantity at the higher price. The hig
price unleashed the forces of supply and demand to the detriment of
Madagascar growers. On the demand side of the market, consumers and f
manufacturers switched to synthetic vanilla, which sells for as little as $15
kilo. On the supply side, the high price encouraged people in other countrie
enter the lucrative market. In India, 10,000 hectares are expected to be
cultivated in the next few years. In East Timor, the world's newest nation, co
growers switched to vanilla beans and harvested their first crop in 2002.

Our discussion of the virtues of exchange and markets in Chapter 3 has set the stage for this chapter, where we explore the mechanics of markets. We use the model of supply and demand—the most important tool of economic analysis—to see how markets work. We'll see how the prices of goods and services are affected by all sorts of changes in the economy, including bad weather, higher income, technological innovation, bad publicity, and changes in consumer preferences. This chapter will prepare you for the applications of supply and demand you'll see in the rest of the book.

The model of supply and demand explains how a perfectly competitive market operates. A **perfectly competitive market** has a very large number of firms, each of which produces the same standardized product in amounts so small that no individual firm can affect the market price. The classic example of a perfectly competitive firm is a wheat farmer, who produces a tiny fraction of the total supply of wheat. No matter how much wheat an individual farmer produces, the farmer can't change the market price of wheat.

This chapter includes many applications of supply and demand analysis. Here are some practical questions we answer:

1 The supply of electricity generated from wind power doubled in 2001. Why?
2 Ted Koppel, host of the ABC news program *Nightline*, once suggested that the price of cocaine had fallen because the supply of cocaine had increased. Was he correct?
3 Over the last few decades the consumption of chicken and turkey has increased. Why?
4 You shop for groceries at a different store each week. At each store, the clerk says, "You saved $12 by shopping here instead of at another store." Is it possible to "save money" wherever you go?

Perfectly competitive market

A market with a very large number of firms, each of which produces the same standardized product in amounts so small that no individual firm can affect the market price.

The Demand Curve

On the demand side of a product market, consumers buy products from firms. The main question concerning the demand side of the market is: How much of a particular product are consumers willing to buy during a particular period? A consumer who is "willing to buy" a particular product is willing to sacrifice enough money to purchase it. The consumer doesn't merely have a desire to buy the good but is willing to sacrifice something to get it. Notice that demand is defined for a particular period, for example, a day, a month, or a year.

We'll start our discussion of demand with the individual consumer. How much of a product is an individual willing to buy? It depends on a number of variables. Here is a list of the variables that affect an individual consumer's decision, using the pizza market as an example:

▶ The price of the product, for example, the price of a pizza
▶ The consumer's income
▶ The price of substitute goods such as tacos or sandwiches
▶ The price of complementary goods such as beer or lemonade
▶ The consumer's tastes and advertising that may influence tastes
▶ The consumer's expectations about future prices

Quantity demanded

The amount of a product consumers are willing to buy.

Together, these variables determine how much of a particular product an individual consumer is willing to buy, the **quantity demanded**. We'll start our discussion of demand with the relationship between the price and quantity demanded, a relationship that is represented graphically by the demand curve.

The Individual Demand Curve and the Law of Demand

Demand schedule

A table of numbers that shows the relationship between price and quantity demanded, *ceteris paribus*.

The starting point for a discussion of individual demand is a **demand schedule**, which is a table of numbers showing the relationship between the price of a particular product and the quantity that an individual consumer is willing to buy. The demand schedule shows how the quantity demanded by an individual changes with the price, *ceteris paribus* ("everything else held fixed"). The variables that are held fixed in the demand schedule are the consumer's income, the prices of substitutes and complements, the consumer's tastes, and the consumer's expectations about future prices.

Table 4.1 shows Al's demand schedule for pizza. At a price of $2, Al buys 13 pizzas per month. As the price rises, he buys fewer pizzas: 10 pizzas at a price of $4, 7 pizzas at a price of $6, and so on, down to only 1 pizza at a price of $10. It's important to remember that in a demand schedule, any change in quantity results from a change in price alone.

Individual demand curve

A curve that shows the relationship between price and quantity demanded by an individual consumer, *ceteris paribus*.

The **individual demand curve** is a graphical representation of the demand schedule. By plotting the numbers in Al's demand schedule—various combinations of price and quantity—we can draw his demand curve for pizza. The demand curve shows the relationship between the price and the quantity demanded by an individual consumer, *ceteris paribus*. To get the data for a single demand curve, we change only the price of pizza, and observe how a consumer responds to the price change. In Figure 4.1, Al's demand curve shows the quantity of pizzas he is willing to buy at each price.

OneKey
OneKey is
all you need

TABLE 4.1

Al's Demand Schedule for Pizzas

Price	Quantity of pizzas per month
$ 2	13
4	10
6	7
8	4
10	1

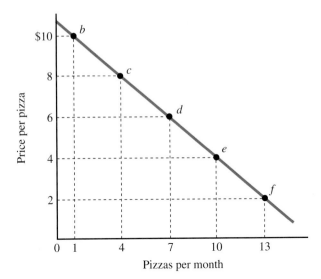

FIGURE 4.1

The Individual Demand Curve
According to the law of demand, the higher the price, the smaller the quantity demanded, everything else being equal. Therefore, the demand curve is negatively sloped: When the price increases from $6 to $8, the quantity demanded decreases from 7 pizzas per month (point *d*) to 4 pizzas per month (point *c*).

Notice that Al's demand curve is negatively sloped, reflecting the **law of demand**. This law applies to all consumers:

Law of demand
The higher the price, the smaller the quantity demanded, *ceteris paribus*.

■ Law of Demand

The higher the price, the smaller the quantity demanded, *ceteris paribus*.

The words *ceteris paribus* remind us that to isolate the relationship between price and quantity demanded, we *must* assume that income, other prices, and tastes are unchanged. As the price of pizza increases and nothing else changes, Al moves upward along his demand curve and buys a smaller quantity of pizza. For example, if the price increases from $8 to $10, Al moves upward along his demand curve from point *c* to point *b*, and he buys only 1 pizza per month, down from 4 pizzas at the lower price. A movement along a single demand curve is called a **change in quantity demanded**, a change in the quantity a consumer is willing to buy when the price changes.

To see why the law of demand is sensible, think about how Al might react to an increase in the price of pizza.

Change in quantity demanded
A change in the quantity consumers are willing to buy when the price changes; represented graphically by movement along the demand curve.

▶ **Substitution effect**. The more money Al spends on pizza, the less he has to spend on other products such as tacos, music, books, and travel. The price of pizza determines exactly how much of these other goods he sacrifices to get a pizza. If the price of pizza is $6 and the price of tacos is $1, Al will sacrifice 6 tacos for each pizza he buys. If the price of pizza increases to $8, he'll now sacrifice 8 tacos for each pizza. Given the larger sacrifice associated with buying pizza, he is likely to buy fewer pizzas, substituting tacos for pizza.

Substitution effect
The change in consumption resulting from a change in the price of one good relative to the price of another good.

▶ **Income effect**. Suppose Al has a food budget of $100 per month and buys 10 pizzas at a price of $6 each (for a total cost of $60) and spends $40 on other food. If, for example, the price of a pizza rises to $7, the cost of Al's original food choices will be

Income effect
The change in consumption resulting from a change in purchasing power caused by a price change.

$110—$70 for pizza and $40 for other items. This is well above his $100 total food budget. To avoid exceeding his budget, Al must cut back on something. That might end up being pizzas as well as other items. This is called the *income effect* because when the price of pizza increases, the purchasing power of Al's income (and budget) decreases.

From Individual Demand to Market Demand

Market demand curve

A curve showing the relationship between price and quantity demanded, *ceteris paribus*.

The **market demand curve** shows the relationship between the price of the good and the quantity that *all* consumers—you, me, Al, and everyone else—together are willing to buy, *ceteris paribus*. As in the case of the individual demand curve, when we draw the market demand curve, we assume that the other variables that affect individual demand (income, the prices of substitute and complementary goods, tastes, and price expectations) are fixed. In addition, we assume that the number of consumers is fixed. The market demand curve shows the relationship between price and the quantity demanded by all consumers, everything else being equal.

Figure 4.2 shows how to derive the market demand curve when there are only two consumers. Panel A shows Al's demand curve for pizza, and panel B shows Bea's demand curve for pizza. At a price of $8, Al will buy 4 pizzas (point *c*) and Bea will buy 2 pizzas (point *g*), so the total quantity demanded at this price is six pizzas (4 + 2). In panel C, point *j* shows the point on the market demand curve associated with a price of $8. At this price, the market quantity demanded is 6 pizzas. At a price of only $4, Al buys 10 pizzas and Bea buys 6 pizzas, for a total of 16 pizzas (shown by point *k* on the market demand curve).

The market demand is negatively sloped, reflecting the law of demand. This is sensible because if each consumer obeys the law of demand, consumers as a group will

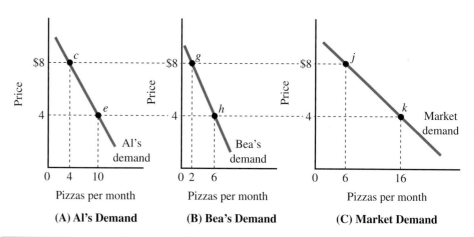

(A) Al's Demand   **(B) Bea's Demand**   **(C) Market Demand**

FIGURE 4.2 From Individual to Market Demand

The market demand equals the sum of the demands of all consumers. In this case there are only two consumers, so at each price, the market quantity demanded equals the quantity demanded by Al plus the quantity demanded by Bea. At a price of $8, Al's quantity is 4 pizzas (point *c*) and Bea's quantity is 2 pizzas (point *g*), so the market quantity demanded is 6 pizzas (point *j*). Each consumer obeys the law of demand, so the market demand curve is negatively sloped.

too. When the price increases from $4 to $8, there is a change in quantity demanded as we move along the demand curve from point *k* to *j*. The movement along the demand curve occurs if the price of pizza is the only determinant of demand that has changed.

Saving Money Wherever You Shop?

Grocery stores often boast that they have lower prices than their competitors. One boasting strategy happens at the checkout stand. After a clerk computes your bill, he or she uses data on a competitor's prices to compute how much you would have paid if you had purchased your basket of goods at the other store. Then the clerk says, "You saved $12 by shopping with us instead of with our competitor." It seems that wherever you shop, you get the same message: "You save by shopping with us." It appears that each store has lower prices than its competitors. Is this possible, or are the clerks dishonest?

  It turns out that the clerks are being honest. To see how you would "save money" no matter where you shop, consider Frieda, who each week picks a store at random for her fruit shopping. She buys exactly six pounds of fruit per week but is flexible about the variety of fruit she buys. In week one, she shops at Alpha market, where the price of apples is $1 per pound and the price of bananas is $3 per pound. She buys six pounds of apples, spending $6. At Beta market across town, the prices are reversed, with apples at $3 per pound and bananas at $1 per pound. If Frieda had purchased six pounds of apples at Beta, she would have spent $18, so the clerk at Alpha correctly observes, "Frieda, you saved $12 by shopping at Alpha instead of Beta." In week two, Frieda shops at Beta market and buys the cheaper fruit (bananas) instead of apples, spending $6 on fruit that would have cost her $18 at the other market. In two successive weeks, she "saves money" at each store. This is possible because she obeys the law of demand, purchasing the less expensive product at each store. ∎

The Supply Curve

On the supply side of a market, firms sell their products to consumers. Suppose you ask the manager of a firm, "How much of your product are you willing to produce and sell?" The answer is likely to be "it depends." The manager's decision about how much to produce depends on many variables, including the following (using pizza as an example):

▶ The price of the product—in this case, the price per pizza
▶ The cost of the inputs used to produce the product, for example, wages paid to workers, the cost of dough and cheese, and the cost of the pizza oven
▶ The state of production technology, such as the knowledge used in making pizza
▶ The number of producers—in this case, the number of pizzerias
▶ Producers' expectations about the future price of pizza
▶ Taxes paid to the government or subsidies received from the government

Together, these variables determine how much of a product will be produced and offered for sale, the **quantity supplied**. We'll start our discussion of market supply with the relationship between price of a good and quantity of that good supplied, a relationship that is represented graphically by the supply curve.

Quantity supplied
The amount of a product firms are willing to sell.

The Individual Supply Curve and the Law of Supply

Supply schedule

A table of numbers that shows the relationship between price and quantity supplied, *ceteris paribus*.

Consider the decision of an individual producer. The starting point for a discussion of individual supply is a **supply schedule**, a table of numbers that shows the relationship between the price of a particular product and the quantity that an individual producer is willing to sell. The supply schedule shows how the quantity supplied by an individual producer changes with the price, *ceteris paribus*. The variables that are held fixed in the supply schedule are input costs, technology, expectations, and government taxes or subsidies.

Table 4.2 shows Nora's supply schedule for pizza. At a price of $4, she supplies 100 pizzas per month. As the price rises, she supplies more pizza: 200 pizzas at a price of $6, 300 pizzas at a price of $8, and so on, up to 500 pizzas at a price of $12. It's important to remember that in a supply schedule, a change in quantity results from a change in price alone.

Individual supply curve

A curve showing the relationship between price and quantity supplied by a single firm, *ceteris paribus*.

The **individual supply curve** is a graphical representation of the supply schedule. By plotting the numbers in Nora's supply schedule—various combinations of price and quantity—we can draw her supply curve for pizza. The supply curve shows the relationship between the price of a product and the quantity supplied by a single firm, *ceteris paribus*. To get the data for a single supply curve, we change only the price of pizza and observe how a producer responds to the price change. In Figure 4.3, Nora's supply curve shows the quantity of pizzas she is willing to sell at each price.

Nora's supply curve is positively sloped, reflecting the law of supply, a pattern of behavior that we observe in producers.

■ Law of Supply

The higher the price, the larger the quantity supplied, *ceteris paribus*.

Change in quantity supplied

A change in the quantity firms are willing to sell when the price changes; represented graphically by movement along the supply curve.

The words *ceteris paribus* remind us that to isolate the relationship between price and quantity supplied, we assume that the other factors that influence producers are unchanged. As the price of pizza increases and nothing else changes, Nora moves upward along her supply curve and produces a larger quantity of pizza. For example, if the price increases from $8 to $10, Nora moves upward along her supply curve from point *p* to point *q*, and she produces 400 pizzas per month, up from 300 pizzas at the lower price. A movement along a single supply curve is called a **change in quantity supplied**, a change in the quantity a producer is willing to sell when the price changes.

TABLE 4.2

Nora's Supply Schedule for Pizza

Price	Quantity of pizzas per month
$ 4	100
6	200
8	300
10	400
12	500

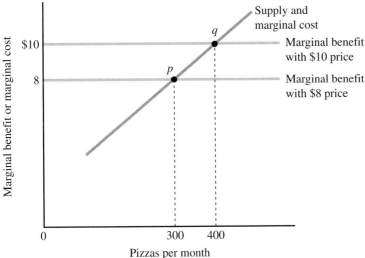

FIGURE 4.3

The Marginal Principle and the Output Decision
The marginal benefit curve is horizontal at the market price. To satisfy the marginal principle, the firm produces the quantity at which the marginal benefit equals the marginal cost. An increase in the price shifts the marginal-benefit curve upward and increases the quantity at which the marginal benefit equals the marginal cost.

Why Is the Individual Supply Curve Positively Sloped?

To see why the law of supply is sensible, think about how Nora might react to an increase in the price of pizza. Suppose the initial price of pizza is $8, and at this price Nora supplies 300 pizzas per month (point *p* on the supply curve). Like other business people, Nora doesn't choose a quantity arbitrarily, but instead picks the quantity that satisfies the marginal principle.

> MARGINAL *Principle*
>
> Increase the level of an activity if its marginal benefit exceeds its marginal cost; reduce the level of an activity if its marginal cost exceeds its marginal benefit. If possible, pick the level at which the activity's marginal benefit equals its marginal cost.

The marginal benefit of selling a pizza is the $8 price Nora gets when she sells it. The fact that Nora chose 300 pizzas at a price of $8 reveals that the marginal cost of producing each of the first 299 pizzas is less than the $8 marginal benefit and the marginal cost of the 300th pizza equals the $8 benefit. Nora stops at 300 pizzas because the marginal cost of one more pizza—the 301st—exceeds the $8 benefit from selling it. For example, if the marginal cost of the 301st pizza is $8.02, Nora would lose $0.02 by producing and selling it.

The supply curve shows that if the price rises above $8, Nora will produce more pizzas. As long as the new price is above the marginal cost of the 301st pizza ($8.02), it will be profitable to produce that pizza. For example, if the price rises to $10, Nora can make a profit of $1.98 on the 301st pizza ($10.00 − $8.02). At a price of $10, the supply curve indicates that she will actually produce 400 pizzas. An increase in price from $8 to $10 raises the marginal benefit above the marginal cost for the 301st through the 400th pizza, and she satisfies the marginal principle by selling 400 pizzas. At this new point, the best Nora can do is produce 400 pizzas because the marginal cost of the 400th pizza is $10 and the marginal cost of one more pizza ($10.02) exceeds the price she can get for it.

Why does the marginal cost of pizzas increase as the quantity produced increases? When Nora produces a relatively small quantity of pizzas, she will have just a few workers for every pizza oven, so workers won't face much competition for oven time. In this environment, Nora's costs will be relatively low. Imagine that Nora had to double her pizza output. To do so, she may be forced to pay overtime to her original workers and pay higher wages to attract more workers. In addition, there would be more workers sharing a fixed number of pizza ovens, and there may be a bottleneck as workers wait to use the oven. Because in the larger operation workers are less productive and more expensive, the cost of making pizzas will be higher. In general, the larger the quantity Nora produces, the higher her marginal cost of producing pizza.

To summarize, the individual supply curve is positively sloped because to get Nora to produce more pizza, the price must increase. To go from 300 pizzas to 400 pizzas, the price must increase from $8 to $10 to cover the higher marginal cost associated with producing more pizzas.

From Individual Supply to Market Supply

Market supply curve

A curve showing the relationship between price and quantity supplied, *ceteris paribus*.

The **market supply curve** for a particular good shows the relationship between the price of the good and the quantity that all producers together are willing to sell, *ceteris paribus*. To draw the market supply curve, we assume that the other variables that affect individual supply are fixed. In addition, we assume that the number of producers is fixed. Panel B of Figure 4.4 shows the market supply curve when there are 100 producers, each of which has the same individual supply curve as Nora. At a price of $8, Nora supplies 300 pizzas per month (point *p*), so the 100 firms together produce 30,000 pizzas (300 pizzas per firm times 100 firms), as shown by point *u*. If the price increases to $10, Nora supplies 400 pizzas (point *q*), so the quantity supplied by the market is 40,000 (point *v*).

The market supply curve is positively sloped, reflecting the law of supply. This is sensible because if each firm obeys the law of supply, firms as a group will too. When the price increases from $8 to $10, there is a change in quantity supplied as we move along the market supply curve from point *u* to point *v*. The movement along the supply curve occurs if the price of pizza is the only determinant of supply that has changed.

TEST Your Understanding

1. Complete the statement with "increase" or "decrease": When a price increases, the law of demand suggests that the quantity demanded will _____, while the law of supply suggests that the quantity supplied will _____.
2. List the variables that are held fixed in drawing a market demand curve.
3. List the variables that are held fixed in drawing a market supply curve.

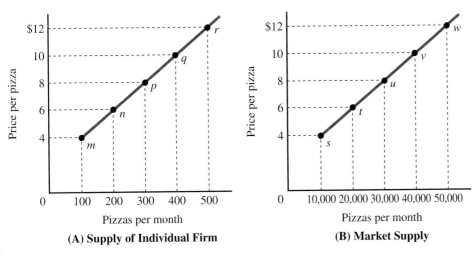

(A) Supply of Individual Firm

(B) Market Supply

FIGURE 4.4 Individual and Market Supply

(A) Supply of an individual firm. Nora supplies 300 pizzas at a price of $8 (point *p*) but 400 pizzas at a price of $10 (point *q*).

(B) Market supply. There are 100 identical pizzerias, so the market quantity equals 100 times the quantity supplied by Nora's, the typical pizzeria. At a price of $8, Nora supplies 300 pizzas (point *p*), so the market quantity supplied is 30,000 pizzas (point *u*).

Market Equilibrium

When the quantity of a product demanded equals the quantity supplied, this is called a **market equilibrium**. When a market reaches an equilibrium, there is no pressure to change the price. For example, if pizza firms produce exactly the quantity of pizza consumers are willing to buy, there will be no pressure for the price of pizza to change. The equilibrium price is shown by the intersection of the supply and demand curves. In Figure 4.5 at a price of $8, the supply curve shows that firms will produce 30,000 pizzas, which is exactly the quantity that consumers are willing to buy at that price.

Market equilibrium
A situation in which the quantity of a product demanded equals the quantity supplied, so there is no pressure to change the price.

OneKey is all you need

Excess Demand Causes the Price to Rise

If the price is below the equilibrium price, there will be excess demand for the product. **Excess demand** (sometimes called a shortage) occurs when consumers are willing to buy more than producers are willing to sell. In Figure 4.5 at a price of $6, there is an excess demand equal to 17,000 pizzas: Consumers are willing to buy 37,000 pizzas (point *d*), but producers are willing to sell only 20,000 pizzas (point *c*). This mismatch between supply and demand will cause the price of pizza to rise. Firms will increase the price they charge for their limited supply of pizza, and anxious consumers will pay the higher price to get one of the few pizzas that are available.

An increase in price eliminates excess demand by changing both the quantity demanded and quantity supplied. As the price increases, the excess demand shrinks for two reasons:

Excess demand
A situation in which, at the prevailing price, consumers are willing to buy more than producers are willing to sell.

▶ The market moves upward along the demand curve (from point *d* toward point *e*), decreasing the quantity demanded.

▶ The market moves upward along the supply curve (from point *c* toward point *e*), increasing the quantity supplied.

Because quantity demanded decreases while quantity supplied increases, the gap between the quantity demanded and the quantity supplied narrows. The price will continue to rise until excess demand is eliminated. In Figure 4.5, at a price of $8, the quantity supplied equals the quantity demanded.

In some cases, government creates an excess demand for a good by setting a maximum price (sometimes called a price ceiling). If the government sets a maximum price that is less than the equilibrium price, the result is a permanent excess demand for the good. We will explore the market effects of such policies in the next chapter.

Excess Supply Causes the Price to Drop

Excess supply

A situation in which, at the prevailing price, producers are willing to sell more than consumers are willing to buy.

What happens if the price is above the equilibrium price? **Excess supply** (sometimes called a surplus) occurs when producers are willing to sell more than consumers are willing to buy. This is shown by points *r* and *s* in Figure 4.5. At a price of $12, the excess supply is 35,000 pizzas: Producers are willing to sell 50,000 pizzas (point *s*), but consumers are willing to buy only 15,000 pizzas (point *r*). This mismatch will cause the price of pizzas to fall as firms cut the price to sell them. As the price drops, the excess supply will shrink for two reasons:

▶ The market moves downward along the demand curve, increasing the quantity demanded.
▶ The market moves downward along the supply curve, decreasing the quantity supplied.

Because the quantity demanded increases while the quantity supplied decreases, the gap between quantity supplied and demanded narrows. The price will continue to

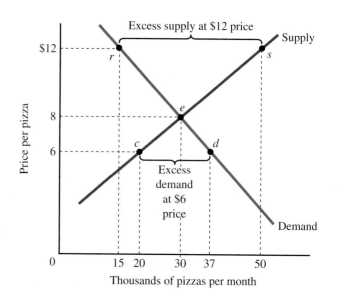

FIGURE 4.5

Market Equilibrium
At the market equilibrium (point e, with price = $8 and quantity = 30,000), the quantity supplied equals the quantity demanded. At a price lower than the equilibrium price ($6), there is excess demand (the quantity demanded exceeds the quantity supplied). At a price above the equilibrium price ($12), there is excess supply (the quantity supplied exceeds the quantity demanded).

drop until excess supply is eliminated. In Figure 4.5, at price of $8, the quantity supplied equals the quantity demanded.

The government sometimes creates an excess supply of a good by setting a minimum price (sometimes called a price floor). If the government sets a minimum price that is greater than the equilibrium price, the result is a permanent excess supply. We'll discuss the market effects of minimum prices in the next chapter.

TEST Your Understanding

4. Complete the statement: The market equilibrium is shown by the intersection of the _____ curve and the _____ curve.
5. Complete the statement with "less" or "greater": Excess demand occurs when the price is _____ than the equilibrium price; excess supply occurs when the price is _____ than the equilibrium price.
6. Complete the statement with "supply" or "demand": A maximum price below the equilibrium price causes excess _____, while a minimum price above the equilibrium price causes excess _____.

Market Effects of Changes in Demand

We've seen that a market equilibrium occurs when the quantity supplied equals the quantity demanded, shown graphically by the intersection of the supply curve and the demand curve. In this part of the chapter, we'll see how changes on the demand side of the market affect the equilibrium price and equilibrium quantity.

Change in Quantity Demanded Versus Change in Demand

Earlier in the chapter, we listed the variables that determine how much of a particular product consumers are willing to buy. One of the variables is the price of the product, and the demand curve shows the negative relationship between price and quantity demanded, *ceteris paribus*. In Panel A of Figure 4.6, when the price increases from $8 to $12, we move along the demand curve from point *b* to point *c*, and the quantity demanded decreases. As noted earlier in the chapter, this is called a *change in quantity demanded*. Now, we're ready to take a closer look at the other variables that affect demand besides price—income, the prices of related goods, tastes, advertising, and the number of consumers—and see how changes in these variables affect the demand for the product and the market equilibrium.

If any of these other variables change, the relationship between the product's price and quantity—shown numerically in the demand schedule and graphically in the demand curve—will change. That means we will have an entirely different demand schedule and an entirely different demand curve. In Panel B of Figure 4.6, for example, this is shown as a *shift* of the entire demand curve from D_1 to D_2. A shift means that at

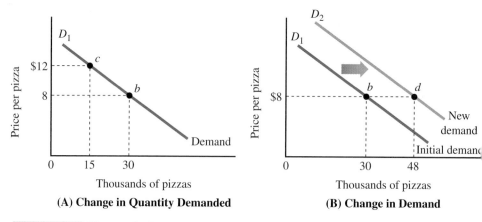

(A) Change in Quantity Demanded   **(B) Change in Demand**

FIGURE 4.6 **Change in Demand Versus Change in Quantity Demanded**
(A) A change in price causes a change in quantity demanded, a movement along a single demand curve. For example, an increase in price causes a move from point *b* to point *c*.
(B) A change in demand (caused by changes in something other than the price of the good) shifts the entire demand curve. For example, an increase in demand shifts the demand curve from D_1 to D_2. For any given price (for example, $8), a larger quantity is demanded (48,000 pizzas instead of $30,000).

Change in demand
A change in the amount of a good demanded resulting from a change in something other than the price of the good; represented graphically by a shift of the demand curve.

As income increases, consumers buy more of a "normal" good like restaurant meals and less of an "inferior" good like Spam.

any price, consumers are willing to buy a larger quantity of the product. For example, at a price of $8, consumers are willing to buy 48,000 pizzas, up from 30,000 with the original demand curve. To convey the idea that changes in these other variables change the demand schedule and the demand curve, we say that a change in any of these variables causes a **change in demand**.

Increases in Demand

We'll start with changes in the pizza market that increase the demand for pizza. An increase in demand means that at each price, consumers are willing to buy a larger quantity. In Figure 4.7, an increase in demand shifts the market demand curve from D_1

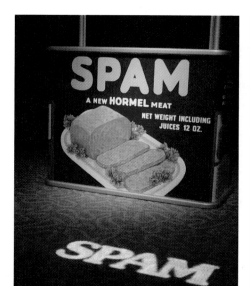

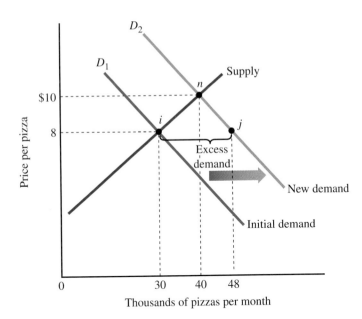

FIGURE 4.7

Market Effects of an Increase in Demand
An increase in demand shifts the demand curve to the right: At each price, the quantity demanded increases. At the initial price ($8), the shift of the demand curve causes excess demand, causing the price to rise. Equilibrium is restored at point *n*, with a higher equilibrium price ($10, up from $8) and a larger equilibrium quantity (40,000 pizzas, up from 30,000 pizzas).

to D_2. At the initial price of $8, the quantity demanded increases from 30,000 pizzas (point *i*) to 48,000 (point *j*). An increase in demand like the one represented in Figure 4.7 can occur for several reasons, which are listed in the first column of Table 4.3:

▶ Increase in income. Consumers use their income to buy products, and the more money they have, the more money they spend. For a normal good there is a positive relationship between consumer income and the quantity consumed. A **normal good** is a good that consumers buy more of when their income *increases*. Most goods fall into this category. New clothes, movies, and pizza are examples of normal goods.
▶ Decrease in income. An **inferior good** is the opposite of a normal good. Consumers buy more of inferior goods when their income *decreases*. For example, if you were laid off from your job, you might resort to buying more used clothing,

Normal good
A good for which an increase in income increases demand.

Inferior good
A good for which an increase in income decreases demand.

TABLE 4.3

Changes in Demand Shift the Demand Curve

An increase in demand shifts the demand curve to the right when:	A decrease in demand shifts the demand curve to the left when:
The good is normal and income increases	The good is normal and income decreases
The good is inferior and income decreases	The good is inferior and income increases
The price of a substitute good increases	The price of a substitute good decreases
The price of a complementary good decreases	The price of a complementary good increases
Population increases	Population decreases
Consumer tastes shift in favor of the product	Consumer tastes shift away from the product
Consumers expect a higher price in the future	Consumers expect a lower price in the future

renting DVDs instead of going to the theatre, and eating more macaroni and cheese. In this case, used clothing, DVDs, and macaroni and cheese are examples of inferior goods.

Substitutes

Two goods that are related in such a way that an increase in the price of one good increases the demand for the other good.

Complements

Two goods related in such a way that a decrease in the price of one good increases the demand for the other good.

▶ Increase in price of a substitute good. When two goods are **substitutes**, an increase in the price of the first good causes some consumers to switch to the second good. Tacos and pizzas are substitutes, so an increase in the price of tacos increases the demand for pizzas as some consumers substitute pizza for tacos, which are now more expensive relative to pizza.

▶ Decrease in price of a complementary good. When two goods are **complements**, they are consumed together as a package, and a decrease in the price of one good decreases the cost of the entire package. As a result, consumers buy more of both goods. Pizza and beer are complementary goods, so a decrease in the price of beer decreases the total cost of a beer-and-pizza meal, increasing the demand for pizza.

▶ Increase in population. An increase in the number of people means that there are more potential pizza consumers—more individual demand curves to add up to get the market demand curve—so market demand increases.

▶ Shift in consumer tastes. Consumers' preferences or tastes can change over time. If consumers' preferences shift in favor of pizza, the demand for pizza increases. The purpose of advertising is to shift consumers' preferences. Therefore, a successful pizza advertising campaign will increase the demand for pizza.

▶ Expectations of higher future prices. If consumers think next month's pizza price will be higher in the future than they had initially expected, they may buy a larger quantity today (and a smaller quantity next month). That means that the demand for pizza today will increase.

We can use Figure 4.7 to show how an increase in demand affects the equilibrium price and equilibrium quantity. An increase in the demand for pizza resulting from one or more of the factors listed in Table 4.3 shifts the demand curve to the right, from D_1 to D_2. At the initial price of $8, there will be excess demand, as indicated by points i and j: Consumers are willing to buy 48,000 pizzas (point j), but producers are willing to sell only 30,000 pizzas (point i). Consumers want to buy 18,000 more pizzas than producers are willing to supply, and the excess demand causes upward pressure on the price. As the price rises, the excess demand shrinks because the quantity demanded decreases while the quantity supplied increases. The supply curve intersects the new demand curve at point n, so the new equilibrium price is $10 (up from $8), and the new equilibrium quantity is 40,000 pizzas (up from 30,000).

Decreases in Demand

What sort of changes in the pizza market will decrease the demand for pizza? A decrease in demand means that at each price, consumers are willing to buy a smaller quantity. In Figure 4.8, a decrease in demand shifts the market demand curve from D_1 to D_0. At the initial price of $8, the quantity demanded decreases from 30,000 pizzas (point i) to 12,000 pizzas (point k). A decrease in demand like the one represented in Figure 4.8 can occur for several reasons, which are listed in the second column of Table 4.3.

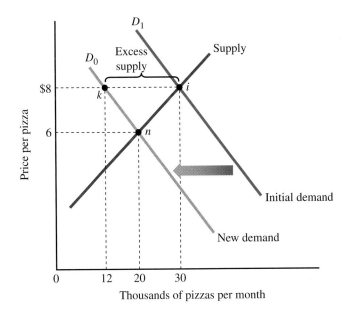

FIGURE 4.8

Market Effects of a Decrease in Demand

A decrease in demand shifts the demand curve to the left: At each price, the quantity demanded decreases. At the initial price ($8), the leftward shift of the demand curve causes excess supply, causing the price to fall. Equilibrium is restored at point n, with a lower equilibrium price ($6, down from $8) and a smaller equilibrium quantity (20,000 pizzas, down from 30,000 pizzas).

▶ Decrease in income. A decrease in income means that consumers have less to spend, so they buy a smaller quantity of each normal good.
▶ Decrease in price of a substitute good. A decrease in the price of a substitute good such as tacos makes pizza more expensive relative to tacos, causing consumers to demand less pizza.
▶ Increase in price of a complementary good. An increase in the price of a complementary good such as beer increases the cost of a beer-and-pizza meal, decreasing the demand for pizza.
▶ Decrease in population. A decrease in the number of people means that there are fewer pizza consumers, so the market demand for pizza decreases.
▶ Shift in consumer tastes. When consumers' preferences shift away from pizza in favor of other products, the demand for pizza decreases.
▶ Expectations of lower future prices. If consumers think next month's pizza price will be lower than they had initially expected, they may buy a smaller quantity today, meaning the demand for pizza today will decrease.

We can use Figure 4.8 to show how a decrease in demand affects the equilibrium price and equilibrium quantity. The decrease in the demand for pizza shifts the demand curve to the left, from D_1 to D_0. At the initial price of $8, there will be an excess supply, as indicated by points i and k: Producers are willing to sell 30,000 pizzas (point i), but given the lower demand, consumers are willing to buy only 12,000 pizzas (point k). Producers want to sell 18,000 more pizzas than consumers are willing to buy, and the excess supply causes downward pressure on the price. As the price falls, the excess supply shrinks because the quantity demanded increases while the quantity supplied decreases. The supply curve intersects the new demand curve at point n, so the new equilibrium price is $6 (down from $8), and the new equilibrium quantity is 20,000 pizzas (down from 30,000).

TEST Your Understanding

7. Which of the following go together?
   a. A change in demand
   b. A change in quantity demanded
   c. A change in price
   d. Movement along the demand curve
   e. A shift in the demand curve
   f. A change in income

8. What's wrong with the following statement? "Demand increased because the demand curve shifted."

9. Complete the statement with "right" or "left": An increase in the price of cassette tapes will shift the demand curve for CDs to the _____; an increase in the price of CD players will shift the demand curve for CDs to the _____.

10. Circle the following variables that change as we move along the demand curve for pencils, and cross out the ones that are assumed to be fixed:
    Quantity of pencils demanded
    Number of consumers
    Price of pencils
    Price of pens
    Consumer income

Market Effects of Changes in Supply

We've seen that changes in demand shift the demand curve and change the equilibrium price and quantity. In this part of the chapter, we'll see how changes on the supply side of the market affect the equilibrium price and equilibrium quantity.

Change in Quantity Supplied Versus Change in Supply

Earlier in the chapter, we listed the variables that determine how much of a particular product firms are willing to sell. Of course, one of the important variables is the price of the product. The supply curve shows the positive relationship between price and quantity, *ceteris paribus*. In Panel A of Figure 4.9, when the price increases from $6 to $8, we move along the supply curve from point *e* to point *f*, and the quantity of the product supplied increases. As noted earlier in the chapter, this is called a *change in quantity supplied*. Now we're ready to take a closer look at the other variables that affect supply— input costs, technology, the number of firms, and price expectations—and see how changes in these variables affect the supply of the product and the market equilibrium.

If any of these other variables changes, the relationship between price and quantity—shown numerically in the supply schedule and graphically in the supply curve— will change. That means that we will have an entirely different supply schedule and a different supply curve. In Panel B of Figure 4.9, this is shown as a shift of the entire

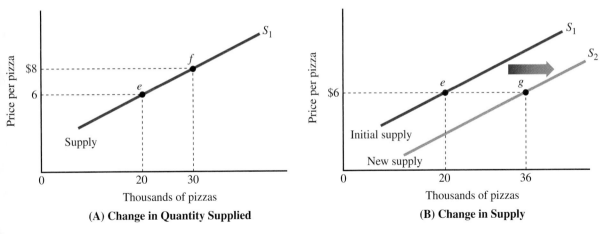

(A) Change in Quantity Supplied

(B) Change in Supply

FIGURE 4.9 **Change in Supply Versus Change in Quantity Supplied**

(A) A change in price causes a change in quantity supplied, a movement along a single supply curve. For example, an increase in price causes a move from point e to point f.
(B) A change in supply (caused by changes in something other than the price of the good) shifts the entire supply curve. For example, an increase in supply shifts the demand curve from S_1 to S_2. For any given price (for example, $6), a larger quantity is supplied (36,000 pizzas instead of 20,000).

supply curve from S_1 to S_2: at any price, producers are willing to sell a larger quantity. For example, at a price of $6, producers are willing to sell 36,000 pizzas, up from 20,000 with the initial supply curve. To convey the idea that changes in these other variables change the supply schedule and the supply curve, we say that a change in any of these variables causes a **change in supply**.

Increases in Supply

We'll start with changes in the pizza market that increase the supply of pizza. An increase in supply means that at each price, producers are willing to sell a larger quantity. In Figure 4.10, an increase in supply shifts the market supply curve from S_1 to S_2.

Change in supply
A change in the amount of a good supplied resulting from a change in something other than the price of the good; represented graphically by a shift of the supply curve.

FIGURE 4.10

Market Effects of an Increase in Supply
An increase in supply shifts the supply curve to the right: At each price, the quantity supplied increases. At the initial price ($8), the rightward shift of the supply curve causes excess supply, causing the price to drop. Equilibrium is restored at point n, with a lower equilibrium price ($6, down from $8) and a larger equilibrium quantity (36,000 pizzas, up from 30,000 pizzas).

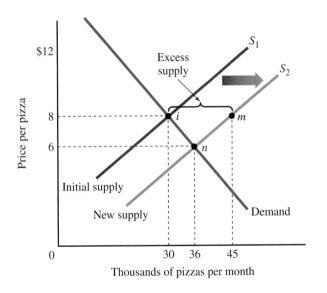

At the initial price of $8, the quantity supplied increases from 30,000 pizzas (point *i*) to 45,000 (point *m*). An increase in supply like the one represented in Figure 4.10 can occur for several reasons, which are listed in the first column of Table 4.4.

▶ A decrease in input costs. A decrease in the cost of labor or some other input will make pizza production less costly and more profitable at a given price, so producers will supply more.

▶ An advance in technology. A technological advance that makes it possible to produce pizza at a lower cost will make pizza production more profitable, so producers will supply more of it.

▶ An increase in the number of producers. The market supply is the sum of the product supplied by all producers, so the larger the number of producers, the greater the supply.

▶ Expectations of lower future prices. If firms think next month's pizza price will be lower than they had initially expected, they may be willing to sell a larger quantity today (and a smaller quantity next month). That means that the supply of pizza today will increase.

▶ Subsidy. If the government subsidizes the production of the product (pays firms some amount for each unit produced), the subsidy will make the product more profitable, so firms will produce more.

We can use Figure 4.10 to show the effects of an increase in supply on the equilibrium price and equilibrium quantity. An increase in the supply of pizza shifts the supply curve to the right, from S_1 to S_2. At the initial price of $8 (the equilibrium price with the initial supply curve), there will be an excess supply, as indicated by points *i* and *m*: Producers are willing to sell 45,000 pizzas (point *m*), but consumers are willing to buy only 30,000 (point *i*). Producers want to sell 15,000 more pizzas than consumers are willing to buy, and the excess supply causes pressure to decrease the price. As the price decreases, the excess supply shrinks because the quantity supplied decreases while the quantity demanded increases. The new supply curve intersects the demand curve at point *n*, so the new equilibrium price is $6 (down from $8) and the new equilibrium quantity is 36,000 pizzas (up from 30,000).

How has technological change in electricity generation affected the supply of electricity from alternative sources, including wind power? To see the effects of technological innovation in the production of wind power, read "A Closer Look: Increasing the Supply of Wind Power."

TABLE 4.4

Changes in Supply Shift the Supply Curve

An increase in supply shifts the supply curve to the right when:	A decrease in supply shifts the supply curve to the left when:
The cost of an input decreases	The cost of an input increases
A technological advance decreases production cost	
The number of firms increases	The number of firms decreases
Producers expect a lower price in the future	Producers expect a higher price in the future
Product is subsidized	Product is taxed

Increasing the Supply of Wind Power

In recent years, the supply of electricity generated from wind power has increased dramatically, doubling in 2001.[1] The rapid increase in wind-generated electricity resulted from technological innovations that decreased production costs. In the 1980s, the cost of wind electricity was about 50 cents per kilowatt hour. Several design innovations—including the replacement of small, rapid rotors with large, slow-moving blades and the development of monitoring systems that permit the turbines to change their direction and blade angle to more efficiently harness the wind—have decreased the cost of maintaining the turbines and increased the electricity output per hour. By 2001, the cost of wind power had dropped to about four cents per kilowatt hour, compared with 2.5 to three cents for electricity generated by conventional sources (natural gas and coal). Because the producers of wind power receive a federal tax credit of 1.5 cents per kilowatt hour, wind power is often competitive with conventional power sources.

In graphical terms, the technological innovations decreased production costs, shifting the supply curve for wind electricity to the right, increasing the equilibrium quantity and decreasing its price.

Decreases in Supply

What sort of changes in the pizza market will decrease the supply of pizza? A decrease in supply means that at each price, producers are willing to supply a smaller quantity. In Figure 4.11, a decrease in supply shifts the market supply curve from S_1 to S_0. At the initial price of $8, the quantity supplied decreases from 30,000 pizzas (point i) to 14,000 pizzas (point p). A decrease in supply like the one represented in Figure 4.11 can occur for several reasons, which are listed in the second column of Table 4.4.

▶ Increase in input costs. An increase in the cost of labor or some other input will make pizza production more costly and less profitable at a given price, so producers will supply less.

▶ A decrease in the number of producers. The market supply is the sum of the supplies of all producers, so a decrease in the number of producers decreases supply.

▶ Expectations of higher future prices. If firms think next month's pizza price will be higher than they had initially expected, they may be willing to sell a smaller quantity today (and a larger quantity next month). That means that the supply of pizza today will decrease.

▶ Taxes. If the government imposes a tax on each unit produced by the firm, the tax will make the product more costly and less profitable. Consequently, firms will supply less of it.

Market Effects of a Decrease in Supply

A decrease in supply shifts the supply curve to the left: At each price, the quantity supplied decreases. At the initial price ($8), the leftward shift of the supply curve causes excess demand, causing the price to rise. Equilibrium is restored at point *n*, with a higher equilibrium price ($10, up from $8) and a smaller equilibrium quantity (23,000 pizzas, down from 30,000 pizzas).

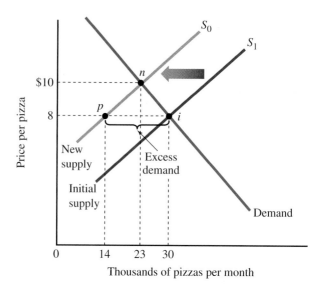

We can use Figure 4.11 to show the effects of a decrease in supply on the equilibrium price and equilibrium quantity. A decrease in the supply of pizza shifts the supply curve to the left, from S_1 to S_0. At the initial price of $8 (the equilibrium price with the initial supply curve), there will be an excess demand, as indicated by points *i* and *p*: Consumers are willing to buy 30,000 pizzas (point *i*), but producers are willing to sell only 14,000 pizzas (point *p*). Consumers want to buy 16,000 more pizzas than producers are willing to sell, and the excess demand causes upward pressure on the price. As the price increases, the excess demand shrinks because the quantity demanded decreases while the quantity supplied increases. The new supply curve intersects the demand curve at point *n*, so the new equilibrium price is $10 (up from $8), and the new equilibrium quantity is 23,000 pizzas (down from 30,000).

Market Effects of Simultaneous Changes in Demand and Supply

What happens to the equilibrium price and quantity when both supply and demand increase? It depends on which change is larger. In Panel A of Figure 4.12, the increase in demand is larger than the increase in supply, meaning the demand curve shifts by a larger amount than the supply curve. The market equilibrium moves from point *i* to point *d*, and the equilibrium price increases from $8 to $9. This is sensible because an increase in demand tends to pull the price up, while an increase in supply tends to push the price down. If demand increases by a larger amount, the upward pull will be stronger than the downward push, and the price will rise.

We can be certain that when supply and demand both increase, the equilibrium quantity will increase. That's because both changes tend to increase the equilibrium quantity. In Panel A of Figure 4.12, the equilibrium quantity increases from 30,000 to 44,000 pizzas.

Panel B of Figure 4.12 shows what happens when the increase in supply is larger than the increase in demand. The equilibrium moves from point *i* to *s*, meaning that

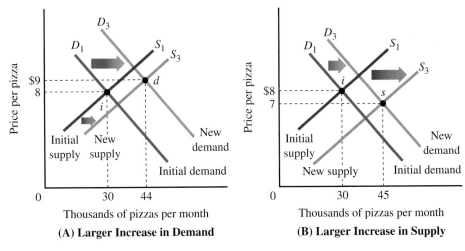

(A) Larger Increase in Demand   **(B) Larger Increase in Supply**

FIGURE 4.12 **Market Effects of Simultaneous Changes in Supply and Demand**

(A) Larger increase in demand. If the increase in demand is larger than the increase in supply (if the shift of the demand curve is larger than the shift of the supply curve), both the equilibrium price and the equilibrium quantity will increase.

(B) Larger increase in supply. If the increase in supply is larger than the increase in demand (if the shift of the supply curve is larger than the shift of the demand curve), the equilibrium price will decrease and the equilibrium quantity will increase.

the price falls from $8 to $7. This is sensible because the downward pull on the price resulting from the increase in supply is stronger than the upward pull from the increase in demand. As expected, the equilibrium quantity rises from 30,000 to 45,000 pizzas.

What about simultaneous decreases in supply and demand? In this case the equilibrium quantity will certainly fall because both changes tend to decrease the equilibrium quantity. The effect on the equilibrium price depends on which change is larger, the decrease in demand, which pushes the price downward, or the decrease in supply, which pulls the price upward. If the change in demand is larger, the price will fall because the force pushing the price down will be stronger than the force pulling it up. In contrast, if the decrease in supply is larger, the price will rise because the force pulling the price up will be stronger than the force pushing it down.

TEST Your Understanding

11. Which of the following items go together?
    a. A change in quantity supplied
    b. A change in an input cost
    c. A change in price
    d. A shift of the supply curve
    e. Movement along the supply curve
    f. A change in supply

(*continued*)

12. An increase in the wage of computer workers will shift the supply curve for computers to the left. True or false? Explain.
13. Circle the following variables that change as we move along the market supply curve for housing, and cross out the variables that are assumed to be fixed:
    a. Quantity of housing supplied
    b. Number of firms
    c. Price of wood
    d. Price of houses
    e. Technology

Using the Model to Predict Changes in Price and Quantity

We've used the model of supply and demand to show how equilibrium prices are determined and how changes in demand and supply affect equilibrium prices and quantities. Table 4.5 summarizes what we've learned about how changes in demand and supply affect equilibrium prices and quantities.

▶ When demand changes and the demand curve shifts, price and quantity change in the *same* direction: When demand increases, both price and quantity increase; when demand decreases, both price and quantity decrease.
▶ When supply changes and the supply curve shifts, price and quantity change in *opposite* directions: When supply increases, the price decreases but the quantity increases; when supply decreases, the price increases but the quantity decreases.

We can use these lessons about supply and demand to predict the effects of various events on the equilibrium price and equilibrium quantity of a product.

Population Growth and Apartment Prices

How will an increase in enrollment at a university affect the equilibrium price of apartments in a university town? An increase in university enrollment will increase the number of students seeking apartments thereby increasing the demand for apartments. As shown in the first row of Table 4.5, we would expect the increase in demand

TABLE 4.5

Market Effects of Changes in Demand or Supply

Change in Demand or Supply	Change in Price	Change in Quantity
Increase in demand	Increase	Increase
Decrease in demand	Decrease	Decrease
Increase in supply	Decrease	Increase
Decrease in supply	Increase	Decrease

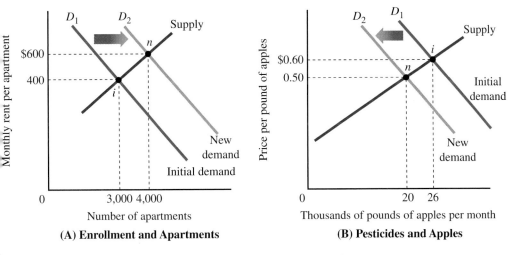

(A) Enrollment and Apartments   (B) Pesticides and Apples

FIGURE 4.13 **Predicting the Effects of Changes in Demand**

A) An increase in university enrollment will increase the demand for apartments, shifting the demand curve to the right. The equilibrium price increases from $400 to $600, and the equilibrium quantity increases from 3,000 to 4,000.

B) A report of pesticide residue on apples decreases the demand for apples, shifting the demand curve to the left. The equilibrium price decreases from $0.60 to $0.50, and the equilibrium quantity decreases from 26,000 to 20,000 pounds.

to increase both the price and quantity of apartments. In Panel A of Figure 4.13, the initial equilibrium in the apartment market is shown by point i, with a monthly rent of $400 per apartment. An increase in university enrollment shifts the demand for apartments to the right, leading to a new equilibrium at point n, with a higher price ($600) and a larger quantity.

Product Safety and Apples

How will public information about the safety of products affect equilibrium prices and quantities? In 1999, a controversial report suggested that pesticide residue on apples made them unsafe for infants and small children. Although many experts disputed the report, it nonetheless decreased the demand for apples. Essentially, the report had the opposite effect of advertising. As shown in the second row of Table 4.5, we would expect the decrease in demand to decrease both the price and quantity of apples. In Panel B of Figure 4.13, the initial equilibrium is shown by point i, with a price of $0.60 per pound and a quantity of 26,000 pounds per month. After the pesticide report is released, the demand curve shifts to the left, leading to a new equilibrium at point n, with a lower price ($0.50) and a smaller quantity (20,000 pounds).

Technological Innovation and Computers

How will technological innovations affect equilibrium prices? Let's look at the market for personal computers. Recent innovations in electronics have decreased the cost of producing personal computers, increasing the supply of computers. As shown in the

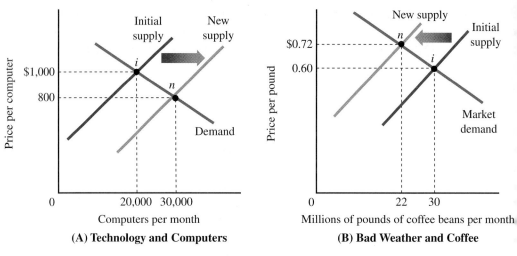

FIGURE 4.14 **Predicting the Effects of Changes in Supply**

(A) Technological innovation decreases production costs, shifting the supply curve to the right. The equilibrium price decreases from $1,000 to $800, and the equilibrium quantity increases from 20,000 to 30,000. Bad weather decreases the supply of coffee beans, shifting the supply curve to the left.
(B) The equilibrium price increases from $0.60 to $0.72, and the equilibrium quantity decreases from 30 million to 22 million pounds.

third row of Table 4.5, we would expect the increase in supply to decrease the price but increase the quantity of computers. In Panel A of Figure 4.14, the initial equilibrium is shown by point i, with a price of $1,000 and a quantity of 20,000 computers. The innovation that decreased production costs shifts the supply curve to the right, generating a new equilibrium at point n, with a lower price ($800) and a larger quantity (30,000).

Weather and Coffee

How will poor weather affect equilibrium prices? In 1992, several events combined to decrease the world supply of coffee. Poor weather and insect infestations in Brazil and Colombia decreased the coffee bean harvest by about 40%. Some farmers lost their entire crop, so the number of producers decreased. In addition, a slowdown by dock-workers at Santos, Brazil's main coffee bean port, decreased the amount supplied to the world market. As shown in the fourth row of Table 4.5, we would expect the decrease in supply to increase the price but decrease the quantity of coffee. In Panel B of Figure 4.14, the initial equilibrium is shown by point i, with a price of $0.60 and a quantity of 30 million pounds. The poor weather, insect infestations, and other supply disruptions shifted the supply curve to the left, generating a new equilibrium at point n, with a higher price ($0.72) and a smaller quantity (22 million pounds).

Explaining Changes in Price or Quantity

We can use the lessons listed in Table 4.5 to explain the reasons for changes in prices or quantities. Suppose we observe changes in the equilibrium price and quantity of a particular good, but we don't know what caused these changes. Perhaps it was a change in demand, or maybe it was a change in supply. We can use the information in Table 4.5 to work backwards, using what we've observed about changes in prices and quantities to determine which side of the market—supply or demand—caused the changes.

An Increase in Poultry Consumption

Why has the consumption of poultry (chicken and turkey) increased so much over the last several decades? One possibility is that consumers have become more health conscious and have switched from red meat to poultry in an effort to eat healthier. In other words, the demand curve for poultry may have shifted to the right, increasing the equilibrium quantity of poultry. Of course, an increase in demand will increase the price too, so if this explanation is correct, we should also observe higher prices for poultry.

According to the U.S. Department of Agriculture, this popular explanation is incorrect.[2] In fact, the increase in poultry consumption was caused by an increase in supply, not an increase in demand. This conclusion is based on the fact that poultry prices have been decreasing, not increasing. Between 1950 and 1990, the real price of poultry (adjusted for inflation) actually decreased by about 75%. As shown in Panel A of Figure 4.15, an increase in supply causes the market equilibrium to shift from point i (where price = $2 and quantity = 50 million pounds) to point n (price = $0.80 and quantity = 90 million pounds). In other words, the increase in supply decreased the equilibrium price. The supply of poultry increased because innovations in poultry processing decreased the cost of producing poultry products. The lesson here is that we shouldn't jump to conclusions based on limited information. A change in the equilibrium quantity could result from either a change in supply or a

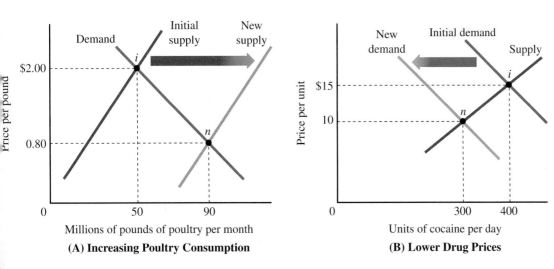

FIGURE 4.15 **Explaining Changes in Price or Quantity**
(A) At the same time the quantity of poultry increased (from 50 million pounds to 90 million), the price decreased from $2.00 to $0.80). Therefore, the increase in consumption resulted from an increase in supply, not an increase in demand.
(B) At the same time the price of cocaine decreased (from $15 to $10), the quantity of cocaine consumed decreased (from 400 units to 300 units). Therefore, the decrease in price was caused by a decrease in demand, not an increase in supply.

change in demand. To draw any conclusions, we need information about both price and quantity.

Nonetheless, there may be a grain of truth in the popular explanation that poultry consumption increased because consumers were trying to eat healthier. It is indeed possible that the demand curve shifted to the right, meaning that both supply and demand increased. Because the price of poultry decreased, however, we know that the shift of the supply curve (which tends to decrease the price) overwhelmed any shift of the demand curve (which tends to increase the price). So although changes in consumer preferences might have contributed to the increase in poultry consumption, the changes in consumption were caused largely by changes on the supply side of the market.

A Decrease in Drug Prices

Ted Koppel, host of the ABC news program *Nightline*, once said, "Do you know what's happened to the price of drugs in the United States? The price of cocaine, way down, the price of marijuana, way down. You don't have to be an expert in economics to know that when the price goes down, it means more stuff is coming in. That's supply and demand."[3] According to Koppel, the price of drugs dropped because the government's efforts to control the supply of illegal drugs had failed. In other words, the lower price resulted from an increase in supply. According to the U.S. Department of Justice, the quantity of drugs consumed actually decreased during the period of dropping prices.[4] Is Koppel's economic detective work sound?

In this case, both the price and the quantity decreased. As shown in the second row of Table 4.5, when both the price and the quantity decrease, that means demand has decreased. For example, in Panel B of Figure 4.15, a decrease in demand shifts the demand curve to the left, and the market moves from point *i* (price = $15 and quantity = 400 units per day) to point *n* (price = $10 and quantity = 300 units per day). Koppel's explanation (an increase in supply) would be correct if the quantity of drugs increased at the same time that the price decreased. However, because the quantity of drugs consumed actually decreased during the period of dropping prices, Koppel's explanation is incorrect. Lower demand—not a failure of the government's drug policy and an increase in supply—was responsible for the decrease in drug prices.

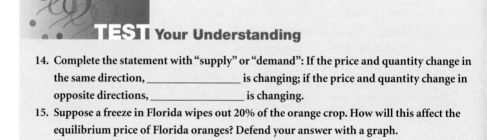

TEST Your Understanding

14. Complete the statement with "supply" or "demand": If the price and quantity change in the same direction, _____ is changing; if the price and quantity change in opposite directions, _____ is changing.
15. Suppose a freeze in Florida wipes out 20% of the orange crop. How will this affect the equilibrium price of Florida oranges? Defend your answer with a graph.

A CLOSER LOOK

Higher Platinum Prices

In early 2003, the price of platinum reached its highest point in 23 years—$700 per ounce—up by 17% from just a year earlier.[5] The precious metal is used for jewelry and in catalytic converters that control air pollution from automobiles. The higher price was caused by changes on both sides of the platinum market. On the supply side, Russia cut its production to almost zero. It appears that the cut in Russian production was motivated by (1) a desire to stockpile platinum in anticipation of a miners' strike and (2) a desire to get automakers to switch from platinum to palladium, another Russian export. On the demand side, a new interest in fuel-cell technology for cars, which relies on platinum to generate cleaner electricity, increased the demand for the precious metal.

Economic Experiment

Market Equilibrium

This simple experiment takes about 20 minutes. We start by dividing the class into two equal groups: consumers and producers.

- The instructor provides each consumer with a number indicating the maximum amount he or she is willing to pay (WTP) for a bushel of apples: The WTP is a number between $1 and $100. Each consumer has the opportunity to buy 1 bushel of apples per trading period. The consumer's score for a single trading period equals the gap between the WTP and the price actually paid for apples. For example, if the consumer's WTP is $80 and he or she pays only $30 for apples, the consumer's score is $50. Each consumer has the option of not buying apples. This will be sensible if the best price the consumer can get exceeds the WTP. If the consumer does not buy apples, his or her score will be zero.
- The instructor provides each producer with a number indicating the cost of producing a bushel of apples (a number between $1 and $100). Each producer has the opportunity to sell 1 bushel per trading period. The producer's score for a single trading period equals the gap between the selling price and the cost of producing apples. So if a producer sells apples for $20, and the cost is only $15, the producer's score is $5. Producers have the option of not selling apples, which is sensible if the best price the producer can get is less than the cost. If the producer does not sell apples, his or her score is zero.

Once everyone understands the rules, consumers and producers meet in a trading area to arrange transactions. A consumer may announce how much he or she is willing to pay for apples and wait for a producer to agree to sell apples at that price. Alternatively, a producer may announce how much he or she is willing to accept for apples and wait for a consumer to agree to buy apples at that price. Once a transaction has been arranged, the consumer and producer inform the instructor of the trade, record the transaction, and leave the trading area.

(continued)

There are several trading periods, each of which lasts a few minutes. After the end of each trading period, the instructor lists the prices at which apples sold during that period. Then another trading period starts, providing consumers and producers another opportunity to buy or sell 1 bushel of apples. After all the trading periods have been completed, each participant computes his or her score by adding the scores from each trading period.

USING THE TOOLS

In this chapter you learned how to use two tools of economics—the supply curve and the demand curve—to find equilibrium prices to predict changes in prices and quantities. Here are some opportunities to use these tools to do your own economic analysis.

1. Using Data to Draw a Demand Curve

The following table shows data on gasoline prices and gasoline consumption in a particular city. Is it possible to use these data to draw a demand curve? If so, draw the demand curve. If not, why not?

Year	Gasoline Price (per gallon)	Quantity Consumed (millions of gallons)
2003	1.20	400
2004	1.40	300
2005	1.60	360

2. Foreign Farm Workers and the Price of Berries

Current law allows thousands of Mexican workers to work on farms in the United States during harvest season. Suppose a new law outlaws the use of foreign farm workers. Assume that the resulting excess demand for labor increases the wage paid to farm workers by 20%. Use a supply–demand graph to predict the effects of the higher wage on the price of berries.

3. Market Effects of an Import Ban on Shoes

Consider a nation that initially imports half the shoes it consumes. Use a supply–demand graph to predict the effect of a ban on shoe imports on the equilibrium price and quantity of shoes.

4. The Puzzle of Free Used Newspapers

In 1987 you could sell a ton of used newspapers for $60. Five years later, you could not sell them at any price. In other words, the price of used newspapers dropped from $60 to zero in just five years. Over this period, the quantity of used newspapers bought and sold increased. What caused the drop in price? Defend your answer with a supply–demand graph.

SUMMARY

In this chapter, we've seen how supply and demand determine prices. We also learned how to predict the effects of changes in demand or supply on prices and quantities. Here are the main points of the chapter.

1 To draw a demand curve, we must be certain that the other variables that affect demand (consumer income, the prices of related goods, tastes, con-sumers' price expectations, and the number of consumers) are held fixed.

2 To draw a market supply curve, we must be certain the other variables that affect supply (such as input costs, technology, the number of producers, their price expectations, and taxes and subsidies) are held fixed.

3 Equilibrium in a market is shown by the intersection of the demand curve and the supply curve. When a market reaches equilibrium, there is no pressure to change the price.

4 A change in demand changes price and quantity in the same direction: An increase in demand increases the equilibrium price and quantity; a decrease in demand decreases the equilibrium price and quantity.

5 A change in supply changes price and quantity in opposite directions: An increase in supply decreases price and increases quantity; a decrease in supply increases price and decreases quantity.

KEY TERMS

change in demand, 72
change in quantity demanded, 63
change in quantity supplied, 66
change in supply, 77
complements, 74
demand schedule, 62
excess demand, 69
excess supply, 70

income effect, 63
individual demand curve, 62
individual supply curve, 66
inferior good, 73
law of demand, 63
market demand curve, 64
market equilibrium, 69
market supply curve, 68

normal good, 73
perfectly competitive market, 61
quantity demanded, 62
quantity supplied, 65
substitutes, 74
substitution effect, 63
supply schedule, 66

PROBLEMS AND DISCUSSION QUESTIONS

1 Figure 4.A shows the supply and demand curves for CD players. Complete the following statements.
   a. At the market equilibrium (shown by point _____), the price of CD players is _____ and the quantity of CD players is _____.

   b. At a price of $100, there would be excess _____, so we would expect the price to _____.
   c. At a price exceeding the equilibrium price, there would be excess _____, so we would expect the price to _____.

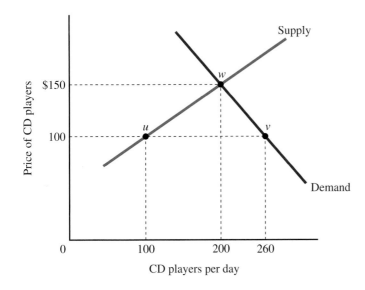

FIGURE 4.A

Supply and Demand for CD Players

2 The following table shows the quantities of corn supplied and demanded at different prices:

Price per Ton	Quantity Supplied	Quantity Demanded	Excess Demand or Excess Supply
$80	600	1,200	_____
$90	800	1,100	_____
$100	1,000	1,000	_____
$110	1,200	900	_____

   a. Complete the table.
   b. Draw the demand curve and the supply curve.
   c. What is the equilibrium price of corn?

3 Consider the market for personal computers. Suppose that the demand is stable: The demand curve doesn't change. Predict the effects of the following changes on the equilibrium price of computers. Illustrate your answer with a supply and demand diagram.
   a. The cost of memory chips (one component of a computer) decreases.
   b. The government imposes a $100 tax on personal computers.

4 Draw a supply–demand diagram to illustrate the effect of an increase in income on the market for restaurant meals.

5 Suppose that the tuition charged by public universities increases. Draw a supply-demand diagram to illustrate the effects of the tuition hike on the market for private college education.

6 Suppose that the government imposes a tax of $1 per pound of fish and collects the tax from fish producers. Draw a supply-demand diagram to illustrate the market effects of the tax.

7 As summer approaches, the equilibrium price of rental cabins increases and the equilibrium quantity of cabins rented increases. Draw a supply-demand diagram that explains these changes.

8 Suppose that the initial price of a mobile phone is $100 and that the initial quantity demanded is 500 phones per day. Depict graphically the effects of a technological innovation that decreases the cost of producing mobile phones. Label the starting point with "*i*" and the new equilibrium with "*n*."

9 The Multifiber Agreement sets import quotas for various apparel products—including shirts—coming into the United States. Use a supply-demand graph to show the effects of the shirt quota on the equilibrium price of shirts in the United States.

10 Suppose a freeze in Florida wipes out 20% of the orange crop. How will this affect the equilibrium price of California oranges? Defend your answer with a graph.

MODEL ANSWERS

Chapter-Opening Questions

1 As explained in "A Closer Look: Increasing the Supply of Wind Power," innovations in the design of wind turbines decreased the cost of generating electricity from wind power, increasing supply.

2 As explained in the last section of the chapter, the equilibrium quantity of drugs decreased at the same time that prices decreased, so the price drop was caused by a decrease in demand, not an increase in supply.

3 As explained in the last section of the chapter, the price decreased while the quantity increased, so the increase in quantity was caused by an increase in supply, not an increase in demand. Supply increased because innovations in poultry processing decreased the cost of producing poultry.

4 As explained in "Economic Puzzle: Saving Money Wherever You Shop," this is possible because you obey the law of demand, choosing low-price products at each store.

Test Your Understanding

1 decrease, increase
2 consumer income, the prices of substitute goods, the prices of complementary goods, consumer tastes, advertising, the number of consumers, and price expectations
3 input costs, technology, price expectations, number of producers, taxes and subsidies
4 supply, demand
5 less, greater
6 demand, supply

7 One group is a, e, and f; another group is b, c, and d.

8 The statement is incorrect because it confuses the direction of causality. The correct statement is: "The demand curve shifted because demand increased." When something other than the price of the product changes, the relationship between price and quantity changes, causing the demand curve to shift.

9 right, left

10 Circle quantity of pencils demanded and price of pencils. Cross out number of consumers, price of pens, and consumer income.

11 One group is a, c, and e; another group is b, d, and f.

12 True. An increase in the wage increases production cost, so fewer computers will be supplied at each price.

13 Circle quantity of housing supplied and price of houses. Cross out number of firms, price of wood, and technology.

14 demand, supply

15 The supply of oranges decreases, shifting the supply curve to the left. The equilibrium price will increase.

NOTES

1. *The News and Observer*, "Raleigh, N.C.-Based Companies Tap Growing Market for Wind Power," January 26, 2001; *Associated Press Online*, "Wind Farm to Power 70,000 Homes," January 10, 2001.

2. Mark R. Weimar and Richard Stillman, "Market Trends Driving Broiler Consumption," *Livestock and Poultry Situation and Outlook Report LPS-44* (Washington, DC: U.S. Department of Agriculture, Economic Research Service, November 1990).

3. Kenneth R. Clark, "Legalize Drugs. A Case for Koppel," *Chicago Tribune*, August 30, 1988, sec. 5, p. 8.

4. U.S. Department of Justice, "Drugs, Crime, and the Justice System" (Washington, DC: U.S. Government Printing Office, 1992), p. 30.

5. "Going Platinum," *The Economist*, February 8, 2003, p. 68.

A Closer Look at Supply and Demand

Elasticity: A Measure of Responsiveness

In every large city in the United States, the public bus system runs a deficit: Operating costs exceed revenues from passenger fares. Suppose your city wants to reduce its bus deficit and is trying to decide whether to increase fares by 10%. Consider the following exchange between two city officials:

Buster: A fare increase is a great idea. We'll collect more money from bus riders, so revenue will increase, and the deficit will shrink.

Bessie: Wait a minute, Buster. Haven't you heard about the law of demand? The increase in the bus fare will decrease the number of passengers taking buses, so we'll collect less money, not more, and the deficit will grow.

Who is right? As we'll see in this chapter, we can't predict how an increase in price will affect total revenue unless we know just how responsive consumers are to an increase in price. Like other consumers, bus riders obey the law of demand, but that doesn't necessarily mean that total fare revenue will fall.

n Chapter 4, we discussed the law of demand, the observation that an increase in price decreases the quantity demanded, *ceteris paribus*. The law of demand is useful, but sometimes we need to know the numbers behind the law of demand, that is, exactly how much less will be demanded at a higher price. In this chapter, we will quantify the law of demand, exploring the responsiveness of consumers to changes in price. Suppose your student group has decided to increase the price for its film series from $2 to $3. You know from the law of demand that you'll sell fewer tickets, but the question is: How many fewer tickets? As we'll see in this chapter, you can use the notion of elasticity to predict how many tickets you'll sell and how much money you'll collect in total. Similarly, in the case of hiking the bus fare, we can use the notion of elasticity to determine whether Buster or Bessie is correct.

Switching to the supply side of the market, the law of supply tells us that an increase in price increases the quantity supplied, *ceteris paribus*. Sometimes the question is: By how much? We'll quantify the law of supply, showing how to predict just how much more of a product will be supplied at a higher price. For example, if the world price of oil increases from $25 to $28 per barrel, we know from the law of supply that domestic producers will supply more oil, but the question is: How much more? We can use the notion of elasticity to predict how much more domestic oil will be supplied at the higher price.

This chapter contains many applications of the concept of elasticity. Here are some practical questions that we answer:

1 How would a tax on beer affect the number of highway deaths among young adults?
2 Why is a bumper crop bad news for farmers?
3 Why do policies that limit the supply of illegal drugs increase the number of burglaries and robberies?
4 If the population of a city increases by 9%, by how much will housing prices increase?

The Price Elasticity of Demand

Price elasticity of demand
A measure of the responsiveness of the quantity demanded to changes in price; computed by dividing the percentage change in quantity demanded by the percentage change in price.

The **price elasticity of demand** (E_d) measures the responsiveness of consumers to changes in price. We compute the price elasticity by dividing the percentage change in quantity demanded by the percentage change in price:

$$E_d = \frac{\text{percentage change in quantity demanded}}{\text{percentage change in price}}$$

For example, if the price of milk increases by 10% and the quantity demanded decreases by 15%, the price elasticity of demand is 1.5:

$$E_d = \frac{\text{percentage change in quantity demanded}}{\text{percentage change in price}} = \frac{15\%}{10\%} = 1.5$$

When we compute the price elasticity of demand, we ignore any minus signs, so the elasticity is always a positive number. The law of demand tells us that price and quantity demanded always move in opposite directions. This means that the percentage change in price will always have the opposite sign of the percentage change in quantity. In our example, a +10% change in price results in a −15% change in quantity. Although the price elasticity could be reported as a negative number, the conventional approach is to ignore the minus sign and always report the elasticity as a positive number: A large positive elasticity number indicates that the demand for the product is very elastic, or very responsive to changes in price; a small positive elasticity number indicates that the demand for a product is very inelastic. As long as we remember the law of demand, there is no harm in dropping minus signs and reporting all price elasticities of demand as positive numbers.

Price Elasticity and the Demand Curve

Figure 5.1 shows five different demand curves, each with a different elasticity. We can divide products into five types, depending on their price elasticities of demand.

Elastic demand

The price elasticity of demand is greater than 1.

▶ **Elastic Demand** (Panel A). In this case, a 20% increase in price (from $5 to $6) decreases the quantity demanded by 40% (from 20 to 12), so the price elasticity of demand is 2.0. When the price elasticity is greater than 1.0, we say that demand is "elastic," or highly responsive to changes in price. Some examples of goods with elastic demand are restaurant meals, air travel, and movies.

Inelastic demand

The price elasticity of demand is less than 1.

▶ **Inelastic Demand** (Panel B). The same 20% increase in price decreases the quantity demanded by only 10% (from 20 to 18), so the price elasticity of demand is 0.50. When the elasticity is less than 1.0, we say that demand is "inelastic," or not very responsive to changes in price. Some examples of goods with inelastic demand are eggs, coffee, cigarettes, and electricity.

Unitary elastic

The price elasticity of demand equals 1.

▶ **Unitary Elastic Demand** (Panel C). A 20% increase in price decreases the quantity demanded by exactly 20%, so the price elasticity of demand is 1.0. Some examples of goods with close to unitary elasticity are housing, gasoline, and recreation.

Perfectly inelastic demand

The price elasticity of demand equals 0.

▶ **Perfectly Inelastic Demand** (Panel D). When demand is perfectly inelastic, the quantity doesn't change as the price changes, so the demand curve is vertical at the fixed quantity. This extreme case is rare because for most products, consumers can either switch to a substitute good or do without. For example, although there are no direct substitutes for household water, as the price of water rises, people install low-flow showerheads, water their lawn less frequently, and drive dirty cars. The rare cases of perfectly inelastic demand are medicines that have no substitutes.

Perfectly elastic demand

The price elasticity of demand is infinite.

▶ **Perfectly Elastic Demand** (Panel E). In this case, the demand curve is horizontal, meaning that only one price is possible. At that price, the quantity demanded could

FIGURE 5.1

Elasticity and Demand Curves

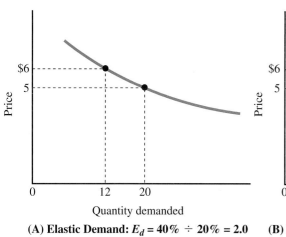

(A) Elastic Demand: $E_d = 40\% \div 20\% = 2.0$

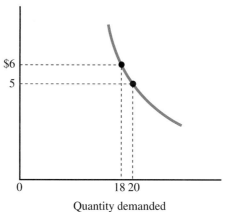

(B) Inelastic Demand: $E_d = 10\% \div 20\% = 0.50$

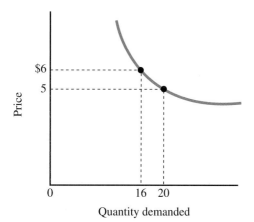

(C) Unitary Elastic Demand: $E_d = 20\% \div 20\% = 1.0$

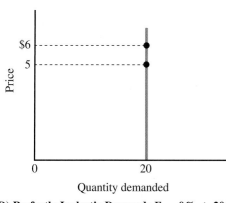

(D) Perfectly Inelastic Demand: $E_d = 0\% \div 20\% = 0$

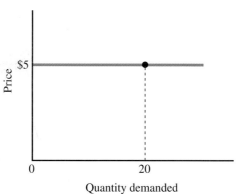

(E) Perfectly Elastic Demand: $E_d = \infty$

be any quantity, from one unit to millions of units. If the price were to increase even a penny, the quantity demanded would drop to zero. As we'll see in Chapter 9, firms in a perfectly competitive market face this sort of demand curve: Each firm can sell as much as it wants at the market price but would sell nothing at any price above the market price.

What Determines the Price Elasticity of Demand?

The price elasticity of demand for a particular product depends on the availability of substitutes. Consider the substitution possibilities for insulin (a medicine for diabetics) and cornflakes. There are no good substitutes for insulin, so consumers are not very responsive to changes in price. The demand for insulin is therefore inelastic. In contrast, there are many substitutes for cornflakes, including different types of corn cereals, as well as cereals made from wheat, rice, and oats. Faced with an increase in price of cornflakes, consumers can easily switch to substitute products, so the demand for cornflakes is relatively elastic.

Table 5.1 shows the price elasticities of demand for various products. The different elasticities illustrate the importance of substitutes in determining the price elasticity of demand. Because there are no good substitutes for water and salt, it is not surprising that the elasticities are small. For example, the price elasticity of demand for water is 0.20, meaning that a 10% increase in price decreases the quantity demanded by 2%. The demand for coffee is inelastic as well. Although there are alternative beverages and caffeine delivery systems (tea, infused soft drinks, and pills), coffee provides a unique combination of taste and caffeine, which explains the relatively low elasticity of 0.30. Although there is an artificial substitute for eggs (for people concerned about dietary cholesterol), there are no natural substitutes, so demand is relatively inelastic, 0.30.

The demand for a specific brand of a product is typically elastic. For example, the elasticity of demand for a specific brand of coffee is 5.6, compared to an overall elasticity for coffee of 0.30. This means that a 10% increase in the price of coffee in general (all brands) will decrease the quantity of coffee sold by 3%, but a 10% increase in the price

---

TABLE 5.1

Price Elasticities of Demand for Selected Products

Product	Price Elasticity of Demand
Salt	0.1
Water	0.2
Coffee	0.3
Eggs	0.3
Cigarettes	0.3
Shoes and footwear	0.7
Housing	1.0
Automobiles	1.2
Foreign travel	1.8
Restaurant meals	2.3
Air travel	2.4
Motion pictures	3.7
Specific brands of coffee	5.6

Sources: Frank Chaloupka, "Rational Addictive Behavior and Cigarette Smoking," Journal of Political Economy, August 1991, pp. 722–742; Gregory Chow, Demand for Automobiles in the United States (Amsterdam: North-Holland, 1957); David Ellwood and Mitchell Polinski, "An Empirical Reconciliation of Micro and Grouped Estimates of the Demand for Housing," Review of Economics and Statistics, vol. 61, 1979, pp. 199–205; H. F. Houthakker and Lester B. Taylor, Consumer Demand in the United States: Analysis and Projections, 2nd ed. (Cambridge, MA: Harvard University Press, 1970); John R. Nevin, "Laboratory Experiments for Estimating Consumer Demand: A Validation Study," Journal of Marketing Research, vol. 11, August 1974, pp. 261–268; Herbert Scarf and John Shoven, Applied General Equilibrium Analysis (New York: Cambridge University Press, 1984).

of a specific brand will decrease the quantity of that brand sold by 56%. This illustrates the importance of substitutability: Each brand is a substitute for the other brands, so consumers are very responsive to a change in the price of a specific brand. Similarly, the demand for specific brands of tires is more elastic than the demand for tires in general.

It often takes time for consumers to respond to price changes, so the short-run price elasticity of demand is typically smaller than the long-run elasticity. For example, when the price of gasoline increases, consumers can immediately drive fewer miles in their existing cars. The longer-term consumer responses to higher prices include buying more fuel-efficient cars and moving closer to workplaces. As time passes, consumers have more options to cut gasoline consumption, so demand becomes more elastic.

Elasticity is generally larger for goods that take a relatively large part of a consumer's budget. If a good represents a small part of the budget of the typical consumer, demand is relatively inelastic. For example, suppose the price of pencils is 20 cents and then increases by 10%, or 2 cents. Because the price change is tiny compared to the income of the typical consumer, we would expect a relatively small decrease in the quantity of pencils demanded. In contrast, if the price of a car is $20,000 and then increases 10% ($2,000), we would expect bigger response because the change in price is large relative to the income of the typical consumer.

International comparisons of the price elasticity of demand for food suggest that demand is more price elastic when the good represents a large part of the consumer's budget. In wealthy countries such as the United States, Canada, and Germany, the price elasticity of demand for food is around 0.15.[1] In poor countries such as India, Nigeria, and Bolivia, people spend a larger fraction of their budget on food, so they are more responsive to changes in food prices. In these countries the price elasticity of demand is around 0.34.

Let's summarize what we know about the determinants of the price elasticity of demand. The demand for a product will be relatively elastic if

- There are good substitutes for the product.
- Consumers have time to respond to the price change.
- The product represents a large fraction of the consumer's budget.

The price elasticity of demand for some products varies with the age of the consumer. For the general population, the demand for cigarettes is inelastic, with $E_d = 0.30$. For teenagers, the demand for cigarettes is elastic, with $E_d = 1.30$. The elasticity is larger for teenagers because cigarettes take up a bigger fraction of a teenager's budget and most teenagers are not yet addicted to them. For the implications for the effort to cut teenage smoking, read "A Closer Look: How to Cut Teen Smoking by 60%."

Computing Price Elasticity: Initial Value Versus Midpoint

To compute the price elasticity of demand from market data, we divide the percentage change in the quantity by the percentage change in price. As explained in the Appendix to Chapter 1, there are two ways to compute a percentage change. The simplest approach is to use the initial value of the variable. Suppose the price of milk increases from $2.00 to $2.20 and the quantity falls from 100 to 85 (shown in Table 5.2). The percentage change in price is the change ($0.20) divided by the initial value ($2.00), or

A CLOSER LOOK

How to Cut Teen Smoking by 60%

Under the 1997 tobacco settlement, if smoking by teenagers does not decline by 60% by the year 2007, cigarette makers will be fined $2 billion.[2] The settlement is expected to increase cigarette prices by about 62 cents per pack, a percentage increase of about 25%. Will that be enough to reduce teen smoking by the target percentage? The answer depends on the price elasticity of demand for cigarettes by teens.

The demand for cigarettes by teenagers is elastic: 1.3. This means that a 10% increase in the price of cigarettes will decrease teen cigarette consumption by 13%.[3] About half the reduction results from fewer teen smokers, and the other half results from fewer cigarettes for each teen smoker. Although the teen demand for cigarettes is relatively elastic, a 25% price hike will not be enough to cut teen smoking by the target amount. Given an elasticity of 1.3, cigarette prices would have to increase by about 46% to reach the 60% reduction required by the settlement (60% divided by 1.3). Recognizing this tobacco companies have taken other measures to reduce teen smoking, including antismoking campaigns aimed at teens.

10%. The percentage change in quantity is the change (15) divided by the initial value (100), or 15%. Using the initial values to compute the percentage changes, the price elasticity of demand is 1.50:

$$E_d = \frac{\text{percentage change in quantity}}{\text{percentage change in price}} = \frac{\dfrac{15}{100}}{\dfrac{\$0.20}{\$2.00}} = \frac{15\%}{10\%} = 1.5$$

Midpoint method

A method of computing a percentage change by dividing the change in the variable by the average value of the variable, or the midpoint between the old value and the new one.

The **midpoint method** provides a more precise way to compute a percentage change: We divide the change in the variable by the average value of the variable, or the midpoint between the old value and the new one. We can use the midpoint approach to compute the price elasticity associated with the changes listed in Table 5.2. The percentage change in price equals the change in price (0.20) divided by the average price ($2.10), for a percentage change of 9.52%:

$$\text{percentage change in price} = \frac{0.20}{(2.00 + 2.20)/2} = \frac{0.20}{2.10} = 9.52\%$$

TABLE 5.2 Computing Percentage Changes and Elasticity

	Old	New	Initial Value Method	Midpoint Value Method
Price	$2.00	$2.20	Percent change: 10% = $0.20 ÷ $2.00	Percent change: 9.52% = 0.20 ÷ 2.10
Quantity	100	85	Percent change: **15%** = 15 ÷ 100 Elasticity: 1.5 = 15% ÷ 10%	Percent change: 16.22% = **15** ÷ 92.5 Elasticity: 1.70 = 16.22% ÷ 9.52%

The percentage change in quantity equals the change in quantity (15) divided by the average quantity (92.5), for a percentage change of 16.22%:

$$\text{percentage change in quantity} = \frac{15}{(100 + 85)/2} = \frac{15}{92.5} = 16.22\%$$

If we plug these percentage changes into the formula for the price elasticity of demand, the computed price elasticity is 1.70:

$$E_d = \frac{\text{percentage change in quantity}}{\text{percentage change in price}} = \frac{16.22\%}{9.52\%} = 1.70$$

Why is this elasticity different from the elasticity computed with the initial values (1.50)? The midpoint approach measures the percentage changes more precisely, so we get a more precise measure of price elasticity. In this case, the percentage changes are relatively small, so the two elasticity numbers aren't too far apart. If the percentage changes were larger, however, the elasticity numbers generated by the two approaches would be quite different, and it would be wise to use the midpoint approach. In this book, we will use the simpler approach (initial value).

Elasticity Along a Linear Demand Curve

If a demand curve is linear—a straight line—does that mean that the elasticity of demand is the same at all points on the line? As shown in Figure 5.2, the price elasticity of demand decreases as we move downward along a linear demand curve.

▶ On the upper part of a linear demand curve, demand is elastic. Moving from point *r* to point *s*, the percentage change in quantity is 20%, equal to the change in quantity (2) divided by the initial quantity (10). The percentage change in price is 5%, equal to the change in price ($4) divided by the initial price ($80). Dividing the 20% change in quantity by the 5% change in price gives us an elasticity of 4.0 on the upper part of the demand curve.

▶ On the lower part of a linear demand curve, demand is inelastic. Moving from point *v* to point *w*, the percentage change in quantity is 5%, equal to the change in

FIGURE 5.2

Price Elasticity Along a Linear Demand Curve
The price elasticity of demand decreases as we move downward along a linear demand curve. Demand is elastic on the upper half of the demand curve and inelastic on the lower half.

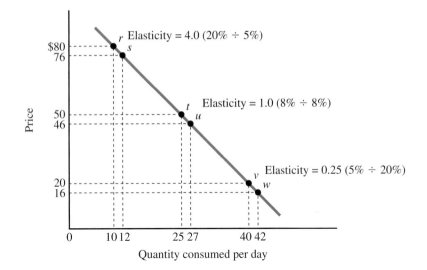

quantity (2) divided by the initial quantity (40). The percentage change in price is 20%, equal to the change in price ($4) divided by the initial price ($20). Dividing the 5% change in quantity by the 20% change in price gives us an elasticity of only 0.25 on the lower part of the demand curve.

Why does the price elasticity vary along a linear demand curve? It's tempting to think the elasticity is constant because a straight line has a constant slope. But that's incorrect, because elasticity is measured by percentage changes, not absolute changes. As we move downward along the demand curve, we're moving in the direction of larger quantities, so the same absolute change in quantity (2 units) becomes a smaller *percentage* change in quantity. Between points *r* and *s*, the percentage change in quantity is 20% (2/10), compared to only 5% (2/40) between points *v* and *w*. At the same time, the movement downward along the curve leads to a larger *percentage* change in price. As a result, the elasticity becomes smaller and smaller.

TEST Your Understanding

1. Complete the statement: To compute the price elasticity of demand, we divide the percentage change in _____ by the percentage change in _____.
2. Complete the statement: If a 10% increase in price decreases the quantity demanded by 12%, the price elasticity of demand is _____.
3. Explain why the demand for movies on DVDs is more elastic in the long run than in the short run.
4. If we are on the upper portion of a linear demand curve and the price increases by 10%, will the quantity demanded decrease by more than 10% or by less than 10%?

Using the Price Elasticity of Demand to Make Predictions

The price elasticity of demand is a very useful tool for economic analysis. If we know the elasticity of demand for a particular good, we can quantify the law of demand, predicting exactly how much more of a product will be sold at a lower price or how much less will be sold at a higher price. We can also predict whether a change in price will increase or decrease total spending on the good.

Predicting Changes in Quantity Demanded

The formula for the elasticity has three variables: The price elasticity of demand (one variable) equals the percentage change in quantity (the second variable) divided by the percentage change in price (the third variable). If we know two of the three variables, we can compute the third. For example, suppose you run a campus film series and you've decided to increase your admission price by 15%. If you know the elasticity of demand for your movies, you could use the elasticity formula to predict how many fewer tickets you'll sell at the higher price. Suppose the elasticity of demand is 2.0, and you increase the price by 15%. Rearranging the elasticity formula, we would predict a 30% decrease in the quantity of tickets demanded:

$$\text{percentage change in quantity demanded} = E_d \cdot \text{percentage change in price}$$
$$= 2.0 \cdot 15\% = 30\%$$

Applications: College Education, Highway Deaths, and Medical Care

How could university officials use the price elasticity of demand? Suppose a university increases its tuition from $4,000 to $4,400 and wants to predict how the price hike will affect enrollment. Suppose the price elasticity of demand for an education at the university is 2.40. In this case, a 10% increase in tuition will decrease enrollment by 24%:

$$\text{percentage change in quantity demanded} = E_d \cdot \text{percentage change in price}$$
$$= 2.40 \cdot 10\% = 24\%$$

How would a tax on beer affect highway deaths among young adults? The price elasticity of demand for beer among young adults is about 1.30, and the number of highway deaths is roughly proportional to the group's beer consumption.[4] If a state imposes a beer tax that increases the price of beer by 20%, what will happen to the number of highway deaths among young adults? Using the elasticity formula, we predict that beer consumption will decrease by 26%:

$$\text{percentage change in quantity demanded} = E_d \cdot \text{percentage change in price}$$
$$= 1.30 \cdot 20\% = 26\%$$

If the number of highway deaths among young adults is proportional to their beer consumption, the number of deaths will also decrease by 26%. Of course, if young adults switch from beer to other alcoholic beverages, the number of highway deaths will decrease by a smaller amount.

If the price of medical care increases, how will consumers respond? The rising cost of medical care has forced many nations to take a closer look at programs that subsidize medical care for their citizens. If prices are increased to cover more of the costs of providing medical care, how will this affect poor and wealthy households? For an answer, read "A Closer Look: Pricing Medical Care in Developing Countries."

Predicting Changes in Total Revenue

If a firm increases the price of its product, will total sales revenue increase or decrease? The answer depends on the price elasticity of demand for the product. If we know the price elasticity, we can determine whether a price hike will increase or decrease the firm's total revenue.

Let's return to the example of the campus film series. Suppose you are thinking about increasing the price of tickets from $4.00 to $4.40. An increase in the ticket price brings good news and bad news:

▶ Good news. You get more money for each ticket sold.
▶ Bad news. You sell fewer tickets.

A CLOSER LOOK   Pricing Medical Care in Developing Countries

Many developing nations subsidize medical care, charging consumers a small fraction of the cost of providing the services. If a nation were to cut its subsidies and thus increase the price of medical care, how would the higher price affect its poor and wealthy households? In Côte d'Ivoire in Africa, the price elasticity of demand for hospital services is 0.47 for poor households and 0.29 for wealthy households.[5] This means that a 10% increase in the price of hospital services would cause poor households to cut back their hospital care by 4.7%, whereas wealthy households would cut back by only 2.9%. In Peru, the differences between poor and wealthy households are even larger: The price elasticity is 0.67 for poor households but only 0.03 for wealthy households. The same pattern occurs in the demand for the medical services provided in outpatient clinics. The poor are much more sensitive to price, so when prices increase, they suffer much larger reductions in medical care.

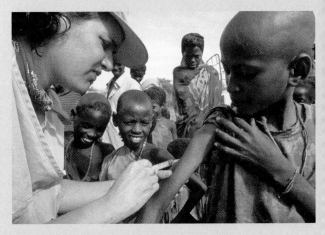

In developing nations, the poor are relatively sensitive to changes in the price of medical care.

TABLE 5.3

**Price and Total Revenue
with Elastic Demand**

Price	Quantity of Tickets Sold	Total Revenue
4.00	100	$400
4.40	80	$352

Your total revenue will decrease if the bad news (fewer tickets sold) dominates the good news (more money per ticket). The elasticity of demand tells us how the good news compares to the bad news. If demand is elastic, consumers will respond to the higher price by purchasing many fewer tickets, so although you will collect more money per ticket, you'll sell so few tickets that your total revenue will decrease. For example, as Table 5.3 shows, if the price elasticity of demand is 2.0, a 10% increase in price will decrease the quantity demanded by 20%, from 100 to 80 tickets. Because the percentage decrease in quantity (the bad news) exceeds the percentage increase in price (the good news), total revenue decreases, from $400 to $352. In general, an elastic demand means that the percentage change in quantity (the bad news from a price hike) will exceed the percentage change in price (the good news), so an increase in price will decrease total revenue.

We get the opposite result if the demand for the good is inelastic: An increase in price increases total revenue. If demand is inelastic, consumers are not very responsive to an increase in price, so the good news (more money per unit sold) dominates the bad news (fewer units sold). For example, suppose that your campus bookstore starts with a textbook price of $50 and a quantity of 100 books. If the bookstore increases its price by 10% (from $50 to $55 per book) and the elasticity of demand for textbooks is 0.40, the quantity of textbooks sold will decrease by only 4% (from 100 to 96). Therefore, the store's total revenue will be $5,280 ($55 × 96), compared to only $5,000 at the lower price ($50 × 100). In general, an inelastic demand means that the percentage change in quantity will be smaller than the percentage change in price, so an increase in price will increase total revenue.

Table 5.4 summarizes the revenue effects of changes in prices for different types of goods:

▶ *Elastic demand.* There is a negative relationship between price and total revenue: An increase in price decreases total revenue; a decrease in price increases total revenue.

TABLE 5.4 Elasticity and Total Revenue

Type of Demand	Value of Price Elasticity of Demand	Change in Quantity Versus Change in Price	Effect of Higher Price on Total Revenue	Effect of Lower Price on Total Revenue
Elastic	Greater than 1.0	Larger percentage change in quantity	Decreases	Increases
Inelastic	Less than 1.0	Smaller percentage change in quantity	Increases	Decreases
Unitary elastic	1.0	Same percentage changes in quantity and price	Does not change	Does not change

▶ *Inelastic demand.* There is a positive relationship between price and total revenue: An increase in price increases total revenue; a decrease in price decreases total revenue.

▶ *Unitary elastic demand.* Total revenue does not vary with price.

The relationship between elasticity and total revenue provides a simple test of whether demand is elastic or inelastic. Suppose that when a music store increases the price of its CDs, its total revenue from CDs drops. The negative relationship between price and total revenue means that demand for the store's CDs is elastic: Total revenue decreases because consumers are very responsive to an increase in price, buying a much smaller quantity. In contrast, suppose that when a city increases the price it charges for water, the total revenue from water sales increases. The positive relationship between price and total revenue suggests that the demand for the city's water is inelastic: Total revenue increases because consumers are not very responsive to an increase in price.

We can use Figure 5.3 to reinforce what we've learned about price elasticity and total revenue. Panel A shows a linear demand curve (the same as the one in Figure 5.2), and Panel B shows the total-revenue curve associated with the demand curve. We know that demand is elastic along the upper half of a linear demand curve; that means that a decrease in price will increase the quantity sold by a larger percentage amount. As a result, total revenue will increase, as shown by the positively sloped total-revenue curve between points *b* and *c*. In contrast, demand is inelastic along the lower half of a linear demand curve; that means that a decrease in price will increase the quantity sold by a smaller percentage amount. As a result, total revenue will decrease, as shown by the negatively sloped total-revenue curve between points *c* and *d*. The total-revenue curve will reach its maximum at the midpoint of the linear demand curve, where demand is unitary elastic. In Figure 5.3, demand is unitary elastic at point *t* on the demand curve, so total revenue reaches its maximum at $1,250 at point *c* on the total-revenue curve.

Applications: Transit Deficits, Property Crime

At the beginning of the chapter, we considered the question of whether increasing the price of bus rides would reduce a city's transit deficit. The price elasticity in the typical city is 0.33, meaning that a 10% increase in fares will decrease ridership by only about 3.3%.[6] Because demand for bus travel is inelastic, the good news associated with a fare hike (10% more revenue per rider) will dominate the bad news (3.3% fewer riders), and total fare revenue will increase. In other words, an increase in fares will reduce the transit deficit.

What's the connection between antidrug policies and property crimes such as robbery, burglary, and auto theft? The government uses search-and-destroy tactics to restrict the supply of illegal drugs. If this approach succeeds, drugs become scarce, and the price of drugs increases. Because the demand for illegal drugs is inelastic, the increase in price will increase total spending on illegal drugs. Many drug addicts support their habits by stealing personal property—robbing people, stealing cars, and burglarizing homes. This means that drug addicts will commit more property crimes to support the higher total spending level associated with pricier drugs.[7] Given the inelas-

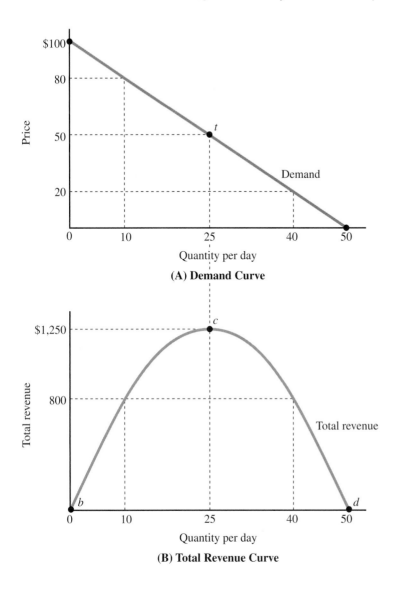

(A) Demand Curve

(B) Total Revenue Curve

FIGURE 5.3
Elasticity and Total Revenue Along a Linear Demand Curve
Demand is elastic along the upper half of a linear demand curve, so an increase in quantity (from a decrease in price) increases total revenue, as shown between points *b* and *c*. Demand is inelastic along the lower half of a linear demand curve, so an increase in quantity (from a decrease in price) decreases total revenue, as shown between points *c* and *d*. Total revenue reaches its maximum at the midpoint of the demand curve (point *t*), where demand is unitary elastic.

tic demand for illegal drugs and the connection between drug consumption and property crime, there is a trade-off: A policy that increases drug prices will slightly reduce drug consumption and the number of drug addicts, but it will also increase property crime committed by addicts who continue to abuse drugs.

DVD Elasticity

The manager of a DVD rental store has asked you to solve a puzzle. According to national studies of the DVD rental market, the price elasticity of demand for DVD rentals is 0.80: A 10% increase in price decreases the quantity of DVDs demanded by about 8%. In other words, the demand for DVDs is inelastic. Based on this information, the manager of the DVD store increased her prices by 20%, expecting her total revenue to increase. She expected the good news (more money per rental) to dominate the bad news (fewer rentals). But in fact her total revenue decreased. Why?

The demand for DVDs at an individual rental store is more elastic than the overall demand for DVDs at all rental stores.

The key to solving this puzzle is to recognize that the manager can't use the results of a national study to predict the effects of increasing her own price. The national study suggests that if all DVD stores in the nation increased their prices by 10%, the nationwide quantity of DVDs demanded would drop by 8%. But when a single DVD store in a city increases its price, consumers can easily rent DVDs at other competing stores in the city. As a result, a 10% increase in the price of DVD rentals at one store will decrease the quantity sold by that store by much more than 8%. The demand facing an individual store is elastic, so an increase in price will decrease total revenue. ■

TEST Your Understanding

5. Complete the statement: If the price elasticity of demand is 0.60, a 10% increase in price will _____ the quantity demanded by _____%. (Fill in the blanks with "increase" or "decrease".)

6. If an increase in the price of accordions does not change total revenue from accordion sales, what can we infer about the price elasticity of demand for accordions?

7. Suppose the price elasticity of demand for vanity license plates in the state of Ohio is 2.60. If the state's objective is to maximize its revenue from vanity plates, should it pick a higher price or a lower one?

Other Elasticities of Demand

We've seen that the price elasticity of demand measures the responsiveness of consumers to changes in the price of a particular good. Of course, the demand for a particular product also depends on other variables such as consumer income and the prices of related goods—substitutes and complements. We can use two other elasticities to measure the responsiveness of consumers to changes in these other variables that affect demand.

We saw in Chapter 4 that the demand for a particular product depends in part on the consumer's income. The **income elasticity of demand** measures the responsiveness of demand to changes in income, indicating how much more or less of a particular product is purchased as income changes. The income elasticity of demand is defined as the percentage change in quantity demanded divided by the percentage change in income:

$$E_i = \frac{\text{percentage change in quantity demanded}}{\text{percentage change in income}}$$

Income elasticity of demand

A measure of the responsiveness of the quantity demanded to changes in consumer income; computed by dividing the percentage change in the quantity demanded by the percentage change in income.

For example, if a 10% increase in income increases the quantity of books demanded by 15%, the income elasticity of demand for books is 1.50 (equal to 15% ÷ 10%).

We can use the income elasticities of demand for various products to categorize the products into different types. Recall from Chapter 4 that when a consumer's income increases, he or she buys more of a "normal" good. If the income elasticity is positive—indicating a positive relationship between income and demand—we say that the good is normal. New cars and new clothes are products that have positive income elasticities and are thus considered normal goods. On the other hand, the consumption of other products, called "inferior" goods, increases as income *decreases.* For these goods, the income elasticity is negative—revealing a negative relationship between income and demand. Some examples are intercity bus travel, used clothing, and used cars.

We saw in Chapter 4 that the demand for a particular product also depends in part on the prices of related goods—substitutes and complements. The **cross elasticity of demand** measures the responsiveness of demand to changes in the prices of other goods, indicating how much more or less of a particular product is purchased as other prices change. The cross elasticity is defined as the percentage change in quantity demanded of one good (*X*) divided by the percentage change in the price of a related good (*Y*):

$$E_{xy} = \frac{\text{percentage change in quantity of } X \text{ demanded}}{\text{percentage change in price of } Y}$$

Cross elasticity of demand

A measure of the responsiveness of the quantity demanded to changes in the price of a related good; computed by dividing the percentage change in the quantity demanded of one good (*X*) by the percentage change in the price of another good (*Y*).

As we saw in Chapter 4, two goods are considered substitutes if there is a positive relationship between the quantity demanded of one good and the price of the other good. For example, an increase in the price of bananas increases the demand for apples as consumers substitute apples for the now relatively expensive bananas. For substitute goods, the cross elasticity is positive. In contrast, two goods are considered complements if there is a negative relationship between the quantity demanded of one good and the price of the other. For example, an increase in the price of ice cream increases the cost of apple pie with ice cream, causing consumers to demand fewer apples. For complementary goods, the cross elasticity is negative.

Estimates of cross elasticity of demand are useful to retailers in their pricing decisions. For example, when a grocery store cuts the price of peanut butter by 10%, the store will sell more peanut butter but will also sell more complementary goods such as jelly and bread. If the cross elasticity of demand for jelly is 0.5, a 10% decrease in the price of peanut butter will increase the demand for jelly by 5%. Retailers use coupons for one product to promote the sales of that good as well as complementary goods. Armed with the relevant cross elasticities, retailers can predict just how much more of a complementary good consumers will buy.

The Price Elasticity of Supply

Price elasticity of supply
A measure of the responsiveness of the quantity supplied to changes in price; computed by dividing the percentage change in quantity supplied by the percentage change in price.

Let's look at elasticity on the supply side of the market. The **price elasticity of supply** measures the responsiveness of producers to changes in price. We compute this elasticity by dividing the percentage change in quantity supplied by the percentage change in price:

$$E_s = \frac{\text{percentage change in quantity supplied}}{\text{percentage change in price}}$$

In Figure 5.4, when the price of milk increases from $2.00 to $2.20, the quantity supplied increases from 100 million gallons to 120 million gallons. In other words, a 10% increase in price increased the quantity supplied by 20%, so using the initial-value formula for percentage change, the price elasticity of supply is 2.0:

$$E_s = \frac{\text{percentage change in quantity supplied}}{\text{percentage change in price}} = \frac{\dfrac{20}{100}}{\dfrac{\$0.20}{\$2.00}} = \frac{20\%}{10\%} = 2.0$$

Time is an important factor in determining the price elasticity of supply for a product. When the price of a particular product increases, the immediate response is that current producers produce more of the product in their existing production facil-

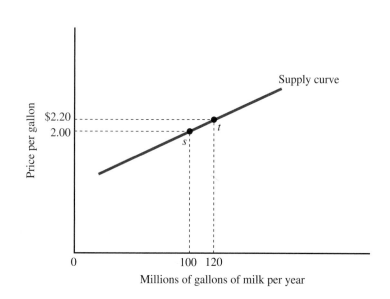

FIGURE 5.4

The Market Supply Curve and Price Elasticity of Supply
A 10% increase in the price of milk (from $2 to $2.20) increases the quantity supplied by 20% (from 100 million gallons to 120 million), so the price elasticity of supply is 2.0 = (20% ÷ 10%).

ities (for example, in their factories, stores, offices, or restaurants). Although a higher price will certainly induce firms to produce more, the response is limited by the limited capacity of the firms' production facilities. Over time, however, new firms can enter the market and old firms can build new production facilities, so there will be a larger response in the long run. As time passes, supply becomes more elastic because more and more firms have the time to build production facilities and produce more output.

The milk industry provides a good example of the difference between the elasticity over a short period of time and a longer period. The price elasticity of supply over a one-year period is 0.12: If the price of milk increases by 10% and stays there for a year, the quantity of milk supplied will rise by only 1.2%.[8] In the short run, dairy farmers can squeeze just a little more output from their existing production facilities. Over a 10-year period, however, the price elasticity is 2.5: The same 10% rise in price will increase the quantity supplied by 25%. In the long run, dairy farmers can expand existing facilities and build new ones, so in the long run, there is a larger response to a higher price.

Predicting Changes in Quantity Supplied

We can use the price elasticity of supply to predict the effect of price changes on the quantity supplied. For example, suppose that the elasticity of supply is 0.80 and the price increases by 5%. Rearranging the elasticity formula, we would predict a 4% increase in quantity supplied:

$$\text{percentage change in quantity supplied} = E_s \cdot \text{percentage change in price}$$
$$= 0.80 \cdot 5\% = 4\%$$

As we saw in Chapter 4, many governments establish minimum prices for agricultural products. The higher the minimum price, the larger the quantity supplied, consistent with the law of supply. If we know the price elasticity of supply, we can predict just how much more will be supplied at a higher minimum price. For example, if the minimum price of cheese increases by 10% and the price elasticity is 0.60, the quantity of cheese supplied will rise by 6%:

$$\text{percentage change in quantity supplied} = E_s \cdot \text{percentage change in price}$$
$$= 0.60 \cdot 10\% = 6\%$$

Extreme Cases: Perfectly Inelastic Supply and Perfectly Elastic Supply

Figure 5.5 shows two supply curves that show the extreme cases of supply elasticity. The supply curve in Panel A of Figure 5.5 is a vertical line, indicating that regardless of price, the quantity supplied is 50 units. This is the case of **perfectly inelastic supply**, with a price elasticity of supply equal to zero. The numerator in the elasticity expression (the percentage change in quantity supplied) is zero, regardless of the percentage change in the price of the good. Land is an example of a product that has a perfectly inelastic supply. In the words of Will Rogers, "The trouble with land is that they're not making it any more."

Perfectly inelastic supply
The price elasticity of supply equals 0.

FIGURE 5.5

Perfectly Inelastic Supply and Perfectly Elastic Supply

In Panel A, the quantity supplied is the same at every price, so the price elasticity of supply is zero. In Panel B, the quantity supplied is infinitely responsive to changes in price, so the price elasticity of supply is infinite.

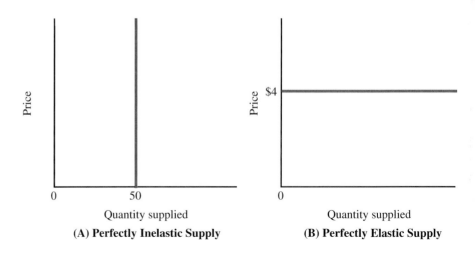

(A) Perfectly Inelastic Supply   **(B) Perfectly Elastic Supply**

Perfectly elastic supply

The price elasticity of supply is infinite.

The supply curve in Panel B of Figure 5.5 is a horizontal line, indicating that the quantity supplied is infinitely responsive to any change in price. This is the case of **perfectly elastic supply**, with a price elasticity of supply equal to infinity. The numerator in the elasticity expression (the percentage change in quantity supplied) is infinite, regardless of the percentage change in the price of the good. One implication of this supply curve is that if the price were to drop from $4 to any lower price, the quantity supplied would fall to zero. Later in the book we'll explain the economics behind a perfectly elastic supply.

Predicting Changes in Price Using Supply and Demand Elasticities

When supply or demand changes—that is, when the supply curve or demand curve shifts—we can draw a supply and demand diagram to predict whether the equilibrium price will increase or decrease. In many cases, the simple diagram will show all we need to know about the effects of a change in supply or demand. But what if we want to predict how much a price will increase or decrease? We can use a simple formula to predict the change in the equilibrium price resulting from a change in supply or a change in demand.

The Price Effects of a Change in Demand

In Figure 5.6, an increase in demand shifts the demand curve to the right and increases the equilibrium price. We explained in Chapter 4 that a demand curve shifts as a result of a change in something other than the price of the product—for example, a change in income, tastes, or the price of a related good. When demand increases, the immediate effect is excess demand: At the original price ($2.00), the quantity demanded exceeds the quantity supplied by 35 million gallons (135 million − 100 million). As the price increases, both consumers and producers help to eliminate the excess demand: Consumers buy less (the law of demand), and firms produce more (the law of supply).

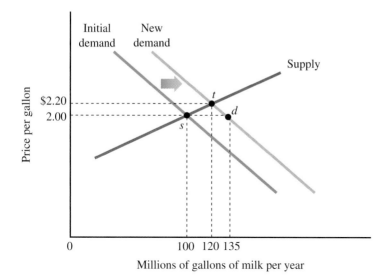

FIGURE 5.6

An Increase in Demand Increases the Equilibrium Price
An increase in demand shifts the demand curve to the right, increasing the equilibrium price. In this case, a 35% increase in demand increases the price by 10%. Using the price-change formula, 10% = 35% ÷ (2.0 + 1.5).

If both consumers and producers are very responsive to changes in price, it will take a small increase in price to eliminate the excess demand. In other words, an increase in demand will cause a small increase in price if both demand and supply are elastic.

We can use the following **price-change formula** to predict the change in the equilibrium price resulting from a change in demand. We divide the percentage change in demand by the sum of the price elasticities of supply and demand:

$$\text{percentage change in equilibrium price} = \frac{\text{percentage change in demand}}{E_s + E_d}$$

Price-change formula
A formula that shows the percentage change in equilibrium price resulting from a change in demand or supply, given values for the price elasticity of supply and the price elasticity of demand.

The numerator is the rightward shift of the demand curve in percentage terms. In Figure 5.6, the initial quantity demanded at a price of $2.00 is 100 million gallons (shown by the initial demand curve), and the new quantity demanded at the same price is 135 million gallons (shown by the new demand curve). The change in demand is 35% (35/100). The two price elasticities appear in the denominator. This is sensible because if consumers and producers are very responsive to changes in price (the elasticities are large numbers), excess demand will be eliminated with a relatively small increase in price.

We can use a simple example to see how to use the price-change formula. Suppose that demand increases by 35% (the demand curve shifts to the right by 35%). If the supply elasticity is 2.0 and the demand elasticity is 1.5, the predicted change in the equilibrium price is 10%:

$$\text{percentage change in equilibrium price} = \frac{35\%}{2.0 + 1.5} = 10\%$$

In Figure 5.6, the equilibrium price increases by 10%, from $2.00 to $2.20. If either demand or supply were less elastic (if either of the elasticity numbers were smaller), the predicted change in price would be larger. For example, if the supply elasticity were 0.25 instead of 2.0, we would predict a 20% increase in price (35% ÷ 1.75).

What about the direction of the price change? We know from Chapter 4 that an increase in demand increases the equilibrium price, and a decrease in demand decreases the equilibrium price. Therefore, the percentage change in price is positive when the change in demand is positive (when demand increases and the demand curve shifts to the right), and negative when the change in demand is negative (when demand decreases and the demand curve shifts to the left). For example, suppose the demand for a product decreases by 15% (the demand curve shifts to the left by 15%). If the supply elasticity is 1.0 and the demand elasticity is 0.50, the price-change formula shows that the equilibrium price will decrease by 10%:

$$\text{percentage change in equilibrium price} = \frac{-15\%}{1.0 + 1.5} = -10\%$$

We can use the price-change formula to predict the effects of changes in demand on equilibrium prices. Suppose a city is expected to grow by 9% in the next few years, and you want to predict the effects of population growth on the equilibrium price of housing. If the price elasticity of supply is 2.0 and the price elasticity of demand is 1.0, the population growth will increase the equilibrium price of housing by 3%:

$$\text{percentage change in equilibrium price} = \frac{9\%}{2.0 + 1.0} = 3\%$$

We could also use the price-change formula to predict the price effects of an increase in the demand for organic produce. Suppose the demand for organic food is expected to increase by 10% in the next two years. If the price elasticity of supply for organic food is 2.0 and the price elasticity of demand is 0.50, we would predict a 4% increase in price:

$$\text{percentage change in equilibrium price} = \frac{10\%}{2.0 + 0.50} = 4\%$$

The Price Effects of a Change in Supply

We can use a slightly different version of the price-change formula to predict the change in the equilibrium price resulting from a change in supply. As explained in Chapter 4, a change in supply results from changes in something other than the price of the product—for example, a change in the cost of labor or raw materials, a change in production technology, or a change in the number of firms. The immediate effect of an increase in supply is excess supply: At the original price, the quantity supplied exceeds the quantity demanded. As the price drops, consumers respond by purchasing more and producers respond by producing less, so the gap between quantity supplied and quantity demanded narrows. If both consumers and producers are very responsive to changes in price, it will take only a small decrease in price to eliminate the excess supply. In other words, an increase in supply will cause a small decrease in price if both demand and supply are elastic.

To predict the change in price resulting from a change in supply, we just substitute the percentage change in supply for the percentage change in demand in the numerator of the price-change formula and add a minus sign. The minus sign indicates that there is a negative relationship between the equilibrium price and supply: When supply increases—that is, when the supply curve shifts to the right—the price drops; when supply decreases, the price rises. For example, suppose the supply of milk increases by 10%. If the price elasticity of demand is 0.6 and the price elasticity of supply is 1.4, the equilibrium price will decrease by 5%:

$$\text{percentage change in equilibrium price} = -\frac{\text{percentage change in supply}}{E_s + E_d}$$

$$\text{percentage change in equilibrium price} = -\frac{10\%}{1.4 + 0.6} = -5\%$$

The price-change formula can be used by firms and government to predict the effects of changes in supply on equilibrium prices. Suppose a city decides to limit the amount of new housing by limiting the amount of land that can be developed and the policy decreases the supply of housing by 6%. If the price elasticity of supply is 2.0 and the price elasticity of demand is 1.0, the policy will increase the equilibrium price of housing by 2%:

$$\text{percentage change in equilibrium price} = -\frac{-6\%}{2.0 + 1.0} = 2\%$$

Similarly, we can use the formula to predict the effects of a war in the Middle East on the equilibrium price of oil. Suppose a war disrupts supply from a major oil exporter, decreasing the world supply of oil by 12.5%. If the price elasticity of supply is 0.50 and the price elasticity of demand is 0.75, the war will increase the equilibrium price of oil by 10%:

$$\text{percentage change in equilibrium price} = -\frac{-12.5\%}{0.50 + 0.75} = 10\%$$

TEST Your Understanding

8. Complete the statement: If a 10% increase in price increases the quantity supplied by 15%, the price elasticity of supply is _____.

9. Suppose the price elasticity of a supply of cheese is 0.80. If the price of cheese rises by 20%, by what percentage will the quantity supplied change?

10. Suppose that the elasticity of demand for chewing tobacco is 0.70 and the elasticity of supply is 2.30. If an antichewing campaign decreases the demand for chewing tobacco by 30%, in what direction and by what percentage will the price of chewing tobacco change?

11. Suppose that the elasticity of demand for motel rooms in a town near a ski area is 1.0 and the elasticity of supply is 0.50. If the population of the surrounding area increases by 30%, in what direction and by what percentage will the price of motel rooms change?

USING THE TOOLS

This chapter introduced several new tools of economics, including four different elasticities and a formula that can be used to predict the change in price resulting from a change in supply or demand. Here are some opportunities to use these tools to do your own economic analysis.

1. Projecting Transit Ridership

As a transit planner, you must predict how many people ride commuter trains and how much money is generated from train fares. According to a recent study,[9] the short-run price elasticity of demand for commuter rail is 0.62, and the long-run elasticity is 1.59. The current ridership is 100,000 people per day. Suppose fares increase by 10%.
a. Predict the changes in train ridership over a one-month period (short run) and a five-year period (long run).
b. Over the one-month period, will total revenue increase or decrease? What will happen in the five-year period?

2. Bumper Crops

Your job is to predict the total revenue generated by the nation's corn crop. Last year's crop was 100 million bushels, and the price was $4.00 per bushel. This year's weather was favorable throughout the country, and this year's crop will be 110 million bushels, or 10% larger than last year's. The price elasticity of demand for corn is 0.50.
a. Predict the effect of the bumper crop on the price of corn, assuming that the entire crop is sold this year.
b. Predict the total revenue from this year's corn crop.
c. Did the favorable weather increase or decrease the total revenue from corn? Why?

3. Price Controls for Medical Care

Suppose that in an attempt to control the rising costs of medical care, the national government imposes price controls on visits to physicians. The maximum price for a physician visit is 10% less than the equilibrium price. Assume that the price elasticity of demand for physician visits is 0.60 and the price elasticity of supply is 1.5.
a. By what percentage will the quantity of medical care supplied decrease?
b. By what percentage will the quantity of medical care demanded increase?
c. Illustrate your answer with a graph.
d. What sort of inefficiencies will occur as a result of the maximum price?
e. Would you expect patients and physicians to find ways around the maximum price?

4. Price Effects of Increased Enrollment

Consider a college town where the initial price of apartments is $400 and the initial quantity is 1,000 apartments. The price elasticity of demand for apartments is 1.0, and the price elasticity of supply of apartments is 0.50.
a. Use supply and demand curves to show the initial equilibrium, and label the equilibrium point *i*.
b. Suppose an increase in college enrollment is expected to increase the demand for apartments in a college town by 15%. Use your graph to show the effects of the increase in demand on the apartment market. Label the new equilibrium point *f*.
c. Predict the effect of the increase in demand on the equilibrium price of apartments.

SUMMARY

This chapter deals with the numbers behind the laws of demand and supply. The law of demand tells us that an increase in the price of a product will decrease the quantity demanded, *ceteris paribus*. If we know the price elasticity of demand for that good, we can determine just how much less of it will be sold at the higher price.

Similarly, if we know the price elasticity of supply for a product, we can determine just how much more of it will be supplied at a higher price. Here are the main points of the chapter.

1 The price elasticity of demand—defined as the percentage change in quantity demanded divided by the percentage change in price—measures the responsiveness of consumers to changes in price.
2 Demand is relatively elastic if there are good substitutes.

3 If demand is elastic, there is a negative relationship between price and total revenue. If demand is inelastic, there is a positive relationship between price and total revenue.
4 The price elasticity of supply—defined as the percentage change in quantity supplied divided by the percentage change in price—measures the responsiveness of producers to changes in price.
5 If we know the elasticities of supply and demand, we can predict the percentage change in price resulting from a change in demand or supply.

KEY TERMS

cross elasticity of demand, 109
elastic demand, 96
income elasticity of demand, 109
inelastic demand, 96
midpoint method, 100

perfectly elastic demand, 96
perfectly elastic supply, 112
perfectly inelastic demand, 96
perfectly inelastic supply, 111
price elasticity of demand, 95

price elasticity of supply, 110
price-change formula, 113
unitary elastic, 96

PROBLEMS AND DISCUSSION QUESTIONS

1 When the price of compact discs (CDs) increased from $10 to $11, the quantity of CDs demanded decreased from 100 to 87. What is the price elasticity of demand for CDs? Is demand elastic or inelastic?
2 Explain why the demand for residential natural gas (gas used for heating, cooling, and cooking) is more elastic than the demand for residential electricity.
3 Would you expect the demand for a specific brand of running shoes to be more elastic or less elastic than the demand for running shoes in general? Why?
4 For each of the following goods, indicate whether you expect demand to be inelastic or elastic, and explain your reasoning: opera, foreign travel, local telephone service, DVD rentals, and eggs.

5 You observe a positive relationship between the price your store charges for CDs and the total revenue from CDs. Is the demand for your CDs elastic or inelastic?
6 Suppose that at the current price, the price elasticity of demand for a campus film series is 1.40. If the objective of the film society is to maximize its total revenue (price times the number of tickets sold), should it increase or decrease its price?
7 As the head of a state chapter of MADD (Mothers Against Drunk Driving), you are to speak in support of policies that discourage drunk driving. The number of highway deaths among young adults, which is roughly proportional to the group's beer consumption, is initially 100 deaths per year. You have scheduled a news conference to express your support for a beer tax that will increase the price of

beer by 10%. The price elasticity of demand for beer is 1.30. Complete the following statement: "The beer tax will decrease the number of highway deaths among young adults by about _____ per year."

8 When the price of paper increases from $100 to $104 per ton, the quantity supplied increases from 200 to 220 tons per day. What is the price elasticity of supply?

9 You are a tax analyst for Washington, D.C., and have been asked to predict how much revenue will be generated by the city's gasoline tax. The initial quantity of gasoline is 100 million gallons per month, and the price elasticity of demand for gasoline in the typical large city is 4.0. The tax, which is $0.10 per gallon, will increase the price of gasoline by 5%.
   a. How much revenue will the gasoline tax generate?
   b. In 1980, tax analysts in Washington, D.C., based their revenue predictions for a gasoline tax on

the elasticity of demand for gasoline in the United States as a whole, which is 1.0. Would you expect the national elasticity to be larger or smaller than the elasticity for the typical large city? Would you expect the analysts to overestimate or underestimate the revenue from the gasoline tax?

10 Suppose that the government restricts logging to protect an endangered species. The restrictions increase the price of wood products and shift the supply curve for new housing to the left by 4%. The initial price of new housing is $100,000, the elasticity of demand is 1.0, and the elasticity of supply is 3.0. Predict the effect of the logging restriction on the equilibrium price of new housing. Illustrate your answer with a graph that shows the initial point (i) and the new equilibrium (f).

MODEL ANSWERS

Chapter-Opening Questions

1 A beer tax will increase the price of beer, decreasing beer consumption. Highway deaths are roughly proportional to beer consumption, so the tax will also decrease highway deaths. The actual change in highway deaths depends on the price elasticity of demand for beer.

2 As shown in "Using the Tools: Bumper Crops," a bumper crop of corn decreases the equilibrium price of corn by a relatively large amount because the demand for corn is inelastic. Although corn farmers will sell more bushels, they will receive much less per bushel, so total revenue will drop.

3 The policies increase the price of the illegal drug, which increases total spending on the drug because demand is inelastic. If drug addicts support their habits with property crime, they commit more crime to support their more expensive habits.

4 As explained in the section "The Price Effects of a Change in Demand," if the elasticity of demand is 1.0 and the elasticity of supply is 2.0, a 9%

increase in demand will increase the equilibrium price by 3%.

Test Your Understanding

1 Quantity, price.

2 1.20.

3 A decrease in the price of DVDs will cause some consumers to buy DVD players and switch from videocassettes to DVDs, but this takes some time.

4 On the upper portion, demand is elastic, so quantity will decrease by more than 10%.

5 Decrease, 6.

6 The price elasticity is 1.0 (neither elastic nor inelastic).

7 Demand is elastic, so a decrease in price would increase total revenue.

8 $1.50 = 15\% \div 10\%$.

9 The quantity supplied will increase by 16%.

10 Using the price-change formula, the price will decrease by 10% = 30% ÷ 3.

11 Using the price-change formula, the price will increase by 20% = 30% ÷ 1.50.

NOTES

1. Chin-Fun Cling and James Peale, Jr., "Income and Price Elasticities," in *Advances in Econometrics Supplement*, edited by Henri Theil (Greenwich, CT: JAI Press, 1989).

2. Michael M. Phillips and Suein L. Hwang, "Why Tobacco Pact Won't Hurt Industry," *Wall Street Journal*, September 12, 1997, p. A2.

3. Frank J. Chaloupka and Michael Grossman, "Price, Tobacco Control Policies, and Smoking among Young Adults," *Journal of Health Economics*, vol. 16, 1997, pp. 359–373.

4. Henry Saffer and Michael Grossman, "Beer Taxes, the Legal Drinking Age, and Youth Motor Vehicle Fatalities," *Journal of Legal Studies*, vol. 16 , June 1987, pp. 351–374.

5. Paul Gertler and Jacques van der Gaag, *The Willingness to Pay for Medical Care: Evidence from Two Developing Countries* (Baltimore, MD: Johns Hopkins University Press, 1990.)

6. Kenneth A. Small, *Urban Transportation Economics* (Philadelphia, PA: Harwood Academic Publishers, 1992).

7. L. P. Silverman and N. L. Sprull, "Urban Crime and the Price of Heroin," *Journal of Urban Economics*, vol. 4, 1977, pp. 80–103.

8. Richard Klemme and Jean-Paul Chavas, "The Effects of Changing Milk Price on Milk Supply and National Dairy Herd Size," *Economic Issues*, No. 92 University of Wisconsin, June 1985.

9. Richard Voith, "The Long Run Elasticity of Demand for Commuter Rail Transportation," *Journal of Urban Economics*, vol. 30, 1991, pp. 360–372.

Consumer Choice

In 2003, Apple Computer started selling music online, with a price of $0.99 per song. This was a dramatic departure from the traditional way of selling music on CDs, with each "bundle" of songs on a CD selling for between $15 and $20. In the first year, Apple sold 70 million songs through its online music service, and other firms entered the market with their own online music stores. One of the purposes of launching the service was to provide an alternative to Internet music piracy for people who wanted just a few songs, not an entire CD. In designing the online music store, the folks at Apple applied some of the basic concepts of consumer choice, although they might not have realized it.

Consumer choice theory is based on the notion that consumers do the best they can, given the limitations dictated by their incomes and consumer prices. The first step in consumer choice is to figure out your options: Given your income or budget, what are the alternative ways you can spend your budget? In other words, you can develop a sort of "menu" of options for spending your money. The menu reveals that there are trade-offs: If you spend more on music, you'll have less for books, movies, and other products. The second step in consumer choice is to pick the best item on your menu of affordable options, the one that generates the highest level of satisfaction.

Why study consumer choice? We are all consumers, and a discussion of consumer choice could help us spend our money in more fruitful ways. Consumer theory also provides insights into how consumers make decisions, and these insights are useful to firms and other organizations that sell products to consumers. Consumer theory also helps us understand why consumption patterns change. For example, the theory helps us understand the trend away from home cooking and toward restaurant meals, and the success of online music stores. Finally, consumer theory provides a decision-making framework that can be applied to a wide variety of decisions.

Consumer choice is really about doing the best with limited resources. Here are some of the practical questions we answer:

1 If you want to determine whether a consumer is doing the best she can, what single question can you ask?
2 Does inflation make the typical consumer better off, worse off, or just as well off?
3 In an attempt to curb teen drinking, New Zealand imposed a special tax on the favorite alcoholic beverage of teens. How did teens respond?

Consumer Constraints and Preferences

Let's consider the decisions of Maxine, a consumer who must decide how many movies and paperback books to buy each month. Maxine has a fixed income per month to spend on the two goods, so her options are limited by her budget. To decide how to spend her money, Maxine takes two steps:

1 She figures out her menu of options, the list of alternative combinations of books and movies her budget allows.
2 She picks the combination of movies that generates the highest level of satisfaction. To pick a combination from the menu, Maxine will carefully consider her own personal preferences and tastes.

We'll start with a discussion of Maxine's budget options, and then discuss her preferences.

Consumer Constraints: The Budget Line

Consider first the constraints faced by a consumer. Maxine's ability to purchase movies and other goods is limited by her income and the prices of movies and other products. Suppose Maxine has a fixed income of $30 per month, which she spends entirely on movies and used paperback books. The price of movies is $3 and the price of books is $1.

Budget line

The line connecting all the combinations of two goods that exhaust a consumer's budget.

A consumer's **budget line** shows all the combinations of two goods that exhaust the consumer's budget. In Figure 6.1, if Maxine spends her entire $30 budget on books, she gets 30 books and no movies (point *y*). At the other extreme, she can spend her entire budget on movies, getting 10 of them (point *x*). The points between these two extremes are possible too. For example, she could reach point *b* (1 movie and 27 books) by spending $3 on movies and $27 on books, or point *c* (2 movies and 24 books) by spending $6 on movies and $24 on books. Although the budget line may look similar to a consumer's demand curve, they are very different graphical tools. The budget line shows the different combinations of two goods that a consumer can buy. The demand curve, on the other hand, shows the quantity of a single good that a consumer is willing to buy at different prices.

Budget set

A set of points that includes all the combinations of goods that a consumer can afford, given the consumer's income and the prices of the goods.

A consumer's **budget set** is the set of all the affordable combinations of two goods. The budget set includes the budget line (combinations that exhaust the budget) as well as combinations that leave the consumer with leftover money. In Figure 6.1, Maxine's budget set is shown as a shaded triangle. She can afford any combination below the budget line, but cannot afford combinations above it.

FIGURE 6.1

Budget Set and Budget Line

The budget set (the shaded triangle) shows all the affordable combinations of books and movies, and the budget line (with endpoints *x* and *y*) shows the combinations that exhaust the budget.

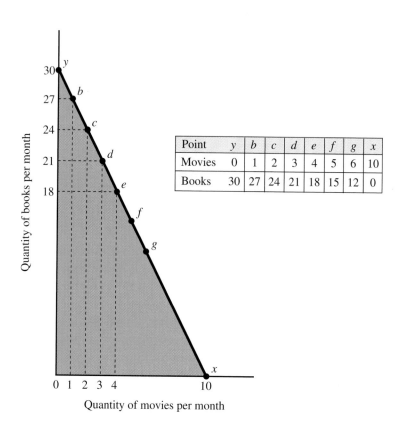

Point	*y*	*b*	*c*	*d*	*e*	*f*	*g*	*x*
Movies	0	1	2	3	4	5	6	10
Books	30	27	24	21	18	15	12	0

Quantity of books per month

Quantity of movies per month

The budget line shows the market trade-off between books and movies. Starting from any point on the budget line, if Maxine buys one more movie, she diverts $3 from book purchases, reducing the number of $1 books she can purchase by 3. The market trade-off equals the **price ratio**, the price of movies ($3) divided by the price of books ($1), or 3 books per movie. The market trade-off also equals the slope of the budget line, the "rise" (the change in books) divided by the "run" (the change in movies). Because all consumers pay the same price for the two goods, they all have the same market trade-off of 3 books per movie.

Price ratio

The ratio of the price of one good to the price of a second good; the market trade-off.

Consumer Preferences: Indifference Curves

We've seen the consumer's budget set, which shows what the consumer can afford. The next step in our discussion of consumer choice is to look at what the consumer wants, what makes the consumer happy. Once we have a means of representing consumer preferences, we can show how a consumer makes her choice, picking the best of the combinations shown by the budget set.

We can represent the consumer's preferences or tastes with **indifference curves**. An indifference curve represents the fundamental idea that there are different ways for a consumer to reach a particular level of satisfaction, or what economists call **utility**. An indifference curve shows the different combinations of two goods that generate the same level of utility or satisfaction. In Figure 6.2, the indifference curve passing through points *b*, *z*, *m*, and *n* separates the combinations of books and movies into three groups.

Indifference curve

A curve showing the different combinations of two goods that generate the same level of utility or satisfaction.

Utility

The satisfaction experienced from consuming a product.

▶ *Superior combinations.* All the combinations above the indifference curve generate higher utility than combinations on the curve. Maxine would prefer point *h* to point *z* because she gets more of both goods with point *h*.

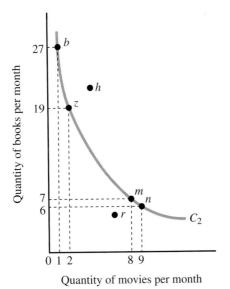

FIGURE 6.2

Indifference Curve and the Marginal Rate of Substitution

The indifference curve shows the different combinations of books and movies that generate the same utility level. The slope is the marginal rate of substitution (*MRS*) between the two goods. The *MRS* is eight books per movie between points *b* and *z*, but only one book per movie between points *m* and *n*.

> ▶ *Inferior combinations.* All the combinations below the indifference curve generate lower utility than combinations on the curve. Maxine would prefer point *m* to point *r* because she gets more of both goods with point *m*.
>
> ▶ *Equivalent combinations.* All combinations along the indifference curve generate the same utility as combination *u*. Maxine is therefore indifferent between combinations *b*, *z*, *m*, and *n*.

An indifference curve shows the preferences of an individual consumer, so indifference curves vary from one consumer to another. Nonetheless, the indifference curves of all consumers share two characteristics: They are negatively sloped, and they become flatter as we move downward along an individual curve.

Why is the indifference curve negatively sloped? If we increased Maxine's movie consumption by one unit without changing her book consumption, her utility would increase. To restore the original utility level, we must take away some books, and that's what happens along an indifference curve. To keep utility constant, there is a negative relationship between books and movies, so the indifference curve is negatively sloped. The slope of the curve is called the **marginal rate of substitution (MRS)** between the two goods; it is the rate at which a consumer is willing to substitute one good for another. The *MRS* is the consumer's trade-off between the two goods, the number of books we must take from Maxine to offset the effect of giving her 1 more movie. In Figure 6.3, if Maxine starts at point *b* and we give her 1 more movie, we take away 8 books to keep her on the same indifference curve. Therefore, starting from point *b*, her marginal rate of substitution is 8 books per movie. When she starts with many books and only 1 movie, she is willing to trade a lot of books to get 1 more movie.

The indifference curve becomes flatter as we move downward along the curve. This reflects the assumption that consumers prefer balanced consumption to extremes. As we move down Maxine's indifference curve, movie consumption increases while book consumption decreases. Starting from one extreme (few movies and many books), she is willing to sacrifice many books to get another movie: The *MRS* is large and the indifference curve is steep. For example, starting from point *b*, her *MRS* is 8

Marginal rate of substitution (*MRS*)

The rate at which a consumer is willing to trade or substitute one good for another.

FIGURE 6.3

Indifference Map

An indifference map shows a set of indifference curves, with utility increasing as we move northeasterly to higher indifference curves (from C_1 to C_2 to C_4).

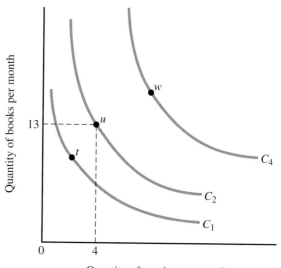

books per movie. But as she gets more and more movies (and fewer and fewer books), she isn't willing to sacrifice as many books to get more movies. As a result, her *MRS* decreases, and the indifference curve becomes flatter. For example, between points *m* and *n*, the *MRS* is 1 book per movie.

An **indifference map** is a set of indifference curves, each with a different level of utility. Figure 6.4 shows three indifference curves: C_1, C_2, and C_4. As Maxine moves from a point on indifference curve C_1 to any point on C_2, her utility increases. This is sensible because she can get more of both goods on C_2, so she will be better off. In general, Maxine's utility increases as she moves in the northeasterly direction to a higher indifference curve (from C_1 to C_2 to C_4, and so on).

Indifference map

A set of indifference curves, each with a different utility level.

TEST Your Understanding

1. Rob consumes muffins (shown on the horizontal axis) and bagels (shown on the vertical axis). He has a budget of $20; the price of bagels is $1 and the price of muffins is $2. Draw his budget line.
2. Draw a representative indifference curve for Rob. Provide enough numbers to show that when he consumes three muffins and 14 bagels, his *MRS* is six bagels per muffin.
3. Why does the marginal rate of substitution decrease as a consumer moves downward along an indifference curve?

Maximizing Utility

Maxine's objective is to maximize her utility, given her budget and the prices of movies and books. Maxine can pick from many affordable combinations of books and movies, and she should pick the one that generates the highest level of utility or satisfaction. In graphical terms, Maxine will reach the highest indifference curve possible, given her budget set.

The Tangency Condition

In Figure 6.4, Maxine maximizes her utility at point *e*, with 4 movies and 18 books. She achieves the utility level associated with indifference curve C_3. Why does she choose point *e* instead of other points such as *z*, *b*, or *w*?

▶ Point *z*. Maxine doesn't choose this point for two reasons. First, it is not on the budget line, so it does not exhaust her budget: She would have some money left over. Second, it is on a lower indifference curve—and thus generates less utility—than point *e*.
▶ Point *b*. Although point *b* exhausts Maxine's budget, it lies on a lower indifference curve than *e*, so it generates less utility than point *e*. Starting from point *b*, Maxine could reallocate her budget and buy more movies and fewer books. As she moves down her budget line, she moves to progressively higher indifference curves, ultimately reaching point *e* on indifference curve C_3.

Maximizing Utility

To maximize utility, the consumer finds the combination of books and movies where an indifference curve is tangent to the budget line. At the utility-maximizing combination, the marginal rate of substitution (the consumer's own trade-off) equals the price ratio (the market trade-off).

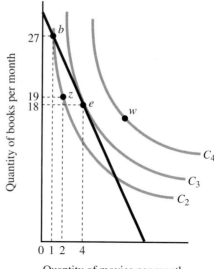

▶ Point *w*. Although point *w* is on a higher indifference curve and thus would generate a higher utility level than point *e*, it lies outside Maxine's budget set, so she cannot afford it.

At point *e*, Maxine reaches the highest indifference curve possible, given her budget set. Notice that at point *e*, the indifference curve touches—but does not pass through—the budget line. In other words, the indifference curve is tangent to the budget line.

Utility-maximizing rule

Pick the affordable combination that makes the marginal rate of substitution equal to the price ratio.

The Utility-Maximizing Rule: MRS = Price Ratio

What is the economic interpretation of the tangency condition? At the point of tangency, the slope of the indifference curve equals the slope of the budget line. The slope of the budget line equals the opportunity cost of movies, computed as the movie price ($3) divided by the book price ($1), or 3 books per movie. The slope of the indifference curve is the marginal rate of substitution (*MRS*), so if the two curves are tangent at point *e*, the *MRS* is also 3 books per movie. In other words, the consumer's trade-off between the two goods (the *MRS*) equals the market trade-off (the price ratio) between the two goods.

■ Utility Maximizing Rule

$$MRS = \frac{\text{price of movie}}{\text{price of book}}$$

To show why the tangency point is best, suppose Maxine tentatively chooses a point where the *MRS* is not equal to the price ratio. For example, starting at point *b*, the indifference curve is relatively steep, and the *MRS* is eight books per movie: She is willing to give up eight books to get a single movie. But given market trade-off, she can actually get that movie by sacrificing only three books, so she will move down her budget line and consume more movies. The same argument applies to any combination for which the *MRS* (the consumer's own trade-off) is not equal to the price ratio (the market trade-off). Anytime Maxine is willing to trade at a rate that is different from market trade-off, it will be in her best interest to do so. The benefits of trading will be exhausted only when the *MRS* equals the price ratio. In Figure 6.4, this happens at point *e*.

Drawing the Demand Curve

We can use the budget line and indifference curve for movies and books to draw Maxine's demand curve for just one of those products—say, movies. We've already derived one point on her demand curve. In Figure 6.5, the upper panel shows the consumer-choice model, with indifference curves and a budget line. When the price of movies is $3, she maximizes utility at point *e*, with 4 movies. The lower panel shows Maxine's demand curve for movies, with the number of movies shown on the horizontal axis and the price of movies on the vertical axis. When the price is $3, her utility-maximizing choice is shown as point *e* in the upper panel and point *E* in the lower panel. In other words, the demand curve shows her utility-maximizing choice.

With so many curves floating around, it is worth reviewing their roles in consumer decision-making.

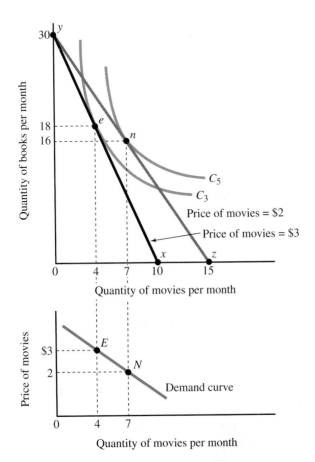

FIGURE 6.5

Drawing the Demand Curve

A decrease in the price of movies tilts the budget line outward. The indifference curve is tangent to the budget line at a larger quantity of movies (7 instead of 4). This is the law of demand: The higher the price, the smaller the quantity demanded.

1 The budget line shows the affordable combinations of two goods, representing the consumer's constraints.

2 An indifference curve shows the different combinations of two goods that generate the same utility level, and thus shows the consumer's preferences.

3 The demand curve shows how much of a *single* product a consumer is willing to buy at a particular price. To get the demand curve, we use both the budget line and indifference curves.

The upper panel Figure 6.5 shows what happens to the budget line when the price of movies decreases to $2. The decrease in price tilts the budget line outward. The original vertical intercept (point *y*) is still in the budget set because if the entire budget is spent on books, the price of movies is irrelevant. The horizontal intercept moves outward from *x* (10 movies) to *z* (15 movies) because with a lower movie price, a given budget will buy more movies. If Maxine buys both books and movies, she will choose a point on the new budget line between points *y* and *z*. In general, the decrease in the movie price makes more combinations affordable.

How will Maxine respond to the lower price of movies? Given the new budget line and the same set of indifference curves, Maxine picks point *n*, where one of her indifference curves is tangent to the new budget line. Maxine responds to the decrease in the movie price by consuming 7 movies instead of 4. With this combination, her *MRS* is equal to the new price ratio of 2 books per movie. The decrease in price means that the market trade-off is lower, and so to satisfy the utility-maximizing rule, Maxine picks a combination of movies and books with a lower *MRS*—2 books per movie, down from 3 books per movie.

The lower panel of Figure 6.5 shows the point on the demand curve associated with a movie price of $2 (point *N*). When the price is $2, Maxine consumes 7 movies. This is consistent with the law of demand: The lower the price, the larger the quantity demanded, *ceteris paribus*. Recall that when we draw a demand curve, we use the *ceteris paribus* assumption that everything except the *price* of the product is fixed. To draw Maxine's demand curve for movies, we change the price of movies, holding fixed the other variables that affect her consumption of movies. These other variables include her income (fixed at $30) and the price of related goods like books, with a fixed price of $1. We also hold fixed her personal preferences for the two goods, meaning that we use a single set of indifference curves.

We've used the consumer choice model to find two points on the individual demand curve. We could repeat the process for other prices to find other points on the demand curve. For each price, we find the quantity of movies that generates the highest possible utility level, given the consumer's budget and the price of the other good. Each point on the demand curve satisfies the utility-maximizing rule that the *MRS* (the consumer's own trade-off) equals the price ratio (the market trade-off).

Do Consumers Actually Do This?

We've used the consumer choice model to find a point on the demand curve of one consumer, given the consumer's budget and her personal preferences. A consumer with a different budget would have a different budget line and by following the utility-maximizing rule (*MRS* = price ratio) would choose a different point on his or her budget line. Similarly, a consumer with different personal preferences would have different indifference curves and would maximize utility with a different combination of movies and books.

Do consumers actually use the consumer choice model to make decisions? When you think about going to the movies, do you compute your *MRS*, and then go only if the *MRS* exceeds the price ratio? Although consumers don't actually base their decisions on *MRS* computations, most consumer choices are consistent with the consumer choice model.

To see how consumers act as if they are using consumer choice model, consider the billiard (pool) play of Minnesota Fats, a legendary player from the 1950s and 1960s. The movement of balls on a pool table obey various laws of physics, including the laws of inertia and friction. Although Minnesota Fats could not state the relevant laws of physics, he played pool as if he applied the laws to every shot. Similarly, although consumers may not compare their *MRS* to the price ratios, they act as if they are applying the utility-maximizing rule.

TEST Your Understanding

4. Recall Rob's situation from an earlier question. He has a $20 budget to spend on muffins (price = $2) and bagels (price = $1). At his current consumption bundle of 3 muffins and 14 bagels, Rob is willing to sacrifice 6 bagels to get 1 muffin. Is he maximizing utility? If not, should he buy more or fewer muffins?
5. What is the difference between the budget line and the demand curve?

Applications of the Consumer Choice Model

We can use the consumer choice model to explore two questions. First, how is the development of online music stores related to Internet music piracy? Second, how does inflation affect a consumer's buying habits and well-being? Third, how is the notion of utility maximization related to the commonsense notion that a person should choose the action with the largest bang per buck?

Music Piracy and Online Music Stores

The chapter opener described the new online music stores, which provide an alternative to the traditional method of buying bundles of songs on CDs. We can use the consumer choice model to explain the logic behind this new development in the music business.

Consider Sam, who has $30 to spend on music and arcade games. In an ideal world, he could buy music by the song, just as he buys arcade games individually.

A
CLOSER
LOOK

Modern Consumer Theory Versus Old Utility Theory

This chapter presents modern consumer theory, which is based on indifference curves and the marginal rate of substitution. This theory does not require a measure of the actual *utility* or satisfaction a consumer gets from a product. It simply requires a measure of the consumer's personal trade-off between two goods, the consumer's marginal rate of substitution. To decide if a consumer could do better, we simply compare the *MRS* to the price ratio.

In contrast, utility theory of the nineteenth century was based on the idea that we could actually measure the utility people get from consuming products. Some social scientists thought it would even be possible to hook people up to a "utility meter" and then see what happens when they consumed a product. The following figure shows the framework for utility theory. The horizontal axis measures the quantity of a product consumed, and the vertical axis measures the person's total utility, in "utils." The slope of the utility curve decreases as consumption increases, reflecting the assumption that the more of a product a person consumes, the lower the marginal utility of the product. Although this theory provides some insights into consumer choice, the assumption of "measurable" utility is troublesome to most economists. Instead, we use budget lines and indifference curves to model consumer choice.

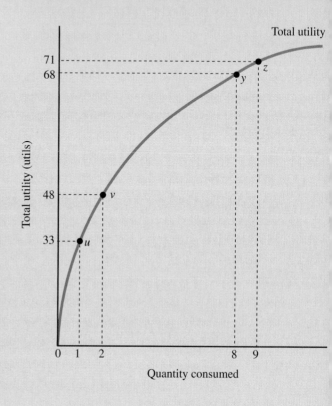

Suppose the price of music in this ideal world is $1 per song and the price of arcade games is $0.50 per game. In Figure 6.6, Sam's budget line is the line connecting points *y* and *x*. He can spend his entire budget on games, getting 60 games (point *y*), or spend it all on songs, getting 30 songs (point *x*). Alternatively, he could split his budget between the two goods. With a price ratio of 2 games per song, the market trade-off is 2 games per song. Suppose that in this ideal world, Sam's best point is *i*, where an indifference curve is tangent to his budget line, meaning that his *MRS* equals the price ratio. At point *i*, Sam would have 6 songs and 48 arcade games.

Suppose that music cannot be purchased by the song but instead must be purchased on CDs. Each CD carries 15 songs and has a price of $15. In this case, Sam has only three options: He can spend his entire budget on games (60 games, as shown by point *y*), or he can get one CD with 15 songs and also get 30 games (point *j*), or he can spend his entire budget on two CDs (30 songs, point *x*). All of these points are

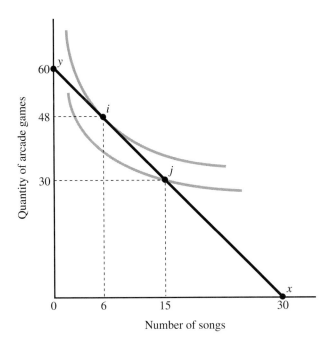

FIGURE 6.6

Internet Music Piracy and iTunes

When music is sold as 15-song bundles on CDs, the consumer has three budget points (y, j, and x) rather than an entire budget line. If songs are sold individually, the consumer has a full budget line and can legally reach his or her ideal combination of 6 songs and 48 arcade games (point i).

below the indifference curve associated with point *i*, so his utility is lower at any of these other points. He'd prefer point *i* (6 songs and 48 games) to any of these other points.

In the world of CDs and Internet file sharing, Sam actually has another option. He can use a swapping service to get songs for free. Of course, this is illegal, and Sam risks a penalty and may also feel bad about breaking the law. If the benefit (free songs) exceeds the cost (risk and bad feelings about law breaking), he will engage in piracy.

Consider next the effects of iTunes and other online music services that sell single songs. Now Sam has a third alternative to buying an entire CD or stealing songs. Sam can get his ideal combination of goods without any risk of criminal penalties, and he may prefer paying for his music to engaging in piracy. One motivation for online music stores is to reduce music piracy by people who want just a few songs off a particular CD. Of course, there are other motives for piracy, and it is expected to continue. But the early experience with online music stores suggest that many consumers prefer the flexibility of buying music by the song and are willing to pay for it.

Inflation, the Real–Nominal Principle, and Consumer Choice

We can use our model of consumer decision-making to address the issue of inflation, defined as a general increase in all prices, including the price of labor. Consider the effects of a doubling of all prices. Using our example, the prices of movies and books would double, along with wages and salaries paid to workers. If Maxine's income comes from a job, the doubling of wages would cause her income to double. How would she respond to inflation?

Online music services that sell single, downloadable songs help consumers achieve maximum utility and avoid music-piracy penalties.

Inflation will not affect Maxine's consumer decision. If consumer prices double, the price of movies doubles to $6 and the price of books doubles to $2, but Maxine's income doubles too, from $30 to $60. Consequently, she will continue to purchase 4 movies, just as she did before inflation. Inflation doesn't affect her consumer decision because it doesn't affect her budget set: Her new budget set, with doubled prices and income, is identical to the old one. To see this, think about the horizontal and vertical intercepts of the budget line—the point where Maxine's budget line crosses the x and y axes. The horizontal intercept shows how many movies Maxine can buy if she spends her entire income on movies. Before inflation, her $30 income could buy 10 movies at $3; after inflation, her $60 income can buy 10 movies at $6 each. Similarly, when the price of books and income both double, the vertical intercept doesn't change.

The implication of this analysis is that inflation doesn't harm or help Maxine. Inflation doesn't affect her budget set or her consumer choices, so she is just as well off as she was before inflation. This is an application of one of the five key principles.

THE REAL–NOMINAL *Principle*

What matters to people is the real value of money or income, not the nominal value.

In our example, what matters to Maxine is her real income, or the purchasing power of her income. Although inflation doubles her income, it also doubles prices, leaving her real income the same.

The Equimarginal Rule

The utility-maximizing rule tells consumers how to pick the best mix of two goods. The logic behind this rule can be used to find the best mix of other things, such as the best mix of skilled and unskilled labor or the best mix of radio and television advertising. For these types of decisions, we can use the **equimarginal rule**, which is a variation on the utility-maximizing rule.

Equimarginal rule

Pick the combination of two things that equalizes the marginal benefit per dollar spent.

■ Equimarginal Rule

If the marginal benefit per dollar spent on one thing exceeds the marginal benefit per dollar spent on a second, do more of the first and less of the second. To get the best possible combination of the two things, pick the mix that equalizes the marginal benefit per dollar spent.

Recall that Maxine picks the mix of movies and books where the *MRS* is 3 books per movie, the same as the price ratio. Maxine is willing to sacrifice 3 books to get 1 movie, meaning that her benefit from 1 movie equals her benefit from 3 books. In other words, the marginal benefit per movie is three times the marginal benefit per book. Compared to books, movies have three times the marginal benefit and *exactly* three times the price, so Maxine's mix of movies and books satisfies the equimarginal principle: She has equalized the marginal benefit per dollar spent on the two goods.

A firm can use the equimarginal principle to pick the best mix of skilled and unskilled workers. Skilled workers are expensive and highly productive, whereas unskilled workers are cheaper but produce less. The firm should pick the worker type with the largest marginal benefit (output produced) per dollar spent. If skilled workers produce $120 worth of output and receive a wage of $20, the benefit per dollar spent is $6 ($120 worth of output divided by the $20 wage). If an unskilled worker produces $30 worth of output and receives a wage of $10, the benefit per dollar spent is only $3 ($30 divided by the $10). Although skilled workers are twice as expensive, they are actually a better deal because they are *four* times as productive. In other words, skilled workers give the firm more bang (output) per buck.

A firm could also use the equimarginal principle to pick the best mix of radio and television advertising. The marginal benefit of advertising is the increase in sales from one more minute of airtime. If a minute of television advertising increases sales by $18,000 and costs $6,000, the marginal benefit per dollar is $3. If a minute of radio advertising increases sales by $2,000 and costs $1,000, the marginal benefit per dollar is only $2. In this case, television gives a bigger bang per buck, so television is a better choice.

Should our hypothetical firm allocate all of its advertising budget to television? We would expect the first television advertisement to be more effective in increasing sales than the second, and the second to be more effective than the third. In general, the marginal benefits of television advertising will decrease as the number of ads increases and so will the marginal bang per buck. Eventually, the marginal bang per buck from television may drop to the point where it is less than

A CLOSER LOOK

The Bang per Buck of Light Spirits

To illustrate the relevance of the equimarginal rule, consider New Zealand's recent experiences with taxing alcoholic beverages. Policymakers who were concerned about teen drinking discovered that the favored beverages among teens were "light spirits"—beverages with alcohol content between 14% and 24%. These light spirits provided the biggest alcoholic bang per buck for teens. For example, cheap rum with an alcohol content of 23% sold for $8, generating a bang per buck of $23 \div 8 = 2.88$.

The government imposed a special tax on light spirits, nearly doubling the price of teens' favorite beverages, from $8 to $14. The bang per buck of light spirits therefore decreased to 1.64, and teens responded by cutting back on light spirits. Producers responded by changing their beverage recipes, cutting the alcohol content to 13.9% to avoid the tax. Moreover, they priced these new "super-light" beverages below the prices of the original light beverages. For example, super-light rum with an alcohol content of 13.9% was priced at $7, yielding a bang per buck of 2.25—bigger than the 1.64 bang per buck from light beverages subject to the tax. Given the equimarginal principle, we would expect many teens to switch to super-light beverages,

and that's exactly what happened. In addition, some teens went the other direction, switching to beverages that were too potent to be subject to the light-spirits tax.

The simple lesson is that consumers respond to price changes and taxes. A tax decreases the bang per buck of the taxed good, causing consumers to switch to products that now have a higher bang per buck than the taxed good. In this case, the tax increased the consumption of beverages with both lower and higher alcohol content.

the marginal bang per buck for the first radio advertisement. At that point, the firm will buy some radio time. For the best mix of radio and television, the marginal benefit per dollar spent on television will equal the marginal benefit per dollar spent on radio.

TEST Your Understanding

6. In the labor example, suppose the wage of skilled workers increases to $60. Which type of worker has a bigger bang per buck?
7. Explain how you would use the equimarginal rule to allocate a fixed amount of time to study for two exams, one in history and one in psychology.

In this chapter, we use some of the key principles of economics to explain the logic behind consumer choice and the law of demand. Here are some opportunities to do your own economic analysis.

1. Utility Maximization for Holiday Party

At your company's annual holiday party, people eat food (price per unit = $1) and drink punch (price per unit = $2), and the firm pays for everything. This year, the firm spent $20 per employee, with equal quantities of food and punch. Your job is to determine whether the company spent this year's party budget wisely, given its objective of maximizing the utility of the typical employee. To simplify matters, assume that all employees have identical tastes for food and punch, so data from a single person will apply to every employee. You can ask the typical employee a single question.
a. What's your question?
b. Provide an answer to your question that would suggest that the firm should have spent more on punch and less on food. Illustrate your answer with a completely labeled graph.

2. Product Design: Horsepower Versus Cubic Feet

Carla has a fixed budget for a new car and has tentatively decided to buy a car with 80 horsepower (hp) and 100 cubic feet (cf) of interior space. Given the current selection of cars and their prices, the price of horsepower is one-third the price of cubic

feet. After some prompting from the used-car salesperson, Carla said, "To get an additional unit of horsepower, I would be willing to sacrifice two cubic feet of interior space." Does her tentative choice (80 hp and 100 cf) maximize her utility subject to her auto budget? If not, should she choose an auto with more or less horsepower?

3. Allocating an Advertising Budget to Different Markets

You are responsible for allocating a fixed advertising budget for your firm in various markets. Your budget is $12 million. The benefits and costs of advertising in the markets are shown in the following table (in millions of dollars):

Market	B	C	D	E	F	G	H
Benefit of campaign	$3	$14	$6	$15	$40	$30	$48
Cost of campaign	$1	$2	$2	$3	$4	$5	$6

a. How would you allocate the budget?
b. How would the total benefits change if you spent the $12-million budget on the least expensive campaigns?

SUMMARY

We've used modern consumer theory to explore the decision-making process of a rational consumer. The consumer's objective is to maximize utility, given her income and the prices of consumer goods. Here are the main points of the chapter.

1 To maximize utility, the consumer finds the point at which one of her indifference curves is tangent to her budget line.

2 At the utility-maximizing combination of two goods, the marginal rate of substitution (the consumer's own trade-off between the two goods) equals the price ratio (the market trade-off).

3 According to the equimarginal rule, you should pick the mix of two things at which the marginal benefit per dollar spent on the first equals the marginal benefit per dollar spent on the second.

PROBLEMS AND DISCUSSION QUESTIONS

1 Suppose the price of amusement rides is $2 and the price of a video arcade game is $1. The following table shows points on the budget line (given an income of $30) and the associated *MRS*:

	b	c	d	e
Quantity of rides	1	2	3	4
Quantity of video games	28	26	24	22
Marginal rate of substitution	5	3	2	1

   a. Explain why point b is not the best the consumer can do.
   b. What is the utility-maximizing combination of rides and games?

2 Suppose you have a fixed budget of $3,000 per year to spend on food and music. The price of food is $1 per pound, and the price of music is $10 per CD. You currently spend $2,400 on food and $600 on music.
   a. If you want to determine whether you are spending your money wisely, what question must you ask yourself?
   b. Provide an answer such that you should spend less on CDs and more on tapes.

3 Suppose you have a fixed monthly budget for audiotapes and CDs. The price of CDs is $15, and the price of tapes is $5. Given your current choice of CDs and tapes, your marginal rate of substitution is one tape per CD. Are you doing the best you can with your music budget? If not, should you buy more CDs (and fewer tapes) or more tapes (and fewer CDs)? Relate your answer to the utility-maximizing rule and illustrate with a completely labeled graph.

4 Consider a person who spends a total of $200 on hats and violets. The price of hats is $20, and the price of violets is $5. Draw a budget line with hats on the horizontal axis and violets on the vertical axis.
   a. What is the slope of the budget line?
   b. Draw a conventional indifference curve (negatively sloped and convex to the origin) that intersects the budget line. Explain why the consumer can reach a higher utility level than the level shown by this indifference curve.
   c. Draw a second indifference curve that shows the highest possible utility level.
   d. Complete the statement: To maximize utility, the consumer finds the combination of hats and violets such that _____ equals four.

5 Biff consumes two entertainment goods, arcade games and CDs. When you ask him in week one, "How many arcade games are you wiling to sacrifice for one more CD?" he says, "two." When you ask him the same question a week later (week two), he says, "five." Over this period, his underlying preferences for arcade games and CDs haven't changed.
   a. What could explain the change in his trade-off from week one to week two? Illustrate with a completely labeled graph, with CDs on the horizontal axis and arcade games on the vertical axis.
   b. Suppose Biff reached the same utility levels in weeks one and two. In week three, you offer to provide Biff his average consumption bundle from weeks one and two, that is, the average number of CDs and the average number of arcade games. Will he be better off, worse off, or equally well off compared to weeks one and two? Illustrate with a completely labeled graph.

6 Wolfgang has a fixed budget for a new car and has tentatively decided to buy a car that gets 20 miles per gallon (mpg) and has a performance level of 60 ms (the maximum speed at which a turntable can play Mozart's first symphony without skipping). A salesperson recently asked Wolfgang about his attitudes toward cars with different combinations of mpg and ms. Wolfgang would prefer a car with 19 mpg and 64 ms to his tentative choice but would prefer his tentative choice to a car with 19 mpg and 62 ms. Suppose that the cost of an additional mpg is six times the cost of an additional unit of ms.

a. Does Wolfgang's tentative choice (20 mpg and 60 ms) maximize his utility subject to his auto budget? If not, should he choose an auto with more or fewer mpg?

b. Illustrate your answer with a completely labeled graph. Label Wolfgang's tentative choice with a "*T*" and his utility-maximizing choice with a "*U*."

7 Consider the following statement: "My car can use either gasoline or gasohol (a mixture of methanol and gasoline). I use whatever fuel has a lower price per gallon." Is this a good rule for deciding what type of fuel to use in a car? If not, develop a rule that is consistent with the utility-maximizing rule.

MODEL ANSWERS TO QUESTIONS

Chapter-Opening Questions

1 What's your marginal rate of substitution between two goods? If her *MRS* equals the price ratio, she is maximizing her utility.

2 A doubling of prices and incomes does not affect the consumer's budget line, so the consumer is just as well off.

3 As explained in "A Closer Look: The Bang per Buck of Light Spirits," teens switched to super-light and heavy beverages.

Test Your Understanding

1 The vertical intercept is 20 bagels, and the horizontal intercept is 10 muffins. The slope (the market trade-off) is two bagels per muffin.

2 One point on the indifference curve is {three muffins, 14 bagels}. Given an *MRS* = 6, another point is {four muffins, eight bagels}. If Rob is like other consumers, who prefer balanced consumption to extremes, his *MRS* decreases as he consumes more muffins and fewer bagels.

3 Consumers prefer balanced consumption of two goods to extremes.

4 The price ratio (the market trade-off) is two bagels per muffin. His *MRS* exceeds the price ratio, so he should consume more muffins and fewer bagels.

5 The budget line shows the affordable combinations of *two* goods, and the demand curve shows how much of a *single* good a consumer is willing to buy at a particular price.

6 For skilled workers, the marginal benefit per dollar is now $2, which is less than the marginal benefit per dollar for unskilled workers ($3).

7 Allocate time to the exam that has the largest bang (increase in score) per minute of study time.

Market Efficiency and Government Intervention

A group of citizens in College Town recently proposed a rent-control law under which the monthly rent on apartments would decrease from $400 to $300. The mayor of College Town, who has the power to approve or disapprove the proposed law, recently made the following statement to the citizens of the city:

> I know that some of you would be harmed by rent control, and others would be helped. To help me decide whether to approve the proposed law, send me a note stating whether you favor or oppose rent control, along with a campaign contribution equal to just 1% of your cost or benefit from rent control. If the total contributions of citizens favoring rent control exceed the contributions of those who oppose it, I will approve the proposed law. Otherwise, I won't.

If everyone follows the mayor's directions, she will not approve rent control.

I n Chapter 3, we discussed the exchange principle, which conveys the simple idea that transactions make both buyer and seller better off:

THE *Principle* OF VOLUNTARY EXCHANGE

A voluntary exchange between two people makes both people better off.

In this chapter, we will take a closer look at the benefits of exchange, examining the experiences of both buyers and sellers. We will see how to compute the surplus or net benefit from a market and see why the market equilibrium—where the quantity demanded equals the quantity supplied—*may* generate the largest possible surplus. We'll explore the logic behind Adam Smith's metaphor of the invisible hand, the idea that individual buyers and sellers, each acting in his or her own self-interest, *may* promote the social interest.

You'll notice that we use the word "may" in noting the virtues of markets and the invisible hand. A market equilibrium will generate the largest possible surplus and thus be efficient when four conditions are met:

▶ *No external benefits:* The benefits of a product are confined to the person who pays for it.
▶ *No external costs:* The cost of producing a product is confined to the person who sells it.
▶ *Perfect information:* Buyers and sellers know enough about the product to make informed decisions about whether to buy or sell it.
▶ *Perfect competition:* Each firm produces such a small quantity that the firm cannot affect the price.

In this chapter, we discuss markets that meet these four conditions. As we'll see later in the book, when these conditions are not satisfied, free markets are not efficient.

Governments around the world intervene in markets, sometimes promoting efficiency and other times preventing it. In this chapter, we'll see that when the four efficiency conditions are met, government intervention is inefficient in the sense that it decreases the total surplus of the market. Here are some of the practical questions we answer:

1 If a college town uses a rent-control policy to cut the monthly rent on apartments, will some students be harmed by the policy?

2 If you want to operate a taxi in New York City, Toronto, or Boston, you must first buy a taxi medallion for over $100,000. Why does the medallion cost so much?

3 Why is there a shortage (excess demand) for human organs for transplanting?

4 Who bears the cost of restrictions on textile imports, and what is the cost per textile job saved?

5 How would a monthly apartment tax of $100 affect monthly rents?

Consumer Surplus and Producer Surplus

We'll begin our discussion of market efficiency by showing how to measure the benefits experienced by consumers and producers. We'll start with consumers, and then we'll look at producers.

The Demand Curve and Consumer Surplus

Willingness to pay

The maximum amount a consumer is willing to pay for a product.

Consumer surplus

The difference between a consumer's willingness to pay for a product and the price that he or she pays for the product.

If you said "thank you" the last time you purchased a CD, did you mean it? If you were willing to pay more for the CD than the price you actually paid, you probably really *did* mean it when you said "thank you" because you got what you consider to be a good deal. Your **willingness to pay** for a product is the maximum amount you are willing to pay for the product. Your **consumer surplus** is the difference between your willingness to pay and the price you actually pay for it. For example, if you are willing to pay $21 for a CD that you buy for $10, your consumer surplus is $11.

The market demand curve shows consumers' willingness to pay for a product. Consider the demand for lawn cutting in a small town, with the market demand curve shown in Figure 7.1. The demand curve shows that at a price of $25, no one will pay to have the lawn cut (point *t*), but if the price drops to $22, the first consumer (Juan) will pay for a lawn cut. This suggests that Juan is willing to pay up to $22 to have his lawn cut, but no more. Moving down the demand curve, the second consumer (Tupak) will pay for a lawn cutting when the price drops to $19, meaning that his willingness to pay is $19. As we continue to move downward along the demand curve, the price drops below the willingness to pay for more and more consumers, so more people have their lawns cut.

We can use the demand curve to measure just how much of a net benefit or surplus consumers get. Suppose that the price of a lawn cut is $10, and everyone in town pays this price. Juan's consumer surplus is $12, equal to his willingness to pay ($22) minus the price. Similarly, Tupak's consumer surplus is $9, equal to the difference between his willingness to pay ($19) and the market price. To compute the total consumer surplus in the lawn-cutting market, we simply add up the surpluses for each of the five consumers who buy lawn cutting at a price of $10. In this example, the market consumer surplus is $30, equal to $12 (Juan) + $9 (Tupak) + $6 (Thurl) + $3 (Forest) + $0 (Fivola). The fifth consumer (Fivola) gets no consumer surplus because the price equals her willingness to pay. The sixth person (Siggy) doesn't have his lawn cut because the amount he is willing to pay is less than the price.

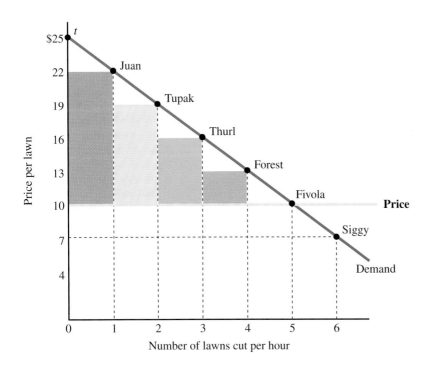

FIGURE 7.1

The Demand Curve and Consumer Surplus
Consumer surplus equals the maximum amount a consumer is willing to pay (shown by the demand curve) minus the price paid. Juan is willing to pay $22, so if the price is $10, his consumer surplus is $12. The market consumer surplus equals the sum of the surpluses earned by all consumers in the market. In this case, the market consumer surplus is $30 = $12 + $9 + $6 + $3 + $0.

The Supply Curve and Producer Surplus

Like consumers, the people who produce goods and services say "thank you" when they sell their products. This suggests that they too receive a net benefit or surplus from voluntary transactions. A seller's **willingness to accept** is the minimum amount he or she is willing to accept as payment for a product and is equal to the marginal cost of production. For example, if your marginal cost of cutting a lawn is $4, you will be willing to accept any amount greater than or equal to $4. Of course, you'd prefer $10 to $4, but you'll accept as little as $4 because the lower amount covers all your costs, including the opportunity cost of your time. **Producer surplus** is the difference between the price a producer receives for a product and the willingness to accept, or the difference between the price and marginal cost. For example, if your marginal cost for cutting a lawn is $4 and you do it for $10, your producer surplus is $6.

Figure 7.2 shows the market supply curve for lawn cutting in our small town. Let's imagine that six people are willing to cut lawns if the price is right, and each person can cut one lawn per hour. Each person incurs the same cost for renting a lawn mower but has a different opportunity costs for his or her time. The first producer (Abe) incurs a cost of $2, so he is willing to accept as little as $2 to cut a lawn. On the supply curve, if the price is $2, one person—Abe—will cut lawns. Bea has a higher opportunity cost of time, so her cost is $4, meaning that she won't cut a lawn unless she is paid at least $4. So if the price is $4, two people—Abe and Bea—will cut lawns. Moving upward along the supply curve, the other potential lawn cutters have even higher costs, so they don't start cutting until the price reaches their higher willingness to pay: $6 for Cecil, $8 for Dee, and so on. The higher the price, the larger the number of people willing to cut lawns.

Willingness to accept
The minimum amount a producer is willing to accept as payment for a product; equal to the marginal cost of production.

Producer surplus
The difference between the price a producer receives for a product and the producer's willingness to accept for the product.

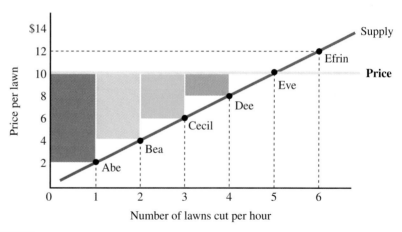

FIGURE 7.2 **The Supply Curve and Producer Surplus**

Producer surplus equals the market price minus the producer's willingness to accept or marginal cost (shown by the supply curve). Abe's marginal cost is $2, so if the price is $10, his producer surplus is $8. The market producer surplus equals the sum of the surpluses earned by all producers in the market. In this case, the market producer surplus is $20 = $8 + $6 + $4 + $2 + $0.

We can use the supply curve to measure just how much of a net benefit or surplus producers get. If the price of lawn cutting is $10, Abe's producer surplus for cutting the lawn is $8, the price he receives minus his cost ($2). Similarly, Bea's producer surplus is $6, equal to the difference between the price and her cost ($4). To compute the total producer surplus in the lawn-cutting market, we simply add up the surpluses for each of the five producers who cut lawns at a price of $10. In this example, the market producer surplus is $20, equal to $8 (Abe) + $6 (Bea) + $4 (Cecil) + $2 (Dee) + $0 (Eve). The fifth producer (Eve) gets no producer surplus because the price equals her cost, and the sixth potential producer (Efrin) doesn't cut any lawns because the price is less than his cost.

Market Equilibrium and Efficiency

Total surplus

The sum of consumer surplus and producer surplus.

Figure 7.3 puts the demand and supply curves together to show the equilibrium in the market for lawn cutting. The demand curve intersects the supply curve at a price of $10 per lawn. At this price, five lawns are cut, meaning that there are five buyers and five sellers. The **total surplus** of a market is the sum of consumer surplus and producer surplus. In Figure 7.3, the consumer surplus is $30 and the producer surplus is $20, so the total surplus of the market—shown by the shaded area—is $50. As we'll see in this part of the chapter, the market equilibrium generates the highest possible total surplus. That's why we say that the market equilibrium is efficient: We can't do any better in terms of the total surplus.

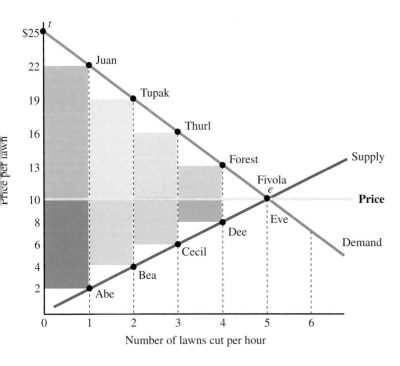

FIGURE 7.3

Market Equilibrium and the Total Market Surplus

The total surplus of the market equals consumer surplus (the lightly shaded areas) plus producer surplus (the darkly shaded areas). The market equilibrium generates the highest possible total market value, equal to $50 = $30 (consumer surplus) + $20 (producer surplus).

Total Surplus Is Lower with a Price Below the Equilibrium Price

To see why the market equilibrium maximizes the total surplus of the market, let's look at the total surplus of the market when the price is less than the equilibrium price. Suppose the government imposes a maximum price of $4 on lawn cutting. As shown in Panel A of Figure 7.4, at this price only two people cut lawns—Abe and Bea. Abe's producer surplus is shown by the darkly shaded area between the price line and the supply curve. For Bea, the price equals her willingness to accept, so she participates in the market but gets no producer surplus, receiving a price just high enough to keep her in the market. Consumers can buy only as much as producers are willing to sell, so the market consumer surplus equals the surpluses of just the first two consumers—Juan and Tupak. This is shown as the lightly shaded areas between the price line and the demand curve. By comparing Panel A in Figure 7.4 to Figure 7.3, we see that the maximum price reduces the total surplus of the market. For the first two lawns, consumers simply gain at the expense of producers. The maximum price also eliminates the surpluses from the third and fourth lawns because these transactions don't happen, so the total surplus decreases.

The maximum price reduces the total surplus of the market because it prevents some mutually beneficial transactions. For example, the third consumer, Thurl, is willing to pay $16 to have his lawn cut, and the third producer, Cecil, is willing to cut a lawn if he is paid at least $6. Thurl is willing to pay more than Cecil requires, so cutting Thurl's lawn would generate a net benefit of $10. If they split the difference, agreeing

**A Maximum Price
or a Minimum Price
Decreases the Total
Surplus of the Market**
(A) A maximum price of $4
reduces the total surplus of
the market. The first two
consumers gain at the
expense of the first two
producers. The consumer
and producer surpluses for
the third and fourth lawns
are lost entirely, so the
total value of the market
decreases.
(B) A minimum price of $19
reduces the total surplus of
the market. The first two
producers gain at the
expense of the first two
consumers. The consumer
and producer surpluses for
the third and fourth lawns
are lost entirely, so the total
value of the market
decreases.

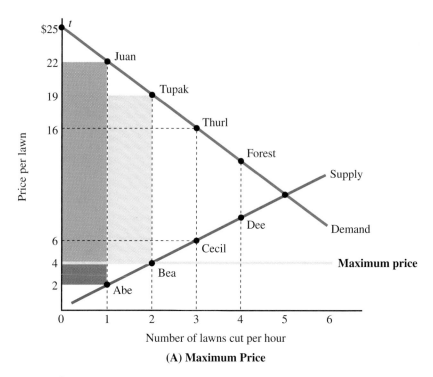

(A) Maximum Price

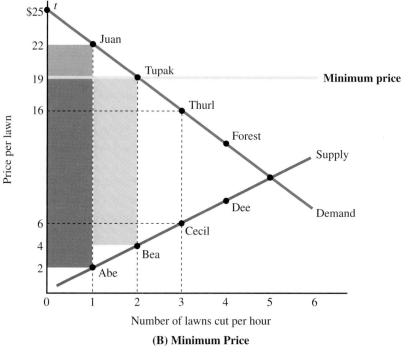

(B) Minimum Price

on a price of $11, each would get a surplus of $5. The maximum price prevents Thur
and Cecil from executing their transaction. The same logic applies to the fourth lawn
The maximum price prevents Forest and Dee from executing a transaction that would
generate a net benefit of $5, equal to Forest's willingness to pay ($13) minus Dee's mar
ginal cost ($8).

Total Surplus Is Lower with a Price Above the Equilibrium Price

What happens when the government imposes a minimum price instead of a maximum price? If the minimum price is $19, as shown in Panel B of Figure 7.4, the demand curve indicates that only two consumers, Juan and Tupak, will have their lawns cut. The total surplus of the market is the sum of consumer and producer surplus for these first two lawns, the same as it was under the maximum price. Again, this is lower than the total surplus that could have been gained, as shown by Figure 7.3. The difference between the two pricing policies is that under a maximum price, the first two consumers gain at the expense of the first two producers, whereas under the minimum price, the first two producers gain at the expense of the first two consumers. Like the maximum price, the minimum price prevents mutually beneficial transactions for the third, fourth, and fifth lawns.

Efficiency and the Invisible Hand

The market equilibrium maximizes the total surplus that can be squeezed out of the market because it guarantees that all mutually beneficial transactions will happen. Once we reach the market equilibrium at point *e* in Figure 7.3, there are no more transactions that would benefit a buyer and a seller. The market demand curve tells us that the potential buyer of the sixth lawn cut (Siggy) is willing to pay only $7, and the supply curve tells us that the potential seller of the sixth lawn cut (Efrin) has a marginal cost of $12. This transaction doesn't happen because the potential buyer is not willing to pay the cost of producing the good.

Our little example of the market for lawn cutting illustrates a general lesson about markets. The typical market has thousands of buyers and thousands of sellers, each acting in his or her own self-interest. If the market has no externalities, the market reaches the quantity that maximizes the total surplus of the market and is therefore efficient. Instead of using a bureaucrat to coordinate the actions of everyone in the market, we can rely on the actions of individual consumers and individual producers, each guided only by self-interest. This is the invisible hand in action.

The experience of the former Soviet Union demonstrates the importance of prices and the power of Adam Smith's ideas as embodied in the metaphor of the invisible hand. The Soviet economy was a planned economy in the sense that bureaucrats—not individual producers—decided how much of each good to produce and at what prices to sell them. There were no market prices to guide the decisions of consumers and producers. When the Soviets discovered a persistent mismatch between what they were producing and what consumers wanted, they asked a team of experts to propose a solution to the problem. The experts told the bureaucrats to figure out the prices that would have occurred if the Soviet economy were a market economy instead of a planned one. Once the bureaucrats predicted the prices, they could then base their production decisions on them. In other words, the experts told the bureaucrats to base their decisions on the prices that would have emerged from a market economy.

The Soviet economy relied on bureaucrats—not markets—to decide how much of each product to produce, resulting in widespread shortages.

TEST Your Understanding

1. Complete the statement: Consumer surplus equals _____ minus _____, whereas producer surplus equals _____ minus _____.

2. You are willing to pay $2,000 to have your house painted, and Pablo's marginal cost of painting a house is $1,400. If you split the difference, what's your consumer surplus? What's Pablo's producer surplus?

3. Looking back at Figure 7.4, how much is Forest willing to pay for the fourth cut lawn? What is Dee's marginal cost for cutting the fourth lawn? Describe a mutually beneficial transaction that would be blocked by a maximum price of $4.

Government Intervention in Markets

In most modern economies, governments take an active role in the economy. Government action can be justified on efficiency grounds when one of the four efficiency conditions listed at the beginning of the chapter is not met.

▶ *External benefit.* When a person who doesn't pay for a product benefits from it, the government can intervene to ensure that all the people who benefit share in its cost. For example, the government could intervene to build a dam to provide flood protection for everyone in a valley and use taxes to pay for the dam. Later in the book, we explore government intervention in response to external benefits.

- *External cost.* When the cost of producing a product is incurred by people who don't sell the product, the government can intervene to "internalize the external cost, forcing sellers to bear the full cost of production. In a later chapter, we'll explore government intervention in response to the external costs associated with air and water pollution.
- *Imperfect information.* When one side of the market has better information than the other, the government can intervene to provide information. Later in the book, we look at the problems experienced in markets with imperfect information and explore government responses to these problems.
- *Imperfect competition.* When a market is dominated by few large firms, the government can intervene, directly controlling the prices monopolies can charge and promoting competition. Later in the book, we look at a wide range of policies to deal with imperfect competition.

These are cases of **market failure**, situations in which markets, if left on their own, will fail to generate socially efficient outcomes.

> **Market failure**
>
> A situation in which a market fails to be efficient because of external benefits, external costs, imperfect information, or imperfect competition.

In some markets, government intervention cannot be justified on efficiency grounds. For a market that meets the four efficiency conditions, the market equilibrium generates the largest possible total surplus, so government intervention can only decrease the surplus and cause inefficiency. A government motivated exclusively by efficiency would not intervene in such a market, but instead would permit the invisible hand to guide consumers and producers to the market equilibrium.

So why would a government intervene in an efficient market? Sometimes the government's objective is not to promote efficiency—maximize the size of the pie—but instead to slice the pie in favor of one group or another. For example, a government that restricts shoe imports prevents some domestic workers from losing their shoe-making jobs. Of course, limiting imports will decrease the supply of shoes, and consumers will pay higher prices. As we'll see, when the government intervenes in a market to slice the pie in favor of one group, the pie shrinks, so there is a trade-off between efficiency (maximizing the size of the pie) and distributional concerns (slicing the pie).

What is the role of economic analysis in exploring government intervention in efficient markets? We will focus our attention on the inefficiencies of government intervention, looking at how much the pie shrinks. We will briefly discuss some of the distributional consequences of intervention—how the slices change. The decision about whether intervention in an efficient market is worthwhile—whether the changes in the slices are worth losing part of the pie—is made in the political sphere. The economic analysis you learn in this book will help you understand the trade-offs associated with various public policies.

There are circumstances under which groups of people who fare poorly in the market economy deserve special consideration. If a society decides that a particular group merits special treatment—for example, workers who lose their jobs because of imports—a more direct form of assistance is generally superior than intervention in efficient markets by the government. One alternative would be for the government to retrain workers for new jobs.

Controlling the Price

We'll start with government policies that control product prices, setting either a maximum or a minimum price. In both cases, if the market meets the four efficiency conditions, government intervention reduces the total surplus of the market and causes inefficiency.

Setting Maximum Prices

We've already seen two different effects of a maximum price, sometimes known as a price ceiling. In Chapter 4, we saw that when the government sets a maximum price that is less than the equilibrium price, the result is permanent excess demand for the product. The decrease in price reduces the quantity supplied and increases the quantity demanded, so at the controlled price, consumers want to buy more than producers want to sell. In this chapter, we saw from Panel A in Figure 7.4 that a maximum price decreases the total surplus of the market: Some consumers gain at the expense of producers, and the total surplus decreases. Here are some examples of goods that have been subject to maximum prices or may be subject to maximum prices in the near future:

▶ Rental housing. During World War II, the federal government instituted a national system of rent controls. Although only New York City continued rent control after the war, during the 1970s, rent control spread to dozens of cities.
▶ Gasoline. In response to sharp increases in the price of gasoline in the 1970s, the national government set a maximum price on gasoline.
▶ Medical goods and services. Some proposals to control medical costs include price controls for prescription drugs.

In all three cases, a maximum price will cause excess demand and reduce the total surplus of the market.

Application: Rent Control

Figure 7.5 shows the effects of rent control on consumer and producer surplus. Panel A shows the market equilibrium, with a price (monthly rent) of $400 per apartment and a quantity of 1,000 apartments. The total surplus is the sum of the consumer surplus and producer surplus, shown as the area between the demand curve and the supply curve. Panel B shows the effect of a maximum price of $300 per apartment. The decrease in price causes movement downward along the supply curve to point s, and the quantity of apartments supplied decreases to 700. Because the policy decreases the number of apartments from 1,000 to 700, the total surplus of the market decreases. For the first 700 apartments, consumers gain at the expense of producers, paying $300 per apartment rather than $400. The 701st through the 1,000th apartments disappear from the market, so the surpluses associated with these apartments are lost entirely. The decrease in total surplus means that the market is inefficient.

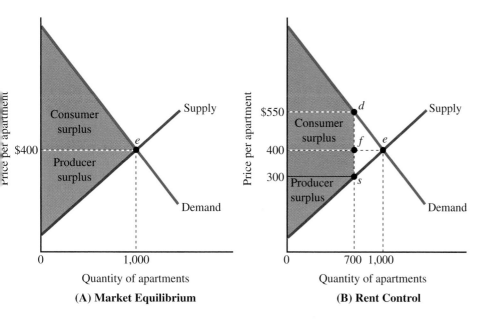

(A) Market Equilibrium

(B) Rent Control

FIGURE 7.5

Rent Control Decreases Total Surplus
(A) In the market equilibrium, with a price of $400 and 1,000 apartments, the total surplus is the area between the demand curve and the supply curve.
(B) Rent control, with a maximum price of $300, reduces the quantity to 700 apartments and decreases the total surplus.

Because rent control decreases the total surplus of the market, the policy generates a **deadweight loss**. In Figure 7.5, the deadweight loss is shown by the triangle *des*, the decrease in the total surplus of the market. This is a deadweight loss in the sense that it is not offset by a gain to anyone else. The consumers and producers who are excluded from the market by rent control lose the surpluses they could have received in the market.

Let's return to the chapter opener about the mayor's curious strategy for deciding whether to approve a rent-control policy. Recall that the mayor announced that if the supporters of rent control contributed more money than the opponents, she would approve rent control. As a start, we know from Figure 7.5 that rent control decreases the total surplus of the rental market because the losses of the losers exceed the gains of the winners. Therefore, if everyone contributes 1% of his or her loss to the mayor, the contributions in opposition to rent control will be larger, and the mayor will not approve rent control.

Table 7.1 provides a detailed look at the winners and losers and their campaign contributions. For the 700 apartments that would remain in the market even after rent control, each consumer gets a $100 benefit, for a consumer benefit of $70,000 (700 consumers times $100). If each of these consumers contributes 1% of the potential

Deadweight loss
The decrease in the total surplus of the market.

TABLE 7.1 College Town's Campaign Contributions

	Benefit	Cost	Contribution
Consumers 1–700	$70,000 = $100 × 700		+$700 = 1% of $70,000
Producers 1–700		$70,000 = $100 × 700	–$700 = 1% of $70,000
Consumers 701–1,000		$22,500 = 1/2($150 × 300)	–$225 = 1% of $22,500
Producers 701–1,000		$15,000 = 1/2($100 × 300)	–$150 = 1% of $15,000
TOTAL	$70,000	$107,500	–$375

benefit, the consumer contributions in support of rent control will be $700. But these consumers would gain at the expense of the suppliers of the 700 apartments: Each supplier would lose $100, so their total losses would be $70,000, and their contributions in opposition to rent control will be $700. The two groups who would be excluded from the market under rent control—consumers and producers knocked out of the market when the transactions from apartments 701 through 1,000 disappear—will contribute in opposition. The loss of the excluded consumers is shown by triangle *def* in Panel B of Figure 7.5 and totals $22,500. These consumers will therefore contribute $225. The loss of the excluded producers is shown by triangle *fes* ($15,000); these producers will contribute $150. The contributions opposing rent control exceed the contributions favoring it by $375. Therefore, the mayor will not approve rent control.

Another way to see the inefficiency of rent control is to look at the consumers and producers who are excluded from the market. As shown by the points between *d* and *e* on the demand curve, 300 consumers are willing to pay between $400 and $550 for an apartment. As shown by the points between *s* and *e* on the supply curve, there are 300 producers who are willing to rent out an apartment for amounts between $300 and $400. Although the 300 excluded consumers are willing to pay more than these suppliers require to provide an apartment, the transactions are illegal under rent control. Because rent control outlaws transactions that would make both parties better off, it causes inefficiency.

There are three more subtle effects associated with rent control. First, at the artificially low maximum price, the number of people seeking apartments exceeds the number of apartments available. Consumers will spend more time searching for apartments, and an additional cost of rent control is the opportunity cost of the extra time spent searching for apartments. Second, because rent control outlaws mutually beneficial transactions, many people violate the spirit and the letter of the law by executing transactions of dubious legal merit. In some rent-control cities, consumers pay extra money to property owners to outbid other consumers. These extra payments are often disguised as "nonrefundable security deposits" or as "key money"—thousands of dollars to get the keys to an apartment. Third, given the lower payoff from providing apartments for rent, property owners will have less incentive to spend money on repair and maintenance, so the quality of apartments will decrease. In other words, lower rent is offset in part by lower housing quality.

Is rent control good for the poor? Rent control specifies a maximum rent for an apartment, regardless of who lives there. Rent-controlled apartments are occupied by the rich and the poor, so many wealthy people benefit from rent control. In other words, rent control is a very blunt instrument for helping the poor. As we explain later in the book, the government could use other policies to more effectively improve the economic circumstances of the poor.

Setting Minimum Prices

We've already seen two different effects of a minimum price (sometimes called a price floor). In Chapter 4, we saw that when the government sets a minimum price that exceeds the equilibrium price, the result is permanent excess supply. The increase in price increases the quantity supplied because it encourages producers to produce more at the artificially high price. At the same time, the increase in price decreases the quan-

A CLOSER LOOK

Milk Mountains

In the United States, the minimum price for powdered milk is $9.90 per hundredweight. To prevent the market price from falling below $9.90, the U.S. government purchases any resulting surpluses at this price. In recent years, the market demand for powdered milk has been relatively low, so the government has purchased millions of pounds of powdered milk each year. By 2003, the government's stockpile of powdered milk reached 1.28 billion pounds.[1] In fact, mountains of dried milk are stored in warehouses across the United States and even in caves near Kansas City. Why doesn't the government just give all of its powdered milk away? Why stockpile it? The problem is that giving it away would ultimately reduce the amount of powder that farmers could sell to consumers. The government would then be forced to buy more unsold powder from farmers.

tity demanded as consumers buy less. At a minimum price above the equilibrium price, producers want to sell more than consumers want to buy, so there is excess supply. Earlier in this chapter, we saw the effects of a minimum price on the market surplus and its distribution between consumers and producers. As shown in Panel B of Figure 7.4, a minimum price for lawn cuts decreases the total surplus of the market as some producers and consumers are excluded from the market. The remaining producers gain at the expense of consumers.

Governments around the world establish minimum prices for agricultural goods. Under a price-support program, a government sets a minimum price for an agricultural product and then buys any resulting surpluses at that price. For an example of what can happen under agricultural price supports, read "A Closer Look: Milk Mountains."

Controlling the Quantity—
Licensing and Import Restrictions

What happens when the government controls the quantity of a particular product instead of its price? We'll consider two policies that control quantities. In the domestic economy, many state and local governments limit the number of firms in particular markets by limiting the number of business licenses to operate in those markets. Many national governments restrict imports, using import bans or quotas on the quantity of a product—for example, shoes or cheese—that can be imported.

You may be surprised by the sheer number of state and local government business licensing programs. For example, many cities and states limit the number of taxicabs, dry cleaners, tobacco farms, liquor stores, bars, and even dog groomers. Some people defend licensing programs on the grounds that they protect consumers from low-quality products and poor service. But studies have shown that most licensing programs increase prices without improving the quality of products and service.[2] Another motive for cities to issue licenses is to limit the number of establishments that could be considered nuisances to some citizens, for example, bars, convenience stores, and gas stations.

Application: Taxi Medallions

We can use the licensing of taxis to explain how the practice affects the market for taxi service and other markets in which licenses are common. Panel A of Figure 7.6 shows the market equilibrium in the taxi market. The demand curve intersects the supply curve at point *e*. The industry provides 10,000 miles of taxi service per day at a price of $3.00 per mile. Each taxi is capable of producing a maximum of 100 miles of service per day, and there are 100 taxicabs in the market. The total surplus of the market equals the sum of consumer surplus and producer surplus, shown by the area between the demand curve and the supply curve.

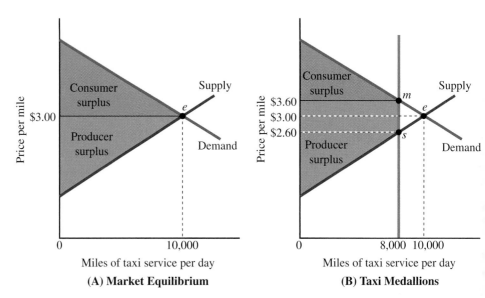

FIGURE 7.6 **The Market Effects of Taxi Medallions**
(A) The market equilibrium is shown by point *e*, with a price of $3.00 and a quantity of 10,000 miles of service per day. The total surplus is the area between the demand and supply curves.
(B) A medallion policy that fixes the number of taxis at 80 fixes the quantity of taxi service at 8,000 miles per day (100 miles per taxi) and increases the price to $3.60 (point *m*). The producers of the first 8,000 miles gain at the expense of consumers, but the surpluses that could have been gained between 8,000 and 10,000 miles are lost entirely, so the total surplus decreases.

Now suppose that the city passes a law requiring each taxicab to have a license—also known as a taxi "medallion"—and limits the number of medallions to 80. The city then gives taxi medallions to the first 80 people who show up at City Hall. In Panel B of Figure 7.6, the vertical line at 8,000 miles of service shows that this policy fixes the quantity of taxi service at 8,000 miles per day (80 taxis times 100 miles per taxi per day). The medallion policy creates an excess demand for taxi service: At the original price ($3.00), the quantity demanded is 10,000 miles, but the city's 80 taxicabs provide only 8,000 miles of service. As a result, the market moves upward along the demand curve to point m, where the price is $3.60 per mile of service. The medallion policy increases the price and decreases the quantity of taxi services.

Licensing and Market Efficiency

The medallion policy decreases the total surplus of the taxi market. In Figure 7.6, we see that the total surplus in Panel B is less than the total surplus in Panel A. The medallion policy decreases consumer surplus, a result of the higher price and the smaller quantity supplied. Producer surplus could increase or decrease, depending on the shapes of the market supply and market demand curves. In this example, the producer surplus of taxi drivers with medallions actually increases by a small amount. As in the cases of a maximum price or a minimum price, the medallion policy decreases the quantity of goods sold, decreasing the total surplus of the market. The producers of the first 8,000 miles of service gain at the expense of consumers, but the surpluses that could have been gained between 8,000 and 10,000 miles are lost entirely, so the total surplus of the market decreases. The deadweight loss is shown by the area of triangle mes.

Another way to see the inefficiency of taxi medallions is to look at just the consumers and producers who are excluded from the market and what they would lose. Some of the excluded consumers would gladly pay the cost of providing taxi service. As shown by the points between m and e on the demand curve, many consumers are willing to pay between $3.00 and $3.60 per mile for taxi service. Although there are plenty of drivers who would be willing to provide taxi service at these prices, they can't do so without a medallion. Because the medallion policy prevents these riders and drivers from executing mutually beneficial transactions, the policy causes inefficiency.

Our analysis of taxi medallions applies to any market subject to quantity controls. State and city governments use licensing to limit many types of small businesses. When an establishment such as a convenience store or dry cleaner would cause a nuisance to its neighbors, the inefficiency of the sort shown in Figure 7.6 may be at least partly offset by the benefit of controlling nuisances. Of course, the alternative policy is to control nuisance directly by restricting the location of the establishment rather than simply limiting the number of establishments. In general, a policy that limits entry into a market increases price, decreases quantity, and causes inefficiency in the market. In evaluating such a policy, we must compare the possible benefits from controlling nuisances to the losses of consumer and producer surplus.

Winners and Losers from Licensing

Who benefits and who loses from licensing programs like the city's medallion policy? The losers are consumers, who pay more for taxi rides. The winners are the people who receive a free medallion and the right to charge an artificially high price for taxi service. In some cities, people buy and sell taxi medallions. The market value of a medallion reflects the profits it can earn its owner. For example, the market price of a medallion is over $150,000 in New York City, $140,000 in Boston, and $100,000 in Toronto.[3] In cities such as Chicago, where medallions are more plentiful, the market price is much lower.

Why don't governments simply eliminate the taxi medallion system and allow free entry into the taxi market? Because doing so would drop the price of taxi service and reduce the market value of medallions to zero. Some city governments are reluctant to eliminate medallions because owners wield a lot of political power to keep the system (and the value of their medallions) in place.

Shortfall from Medallion Sale

Economic Puzzle

Last month, a city decided to increase its number of taxi medallions from 500 to 600 and to auction off the new medallions to the highest bidders. Before the new medallions were issued, the market price of a medallion was $40,000, so the mayor figured that the medallion auction would generate about $4 million (100 medallions times $40,000 per medallion). The mayor was surprised when the auction raised only $3 million. What happened?

The key to solving this puzzle is that the market price of medallions is affected by the price of taxi service, which in turn is affected by the number of taxi medallions. An increase in the number of medallions—an increase in supply—will lead to lower prices for taxi rides. Restricting the number of taxis leads to higher prices, so loosening the restrictions will lead to lower prices. Lower prices means lower profits from operating taxis, so investors are willing to pay less for a taxi medallion. In this example, the market price drops from $40,000 to $30,000. ■

Restricting Imports

We've seen that the government can control the quantity of a good produced by issuing a limited number of business licenses to producers. Another way to control quantity is to limit the imports of a particular good. Like a licensing policy, an import restriction increases the market price and decreases the total surplus of the market.

To show the market effects of import restrictions, let's start with an unrestricted market. Panel A of Figure 7.7 shows the market equilibrium in the sugar market when there is free trade. The domestic supply curve shows the quantity supplied by domestic (U.S.) firms at different prices. Looking at point *m*, we see that U.S. firms will not supply any sugar unless the price is at least $0.26 per pound. The total supply curve, which shows the quantity supplied by both domestic and foreign firms, lies to the right of the domestic curve. At each price, the total supply exceeds the domestic supply because foreign firms also supply sugar. Point *i* shows the free-trade equilibrium: The domestic demand curve (which shows the demand by U.S. consumers) intersects the total sup-

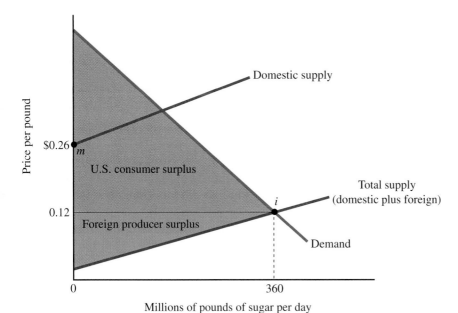

(A) **Free Trade with No Domestic Production**

FIGURE 7.7

The Effects of an Import Ban on U.S. Prices and Consumer and Producer Surplus
(A) With free trade, demand intersects the total supply curve at point *i*, with a price of $0.12 and a quantity of 360 million pounds. This price is below the minimum price of domestic suppliers ($0.26, as shown by point *m*), so domestic firms do not participate in the market. The total surplus is shown by the shaded areas (U.S. consumer and foreign producer surplus).
(B) If sugar imports are banned, the equilibrium is shown by the intersection of the demand curve and the domestic (U.S.) supply curve (point *d*). The price increases to $0.30. Although the ban generates a producer surplus for domestic producers, their gain is less than the loss of domestic consumers.

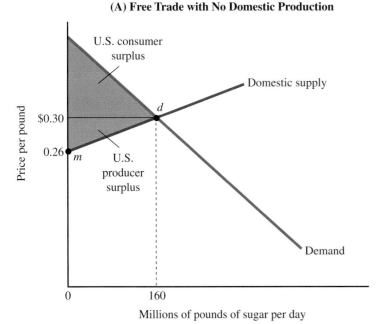

(B) **Import Ban and Domestic Production**

ply curve at a price of $0.12 per pound and a quantity of 360 million pounds per day. Because this price is below the minimum price for domestic firms, domestic firms do not supply any sugar to the U.S. markets.

What would happen if the United States banned sugar imports? Foreign suppliers would disappear from the market, so the total supply of sugar would consist of only the domestic supply. In Panel B of Figure 7.7, the new equilibrium would be shown by point *d*: The demand curve would intersect the domestic supply curve at a price of $0.30 per pound and a quantity of 160 million pounds. The decrease in supply resulting from the import ban would increase the price and decrease the quantity. As a result, domestic firms would produce all the sugar for the domestic market.

The import ban would ultimately decrease the total surplus in the sugar market. The shaded areas in the two graphs show the consumer and producer surpluses that would result with and without free trade. As you can see, the import ban would reduce U.S. consumer surplus, as shown by the two rust triangles in the two graphs. The ban would also eliminate the producer surplus of foreign suppliers (shown by the blue triangle in Panel A of Figure 7.7) and generate a producer surplus for domestic suppliers (shown by the blue triangle in Panel B of Figure 7.7). Therefore, the import ban would cause domestic producers to gain at the expense of domestic consumers. Since consumers would lose more than domestic producers would gain, the import ban would cause a net loss for people in the United States.

Import restrictions are often defended on the grounds that they increase employment in the "protected" industries, such as apparel and steel. But the protection of these jobs increases consumer prices, so there is a trade-off: More jobs in the protected industry, but higher prices for consumers. According to one study, import restrictions in 1993 protected 56,464 jobs in the U.S. textile and apparel industries at a cost to consumers of about $178,000 per job and protected 3,419 jobs in the motor vehicle industry at a cost of about $271,000 per job.[4] A recent study commissioned by the Swedish Ministry for Foreign Affairs concluded that import quotas imposed by the European Union increased the cost of clothing for the typical family in the European Union by about 270 euros (about $270) per year.[5] The quotas protected jobs in the domestic clothing industry, but the cost per job saved is about 41,000 euros per year.

We've just explored two types of policies that influence markets by controlling the quantity produced: license restrictions and import limits. Sometimes governments go beyond simply reducing the quantity produced and outlaw market transactions entirely. For an example, read "A Closer Look: A Market for Used Human Organs?"

A CLOSER LOOK   A Market For Used Human Organs?

Each year, thousands of Americans die waiting for replacement kidneys, hearts, livers, pancreases, and lungs. In the last decade, improvements in the effectiveness of organ transplants have increased the demand for used human organs. Because the supply hasn't increased along with demand, there are shortages of transplantable organs. In a normal market, the price would rise to eliminate the shortage, but because it is illegal to buy and sell human organs, there is no pricing mechanism to close the gap between the quantity supplied and the quantity demanded. The conventional approach to the organ shortage is to appeal to people's generosity, urging them to commit their organs to the transplant program. The failure of this approach led Nobel-winning economist Gary Becker to suggest monetary incentives for organ donors.[6] Under his proposal, the federal government would pay donors and their survivors for the organs they donate and would distribute the organs to hospitals for transplanting. This proposal raises all sorts of ethical questions and has not been embraced by many policymakers or health experts.

TEST Your Understanding

4. Why do tenants in cities with rent control voluntarily pay extra money for nonrefundable cleaning deposits and keys?

5. In Figure 7.6, consider a consumer who is represented by a point on the demand curve halfway between point *m* and point *e*. How much is the consumer willing to pay for a mile of taxi service? Consider a producer who is represented by a point on the supply curve halfway between point *s* and point *e*. What is the producer willing to accept for a mile of taxi service? Describe a mutually beneficial transaction between the consumer and the producer.

6. In Figure 7.7, how much sugar will domestic firms produce at a price of $0.15?

7. Complete the statement with "increases" or "decreases": An import ban _____ the price of sugar, _____ the quantity of sugar, and _____ the output of the domestic sugar industry.

Who Really Pays Taxes?

In this part of the chapter, we'll look at the market effects of taxes and answer two important questions. First, who really bears the burden of a tax? As we'll see, it is not necessarily the person who actually pays the tax to the government. Second, is the total burden of a tax equal to the revenue collected by the government? As we'll see, a tax changes people's behavior, so the total burden actually exceeds the revenue collected.

Figure 7.8 shows the revenue sources for local governments (including cities and counties), states, and the federal government. The major revenue source for local governments is the property tax, which is a fixed percentage of the value of residential, commercial, or industrial property. The sales tax is a fixed percentage of the purchase price of a consumer good. A person's state income tax liability is based on how much he or she earns, with tax rates that typically increase as income increases. The major revenue sources for the federal government are individual income taxes and "social insurance and retirement receipts," which are taxes collected to support Social Security, Medicare, and workers' compensation.

Tax Shifting: Forward and Backward

We can use supply and demand curves to look at the market effects of taxes. Suppose that your city imposes a tax of $100 per apartment and collects the tax from housing firms. You may think the burden of the tax falls exclusively on the housing firm, since that's who mails the check to the government. But some simple supply and demand analysis will show why this is incorrect. The housing firm will charge more for apartments and pay less for its inputs such as labor and land, so the tax will actually be paid by consumers and input suppliers.

FIGURE 7.8

**Revenue Sources
for Local, State, and
Federal Governments**

Source: *Statistical Abstract
of the United States*, 2002.

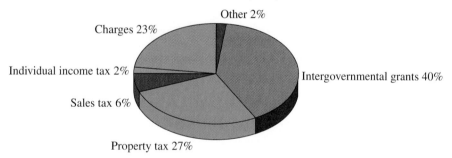

Local Government (1999)

Other 2%

Charges 23%

Individual income tax 2%

Sales tax 6%

Property tax 27%

Intergovernmental grants 40%

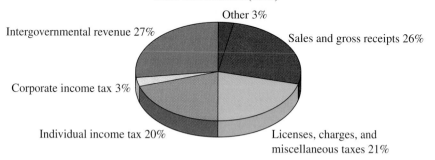

State Government (2000)

Other 3%

Intergovernmental revenue 27%

Sales and gross receipts 26%

Corporate income tax 3%

Individual income tax 20%

Licenses, charges, and
miscellaneous taxes 21%

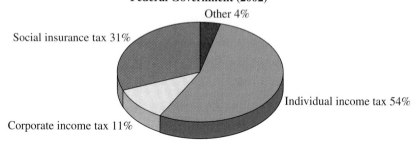

Federal Government (2002)

Other 4%

Social insurance tax 31%

Individual income tax 54%

Corporate income tax 11%

Figure 7.9 shows the market effects of a $100 tax on apartments As we saw earlier
in the chapter, the market supply curve tells us how high the price must be to get producers to supply a particular quantity of output. The price must be high enough to
cover all the costs of production. A unit tax increases the cost of production, so we
need a higher price to get firms to produce any given quantity. In other words, the supply curve shifts upward by the amount of the tax. A unit tax of $100 per apartment
increases a property owner's cost per apartment by $100, so the supply curve shifts up
by $100.

   The shift of the supply curve increases the equilibrium price of apartments. At the
$300 price, there will be an excess demand for apartments, and the price will increase
to eliminate the excess demand. In Figure 7.9 the market moves from point *i* to point *f*.
The demand curve intersects the new supply curve at a price of $360, compared to
$300 before the tax. In other words, housing firms shift part of the tax forward on to
consumers, who pay $60 of the $100 tax. Although housing firms pay the entire $100

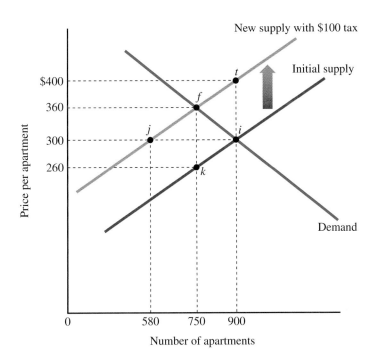

FIGURE 7.9

**The Market Effects
of an Apartment Tax**
A tax of $100 per apartment
shifts the supply curve up,
moving the market
equilibrium from point *i* to
point *f*. The equilibrium
price increases from $300
to $360, and the equilibrium
quantity decreases from
900 to 750 apartments.

tax in a legal sense, they get some of the money to pay the tax by charging consumers $60 more for apartments.

The apartment tax also affects the people who supply inputs like land and labor to the housing industry. The tax decreases the output of the industry, so the industry needs smaller quantities of the inputs used to produce apartments. The resulting excess supply of inputs like labor and land will decrease land and labor prices, decreasing the cost of producing apartments. As a result, part of the $100 tax gets shifted backward on to input suppliers. Although housing firms pay the apartment tax in a legal sense, they get some of the money to pay the tax by paying less to workers and landowners.

Predicting the Amount Shifted Forward and Backward

The amount of the tax shifted forward to consumers depends on the price elasticity of demand for the taxed good. If the demand for a taxed good is inelastic—meaning that consumers are not very responsive to price changes—we need a large price hike to eliminate the excess demand caused by the tax. Therefore, consumers will be hit by a large increase in price, and so they will pay the bulk of the tax. This is shown in Panel A of Figure 7.10. Demand is inelastic—that is, the demand curve is steep—so a $5 tax increases the equilibrium price by $4 (from $10 to $14). In other words, consumers pay four-fifths of the tax. In Panel B of Figure 7.10, demand is elastic—that is, the demand curve is relatively flat—so consumers pay just a small part of the tax. A $5 tax increases the equilibrium price by only $1 (from $10 to $11). In this case, consumers pay only one-fifth of the tax.

Elasticities of Demand and Tax Effects

If demand is inelastic (Panel A), a tax will increase the market price by a large amount, so consumers will bear a large share of the tax. If demand is elastic (Panel B), the price will increase by a small amount and consumers will bear a small share of the tax.

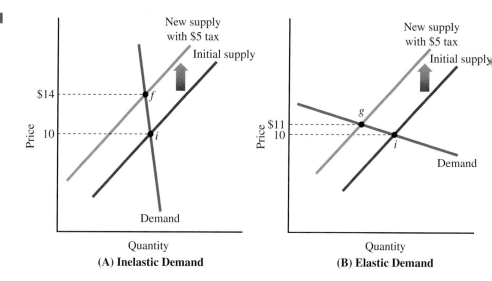

(A) Inelastic Demand   **(B) Elastic Demand**

Why should we care about tax shifting? We've seen that a tax increases consumer prices and decreases input prices, so to determine who actually pays a tax, we must look beyond the actual taxpayer. The subtleties of tax shifting are often missed by the people who design our tax policy and the media folks who report on it, as the following applications illustrate.

Applications: Cigarette and Luxury Taxes

We can use what we've learned about tax shifting to discuss some recent episodes in tax policy. In 1994, President Clinton proposed an immediate $0.75 per pack increase in the cigarette tax. The tax had two purposes: to generate revenue for Clinton's health care reform plan and to decrease medical costs by discouraging smoking. Based on our discussion of the market effects of a tax, we would predict that the tax would be shared by consumers, who would pay higher prices, and the owners of land where tobacco is grown. It appears tobacco farmers and landowners understand the economics of cigarette taxes. Led by a group of representatives and senators from tobacco-growing areas in North Carolina, Kentucky, and Virginia, the Congress scaled back Clinton's proposed tax hike from $0.75 to $0.05. Although the government would have collected the tax from cigarette manufacturers, savvy tobacco farmers realized the tax would decrease the price of their tobacco-growing land.

Another lesson on backward shifting occurred when Congress passed a steep luxury tax on boats and other expensive goods in 1990. Under the new luxury tax, a person buying a $300,000 boat had to pay an additional $20,000 in taxes. The burden of the tax was actually shared by consumers and input suppliers, including people who worked in boat factories and boatyards. Because the demand for luxury goods is elastic, the tax caused demand for the boats to fall sharply. The boat industry produced fewer boats, and the resulting decrease in the demand for boat workers led to layoffs and lower wages for those who managed to keep their jobs. Although the idea behind the luxury tax was to "soak the rich," the tax actually harmed low-income workers in the boat industry. It was repealed a few years later.

Tax Burden and Deadweight Loss

We've seen that people respond to a tax by changing their behavior. As a result, the total burden of a tax will exceed the total amount of money the government actually collects from the tax. To see why, suppose the government imposes a tax on No. 3 pencils, and the tax is large enough that everyone who initially used No. 3 pencils switches to other types of pencils or other writing implements. If no one purchases No. 3 pencils, the tax won't raise any revenue for the government, but the tax still generates a burden because some people who would prefer to use No. 3 pencils have switched to other writing implements.

We'll use the fish market to explore the total burden of a tax. To simplify matters, let's assume that the supply curve for fish is horizontal, as shown in Figure 7.11. As we'll see later in the book, a supply curve will be horizontal if the prices of the inputs used in the industry don't change as the total output of the industry changes. For the fish market, this means that wages and the cost of bait and fuel don't change as the total fish harvest changes. The demand curve intersects the initial supply curve at point *i*, so the price is $2 per pound and the quantity is 60,000 pounds of fish per day.

Suppose the government imposes a tax of $1 per pound of fish, and the tax is paid in legal terms by producers. As we saw earlier, a unit tax shifts the market supply upward by the amount of the tax. As shown in Figure 7.11, a $1 tax on fish producers shifts the supply curve up by $1: Each firm now needs $3, not $2, to cover all of its costs, including the tax.

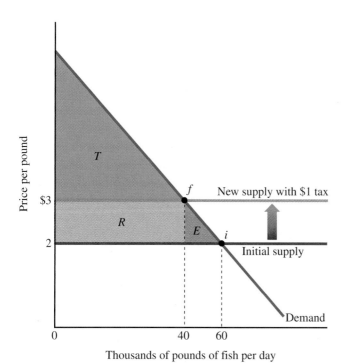

FIGURE 7.11

The Deadweight Loss or Excess Burden of a Tax

When the supply curve is horizontal, a tax increases the equilibrium price by the tax ($1 per pound in this example). Consumer surplus decreases by areas *R* and *E*. Total tax revenue collected is shown by rectangle *R*, so the total burden exceeds tax revenue by triangle *E*. Triangle *E* is sometimes known as the deadweight loss or excess burden of the tax

In Figure 7.11 the fish tax increases the equilibrium price of fish from $2 to $3. Why does the price increase by an amount equal to the tax? The supply curve is horizontal because input prices are fixed, regardless of how much output is produced. There is no opportunity to shift the tax backward onto input suppliers, so consumers bear the full cost of the tax.

We can use the concept of consumer surplus to determine just how much consumers lose as a result of the tax. Before the fish tax, the consumer surplus is shown by the area between the initial supply curve and the demand curve, or areas *T*, *R*, and *E*. When the price increases to $3, the consumer surplus shrinks to the area of triangle *T*, so the loss of consumer surplus (the total burden of the tax) is shown by rectangle *R* and triangle *E*. Let's take a closer look at these two areas.

▶ Rectangle *R* shows the extra money consumers must pay for the 40,000 pounds of fish they purchase. The tax increases the price by $1 per pound, so consumers pay an extra $40,000.

▶ Triangle *E* shows the loss of consumer surplus on the fish that are not consumed because of the tax. Consumers obey the law of demand, so when the price rises, they cut their purchases, buying 20,000 fewer pounds of fish. As a result, they give up the consumer surplus they would have received on these 20,000 pounds of fish.

How does the total burden of the tax compare to the tax revenue raised by the government? The total tax revenue is the tax per pound ($1) times the quantity consumed (40,000 pounds), or $40,000. This is shown by rectangle *R*: Part of the loss experienced by consumers is the revenue gain for government. But in addition to losing rectangle *R*, consumers also lose triangle *E*, so the consumer's total burden of the tax exceeds the tax revenue. Triangle *E* is sometimes known as the **deadweight loss** from taxation or the **excess burden** of a tax.

In the example shown in Figure 7.11, we used a horizontal supply curve to simplify matters and make the analysis of deadweight loss transparent. In a market with a positively sloped supply curve, a tax generates a deadweight loss, but the analysis is a bit more complex. For students interested in a challenge, one of the problems at the end of the chapter deals with deadweight loss for the apartment market, a market with a positively sloped supply curve.

The essential reason for excess burden is that taxes cause people to change their behavior, making choices to avoid taxes. For another example of changes in behavior in response to taxes, read "A Closer Look: Taxes and December Babies."

Deadweight loss from taxation

The difference between the total burden of a tax and the amount of revenue collected by the government.

Excess burden of a tax

Another name for deadweight loss.

TEST Your Understanding

8. Suppose a city proposes tax on hotel stays, equal to $20 per person per night. What sort of people would you expect to oppose the tax?
9. The demand for coffee is relatively inelastic. Therefore, we would expect _____ to pay a relatively large share of a tax on coffee.
10. Explain why a tax that generates zero tax revenue can be costly to society.

A CLOSER LOOK

Taxes and December Babies

The current tax law includes a tax credit for children: A child born on or before December 31 reduces the household's tax liability in that year and every subsequent year until the child reaches 18. A recent study shows that the higher the tax credit, the larger the percentage of children born in the last week of the year and the smaller the percentage of children born in the first week of the year.[7] It appears that couples time the births of their children to take advantage of the tax credit. The authors estimate that increasing the tax benefit of having a child by $500 raises the probability of having the child in the last week of December by about 27%.

Economic Experiment

Government Intervention

Recall the market equilibrium experiment from Chapter 4. We can modify that experiment to show the various forms of government intervention in the market. After several trading periods without any government intervention, you can change the rules as follows:

- The instructor sets a maximum price for apples.
- The instructor sets a minimum price for apples.
- The instructor issues licenses to a few lucky producers.
- The instructor divides producers into domestic producers and foreign producers, and some of the foreign producers are excluded from the market. ●

USING THE TOOLS

In this chapter, we used two of the tools of economics—the supply curve and the demand curve—to study the effect of government intervention in markets without externalities. Here are some opportunities to use these tools to do your own economic analysis.

1. Price Controls for Medical Care

Consider a town where the equilibrium price of a doctor's visit is $60 and the equilibrium quantity supplied is 90 patient visits per hour. For suppliers (doctors), each $1 increase in price increases the quantity supplied by two visits. For consumers, each $1 increase in price decreases the quantity demanded by one visit. Suppose that in an attempt to control the rising costs of medical care, the government imposes price controls, setting a maximum price of $50 per visit.

a. Use a completely labeled graph to show the effects of the maximum price on (i) the quantity of visits to doctors and (ii) the total surplus of the market.

b. What sort of inefficiencies does the price control cause?

c. Would you expect patients and doctors to find ways around the maximum price?

2. Barber Licensing

Consider the market for haircuts in a city. In the market equilibrium, the price per haircut is $6 and the quantity is 240 haircuts per day. For consumers, each $1 increase in price decreases the quantity demanded by 20 haircuts. For producers, each $1 increase in price increases the quantity supplied by 60 haircuts. In the market equilibrium, there are 24 barbers, each of whom produces 10 haircuts per day. Suppose the city passes a law requiring all barbers to have a license and then issues only 18 barber licenses. Each licensed barber continues to provide 10 haircuts per day. Use a completely labeled graph to show the effects of licensing on (i) the price of haircuts and (ii) the total surplus in the haircut market.

3. Bidding for a Boston Taxi Medallion

In 1997, there were 1,500 taxi medallions in the city of Boston, and each medallion generated a profit of about $14,000 per year. In 1998, the city announced that it would issue 300 new taxi medallions, auctioning the new medallions to the highest bidders.[7] Even with the new medallions, the number of taxis in the city would still be less than the number that would occur in an unregulated market. Your job is to predict the annual profit from a

medallion after the new medallions were issued. To predict the new annual profit, assume the following:

- The cost of providing taxi service is constant at $2.00 per mile of service.
- The initial price of taxi service (with 1,500 medallions issued) is $2.14 per mile.
- Each taxi (or medallion) provides 100,000 miles of service per year, so issuing the 300 new medallions increases the total quantity of taxi service from 150 million miles to 180 million miles.
- For consumers, each $0.01 decrease in the price of taxi service increases the quantity demanded by 10 million miles.

a. Compute the new price of taxi service.

b. Compute the new profit per medallion.

4. Shifting a Housecleaning Tax

Consider a city where poor people clean the houses of rich people. Initially, housecleaning firms charge their customers $10 per hour, keep $1 per hour for administrative costs, and pay their workers $9 per hour. Like many luxury goods, the demand for housecleaning service is very elastic. Housecleaning workers are not very responsive to changes in the wage.

a. Use supply and demand curves to show the initial equilibrium in the market for cleaning services (price = $10 per hour; quantity = 1,000 hours of cleaning per week), and label the equilibrium point with an *i*.

b. Suppose the city imposes a tax of $3 per hour of cleaning services, and one-third of the tax is shifted forward to consumers. Use your graph to show the effects of the tax on the housecleaning market. Label the new equilibrium point with an *f*. What is the new price?

c. Is it reasonable that only one-third of the tax is shifted forward? Explain.

d. Suppose that firms continue to keep $1 per hour for administrative costs. Predict the new wage.

e. Who bears the bulk of the housecleaning tax, wealthy households or poor ones?

SUMMARY

n this chapter, we discussed the efficiency of markets and he consequences of government intervention in perfectly ompetitive markets. Government intervention in a market without externalities prevents consumers and producers from executing beneficial transactions, meaning that ntervention reduces the total surplus of the market and causes inefficiency. We also saw that taxes affect the prices of consumer goods and inputs and that we must look beyond the taxpayer to determine who actually bears the cost of a tax. Here are the main points of the chapter:

1 The total surplus of a market equals the sum of consumer surplus and producer surplus.

2 In a market that meets the four efficiency conditions (no external cost, no external benefits, perfect information, perfect competition), the market equilibrium maximizes the total surplus and is therefore efficient.

3 Price controls reduce the total surplus of a market because they prevent mutually beneficial transactions.

4 Quantity controls (like licensing and import restrictions) decrease consumer surplus and the total surplus of the market.

5 A tax on a good will be shifted forward onto consumers and backward onto input suppliers.

6 Because a tax causes people to change their behavior, the total burden of the tax exceeds the revenue generated by the tax.

KEY TERMS

consumer surplus, 140
deadweight loss, 149
deadweight loss from taxation, 162

excess burden of a tax, 162
market failure, 147
producer surplus, 141

total surplus, 142
willingness to accept, 141
willingness to pay, 140

PROBLEMS AND DISCUSSION QUESTIONS

1 List the four assumptions that ensure a market equilibrium is efficient. For each assumption, provide an example of a good for which the assumption is likely to be violated.

2 According to Ida, "I'm willing to buy a CD player for $50, but I can't find anyone willing to sell me one for that price." Does that mean that the market for CD players is inefficient?

3 Figure 7.A shows a supply curve and a demand curve and several areas between the curves. Identify the areas on the figure that represent the following:
   a. Consumer surplus in the market equilibrium
   b. Producer surplus in the market equilibrium
   c. Total surplus in the market equilibrium
   d. Consumer surplus under a maximum price of $10

   e. Producer surplus under a maximum price of $10
   f. Total surplus under a maximum price of $10
   g. Consumer surplus under a maximum quantity of 70
   h. Producer surplus under a maximum quantity of 70
   i. Total surplus under a maximum quantity of 70

4 In your city, the market equilibrium price of apartments is $500 per month, and the equilibrium quantity is 1,000 apartments. Under a new rent-control program, the maximum price for apartments will be $400 per month. For producers, each $1 increase in price increases the quantity supplied by two apartments.
   a. Use a supply–demand diagram to show the effects of the rent-control program on the rental

FIGURE 7.A

**Identifying the
Surpluses**

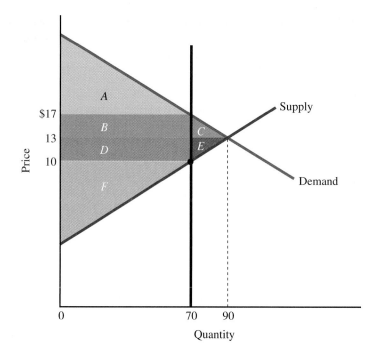

housing market. Label the initial equilibrium point with *i* and the point that shows the quantity supplied under rent control with *r*.

b. How many apartments are lost to rent control?

5 Why are rent controls in cities more common than maximum prices on food or clothing?

6 In the gasoline market, the equilibrium price is $2 and the equilibrium quantity is 100 million gallons per day. Suppose the government sets a maximum price of $1.90. For producers, each $0.01 increase in price increases the quantity supplied by three million gallons.

a. Use a supply–demand diagram to show the effects of the maximum price on the gasoline market. Label the initial equilibrium point with *i* and the point that shows the quantity supplied under the maximum price with *m*.

b. How does the maximum price affect the quantity of gasoline sold?

7 In the example in the text of taxi medallions (see Figure 7.6), suppose the city announces that it will issue 110 medallions instead of 80. Predict the market price of taxi service and the market price of medallions.

8 Using Figure 7.6 as a starting point, suppose the demand for taxi service decreases and the new

demand curve intersects the supply curve at a quantity of 7,000 miles per day. If the government doesn't change the number of medallions, what happens to the price of a medallion?

9 Predict the effect of each of the following policies on the price of the relevant good. Then draw a supply–demand diagram to defend your answer.

a. Licenses for dry cleaners

b. Limits on building permits for housing

c. Import restrictions on clothing

10 Suppose that initially there are no restrictions on importing kiwi fruit. The supply curves are the same as the supply curves for sugar shown in Figure 7.7. The initial price of kiwi fruit is 12 cents per piece. When imports are banned, the equilibrium price increases to 22 cents. Draw a market demand curve consistent with these numbers.

11 Under a special luxury tax passed by Congress, buyers of expensive cars pay a 10% tax on the portion of the purchase price above $30,000.

a. Will the luxury car tax be paid exclusively by the wealthy consumers who buy expensive cars?

b. What information do you need to determine the share of the taxes paid by wealthy consumers?

12 In the words of Will Rogers, "The trouble with land is that they're not making it any more." In other words, the supply of land is fixed and the supply curve is a vertical line.

a. If the government imposes a tax on land, which side of the market—land consumers or landowners—will pay a larger part of the tax?

b. Will the land tax generate a deadweight loss?

13 Consider the market effect of a tax on hotel rooms. The initial equilibrium price is $50 per night, and the initial equilibrium quantity is 100 rooms rented out per day. Draw a supply and demand graph so that a $10 tax per room increases the equilibrium price from $50 to $56 and decreases the equilibrium quantity from 100 rooms to 80 rooms. How is the tax divided between consumers and input suppliers?

14 Consider the analysis of the $100 apartment tax shown in Figure 7.9.

a. Use the graph to show the following after the tax: Consumer surplus (the triangle between the demand curve and the new price), producer surplus (the triangle between the initial supply curve and the price received by an apartment firm after paying the $100 tax), and total tax revenue (the rectangle with height of $100 and width of the new equilibrium number of apartments).

b. The new total value of the market is the sum of the consumer surplus, producer surplus, and tax revenue. How does it compare to the total value (consumer surplus plus producer surplus) before the tax?

c. Use your graph to show the deadweight loss from taxation (a triangle).

15 After 20 years of dog haircuts, perms, and pedicures, Doug wants to sell his pet-grooming salon. Several months earlier, a similar pet salon sold for $50,000. But Doug hasn't found anyone willing to buy his salon for more than $20,000. He suspects that the city has quietly increased the number of pet-grooming licenses, and that's why the price of grooming services has dropped, pulling down the market price of pet salons like his. According to Doug's local pet-grooming association, the quantity of grooming services in the area (the number of pet haircuts, perms, pedicures, and so forth) has not changed in recent years. So why has the market price of a pet salon decreased so much? Has the city issued more licenses, or is there another explanation?

16 In the Economic Puzzle, when the city increased the number of medallions from 400 to 500, the market price of the medallions dropped from $40,000 to $30,000. Assume that the supply curve for taxi service is horizontal. What's the implied price elasticity of demand for taxi service?

MODEL ANSWERS TO QUESTIONS

Chapter-Opening Questions

1 The rent-control policy decreases the quantity of apartments supplied, forcing some students out of the market.

2 The city limits the number of taxi licenses or medallions, leading to higher taxi prices and large profits for people who own the medallions.

3 It is illegal to buy or sell human organs, so there is no pricing mechanism to close the gap between quantity demanded and quantity supplied.

4 Consumers pay higher prices, and the cost per job saved is about $178,000.

5 The housing firm will collect more money from consumers (the price of apartments will be higher) and pay less money to input suppliers (the prices of inputs will be lower), so consumers and input suppliers will indirectly pay the tax.

Test Your Understanding

1 The willingness to pay, price, price, marginal cost.

2 The price would be $1,700, giving you and Pablo each a surplus of $300.

3 Forest is willing to pay $13, and Dee's marginal cost is $8. If they split the difference, the price would be $10.50, and each would get a surplus of $2.50.

4 Many consumers are willing to pay more than the controlled price for an apartment, and deposits and key money allow them to do so and get an apartment they could otherwise not get.

5 The consumer is willing to pay $3.30, and the producer's willingness to accept is $2.80. If they split the difference, agreeing on a price of $3.05, each will get a surplus of $0.25.

6 Zero. This is below the minimum domestic price.

7 Increases, decreases, increases.

8 The tax will be shifted forward to consumers and backward to input suppliers such as landowners (less land will be needed for hotels), construction workers (fewer will be needed to build new hotels), and housekeeping workers (fewer will be needed to clean rooms).

9 The inelastic side of the market (coffee consumers) will pay a larger share of the tax.

10 If a tax changes people's behavior, it generates a deadweight loss or excess burden.

NOTES

1. Tom Webb, "As Powdered Milk Piles Up, U.S. Taxpayers pay $1 Billion," *Oregonian*, August 24, 2003, p. 1.

2. J. K. Smith, "An Analysis of State Regulations Governing Liquor Store Licensees," *Journal of Law and Economics,* October 1982, pp. 301–319; David Kirp and Eileen Soffer, "Taking Californians to the Cleaners," *Regulation,* September/October 1985, pp. 24–26

3. D. W. Taylor, "The Economic Effects of Direct Regulation of Taxicabs in Metropolitan Toronto," *Logistics and Transportation Review,* June 1989, pp. 169–182; Laura Brown, "Hub Cabbie Hopefuls Cry: The Russians Are Coming!" *Boston Herald,* December 16, 1998, p. 1.

4. *The Economic Effects of Significant U.S. Import Restraints* (Washington, DC: U.S. International Trade Commission, initial report in 1993; update in 1996).

5. Joseph F. François, Hans-Hinrich Glismann, Dean Spinanger, "The Cost of EU Trade Protection in Textiles and Clothing", March 2000, p. 49.

6. Gary S. Becker, "How Uncle Sam Could Ease the Organ Shortage," *Business Week,* January 20, 1997, p. 18.

7. Stacy Dickert-Conlin and Amitabh Chandra, "Taxes and the Timing of Births," *Journal of Political Economy*, vol. 107, February 1999, pp. 161–77.

uses more sophisticated and costly means to reduce pollution further.

2 A pollution tax transfers an external cost, borne by people outside the firm, to the firm itself.

3 A tax increases the equilibrium price of the polluting good, and consumers buy less of it.

4 The policy increases production costs by a larger amount because it does not exploit differences in abatement costs and may employ relatively inefficient abatement technology.

5 High, low.

6 Low-cost firms sell some of their permits to high-cost firms, and the extra abatement cost incurred by the low-cost firms is less than the abatement cost saved by the high-cost firms.

7 The quantity demanded decreases by 2.8% (= 10% times 0.28).

8 Driving less frequently to the mall or grocery store; ridesharing for work trips; switching to mass transit, walking, or biking; moving closer to work or other frequent destinations; buying a more fuel-efficient car; getting more frequent tune-ups.

9 A tree decreases the volume of carbon dioxide in the atmosphere and diminishes the problem of global warming, so there is an external benefit. A subsidy could internalize the externality, encouraging people to plant and maintain trees.

NOTES

1. Spencer Banzhaf, Dallas Burtraw, and Karen Palmer, "Efficient Emission Fees in the U.S. Electricity Sector," Resources for the Future Discussion Paper 02-45, October 2002.

2. Abigail Van Buren, "Aid for Reader's Winter Woe," Sacramento Bee, February 15, 1984.

3. Gary Polakovic, "Cost of Clean Air Credits Soars in Southland," Los Angeles Times, September 5, 2000, page B.

4. 1990 Integrated Assessment Report (Washington, DC: U.S. National Acid Precipitation Assessment Program, 1991).

5. Environmental Protection Agency, "EPA Announces Results of Acid Rain Reduction Auction," Environmental News, March 28, 2002.

6. HWS helps clear air, Syracuse Herald-American, April 8, 2001.

7. National Academy of Science, Climate Change Science: An Analysis of Some Key Questions (Washington, DC: National Academy Press, 2001).

8. William D. Nordhaus, "Economic Approaches to Global Warming, in Global Warming: Economic Policy," Responses, edited by Rudiger Dornbush and James M. Poterba (Cambridge, MA: MIT Press, 1991).

9. Graeme Peters, "New Zealand Plans Carbon Tax to Meet Kyoto Targets," Reuters News Service October 18, 2002.

10. Sigurd Lauge Pedersen, "The Danish CO2 Emissions Trading System," RECIEL vol. 9, no. 3, 2000, pp. 223–231; "Domestic Emissions Trading: Denmark," National Round Table on the Environment and the Economy (*http://www.nrtee-trnee.ca/EmissionsTrading*).

11. Thomas Kellner, "Got Gas?" Forbes, March 17, 2003, p. 56.

12. "Greenhouse Gas Trading Doubled in 2003—World Bank," Reuters News Service, December 4, 2003.

13. Nina Sovich, "Selling Smoke," Time Inside Business April 2003.

14. South Coast Air Quality Management District, "New Mobile Asthma Clinic to Serve L.A." County Children, May 12, 2000.

15. Edwin S. Mills and Lawrence J. White, "Government Policies Towards Automobile Emissions Control," in Approaches to Air Pollution Control, edited by Anne Frielaender (Cambridge, MA: MIT Press, 1978).

Public Goods and Public Choice

ere is the text from a TV newscast in the year 2070:

Boomer, the 200-meter asteroid on a collision path with the earth, is expected to land at about 10:00 tomorrow morning in the heart of the world's breadbasket, the American Midwest. The energy expected to be released by the impact will exceed the total explosive yield of all the nuclear weapons on the planet. Although Boomer is much smaller than the asteroid that caused the extinction of the dinosaurs about 65 million years ago, it is large enough to cause significant changes in the world's climate. The collision will generate a stratospheric dust cloud that will inhibit photosynthesis and retard plant growth, resulting in lower agricultural yields and higher food prices throughout the world.

Could this catastrophe have been averted? Yes, according to scientists at the National Aeronautics and Space Administration. In 1996, scientists developed the technology for an asteroid-diversion system: Large optical telescopes would detect an asteroid on a collision course with the earth, and an orbiting gossamer mirror of coated polyester would focus a tight beam of sunlight on the asteroid, vaporizing enough of its surface to change its path. In a U.N. debate over the asteroid-diversion system, everyone agreed that the potential benefits of the system would outweigh the costs, but no one was willing to pay for the system. Why couldn't the nations of the world agree on such an important program, one that would have prevented tomorrow's catastrophe?

In this chapter, we'll see that if a particular good generates external benefits, government intervention can make beneficial transactions happen. For example, the cost of an asteroid-diversion program is so high that no single person would provide such a program. We will never have such a program—even if its benefits exceed its costs—unless we make a collective decision about what sort of diversion program to develop and how to pay for it. The purpose of government is to help make this sort of collective decision. The hypothetical newscast suggests that some sort of multinational arrangement will be necessary to launch an asteroid-diversion program.

This chapter explores the economic challenges associated with providing—and paying for—goods that generate external benefits. We'll also take a look at some alternative theories on government decision-making. Here are some practical questions that we'll answer:

1 What would happen if we eliminated taxes and paid for government programs with voluntary contributions instead?

2 Is it sensible to pay landowners to host endangered wildlife such as wolves and spotted owls?

3 It often seems there is little difference between candidates running for election. Why?

An Overview
of Government Spending and Taxes

Although it's convenient to talk about "the" government, there are thousands of governments in the United States, and each citizen deals with at least three different levels of government. Figure 10.1 shows the budget breakdown for the three levels of government. There are more than 80,000 local governments in the United States, including municipalities (city governments), counties, school districts, and special districts responsible for providing services such as water, fire protection, and libraries. Local governments spend most of their money on education (kindergarten through high school), public welfare and health (payments to poor households and support for public hospitals), highways, fire protection, and police and corrections. For states, the biggest spending programs are education (including colleges and universities), public welfare, highways, health and hospitals, and corrections (state courts and prisons). For the federal government, the biggest spending programs are programs for the elderly (Social Security and Medicare), national defense, income security (payments to the poor), and interest on the national debt.

FIGURE 10.1

Percentages of Government Spending on Various Programs

Source: Statistical Abstract of the United States, 2002.

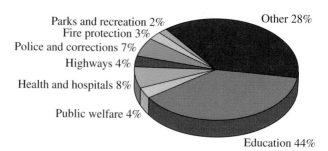

Local Government (1999)

Parks and recreation 2%
Fire protection 3%
Police and corrections 7%
Highways 4%
Health and hospitals 8%
Public welfare 4%
Education 44%
Other 28%

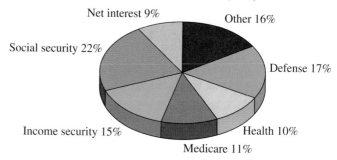

Federal Government (2002)

Net interest 9%
Social security 22%
Income security 15%
Medicare 11%
Health 10%
Defense 17%
Other 16%

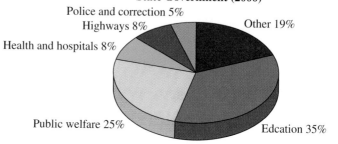

State Government (2000)

Police and correction 5%
Highways 8%
Health and hospitals 8%
Public welfare 25%
Edcation 35%
Other 19%

External Benefits and Inefficiency

In Chapter 5, we saw that when there are neither external benefits nor external costs, the market equilibrium is efficient. When a government intervenes in an efficient market, the result is inefficiency. In this chapter, we'll see that a market with external benefits is inefficient, so there is an opportunity for government to promote efficiency.

To illustrate the idea of external benefits and inefficiency, consider a dam built for flood-control purposes. There are 100,000 people in the valley below the dam, and each person gets a $5 benefit from the dam. The total benefit of the dam is $500,000 (equal to 100,000 people times $5 per person), which exceeds the $200,000 total cost of the dam. Because the total benefit exceeds the total cost, the dam should be built. The problem is that no single person will build the dam because the $200,000 cost exceeds the $5 personal benefit. In other words, if we rely on the forces of supply and demand, with each person considering only personal benefits and costs of a dam, it won't be built.

The government can solve this problem by collecting enough taxes to pay for the dam. Suppose the government proposes to collect $2 per person to pay for the dam. The tax raises $200,000 in tax revenue ($2 per person times 100,000 people), which is just high enough to pay the $200,000 cost of the dam. Most people will support this proposal because the $2 tax per person is less than the $5 benefit per person. The government can use its taxing power to provide a good that would otherwise not be provided.

Public Goods and External Benefits

The dam is an example of a **public good**. A public good is available for everyone to utilize, regardless of who pays for it and who doesn't. In contrast, each unit of a **private good** is consumed by a single person or household. For example, only one person can eat a hot dog. If a government hands out free cheese to the poor, is the free cheese a public good or a private good? Although anyone can get in line for the cheese, only one person can actually consume a particular piece of cheese, so the free cheese is a private good that happens to be available free of charge from the government. Similarly, an apartment in a public housing project can be occupied by a single household, so it is a private good provided by the government.

We can be more precise about the difference between public and private goods. Private goods are *rival* in consumption (only one person can consume the good) and *excludable* (a person who does not pay for the good can be prevented from consuming it). Public goods are *nonrival* in consumption: The fact that one person benefits from a good does not prevent another person from benefiting, too. For example, the fact that I benefit from a flood-control dam doesn't reduce your benefit from the dam. Public goods are also *nonexcludable*: It is impractical to exclude people who don't pay. Some examples of public goods are national defense, law enforcement, space exploration, the preservation of endangered species, the protection of the earth's ozone layer, and fireworks shows. If someone refuses to pay for one of these public goods, it would be impractical to prevent that person from consuming or benefiting from the good.

Private Goods with External Benefits

In contrast to a public good, a private good can be utilized by a single person or household. But some private goods generate benefits for people who are not directly consuming the good. For example, suppose if I replace the peeling paint on my house with a fresh coat of paint. I benefit from the new paint because it protects my house from decay and my house will look better, at least to me. Assuming that I've avoided an obnoxious color, my neighbors will also benefit from the improved appearance of the neighborhood.

As another example of a private good with external benefits, consider LoJack, the system used to recover stolen vehicles. A small, silent transmitter hidden in a vehicle allows police to track a stolen car. A thief who steals a LoJack-equipped car won't keep the car for long and is likely to get caught, so LoJack is an effective deterrent to car theft. Car thieves cannot distinguish between cars with and without LoJack, so the system decreases the payoff from car theft in general, decreasing the number of thefts. Therefore, people who install LoJack systems generate benefits for themselves and for other car owners who don't have LoJack.

Public good

A good that is available for everyone to consume, regardless of who pays and who doesn't.

Private good

A good that is consumed by a single person or household.

Another example of a private good with external benefits is education. Most of the benefits of education go to the student because education increases his or her productivity and potential earnings, and presumably makes everyday life easier and more interesting. There are two sorts of external benefits from education:

1 **Workplace externalities.** In most workplaces, people work in groups and teamwork is important. A well-educated person understands instructions readily and is more likely to suggest ways to improve the production process. As a result, when a well-educated person joins a work team, the productivity of everyone on the team increases. Higher productivity generally leads to higher profits for firms, and members of the team are more likely to earn higher salaries.

2 **Civic externalities.** Citizens in a democratic society make collective decisions by voting in elections, and each citizen must live with these decisions. A well-educated person is more likely to vote intelligently, so there are external benefits for other citizens.

Because of these external benefits from education, the government uses various policies to encourage people to become educated. Local governments provide free education through high school. States subsidize students at public colleges and universities, providing college education at a fraction of its actual cost. In addition, the federal government provides financial aid to students in both public and private schools.

The government subsidizes other goods that generate external benefits. Subsidies for on-the-job training and education encourage workers and firms to invest in human capital and increase labor productivity. It is sensible for the government to subsidize training and education because some of the benefits are transferred to other firms when workers change employers. Another example is research at universities and other nonprofit organizations. If a research project provides knowledge or technology that leads to the development of new products or the improvement of old ones, the benefits from the project spill over onto consumers and producers. When there are external benefits, the government can encourage people to take actions that benefit other people. By making beneficial transactions happen, the government can increase efficiency.

Public Goods and the Free-Rider Problem

Most public goods are supported by taxes. What would happen if we eliminated taxes and asked people to contribute money to pay for national defense, dams, city streets, and the police? Would people contribute enough money to support these programs at their current levels?

Free-rider problem

A problem that occurs when people try to benefit from a public good without paying for it.

The problem with using voluntary contributions to support public goods is known as the **free-rider problem**. Each person has a financial incentive to try to get the benefits of a public good without paying for it. That is, some people will try to get a "free ride" at the expense of others who do pay. Of course, if everyone tries to get a free ride, there will be no money to support the public good, so it won't be provided. The flip side of the free-rider problem is the chump problem: No one wants to be the chump—the person who gives free rides to other people—so no one contributes any money. The free-rider problem suggests that if taxes were replaced with voluntary contributions, the government would be forced to cut back or eliminate many programs.

Why Build a Three-Faced Clock Tower?

Economic **Puzzle**

Back in the days before inexpensive wristwatches, most people did not carry their own timepieces. Many towns built clock towers to help their citizens keep track of time. The towns paid for the clock towers with voluntary contributions from citizens. One town in the northeastern United States built a four-sided tower but put clock faces on only three sides of the tower. To most people, this seems bizarre. If you build a clock tower, why not put clock faces on all four sides?

The key to solving this puzzle is the free-rider problem. It turns out that one of the town's wealthy citizens refused to contribute money to help build the clock tower. The town officials decided not to put a clock face on the side of the tower facing the wealthy citizen's house. In other words, the citizen tried—unsuccessfully—to get a free ride. The problem is that other citizens on the same side of town also suffered from not seeing the clock. In this case, preventing a free ride by one citizen caused problems for other citizens. ∎

Overcoming the Free-Rider Problem

Many organizations, including public radio and television, religious organizations, and charitable organizations, raise money through voluntary contributions. So it appears that some people overcome their inclination to be free riders and contribute voluntarily to organizations that provide public goods. The successful organizations use a number of techniques to encourage people to contribute.

► Giving contributors private goods such as coffee mugs, books, musical recordings, and magazine subscriptions. People are more likely to contribute if they get something for it.
► Arranging matching contributions. You are more likely to contribute if you know that your $30 contribution will be matched with a contribution from another person.
► Appealing to people's sense of civic or moral responsibility.

It's important to note, however, that these organizations are only partly successful in mitigating the free-rider problem. Public radio is one of the success stories, even though the typical public-radio station gets contributions from fewer than a quarter of its listeners.

TEST Your Understanding

1. Explain why the free-rider problem occurs for public goods but not for private goods.
2. Is admission to a nearly empty movie theater a public good or a private good?
3. Is painting your house a public good, a private good, or a private good with external benefits?

Applications: Asteroids and Wildlife

Now that we've discussed some of the economic challenges associated with providing public goods, let's think about two unconventional public goods: The diversion of asteroids and the preservation of wolves.

Asteroid Diversion

How do we apply the concepts of public goods to the issue of protecting the earth from catastrophic collisions with asteroids? On average, the earth is hit by a 200-meter asteroid every 10,000 years, by a 2-kilometer asteroid every million years, and by a 10-kilometer asteroid every 100 million years.[1] As was explained at the beginning of the chapter, we have the technology to divert approaching asteroids.

The diversion of asteroids is a public good in the sense that it is available for everyone's benefit, regardless of who pays and who doesn't. As with any public good, the key to developing an asteroid-diversion program is to collect money to pay for the program. According to NASA scientists, the program would require several new telescopes, which would cost about $50 million to install and about $10 million per year to operate.[2] The cost of the gossamer mirror or the nuclear weapons required to change the path of the asteroid would be $100 million to $200 million. Although it would be sensible to finance the program with contributions from all earthlings, it may be impossible to collect money from everyone. A more likely outcome is that one or more developed countries will finance their own diversion systems.

Preservation of Wolves

We can also apply the concepts of public goods and free riding to the issue of preserving wildlife. There are some trade-offs associated with preserving wolves and other wildlife in Yellowstone Park. To environmentalists, wolves are a part of the natural ecosystem. To ranchers, whose livestock is often eaten by wolves, wolves are pests that should be eliminated or tightly controlled. In other words, there are costs as well as benefits associated with the preservation of wolves, just as there are costs and benefits associated with other public goods such as dams, fireworks, national defense, and space exploration.

One response to the wolf-preservation problem comes from Defenders of Wildlife, an environmental group in Montana. The organization collects money from its members and uses the money to reward landowners who allow wolves to live on their properties. The host landowner receives a payment of $5,000 for each litter of wolf pups reared on the property.[3] In addition, the organization compensates ranchers for livestock killed by wolves. As a result of these programs, ranchers in the Yellowstone area are more likely to support efforts to maintain the wolves as part of Yellowstone Park's ecosystem. The programs treat preservation as a public good, one

Innovative programs that compensate ranchers for livestock lost to wolves help preservation efforts.

that is supported by money contributed by people who benefit from preservation. The organization has collected contributions from thousands of people despite the free-rider problem.

Public Choice

We have discussed the challenges associated with providing and paying for goods that generate external benefits. In this part of the chapter, we look at how governments actually operate, exploring some contrasting views of government that have emerged from a field of study known as **public choice economics**. We'll start with a model of government decisions based on voting and then look at some alternative models.

Public choice economics

A field of economics that explores how governments actually operate.

Voting and the Median-Voter Rule

As citizens in a democracy, we pick people to make public decisions. We vote for people to represent our viewpoints in legislative bodies (city council members, state legislators, and congressional representatives), and we vote for people in executive positions (mayors, governors, and presidents). The basic idea of a democracy is that the government will take actions that are approved by the majority of citizens. If governments are responsive to voters, the voting public ultimately makes all the important decisions, and the actions of the government will reflect their preferences.

One finding of public choice economics is known as the **median-voter rule**. According to the median-voter rule, the choices made by government will reflect the preferences of the median voter, defined as the voter whose preferences lie in the

Median-voter rule

A rule suggesting that the choices made by government will reflect the preferences of the median voter.

middle of the set of all voters' preferences; half the voters want more of something (for example, a larger government budget) and half want less (a smaller government budget). As we'll see, this rule has some interesting implications for decision-making and politics.

To see the logic of this rule, consider a state where there are two candidates for governor—Penny and Buck—and the only issue in the election is how much the state should spend on education. Each citizen will vote for the candidate whose proposed education budget is closest to the citizen's preferred budget. Figure 10.2 shows citizens' preferences for education spending, with different preferred budgets on the horizontal axis and the number of voters on the vertical axis. For example, two citizens have a preferred budget of $1 billion, four have a preferred budget of $2 billion, and so on. The median budget, which splits the rest of the voters into two equal groups (20 voters on either side), is $5 billion.

Suppose the two candidates start out with very different proposed education budgets. Penny proposes a budget of $3 billion, and Buck proposes $7 billion. The 20 citizens with preferred budgets less than or equal to $4 billion will vote for Penny because her proposed budget is closest to their preferred budgets. Buck's supporters include the 20 citizens with preferred budgets greater than or equal to $6 billion. The two candidates will split the 10 voters with a preferred budget of $5 billion (halfway between the two proposed budgets), so each candidate will get a total of 25 votes, resulting in a tie.

Penny could increase her chance of being elected by increasing her proposed budget. Let's say she proposes $4 billion instead of $3 billion. The voters with a preferred budget of $5 billion will switch to Penny because Penny's $4 billion proposal is now closer to their $5 billion preferred budget than Buck's $7 billion. Penny won't lose any of her other votes either, so she will win the election by a vote of 30 (2 + 4 + 6 + 8 + 10) to 20 (8 + 8 + 4). If Buck is smart, he will realize that he could get more votes by moving toward the median budget. For example, if he decreases his proposed budget to $6 billion, the election would result in a tie vote again. Penny

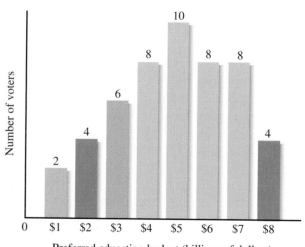

FIGURE 10.2

The Median-Voter Rule

If Penny proposes a $3 billion budget and Buck proposes a $7 billion budget, the election will result in a tie. By moving toward the median budget, Penny can increase her chance of being elected. Both candidates will propose a budget close to the $5 billion preferred budget of the median voter.

and Buck will continue to move their proposed budgets toward the median budget ($5 billion) until they both propose budgets that are very close to the median budget.

There are powerful forces pulling the two candidates toward the preferences of the median voter. As long as Penny proposes a smaller budget than Buck, the people with small preferred budgets will continue to vote for her. The benefit of moving toward the median is that she can take some votes from Buck. Similarly, Buck doesn't have to worry about people with large preferred budgets but can concentrate instead on the battle for voters in the middle. The result is that by election day, the two candidates have adopted virtually the same position: The position of the median voter. Voters trying to choose between two candidates may feel they don't have much choice. In fact, the median-voter rule says that the choices made by government will reflect the preferences of the median voter, regardless of who wins the election.

The logic of the median-voter result also applies to competition among some types of sellers. Read "A Closer Look: Are Politicians Like Ice-Cream Vendors?"

Although we usually think that people make political decisions by voting in elections, it is also possible to "vote with your feet." In 1956, economist Charles M. Tiebout suggested that a household's choice of which community to live in is based in part on the tax and spending policies of different communities. Households express their preferences by moving to communities that offer the best package of services and taxes. A community with inefficient public services will experience a

A CLOSER LOOK

Are Politicians Like Ice-Cream Vendors?

Imagine a one-mile stretch of beach with 120 swimmers and sunbathers distributed evenly along the beach. Suppose each person on the beach will purchase one ice-cream cone. If there are two ice-cream vendors on the beach selling an identical product, where will they locate? The most efficient arrangement would be to divide the beach into two half-mile territories and locate each vendor at the middle of his or her territory. As shown in Panel A of Figure 10.3, Lefty would be at the quarter-mile mark, and Righty would be at the three-quarter-mile mark. If beachgoers patronize the closest vendor, each vendor would sell 60 ice-cream cones. This arrangement will minimize the total travel costs of ice-cream patrons.

Is this an equilibrium arrangement? If Lefty were to move to the right—to the half-mile mark, the median location that splits consumers into two equal halves—he would not lose any of his customers to his left but would capture part of Righty's market. As shown in Panel B of Figure 10.3, Lefty would then be the closest vendor for the people located between the half-mile mark and the five-eighths mark. Therefore, Lefty would sell 75 cones (up from 60) and Righty would sell only 45 cones. To protect her market, Righty would move to the median location too, locating right next to Lefty. By doing so, Righty can recover her 50% share of the market, again serving the consumers on the right half of the beach. At any other location, she would get less than half the market, given Lefty is at the median location. In equilibrium, shown in Panel C of Figure 10.3, both vendors pick the median location and each serves half the market.

The outcome of the ice-cream vendors' game is the same as the politicians' game. Like the politicians, the vendors have an incentive to move to the median location, so there is no real difference between the two vendors.

FIGURE 10.3

Competition on a Beach Leads to a Median Location for Both Sellers

A: If the two sellers start at the one-quarter- and three-quarter-mile marks, each has a territory of one-half mile and sells 60 cones.
B: If Lefty moves to the median location, his territory increases to the 5/8 mile mark, and he sells 75 cones, compared to 45 for Righty.
C: Righty can recover her lost territory by moving to the median location. In equilibrium, both sellers locate at the median location and each has half the market.

If the two sellers start at the 1/4 and 3/4 mile marks, each has a territory of 1/2 mile and sells 60 cones:

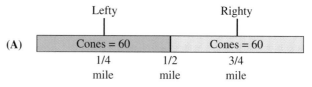

If Lefty moves to the median location, his territory increases to the 5/8 mile mark, and he sells 75 cones, compared to 45 for Righty:

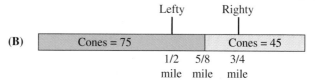

Righty can recover her lost territory by moving to the median location. In equilibrium, both sellers locate at the median location and each has half the market:

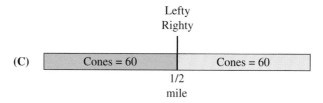

loss in population, perhaps causing the local officials to make the public services more efficient.

It is clear that people vote with their ballots *and* with their feet. In both cases, citizens can express their preferences for public goods, taxes, and public policies. These two sources of citizen power limit the ability of governments to take actions that are inconsistent with the preferences of most voters.

Alternative Models of Government: Self-Interests and Special Interests

Several economists, including Nobel laureate James Buchanan, have suggested a model of government that focuses on the selfish behavior of government officials. According to this view, politicians and bureaucrats pursue their own narrow interests, which, of course, may differ from the public interest. For example, politicians or bureaucrats may gain prestige from starting a new spending program even if the cost of the program exceeds its social benefit. Because voters don't have much information about the costs and benefits of public services, they may not be in a position to evaluate the actions of politicians or bureaucrats and vote accordingly.

The self-interest theory of government explains why voters sometimes approve explicit limits on taxes and government spending. For example, most states have limits on the amount of property taxes that can be raised, and many states also limit total government spending. According to the self-interest theory of government, limitations on taxes and spending are necessary safeguards against politicians and bureaucrats who benefit from larger budgets.

Another model of government is based on the idea that small groups of people manipulate government for their own gain. Suppose the total benefit of a dam is less than its total cost, so the project is inefficient, but a few farmers reap large benefits from the dam, while the costs are spread over a million taxpayers. The farmers have a strong incentive to spend time and money to convince policymakers to build the dam. In contrast, if the tax is only $1 per person, not many taxpayers will make their preferences known to policymakers because the marginal benefit (the $1 tax savings) is less than the marginal cost (the opportunity cost of their time). If politicians listen to people who express their preferences and contribute money to political campaigns, the inefficient project may be approved. This is an example of a special-interest group (farmers) manipulating the government at the expense of a larger group (all taxpayers). In general, when a few people share the benefit from a project and a large number of people share the cost, the government is more likely to approve inefficient projects.

In general, whenever benefits are concentrated on a few citizens but costs are spread out over many citizens, we expect special-interest groups to form. Special-interest organizations often use lobbyists to express their views to government officials and policymakers.

Which Theory or Viewpoint Is Correct?

Which of these theories or viewpoints best describes the actual practices of governments? This is a very difficult question. Economists and political scientists have studied many dimensions of the decision-making processes underlying tax policies and spending policies. There is evidence that people do vote with ballots and with their feet, and that these two forms of voting make a difference. There is also evidence that government officials sometimes pursue their own interests and those of special-interest groups. The field of public choice is a very active area of research involving both economists and political scientists.

TEST Your Understanding

4. In Figure 10.2, suppose that 32 additional citizens appear, and each has a preferred budget of $2 billion. How will the new citizens affect the election?
5. Do you think all citizens have the same opportunity to vote with their feet, picking the communities with the best combination of public services and taxes?
6. Does your ability to vote with your feet vary with the level of government? Compared to the municipal level, is foot voting more or less likely at the state level? What about the national level?

Economic Experiment

Voluntary Contributions

Do people really try to get free rides? Or would most people contribute at least some money to support a public good? Here is a classroom experiment that helps to answer this question.

- The instructor selects 10 students at random and gives each student 10 dimes (or play money).
- Each student can contribute money to support a public good by dropping 1, 2, or 3 dimes into a public-good pot. Each student has the option of keeping all the dimes and not contributing anything. The contributions are anonymous; none of the students knows how much the other students contribute.
- For each dime in the pot, the instructor adds 2 dimes. For example, if the students contribute a total of 40 dimes, the instructor adds 80 dimes, for a total of 120 dimes in the pot. The 2-for-1 match represents the idea that the benefits of public goods exceed the costs. In this case, the benefit–cost ratio is 3 to 1.
- The instructor divides the money in the public-good pot equally among the 10 students. For example, if there are 120 dimes in the pot, each student receives 12 dimes.
- Steps 2 through 4 can be repeated 4 or 5 times.

We can change the experiment to mimic the compulsory tax system. The instructor could require each student to contribute 3 dimes, the maximum amount, each round. Would a switch to a compulsory tax system make the students better off or worse off? ●

USING THE TOOLS

In this chapter, we explained why the government provides public goods. Because of the free-rider problem, we can't rely on voluntary contributions to support public goods and subsidies, so we use taxes to support public programs. Here are some opportunities to do your own economic analysis of public goods and taxes.

1. Stream Preservation

Consider a trout stream that is threatened with destruction by a nearby logging operation. Each of the 10,000 local fishers would be willing to pay $5 to preserve the stream. The owner of the land would incur a cost of $20,000 to change the logging operation to protect the stream.
a. Is the preservation of the stream efficient from the social perspective?
b. If the landowner has the right to log the land any way he wants, will the stream be preserved?
c. Propose a solution to this problem. Describe a transaction that would benefit the fishers and the landowner.
d. Will your proposed solution work?

2. Marginalism and Contributions

Consider the voluntary contributions experiment described at the end of the chapter. Margie, one of the students participating in the free-rider experiment, thinks in marginal terms and asks the following question: "If I contribute one dime, how will that affect my payoff from the experiment?"
a. Answer her question, assuming that her contribution does not affect the contribution of other students.
b. Suppose Margie uses the marginal principle to make all her decisions. Will she contribute the extra dime?

SUMMARY

In this chapter, we've seen that governments can solve the problems caused by external benefits. We've also examined different views on how governments really make decisions. Here are the main points of the chapter:

1 We can use government—with its taxing authority—to make collective decisions about the provision of public goods.

2 A system of voluntary contributions suffers from the free-rider problem: People do not have a financial incentive to contribute to the support of public goods.

3 The choices made by government will reflect the preferences of the median voter, defined as the voter whose preferences lie in the middle of the set of all voters' preferences.

KEY TERMS

free-rider problem, 222
median-voter rule, 225

private good, 221
public choice economics, 225

public good, 221

PROBLEMS AND DISCUSSION QUESTIONS

1 A three-person city is considering a fireworks display. Bertha is willing to pay $100 for the proposed fireworks display, Marian is willing to pay $30, Sam is willing to pay $20. The cost of the fireworks display is $120.
   a. Will any single citizen provide the display on his or her own?
   b. If the cost of the fireworks display is divided equally among the citizens, will a majority vote in favor of the display?
   c. Describe a transaction that would benefit all three citizens.

2 Churches collect substantial sums of money through voluntary contributions. What explains their ability to overcome the free-rider problem at least partially?

3 Consider the voluntary contributions experiment described at the end of the chapter. Suppose the participants make the following agreement: If any single person does not contribute 3 dimes, all the contributions will be returned, and each contributor will receive a refund equal to the amount he or she contributed. How will this agreement affect the outcome of the experiment?

4 The spotted owl is an endangered species that lives in old-growth forests. Logging destroys the habitat of spotted owls. Explain how the lessons from the wolf-preservation program might be applied to the issue of preserving the spotted owl.

5 Each of the 80,000 citizens in a particular county would be willing to pay $0.10 to increase the number of wolf litters by one. Each litter of wolves imposes costs on ranchers (from livestock losses) of $5,000.
   a. Is the provision of an additional litter of wolves efficient from the social perspective?
   b. If ranchers have the right to kill any wolves on their property, will an additional litter be protected?
   c. Propose a solution to this problem. Describe a transaction that would benefit the wolf lovers and the ranchers.

6 Contributions to organizations such as the United Way and the American Cancer Society are tax deductible: For each dollar contributed, a person's tax liability decreases by $0.15 to $0.31. Explain the rationale for this tax policy.

7 Consider the example of the governor's election shown in Figure 10.2. Suppose 18 new people move

into the state and each newcomer has a desired education budget of $9 billion.

a. Will the two candidates change their proposed education budget? If so, how much will each candidate propose?

b. How would your answer to part (a) change if each newcomer had a desired budget of $15 billion instead of $9 billion?

MODEL ANSWERS TO QUESTIONS

Chapter-Opening Questions

1 A system based on voluntary contributions would suffer from the free-rider problem, with few people contributing money to support the public good.

2 The payments to host landowners treat preservation as a public good supported by money collected from the people who benefit from preservation.

3 A liberal candidate who moves toward the center won't lose the votes of liberal citizens, but will gain some votes from moderate citizens. A conservative candidate who moves toward the center won't lose conservative votes, but will gain moderate votes. Both candidates are likely to adopt the position favored by the median voter.

Test Your Understanding

1 The producer of a private good collects money from each consumer. If you don't pay, you don't get the good. In contrast, it is impossible to prevent people who don't pay from consuming a public good.

2 Although movie admission is nonrival if the theater is nearly empty, it is excludable, so it is a private good.

3 It is a private good with external benefits. Your neighbors benefit from looking at a nicely painted house.

4 The median voter now has a preferred budget of $3 billion: A total of 38 voters have a lower preferred budget ($1 or $2 billion), and a total of 38 voters have a higher preferred budget. Both candidates will propose the median budget ($3 billion).

5 Low-income households cannot afford housing in many neighborhoods, so they have fewer options. Many suburban communities have zoning policies that limit high-density housing, restricting the choices of low-income households. If there is racial discrimination, minority households will have fewer options.

6 At the local level, the typical metropolitan area has many municipalities to choose from, so foot voting is not very costly. At the national level, voting with your feet means renouncing your citizenship and moving far away, so it is more costly.

NOTES

1. Carl Sagan, "A Warning for Us?" *Parade*, June 5, 1994, p. 8; John Boudreau, "Collision Course: Scientists Say There's a Big Asteroid Bang in Our Future," *Washington Post*, April 6, 1994, p. C1.

2. "Mirror Beam Could Deflect Killer Asteroid, Theory Says," *New York Times*, November 9, 1994, p. C6.

3. Terry L. Anderson, "A Carrot to Save the Wolf," *The Margin*, Spring 1992, p. 28.

Part 4

Market Structures and Pricing

Production Technology and Cost

A few years ago the price of a hardback version of Encyclopedia Britannica, the world's leading encyclopedia, was $1,600. Now you can get a CD version of the encyclopedia, along with a dictionary, thesaurus, and world atlas, for only $69.95. Why did the price drop to less than 1/20th of its former value?

An encyclopedia is an information good, and its production involves collecting information—facts, figures, and images—and packaging them for use by consumers. The cost of compiling the information for the first copy of an encyclopedia is huge, but the cost of reproducing the encyclopedia in digital format (CDs) is tiny. The move from hardback encyclopedias to digital ones decreased the cost of production, pulling down the price. In addition, heated competition among rival encyclopedia firms pulled the price down further.

This chapter is about how the cost of producing a particular product varies with the quantity of output produced. As we'll see, the cost of producing a product is determined by production technology—the way a firm combines inputs like capital and labor to produce output. After explaining the link between technology and costs, we'll look at the actual cost curves of several products, including aluminum, hospital services, wind power, and freight services.

In later chapters, we'll use the cost curves discussed in this chapter to explore firms' decisions about whether to enter a market and how much output to produce once they enter. In this chapter, we'll see how to use cost curves to answer the following practical questions:

1 Why is the typical *short-run* average-cost curve shaped like the letter U, while the typical *long-run* average-cost curve is shaped like the letter L?

2 If the short-run average cost of production is the same for two different quantities of output, can it be the same for three different quantities?

3 The cost of producing the first fake killer whale is about three times the cost of producing the second. Why?

4 How does the cost of electricity vary with the size of the wind turbine used to generate it?

Introduction

Why study production costs? The ultimate goal of a firm is to maximize its profit, where profit equals total revenue minus total cost. For most firms, total revenue exceeds total cost by a small margin. For example, the typical convenience store has monthly sales (total revenue) of $76,400, and the cost of sales clerks, utilities, building rent, and merchandise add up to $74,100.[1] The store therefore has $2,300 left over after paying all these costs ($76,400 − $74,100), meaning that the reward for the entrepreneur is just $2,300 per month. Of course, the opportunity cost of the entrepreneur's time is a cost of doing business, too. If this opportunity cost is $2,000 per month, the store's actual profit is only $300 per month. Because this profit margin is so slim, the typical convenience store has a strong incentive to control its costs. If it doesn't, it might actually end up losing money.

In this chapter, we'll look at several ways to measure a firm's cost of production. Given the importance of costs in determining a firm's profit, firms spend a great deal of time and money in computing their costs. They use this information to decide how much to produce and how much to charge for their products. In the chapters following this one, we'll use what we learn about production costs to explore firm's production and pricing decisions.

Economic Cost Is Opportunity Cost

Economic cost

The opportunity cost of production, including both explicit and implicit costs.

Our discussion of the firm's cost is based on the notion of **economic cost**. The computation of economic cost is based on the principle of opportunity cost.

 Principle OF OPPORTUNITY COST

The opportunity cost of something is what you sacrifice to get it.

Explicit cost

The firm's actual cash payments for its inputs.

Implicit cost

The opportunity cost of nonpurchased inputs.

A firm's economic cost includes all of its opportunity costs, which can be divided into two types, explicit costs and implicit costs. A firm's **explicit cost** is defined as its actual cash payments for inputs. For example, if a firm spends a total of $3,000 per month on labor, materials, rent, and machinery, its explicit cost is $3,000. This is an opportunity cost because money spent on these inputs cannot be used to buy something else. The firm's **implicit cost** is defined as the opportunity cost of nonpurchased inputs such as the entrepreneur's time or money:

▶ Opportunity cost of the entrepreneur's time. An entrepreneur's economic cost includes the opportunity cost of the time spent running the firm. If an entrepreneur could earn $5,000 per month in another job, the opportunity cost of his or her time is $5,000 per month.

▶ Opportunity cost of the entrepreneur's funds. Many entrepreneurs use their own funds to set up and run their businesses. If an entrepreneur starts a business with money withdrawn from a savings account, the opportunity cost of using these funds is the interest the funds could have earned, for example $1,000 per month.

As shown in Table 11.1, the economic cost for our example is $9,000, including $3,000 in explicit costs and $6,000 in implicit costs.

Short-Run Versus Long-Run Costs

As we saw in Chapter 2, economists distinguish between the short run and the long run in production. The long run is a period long enough that a firm is perfectly flexible in its choice of all inputs, including its production facility. In contrast, when a firm can-

TABLE 11.1

Economic Cost

Explicit cost (purchased inputs)	$3,000
Implicit cost: opportunity cost of entrepreneur's time	5,000
Implicit cost: opportunity cost of funds	1,000
Economic cost	$9,000

not modify its facility, it is operating in the short run. In this chapter, we'll explore both short-run and long-run cost curves. In later chapters, we'll see how firms use these cost curves to make two types of decisions:

▶ A firm with a fixed production facility must decide how much output to produce in that facility. This is a short-run decision because one of the factors of production (the facility) is fixed.

▶ A firm that has decided to enter a market must decide how large a facility to build. This is a long-run decision because none of the factors of production are fixed. The firm starts from scratch and can choose a production facility of any size.

The time required to reach the long run varies across industries. If it takes one day to get a hot-dog cart and start selling hot dogs, the long run for a hot-dog vendor is one day. In contrast, it takes several years to design and build a computer-chip factory, so the long run for a computer-chip producer is several years.

In the last part of the chapter, we'll look at the cost curves for information goods such as music CDs, books, and movie DVDs. The production of these goods requires a substantial expense before any output is produced, but the additional cost to produce the first unit of output is relatively low. For example, producing a movie requires millions of dollars for writers, actors, camera operators, and other crew members, but once the images and sounds are stored in digital format, the cost of burning them onto a DVD is less than a dollar. Similarly, to produce a book, thousands of dollars must be paid to authors, illustrators, and editors. However, once all the words and images are compiled, the cost of printing the book is just a few dollars per unit. As we'll see, the cost curves for information goods are very different from those for other products.

The Fixed Production Facility: Short-Run Costs

Consider first the case of producing with a fixed production facility. Suppose that you have decided to start a small firm to produce plastic paddles for rafts. The production of paddles requires a workshop where workers use molds to form plastic material into paddles. Before we can discuss the cost of production, we need information about the nature of the production process.

Production and Marginal Product

Table 11.2 shows how the quantity of paddles produced varies with the number of workers. A one-worker operation produces one paddle per day, while a two-worker operation produces 5 paddles. The **marginal product of labor** is the change in output from one additional unit of labor. In Table 11.2, the marginal product of the first worker is 1 paddle, compared to a marginal product of 4 paddles for the second worker.

Marginal product of labor
The change in output from one additional unit of labor.

TABLE 11.2

Labor, Output, and
Marginal Product

Labor	Quantity of Output Produced	Marginal Product of Labor
1	1	1
2	5	4
3	8	3
4	10	2
5	11	1
6	11.5	0.50

Why does the marginal product increase as output increases? As we saw earlier in the book, when a firm increases its workforce, individual workers can specialize in particular production tasks. Productivity increases because of the benefits of continuity (less time switching between production tasks) and repetition (each worker becomes more proficient at the assigned task). A two-worker operation produces more than twice as many paddles as a one-person operation because the two workers can specialize, one being responsible for preparing the plastic for the mold and the other responsible for working the mold.

Starting with the third worker, the production process is subject to **diminishing returns**, one of the key principles of economics.

Diminishing returns

As one input increases while the other inputs are held fixed, output increases at a decreasing rate.

Principle OF DIMINISHING RETURNS

Suppose that output is produced with two or more inputs and we increase one input while holding the other inputs fixed. Beyond some point—called the point of diminishing returns— output will increase at a decreasing rate.

The third worker adds 3 paddles to total output, down from 4 paddles for the second worker. As the firm continues to hire more workers, the marginal product drops to 2 paddles for the fourth worker and 1 paddle for the fifth worker. As we saw earlier in the book, diminishing returns occurs because workers share a production facility, and with a larger workforce, each worker gets a smaller share of the production facility. In the paddle example, the workers share a mold, and as the number of workers increases, they will spend more time waiting to use the mold.

Figure 11.1 provides a graphical representation of this production relationship. The firm's **total product curve** shows the relationship between number of workers (on the horizontal axis) and output (on the vertical axis), *ceteris paribus*. The total-product curve shows the effects of labor specialization as well as diminishing returns. For the first two workers, output increases rapidly because labor specialization increases the marginal product of labor. Starting with the third worker, however, total output increases at a decreasing rate because of diminishing returns.

Total product curve

A curve showing the relationship between the quantity of labor and the quantity of output produced.

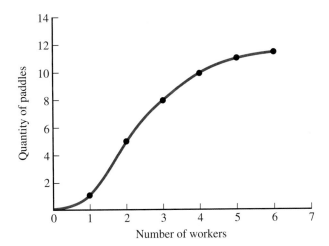

FIGURE 11.1

Total Product Curve
The total product curve shows the relationship between the quantity of labor and the quantity of output, given a fixed production facility. For the first 2 workers, output increases at an increasing rate, a result of labor specialization. Hiring additional workers generates diminishing returns, and output then increases at a decreasing rate.

Short-Run Total Cost

We've seen the production relationship between labor and output, so now we're ready to show the relationship between output and production cost. The first step is to specify some numbers for the inputs used in paddle production. Suppose your opportunity cost is $50 per day, and you can hire workers for your workshop at the market wage of $50 per day. Further suppose you can purchase your workshop, including the building and the paddle mold, for $365,000. If the interest rate you could have earned on that money is 10% per year, the opportunity cost of tying up your $365,000 in the workshop is $36,500 per year, or $100 per day.

In the short-run analysis of costs, we divide production costs into two types, fixed cost and variable cost.

▶ **Fixed cost (FC)** is defined as the cost that does not vary with the quantity produced. In our example, the fixed cost is the cost of the workshop, including the cost of the building and the mold. As shown in the third column of Table 11.3, the fixed cost is $100 per day, regardless of how much output is produced.

▶ **Variable cost (VC)** is defined as a cost that varies with the quantity produced. For example, to produce more paddles, you must hire more workers. If the cost per worker is $50 per day, the total variable cost per day is $50 times the number of workers, including you. As shown in the fourth column of Table 11.3, variable cost is $50 for a one-worker operation, $100 for a two-worker operation, and so on.

Fixed cost (FC)
Cost that does not depend on the quantity produced.

Variable cost (VC)
Cost that varies as the firm changes its output.

The firm's **short-run total cost (TC)** equals the sum of fixed and variable costs:

$$TC = FC + VC$$

The total costs for different output levels are shown in the fifth column of Table 11.3.

Figure 11.2 shows the three short-run cost curves. They correspond to columns 3, 4, and 5 in Table 11.1. The horizontal line on the graph shows the fixed cost of $100.

Short-run total cost (TC)
The total cost of production in the short run, when one or more inputs (for example, the production facility) is fixed; equal to fixed cost plus variable cost.

TABLE 11.3 Short-Run Costs

1	2	3	4	5	6	7	8	9
Labor	Output	Fixed Cost (*FC*)	Variable Cost (*VC*)	Total Cost (*TC*)	Average Fixed Cost (*AFC*)	Average Variable Cost (*AVC*)	Average Total Cost (*ATC*)	Marginal Cost (*MC*)
0	0	$100	$0	$100				
1	1	100	$50	150	$100.00	$50.00	$150.00	$50.00
2	5	100	100	200	20.00	20.00	40.00	12.50
3	8	100	150	250	12.50	18.75	31.25	16.67
4	10	100	200	300	10.00	20.00	30.00	25.00
5	11	100	250	350	9.09	22.73	31.82	50.00
6	11.5	100	300	400	8.70	26.09	34.78	100.00

The lower of the two positively sloped curves shows the variable cost. The higher of the two positively sloped curves is total cost, which is the sum of fixed cost and variable cost. The vertical distance between the *TC* curve and the *VC* curve equals the firm's fixed cost. Notice that this distance is the same at any level of output.

Short-Run Average Costs

Average fixed cost (AFC)

Fixed cost divided by the quantity produced.

There are three types of average cost. **Average fixed cost (AFC)** equals the fixed cost divided by the quantity produced:

$$AFC = \frac{FC}{Q}$$

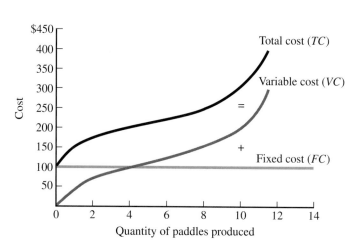

FIGURE 11.2 Short-Run Costs: Fixed Cost, Variable Cost, and Total Cost

The short-run total-cost curve shows the relationship between the quantity of output and production costs given a fixed production facility. Short-run total cost equals fixed cost (the cost that does not vary with the quantity produced) plus variable cost (the cost that varies with the quantity produced).

To compute *AFC* for our paddle company, we simply divide the fixed cost by the quantity of paddles produced. In Table 11.2, we divide the number in column 3 by the number in column 2. This gives us the values for *AFC*, which are shown in column 6. Notice that *AFC* decreases from $100 for the first paddle, to $20 for five paddles, and so on. As output increases, the fixed cost is spread over more units, so *AFC* decreases. In Figure 11.3, the *AFC* curve is negatively sloped, reflecting the spreading of a fixed amount over more and more units.

A firm's **average variable cost (AVC)** incorporates the costs that vary with the quantity produced. Average variable cost equals the variable cost divided by the quantity produced:

$$AVC = \frac{VC}{Q}$$

To compute *AVC* for our paddle company we simply divide the number in column 4 of Table 11.3 by the number in column 2. That gives us the values for *AVC*, shown in column 7. Notice that for small quantities of output, the *AVC* decreases as the quantity produced increases—from 50 for one paddle, $20 for two paddles, and so on. The declining *AVC* reflects the benefits of labor specialization. Adding workers to a small workforce makes workers more productive on average, so the amount of labor required per unit of output drops, pulling down the average variable cost. By contrast, for large quantities of output, average variable cost increases as output increases, reflecting diminishing returns. Adding workers to a large workforce makes workers less productive on average, pulling up the average variable cost. In Figure 11.3, the *AVC* curve is negatively sloped for small quantities and positively sloped for large quantities.

Average variable cost (AVC)

Total variable cost divided by the quantity produced.

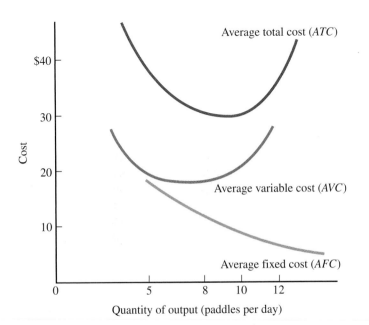

FIGURE 11.3

Short-Run Average Costs

The short-run average-total-cost curve (*ATC*) is U-shaped, a result of spreading fixed cost (which pulls down the average total cost) and diminishing returns (which pulls up the average total cost).

Short-run average total cost (ATC)

Short-run total cost divided by the quantity of output; equal to AFC plus AVC.

Total cost is the sum of fixed cost and variable cost, so the **average total cost (ATC)**, or what we'll simply call "average cost," is the sum of the average fixed cost and the average variable cost:

$$ATC = \frac{TC}{Q} = \frac{FC}{Q} + \frac{VC}{Q}$$

For small quantities of output, the *ATC* curve is negatively sloped, a result of two forces that work together to pull *ATC* down as output increases:

▶ Spreading the fixed cost. For small quantities of output, a one-unit increase in output reduces *AFC* by a large amount because the fixed cost is pretty "thick," being spread over just a few units of output. For example, going from one paddle to five paddles decreases *AFC* from $100 to $20 per paddle.
▶ Labor specialization. For small quantities of output, *AVC* decreases as output increases, a result of labor specialization that increases worker productivity.

These two forces both pull *ATC* downward as output increases, so the curve is negatively sloped for small quantities of output.

What happens once the firm reaches the point at which the benefits of labor specialization are exhausted? As the firm continues to increase output, the average variable cost increases because of diminishing returns. There is a tug-of-war between two forces: The spreading of fixed cost continues to pull *ATC* down, while diminishing returns and rising average variable cost pushes *ATC* up. The outcome of the tug-of-war depends on the quantity produced, giving the *ATC* curve its U shape.

▶ Intermediate quantities of output (between 3 and 10 paddles). The tug-of-war is won by the spreading of fixed cost, because the fixed cost is still relatively "thick" and diminishing returns are not yet very strong. As a result, *ATC* decreases as output increases.
▶ Large quantities of output (11 or more paddles). The tug-of-war is won by diminishing returns and rising average variable cost. In this case, the reductions in *AFC* are relatively small because the fixed cost is already spread pretty thinly and diminishing returns are severe. As a result, *ATC* increases as output increases.

Short-Run Marginal Cost

Short-run marginal cost (MC)

The change in short-run total cost resulting from producing one more unit of the good.

The **short-run marginal cost (MC)** is the change in short-run total cost per unit change in output. In other words, it is the increase in total cost associated with a one-unit increase in output. Mathematically, marginal cost is calculated by dividing the change in total cost (ΔTC) by the change in output (ΔQ):

$$MC = \frac{\Delta TC}{\Delta Q} = \frac{\text{change in } TC}{\text{change in output}}$$

The marginal cost of the first paddle is the increase in cost associated with hiring the single worker the firm needs to produce the first paddle, or $50. The ninth column n Table 11.3 shows the marginal cost for different output levels. When you hire the second worker for $50, output increases to 5 paddles. A $50 increase in total cost increases output by 4 paddles, so the marginal cost is $12.50:

$$MC = \frac{\Delta TC}{\Delta Q} = \frac{\text{change in } TC}{\text{change in output}} = \frac{\$50}{4} = \$12.50$$

In this case, marginal cost decreases as output increases because of labor specialization and rising worker productivity. The first worker produces just 1 paddle, but adding a second worker increases output by 4 paddles. The $50 expense of adding the second worker translates into a $12.50 expense for each of the 4 extra paddles produced. We saw earlier that specialization leads to increasing marginal productivity; now we know that it also leads to decreasing marginal cost. In Figure 11.4, the short-run marginal-cost curve is negatively sloped for the first 5 paddles.

Eventually, the marginal-cost curve is positively sloped. Starting with the fifth paddle, the short-run marginal cost increases as the output increases. When you hire the third worker, output increases from 5 to 8, so the $50 expense translates into a $16.67 expense for each of the three extra paddles produced. Diminishing returns has set in, and marginal cost increases as output increases. The marginal cost increases to $25 for between 8 and 10 paddles ($50/2 paddles), $50 for between 10 and 11 paddles ($50/1 paddle), and so on. In general, decreasing labor productivity causes rising marginal cost.

The Relationship Between Marginal Cost and Average Cost

Figure 11.4 shows the relationship between short-run marginal cost and short-run average total cost. Whenever the marginal cost is less than the average cost (for fewer than 10 paddles), the average cost is falling. In contrast, whenever the marginal cost

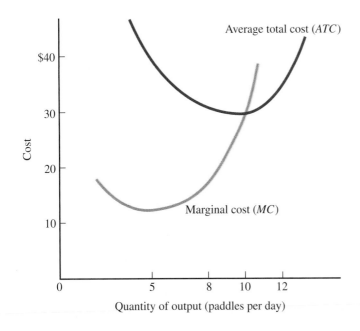

Quantity of output (paddles per day)

FIGURE 11.4

Short-Run Marginal and Average Cost

The marginal cost curve (*MC*) is negatively sloped for small quantities of output, reflecting the benefits of labor specialization, and positively sloped for large quantities, reflecting diminishing returns. The *MC* curve intersects the average-cost curve (*ATC*) at the minimum point of the average curve. At this point *ATC* is neither falling nor rising.

exceeds the average cost (for more than 10 paddles), the average cost is rising. Finally when the marginal cost equals the average cost, the average cost is neither rising nor falling. This is where the marginal-cost curve intersects the short-run average total-cost curve at its minimum point.

We can use some simple logic to explain the relationship between average cost and marginal cost. Suppose that you start the semester with a cumulative GPA of 3.0 (a B average) and enroll in a single course that semester—a history course. If you receive a grade of C in history (2.0 for computing your GPA), your GPA will drop below 3.0. Your GPA decreases because the grade in the "marginal" course (the history course) is less than the "average" grade (the starting cumulative GPA), so the marginal grade pulls down your GPA. Suppose that you take an economics class the following semester and get a grade of A (4.0 for computing your GPA). In this case, your GPA will increase because the marginal grade (in economics) is higher than your average (your GPA), so the marginal grade pushes up your GPA. If you were to take a course the following semester and your grade in the course was the same as your GPA, your GPA wouldn't change. To summarize, whenever the marginal grade is less than the average grade, the average will fall; whenever the marginal grade exceeds the average grade, the average will rise; whenever the marginal grade equals the average grade, the average will not change.

Same Average Cost at Two or Three Quantities?

Mr. Large wants to enter the pencil-making business. He gathered some information from two existing pencil manufacturers: Ms. Small and Ms. Medium. The two firms have identical production facilities—identical factories and equipment—but Medium has

more workers. The two firms also pay the same wage to each of their workers and pay the same prices for materials. Although Small produces 1,000 pencils per minute and Medium produces 2,000 per minute, each firm has an average total cost of 10 cents per pencil. The first puzzle is, How can two firms producing different quantities have the same average cost?

We can solve this first puzzle with a quick look at the U-shaped average-cost curve in Figure 11.5. For a small quantity of output (1,000 pencils), the average fixed cost is relatively large (the fixed cost is spread over a small quantity), but the average variable cost is relatively low (diminishing returns are not yet severe). For a medium quantity (2,000 pencils), the average fixed cost is lower, but average variable cost is higher (more severe diminishing returns). Moving from the small quantity to the medium quantity, average fixed cost decreases while average variable cost increases, so it is possible to have the same average cost (10 cents) at the two quantities.

Based on the information about Small and Medium, Large built a production facility identical to the ones used by the other firms. He hired enough workers and bought enough materials to produce 2,500 pencils per minute. Based on the experience of Small and Medium, he expected to produce at the same average cost, 10 cents per pencil. After all, he thought, that's the average cost for 1,000 pencils and 2,000 pencils, so it should also be the average cost for 2,500 pencils. Much to his dismay, his average cost was 14 cents per pencil. The second puzzle is, Why didn't Large have the same average cost as the two other firms?

We can solve this second puzzle with another look at the average total cost curve. In Figure 11.5, Large produces 2,500 pencils at an average cost of 14 cents. With a U-shaped curve, it is possible to have the same average cost with two different quantities, but not three. Moving from 2,000 pencils to 2,500 pencils, diminishing returns become even more severe, pulling up average cost. Although the spreading of fixed costs decreases the average fixed cost, the fixed costs are so "thin" that the advantages of spreading the fixed costs are overwhelmed by diminishing returns and higher average variable cost. ∎

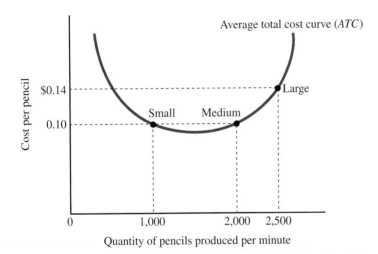

FIGURE 11.5

Different Quantities and the Same Average Cost?

Because the short-run average-total-cost curve is U-shaped, it is possible to have the same short-run average cost at two—but not three—different quantities of output.

TEST Your Understanding

1. What key principle explains the positively sloped portion of the short-run marginal-cost curve?
2. Comment on the following statement: "We're planning on increasing the output of our rubber-chicken factory by 10%. It's obvious that our short-run average total cost will decrease because we'll spread our fixed costs over more chickens."
3. According to the foreman in your chair factory, the marginal cost of chairs is less than the average cost. If you increase your output of chairs, will your average cost increase or decrease?
4. Complete the statement with "average" or "marginal": The short-run marginal-cost curve intersects the short-run average-cost curve at the minimum point of the _____ cost curve.

Production and Cost in the Long Run

Up to this point, we've been exploring short-run cost curves, which show the cost of producing different quantities of output in a given production facility. We turn next to long-run cost curves, which show production costs in facilities of different sizes. The long run is defined as the period of time over which a firm is perfectly flexible in its choice of all inputs. In the long run, a firm can build a new production facility (factory, store, office, or restaurant) or modify an existing facility.

The key difference between the short run and the long run is that there are no diminishing returns in the long run. Recall that diminishing returns occur because workers share a fixed production facility, so the more workers in the facility, the smaller the share of the facility available for each worker. In the long run, a firm can expand its production facility as its workforce grows, so there are no diminishing returns.

Expansion and Replication

Continuing the example of paddle production, suppose that you have decided to replace your existing workshop with a new one. You have been producing 10 paddles per day at a total cost of $300 per day, or an average cost of $30 per paddle. If you want to produce twice as much output in your new facility, what should you do?

Long-run total cost (LTC)
The total cost of production in the long run when a firm is perfectly flexible in its choice of all inputs and can choose a production facility of any size.

One possibility is simply to double the original operation. You could build two workshops that are identical to the original shop and hire two workforces, each identical to the original workforce. In this case, your total cost will double with your output: Each new shop will produce 10 paddles per day at a cost of $300, so you can produce a total of 20 paddles per day at twice the total cost, $600. A firm's **long-run total cost** is

TABLE 11.4
Long-Run Average Cost

1	2	3	4	5	6
Labor	Output	Labor Cost	Capital Cost	Long-Run Total Cost	Long-Run Average Cost (*LAC*)
3	5	$150	$100	$250	$50
4	10	200	100	300	30
8	20	400	200	600	30
12	30	600	300	900	30

defined as the total cost of production when the firm is perfectly flexible in its choice of all inputs and can choose a production facility of any size. Column 5 in Table 11.4 shows the long-run total cost for different quantities, including 10, 20, and 30 paddles per day. The replication process means the long-run total cost increases proportionately with the quantity produced, from $300 for 10 paddles, to $600 for 20 paddles, to $900 for 30 paddles.

The **long-run average cost of production (LAC)** equals the long-run cost divided by the quantity produced. In column 6 of Table 11.4, the long-run average cost is $30 per paddle for 10 or more paddles. Because long-run total cost is proportional to the quantity produced, the long-run *average* cost (*LAC*) doesn't change as output increases. In Figure 11.6, the long-run average-cost curve is horizontal for 10 or more paddles per day.

We've seen that if a firm wants to double its output in the long run, replication is one option. By simply replicating an existing operation, a firm can double its output and its total costs, leaving average cost unchanged. Another possibility is to build a single larger workshop, one that can produce twice as much output at a lower cost than

Long-run average cost of production (LAC)
Long-run total cost divided by the quantity of output produced.

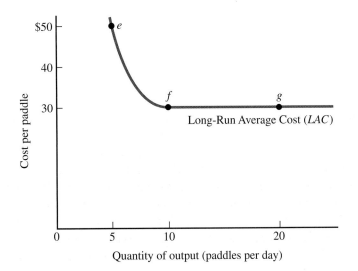

FIGURE 11.6
The Long-Run Average-Cost Curve and Scale Economies
The long-run average-cost curve (*LAC*) is negatively sloped for up to 10 paddles per day, a result of indivisible inputs and the effects of labor specialization. If the firm replicates the operation that produces 10 paddles per day, the long-run average-cost curve will be horizontal beyond 10 paddles per day.

Long-run marginal cost (LMC)

The change in long-run cost from producing one more unit of output.

would be possible by simply building two facilities identical to the original. If so, the long-run average cost of producing the larger quantity (for example, 20 paddles) would be less than $30 per paddle.

A firm's **long-run marginal cost (LMC)** is the change in long-run cost resulting from producing one more unit of output. In the long run, the firm is perfectly flexible in choosing its inputs. Therefore, the LMC is the increase in cost when the firm can change its production facility as well as its workforce.

Scaling Down and Indivisible Inputs

What would happen if you decided to scale down your operation, producing only 5 paddles per day instead of 10? Although it's tempting to think that your total costs would be cut in half, that's not necessarily the case. Remember that you use a single mold to produce 10 paddles per day. If you cut your output in half, you would still need the mold, so your capital costs won't be cut in half. If each mold requires a fixed amount of floor space, you would also need the same floor space, so cutting output in half wouldn't decrease the cost of your production facility at all. You would still have a cost of $100 per day for the mold and the workspace. Because cutting output in half doesn't cut capital costs in half, the average cost of 5 paddles will exceed the average cost of 10 paddles.

Indivisible input

An input that cannot be scaled down to produce a smaller quantity of output.

The mold is an example of an **indivisible input**, one that cannot be scaled down to produce a smaller quantity of output. When a production process requires the use of indivisible inputs, the average cost of production increases as output decreases, because the cost of the indivisible inputs is spread over a smaller quantity of output.

The production of many goods and services involves inputs, such as this large ship for ocean cargo service.

Most production operations use some indivisible inputs, but the costs of these inputs vary. Here are some examples of firms and their indivisible inputs:

- A railroad company providing freight service between two cities must lay a set of tracks between them. The company cannot scale down the tracks by laying a half set of tracks (a single rail).
- A shipping firm uses a large ship to carry TV sets from Japan to the United States.
- A steel producer uses a large blast furnace.
- A hospital uses imaging machines (for X rays, CAT scans, and MRIs).
- A pizzeria uses a pizza oven.

These indivisible inputs cannot be scaled down to produce a smaller quantity of output. For example, it is impractical to produce steel in a toaster oven, just as it is impractical to transport a single TV set across the ocean in a rowboat. For another example of indivisible inputs, read "A Closer Look: Indivisible Inputs and the Cost of Fake Killer Whales."

A CLOSER LOOK

Indivisible Inputs and the Cost of Fake Killer Whales

Sea lions off the Washington coast eat steelhead and other fish, depleting some species threatened with extinction and decreasing the harvest of the commercial fishing industry. Rick Funk, a plastics manufacturer, thinks that a variation on the scarecrow would solve the sea lion problem. Killer whales love to eat sea lions. Funk says that he could build a life-sized fiberglass killer whale, mount it on a rail like a roller coaster, and then send the whale diving through the water to scare off the sea lions. According to Funk, it would cost about $16,000 to make the first whale.[2] Once the mold is made, however, each additional whale would cost an additional $5,000. That means two whales would cost $21,000, three whales would cost $26,000, and so on.

This little story illustrates the effects of indivisible inputs on the firm's cost curves. The mold is an indivisible input, because it cannot be scaled down and still produce whales. If Funk wants to cut his production from two whales per month down to one, he still needs the mold; he cannot simply produce half as many whales with a mold that is half the size. The cost of producing the first whale ($16,000) includes the

How much would it cost to make fake killer whales to scare away sea lions that feast on steelhead and other fish?

cost of the mold, the indivisible input. Once the firm has the mold, the marginal cost for each whale is only $5,000, so the average cost per whale decreases as the number of whales increases.

Scaling Down and Labor Specialization

A second reason for higher average long-run costs in a smaller operation is that labor will be less specialized in the small operation. As we saw earlier in the book, the labor specialization—each worker specializing in an individual production task—makes workers more productive because of continuity (less time switching from one task to another) and repetition (each worker becomes more proficient). Reversing this process, when we reduce the workforce, each worker will become less specialized, performing a wider variety of production tasks. The loss of specialization will decrease labor productivity, so you'll need more than half the original workforce to produce half as much output.

The first row in Table 11.4 shows labor and capital costs in the smaller operation. Suppose that to produce 5 paddles, you'll need 3 workers (including yourself). In this case, your labor cost will be $150. Adding the $100 cost of the indivisible input (the mold and shop space), the total cost of producing 5 paddles per day will be $250, or $50 per paddle. This exceeds the average cost of 10 paddles because in the smaller operation you still need the same amount of capital and your workers are less productive. In Figure 11.6, the average cost of 5 paddles per day exceeds the average cost for larger quantities.

Economies of Scale

Economies of scale

A situation in which an increase in the quantity produced decreases the long-run average cost of production.

A firm experiences **economies of scale** if its long-run average-cost curve is negatively sloped. In Figure 11.6, the paddle producer experiences economies of scale between points *e* and *f*. For example, at point *e*, the long-run average cost of producing 5 paddles per day is $50, compared to $30 for 10 paddles (point *f*) and larger quantities. An increase in output from 5 to 10 paddles decreases the long-run average cost of production because (1) the firm spreads the cost of an indivisible input over a larger quantity and (2) labor specialization increases worker productivity, decreasing average cost. In other words, there are some economies (that is, cost savings) associated with scaling up the firm's operation.

As we will see later in the book, recent technological innovations have decreased the cost of producing electricity from the wind, leading to the development of wind farms. There are scale economies in the production of electricity from wind because although large wind turbines are more costly than small ones, the higher cost is more than offset by greater generating capacity. For the details, read "A Closer Look: Scale Economies in Wind Power."

One way to quantify the extent of scale economies in the production of a particular good is to determine the minimum efficient scale for producing the good. The **minimum efficient scale** is defined as the output at which scale economies are exhausted. In graphical terms, the minimum efficient scale is the quantity at which the long-run average-cost curve becomes horizontal, for example, point *f* in Figure 11.6. If a firm starts out with a quantity of output below the minimum efficient scale, an increase in output will decrease its long-run average cost. Once the minimum efficient scale has been reached, an increase in output no longer decreases the long-run average cost. In Britain, the minimum efficient scale for an

Minimum efficient scale

The output at which the long-run average-cost curve becomes horizontal.

A CLOSER LOOK

Scale Economies in Wind Power

There are scale economies in the production of electricity from wind because the cost of purchasing, installing, and maintaining a wind turbine increases less than proportionately with the generating capacity of the turbine. The table shows the various costs of a small turbine (150 kilowatt capacity) and a large turbine (600 kilowatt capacity), each with an assumed lifetime of 20 years.[3]

Costs of Wind Turbines

	Small Turbine (150 kilowatt)	Large Turbine (600 kilowatt)
Purchase price of turbine	$150,000	$420,000
Installation cost	**$100,000**	$100,000
Operating and maintenance cost	$75,000	$126,000
Total cost	$325,000	$646,000
Electricity generated (kilowatt hours)	5 million	20 million
Average cost (per kilowatt hour)	$0.065	$0.032

The larger turbine has four times the generation capacity (20 million kilowatt hours versus 5 million kilowatt hours), but its purchase price is less than three times as much, its installation cost is the same, and its operating and maintenance costs are less than twice as much. The average cost per kilowatt hour is only $0.032 for the large turbine, compared to $0.065 for the smaller turbine.

oil refinery is 10 million tons of oil per year (about 10% of the British market).[4] In the United States, the minimum efficient scale for automobiles is between 200,000 and 400,000 autos per year.[5] This means that a production facility serving between 3% and 6% of the U.S. market would be large enough to fully exploit the economies of scale in auto production.

Dieseconomies of Scale

If a firm's long-run average cost curve is positively sloped, the firm experiences **diseconomies of scale**, meaning that when the firm increases its output, its long-run average cost of production increases. Diseconomies of scale can occur for two reasons:

▶ *Coordination problems.* One of the problems of a large organization is that it requires several layers of management (a bureaucracy) to coordinate the activities of the different parts of the organization. If an increase in the firm's output requires additional layers of management, the long-run average-cost curve may be positively sloped.
▶ *Increasing input costs.* When a firm increases its output, it will demand more of each of its inputs and *may* be forced to pay higher prices for some of these inputs. For example, a construction firm may be forced to pay more for workers to attract more of them. Alternatively, a firm may have to hire workers who are less skilled. An increase in input prices will increase the long-run average cost of production, generating a positively sloped long-run average-cost curve.

The experience of General Motors suggests there are diseconomies of scale in the production of automobiles, largely because of coordination problems.[6] General Motors is one-third bigger than Ford and larger than the two biggest Japanese automakers combined (Toyota and Nissan). Nonetheless, the average cost of a GM automobile is $200 to $2,000 higher than the average cost of automobiles produced by other firms.

Firms recognize the possibility of diseconomies of scale and adopt various strategies to avoid them. An example of a firm that adjusts its operations to do so is 3M. According to Gordon Engdahl, the company's vice president for human resources, "We made a conscious effort to keep our units as small as possible because it keeps them flexible and vital. When one gets too large, we break it apart. We like to say that our success in recent years amounts to multiplication by division."[7]

Actual Long-Run Average-Cost Curves

Figure 11.7 shows the actual long-run average-cost curves for several products: Aluminum production, truck freight, and hospital services.[8] Each long-run average-cost curve is negatively sloped for small quantities of output and relatively flat (almost horizontal) over a large range of output. In addition, each curve has a slight positive slope for large quantities of output. In other words, these curves are L-shaped. Other studies suggest that the long-run cost curves of a wide variety of goods and services have the same shape.

Why is the typical long-run average-cost curve L-shaped? The long-run average-cost curves are negatively sloped for small quantities of output because there are economies of scale resulting from indivisible inputs and labor specialization. They then level off and are horizontal over a wide range of output because once a firm reaches a certain scale, its long-run total cost increases proportionately with its output, reflecting its ability to increase inputs and outputs proportionately. This leads to a constant long-run average total cost (*LAC*).

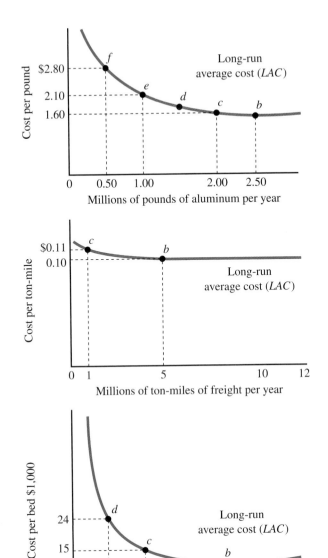

FIGURE 11.7

Actual Long-Run Average-Cost Curves for Three Products: Aluminum, Truck Freight, and Hospital Services

Short-Run Versus Long-Run Average Cost

Why is the firm's short-run average-cost curve U-shaped, while the long-run average-cost curve is L-shaped? For large quantities of output, the short-run curve is positively sloped because of diminishing returns and the resulting increases in the labor cost per unit of output. In the long run, the firm can scale up its operation by building a larger production facility, so the firm does not suffer from diminishing returns. If there are no diseconomies of scale, the long-run average-cost curve will be negatively sloped or horizontal. If the firm experiences some diseconomies of scale, the long-run average-cost curve will eventually be positively sloped, but the short-run average-cost curve will be much steeper.

5. Draw a line connecting each item on the left with the appropriate item on the right.

   Diseconomies of scale   Negatively sloped long-run average-cost curve

   Economies of scale   Positively sloped long-run average-cost curve

   Indivisible inputs

   Labor specialization

   Coordination problems

6. When you mention that most firms have L-shaped long-run average-cost curves, your new boss says, "You're wrong. Haven't you heard of diminishing returns?" How should you respond?

7. What portion of a long-run average-cost curve is explained by the notion of replication?

Information Goods and First-Copy Cost

We've discussed costs in the short run, when a firm cannot change its production facility, and the long run, when a firm can pick a facility of any size. Consider next the special case of producing an information good such as a music CD, a movie on DVD, or a book. In all three cases, the cost of producing the first copy is very high, but the marginal cost of reproduction is very low.

We'll illustrate the production costs of information goods with a music CD. Suppose that your band, Adam Smith and the Invisible Hands, has decided to produce a music CD. The cost of recording a set of songs is $100,000. This amount includes the band's opportunity cost of time spent in the recording studio and the cost of studio time ($200 per hour). Once the tracks are recorded and put in a digital format, you can have CDs burned at a cost of $1 per CD, regardless of the number burned.

Table 11.5 shows the relationships between the quantity of CDs produced and production cost. In this case, you are using the production facilities of other firms, so the distinction between short run and long run is unimportant. The marginal cost is constant at $1, but the average cost decreases with the quantity produced. For example, the cost of the first CD is a whopping $100,001, but the average cost drops to $11 for the 10,000th CD and

TABLE 11.5 Average Cost of an Information Good

Quantity of CDs	Recording Cost	Burning Cost	Total Cost	Average Cost	Marginal Cost
0	$100,000	0	$100,000		
1	100,000	$1	100,001	$100,001	$1
1,000	100,000	1,000	101,000	101	1
5,000	100,000	5,000	105,000	21	1
10,000	100,000	10,000	110,000	11	1
50,000	100,000	50,000	150,000	3	1

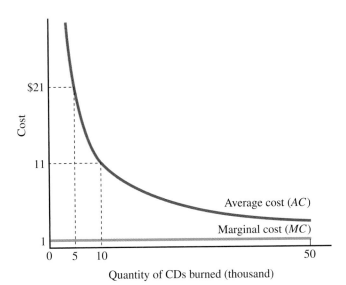

FIGURE 11.8

Average-Cost Curve for an Information Good
For an information good such as a music CD the cost of producing the first copy is very high, but the marginal cost of reproduction is low and constant.

$3 for the 50,000th CD. In Figure 11.8, the average-cost curve is negatively sloped and gets closer and closer to the horizontal marginal-cost curve as the quantity produced increases, reflecting the spreading of the fixed recording cost over a larger number of CDs.

With this production technology, the "first-copy" cost is relatively large because it is costly to generate the digital information to be burned onto CDs. The first-copy cost is the $100,001 required to generate the information and then make the first copy. There are many other examples of products with large first-copy costs, including software, phone books, business directories, maps, and the book you are holding. To produce a book, a publisher must first arrange all the words and images into a coherent manuscript. The cost of producing this information—including the opportunity costs of the authors, editors, photographers, graphic artists, and typesetters—is very large. Once the stream of words and images—on pages or in digital format—is generated, the publisher can reproduce the information, with a relatively low marginal cost for paper, ink, and printing-press time. Most publishers use outside presses to actually print their books, with a constant marginal cost per book produced.

USING THE TOOLS

This chapter has explained the economics behind the firm's short- and long-run cost curves. Here are some opportunities to use those curves as graphical tools in your own economic analysis.

1. Changing Costs

Return to the paddle production example and refer to Table 11.2. Compute the short-run average cost for 10 paddles with the following changes: (a) your opportunity cost of work time triples, from $50 to $150; (b) the interest rate for invested funds is cut in half, from 10% to 5%; (c) labor productivity doubles (the quantity produced by each workforce doubles).

2. The Cost of Breaking Up an Aluminum Firm

Consider a large aluminum firm that initially produces two million pounds of aluminum per year. Suppose that an antitrust action breaks up the firm into two smaller firms, each of which produces half as much as the original firm. Use the information in Figure 11.7 to predict the effects on the long-run average cost of producing aluminum.

3. Popularity and Information Goods

You are the manager of the band whose CD production costs are shown in Table 11.5. Your objective is to sell as many CDs as you can and break even (the break-even point is where your total revenue just equals your total cost). If you pick a price of $21, you will sell 5,000 CDs. The slope of the demand curve is –$0.002 per CD sold.
a. If you want to maximize sales while breaking even, what price should you choose? Illustrate with a completely labeled graph.
b. Suppose an interview in *Rolling Stone* makes more people aware of your music and the demand curve shifts to the right. If you still want

to break even and maximize sales, will you increase or decrease your price? Illustrate with a completely labeled graph.

4. Deregulation and the Cost of Trucking

Assume that the market for truck freight is initially served by a single regulated firm. If the market is deregulated, several new firms, unconstrained by regulations, will enter the market. At a public hearing on the issue of deregulation, the manager of the regulated firm issued a grim warning to the regulatory authorities: "If you deregulate this market, four or five firms will enter the market, and the unit cost of truck freight will at least triple. There are big economies of scale in trucking services, so a single large firm is much more cost-efficient than several small firms would be. If you want firms in your city to pay three times as much for their truck freight, go ahead and deregulate this market." Use the information in Figure 11.7 to comment on this statement.

SUMMARY

In this chapter, we explored the cost side of a firm, explaining the shapes of the firm's short-run cost curves and long-run cost curves. Here are the main points of the chapter:

1 The positively sloped portion of the short-run marginal-cost curve (*MC*) results from diminishing returns.

2 The short-run average-total-cost curve (*ATC*) is U-shaped because of the conflicting effects of (a) fixed costs being spread over a larger quantity of output and (b) diminishing returns.

3 The long-run average-cost curve (*LAC*) is horizontal over some range of output because replication is an option, so doubling output will no more than double long-run total cost.

4 The long-run average-cost curve (*LAC*) is negatively sloped for small quantities of output because there are indivisible inputs that cannot be scaled down and a smaller operation has limited opportunities for labor specialization.

5 Diseconomies of scale arise if there are problems in coordinating a large operation or higher input costs in a larger organization.

KEY TERMS

PROBLEMS AND DISCUSSION QUESTIONS

1 Suppose that the indivisible inputs used in the production of shirts have a cost per day of $400. To produce one shirt per day, the firm must also spend a total of $5 on other inputs (labor, materials, and other capital). For each additional shirt, the firm incurs the same additional cost ($5). Compute the average cost for 40 shirts, 100 shirts, 200 shirts, and 400 shirts. Draw the long-run average-cost curve for 40 to 400 shirts per day.

2 Consider a firm with the following short-run costs:

Quantity	Variable Cost (*VC*)	Total Cost (*TC*)
1	30	90
2	50	110
3	90	150
4	140	200
5	200	260

a. What is the firm's fixed cost?

b. Compute short-run marginal cost (*MC*), short-run average variable cost (*AVC*), and short-run average total cost (*ATC*) for the different quantities of output.

c. Draw the three cost curves. Explain the relationship between the *MC* curve and the *ATC* curve and the relationship between the *AVC* curve and the *ATC* curve.

3 Given the following relationship between labor input and the quantity produced, compute the marginal product of labor for the different input levels. Then draw the total product curve and the marginal-product curve.

Labor	Output
0	0
1	5
2	11
3	15
4	18
5	19

4 Consider a firm that has a fixed cost of $60 per minute. Complete the following table:

Output	FC	VC	TC	MC	AFC	AVC	ATC
1	——	10	——	——	——	——	——
2	——	18	——	——	——	——	——
3	——	30	——	——	——	——	——
4	——	45	——	——	——	——	——
5	——	65	——	——	——	——	——
6	——	90	——	——	——	——	——

5 Consider a firm that has constant marginal returns. That means that the first worker is just as productive as the second, who is just as productive as the third, and so on. The same is true for all the firm's inputs.

a. Draw the firm's short-run marginal cost curve (*MC*).

b. Explain why this firm's cost curve differs from the short-run marginal-cost curve for paddle production.

6 Beaverduck Bus Company wants to compute the cost of adding a third daily bus between Eugene and Corvallis, Ore. Comment on the following statement of Abby Abacus, the company's accountant: "If we add the third bus, our total cost would increase from $700 to $780. Therefore, the marginal cost of the third bus is $260 ($780 divided by 3)."

7 You want to know the short-run marginal cost of producing a Chevrolet Caprice. Comment on the following statement from an analyst in the production department: "The marginal cost of a Caprice, given our current volume, is $12,500. Of course, the actual marginal cost depends on the number of cars produced. The larger the number produced, the lower the unit cost because we will spread out our design and tooling costs over more cars."

8 Explain the difference between diseconomies of scale and diminishing returns. Based on the cost curves you've seen in this chapter, which is more pervasive?

9 Suppose that one firm generates 30 billion kilo-watthours of electricity, which is about three times the output of a second electricity firm. Which firm will have a higher cost per kilowatthour? Use the information in Figure 11.7 to predict the difference in the average costs of the two firms.

10 As a child, you recorded the costs of your lemonade stand and drew your long-run average-cost curve. Now you work in a computer-chip factory. Would you expect any similarities between the long-run average-cost curve for lemonade and the long-run average-cost curve for the chip factory? Would you expect any differences?

11 A hammer manufacturer has just hired you to advise the firm on its production costs. In your first meeting with production managers, you hear the following statements. Are they true or false? Explain.

a. "If the production process is subject to diminishing returns, the long-run average-cost curve will be positively sloped."

b. "At the current output level, this factory is subject to diminishing returns. Therefore, the firm is operating along the upward-sloping portion of its short-run marginal-cost (MC) curve."

c. "At the current output level, this factory is subject to diminishing returns. Therefore, the firm is operating along the upward-sloping portion of its short-run average-total-cost (ATC) curve."

d. "The short-run average total cost of producing 250 hammers is less than the short-run average cost of producing 260 hammers. Therefore, the short-run marginal cost of 260 hammers is less than the short-run average cost of 260 hammers."

MODEL ANSWERS TO QUESTIONS

Chapter-Opening Questions

1 The short-run average-cost curve reflects diminishing returns, which pulls up short-run average cost as output increases. There are no diminishing returns in the long run.

2 As explained in the "Economic Puzzle: Same Average Cost at Two or Three Quantities," a U-shaped average cost curve has the same average cost for two quantities.

3 As explained in "A Closer Look: Indivisible Inputs and the Cost of Fake Killer Whales," the cost of the first whale includes the cost of the mold, an indivisible input.

4 As shown in "A Closer Look: Scale Economies in Wind Power," the average cost with a large turbine (600 kilowatts) is about half the average cost with a smaller one (150 kilowatts).

Test Your Understanding

1 The principle of diminishing returns.

2 If the firm is operating in the region of diminishing returns, an increase in output will have two conflicting effects: Diminishing returns pull up average cost, while spreading the fixed costs pulls it down. If the initial quantity of output is large enough, diminishing returns will be more powerful than spreading the fixed cost, so ATC will increase.

3 The marginal cost is less than the average cost, so the marginal cost pulls down the average cost. ATC will decrease, at least for small increases in output.

4 Average.

5 Draw lines from "diseconomies of scale" and "coordination problems" to "positively sloped long-run average-cost curve." Draw lines from "economies of scale," "indivisible inputs," and "labor specialization" to "negatively sloped long-run average-cost curve."

6 Diminishing returns occur when we increase output in an existing production facility. The principle of diminishing returns is applicable in the short run, not in the long run. To draw the long-run cost curve, we assume that we can change the size of the production facility.

7 The horizontal portion of the LAC curve.

NOTES

1. Emily Lambert and John Turrettine, "Unplugged," *Forbes Magazine*, November 25, 2002, pp. 239–232.

2. Sandi Doughton, "Killer Whale Latest Idea on Sea Lions," *The Oregonian*, January 7, 1995.

3. Danish Wind Turbine Manufacturers Association. Guided Tour of Wind Energy (http://www.windpower.dk).

4. Aubrey Silberson, "Economies of Scale in Theory and Practice," *Economic Journal*, vol. 82, 1972, pp. 369–391.

5. Walter Adams and James W. Brock, "Automobiles," Chapter 4 in *The Structure of the American Economy*, 9th ed., edited by Walter Adams and James W. Brock (Upper Saddle River, NJ: Prentice Hall, 1995).

6. Walter Adams and James W. Brock, "Automobiles," Chapter 4 in *The Structure of the American Economy*, 9th ed., edited by Walter Adams and James W. Brock (Upper Saddle River, NJ: Prentice Hall, 1995).

7. Frederick C. Klein, "At 3M Plants, Workers Have Flexibility, Involvement—And Their Own Radios," *Wall Street Journal*, February 5, 1982, p. 1.

8. Laurits Christensen and William H. Greene, "Economies of Scale in U.S. Electric Power Generation," *Journal of Political Economy*, vol. 84, 1976, pp. 655–676. Reprinted by permission of The University of Chicago Press; Joel P. Clark and Merton C. Flemings, "Advanced Materials and the Economy," *Scientific American*, vol. 255, October 1986, pp. 51–60. Copyright © 1986 by Scientific American, Inc. All rights reserved; Roger Koenker, "Optimal Scale and the Size Distribution of American Trucking Firms," *Journal of Transport Economics and Policy*, January 1977, p. 62; Harold A. Cohen, "Hospital Cost Curves with Emphasis on Measuring Patient Care Output," in *Empirical Studies in Health Economics*, edited by Herbert E. Klarman (Baltimore, MD: Johns Hopkins University Press, 1970); John Johnson, *Statistical Cost Analysis* (New York: McGraw-Hill, 1960).

Perfect Competition

n 1992, Hurricane Andrew struck the
southeastern United States, leaving million
people without electricity for several days.
Refrigerators stopped working, and thousands c
people suddenly needed a lot of ice to cool and
preserve their food. The price of a bag of ice immediate
rose from $1 to $5. The same sort of price hikes occurred
chain saws (for clearing downed trees), bottled water, tarpaper
repairing roofs), and plywood. If you had been the governor of Florida in
1992, what would you have done about the price hikes?

This is the first of four chapters exploring the decisions made by firms in different types of markets. Markets differ in the number of firms that compete against one another for customers. At one extreme is a monopoly, a market with a single seller. In this chapter, we'll look at the other extreme—a perfectly competitive market. In a **perfectly competitive market**, hundreds or even thousands of firms sell a standardized or homogeneous product. Each firm realizes that it cannot affect the market price, so each firm takes the market price as given. A firm has no reason to cut its price to sell more because it can sell as much as it wants at the market price. A firm has no reason to increase its price because it would lose all its customers to one of the other firms selling at the market price.

Perfectly competitive market

A market with hundreds or thousands of sellers and buyers of a standardized good. Each buyer and seller takes the market price as given. Firms can easily enter or exit the market.

Perfectly competitive market has two other features. First, on the demand side of the market, there are hundreds or even thousands of buyers, each of whom takes the market price as given. Second, there are no barriers to market entry, so firms can easily enter or exit the market. To summarize, here are the five features of a perfectly competitive market:

▶ There are many sellers (hundreds or even thousands).
▶ There are many buyers (hundreds or even thousands).
▶ The product is standardized or homogeneous.
▶ Firms can freely enter or leave the market.
▶ Both buyers and sellers take the market price as "given."

If you're thinking that the model of perfect competition is not very realistic, you're right. Most firms have some flexibility over their prices. When a firm increases its price slightly, it will certainly sell less, but the quantity sold will probably not drop to zero. Although perfect competition is rare, it's a good starting point for analyzing a firm's decisions because a price-taking firm's decisions are easy to understand. The firm doesn't have to pick a price; it just decides how much to produce, given the market price. Once you understand this simple case, you will be ready to tackle the more complex decisions that must be made when firms choose their own prices. We'll discuss this scenario in later chapters.

In this chapter, we'll see how perfectly competitive firms use information on revenues and costs to decide how much output to produce when the price is a given. We'll see how the law of supply applies to firms in a perfectly competitive market, both in the short run and the long run. Here are some practical questions that we answer:

1 You and some fellow students have a firm that delivers packages by bicycle. If you want to determine whether you are maximizing your profit, what information do you need?
2 If a firm is losing money, when does it make sense to operate at a loss?

3 If you want to provide phone service in the United States, you must first invest millions of dollars. In Pakistan, you can start providing phone service after an investment of only $310. What explains the difference?

Preview: Alternative Market Structures

Before we delve into perfect competition, it will be useful to see how our discussion of perfect competition fits into the general scheme of the book. After discussing perfect competition in this chapter, we'll look at three other market structures in the next three chapters. The key difference between perfect competition and these other market structures is the assumption of price-taking by perfectly competitive firms.

Let's start by distinguishing between a market demand curve and the demand curve for an individual firm. As we saw earlier in the book, the market demand curve shows the relationship between the price and the quantity that can be sold in the market, assuming that all firms charge the same price. In contrast, the **firm-specific demand curve** shows the relationship between the price charged by a specific firm and the quantity that can be sold by that firm. In a monopoly, a single firm serves the entire market, so the firm-specific demand curve is the same as the market demand curve. There is a single price in the market, and everything is sold by the single firm. As shown in Panel A of Figure 12.1, the monopolist can choose any point on the market demand curve, recognizing that the higher the price, the smaller the quantity it will sell.

As shown in Panel B of Figure 12.1, things are different for a perfectly competitive firm. The firm-specific demand curve is horizontal—perfectly elastic. A perfectly competitive firm can sell as much as it wants at the market price of $12, but if it raises its price even a penny, it will sell nothing.

Most markets lie between the extremes of monopoly and perfect competition. Table 12.1 provides a preview of three alternative market structures.

Firm-specific demand curve

A curve showing the relationship between the price charged by a specific firm and the quantity that can be sold by that firm.

FIGURE 12.1

Monoply Versus Perfect Competition

In Panel A, the demand curve facing a monopolist is the market demand curve. In Panel B, a perfectly competitive firm takes the market price as given, so the firm-specific demand curve is horizontal. The firm can sell all it wants at the market price, but would sell nothing if it charged a higher price.

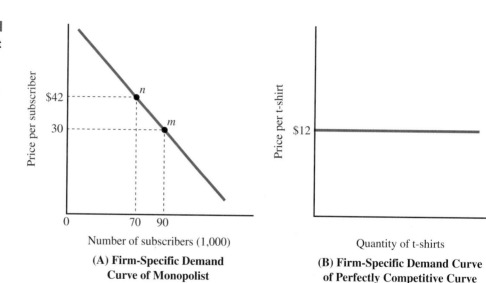

(A) Firm-Specific Demand Curve of Monopolist

(B) Firm-Specific Demand Curve of Perfectly Competitive Curve

TABLE 12.1 Characteristics of Different Types of Markets

	Perfect Competition	Monopolistic Competition	Oligopoly	Monopoly
Number of firms	Very large number (hundreds or more)	Many	Few	One
Type of product	Standardized (homogeneous)	Differentiated	Standardized or differentiated	Unique
Firm-specific demand curve	Price-taker: Demand is perfectly elastic	Demand is price elastic but not perfectly elastic	Demand is less elastic than demand facing monopolistically competitive firm	Firm faces market demand curve
Entry conditions	No barriers	No barriers	Large barriers from economies of scale or government policies	Large barriers from economies of scale or government policies
Examples	Corn, plain T-shirts	Toothbrushes, music stores, groceries	Air travel, automobiles, beverages, cigarettes, long-distance phone services	Local phone service, patented drugs

▶ Chapter 13: Monopoly. A single firm serves the entire market. A monopoly occurs when the barriers to market entry are very large. This can result from very large economies of scale or a government limit on the number of firms. Some examples of goods with large-scale economies are local phone service, cable TV, and electric power transmission. Some examples of monopolies established by government policy are drugs covered by patents and the selling of food and firewood in national parks.

▶ Chapter 14: Monopolistic competition. There are many firms, each selling a slightly different product. Some examples are restaurants, gas stations, and drug stores. There are no barriers to entering the market, so there are many firms.

▶ Chapter 15: Oligopoly. There are just a few firms in the market, which can be a result of the same two barriers to entry we discussed with monopoly: economies of scale and government policies limiting the number of firms in the market. Some product examples are automobiles, airline travel, and breakfast cereals. The large economies of scale in automobile production result from the large start-up costs, with billions of dollars required to build factories and assembly plants. In contrast, a person can start producing corn with a much smaller initial investment.

The Firm's Short-Run Output Decision

We'll start our discussion of perfect competition with an individual firm's decision about how much to produce. The firm's objective is to maximize its **economic profit** which equals its **total revenue** minus its total economic cost. Recall that economic cost includes all the opportunity costs of production, including both explicit costs

Economic profit

Total revenue minus total economic cost.

Total revenue

The money the firm gets by selling its product; equal to the price times the quantity sold.

(cash payments) and implicit costs (the entrepreneur's opportunity costs). In Chapter 11, we saw that the cost of production varied with the quantity produced. In this chapter, we'll see how economic profit varies with the quantity produced and how a firm can pick the quantity that maximizes its economic profit.

It's important to note that economic profit differs from the conventional notion of profit. When accountants compute a firm's cost, they include explicit costs, but ignore implicit costs. Accountants focus on the flow of money into and out of a firm, so they ignore costs that do not involve explicit transactions. **Accounting profit** equals total revenue minus explicit costs. Because accountants ignore implicit costs, accounting profit usually exceeds economic profit.

Accounting profit

Total revenue minus explicit costs.

We will use the market for plain T-shirts to illustrate decision-making in a perfectly competitive market. Some plain T-shirts are sold directly to consumers, and others are sold to firms that imprint words and images on the T-shirts and then sell the finished shirts to consumers. Plain T-shirts are produced in countries around the world, by a large number of producers.

The Total Approach: Computing Total Revenue and Total Cost

One way to decide how much to produce involves computing the total revenue and total cost of different quantities of output. We looked at the cost side of the profit equation in Chapter 11, and the revenue side for a perfectly competitive market is straightforward. A firm's total revenue is the money it gets by selling its product. Total revenue is equal to the price of the product times the quantity sold. For example, if a firm sells 8 T-shirts at $12 per shirt, total revenue is $96. If our T-shirt producer has an economic cost of $63, the firm's profit would be $33 (equal to $96 − $63).

Table 12.2 shows the total revenue and total costs of a hypothetical producer of plain cotton T-shirts. As shown in the second and third columns, there is a fixed cost of $17, and variable cost increases with the amount produced. The fourth column shows total

TABLE 12.2

Deciding How Much to Produce When Price = $12

1 Output: Shirts per Minute	2 Fixed Cost	3 Variable Cost	4 Total Cost	5 Total Revenue	6 Profit	7 Marginal Revenue (Price)	8 Marginal Cost
0	$17	$0	$17	$0	−$17		
1	17	5	22	12	−10	$12	$5
2	17	6	23	24	1	12	1
3	17	9	26	36	10	12	3
4	17	13	30	48	18	12	4
5	17	18	35	60	25	12	5
6	17	25	42	72	30	12	7
7	17	34	51	84	33	12	9
8	**17**	**46**	**63**	**96**	**33**	**12**	**12**
9	17	62	79	108	29	12	16
10	17	83	100	120	20	12	21

cost, the sum of fixed and variable costs. As shown in the fifth column, with a price of $12 per shirt, the firm's total revenue is $12 times the number of shirts produced. The sixth column shows economic profit, defined as total revenue minus total cost.

Figure 12.2 shows one way to choose the quantity of output that maximizes profit. We're looking for the largest profit, the biggest gap between total revenue and total cost. For example, for 5 shirts, the gap is $25 (total revenue equals $60, and total cost equals $35). Moving down the table and across the figure, we see that profit increases to $30 for 6 shirts, and profit is maximized at $33 when the firm produces either 7 or 8 shirts. When profit reaches its highest level with two different quantities (7 and 8 shirts in this example), we assume that the firm produces the larger quantity. When the firm produces 8 shirts, its total revenue is $96 and its total cost is $63, leaving a profit of $33.

The Marginal Approach

The other way to decide how much output to produce involves the marginal principle, the general decision-making rule that is one of the key principles of economics.

MARGINAL *Principle*

Increase the level of an activity if its marginal benefit exceeds its marginal cost, but reduce the level if the marginal cost exceeds the marginal benefit. If possible, pick the level at which the marginal benefit equals the marginal cost.

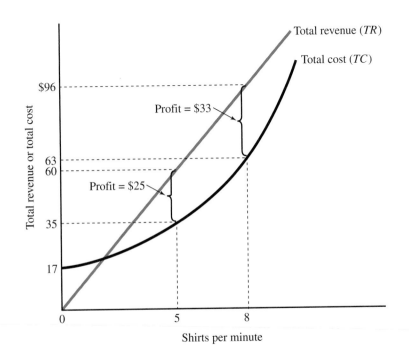

FIGURE 12.2

Using the Total Approach to Choose an Output Level
Economic profit is shown by the vertical distance between the total-revenue curve and the total-cost curve. To maximize profit, the firm chooses the quantity of output that generates the largest vertical difference between the two curves.

Marginal revenue

The change in total revenue that results from selling one more unit of output.

Since our firm is in the business to make money, the "benefit" it gets from producing shirts is revenue. The *marginal* benefit—or **marginal revenue**—of producing shirts is the change in total revenue that results from selling one more shirt. A perfectly competitive firm takes the market price as given, so the marginal revenue—the change in total revenue from one more shirt—is simply the price.

$$\text{marginal revenue} = \text{price}$$

The marginal principle tells us that the firm will maximize its profit by choosing the quantity at which price equals marginal cost:

To maximize profit, produce the quantity where price = marginal cost

In Figure 12.3, the horizontal line shows the market price for T-shirts, which our shirt producer takes as given. The price line intersects the marginal-cost curve at 8 shirts per minute, so that's the quantity that satisfies the marginal principle and maximizes profit.

To see that an output of 8 shirts per minute maximizes the firm's profit, imagine the firm produced only 5 shirts per minute. Could the firm make more profit by producing more—that is 6 shirts instead of 5?

▶ From the seventh row of numbers in Table 12.2 and point *b* in Figure 12.3, we know that the marginal cost of the sixth shirt is $7.
▶ The price of shirts is $12, so the marginal revenue is $12.

Because the extra revenue from the sixth shirt (price = $12) exceeds the extra cost (marginal cost = $7), the production and sale of the sixth shirt increases the firm's total

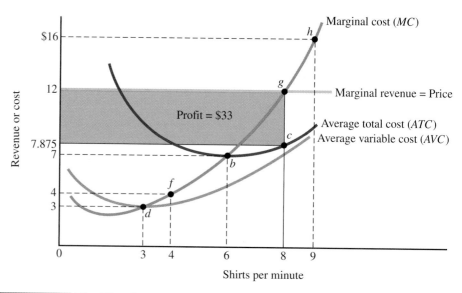

FIGURE 12.3 **The Marginal Approach to Picking an Output Level**
A perfectly competitive firm takes the market price as given, so the marginal benefit, or marginal revenue, equals the price. Using the marginal principle, the typical firm will maximize profit at point *g*, where the market price ($12) equals the marginal cost. Economic profit equals the difference between the price and the average cost ($4.125 = $12 − $7.875) times the quantity produced (8 shirts per minute), or $33 per minute.

profit by $5 (equal to $12 − $7). Therefore, it is sensible to produce the sixth shirt. The same logic applies, with different numbers for marginal cost, for the seventh shirt. For the eighth shirt, marginal revenue equals marginal cost, so the firm's profit doesn't change. To be consistent with the marginal principle, we'll assume that the firm produces to the point at which marginal revenue equals marginal cost. In this case, the firm produces the eighth shirt.

If the firm produced more than 8 shirts, it would earn less than the maximum profit. Imagine the firm initially produced 9 shirts. From Table 12.2 and the marginal-cost curve in Figure 12.3, we see that the marginal cost of the ninth shirt is $16 (point *h*), which exceeds the marginal revenue (the market price) of $12. The ninth shirt adds more to cost ($16) than it adds to revenue ($12), so producing the shirt decreases the firm's profit by $4. The marginal principle suggests that the firm should choose point *g*, with an output of 8 shirts. As you can see, the output decision is the same whether we use the marginal approach or the total approach.

The advantage of the marginal approach is that it is easier to apply. To use the total approach, a firm needs information on the total revenue and total cost for all possible output levels. In contrast, a firm can apply the marginal principle by simply increasing its output by one unit and computing the marginal revenue (the price) and the marginal cost. Using the marginal principle, the firm should produce more output if the price exceeds the marginal cost, or produce less if the opposite is true. The firm can use the marginal principle to fine-tune its decision until the price equals the marginal cost.

Economic Profit and the Break-Even Price

We've seen that the perfectly competitive firm maximizes its profit by producing the quantity at which its marginal revenue (price) equals its marginal cost. How much profit does the firm earn? The firm's economic profit equals its total revenue minus its total cost. One way to compute a firm's total economic profit is to multiply the average profit per unit produced (the gap between the price and the average cost) by the quantity produced:

$$\text{economic profit} = (\text{price} − \text{average cost}) \cdot \text{quantity produced}$$

In Figure 12.3, the average cost of producing 8 shirts is $7.875 (point *c*), so the economic profit is $33:

$$\text{economic profit} = (\$12 − \$7.875) \cdot 8 = \$33$$

In Figure 12.3, the firm's profit is shown by the area of the shaded rectangle. The area of a rectangle is the height of the rectangle times its width. In Figure 12.3, the height of the profit rectangle is the average profit ($12 − $7.875 = $4.125 per shirt), and the width is the quantity produced (8 shirts), so the profit is $33.

How will a decrease in price affect the firm's output decision and its profit? A decrease in price shifts the marginal-revenue (price) line downward, so it will intersect the marginal-cost curve at a smaller quantity. For example, if the price drops to

$9, the firm will satisfy the marginal principle by producing 7 shirts per minute (where marginal cost = $9, as shown in Table 12.2). If the price drops to $7, profit would be maximized at point *b*, where the marginal cost equals $7. Point *b* is the minimum point of the *ATC* curve, where marginal cost equals average total cost. This is **the break-even price**, defined as the price at which the firm will have zero economic profit. At this price, the average total cost equals the price, so the economic profit per shirt is zero. Remember that zero economic profit means that the firm is making just enough money to cover all its costs, including the opportunity costs of the entrepreneur.

Break-even price

The price at which the economic profit is zero; price equals average total cost.

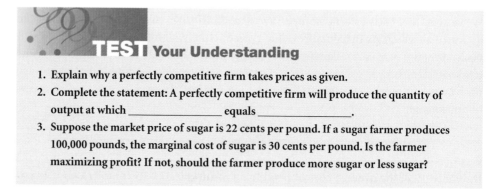

Fewer Deliveries and More Profit?

Consider a student-run delivery firm that delivers packages by bicycle, charging $13 per package and paying each of its workers $12 per hour. One day, one of the workers was two hours late to work, and the number of packages delivered that day decreased by 1 package. According to a worker enrolled in an economics course, this was actually beneficial to the firm: Less output means more profit. Why?

The key to solving this puzzle is the marginal principle. The marginal benefit (revenue) of a delivery is the market price of $13. When the worker was late, output dropped by one unit, resulting in $13 less in revenue, but costs dropped by $24 (two hours times $12 per hour). In other words, the marginal cost of a package delivered ($24), exceeds the marginal revenue of delivering it ($13), so the firm will earn more profit if it hires less labor and delivers fewer packages. ■

TEST Your Understanding

1. Explain why a perfectly competitive firm takes prices as given.
2. Complete the statement: A perfectly competitive firm will produce the quantity of output at which _____ equals _____.
3. Suppose the market price of sugar is 22 cents per pound. If a sugar farmer produces 100,000 pounds, the marginal cost of sugar is 30 cents per pound. Is the farmer maximizing profit? If not, should the farmer produce more sugar or less sugar?

The Firm's Shut-Down Decision

Consider next the decisions faced by a firm that is losing money. Suppose the price of shirts drops to $4, which is so low that the firm's total revenue is less than its total cost. In Table 12.3, the marginal principle tells the firm to produce 4 shirts at this price, but the firm's total cost of $30 exceeds its total revenue of $16, so the firm will lose $14 per minute. For an unprofitable firm like this one, the question is, Should the firm continue to operate at a loss, or shut down?

TABLE 12.3
Deciding How Much to
Produce When Price = $4

1	2	3	4	5	6	7	8
Output: Shirts per Minute	Fixed Cost	Variable Cost	Total Cost	Total Revenue	Profit	Marginal Revenue (Price)	Marginal Cost
$0	$17	$0	$17	$0	-$17	$4	$0
1	17	5	22	4	-18	4	5
2	17	6	23	8	-15	4	1
3	17	9	26	12	-14	4	3
4	**17**	**13**	**30**	**16**	**-14**	**4**	**4**
5	17	18	35	20	-15	4	5
6	17	25	42	24	-18	4	7

Total Revenue, Variable Cost, and the Shut-Down Decision

The decision to shut down is a short-run decision, a day-to-day decision to temporarily halt production in response to market conditions. Suppose our shirt factory hires workers by the day, so the shut-down decision is made at the beginning of each day. The decision-making rule is:

operate if total revenue > variable cost
shut down if total revenue < variable cost

As we saw in Chapter 11, a firm's variable cost includes all the costs that vary with the quantity produced. In the case of the shirt firm, it would include the costs of workers, raw materials (cotton, thread), and the cost of heating and powering the factory for the day. It does not include the $17 fixed cost of the production facility—for example, the cost of the machines or the factory itself—because these costs are not affected by the decision to operate or shut down.

Although the decision is made at the beginning of each day, we can use the revenue and costs per minute to compare total revenue to variable cost. From Table 12.3, for a quantity of 4 shirts per minute (the best quantity, given a price of $4), the variable cost is $13 per minute, so total revenue ($16) exceeds variable cost ($13). The firm is better off operating the facility because its total revenue of $16 exceeds the cost of operating the facility for each minute of the day. The firm cannot do anything about the $17 fixed cost, but by paying an additional $13 to operate the factory, the firm can get $16 in revenue. The benefit of operating the facility exceeds the variable cost, so it is sensible to produce 4 shirts per minute.

Of course, the firm will not operate the factory at any price. If the price drops to $1, the firm would be better off shutting the factory down for the day. In this case, the quantity that satisfies the marginal principle is 2 shirts per day (see the third row of numbers in Table 12.3, where marginal cost = $1), with a variable cost of $6 per minute. Total revenue in this case would be $2 per minute ($1 per shirt times 2 shirts), which is less than the variable cost, so the firm is better off shutting down. With this low price, the firm's total revenue is not high enough to cover the variable cost associated with operating the facility let alone any of the fixed costs, so it is better to shut down for the day.

The Shut-Down Price

Instead of calculating total revenue and comparing it to variable cost, we can use a shortcut to determine whether it is sensible to continue to operate—look at the price. Total revenue equals the price times the quantity produced, and variable cost equals the average variable cost times the quantity produced. Therefore, total revenue will exceed variable cost if the price exceeds the average variable cost. The firm should continue to operate if price exceeds the average variable cost; otherwise, it should shut down.

operate: price > average variable cost
shut down: price < average variable cost

In Figure 12.3, with a price of $4, the marginal principle is satisfied at point *f*, and this price exceeds the average variable cost of producing 4 shirts. Therefore, it is sensible to continue operating, even at a loss.

The firm's **shut-down price** is the price at which the firm is indifferent between operating and shutting down. To find the shut-down price, we find the minimum point on the *AVC* curve. In Figure 12.3, the minimum *AVC* is $3 at a quantity of 3 shirts per minute, so the shut-down price is $3 (shown by point *d*). The average variable cost never drops below $3, so if the price drops below $3, it would be impossible to generate enough revenue to even cover the firm's variable cost. When the price equals the shut-down price, the firm is generating just enough revenue to cover its variable costs, so it is just as well off either operating or shutting down.

Shut-down price

The price at which the firm is indifferent between operating and shutting down; equal to the minimum average variable cost.

A firm will shut down an unprofitable factory if the total revenue from the factory is less than the variable cost of operating it.

THIS G M FACILITY IS CLOSED

How long will a firm continue to operate at a loss? Let's think about what happens when the firm must decide whether or not to build a new production facility. The firm will build a new facility—and stay in the market—only if the price of shirts exceeds the average total cost of production. In other words, the firm will stay in the market only if the market price is high enough for its total revenue to cover *all* the costs of production, including the cost of the new facility. In other words, the price must be greater than or equal to the firm's break-even price. Although a firm might operate an existing facility at a loss (a short-run decision), it won't replace it if the new facility will be unprofitable too (a long-run decision).

Fixed Costs and Sunk Costs

It's important to note that the decision whether to operate or shut down does not incorporate the fixed costs of the production facility. If we assume that the facility cannot be rented out to some other firm while the shirt firm isn't using it, the fixed cost is a **sunk cost**. A sunk cost is an expenditure that has already been made and cannot be recovered. Once the firm incurs this cost, it cannot be avoided by shutting down the factory. Therefore, the firm should ignore the cost of the facility when deciding whether to operate or shut down.

Sunk cost
A cost a firm has already paid or has agreed to pay some time in the future.

This is just one example of the notion that sunk costs are irrelevant. The marginal principle tells us that what matters is the costs that depend on what we do, not costs that we can do nothing about. Suppose a dairy farmer spills two-thirds of a 300-gallon load of milk on the way to an ice-cream plant. Should the farmer return to the farm, or deliver the remaining 100 gallons? As long as the marginal cost of delivering the milk (the opportunity cost of the farmer's time and the cost of fuel) is less than the amount the farmer will be paid for the remaining 100 gallons, it is sensible to deliver the milk. The spilt milk is a sunk cost that is irrelevant to the delivery decision. The farmer should not cry over spilt milk, but deliver the rest.

Application: Break-Even and Shut-Down Prices for Corn Farmer

To illustrate the notions of break-even and shut-down prices, let's look at these prices for the typical corn farmer. The break-even or zero-profit price is $0.72 per bushel.[1] At this price, the farmer will produce at the minimum point of the average total-cost curve, with the average cost equal to the market price of $0.72. At a higher price, the farmer will make a positive economic profit. For example, if the price is $0.92 per bushel and the farmer produces 50,000 bushels, the economic profit will be $10,000 (equal to the output of 50,000 bushels times the profit margin of $0.20 = $0.92 − $0.72).

The corn farmer's shut-down price is $0.44. At this price, total revenue equals the farmer's variable cost, so the farmer is indifferent about operating as opposed to shutting down. At a price between the shut-down price ($0.44) and the break-even price ($0.72), the farmer will lose money but will continue to operate at a loss because total revenue will exceed the variable cost of growing corn. For example, if the price is $0.50, the farmer will operate at a loss in the short run. However, if the price drops below the shut-down price of $0.44, the farmer will shut down, not bringing any crops to market in a particular year.

In the long run, farmers will exit the corn market if the price is not high enough to cover all the costs of growing corn, including the costs of the production facility. In the long run, the price must be high enough to cover the costs of land, machinery, and vehicles. In other words, farmers will exit the market if the price stays below the break-even price of $0.72. If the price is below this level, the farmer will not raise enough revenue to cover all the costs of growing corn and will exit the market.

TEST Your Understanding

4. Complete the statement with a number: If a lamp producer can sell 40 lamps per day at a price of $20 per lamp, the benefit of operating its production facility is _____ per day.
5. Complete the statement with "operate" or "shut down": Consider a firm with total revenue of $500, total cost of $700, and variable cost of $400. The firm should _____ its production facility.
6. Complete the statement: A firm that is losing money should continue to operate if the market price exceeds _____.

Short-Run Supply Curves

Now that we've explored the output decision of a price-taking firm, we're ready to show how a firm responds to changes in the market price of its product. We'll represent the relationship between price and quantity supplied with two short-run supply curves, one for the individual firm and one for the entire market.

The Firm's Short-Run Supply Curve

Firm's short-run supply curve

A curve showing the relationship between the price of a product and the quantity of output supplied by a firm in the short run.

The **firm's short-run supply curve** shows the relationship between the market price and the quantity supplied by the firm over a period of time during which one input—the production facility—cannot be changed. In the case of shirt producers, the firm's supply curve answers the following question: At a given market price for shirts, how many shirts will the firm produce? We have already used the marginal principle to answer this question for several different prices. At a price of $12, marginal revenue (price) equals marginal cost when the firm produces 8 shirts per minute (shown by point g in Figure 12.3). The firm will produce 6 shirts when the price is $7 (point b) and 4 shirts when the price is $4 (point f).

The firm's short-run supply curve is the part of the firm's short-run marginal-cost curve above the shut-down price. The shut-down price for the shirt firm is $3, so as shown in Figure 12.4, the short-run supply curve is the marginal-cost curve starting at $3. For any price above the shut-down price, the firm will choose the quantity at which price equals marginal cost, so we can read the firm's quantity supplied directly from its

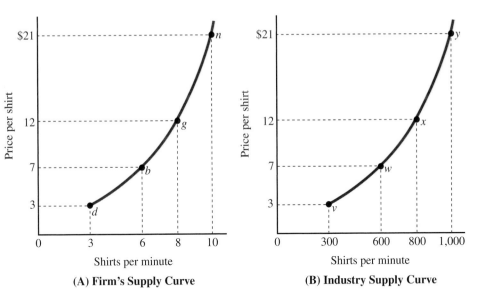

FIGURE 12.4

**Short-Run Supply
Curves**
In Panel A, the firm's short-
run supply curve is the part
of the marginal-cost curve
above the shut-down price.
In Panel B, there are 100
firms in the market, so the
market supply at a given
price is 100 times the
quantity supplied by the
typical firm. At a price of $7,
each firm supplies 6 shirts
per minute (point *b*), so the
market supply is 600 shirts
per minute (point *w*).

marginal-cost curve. If the price is $7, the firm will supply 6 shirts per minute (point
b). As the price increases, the firm responds by supplying more shirts: 8 shirts at a price
of $12 (point *g*) and 10 shirts at a price of $21 (point *n*).

What about prices below the shut-down price? If the price drops below the shut-
down price, the firm's total revenue will not be high enough to cover its total variable
cost, so the firm will shut down and produce no output. In Panel A of Figure 12.4, the
firm's supply curve starts at point *d*, indicating that the quantity supplied is zero for
any price less than $3.

The Short-Run Market Supply Curve

The **short-run market supply curve** shows the relationship between the market
price and the quantity supplied by all firms in the short run. Panel B of Figure 12.4
shows the short-run market supply curve when there are 100 identical shirt firms. For
each price, we get the quantity supplied for the entire market by multiplying the quantity supplied by the typical firm (from the individual supply curve) by 100. At a price of
$7, each firm produces 6 shirts (point *b* in Panel A), so the market supply is 600 shirts
(point *w* in Panel B). If the price increases to $12, each firm produces 8 shirts (point *g*
in Panel A), so the market supply is 800 shirts (point *x* in Panel B).

What happens if firms are not identical but instead have different individual supply curves? To compute the market supply in this case, we would add the quantities
supplied by the hundreds of firms in the market. The assumption that firms are identical is harmless: It makes it easier to derive the market supply curve from the supply
curve of the typical firm, but it does not change the analysis.

For another example of a competitive market, consider phone service in the developing world. In many parts of the developing world, people cannot afford their own
phones and have traditionally relied on pay phones. The recent development of mobile
phones has generated a new competitive industry in many developing nations. Read "A
Closer Look: Wireless Women."

**Short-run market supply
curve**

A curve showing the
relationship between price and
the quantity supplied in the
short run.

Market Equilibrium

Figure 12.5 shows a perfectly competitive market in equilibrium. For a short-run equilibrium, two conditions are satisfied.

1 At the market level, the quantity of the product supplied equals the quantity demanded. The demand curve intersects the short-run market supply curve at a price of $7 and a quantity of 600 shirts per minute (Panel A).

2 The typical firm in the market maximizes its profit, given the market price. Given the market price of $7, each of the 100 firms maximizes profit by producing 6 shirts per minute (Panel B).

In Figure 12.5, the market has reached a short-run equilibrium because the price of $7 generates a total of 600 shirts per minute, exactly the quantity demanded by consumers at this price.

In the long run, firms can enter or leave an industry, and existing firms can modify their facilities or build new facilities. The market reaches a long-run equilibrium when the two conditions for short-run equilibrium are met, and a third long-run condition holds as well.

3 Each firm in the market earns zero economic profit, so there is no incentive for other firms to enter the market.

In Figure 12.5, at the quantity chosen by the typical firm (6 shirts), the price ($7) equals the average total cost, so each firm makes zero economic profit, with total revenue equal to total cost. In other words, the market price equals the break-even price. When economic profit is zero, the firm's revenue is high enough to cover all its costs—

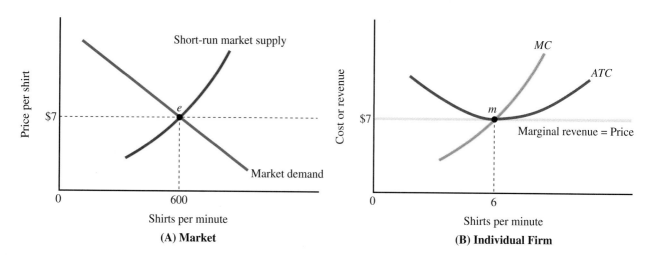

FIGURE 12.5 **Market Equilibrium**

In Panel A, the market demand curve intersects the short-run market supply curve at a price of $7. In Panel B, given the market price, the typical firm satisfies the marginal principle at point *m*, producing 6 shirts per minute. The $7 price equals the average cost at the equilibrium quantity, so economic profit is zero, and no other firms will enter the market.

including the opportunity costs of the entrepreneur—but not high enough to cause additional firms to enter the market. Each firm that is already in the market makes just enough money to stay in business, so there is no incentive for new firms to enter the market, and no incentive for existing firms to leave.

TEST Your Understanding

7. Complete the statement: The firm's short-run supply curve shows the relationship between _____ and _____.
8. Suppose that you want to draw the firm's short-run supply curve. What information do you need?
9. Suppose there are 100 identical firms in a perfectly competitive industry. At a price of $22, the typical firm supplies 50 units of output. What is the market quantity supplied at a price of $22?

A CLOSER LOOK

Wireless Women

In Pakistan, many poor villagers cannot afford their own phones, and phone service is provided by thousands of "wireless women," entrepreneurs who invest $310 in wireless phone equipment (transceiver, battery, charger), a signboard, a calculator, and a stopwatch. Then they sell phone service to their neighbors, charging by the minute and second. On average, their net income is about $2 per day, about three times the average per capita income in Pakistan.[2] The market for phone service has the features of a perfectly competitive market, with easy entry, a standardized good, and a large enough number of suppliers that each takes the market price as given.

The Long-Run Supply Curve
for an Increasing-Cost Industry

Long-run market supply curve

A curve showing the relationship between the market price and quantity supplied in the long run.

Increasing-cost industry

An industry in which the average cost of production increases as the total output of the industry increases; the long-run supply curve is positively sloped.

Let's look at the **long-run market supply curve**, which shows the relationship between the market price and the quantity supplied by all firms in the long run, a period long enough that firms can enter or leave the market. Suppose the typical shirt firm produces 6 shirts per minute, using a standard set of inputs, including a factory, some workers, and raw materials (cotton and thread). In a perfectly competitive industry, there are no restrictions on entry, so anyone can use the standard set of inputs to produce 6 shirts per minute.

We'll start with the case of an **increasing-cost industry**, defined as an industry in which the average cost of production increases as the total output of the industry increases. The average cost increases as the industry grows for two reasons:

▶ *Increasing input price.* As an industry grows, it competes with other industries for limited amounts of various inputs, and this competition drives up the prices of these inputs. For example, suppose that the shirt industry competes against other industries for a limited amount of cotton. To get more cotton to produce more shirts, firms in the shirt industry must outbid other industries for the limited amount available, and this drives up the price of cotton.

▶ *Less productive inputs.* A small industry will use only the most productive inputs, but as the industry grows, firms may be forced to use less productive inputs. For example, a small shirt industry will use only the most skillful workers, but as the industry grows, it will hire less skillful workers. As the average skill level of the industry's workforce decreases, the average cost of production increases: A firm will require more labor time—and pay more in labor costs—to produce each shirt. Another example of progressively less productive inputs is the production of agricultural products such as sugar. Because of variation in climate and soil conditions, it is cheaper to grow sugar in some areas than in others. As the quantity of sugar produced increases, growers are forced to produce sugar in areas with less favorable climates and soil conditions, and this results in higher costs.

Production Cost and Industry Size

Table 12.4 shows hypothetical data on the cost of producing shirts. Let's start with the first row, which shows the firm's production costs in an industry with 100 firms and a total of 600 shirts produced per day (6 shirts per firm). To compute the total cost for the typical firm, we add the cost of the firm's production facility (the cost of the shirt factory), the cost of labor, and the cost of materials. In the first row, the total cost of the typical firm producing 6 shirts per minute is $42, and the average cost is $7 per shirt ($42 divided by 6 shirts). In the second row, if the number of firms doubles to 200 and each firm continues to produce 6 shirts per minute, the total output of the industry will double to 1,200 shirts per minute. For the two reasons listed earlier (higher input prices and less productive inputs), the total cost per firm increases to $60, so the average cost per shirt increases to $10. In the last row, when the total output of the industry increases to 1,800 shirts per minute, the average cost per shirt increases to $13.

TABLE 12.4

Industry Output and
Average Production Cost

Number of Firms	Industry Output	Shirts per Firm	Total Cost for Typical Firm	Average Cost per Shirt
100	600	6	$42	$7
200	1,200	6	60	10
300	1,800	6	78	13

The shirt industry is an example of an increasing-cost industry. In the last column of Table 12.4, the average cost increases from $7 for an industry that produces 600 shirts, to $10 for an industry that produces 1,200 shirts, and so on. The increase in average cost reflects the higher input prices and less productive inputs in a larger industry.

Drawing the Long-Run Market Supply Curve

The long-run supply curve tells us how much output will be produced at each price in the long run, when the number of firms in the market can change. Recall that in the long-run equilibrium, each firm makes zero economic profit, meaning that the price equals the average cost of production:

long-run equilibrium: price = average cost

The data in Table 12.4 shows three points on the long-run supply curve. At a price of $7, a total of 100 firms will be in the market, with each producing 6 shirts per hour. This combination (price = $7 and quantity = 600 shirts) is on the long-run supply curve because the price equals the average cost. Each firm makes zero economic profit, so there is no incentive for firms to either enter or exit the market. This is shown by point *e* in Figure 12.6. Suppose the price of shirts increases. At the higher price, shirt making will be more profitable, and firms will enter the market, increasing total output. Firms will continue to enter the market until the economic profit becomes zero again, which happens when the average cost again equals the price. From Table 12.4, we see that entry will continue until the market reaches 200 firms producing 1,200 shirts at an average cost and price of $10. This is shown by point *h* in Figure 12.6. Point *j* shows another point on the long-run supply curve, with a price of $13 and a quantity of 1,800 shirts.

The long-run supply curve in Figure 12.6 is positively sloped, as it will be for any increasing-cost industry. This is another example of the law of supply. An increase in the price of shirts initially makes shirt production profitable, so firms enter the market and produce more shirts. As industry-wide output increases, the greater demand for cotton and labor pulls up input costs, pulling up the average cost of producing shirts. Firms will continue to enter the market until the average cost rises to the point where it equals the price of shirts. The positively sloped supply curve tells us that the market won't produce a larger quantity of shirts unless the price rises to cover the higher average cost associated with the larger industry.

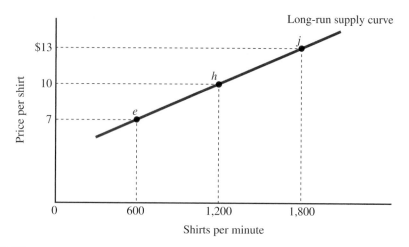

FIGURE 12.6 **Long-Run Market Supply Curve**
The long-run market supply curve shows the relationship between the price and quantity supplied in the long run, when firms can enter or leave the industry. At each point on the supply curve, the market price equals the long-run average cost of production. Because this is an increasing-cost industry, the market supply curve is positively sloped.

Application: Increasing-Cost Industries—Wolfram, Sugar, Rental Housing

For an example of the law of supply with market entry, consider the market for wolfram during World War II. Wolfram is an ore of tungsten, an alloy required to make heat-resistant steel for armor plate and armor-piercing shells. During World War II, the United States and its European allies bought up all the wolfram produced in Spain, thus denying the Axis powers, Germany and Italy, this vital military input. However, the wolfram buying program was very costly to the Allied powers for two reasons:[3]

▶ The Allied powers had to outbid the Axis powers for the wolfram, so the price increased from $1,144 per ton to $20,000 per ton.
▶ Spanish firms responded to the higher prices by supplying more wolfram. Workers poured into the Galatia area in Spain, where they used simple tools to gather wolfram from the widely scattered outcroppings of ore. Because of this market entry, the quantity of wolfram supplied increased tenfold. Because wolfram miners obeyed the law of supply, the Allied powers were forced to buy a huge amount of wolfram, much more than they had expected.

The sugar industry is another example of an increasing-cost industry. If the price of sugar is only 11 cents per pound, sugar production is profitable in areas with relatively low production costs, including the Caribbean, Latin America, Australia, and South Africa.[4] At a price of 11 cents, the world supply of sugar equals the amount produced in these areas. As the price increases, sugar production becomes profitable in areas where production costs are higher, and as these areas enter the world market, the quantity of sugar supplied increases. For example, at a price of 14 cents per pound, sugar production is profitable in the European Community, too. At a price of 24 cents, production is profitable even in the United States.

In many communities, the rental-apartment industry is an increasing-cost industry. Most communities use zoning laws to restrict the amount of land available for apartments. Consequently, when housing firms announce plans to build more apartments, there is fierce competition for the small amount of zoned land available for apartments. As a result, the cost of land for apartments—and the rent that a housing firm must charge to cover its production costs—increases by a large amount.[5]

TEST Your Understanding

10. Complete the statement: The long-run supply curve shows the relationship between _____ (on the horizontal axis) and _____ (on the vertical axis).

11. Use Table 12.4 to compute the average cost in a 400-firm industry, assuming the total cost of the typical firm in such an industry is $96.

12. Circle the three items in the following list that go together: Positively sloped supply curve, horizontal supply curve, increasing-cost industry, increasing average cost of production, constant average cost of production.

Short-Run and Long-Run Effects of Changes in Demand

We can use what we've learned about the short-run and long-run supply curves to get a deeper understanding of perfectly competitive markets. Let's use the two supply curves to explore the short-run and the long-run effects of a change in demand in a perfectly competitive market.

The Short-Run Response to an Increase in Demand

Figure 12.7 shows the short-run effects of an increase in the demand for shirts. Panel A shows what's happening at the market level. Let's start with the initial equilibrium shown by point *i*: The original demand curve intersects the short-run market supply curve at a price of $7 per shirt and a quantity of 600 shirts. When demand increases, the new demand curve intersects the supply curve at a price of $12 and a quantity of 800 shirts (point *s*). In Panel B, an increase in price from $7 to $12 increases the output per firm from 6 shirts to 8 shirts. At this quantity, the $12 price now exceeds the average total cost, so the typical firm makes an economic profit (shown by the shaded rectangle).

This is not a long-run equilibrium, because each firm is making a positive economic profit. Firms will enter the profitable market, and as they compete for

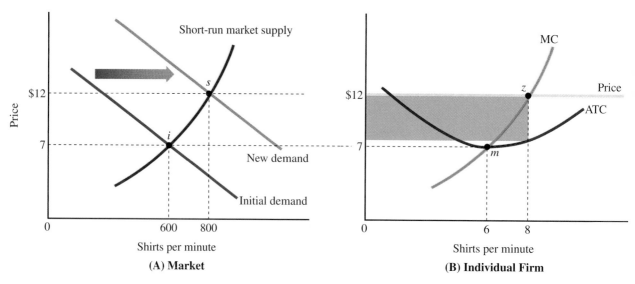

FIGURE 12.7 **Short-Run Effects of an Increase in Demand**

An increase in demand increases the market price to $12, causing the typical firm to produce 8 shirts instead of 6. Price exceeds the average total cost at the 8-shirt quantity, so economic profit is positive. Firms will enter the profitable market.

customers, the price of shirts will decrease. New firms will continue to enter the mar-ket until the price drops to the point at which economic profit is zero. The question is, How far does the price drop?

The Long-Run Response to an Increase in Demand

We can use the long-run supply curve to determine the long-run price after an increase in demand. In Figure 12.8, the short-run effect of the increase in demand is shown by the move from point *i* to point *s*: The price increases from $7 to $12, and the quantity increases from 600 to 800. Economic profit is positve, so firms will enter the market. Entry will continue until the price drops to $10 and the quantity is 1,200 shirts per minute. The new long-run equilibrium is shown by point *f*, where the new demand curve intersects the long-run supply curve. At this price and quantity, each of the 200 firms produces 6 shirts per minute and earns zero economic profit.

Figure 12.8 shows how the price of shirts changes over time. An increase in demand causes a large upward jump in the price (from point *i* to point *s*) in the short run, followed by a slide downward to the new long-run equilibrium price (from point *s* to point *f*). In the short run, firms respond to an increase in price by squeezing more output from their existing production facilities. Because of diminishing returns, it is very costly to increase output in the short run, so the price must increase by a large amount to cover these much higher production costs. Consequently, the short-run supply curve is very steep.

The higher price causes new firms to enter the market, and as they enter, the price gradually drops to the point at which each firm makes zero economic profit. The long-run supply curve is relatively flat because firms enter the industry and build new facto-ries, so there are no diminishing returns to pull up costs.

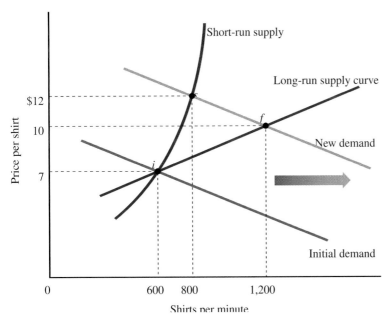

FIGURE 12.8 Short-Run and Long-Run Effects of an Increase in Demand
The short-run supply curve is steeper than the long-run supply curve because production facilities are fixed, and there are diminishing returns in the short run. In the short run, an increase in demand increases the price from $7 (point *i*) to $12 (point *s*). But in the long run, firms can enter the industry and build more plants, so the price eventually drops to $10 (point *f*). The large initial upward jump in price after an increase in demand is followed by a downward slide to the new long-run equilibrium price.

Long-Run Supply for a Constant-Cost Industry

So far we have examined products that are produced by increasing-cost industries, whose average cost increases as the industry expands. We turn next to a **constant-cost industry**. In a constant-cost industry, average cost doesn't change as the industry expands. That is, the prices of inputs such as labor and materials do not change as the total output of the industry increases. This will happen if the industry consumes only a small amount of the input available, meaning that events in the industry—increases or decreases in output—do not affect the price of the input. As a result, the average cost of production for the typical firm doesn't change as the industry grows. In Table 12.3, the shirt industry would be a constant-cost industry if the average cost of shirts were constant at $7, regardless of how many shirts were produced.

Constant-cost industry
An industry in which the average cost of production is constant; the long-run supply curve is horizontal.

Long-Run Supply Curve for a Constant-Cost Industry

As an example of constant-cost industry, consider the production of birthday-cake candles. As the industry grows, it will use more workers and materials (for wicks, wax, and dyes), but because the industry is such a small part of the markets for labor and materials, the prices of these inputs won't change. As a result, the average cost of production won't change as the industry grows.

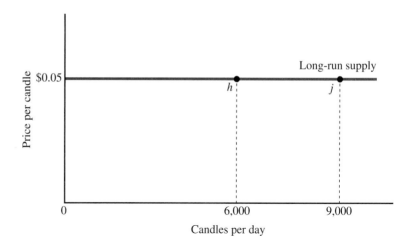

Long-Run Supply Curve for a Constant-Cost Industry

In a constant-cost industry, input prices do not change as the industry grows, so the average production cost is constant, and the long-run supply curve is horizontal. For the candle industry, the cost per candle is constant at $0.05, so the supply curve is horizontal at $0.05 per candle.

The long-run supply curve for a constant-cost industry is horizontal at the constant average cost of production. If the average cost of birthday-cake candles is $0.05 per candle (including the cost of materials and labor), the long-run supply curve for candles will be horizontal at $0.05, as shown by Figure 12.9. At any lower price, the quantity of candles supplied would be zero because in the long run, no rational firm would provide candles at a price less than the average cost of production. At any higher price, firms would enter the candle industry in droves, and entry would continue until the price dropped to the constant average cost of candles ($0.05).

Application: Hurricane Andrew and the Price of Ice

For an example of the effects of an increase in demand in a constant-cost industry, let's look at the short-run and long-run effects of a hurricane. In 1992, Hurricane Andrew struck the southeastern United States, leaving millions of people without electricity for several days. Figure 12.10 shows the short- and long-run effects of the hurricane on the price of ice, which was used to cool and preserve food in areas without electricity. Before the hurricane, the market was at point *i*, with a price of $1 per bag of ice. The long-run supply curve is horizontal, indicating that the ice industry is a constant-cost industry.

In the short run (a day or two), the number of ice suppliers is fixed. The increase in demand caused by the hurricane moved the market from point *i* to point *s*, and the price rose to $5 per bag of ice. In the long run, firms responded to the higher price by entering the market. Many people trucked ice from distant locations and sold it from trucks parked on streets and highways. As these firms entered the ice market in the days after the hurricane, the price of ice gradually dropped, and the market eventually reached the intersection of the new demand curve and the long-run supply curve (point *f*), with a price equal to the prehurricane price. In the case of the retail ice industry, the long run is just a few days.

This pattern of price changes following the hurricane was observed in other markets. Immediately after the hurricane, $200 chain saws were sold for $900, but the price dropped steadily as new roadside firms entered the market. The same sort of price changes occurred for bottled water, tarpaper, and plywood. The basic pattern was a large upward jump in price followed by a downward slide to the long-run equilibrium price.

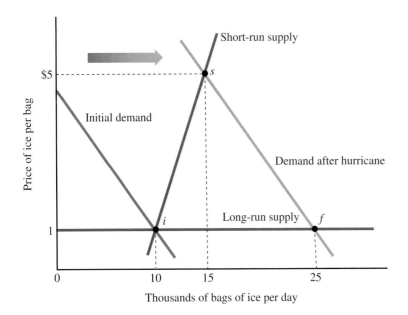

FIGURE 12.10

Hurricane Andrew and the Price of Ice
A hurricane increases the demand for ice, shifting the demand curve to the right. In the short run, the supply curve is relatively steep, so the price rises by a large amount—from $1 to $5. In the long run, firms enter the industry, pulling the price back down. Because ice production is a constant-cost industry, the supply curve is horizontal, and the large upward jump in price is followed by a downward slide back to the original price.

Public officials are often tempted to pass laws prohibiting what's called price gouging, charging high prices for scarce goods after a natural disaster. One effect of such laws is to slow the transition from the short run to the long run. The people who set up roadside stands to sell ice were motivated by the high price. If the price were controlled at $1 per bag, few people would have incurred the large expenses associated with trucking the ice from distant locations and setting up roadside stores. The result would have been less ice and more spoiled food. An alternative to a law regulating prices is to leave prices to the market and help to ease the transition from short run to long run by making it easier for entrepreneurs to enter the market.

Butter Prices

Several years ago, people became concerned about the undesirable health effects of eating butter. The demand for butter dropped, decreasing its price. Some time later, the price of butter started rising steadily, although demand hadn't been changing. After several months of price hikes, the price of butter reached the price observed before demand decreased. According to a consumer watchdog organization, the rising price of butter was evidence of a conspiracy on the part of butter producers. Is there some other explanation for the rising price of butter?

The key to solving this puzzle is the distinction between the short run and the long run. In Figure 12.11, the short-run effect of a decrease in demand is shown by the move from point i (price = $2.00) to point s (price = $1.44). In the short run, not many firms will leave the market when the price drops, so the decrease in demand will cause a large price drop. Although many of the remaining firms will lose money, they will stay in the market if their total revenue covers their total variable cost. In the long run, however, unprofitable firms will leave the market, causing the price to rise. In Figure 12.11, the new long-run equilibrium is shown by point f, with a price of $2.00. The pattern of a large price drop followed by a gradual increase in price is a normal pattern for a perfectly competitive market. ∎

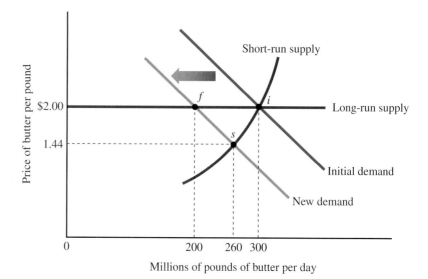

The Short-Run and Long-Run Effects of a Decrease in the Demand for Butter

In the short run, a decrease in demand for butter decreases the price from $2.00 (point *i*) to $1.44 (point *s*). In the long run, firms leave the industry, and the price rises, reaching the original price (point *f*). In a constant-cost industry, changes in demand do not affect the long-run price.

TEST Your Understanding

13. Explain why the short-run supply curve is steeper than the long-run supply curve.
14. Suppose the demand for shirts decreases. Describe the short-run and the long-run effects on the price of shirts.
15. Under what circumstances would an increase in demand for a particular good not affect the price of the good in the long run?

USING THE TOOLS

We've seen how a perfectly competitive firm can use its cost curves to decide how much to produce and whether to continue operating an unprofitable operation. We've also explored the short- and long-run effects of changes in demand. Here are some opportunities to do your own economic analysis.

1. Advice for an Unprofitable Firm

You've been hired as an economic consultant to a price-taking firm that produces baseball caps. The firm already has a factory, so it is operating in the short run. The price of caps is $5, the hourly wage is $12, and each cap requires $1 worth of material. At the current level of output (15 workers and 60 caps), the firm is losing money: Its total cost exceeds its total revenue. The firm has experimented with different workforces and discovered that 14 workers

would produce only 57 caps. Your job is to tell the firm which of these four options to take:

- Option 1: Shut down the unprofitable operation.
- Option 2: Continue to produce 60 caps per hour.
- Option 3: Produce more caps.
- Option 4: Produce fewer caps.

2. Maximizing the Profit Margin

According to the marginal principle, the firm should choose the quantity of output at which price equals marginal cost. A tempting alternative is to maximize the firm's profit margin, defined as the difference between price and short-run average total cost. Use the firm's short-run cost curves to evaluate this approach. Draw the firm's short-run supply curve and compare it to the supply curve of a firm that maximizes its profit.

3. Market Effects of an Increase in Housing Demand

Consider the market for apartments in a small city. In the initial equilibrium, the monthly rent (the price) is $500, and the quantity is 10,000 apartments. Suppose that the population of the city suddenly increases by 24%. The price elasticity of demand for apartments is 1.0. The short-run price elasticity of supply is 0.20, and the long-run price elasticity of supply is 0.50.

a. Depict graphically the short- and long-run effects of the increase in population.
b. By what percentage will the price increase in the short run? (Use the price-change formula from Chapter 5.)
c. By what percentage will the price increase in the long run?

SUMMARY

In this chapter, we explored the decisions made by perfectly competitive firms and the implications of these decisions for the supply side of the market. In the short run, a firm uses the marginal principle to decide how much output to produce. In the long run, a firm will enter a market if the price exceeds the average cost of production. Here are the main points of this chapter:

1 A price-taking firm should produce the quantity of output at which the marginal revenue (the price) equals the marginal cost of production.

2 An unprofitable firm should continue to operate if its total revenue exceeds its total variable cost.

3 The long-run supply curve will be positively sloped if the average cost of production increases as the industry grows.

4 The long-run supply curve is flatter than the short-run supply curve because there are diminishing returns in the short run, but not in the long run.

5 An increase in demand causes a large upward jump in price, followed by a downward slide to the new long-run equilibrium price.

KEY TERMS

accounting profit, 264
break-even price, 268
constant-cost industry, 281
economic profit, 263
firm-specific demand curve, 262

increasing-cost industry, 276
long-run market supply curve, 276
marginal revenue, 266
perfectly competitive market, 261
short-run supply curve, 272

short-run market supply curve, 273
shut-down price, 270
sunk cost, 271
total revenue, 263

PROBLEMS AND DISCUSSION QUESTIONS

1 In the following table, provide the numbers for marginal cost. Then use the data to draw the short-run supply curve for tables.

Tables per Hour	Total Cost	Marginal Cost
3	120	—
4	155	—
5	200	—
6	270	—

2 The following table shows short-run marginal costs for a perfectly competitive firm:

Output	100	200	300	400	500
Marginal cost	$5	$10	$20	$40	$70

   a. Use this information to draw the firm's marginal-cost curve.
   b. Suppose the shut-down price is $10. Draw the firm's short-run supply curve.
   c. Suppose there are 100 identical firms with the same marginal-cost curve. Draw the short-run industry supply curve.

3 Consider the choices facing an unprofitable (and perfectly competitive) firm. The firm currently produces 100 units per day and sells them at a price of $22 each. At the current output quantity, the firm's total cost is $3,000 per day, its variable cost is $2,500 per day, and its marginal cost is $45.
   a. Evaluate the following statement from the firm's accountant: "Given our current production level, our variable cost ($2,500) exceeds our total revenue ($2,200). We should shut down our production facility."
   b. Illustrate your answer with a graph showing short-run cost curves and the revenue curve of a perfectly competitive firm.

4 You've been hired by an unprofitable firm to determine whether it should shut down its unprofitable operation. The firm currently uses 70 workers to produce 300 units of output per day. The daily wage (per worker) is $100, and the price of the firm's output is $30. Although you don't know the firm's fixed cost, you know that it is high enough that the firm's total cost exceeds its total revenue. Should the firm continue to operate at a loss?

5 Consider the following statement from a wheat farmer to his workers: "The price of wheat is very low this year, and the most I can get from the crop is $35,000. If I paid you the same amount as I paid you last year ($30,000), I'd lose money because I also have to worry about the $20,000 I paid three months ago for seed and fertilizer. I'd be crazy to pay a total of $50,000 to harvest a crop I can sell for only $35,000. If you are willing to work for half as

much as last year ($15,000), my total cost will be $35,000, so I'll break even. If you don't take a pay cut. I won't harvest the wheat." Is the farmer bluffing, or will the farm workers lose their jobs if they reject the proposed pay cut?

6 Consider a firm that uses the following rule to decide how much output to produce: If the profit margin (price minus short-run average total cost) is positive, the firm will produce more output. Use the firm's short-run cost curves to evaluate this approach. Draw the firm's short-run supply curve and compare it to the short-run supply curve of a profit-maximizing firm.

7 Consider the following data on the relationship between the price of gasoline (in real terms, adjusted for inflation) and the quantity of gasoline sold per day in the city of Ceteris Paribus:

Year	Price	Gallons per Day
1995	1.00	50,000
1996	1.10	53,000

If possible, draw the industry supply curve and compute the price elasticity of supply.

8 Between 1995 and 2005, the number of U.S. households with DVD players increased dramatically. Predict the implications for the price of DVD rentals in the short run and the long run.

9 Suppose each lamp manufacturer produces 10 lamps per hour. In the following table, fill in a number wherever you see a _____. Then use the data in the table to draw the long-run supply curve for lamps.

Number of Firms	Industry Output	Total Cost for Typical Firm	Average Cost per Lamp
40	_____	$300	$_____
80	_____	$360	$_____
120	_____	$420	$_____

10 Suppose that a new technology decreases the amount of labor time required to produce a particular good. Would you expect all firms eventually to adopt the new technology?

11 Draw a long-run supply curve for haircutting that is consistent with the following statement: "The haircutting industry in our city uses a tiny fraction of the electricity, scissors, and commercial space available on the market. In addition, the industry uses only about 100 of the 50,000 people who could cut hair."

12 Draw a long-run supply curve for pencils and explain why you drew it as you did.

MODEL ANSWERS TO QUESTIONS

Chapter-Opening Questions

1 To use the marginal principle, you need information on marginal cost and marginal revenue (the price). As explained in "Economic Puzzle: Fewer Deliveries and More Profit?" you could use data on labor input and output, along with the wage, to compute the marginal cost.

2 It would be sensible to shut down if your total revenue is less than your variable cost. Otherwise, it would be sensible to continue operating.

3 As explained in "A Closer Look: Wireless Women," individuals can enter the market for phone service by investing $310 in mobile phone equipment. They provide phone service for villagers who lack home phones, charging by the minute or second of usage.

Test Your Understanding

1 The firm is such a tiny part of the market that no matter how much output it produces, it will not affect the market price.

2 Marginal revenue (or price), marginal cost.

3 The farmer is not maximizing profit because the marginal revenue (price) is less than the marginal cost. The farmer should produce less sugar.

4 $800 ($20 per lamp times 40 lamps).

5 Operate.

6 Average variable cost.

7 Price, quantity supplied.

8 You need the short-run marginal-cost curve and the shut-down price. If you have the average variable-cost curve and the marginal-cost curve, you can figure out the shut-down price by finding the price at which the two curves intersect.

9 5,000 units (50 units per firm times 100 firms).

10 Quantity supplied, price.

11 The average cost per shirt is $16 ($96 ÷ 6 shirts).

12 The related terms are positively sloped supply curve, increasing-cost industry, and increasing average cost of production.

13 There are diminishing returns in the short run, so production costs increase rapidly as a firm increases its output.

14 In the short run, the price would drop by a large amount. Then the price would start to rise. If the shirt industry is an increasing-cost industry, the new long-run price would be less than the original price.

15 If the good is produced by a constant-cost industry, one with a horizontal long-run supply curve.

NOTES

1. Walter Adam, *The Structure of the American Economy*, 8th ed. (Upper Saddle River, NJ: Prentice Hall, 1990).

2. TeleCommons Development Group, "Grameen Telecom's Village Phone Programme: A Multi-Media Case Study," (http://www.telecommons.com/villagephone).

3. D. I. Gordon and R. Dangerfield, *The Hidden Weapon* (New York: Harper & Brothers, 1947), pp. 105–116.

4. Frederic L. Hoff and Max Lawrence, "Implications of World Sugar Markets, Policies, and Production Costs for U.S. Sugar," *Agricultural Economic Research Report* 543 (Washington, DC: U.S. Department of Agriculture, Economic Research Service, November 1985).

5. Frank De Leeuw and Nkanta Ekanem. "The Supply of Rental Housing," *American Economic Review*, vol. 61, 1971, pp. 806–817.

Monopoly and Price Discrimination

The Coca-Cola Company recently built a new football scoreboard for a large state university. Now football fans can enjoy the latest in scoreboard graphics as they watch the game. In addition, Coca-Cola gave $2.3 million dollars to remodel the university's student center,[1] providing students with a comfortable place to meet, eat, talk, and relax. What explains this outburst of apparent generosity? Does it have anything to do with the fact that Coca-Cola was recently given the exclusive right to sell beverages on campus—a monopoly? Who is really paying for the scoreboard and the student center?

Monopoly
A market in which a single firm serves the entire market.

Market power
The ability to affect the price of a product

In Chapter 12, we explored the decisions made by firms in a perfectly competitive market, a market where there are hundreds or thousands of firms. This chapter deals with the opposite extreme: a **monopoly**, a market served by a single firm. In contrast with a perfectly competitive or price-taking firm, a monopolist controls the price of its product, so we can refer to a monopolist as a "price maker." A monopolist has **market power**, the ability to affect the price of a product. Of course, consumers obey the law of demand, and the higher the price a monopolist charges, the smaller the quantity it will sell.

A monopoly occurs when something prevents more than one firm from entering the market. Among the possible barriers to entry are patents, government licensing, and large economies of scale in production.

Patent
The exclusive right to sell a particular good for some period of time.

▶ A **patent** grants an inventor the exclusive right to sell a new product for some period of time, currently 20 years under international rules.
▶ Under a licensing policy, the government chooses a single firm to sell a particular product. Some examples are licensing for radio and television stations, off-street parking in cities, and vendors in national parks.

Natural monopoly
A market in which the economies of scale are so large that only a single large firm can survive.

▶ A **natural monopoly** occurs when the scale economies in production are so large that only a single large firm can survive. In other words, the market can support only one firm. Some examples are cable TV service, electricity transmission, and water systems. In such a market, a single firm will be profitable, but the entry of a second firm will ensure that both firms lose money.

In this chapter we will discuss "unnatural" monopolies, which result from artificial barriers to entry. Later in the book, we'll explore the reasons for natural monopolies and the public-policy responses to them.

This chapter examines the production and pricing decisions of a monopoly and the implications for society as a whole. As we'll see, monopoly is inefficient from society's perspective because it produces too little output. We'll also discuss the trade-offs with patents, which lead to monopoly and higher prices but also encourage innovation. We'll also explore the issue of price discrimination. Price discrimination (which is perfectly legal although not always popular) occurs when firms charge different prices to different types of consumers. Although we discuss price discrimination by a monopolist, it also happens in markets with more firms (oligopoly and monopolistic competition). Here are some of the practical questions that we consider:

1 What are the trade-offs associated with patents and other policies that grant monopoly power?
2 When the patent on a popular pharmaceutical drug expires, what happens to the price of the drug?
3 Why are hardback books so much more expensive than paperback books?
4 Why do senior citizens typically pay less than everyone else for admission to a movie, but pay the same as everyone else for popcorn?

The Monopolist's Output Decision

Like other firms, a monopolist must decide how much output to produce, given it objective of maximizing profit. We learned about production costs in an earlier chap ter, so we start our discussion with the revenue side of the monopolist's profit picture Then we show how a monopolist picks a price and a quantity.

Total Revenue and Marginal Revenue

A firm's total revenue—the money it gets by selling its product—equals the price time the quantity sold. In this part of the chapter, we'll assume that the firm charges the same price to all of its customers. Table 13.1 shows how to use a demand schedule (in the first two columns) to compute a firm's total revenue (in the third column). At a price of $16, the firm doesn't sell anything, so its total revenue is zero. To sell 1 unit, the firm must cut its price to $14, so its total revenue is $14. To get consumers to buy 2 units instead of just 1, the firm must cut its price to $12. The total revenue associated with selling 2 units is $24. As the price continues to drop and the quantity sold increases, total revenue increases for a while, but then starts falling. To sell 5 unit instead of 4, the firm cuts its price from $8 to $6, and total revenue decreases from $3: to $30. The total revenue associated with selling 6 units is even lower ($24). The top panel in Figure 13.1 shows the relationship between quantity sold and total revenue.

The firm's marginal revenue is defined as the change in total revenue that result from selling 1 more unit of output. In Table 13.1, we compute marginal revenue by taking the difference between the total revenue from selling a certain quantity of out put (for example, 3 units), and the total revenue from selling 1 fewer unit of outpu (for example, 2 units). As shown in the fourth row in the table, the total revenue from selling 3 units is $30 and the total revenue from selling 2 units is only $24, so the mar ginal revenue from selling the third unit is $6. As shown in the table and in the lowe panel of Figure 13.1, marginal revenue is positive for the first 4 units sold. Beyond units, selling an additional unit results in lower total revenue, so marginal revenue i negative. For example, the marginal revenue for the fifth unit is −$2, and the margina revenue for the sixth unit is −$6.

TABLE 13.1

Demand, Total Revenue, and Marginal Revenue

Price	Quantity Sold	Total Revenue	Marginal Revenue
$16	0	0	—
$14	1	$14	$14
$12	2	$24	10
$10	3	$30	6
$8	4	$32	2
$6	5	$30	−2
$4	6	$24	−6

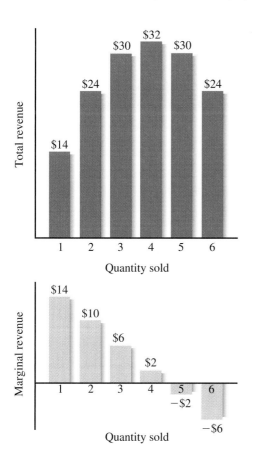

FIGURE 13.1

Total Revenue and Marginal Revenue
As the firm cuts its price to sell more output, its total revenue rises for the first 4 units sold, but then decreases for the fifth and sixth units. Therefore, marginal revenue (the change in total revenue from selling one more unit) is positive for the first 4 units sold and then becomes negative.

Table 13.1 and Figure 13.1 illustrate the trade-offs associated with cutting a price to sell a larger quantity. When the firm cuts its price from $12 to $10, there is good news and bad news:

- Good news: The firm collects $10 from the new customer (the third), so revenue increases by $10.
- Bad news: The firm cuts the price for all its customers, so it gets less revenue from the customers who would have been willing to pay the higher price ($12). Specifically, the firm collects $2 less from each of the two original customers, so revenue decreases by $4.

The combination of good news and bad news leads to a net increase in total revenue of only $6, resulting from the $10 gained from the new customer minus the $4 lost on the first two customers. In other words, the marginal revenue from the third unit ($6) is less than the price ($10).

We can use a simple formula to compute marginal revenue. The formula quantifies the good news and bad news from selling one more unit.

marginal revenue = new price − (old quantity × slope of demand curve)

The first part of the formula is the good news, the new price ($10 in our example) received for the extra unit sold. The second part of the formula is the bad news from selling one more unit, the revenue lost by cutting the price for the original customers. The revenue loss is equal to the old quantity (2 units in our example) times the slope of the demand curve (the change in price required to sell one more unit of output ($2 in our example):

$$\text{marginal revenue} = \$10 - (2 \text{ units} \times \$2 \text{ per unit}) = \$6$$

Similarly, to sell the fifth unit, the firm would cut the price from $8 to $6, and marginal revenue is actually negative:

$$\text{marginal revenue} = \$6 - (4 \text{ units} \times \$2 \text{ per unit}) = -\$2$$

Notice that for all but the first unit sold, the marginal revenue is less than the price. Marginal revenue equals the price (the good news) minus the revenue lost on previous units sold at a lower price (the bad news). The firm must cut the price to sell more, and the bad news guarantees that the marginal revenue is less than the price. As the quantity sold increases, the revenue loss (bad news) increases as well because the firm must cut the price for more consumers. Therefore, the larger the quantity sold, the larger the gap between price and marginal revenue. The only time marginal revenue equals price is for the first unit sold: There is no bad news because the firm didn't have any customers before cutting the price to sell the first unit.

You may recall from the previous chapter that things are different for a perfectly competitive firm, which can sell as much as it wants at the market price. If a perfectly competitive firm sells one unit at $12, it can sell a second unit at the same price, so its marginal revenue is $12 for the second unit sold, just as it was $12 for the first unit sold. For a perfectly competitive firm, marginal revenue is always equal to the price, no matter how many units the firm sells. A perfectly competitive firm does not cut the price to sell more, so there is no bad news associated with selling more. In contrast, a monopolist must cut the price to sell more, so marginal revenue is less than price.

Figure 13.2 shows the demand curve and marginal-revenue curve for the data shown in Table 13.1. Because the firm must cut its price to sell more output, the marginal-revenue curve lies below the demand curve. For example, the demand curve shows that the firm will sell 3 units at a price of $10 (point *d*), but the marginal revenue for this quantity is only $6 (point *i*). For quantities of 5 units and greater, marginal revenue is negative because when the firm cuts its price to sell 1 additional unit, the bad news dominates the good news: The amount the firm loses on its original customers exceeds the amount it gains on the new one, so total revenue drops.

The Marginal Principle and the Output Decision

We use a simple example to explain how a monopolist can use the marginal principle to decide how much output to produce. Sneezy, who holds a patent on a new drug that cures the common cold, must decide how much of the drug to produce. Sneezy can use the marginal principle to make this decision.

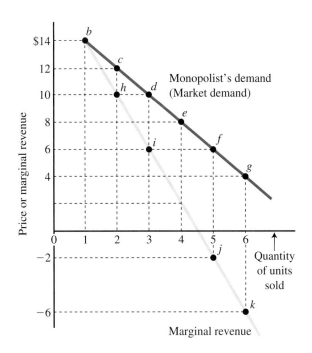

FIGURE 13.2

The Demand Curve and the Marginal-Revenue Curve
Marginal revenue is equal to the price for the first unit sold but is less than the price for all other units sold. To increase the quantity sold, a firm cuts its price and receives less revenue on the units that could have been sold at the higher price. Therefore, beyond the first unit sold, the marginal-revenue curve lies below the demand curve.

MARGINAL *Principle*

Increase the level of an activity if its marginal benefit exceeds its marginal cost, but reduce the level if the marginal cost exceeds the marginal benefit. If possible, pick the level at which the marginal benefit equals the marginal cost.

Sneezy's activity is producing the cold drug, and he will pick the quantity at which the marginal revenue from selling one more unit (the marginal benefit) equals the marginal cost associated with that unit.

The first two columns in Table 13.2 show the relationship between the price of the cold drug and the quantity demanded. We can use these numbers to draw the market demand curve, as shown in Figure 13.3. Because Sneezy is a monopolist—the only

OneKey is
all you need

TABLE 13.2

Using the Marginal Principle to Pick a Price and Quantity

Price (per Dose)	Quantity Sold (Doses)	Marginal Revenue	Marginal Cost	Total Revenue	Total Cost	Profit
$18	600	$12	$4.00	$10,800	$5,710	$5,090
$17	700	$10	$4.60	$11,900	$6,140	$5,760
$16	800	$8	$5.30	$12,800	$6,635	$6,165
$15	900	$6	$6.00	$13,500	$7,200	$6,300
$14	1,000	$4	$6.70	$14,000	$7,835	$6,165
$13	1,100	$2	$7.80	$14,300	$8,560	$5,740
$12	1,200	0	$9.00	$14,400	$9,400	$5,000

The Monopolist Picks a Quantity and a Price
To maximize profit, the monopolist picks point *n*, where marginal revenue equals marginal cost. The monopolist produces 900 doses per hour at a price of $15 (point *m*). The average cost is $8 (point *c*), so the profit per dose is $7 (equal to the $15 price minus the $8 average cost) and the total profit is $6,300 (equal to $7 per dose times 900 doses). The profit is shown by the shaded rectangle.

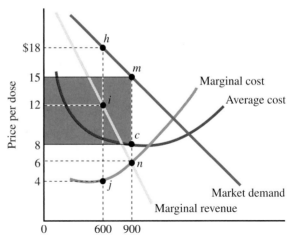

seller of the drug—the market demand curve shows how much he will sell at each price. The demand curve is negatively sloped, consistent with the law of demand. For example, at a price of $18 per dose, the quantity demanded is 600 doses per hour (point *h*), compared to 900 doses at a price of $15 (point *m*).

Like other monopolists, Sneezy must cut his price to sell a larger quantity, so marginal revenue is less than price. This is shown in the third column of Table 13.2 and in Figure 13.3. We can use the marginal-revenue formula explained earlier to compute marginal revenue for different quantities of output. The slope of the demand curve is $0.01 per dose. To simplify the arithmetic, rather than using the "new" price and "old" quantity, we can use a matched pair of price and quantities from the demand curve to get an approximation of marginal revenue. When the change in price is relatively small (for example, $0.01), the difference between the new and old price is small enough to be ignored. For example, at a price of $18, the quantity sold is 600 doses, so marginal revenue is $12:

$$\text{marginal revenue} = \$18 - (600 \text{ doses} \times \$0.01) = \$12$$

Similarly, at a price of $15, the quantity is 900 doses and marginal revenue is $6:

$$\text{marginal revenue} = \$15 - (900 \text{ doses} \times \$0.01) = \$6$$

Using the Marginal Principle to Pick the Profit-Maximizing Quantity and Price

We're ready to show how a monopolist can use the marginal principle to pick a quantity to produce. To maximize his profit, Sneezy should produce the quantity at which the marginal revenue equals marginal cost. By looking at the numbers in Table 13.2, we can see that this happens with a quantity of 900 doses, as shown in the fourth row. In

Figure 13.3, the marginal-revenue curve intersects the marginal-cost curve at point n with a quantity of 900 doses, so that's the quantity that maximizes profit. To get consumers to buy this quantity, the price must be $15 (point m on the demand curve). The average cost of production is $8 per dose (shown by point c), so the profit per dose is $7 ($15 minus $8). Sneezy's profit equals the profit per dose ($7) times the quantity sold (900 doses), or $6,300 per hour.

To show that a quantity of 900 doses maximizes Sneezy's profit, let's see what would happen if he picked some other quantity. Suppose he decided to produce 599 doses per hour at a price just above $18 (just above point h on the demand curve). Could he make more profit by cutting his price by enough to sell one more dose? Sneezy should answer two questions:

▶ What is the extra cost associated with producing dose number 600? As shown by point j on the marginal-cost curve, the marginal cost of the 600th dose is $4.
▶ What is the extra revenue associated with dose number 600? As shown by point i on the marginal-revenue curve, the marginal revenue is $12.

If Sneezy wants to maximize his profit, he should produce the 600th dose because the $12 extra revenue exceeds the $4 extra cost, so his total profit will increase by $8. The same argument applies, with different numbers for marginal revenue and marginal cost, for doses 601, 602, and so on, up to 900 doses. Sneezy should continue to increase the quantity produced as long as the marginal revenue exceeds the marginal cost. The marginal principle is satisfied at point n, with a total of 900 doses.

Why should Sneezy stop at 900 doses? Beyond 900 doses, the marginal revenue from an additional dose will be less than the marginal cost associated with producing it. Although Sneezy could cut his price and sell a larger quantity, an additional dose would add less to revenue than it adds to cost, so his total profit would decrease. As shown in the fifth row in Table 13.2, Sneezy could sell 1,000 doses at a price of $14, but the marginal revenue at this quantity is only $4, while the marginal cost at this quantity is $6.70. Producing the 1,000th dose would decrease Sneezy's profit by $2.70. For any quantity exceeding 900 doses, the marginal revenue is less than the marginal cost, so Sneezy should produce exactly 900 doses.

Let's review what we've learned about how a monopolist picks a quantity and how to compute the monopoly profit. The three-step process is as follows.

1 Find the quantity that satisfies the marginal principle, that is, the quantity at which marginal revenue equals marginal cost. In the drug example shown in Figure 13.3, marginal revenue equals marginal cost at point n, so the monopolist produces 900 doses.
2 Using the demand curve, find the price associated with the monopolist's chosen quantity. In Figure 13.3, the price associated with 900 doses is $15 (point m).
3 Compute the monopolist's profit. The profit per unit sold equals the price minus the average cost, and the total profit equals the profit per unit times the number of units sold. In Figure 13.3, the profit is shown by the shaded rectangle, with height equal to the profit per unit sold and width equal to the number of units sold.

The Social Cost of Monopoly

Why should we as a society be concerned about monopoly? Most people are not surprised to hear that a monopolist uses its market power to charge a relatively high price. If this were the end of the story, a monopolist would simply gain at the expense of consumers. In other words, a monopoly would change how we slice the economic "pie," with a bigger slice for producers and a smaller slice for consumers. As we'll see in this part of the chapter, the social consequences of monopoly go beyond the redistributional effects associated with a different slicing of the pie: A monopoly causes inefficiency and actually reduces the size of the pie, so there is less in total to divide among consumers and producers.

Deadweight Loss from Monopoly

How does a monopoly differ from a perfectly competitive market? To show the difference, let's consider an example of an arthritis drug that could be produced by a monopoly or a perfectly competitive industry. Let's take the long-run perspective—a period of time long enough that a firm is perfectly flexible in its choice of inputs and can enter or leave the market.

Consider the monopoly outcome first. Let's assume that the long-run average cost of producing the arthritis drug is constant at $8 per dose. As we saw in Chapter 11, if average cost is constant, the marginal cost equals average cost. In Panel A of Figure 13.4, the long-run marginal-cost curve is the same as the long-run average-cost curve. Given the demand and marginal-revenue curves in Panel A of Figure 13.4, the monopolist will maximize profit where marginal revenue equals marginal cost (point n), producing 200 doses per hour at a price of $18 per dose. The monopolist's profit is $2,000 per hour —a $10 profit per dose ($18 − $8) times 200 doses.

Consider next the market for the arthritis drug under perfect competition. We're assuming that the arthritis drug industry is a constant-cost industry: Input prices do not change as the industry grows, so the long-run market supply curve is horizontal at the long-run average cost of producing the drug ($8 per dose). In Panel B of Figure

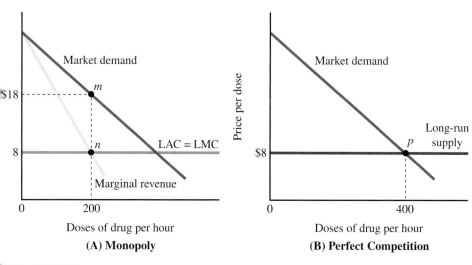

FIGURE 13.4 **Monopoly Versus Perfect Competition: Its Effect on Quantity and Price**

(A) Monopoly The monopolist picks the quantity at which long-run marginal cost equals marginal revenue (200 doses per hour, as shown by point *n*). As shown by point *m* on the demand curve, the price associated with this quantity is $18 per dose.

(B) Perfect Competition The long-run supply curve of a perfectly competitive, constant-cost industry intersects the demand curve at point *p*. The equilibrium price is $8, and the equilibrium quantity is 400 doses per hour.

13.4, the horizontal long-run supply curve intersects the demand curve at point *p*, with an equilibrium price of $8 and an equilibrium quantity of 400 doses per hour. Compared to a monopoly outcome, the perfectly competitive outcome has a lower price ($8 instead of $18 per dose) and a larger quantity (400 doses instead of 200).

To examine the social cost of monopoly power, let's imagine that we start with a perfectly competitive market and then switch to a monopoly. Consumers will be worse off under monopoly, and we can use the concept of consumer surplus to determine just how much worse off they will be. As we saw in Chapter 7, consumer surplus is shown by the area between the demand curve and the horizontal price line. In Figure 13.5, the monopoly price is $18, so the consumer surplus associated with the monopoly is shown by triangle *C*. In contrast, the perfectly competitive price is $8, so the consumer surplus with perfect competition is shown by the larger triangle consisting of triangle *C*, rectangle *R*, and triangle *D*. In other words, a switch from perfect competition to monopoly decreases consumer surplus by the areas *R* and *D*.

► *Rectangle R.* The switch to monopoly increases the price by $10 per dose. Consumers buy 200 doses from the monopolist and pay $10 extra on each of these doses, which results in a loss of $2,000 per hour for consumers.
► *Triangle D.* The switch to monopoly decreases the quantity consumed because the price increases and consumers obey the law of demand. Consumers lose consumer surplus on the doses they would have consumed at the lower price. This loss to consumers is shown by triangle *D* and amounts to $1,000—one-half the base of the triangle (200 doses) times the height of the triangle ($10). The total loss of consumers is the sum of the areas of rectangle *R* and triangle *D*, or $3,000.

FIGURE 13.5

The Deadweight Loss from a Monopoly

A switch from perfect competition to monopoly increases the price from $8 to $18 and decreases the quantity sold from 400 to 200 doses. Consumer surplus decreases by an amount shown by the areas *R* and *D*, while profit increases by the amount shown by rectangle *R*. The net loss to society is shown by triangle *D* (the deadweight loss of monopoly).

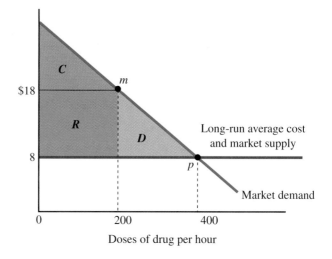

It's clear that consumers lose from monopoly, but what about the monopolist? Under perfect competition, each firm makes zero economic profit. In contrast, the monopolist earns positive economic profit, shown by rectangle *R* in Figure 13.5. The monopolist's profit is $2,000, equal to the quantity produced (200 doses) times the $10 profit per dose (equal to the $18 price minus the $8 average cost). This gain by the monopolist comes at the expense of consumers.

Because only part of the loss experienced by consumers is recovered by the monopolist, there is a net loss from switching to monopoly. Consumers lose rectangle *R* and triangle *D*, but the monopolist gains only rectangle *R*. That leaves triangle *D* as the net loss or **deadweight loss from monopoly**. The word *deadweight* indicates that this loss is not offset by a gain to anyone. In contrast, rectangle *R* is lost by consumers but gained by the monopolist. Consumers lose triangle *D* because in a perfectly competitive market, they would receive some consumer surplus from the 201st through 400th doses, which of course a monopolist would not produce. The lesson is that monopoly is inefficient because, compared to a perfectly competitive market, the monopolist produces less output.

Deadweight loss from monopoly

A measure of the inefficiency from monopoly; with a constant-cost industry, equal to the difference between the consumer-surplus loss from monopoly pricing and the monopoly's profit.

Application: Ending the Monopoly on Internet Registration

For an illustration of the inefficiency of monopoly, we can look at what happens when a government-sanctioned monopoly ends. In February, 1999, the U.S. government announced plans to end the five-year monopoly held by Network Solutions Inc. for registering Internet addresses. Network Solutions had an exclusive government contract to register Web addresses (also known as domain names) ending in .net, .org, .edu, and .com. The company registered almost 2 million names in 1998, collecting $70 for each address and charging an annual renewal fee of $35. The government's plan to introduce competition had some restrictions—an entering firm had to meet strict requirements for security and backup measures and liability insurance. Two new competitors, Register.com and Tucows.com, cut prices to between $10 and $15 per year.[2] In addition, the new firms offered registration periods of up to 10 years (compared to 2 years under the monopoly) and permitted up to 63 characters in each domain name (compared to a limit of 26 characters under the monopoly). Network Solutions, the original monopolist, quickly matched its competitors' lower prices and expanded service options.

Rent Seeking: Using Resources to Get Monopoly Power

Another source of inefficiency from a government-sanctioned monopoly is that firms use resources to acquire monopoly power. Because a monopoly will earn a large profit, firms are willing to spend a great deal of money to persuade the government to erect barriers to entry that grant monopoly power (via licenses, franchises, and tariffs). In Figure 13.5, a firm would be willing to spend up to $2,000 per hour to get a monopoly on the arthritis drug. One way to get monopoly power is to hire lobbyists to persuade legislators and other policymakers to grant monopoly power. This is an example of **rent seeking**.

Rent seeking is inefficient because it uses resources that could be used in other ways. For example, the people employed as lobbyists could instead produce goods and services. In Figure 13.5, if the monopolist spent all its potential profit ($2,000 per hour) on rent-seeking activity, the net loss to society would be areas *R* and *D*, not just area *D*. A classic study of rent seeking by economist Richard Posner found that firms in some industries spent up to 30% of their total revenue to get monopoly power.[3]

At the beginning of this chapter, we saw that Coca-Cola helped a state university to build a new football scoreboard and remodel its student center. Was this an act of generosity? In return for the scoreboard and the remodeled student center, Coca-Cola earned the exclusive right to sell beverages on campus. Like any monopolist, Coca-Cola will use its monopoly power to charge higher prices for beverages, so the cost of

Rent seeking
The process of using governments to obtain economic profit.

Some organizations hire lobbyists to try to persuade legislatures to grant them monopoly power.

the scoreboard and student center actually comes out of the pockets of students. Although Coca-Cola has a monopoly on beverages, some of the profit from the monopoly goes to the university to pay for the scoreboard and the student center.

Monopoly and Public Policy

Given the social costs of monopoly, the government has a number of policies to intervene in markets that are dominated by a single firm or could become a monopoly. We'll examine these policies later in the book. In the case of natural monopoly (a market that can support only a single firm), the government can intervene by regulating the price charged by the natural monopolist. In other markets, the government uses antitrust policies to break up monopolies into smaller companies and prevent corporate mergers that would lead to a monopoly. These policies are designed to promote competition, leading to lower prices and more production.

Patents and Monopoly Power

One source of monopoly power is a government patent that gives a firm the exclusive right to produce a product for 20 years. As we'll see, a patent encourages innovation because the innovators know they will earn monopoly profits on a new product over the period covered by the patent. If the monopoly profits are large enough to offset the substantial research and development costs of a new product, a firm will develop the product and become a monopolist. Granting monopoly power through a patent may be efficient from the social perspective because it may precipitate the development of products that would otherwise not be developed.

Incentives for Innovation

Let's use the arthritis drug to show why a patent encourages innovation. Suppose that Hanna hasn't yet developed the drug, but she believes the potential benefits and costs of developing the drug are as follows:

▶ The economic cost of research and development would be $14 million, including all the opportunity costs of the project.
▶ The estimated annual economic profit from a monopoly would be $2 million (in today's dollars).
▶ Hanna's competitors will need three years to develop and produce their own versions of the drug, so if Hanna isn't protected by a patent, her monopoly will last only three years.

Based on these numbers, Hanna won't develop the drug unless she receives a patent that lasts at least 7 years. That's the length of time she needs to recover her research and development costs of $14 million ($2 million per year times 7 years). If there is no patent and she loses her monopoly in 3 years, she will earn a profit of $6 million, which is less than her research and development costs. On the other hand, with a 20-year patent she will earn $40 million, which is more than enough to recover her costs.

Trade-Offs from Patents

Is the patent for Hanna's drug beneficial from the social perspective? The patent grants monopoly power to Hanna, and she responds by charging a higher price and producing less than the quantity that would be produced in a perfectly competitive market (200 doses per hour instead of 400). From society's perspective, 400 doses would be better than 200 doses, but we don't have that choice. Hanna won't develop the drug unless a patent protects her from competition for at least 7 years. Therefore, society's choice is between 200 doses (the patent and monopoly outcome) and zero doses. Because 200 doses is clearly better than none, the patent is beneficial from society's perspective.

What about a product that would be developed without the protection of a patent? Suppose Marcus could develop a new drug with a research and development project costing $5 million. If Marcus does not have a patent for his new drug, he would earn monopoly profits of $2 million per year for 3 years, a total of $6 million. Because his research and development costs are low relative to the monopoly profit, a 3-year monopoly will generate enough profit to cover his costs, so he will develop the new drug even without a patent. Therefore, if the government issues a 20-year patent, the only effect is to prolong Marcus's monopoly, and that means the patent would be inefficient from society's perspective.

What are the general conclusions about the merits of the patent system? As usual, there are some trade-offs. It is sensible to grant a patent for a product that would otherwise not be developed, but not sensible to grant one for a product that would be developed even without a patent. Unfortunately, no one knows in advance whether a particular product would be developed without a patent, so the government can't be selective in granting patents. Therefore, while the patent system will cause the development of some products that would not occur without patent protection, some patents will merely prolong a firm's monopoly power and generate higher prices.

What happens when a patent expires? New firms will enter the market, and the resulting competition for consumers will decrease prices. The transition from monopoly to competition is not always a smooth one, as you'll see in "A Closer Look: Barriers to Generic Drugs."

TEST Your Understanding

5. True or false: A monopoly is inefficient solely because the monopolist gets a profit at the expense of consumers.
6. Who bears the cost of the scoreboard built by Coca-Cola?
7. How much would you be willing to pay for a monopoly for off-street parking if your average cost is $30 per space per day and you could charge $35 per space per day for 500 spaces?
8. Consider the arthritis example. Will Hanna develop the drug without a patent if she will have a monopoly for five years instead of just three years?

A CLOSER LOOK

Barriers to Generic Drugs

When the patent for a popular pharmaceutical drug expires, other firms introduce generic versions of the drug. The generics are virtually identical to the original branded drug, but they sell at a much lower price. The producers of branded drugs have an incentive to delay the introduction of generic drugs, and sometimes use illegal means to do so.

In 1999, the Federal Trade Commission (FTC) launched a probe of four large pharmaceutical companies to determine whether they unfairly stifled competition from generic producers. The FTC is investigating allegations that the makers of branded drugs made deals with generic suppliers to keep generics off the market. The alleged practices include cash payments and exclusive licenses for new versions of the branded drug.[4]

► Eli Lilly and Company announced a deal under which Sepracor, Inc. would have the exclusive right to sell a purified version of Prozac (the antidepressant with annual sales of $2.8 billion). In effect, this deal would extend Lilly's monopoly over the drug for another 15 years.

► Abbott Laboratories was accused of paying $24 million per year to Ivax Corporation and an undisclosed amount to Novartis AG to delay the launch of their generic versions of Hytrin, Abbott's hypertension drug. Similar allegations of payoffs to generic suppliers have been levied against

Hoechst AG in connection with its annual payment of $40 million to Andrx Corporation, which had produced—but not sold—a generic version of Cardizem, Hoechst's heart medication.

Another tactic used by the producers of branded drugs is to claim that generics are not as good as the branded drug. Dupont has asserted that generic versions of its Coumadin (a blood thinner) are not equivalent to Coumadin, and may pose risks to patients.

Price Discrimination

Up to this point in the book, we've assumed that a firm charges the same price to all its consumers. As we'll see in this part of the chapter, a firm may be able to divide consumers into two or more groups and charge a different price to each group, a practice known as **price discrimination**. For example, airlines offer discount tickets to travelers who are flexible in their departure times, and movie theaters have lower prices for senior citizens.

Although price discrimination is widespread, it is not always possible. A firm has an opportunity for price discrimination if three conditions are met:

Price discrimination
The process under which a firm divides consumers into two or more groups and picks a different price for each group.

1 *Market power.* The firm must have some control over its price, facing a negatively sloped demand curve for its product. Although we will discuss price discrimination by a monopolist, any firm that faces a negatively sloped demand curve can charge different prices to different consumers. In fact, the only type of firm that cannot engage in price discrimination is a perfectly competitive price-taking firm. Such a firm faces a horizontal demand curve, taking the market price as given. For all other types of markets (monopoly, oligopoly, monopolistic competition), price discrimination is possible.

2 *Different consumer groups.* Consumers must differ in their willingness to pay for the product or in their responsiveness to changes in price (as measured by the price elasticity of demand). In addition, the firm must be able to identify different groups of consumers, for example, business travelers versus tourists, students versus nonstudents, seniors versus nonseniors.

3 *Resale is not possible.* It must be impractical for one consumer to resell the product to another consumer. Airlines prohibit consumers from buying and reselling tickets. If they allowed consumers to sell discount tickets to each other, you could go into the business as a ticket broker, buying discount airline tickets one month ahead and then selling them to business travelers one week before the travel date. In general, the possibility of resale causes price discrimination to break down.

One approach to price discrimination is to offer a discount (resulting in a lower price) to some types of consumers. The firm identifies a group of customers who are not willing to pay the regular price and then offers a discount to people in that group. Here are some examples of price discrimination with discounts for certain groups of consumers:

▶ Discounts on airline tickets. Airlines offer discount tickets to travelers who spend Saturday night away from home because they are likely to be tourists, not business travelers. The typical tourist is not willing to pay as much for air travel as the typical business traveler. Airlines also offer discount tickets to people who plan weeks ahead, because tourists plan longer ahead than business travelers.

▶ Discount coupons for groceries and restaurant food. The typical coupon-clipper is not willing to pay as much as the typical consumer.

▶ Manufacturers' rebates for appliances. A person who takes the trouble to mail a rebate form to the manufacturer is not willing to pay as much as the typical consumer.

▶ Senior-citizen discounts on airline tickets, restaurant food, drugs, and entertainment.

▶ Student discounts on movies and concerts.

The only legal restriction on price discrimination is that a firm cannot use it to drive rival firms out of business.

The challenge for a firm is to figure out which groups of consumers should get discounts. Firms can experiment with different prices and look for groups of consumers that are most sensitive to price. In September of 2000, Amazon.com started charging different prices for different types of consumers. For example, consumers who used Netscape's browser paid $65 for the *Planet of the Apes* DVD, while the users of Explorer paid $75 for the same DVD.[5] Prices also varied with the consumer's Internet service provider and the number of previous purchases from Amazon. An Amazon spokeswoman said that the company varied prices in a random fashion, as part of ongoing tests to see how consumers respond to price changes. In other words, it appears that Amazon was assessing the willingness to pay of different types of consumers. In principle, Amazon could use the data collected to develop systems of price discrimination, giving discounts to the most price-sensitive consumers. After widespread protests of the Amazon pricing experiments, the company stopped the practice and issued refunds to about 7,000 consumers who paid relatively high prices.

Application: Senior Discounts in Restaurants

Consider a restaurant whose patrons can be divided into two groups, senior citizens and others. In Figure 13.6, the demand curve for senior citizens is lower than the demand curve for other citizens, reflecting the assumption that the typical senior is willing to pay less than the typical nonsenior, perhaps because senior citizens have lower income and more time to shop for low prices.

Under a price-discrimination plan, the restaurant will simply apply the marginal principle twice, once for seniors and a second time for non-seniors. This is sensible because the two groups have different demands for restaurant meals, so the restaurant should treat them differently. Panel A of Figure 13.6 shows how to pick a price for senior citizens. The marginal principle (marginal revenue = marginal cost) is satisfied at point e, with 280 senior meals per day. Therefore, the appropriate price for seniors is $3 (point d on the senior demand curve). In Panel B of Figure 13.6, the marginal principle is satisfied at point c for nonseniors, with 260 meals per day and a price of $6 per meal.

We know that the application of the marginal principle maximizes profit in each segment of the market. Therefore, charging different prices ($3 for seniors, $6 for non-seniors) maximizes the restaurant's total profit. If the restaurant were instead to charge a single price for both groups, say $5, the profit from each group would be lower, so the restaurant's total profit would be lower too.

Price Discrimination and the Elasticity of Demand

We can use the concept of price elasticity of demand to explain why price discrimination increases the restaurant's profit. From Chapter 5, we know that when demand is elastic ($E_d > 1$), there is a negative relationship between price and total revenue: When

FIGURE 13.6

The Marginal Principle and Price Discrimination

To engage in price discrimination, the firm divides potential customers into two groups, and applies the marginal principle twice, once for each group. Using the marginal principle, the profit-maximizing prices are $6 for nonseniors (point *f*), and $3 for seniors (point *d*).

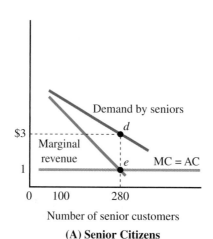

(A) Senior Citizens

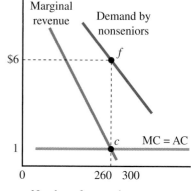

(B) Nonseniors

the price decreases, total revenue (price times quantity sold) increases because the percentage increase in quantity demanded exceeds the percentage decrease in price.

Suppose the restaurant initially has a single price of $5 for both seniors and nonseniors. Compared to other consumers, senior citizens have more elastic demand for restaurant meals, in part because they have lower income and more time to shop for low prices. A price cut for senior citizens brings good news and bad news for the restaurant:

▶ Good news: Demand is highly elastic, so total revenue increases by a large amount.
▶ Bad news: More meals are served, so total cost increases.

If the senior demand for meals is highly elastic (E_d is well above 1.0), the good news will dominate the bad news: The increase in revenue will more than offset the increase in cost. Consequently, a price cut will increase the firm's profit.

For nonseniors, the firm will have an incentive to increase the price above the initial common price of $5. Suppose nonseniors have a mildly elastic demand for meals (E_d is just above 1.0). A price hike for nonseniors brings bad news on the revenue side and good news on the cost side.

▶ Bad news: Demand is mildly elastic, so total revenue decreases by a small amount.
▶ Good news: Fewer meals are served, so total cost decreases.

If the demand by nonseniors is mildly elastic, the good news will dominate the bad news: The savings in production costs will exceed the revenue loss. Consequently, the price hike for nonseniors will increase the firm's profit.

The same logic applies to other cases of price discrimination. A firm will charge a higher price to consumers with relatively inelastic demand. For an example of price discrimination based on weather conditions, read "A Closer Look: Interacting with a Soda Vending Machine on a Hot Day."

A CLOSER LOOK

Interacting with a Soda Vending Machine on a Hot Day

On a hot day, are you willing to pay more for an ice-cold can of Coke? If so, you're the type of consumer Coca-Cola Company had in mind when it developed a high-tech vending machine, complete with heat sensors and microchips, that charges a higher price when the weather is hot.[6] According to Douglas Ivester, the head of Coca-Cola, the desire for a cold drink increases when it is hot, so "it is fair that it should be more expensive. The machine will simply make the process more automatic."

The announcement of the new vending machine led to howls of protest from consumers. In response, Coca-Cola Company said that it would not actually use the new machine, but was "exploring innovative technology and communication systems that can actually improve product availability, promotional activity and even offer consumers an interactive experience when they purchase a soft drink from a vending machine." Based on the reaction to the news of the heat-sensing vending machine, you can imagine the "interactive experience" when a hot and thirsty consumer discovers the higher price for a cold drink on a hot day.

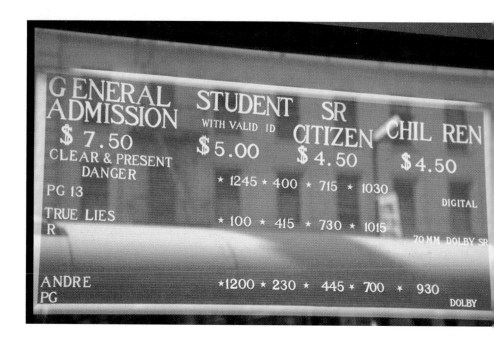

Application: Movie Admission and Popcorn

Recall the chapter-opening question about senior discounts for movies. Why do senior citizens typically pay less to get into movies but pay the same as everyone else for popcorn? A senior discount for movie admission is not an act of generosity by a firm, but part of the firm's pricing strategy designed to increase profit. Senior citizens are typically willing to pay less than other citizens for movies, so a theater divides its consumers into two groups—seniors and others—and offers a discount to seniors. This price discrimination in favor of senior citizens increases the theater's profit. Why don't theaters offer a senior discount for popcorn? Unlike admission to the theater, popcorn can be easily transferred from one customer to another. If senior citizens could buy popcorn at half the regular price, many nonseniors would get seniors to buy popcorn for them, so the theater wouldn't sell as much popcorn at the regular price. Price discrimination for popcorn would not be profitable.

Economic Puzzle

Why Are Hardback Books So Expensive?

Most books are published in two forms—hardback and paperback—the paperback edition being published and available for sale several weeks or months later than the hardback edition. The cost of producing a hardback book is only about 20% higher than the cost of producing the same book as a paperback, but the price of a hardback book is about three times the price of a paperback book. Why?

The key to solving this puzzle is the fact that hardback books are published first, followed by the paperback edition. Booksellers use hardbacks and paperbacks to distinguish between two types of consumers: those who are willing to pay a lot and those who are willing to pay a little. The people who are willing to pay the most are eager to read the book as soon as it comes out, so they pay $18 for a hardback book. The people who are willing to pay less are more patient and are willing to wait a few months for the $6 paperback version. The pricing of hardback and paperback books is another example of price discrimination, with consumers with less elastic demand paying a higher price. ∎

TEST Your Understanding

9. Why is aspirin sold in airports so much more expensive than aspirin sold in grocery stores?
10. Complete the statement with "increase" or "decrease": Suppose a firm starts with a single price and then switches to a price-discrimination scheme. The firm will _____ the price for the group of consumers with the less elastic demand and _____ the group with the more elastic demand.
11. In many lounges and bars, the cover charge for women is less than the charge for men. Why?

Economic Experiment

Price Discrimination

Here is an experiment that shows how a monopolist—a museum—picks different prices for different consumer groups. Some students play the roles of consumers, and others play the roles of museum managers. Here is how the experiment works:

- The instructor picks a small group of students (three to five) to represent the museum. There is a fixed marginal cost of each museum patron (for ticket-takers, guides, cleanup, and other tasks).
- There are 40 consumers (potential museum patrons), and half the consumers are senior citizens with senior-citizen cards. Each consumer receives a number indicating how much he or she is willing to pay for a trip to a museum.

- In each round of the experiment, each museum posts two prices: one for senior citizens and one for nonseniors. Consumers then decide whether to buy a ticket at the relevant posted price.
- A consumer's score in a particular round equals the difference between his or her willingness to pay and the amount actually paid for a museum admission.
- A museum's score equals its profit, equal to its total revenue minus its total cost ($2 times the number of patrons).
- The experiment is run for five rounds. At the end of the experiment, each consumer computes his or her score by adding up the consumer surpluses. The museum's score equals the sum of the profits from the five rounds. ●

USING THE TOOLS

1. Textbook Pricing: Publishers versus Authors

Consider the problem of setting a price for a textbook. The marginal cost of production is constant at $20 per book. The publisher knows from experience that the slope of the demand curve is $0.20 per textbook: Starting with a price of $44, a price cut of $0.20 will increase the quantity demanded by 1 textbook. For example, here are some combinations of price and quantity:

Price per textbook	$44	$40	$36	$32	$30
Quantity of textbooks	80	100	120	140	150

a. What price will the publisher choose?
b. Suppose that the author receives a royalty payment equal to 10% of the total sales revenue from the book. If the author could choose a price, what would it be?
c. Why do the publisher and the author disagree about the price for the book?
d. Design an alternative author-compensation scheme under which the author and the publisher would choose the same price.

2. Payoff for Casino Approval

In 1996, developers interested in building an American Indian casino in Creswell, Oregon, placed a curious announcement in the local newspaper. If local voters approved the casino, the developers promised to give citizens $2 million per year. Given an adult population of about 1,600, each adult in Creswell would receive a cash payment of $1,250 per year.

a. Why did the developers propose this deal? Why aren't similar deals proposed for new clothing stores, music stores, or auto repair shops?
b. If the deal goes through and you moved to Creswell, would you expect to get $1,250 per year?

3. Price Discrimination in a Campus Film Series

You manage a campus film series and charge different prices to students and faculty members. The current prices and numbers of tickets sold are as follows:

	Price	Number of Viewers	Slope of Demand Curve
Students	$3	100	$0.01 per ticket
Faculty	$4	50	$0.10 per ticket

The marginal cost of another viewer is zero. Does the current pricing scheme maximize your total revenue? If not, how should you change your prices?

4. Pricing First-Run Movies and Early Apples

If you see a movie when it first comes out, you pay much more than you would if you waited a month or two for the movie to appear at a second-run movie theater. If you buy apples early in the harvest season, you pay more than you would if you waited until the middle of the harvest season. Are both movies and apples subject to price discrimination?

SUMMARY

In this chapter, we've seen some of the subtleties of monopolies and their pricing policies. Compared to a perfectly competitive market, a monopoly means a higher price, a smaller quantity, and resources wasted when firms seek monopoly power. On the positive side, some of the products we use today might never have been invented without the patent system and the monopoly power it grants. Firms with market power often use price discrimination to increase their profits. Here are the main points of the chapter:

1 Compared to a perfectly competitive market, a market served by a monopolist will have a higher price, a smaller quantity of output, and a deadweight loss to society.

2 Some firms spend money and use resources to acquire monopoly power, a process known as rent seeking.

3 Patents protect innovators from competition, leading to higher prices for new products but greater incentives to develop new products.

4 To engage in price discrimination, a firm divides its customers into two or more groups and charges lower prices to groups with more elastic demand.

5 Price discrimination is not an act of generosity; it's an act of profit maximization.

KEY TERMS

deadweight loss from monopoly, 298
market power, 289
monopoly, 289

natural monopoly, 289
patent, 289

price discrimination, 302
rent seeking, 299

PROBLEMS AND DISCUSSION QUESTIONS

1 Consider a restaurant that charges $10 for all you can eat and has 30 customers at this price. The slope of the demand curve is $0.10 per meal, and the marginal cost of providing a meal is $3. What price will satisfy the marginal principle and maximize the restaurant's profit?

2 The National Park Service grants a single firm the right to sell food and other goods in Yosemite National Park. Discuss the trade-offs associated with this policy.

3 Since 1963, many state governments that outlaw commercial lotteries have introduced state lotteries to raise revenue for state and local governments. In 1994, the net revenue from state lotteries was about $10 billion. Would you expect the state lotteries to have higher or lower paybacks (total prize money divided by the total amount of money collected) than commercial games of chance such as horse racing and slot machines? Explain.

4 Consider the Slappers, a hockey team that plays in an arena with 8,000 seats. The only cost associated with staging a hockey game is a fixed cost of $6,000: The team incurs this cost regardless of how many people attend a game. The demand curve for hockey tickets has a slope of $0.001 per ticket ($1 divided by 1,000 tickets): Each $1 increase in price

decreases the number of tickets sold by 1,000. For example, here are some combinations of price and quantity:

Price per ticket	$4	$5	$6	$7
Quantity of tickets	8,000	7,000	6,000	5,000

The owner's objective is to maximize the profit per hockey game (total revenue minus the $6,000 fixed cost).
  a. What price will maximize profit?
  b. If the owner picks the price that maximizes profit, how many seats in the arena will be empty?
  c. Is it rational to leave some seats empty?

5 The government allows professional sports associations (collections of teams) to restrict the number of teams. How do these barriers to entry affect the price of tickets to professional sporting events and the number of tickets sold? If we eliminated these barriers to entry, what would happen to ticket prices and total attendance at sporting events?

6 Consider a monopolist who owns a natural spring that produces water that, according to nearby residents, has a unique taste and healing properties.

The monopolist has a fixed cost of installing plumbing to tap the water but no marginal cost. The demand curve for the spring water is linear. Depict graphically the monopolist's choice of a price and quantity. At the profit-maximizing quantity, what is the price elasticity of demand? If the spring were owned by an efficiency-minded government, what price would it charge?

7 In the board game Monopoly, when a player gets the third deed for a group of properties (for example, the third orange property: St. James, New York, and Tennessee Avenues), the player doubles the rent charged on each property in the group. Similarly, a player who has a single railroad charges a rent of $25, while a player who has all four railroads charges a rent of $200 for each railroad. Are these rules consistent with the analysis of monopoly in this chapter?

8 Adam Smith predicted that a monopolist would charge "the highest price which can be got." Do you agree?

9 Suppose the drug company Bristol-Meyers-Squibb announces that it will increase the price of Taxol, the cancer-fighting drug, by 10%. According to a consumer advocate, "The price hike will increase Bristol's total revenue from Taxol by 10%." Do you agree? What is the advocate assuming about the price elasticity of demand for Taxol? Is this assumption realistic?

10 Comment on the following statement from a member of a city council: "Several of the merchants in our city offer discounts to our senior citizens. These discounts obviously decrease the merchants' profits, so we should decrease the merchants' taxes to offset their losses on senior-citizen discounts."

11 Consider an airline that initially has a single price ($300) for all consumers. At this price, it has 120 business travelers and 80 tourists. The airline's marginal cost is $100. The slope of the business demand curve is −$2 per traveler, and the slope of the tourist demand curve is −$1 per traveler. Does the single-price policy maximize the airline's profit? If not, how should it change its prices?

12 Why are senior-citizen discounts common for services such as admission to museums and other entertainment events but uncommon for consumer goods such as hardware, appliances, and automobiles?

13 An advertisement for an early-bird sale at a fabric store notes that people who buy fabric between 6:00 and 7:00 A.M. receive a 40% discount, and people who shop between 7:00 and 8:00 A.M. receive a 20% discount. What is the rationale for such a pricing scheme?

14 Car companies offer many options on new cars, including automatic transmissions, CD players, leather trim, and heated seats. The markup on these options (the difference between the price consumers pay and the cost incurred by the car company) is higher for leather trim and CD players than it is for automatic transmissions. Why?

MODEL ANSWERS TO QUESTIONS

Chapter-Opening Questions

1 The bad news is that a monopolist charges a higher price. The good news is that monopoly profits encourage innovation.

2 In response to competition from generic equivalents, the producer of the branded drug usually decreases its price, but the price of the branded drug is still higher than the price of generic drugs.

3 Consumers who are eager to read a book are willing to pay more, so they buy the expensive hardback version because it comes out first. People who are willing to pay less wait for the cheaper paperback version a few months later.

4 If seniors are willing to pay less for movies than others, price discrimination will increase the theater's profits. Because popcorn can easily be purchased for someone else, seniors will pay the same price as everyone else.

Test Your Understanding

1 To sell one more unit, the monopolist must cut the price. Marginal revenue equals the price minus the revenue lost from selling goods at a lower price to the original customers.

2 $MR = \$15 - (80 \text{ units} \times \$0.10 \text{ per unit}) = \$7$.

3 You need the marginal-revenue curve and the marginal-cost curve. The monopolist will pick the quantity at which the two curves intersect.

4 Marginal revenue exceeds marginal cost, so the firm should increase the quantity produced. To increase the quantity, the firm must cut its price.

5 False. The inefficiency (the deadweight social loss) results from a smaller quantity.

6 Campus consumers, who pay more for soft drinks because of the Coca-Cola monopoly.

7 The profit per space is $5 ($35 − $30), so the daily profit is $2,500 ($5 per space × 500 spaces). You are willing to pay up to $2,500 per day for the monopoly.

8 If Hanna's monopoly profit lasts five years, she'll earn a total of $10 million, which is still less than the cost of the research and development project ($14 million). She won't develop the drug.

9 People looking for aspirin in airports usually have a headache or expect one. They are willing to pay more than a headache-free grocery shopper: The airport shopper has a less elastic demand. Firms engage in price discrimination, charging a higher price to the group of consumers with the less elastic demand (airport customers).

10 Increase, decrease.

11 If women are willing to pay less than men for admission into a cocktail lounge or bar (they have a more elastic demand), price discrimination may increase the bar's profit. A discounted cover charge works well because the good purchased (admission) cannot be transferred to men.

NOTES

1. Jeannie Donnelly, "OSU Beverages Will Be Provided Exclusively by Coca-Cola," *The Daily Barometer*, May 27, 1994, p. 1.

2. "Tucows.com to Slash Domain Name Registration Rates," *News Bytes News Network*, January 11, 2000; "Network Solutions Offers 10-Year.Com Registrations," *News Bytes News Network*, January 18, 2000; "Register.com Latest to Offer Long Domain Names," *News Bytes News Network*, January 11, 2000.

3. Richard A. Posner, "The Social Costs of Monopoly and Regulation," *Journal of Political Economy*, vol. 83, 1975, pp. 807–827.

4. Ralph T. King, Jr., "FTC Widens Probe into Generic-Drug Barriers," *Wall Street Journal*, March 9, 1999, p. B8.

5. Linda Rosencrance, "Amazon charging different prices on some DVDs," *Computerworld*, September 5, 2000.

6. Rance Crain, "Is Thirst for Alpha Status behind Coke's High-Tech Talk?" *Advertising Age*, vol. 70, November 22, 1999, p. 26.

Market Entry and Monopolistic Competition

weeter just inherited a lot of money, enough to start her own car-stereo business. Woofer owns the only store in town selling car stereos, and he prices each stereo at $230. Woofer's average cost per stereo is $200, so he earns a profit of $30 on each one he sells. Should Tweeter use her inheritance to open her own car-stereo store? If she does, will she make a profit of $30 per stereo, just like Woofer?

Like entrepreneurs around the world, Tweeter has a difficult decision to make. Before she decides whether or not to enter the car-stereo market, she must predict how much she would be able to charge for her car stereos and how much it would cost her to supply them. Before she enters the market, there is a $30 gap between price and average cost per stereo, but the price is likely to drop when she enters the market and begins competing with Woofer for customers. In addition, Tweeter may have a higher average cost per stereo than Woofer. If the price she can get for her stereos drops below her average cost, Tweeter will lose money and would be better off using her inheritance some other way.

This chapter is about market entry. We explore a firm's decision to enter a market and examine the consequences of entry on prices and profits. Firms are motivated by economic profit and will enter a market as long as there is economic profit to be made. As we'll see, the entry of firms squeezes profit in three ways: The price decreases; the average cost of production increases; and the quantity sold per firm decreases. Eventually, the entry process stops, and we can count the number of firms serving the market. If entry stops at a single firm, we have a natural monopoly, a topic to be covered in Chapter 16. If there are a few firms, we have oligopoly, to be discussed in the next chapter. If many firms enter the market, we have monopolistic competition, the topic of the later part of this chapter.

Monopolistic competition

A market served by many firms selling slightly different products.

Monopolistic competition is a sort of hybrid between monopoly and perfect competition. The label may seem like an oxymoron, similar to "act naturally" and "tight slacks," but it actually conveys the two key features of the market. First, each firm in the market produces a good that is slightly different from the products of other firms, so each firm has a narrowly defined *monopoly*. The products sold by different firms in the market are close substitutes for one another, so there is keen *competition* between firms for consumers. For example, your local grocery store may stock several brands of toothbrushes with different design features. If the price of one brand increases, some loyal customers will continue to buy the brand, but others will switch to different brands that are close substitutes. Some other examples of monopolistic competition are the markets for bread, clothing, restaurant meals, and gasoline. In each case, firms in the market sell products that are close, but not perfect substitutes.

The analysis in this chapter is based on two assumptions. First, we assume there are no barriers to entry: There are no patents or government licensing programs that limit the number of firms. Second, we assume that firms do not act strategically: Each firm acts on its own, taking the actions of other firms as given. This means that firms already in the market do not conspire to fix prices and do not try to prevent other firms from entering the market. In the next chapter, we'll explore several types of strategic behavior in a market with just a few firms, an oligopoly.

The theme of this chapter is that market entry decreases prices and increases the market quantity. Here are some practical questions we answer in the chapter:

1 How did the deregulation of trucking services in the 1980s affect the prices and the profits of trucking firms?
2 If telephone service becomes available on the Internet, what are the implications for traditional providers of phone service?
3 How do restrictions on Internet wine sales affect wine prices?

The Effects of Market Entry

Consider a market served by a single profitable firm, a monopolist. As we saw earlier in the book, a firm in any market can use the marginal principle to decide how much output to produce.

MARGINAL *Principle*

Increase the level of an activity if its marginal benefit exceeds its marginal cost, but reduce the level of the activity if the marginal cost exceeds the marginal benefit. If possible, pick the level of the activity at which the marginal benefit equals the marginal cost.

Consider a firm whose activity is producing toothbrushes. The marginal benefit of producing toothbrushes is the marginal revenue from selling one more brush. In Figure 14.1, if a single firm produces toothbrushes, the firm-specific demand curve is the same as the market demand curve. A firm that is considering entering the toothbrush market must make a long-run decision about what size and type of production facility to build. Therefore, the long-run cost curves—which show production costs for a firm that hasn't committed to a particular production facility—are relevant for the firm's entry decision. In Figure 14.1, the long-run average cost curve is L-shaped, which, as we saw in Chapter 11, is consistent with empirical studies of production costs. If the average cost decreases as output increases (that is, if the average-cost curve is negatively sloped), the marginal cost must be less than the average cost. In Figure 14.1, the marginal-cost curve lies below the negatively sloped average-cost curve.

As we saw in Chapter 13, the monopolist will maximize profit by picking the quantity at which marginal revenue equals marginal cost. In Figure 14.1, this happens at point *n*, with a quantity of 300 toothbrushes. From the market demand curve, we can see that the price associated with this quantity is $2.00. Given an average cost of

FIGURE 14.1

Profit Maximization by a Single Producer
The single toothbrush producer (a monopolist) picks point *n* (where marginal revenue equals marginal cost), supplying 300 toothbrushes per minute at a price of $2.00 (point *m*) and an average cost of $0.90 (point *c*). Economic profit (shown by the shaded rectangle) is $330.

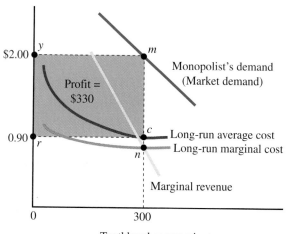

Toothbrushes per minute

$0.90 per toothbrush, the monopolist's profit per unit is $1.10 (equal to $2.00 minus $0.90), so the total profit (shown by the shaded area) is $330. Given the large profits in the toothbrush market, will a second firm enter the market?

Entry Squeezes Profits from Three Sides

Suppose a second firm, producing a nearly identical product, enters the market. When the second firm enters, the firm-specific demand curve for the original firm will shift to the left. At any particular price, some consumers will patronize the new firm, so there will be fewer consumers willing to purchase toothbrushes from the first firm. In other words, the first firm will sell fewer brushes at each price. In Figure 14.2, the firm-specific demand curve for the first firm—the original monopolist—shifts to the left, and profit decreases for three reasons:

1 The market price drops. The marginal principle is satisfied at point x, so the first firm now produces 200 toothbrushes at a price of $1.85 (point e). The competition between the two firms causes the price to drop, from $2.00 to $1.85.

2 The quantity produced by the first firm decreases. The first firm produces only 200 toothbrushes, down from the 300 it produced as a monopolist.

3 The first firm's average cost of production increases. The decrease in the quantity produced causes the firm to move upward along its negatively sloped average-cost curve to a higher average cost per toothbrush (from $0.90 to $1.00).

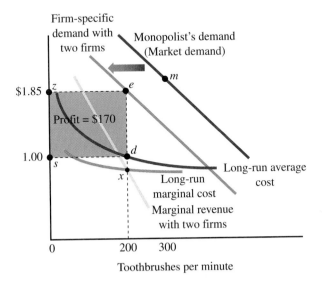

FIGURE 14.2 Entry by Another Firm Decreases Price and Squeezes Profit
The entry of a second toothbrush producer shifts the firm-specific demand curve for the original firm to the left: A smaller quantity is sold at each price. The marginal principle is satisfied at point x, so the firm produces a smaller quantity (200 instead of 300 toothbrushes) at a higher average cost ($1.00 instead of $0.90 per toothbrush) and sells at a lower price ($1.85 instead of $2.00). Economic profit drops to $170.

The combination of a lower price, a higher average cost, and a smaller quantity means that the first firm earns less profit. The profit rectangle (shown by points y, m, c, and r in Figure 14.1 and points z, e, d, and s in Figure 14.2) shrinks because the top of the rectangle (determined by the price) sinks, the bottom of the rectangle (determined by the average cost) rises, and the right side of the rectangle (determined by the quantity) moves to the left. In our example, the profit drops from $330 to $170.

What about the second firm? If we assume that the second firm has access to the same production technology as the first firm and pays the same prices for its inputs, the cost curves for the second firm will be the same as the cost curves for the first firm. If the product of the second firm is nearly identical to the product as the first firm, the firm-specific demand curve for the second firm will be nearly identical to the firm-specific demand curve for the first firm. As an approximation, we can use Figure 14.2 to represent both firms. Each firm produces 200 toothbrushes at an average cost of $1.00 per toothbrush and sells them at a price of $1.85.

Application: Woofer, Tweeter, and the Stereo Business

For an example of the effects of entry on price, cost, and profit, recall Tweeter's hypothetical entry decision described at the beginning of the chapter. Woofer the monopolist initially sells 10 stereos per day at a price of $230 and an average cost of $200 per stereo. Suppose that if Tweeter enters the market, the price will drop to $225 and her average cost will be $205, so she could earn a profit of $20 per stereo. Although Tweeter's entry squeezes profit from both sides—decreasing the market price and increasing the average cost—there is still some profit to be made, so she will enter the market. Of course, other firms may also enter the market, so Tweeter should not count on making a $20 profit per stereo for very long.

Entry Effects in the Real World

Empirical studies of real markets provide overwhelming evidence that entry decreases market prices and firms' profits.[1] In one study of the retail pricing of tires, a market with only two tire stores had a price of $55 per tire, compared to a price of $53 in a market with three stores, $51 with four stores, and $50 with five stores.[2] In other words, the larger the number of stores, the lower the price of tires.

A recent change in public policy shows what happens when the government eliminates artificial barriers to entry. The Motor Carrier Act of 1980 eliminated the government's entry restrictions on the trucking industry, most of which had been in place since the 1930s. New firms entered the trucking market, and freight prices dropped by about 22%.[3] The market value of a firm's trucking license reflects the profit the firm can earn in the market. As a result of increased competition and lower prices from deregulation, the average value of a trucking license dropped from $579,000 in 1977 to less than $15,000 in 1982.[4]

A CLOSER LOOK

Restricting Entry of On-Line Wine Merchants

As electronic commerce has spread to more and more goods and services, there are some products that face online sales restrictions. For example, many states in the U.S. prohibit the direct shipping of wine from winemakers to consumers. In these states, the only way to buy wine directly from a winemaker is to travel to a winery. Other U.S. states require special licenses for consumers buying wine and for firms shipping it.

The Federal Trade Commission (FTC) recently examined the effects of Virginia' direct-shipping ban on the prices and availability of the most popular wines in that state.[5] In Northern Virginia, wine consumers can buy wine from a wide variety of traditional sellers, including specialty wine shops, beverage megastores, and some grocery stores. Yet despite the widespread competition among traditional retailers, online prices were much lower. For wine with prices of $20 or greater, the online prices were between $4.40 and $7.19 lower. All 83 of the most popular wines were available online, but 15 of them were not available at any local store.

Why does the direct-shipping ban persist? Although some people claim that the ban reduces underage drinking, the FTC report debunks this claim. Teenagers looking for alcohol rarely use credit cards to buy expensive wine by the case. It appears that the shipping bans come from the political pressure exerted by traditional merchants, who want to stifle competition. According to Jerry Ellig, an FTC economist who interviewed people about the shipping ban, traditional merchants say that that e-commerce is great in every other market, but not in theirs.

TEST Your Understanding

1. Complete the statement: A firm picks the quantity of output at which
   _____ equals _____.
2. Draw a graph showing the effect of the entry of a second firm on the firm-specific demand curve for the original firm (a monopolist).
3. Complete the statement with "increases" or "decreases": The entry of an additional firm _____ the profit per unit of output because entry _____ the price and _____ the average cost of production.
4. Suppose that when Tweeter enters the car-stereo market, the price drops by $20 and the average cost per unit increases by $15. Is it sensible to enter the market?

Monopolistic Competition

Let's think about how many firms will actually enter a particular market. Under monopolistic competition, many firms enter the market. Here are the characteristics of a market that is subject to monopolistic competition:

1 *Many firms.* Because there are relatively small economies of scale, small firms can produce their products at about the same average cost as large firms. Because even a small firm can cover its costs, the market can support many firms.
2 *A differentiated product.* The firms sell slightly different products. Product differentiation may be in the form of differences in physical characteristics, location, services, and the aura or image associated with the product.
3 *No artificial barriers to entry.* There are no patents or government regulations preventing firms from entering the market.

These characteristics explain the logic behind the label "monopolistic competition." Because of product differentiation, each firm is the sole seller of a narrowly defined good. For example, each firm in the toothbrush market uses a unique design for its toothbrushes, so each is a monopolist for its unique toothbrush. Because the products from different firms are close substitutes, there is keen competition for consumers. When one firm increases its price, many of its consumers will switch to the products of other firms because they are close substitutes. In other words, the demand for the product of a monopolistically competitive firm is very price elastic: An increase in price decreases the quantity demanded by a relatively large amount because consumers can easily switch to another firm selling a similar product.

Product differentiation

A strategy monopolistic firms use to distinguish their products from competitors'.

Let's take a closer look at the notion of **product differentiation**, one of the key features of monopolistic competition. Firms in such a market differentiate their products in several ways:

▶ *Physical characteristics.* A firm can distinguish its products from the products of other firms by offering a different size, color, shape, texture, or taste. For example, toothpastes differ in flavor, color, texture, whitening capability, and alleged ability to fight decay and plaque. Some other examples of goods that are differentiated by their physical characteristics are athletic shoes, dress shirts, appliances, and pens.
▶ *Location.* Some products are differentiated by where they are sold. Some examples are gas stations, music stores, video stores, grocery stores, movie theaters, and ice-cream parlors. In each case, firms sell the same product but at different locations.
▶ *Services.* Some products are distinguished by the services that come with them. For example, some stores provide informative and helpful salespeople, whereas others require consumers to make decisions on their own. Other examples of services that can differentiate products are home delivery (for appliances and pizza) and free technical assistance (for computer hardware and software).
▶ *Aura or image.* Some firms use advertising to make their products stand out from a group of nearly identical products. In this case, product differentiation is a matter of perception rather than reality. Some examples are aspirin, designer jeans, and motor oil.

When Entry Stops: Long-Run Equilibrium

We'll use the toothbrush example to illustrate the features of monopolistic competition. The producers of toothbrushes differentiate their products with respect to color, bristle design, handle size and shape, and durability. We saw earlier that after a second firm enters the toothbrush market, both firms still make a profit. Will a third firm enter this lucrative market? The entry of a third firm will shift the firm-specific demand curve for each firm farther to the left, decreasing the market price, decreasing the quantity produced per firm, and increasing the average cost per toothbrush. If after the third firm enters the market profit is still positive for all three firms, a fourth firm will enter.

Because there are no barriers to entering the toothbrush market, firms will continue to enter the market until each firm makes zero economic profit. Figure 14.3 shows the long-run equilibrium from the perspective of the typical firm in a monopolistically competitive market. As more firms enter the market, the market share of the typical firm decreases, so its firm-specific demand curve shifts to the left to the position shown in Figure 14.3. After the shift, the typical firm satisfies the marginal principle at point *g* by selling 55 brushes per minute at a price of $1.35 (point *h*) and an average cost of $1.35. Since the price equals the typical firm's average cost, the typical firm makes zero economic profit. Each firm's revenue is high enough to cover all its costs—including the opportunity cost of all its inputs—but not enough to cause additional firms to enter the market. In other words, each firm makes just enough money to stay in business.

Trade-Offs Between Average Cost and Variety

We've seen that market entry leads to lower prices and a larger total quantity in the market. At the same time, entry decreases the output per firm and increases the average cost of production. But the higher average cost comes from having more firms in the market, and more firms means more product variety. In a toothbrush market with a dozen firms, consumers can choose from at least a dozen types of differentiated

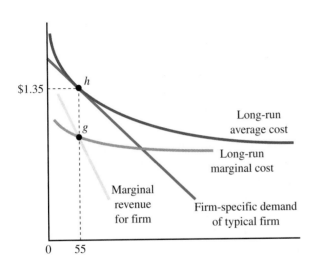

FIGURE 14.3

Long-Run Equilibrium with Monopolistic Competition

In a monopolistically competitive market, new firms will continue to enter the market until economic profit is zero. The typical firm picks the quantity at which its marginal revenue equals its marginal cost (point *g*). Economic profit is zero because the price equals the average cost (shown by point *h*).

toothbrushes. Consumers value variety, and so it is impossible to make a clear-cut case for or against monopolistic competition.

For another example of the trade-offs between average cost and variety, consider restaurant meals. The typical large city has dozens of Italian restaurants, each of which has a slightly different menu and prepares its food in slightly different ways. In this example, the benefit of product differentiation is variety: Consumers can pick from restaurants offering a wide variety of menus and preparation techniques. Although a city with a single Italian restaurant would have a lower average cost of preparing Italian meals—a result of scale economies in producing meals—there would be less variety for restaurant patrons. In addition, a single restaurant would have monopoly power and would charge higher prices.

The same logic applies to articles of clothing such as jeans and shirts, which are differentiated according to their fit, color, design, and durability and the aura associated with the label. There is a trade-off between production cost and variety: If we all wore uniforms, the average cost of producing clothing would be lower, but most people prefer to wear a variety of clothes.

Application: Location and Consumer Travel Costs

Your city probably has several video stores, each of which sells a particular DVD at about the same price. Everything else being equal, you are likely to purchase DVDs from the most convenient store, but if a store across town offers lower prices, you might purchase your DVD there instead. In other words, each video store has a monopoly in its own neighborhood but competes with video stores in the rest of the city.

Figure 14.4 shows the long-run equilibrium in the market for DVDs. Because there are no barriers to entering the market, new video stores will enter the market

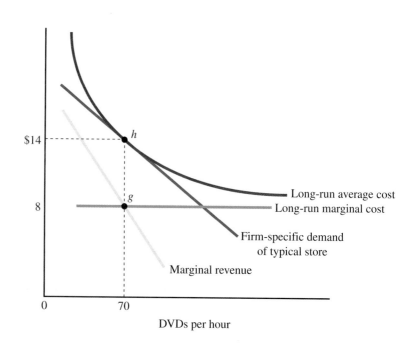

FIGURE 14.4

Long-Run Equilibrium with Spatial Competition: Video Stores
Video stores and other retailers differentiate their products by selling them at different locations. The typical firm chooses the quantity of DVDs at which its marginal revenue equals its marginal cost (point *g*). Economic profit is zero because the price equals average cost (shown by point *h*).

until each store makes zero economic profit. The typical video store satisfies the marginal principle at point g, selling 70 DVDs per hour at a price of $14 per DVD (point h) and an average cost of $14 per DVD. The price equals the store's average cost, so the typical store makes zero economic profit. Each store's revenue is high enough to cover all its costs—including the opportunity cost of all its inputs—but not enough to cause additional stores to enter the market. In other words, the firm makes just enough money to stay in business.

When firms differentiate their products by offering them at more locations, the benefit of having more firms is that consumers travel shorter distances to get the product. If a large metropolitan area had only one video store, the average cost of production would be lower, but prices would be higher and video consumers would spend much more time traveling to buy DVDs.

Lower Profit per Unit Sold?

Economic Puzzle

Consider a local phone company that initially has 1 million customers, each paying $25 per month. The average production cost per customer is $20 per month, so the firm's profit per customer is $5 (equal to $25 – $20), and its total profit is $5 million per month. Suppose a new firm enters the market, providing phone communication over the Internet. The original phone company decided to hold the line on price, maintaining its original $25 price after the new firm entered the market. The firm's objective was to keep the same $5 profit from each of its customers. Although the company expected to lose customers to the new competitor, it still expected to make the same profit per customer. The reality was different from the firm's expectations: Not only did the company lose customers, its profit per customer dropped. Why?

The key to solving this puzzle is to recognize that entry normally squeezes profit in three dimensions: Lower price, smaller quantity, and higher average cost. If a firm maintains its original price after entry, it can get the same revenue per customer, but if there are scale economies in production, the decrease in the number of customers will increase the average cost per customer. That's because the phone company will have fewer customers to share its fixed costs, so the average cost per customer increases. For example, if the company loses 20% of its customers and its average cost increases to $22, its profit per customer will drop to $3. ■

TEST Your Understanding

5. Explain the logic behind the label monopolistic competition. What is monopolistic, and what form does the competition take?
6. List the two conditions required for long-run equilibrium in monopolistic competition.
7. Suppose each new firm entering the car-stereo market in Tweeter's town decreases the price by $5 per stereo and increases the average cost per stereo by $5. How many firms will enter the market?

Economic Experiment

Fixed Costs and Entry

Here is an experiment that shows the implications of entry for prices and profits. Students play the role of entrepreneurs who must decide whether to enter the market for lawn cutting. If they decide to enter the market, they must then decide how much to charge for cutting lawns.

- There are eight potential lawn-cutting firms (each represented by one to three students). There are two sorts of costs for firms: a fixed cost per day and a marginal cost of cutting each lawn. Each firm can cut up to two lawns per day.
- There are 16 potential consumers who are willing to pay different amounts to have their lawns cut.
- The experiment has two stages. In the first stage, each potential firm decides whether to enter the market. The entry decision is sequential: The

instructor will go down the list of potential firms, one at a time, and give each firm the option of entering the market. The entry decisions are public knowledge. When a firm enters the market, it incurs a fixed cost of $14.

- Each firm in the market posts a price for lawn cutting, and consumers shop around and decide whether to purchase lawn care at the posted prices. Each trading period lasts several minutes, and each firm can change its posted price up to three times each period.
- A consumer's score in a trading period equals the difference between the amount that the consumer is willing to pay for lawn care and the price actually paid.
- A firm's score equals its profit, which is its total revenue minus its total cost (the fixed cost of $14 plus the variable cost, equal to $3 per lawn times the number of lawns cut. ●

USING THE TOOLS

We've used the tools of economics to explore the firm's entry decision, showing that a firm will enter a market if the price will exceed the average cost of production. Here are some opportunities to use these tools to do your own economic analysis of markets.

1. How Many Music Stores?

Consider the city of Discville, where zoning laws allow for only one music store. The city's music store sells CDs at a price of $20 with an average cost of $12. Suppose the city eliminates its restrictions on music stores, allowing additional stores to enter the market. According to an expert in the music market, "Each additional music store will decrease the price of CDs by $2 per CD and

increase the average cost of selling CDs by $1 per CD." How many music stores will enter the market?

2. How Many Gas Stations?

Consider a city that initially allowed only one gasoline station to operate. When Jane, a staff member of a local employment agency, heard that the city had decided to relax its restrictions and allow more gasoline stations to operate in the city, she decided to identify some unemployed workers who could apply for the new station manager jobs. She knew that the city's single gas station pumped 20,000 gallons of gasoline per hour and its long-run average-cost curve reaches its minimum point with an output of 5,000 gallons per hour. Therefore, Jane reasoned, the city would soon have a total of four gas stations (20,000 gallons divided by 5,000 gallons per station) and would need three new station managers. You can imagine Jane's surprise when she discovered that there would be five new gas stations instead of three. Why did Jane underestimate the number of new gasoline stations?

3. Opposition to a New Drugstore

The city of Drugville is evaluating a request by a drugstore chain to open a new drugstore in the city. Consider the following statement from a citizen at a public hearing: "The output of the typical drugstore in our city is about 80% of the output at which its long-run average cost is minimized, so the average cost of drugs is higher than the minimum cost. The new drugstore would increase the average cost even further, so all our drugstores—including the new one—would be unprofitable, and consumers would pay higher prices for drugs." Assume that the citizen is correct in stating that the typical drugstore produces at 80% of the output at which average cost is minimized. Do the citizen's conclusions (all stores will be unprofitable and consumers will pay higher prices) follow logically from the facts?

4. Business Licenses

The following table shows how the market price, the quantity per firm, and the average cost of production vary with the number of firms in the market.

Number of Firms	Price	Quantity per Firm	Average Cost
1	$20	38	$ 9
2	$18	35	$10
3	$16	32	$11
4	$14	29	$12
5	$12	26	$13
6	$10	23	$14
7	$ 8	20	$15

A business license allows a firm to operate the business for one day. Each license will be auctioned to the highest bidder. Each firm can buy only one license. The auctioneer will auction up to seven business licenses, and the auction will continue as long as someone bids a positive amount for one of the licenses. How much would you be willing to pay for a license?

SUMMARY

This chapter is about market entry and monopolistic competition. In a monopolistically competitive market, entry continues until each firm in the market makes zero economic profit. Firms can differentiate their products by picking a distinct physical design, level of service, location, or product aura. Here are the main points of the chapter:

1 As firms enter a market, the market price drops and the average cost of production increases because each firm produces less output over which to spread its fixed costs.

2 In a monopolistically competitive market, firms compete for customers by producing differentiated products.

3 In the long-run equilibrium with monopolistic competition, price equals average cost and economic profit is zero.

KEY TERMS

monopolistic competition, 313   product differentiation, 318

PROBLEMS AND DISCUSSION QUESTIONS

1 Consider the city of Discville, where zoning laws limit the number of video arcades to one. The city's only video arcade has a price of $0.50 per game, with an average cost of $0.34 cents per game. Suppose that the city eliminates its restrictions on video arcades, allowing additional firms to enter the market. According to an expert in the arcade market, "Each additional video arcade will decrease the price of games by $0.02 and increase the average cost of providing video games by $0.03." What is the equilibrium number of video arcades?

2 Jean-Luc owns the only wig store in town and sells 30 wigs per week at a price of $70 per wig, with an average cost of $35 per wig. Some experts have reported the following facts on the wig market: (a) The average cost of wig selling increases by $2 for every one-unit decrease in the number of wigs sold. For example, if Jean-Luc sold only 29 wigs per week, his average cost would be $37. (b) The price of wigs decreases by $1 for every one-unit increase in the number of wigs sold; that is, the slope of the market demand curve is $1. Suppose Sinead opens a second wig store in town and sells her wigs at a price of $60 each. If Jean-Luc sells wigs at the same price as Sinead, will the profit per firm be positive or negative?

3 The city of Zoneville currently uses zoning laws to restrict the number of pizzerias. Under a proposed law, the restrictions on pizzerias would be eliminated. Consider the following statement by an expert in the pizza industry: "A pizzeria reaches the horizontal portion of its long-run average-cost curve at an output of about 1,000 pizzas per day. The city's existing pizzeria sells 3,000 pizzas per day. Based on these facts, I predict that if the city eliminates the restrictions on pizzerias, we will soon have three pizzerias (3,000 pizzas divided by 1,000 pizzas per pizzeria)." If we assume that the expert's facts about production costs are correct, is the expert's conclusion (three pizzerias) correct?

4 A prominent feature of Mao's Communist China was the blue uniform worn by all citizens.
   a. Explain the trade-offs associated with the use of uniforms. What were the benefits, and what were the costs?
   b. Suppose people had a choice among 10 types of uniforms rather than being required to wear a single type. Would you expect the benefits of requiring uniforms to decrease by a little or a lot?

5 Consider the "Fixed Costs and Entry" experiment. Suppose the fixed cost per day is $18 per firm and the marginal cost is $4. Each firm can cut up to three lawns per day. The market demand curve is linear, with a vertical intercept of $70 and a slope of −$1 per lawn. Predict the outcome of the experiment, including the equilibrium price, quantity, and number of firms. Explain the reasoning behind your predictions.

6 Under a franchising arrangement, a firm such as McDonald's sells the right to operate retail outlets. Your job is to determine how many franchises McDonald's should sell in Burgerburg.
   a. List the information you need and explain how you would use it.
   b. Provide a numerical example in which McDonald's should sell four franchises.
   c. If you purchase one of the four franchises, would you be better off if McDonald's sold fewer or more franchises? Use your numerical example to defend your answer.

7 Consider a city that issues licenses to pet groomers. Initially, the city does not allow the licenses to be bought and sold. Shortly after an economist joins the city licensing authority, the city decides to allow the licenses to be bought and sold on the open market. Much to the surprise of the licensers, the price of the licenses was zero: No one was willing to pay a positive amount for a pet grooming license.
   a. Explain why the price of grooming licenses was zero.
   b. Illustrate your answer with a supply–demand diagram.

MODEL ANSWERS TO QUESTIONS

Chapter-Opening Questions

1 Because many firms entered the market, prices dropped by about 22% and the profit per license decreased.

2 Market entry reduces a firm's profit by decreasing the price and quantity sold, and increasing the average cost. As explained in "Economic Puzzle: Lower Profit per Unit Sold," if a local phone company doesn't change its price when another firm enters the market, it will still earn less profit per customer because the average cost per customer will increase.

3 Consumers in states with online wine sales pay lower prices and choose from a wider variety of wines.

Test Your Understanding

1 Marginal revenue, marginal cost.

2 The firm-specific's demand curve shifts to the left: At each price, the firm sells a smaller quantity.

3 Decreases, decreases, increases.

4 No. The new price would be $210 per stereo, which would be less than the new average cost of $215 per stereo.

5 Each firm has a monopoly in the sale of its differentiated product, but the firms compete with others that sell similar products.

6 First, each firm picks the profit-maximizing quantity, where $MR = MC$. Second, profit is zero, meaning price = average cost.

7 With four firms in the market, the price is $215 per stereo and the average cost is $215 per stereo, so each firm makes zero economic profit.

NOTES

1. Leonard W. Weiss, ed., *Concentration and Price* (Cambridge, MA: MIT Press, 1989).
2. Timothy F. Bresnahan and Peter C. Reiss, "Entry and Competition in Concentrated Markets," *Journal of Political Economy*, vol. 99, October 1991, pp. 977–1009.
3. Theodore E. Keeler, "Deregulation and Scale Economies in the U.S. Trucking Industry: An Econometric Extension of the Survivor Principle," *Journal of Law and Economics*, vol. 32, October 1989, pp. 229–253.
4. Thomas Gale Moore, "Rail and Truck Reform—The Record So Far," *Regulation*, November/December 1988, pp 57–62.
5. Virgina Postrel, "Laws that Limit Online Shoppers," *New York Times*, July 17, 2003, p. B1; (*www.ftc.gov*).

Oligopoly and Strategic Behavior

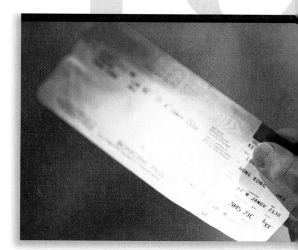

hen Paul Allen, one of the billionaire founders of Microsoft, announced the June 2000 grand opening of the Experience Music Project museum in Seattle, there was an outbreak of messages on the Internet chat site dedicated to Jimi Hendrix, the rock legend. Four Hendrix fanatics who had been exchanging messages on the chat site for several months decided to travel to Seattle to meet each other and celebrate the opening of the museum. They all flew in for the occasion, and the discussion among the Web pals eventually turned to the cost of their airline tickets. Although each of the four traveled about the same distance to Seattle, they paid very different prices for their airline tickets.

▶ Katrina was puzzled and upset: "Brian lives in a city that is served by a single airline, and so do I. But Brian paid $370 and I paid $400." Why is the price lower in Brian's city?

▶ Jason was puzzled and upset, too: "Melissa lives in a city that is served by two airlines, and so do I. But Melissa paid $350 and I paid $400." Why is the price higher in Jason's city?

In this chapter, we explain these puzzling differences in prices. The monopolist in Brian's city could be charging a low price to discourage other firms from entering the market. The two airlines in Jason's city could have agreed upon a price-fixing scheme under which they do not compete with one another but instead collude and charge the same high price.

This is the fourth chapter on decision-making by firms. In earlier chapters, we looked at perfect competition (many firms selling a homogeneous product), monopoly (a market with a single firm), and monopolistic competition (a market with dozens of firms). In this chapter, we look at an **oligopoly**, a market with just a few firms. Given the small number of firms in an oligopoly, the actions of any single firm have a big effect on the other firms, so they act strategically. Before a firm takes a particular action, it considers the possible reactions of its rivals. For example, before Southwest Airlines cuts its fares in an attempt to sell more tickets, it will consider the possible reactions by other airlines. If the rivals maintain their old fares, Southwest's fare cut would increase its sales and profit. But if the rivals match the lower fare, it could be a disaster for Southwest.

We will use some simple concepts from game theory to explore the strategic interactions of oligopolists. **Game theory** is a framework to explore the actions and reactions of interdependent decision-makers. The theory can be applied to the game of chess as well as the decisions of oligopolists. A chess player develops a strategy to win the game, anticipating his opponent's reaction to each of his moves. Similarly, an oligopolist develops a strategy to maximize profit, anticipating the reactions of rival firms. We'll use game theory to discuss three business strategies: price fixing (conspiring to keep prices high), entry deterrence (preventing an additional firm from entering the market), and advertising. Here are some of the practical questions we answer:

Oligopoly
A market served by a few firms.

Game theory
A framework to explore the actions and reactions of interdependent decision-makers.

1 You've probably heard an advertisement that goes like this: "If you buy a stereo from us and find the same stereo for sale somewhere else for a lower price, we'll pay you the difference in price." Does this refund policy lead to higher or lower stereo prices?

2 Suppose two airlines agree to charge the same high price for air travel between two cities. Will this pricing agreement persist?

3 When is it sensible for a monopolist to be passive and let a second firm enter the market?

4 Why might two firms each spend millions of dollars on advertising when both firms would be better off if neither advertised?

What Is an Oligopoly?

Concentration ratio
A measure of the degree of concentration in a market; the four-firm concentration ratio is the percentage of the market output produced by the four largest firms.

In an oligopoly, a few firms have market power—the power to control prices. Economists use **concentration ratios** to measure the degree of concentration in a market. For example, a four-firm concentration ratio is the percentage of total output in a market produced by the four largest firms. In Table 15.1, the four-firm concentration ratio for cigarettes is 99%, indicating that the largest four firms produce 99% of the cigarettes in the United States. According to one rule of thumb, if the four-firm concentration ratio is greater than 40%, the market is considered an oligopoly.

TABLE 15.1			
Concentration Ratios in Selected Manufacturing Industries	Industry	Four-Firm Concentration Ratio (%)	Eight-Firm Concentration Ratio (%)
	Cigarettes	99	Not available
	Primary copper smelting	95	Not available
	Primary battery manufacturing	90	98
	Household laundry equipment	90	Not available
	Breweries	90	94
	Guided missiles and space vehicles	89	99
	Electric lamp bulbs	89	94
	Small arms (weapons)	89	94
	House slippers	85	96
	Military vehicles	85	92
	Breakfast cereals	83	94
	Household refrigerators and freezers	82	97
	Motor vehicles and car bodies	82	92
	Photographic and photocopy equipment	81	85
	Flavoring syrup	81	88
	Soybean processing	80	95
	Chocolate manufacturing from cacao beans	80	93

Source: U.S. Bureau of the Census, 1997 Census of Manufacturing, *Concentration Ratios in Manufacturing* (Washington, DC: U.S. Government Printing Office, 2001).

An alternative measure of market concentration is the Herfindahl-Hirschman Index (HHI). It is calculated by squaring the market share of each firm in the market and then summing the resulting numbers. For example, consider a market with two firms, one with a 60% market share and a second with a 40% share. The HHI for the market is 5,200, computed by adding the square of 60 (3,600) to the square of 40 (1,600). In contrast, for a market with ten firms, each with a 10% market share, the HHI is 1,000 (equal to ten times the square of ten). According to the guidelines established by the U.S. Department of Justice in 1992, a market is "unconcentrated" if the HHI is below 1,000 and "highly concentrated" if the HHI is above 1,800. For example, a market with 5 firms, each with a 20% market share, has a HHI of 2,000 (five times the square of 20), and would be considered highly concentrated.

An oligopoly—a market with just a few firms—occurs for three reasons:

1 *Government barriers to entry.* As we saw in Chapter 13, the government may limit the number of firms in a market by issuing patents or controlling the number of business licenses.
2 *Advertising campaigns.* In some markets, a firm cannot enter a market without a substantial investment in an advertising campaign. For example, the breakfast-cereal oligopoly results from the huge advertising campaigns required to get a foothold in the market. As in the case of economies of scale in production, just a few firms will enter the market.

3 *Economies of scale in production.* As we will see in Chapter 16, a natural monopoly occurs when there are relatively large economies of scale in production, so a single firm produces for the entire market. In some cases, scale economies are not large enough to generate a natural monopoly, but are large enough to generate a natural oligopoly, with a few firms serving the entire market.

Cartel Pricing and the Duopolists' Dilemma

One of the virtues of a market economy is that firms compete with one another for customers, and this leads to lower prices. But in some markets, firms cooperate instead of competing with one another. Eighteenth-century economist Adam Smith recognized the possibility that firms would conspire to raise prices: "People of the same trade seldom meet together, even for merriment and diversion, but the conversation ends in a conspiracy against the public, or in some contrivance to raise prices."[1] We'll see that raising prices is not simply a matter of firms getting together and agreeing on higher prices. An agreement to raise prices is likely to break down unless the firms find some way to punish a firm that violates the agreement.

We'll use a market with two firms—a **duopoly**—to explain the key features of an oligopoly. The basic insights from a duopoly apply to oligopolies with more than two firms. Consider a duopoly in the market for air travel between two hypothetical cities. The two airlines can compete for customers on the basis of price, or they can cooperate and conspire to raise prices. To simplify matters—and to keep the numbers manageable—let's assume that the average cost of providing air travel is constant at $300 per passenger. As shown in Figure 15.1, the average cost is constant, which means that marginal cost equals average cost.

Duopoly
A market with two firms.

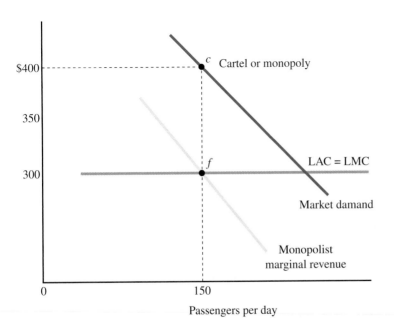

FIGURE 15.1

A Cartel Picks the Monopoly Price
Point *c* shows the outcome with a successful price-fixing arrangement (a cartel). The total output is 150 passengers, and the price is $400 per passenger. Each firm serves 75 passengers at an average cost of $300 per passenger and earns a profit of $7,500 per day.

Cartel

A group of firms that collude explicitly, coordinating their pricing decisions.

Price fixing

An arrangement in which two firms coordinate their pricing decisions.

A **cartel** is a group of firms that collude explicitly, coordinating their pricing deci sions. In our airline example, the two airlines could form a cartel and choose the monopoly price. In Figure 15.1, the firm-specific demand curve for a monopolist is the market demand curve, and the marginal-revenue curve intersects the marginal-cos curve at a quantity of 150 passengers per day (point *f*). If the two airlines act as one they will pick the monopoly price of $400 and split the monopoly output, each serving 75 passengers per day. The average cost per passenger is $300, so each airline earns a daily profit of $7,500 (a profit of $100 per passenger times 75 passengers). An arrange ment under which the two firms act as one, coordinating their pricing decisions, is also known as **price fixing**. As we'll see later in the chapter, cartels and price fixing are ille gal under U.S. antitrust laws.

What would happen if the two firms competed against one another? If they do each firm faces its own demand curve. The firm-specific demand curve is to the left o the market demand curve because consumers are divided between the two firms: At a given price, the number of passengers served by a single firm will be less than the num ber served by both firms together. Panel A in Figure 15.2 shows the perspective of the individual firm. Given the firm-specific demand curve and marginal-revenue curve the marginal principle is satisfied at point *m*, where marginal revenue equals margina cost. This means that each of the two firms in the duopoly serves 100 passengers at a price of $350 (point *n*). Panel B shows the market perspective: The price is $350, and the quantity is 200 passengers (100 passengers for each firm). Given an average cost of $300, each firm earns a profit of $5,000 (the $50 profit per passenger times the 100 pas sengers it carries). In contrast, when the two firms conspire to fix the price as a cartel instead of competing, each earns more ($7,500). As a cartel, they also carry fewer total passengers: 150 passengers versus 200 when they compete.

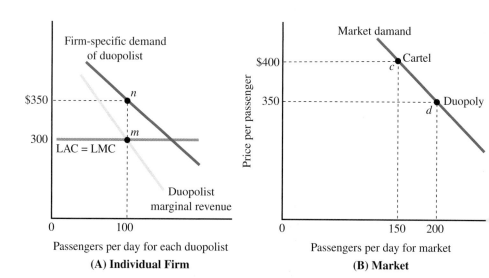

FIGURE 15.2 Competing Duopolists Pick a Lower Price

At the individual firm (duopolist) level, marginal revenue equals marginal cost at point *m*, so each firm serves 100 passengers at a price of $350 per passenger (shown by point *n* in Panel A). Given an average cost of $300 per passenger, each duopolist earns a profit of $5,000 (the $50 profit per passenger times 100 passengers). At the market level (Panel B), the duopoly outcome has a quantity of 200 passengers (100 passengers per firm) at a price of $350 per passenger (point *d*).

Price Fixing and the Game Tree

Clearly, each firm would earn more profit under a price-fixing agreement, but will the firms reach such an agreement? We can answer this question with the help of a **game tree**, a graphical tool that provides a visual representation of the consequences of alternative strategies. Each firm must choose a price for airline tickets, either a high price (the cartel price of $400) or a low price (the duopoly price of $350). Each firm can use the game tree to develop a pricing strategy, knowing that the other firm is also choosing a price.

Figure 15.3 shows the game tree for the price-fixing game. Let's call the managers of the airlines Jack and Jill. The game tree has three components:

> - The squares are decision nodes. For each square, there is a player (Jack or Jill) and a list of the player's options. For example, the game starts at square **X**, where Jill has two options: the high price or the low price.
> - The arrows show the path of the game from left to right. Jill chooses her price first, so we move from square **X** to one of Jack's decision nodes, either square **Y** or square **Z**. If Jill chooses the high price, we move from square **X** to square **Y**. Once we reach one of Jack's decision nodes, he chooses a price (high or low), and then we move to one of the rectangles. For example, if Jack chooses the high price too, we move from square **Y** to rectangle 1.
> - The rectangles show the profits for the two firms. When we reach a rectangle, the game is over, and the players receive the profits shown in the rectangle. There is a profit rectangle for each of the four possible outcomes of the price-fixing game.

We've already computed the profits for two profit rectangles. The first rectangle shows what happens when each firm chooses the high price. This is the cartel or price-fixing outcome, with each firm earning $7,500. The fourth rectangle shows what happens when each firm chooses the low price. This is the duopoly outcome, with each firm earning $5,000.

Game tree
A graphical representation of the consequences of different strategies.

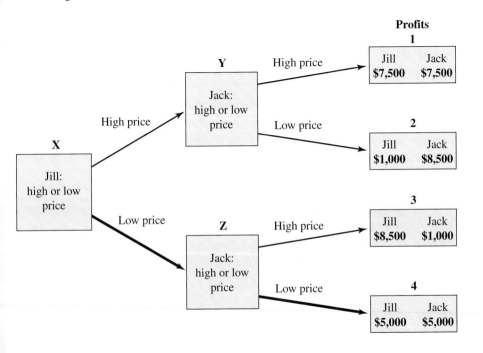

Profits

FIGURE 15.3

Game Tree for a Price-Fixing Game
The path of the game is square **X** to square **Z** to rectangle 4: Each firm picks the low price and earns a profit of $5,000. The duopolists' dilemma is that each firm would make more profit if both picked the high price, but neither firm will do so, fearing that the other firm would pick the low price.

TABLE 15.2
Duopolists' Profits When They Choose Different Prices

	Jill: Low Price	Jack: High Price
Price	$350	$400
Quantity	170	10
Average cost	$300	$300
Profit per passenger	$50	$100
Profit	$8,500	$1,000

What would happen if the two firms chose different prices? If Jill chooses the low price and Jack chooses the high price, Jill will capture a large share of the market and gain at Jack's expense. In the first column of Table 15.2, Jill serves 170 passengers at a price of $350 each and an average cost of $300 per passenger, so her profit is $8,500 (a $50 profit per passenger times 170 passengers). In the second column, Jack serves only 10 passengers at a price of $400 each and the same average cost, so his profit is $1,000 (a $100 profit per passenger times 10 passengers). This is shown by rectangle 3 in Figure 15.3: The path of the game is square **X** to square **Z** to rectangle 3. The other underpricing outcome is shown by rectangle 2. In this case, Jill chooses the high price, and Jack chooses the low price, so Jack gains at Jill's expense. The roles are reversed and so are the numbers in the profit rectangle.

Predicting the Outcome of the Price-Fixing Game

We can predict the outcome of the price-fixing game by a process of elimination. We'll eliminate the rectangles that would require one or both of the firms to act irrationally, leaving us with the rectangle showing the outcome of the game.

▶ If Jill chooses the high price, we'll move along the upper branches of the tree and eventually reach rectangle 1 or 2, depending on what Jack does. Although Jill would like Jack to choose the high price too, this would be irrational for Jack, because he can make more profit by choosing the low price. Therefore, we can eliminate rectangle 1.
▶ If Jill chooses the low price, we'll move along the lower branches of the tree, eventually reaching rectangle 3 or 4, depending on Jack's choice. Jack won't choose the high price because then Jill would gain at his expense. Therefore, we can eliminate rectangle 3.

We've eliminated the two rectangles involving a high price for Jack (1 and 3). This means that the low price is a **dominant strategy** for Jack: Regardless of what Jill does, Jack's best choice is the low price.

There are now two rectangles left (2 and 4), and Jill's action will determine which rectangle we'll reach. Jill knows that Jack will choose the low price regardless of what she does, so she can either choose a high price and allow Jack to gain at her expense (rectangle 2) or choose the low price, too (rectangle 4). It would be irrational for Jill to allow herself to be underpriced, so we can eliminate rectangle 2.

Dominant strategy

An action that is the best choice for a player, no matter what an opponent does.

The remaining rectangle shows the outcome of the game: Each player chooses the low price. The thick arrows show the path of the game, from square **X** to square **Z** to rectangle 4.

Both firms will be unhappy with this outcome because each could earn a higher profit with rectangle 1. To get there, however, each firm must choose the high price. The **duopolists' dilemma** is that although both firms would be better off if they both chose the high price, each firm chooses the low price. There is a big payoff from underpricing the other firm and a big penalty from being underpriced, so both firms will pick the low price. As we'll see later, the firms can avoid this dilemma, but only if they find some way to prevent underpricing. For a description of how vitamin producers succeeded in an international price-fixing scheme, read "A Closer Look: Vitamin, Inc. Gets Busted."

Duopolists' dilemma

A situation in which both firms in a market would be better off if both chose the high price but each chooses the low price.

A CLOSER LOOK

Vitamin, Inc. Gets Busted

In April 2000, the U.S. Department of Justice announced that four former executives of drug companies pled guilty to conspiring to fix the prices of bulk vitamins worldwide. It was the largest price-fixing case in history. The leading companies involved in the illegal cartel were Hoffman-La Roche (with 60% of the U.S. vitamin market), BASF AG (with 28% market share), and Rhone-Poulenc (with 7% market share). They were joined by other vitamin producers from Japan, Switzerland, and Canada. The announcement brought the number of Swiss and German executives imprisoned for the case to six, with fines for the individual executives and their companies totaling $1 billion.[2]

For almost a decade, these executives conspired to stifle competition around the globe, by fixing prices on vitamins A, B2, B5, C, E, and beta carotene. The executives called their group "Vitamin, Inc." and met regularly in hotel rooms to carve up the market. Market shares for each region were specified down to a half percentage point, and prices for each vitamin were agreed upon down to the penny. For vitamin "premixes" (used for livestock feed and human food such as breakfast cereals), the executives rigged the bidding process for contracts, specifying a price and designating a "winner" for each contract. To help prevent cheating, they had "budget meetings" to check each other's data on sales

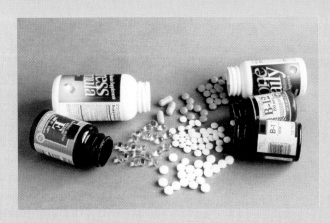

and market shares. The cartel managed to boost the prices of vitamins, with markups averaging about 20%, or even more at the high-end of the vitamin price range. For example, the price of vitamin A nearly doubled, from about $12 per pound to $20.

LaRoche ultimately paid a fine of $500 million, about half of its annual revenue from its vitamin business in the United States. BASF paid a fine of $225 million. Rhone-Poulenc broke ranks early in the investigation, and by cooperating with Justice investigators, avoided any fines. A group of Japanese companies paid a total of $137 million.

Representing a Game with a Payoff Matrix

Table 15.3 shows an alternative way to represent a price-fixing game. The table is a payoff matrix, which shows the payoffs to the players for different combinations of actions (price choices). The payoff matrix is used to represent a **simultaneous decision-making game**, defined as games in which two players make their choices simultaneously. In contrast, a **sequential decision-making game** is typically represented by game trees like the one in Figure 15.3. So if we change the price-fixing game to make the firms' decisions simultaneous rather than sequential, we can use the payoff matrix.

Each cell of the payoff matrix shows the payoffs to the two players for a particular pair of actions, one for each player. In each cell of the matrix, the payoff to Jill (the name that appears on the left side of the matrix) is listed first, followed by the payoff to Jack (the name above the matrix). If both firms pick the low price, each makes a profit of $5,000. In contrast, if both pick the high price, each earns $7,500. If one firm picks the low price and the other picks the high price, the low-price firm earns $8,500 and the high-price firm earns only $1,000.

We can use the payoff matrix to predict the outcome of the price-fixing game. Jill doesn't know whether Jack will pick the low price or the high price. If he picks the low price, Jill's best response is the low price because she can earn $5,000, compared to $1,000 if she picks the high price. If Jack picks the high price, Jill's best action is still the low price, which earns her $8,500 compared to $7,500 for the high price. In other words, the low price is the dominant strategy for Jill. Knowing this, Jack will pick the low price too. Therefore, the outcome is the same as with the game-tree approach: Both firms will pick the low price.

The Prisoners' Dilemma

The duopolists' dilemma is similar to the classic prisoners' dilemma. Consider two people, Bonnie and Clyde, who have been accused of committing a crime. The police give each person an opportunity to confess to the crime, with Bonnie speaking first and Clyde second. The traditional version of the story involves a simultaneous decision-making game: The two are put in separate rooms, and each makes a choice without the other person knowing what that choice is. The results are the same with simultaneous or sequential decision-making. We'll use the sequential approach—the approach we used with Jack and Jill—to emphasize the similarities to the price-fixing scenario.

The police confront Bonnie and Clyde with the game tree shown in Figure 15.4. If both confess, each gets 5 years in prison (rectangle 4). If neither confesses, the police can convict them on a lesser charge, and each gets 2 years (rectangle 1). If only one confesses

---

Simultaneous decision-making game

A game in which each player makes a choice without the other person knowing what that choice is.

Sequential decision-making game

A game in which one player makes a choice before the other.

TABLE 15.3

Payoff Matrix for Simultaneous Game

		Jack			
		Low Price		**High Price**	
Jill	**Low Price**	$5,000	$5,000	$8,500	$1,000
	High Price	$1,000	$8,500	$7,500	$7,500

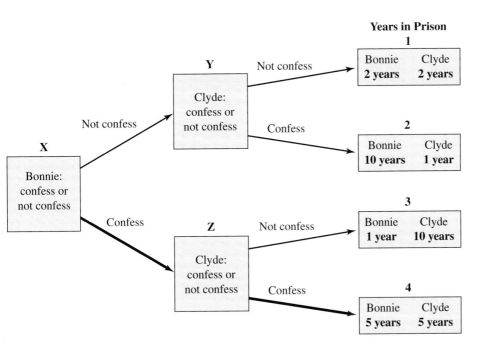

Years in Prison

FIGURE 15.4

Game Tree for a Prisoners' Dilemma
The path of the game is square **X** to square **Z** to rectangle 4: Each person confesses and gets 5 years in prison. The prisoners' dilemma is that each person would be better off if neither confessed, but both actually confess.

and implicates the other, the confessor is rewarded with a 1-year prison sentence and the other gets 10 years. Clyde, who goes second, will confess no matter what Bonnie does:

▶ If she does not confess: He will choose rectangle 2 over rectangle 1, getting 1 year in prison instead of 2.
▶ If she confesses: He will choose rectangle 4 over rectangle 3, getting 5 years in prison instead of 10.

Bonnie can predict Clyde's choices, so she realizes that her choice is between rectangle 2 and rectangle 4, and confessing gives her 5 years instead of 10. Although both criminals would be better off if they both kept quiet, they implicate each other because the police reward them for doing so. There is an incentive for squealing, just as there is an incentive for one duopolist to underprice the other.

TEST Your Understanding

1. Complete the statement with *d* or *c*: Rectangle 1 in Figure 15.3 is associated with point _____ in Figure 15.2, while rectangle 4 is associated with point _____.
2. Use Figure 15.3 to complete the statement: If each firm picks the low price, the path of the game is square _____ to square _____ to rectangle _____, and each firm earns a profit of _____.
3. Suppose Jack promises that if Jill chooses the high price, he will too. If Jack's objective is to maximize his profit, what will he do after Jill chooses the high price? If you were Jill, would you believe Jack's promises to choose the high price? Which price would you choose?

Overcoming the Duopolists' Dilemma

The duopolists' dilemma occurs because the two firms are unable to coordinate their pricing decisions and act as one. Each firm has an incentive to underprice the other firm because the low-price firm will capture a larger share of the market and earn a larger profit. There are two ways to avoid this dilemma: guaranteed price matching and playing the pricing game repeatedly, with a system of retaliation for underpricing.

Guaranteed Price Matching

The duopolists' dilemma occurs because of the possibility of underpricing. There is a big payoff from underpricing the other firm, and a big penalty from being under-priced by the other firm. This concern about underpricing causes both firms to pick the low price. As we'll see, guaranteed price matching eliminates the possibility of underpricing, and makes price fixing possible.

Guaranteed price-matching strategy

A strategy where a firm guarantees it will match a lower price by a competitor; also known as a "meet-the-competition" policy.

To eliminate the incentive for underpricing, one firm can guarantee that it will match its competitor's price. Suppose Jill places the following advertisement in the local newspaper: "If you buy a plane ticket from me and then discover that Jack offers the same trip at a lower price, I will pay you the difference between my price and Jack's price. If I charge you $400 and Jack's price is only $350, I will pay you $50." This pricing strategy is known as **guaranteed price matching**: Jill guarantees that she will match Jack's price. It is also known as a "meet-the-competition" policy. Jill's promise to match Jack's lower price is credible because she announces it in the newspaper.

How will Jack respond to Jill's price-matching scheme? In effect, Jill tentatively chooses the high price but will instantly switch to the low price if Jack picks the low price. After a $50 refund, Jill's price will be $350, the same as Jack's. Jack will respond to Jill's price-matching scheme in one of two ways:

▶ *Choose the high price.* If Jack matches Jill's announced high price, each firm will earn a profit of $7,500 (rectangle 1 in the game tree in Figure 15.3).
▶ *Choose the low price.* If Jack tries to underprice Jill, she will switch to the low price, and each will earn a profit of only $5,000 (rectangle 4 in the game tree).

Jack's decision is easy: A pair of high prices is more profitable than a pair of low prices, so he will choose the high price, just like Jill.

Jill's price-matching scheme eliminates the duopolists' dilemma and makes cartel pricing possible, even without creating a formal cartel. The duopolists' dilemma disappears because underpricing is no longer possible. The motto of the price-matching scheme is "High for one means high for all, and low for one means low for all." It would be irrational for Jack to choose the low price because he knows that Jill would match it. Once the possibility of underpricing has been eliminated, the duopoly will be replaced by an informal cartel, each firm charging the price that would be charged by a monopolist.

To most people, the notion that guaranteed price matching can lead to higher prices is surprising. After all, Jill promises to give refunds if her price exceeds Jack's, so we might expect her to keep her price low to avoid giving out a lot of refunds. In fact, she doesn't have to worry about refunds because she knows that Jack will also choose the high price. In other words, Jill's promise to issue refunds is an empty promise. Although consumers might think Jill's refund policy will protect them from high prices, the policy guarantees that they will pay the high price.

Repeated Pricing Games with Retaliation for Underpricing

Up to this point, we've assumed that the price-fixing game is played only once. Each firm chooses a price and sticks with that price for the lifetime of the firm. What happens when two firms play the price-fixing game repeatedly, setting prices over an extended period of time? We'll see that repetition makes price fixing more likely because firms can punish a firm that cheats on a price-fixing agreement, whether it's formal or informal.

Firms use several strategies to maintain a price-fixing agreement. We explore three, all of which involve punishing a firm that underprices the other firm. Continuing our airline example, suppose Jack and Jill choose their prices at the beginning of each month. Jill chooses the cartel price ($400) for the first month and then waits to see what price Jack chooses. Jill could use one of the following strategies to punish Jack if he underprices her:

1 *A duopoly pricing strategy.* Jill continues to choose the high price until Jack underprices her. Once that happens, she chooses the duopoly price ($350 in our example) for the remaining lifetime of her firm. Jill allows herself to be underpriced only once. Then she abandons the idea of cartel pricing and accepts the duopoly outcome, which is less profitable than the cartel outcome but more profitable than being underpriced by the other firm.

2 *A grim-trigger strategy.* When Jack underprices Jill, she responds by dropping her price to a level at which each firm will make zero economic profit forever. This is called the **grim-trigger strategy** because grim consequences are triggered by Jack's underpricing.

3 *A tit-for-tat strategy.* Starting in the second month. Jill chooses whatever price Jack chose the preceding month. As long as Jack chooses the cartel price, the cartel arrangement will persist, but if Jack underprices Jill, the cartel will break down. In Figure 15.5, Jack underprices Jill in the second month, so Jill chooses the low price for the third month, resulting in the duopoly outcome. To restore the cartel outcome. Jack must eventually choose the high price, allowing Jill to underprice him for one month. This happens in the fourth month. In the fifth month, the cartel is restored. So, although Jack can gain at Jill's expense in the second month, if he wants to restore cartel pricing, he must allow her to gain at his expense during the fourth month. This is called a **tit-for-tat strategy**. You do exactly what your opponent did to you in the last round to encourage them to cooperate rather than compete. Several studies have shown that a tit-for-tat is the most effective strategy to promote cooperation.

Grim-trigger strategy
A strategy where a firm responds to underpricing by choosing a price so low that each firm makes zero economic profit.

Tit-for-tat
A strategy where one firm chooses whatever price the other firm chose in the preceding period.

A Tit-for-Tat Pricing Strategy
Under a tit-for-tat retaliation strategy, the leading firm (Jill, the square) chooses whatever price the other firm (Jack, the circle) chose the preceding month.

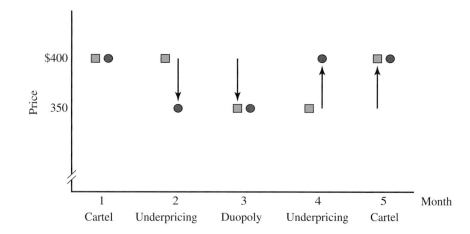

These three pricing schemes promote cartel pricing by penalizing the underpricer. To decide whether to underprice Jill, Jack must weigh the short-term benefit against the long-term cost:

▶ The short-term benefit is the increase in profit in the current period. If Jack underprices Jill, he can increase his profit from $7,500 (Jack's profit if both firms pick the high price) to $8,500 (Jack's profit if he chooses the low price and Jill chooses the high price). Therefore, the short-term benefit of underpricing is $1.000.
▶ The long-term cost is the loss of profit in later periods. Jill will respond to Jack's underpricing by cutting her price, and this decreases Jack's profit. For example, if Jill retaliates with the duopoly price, Jack will lose the opportunity for a monthly profit of $5,000 for the remaining lifetime of his firm.

If the two firms expect to share the market for a long time, the long-term cost of underpricing will exceed the short-term benefit, so underpricing is less likely. The threat of punishment makes it easier to resist the temptation to cheat on the cartel.

Application: Different Airline Ticket Prices

At the beginning of this chapter, we saw that Jason paid more for his plane ticket than Melissa did for hers, even though both live in cities that are served by two airlines. The two airlines in Melissa's city may suffer from the duopolists' dilemma: Although they would prefer the high price ($400), they both choose the low price ($350). In contrast, an airline in Jason's city could use a guaranteed price-matching scheme, promising to refund the difference between its price and the price of the other airline. The price-matching scheme eliminates underpricing, so each airline will choose the high price ($400). Jason pays a higher price because the price-matching scheme allows the airline in his city to engage in cartel pricing (price fixing).

Price Fixing and the Law

Under the Sherman Antitrust Act of 1890 and subsequent legislation, explicit price fixing is illegal. It is illegal for firms to discuss their pricing strategies or their methods of punishing a firm that underprices other firms. In one of the early price-fixing cases (Addyston Pipe, 1899), six manufacturers of cast-iron pipe met to fix prices in certain geographical areas. Several months after the Supreme Court ruled that their cartel pricing was illegal, the firms merged into a single firm, so instead of acting like a monopolist, which was illegal, they became a monopolist. Here are some other examples of price fixing:

1 *Electric generators (1961).* General Electric and Westinghouse were convicted of fixing prices for electrical generators, resulting in fines of over $2 million and imprisonment or probation for 30 corporate executives.

2 *Soft drinks (1986).* The Coca-Cola Bottling Company of North Carolina paid a fine and issued discount coupons to its customers to settle a case involving a conspiracy to fix the prices of soft drinks.

3 *Infant formula (1993).* The three major U.S. producers of infant formula— Abbott Labs, Mead Johnson, and American Home Products—which together served 95% of the market, paid a total of $200 million to wholesalers and retailers to settle lawsuits claiming that they had conspired to fix prices.

4 *Plastic wrap in Japan (1993)* . A Tokyo court found eight Japanese companies guilty of conspiring to fix the prices of the plastic film used for wrapping food. The companies received fines of $54,000 to $73,000, and 15 executives were given suspended jail sentences of six months to one year.

5 *Airline pricing (1994).* In an antitrust lawsuit filed in 1992, the U.S. Justice Department alleged that the nation's airlines used advanced price listing to fix airline ticket prices. Before an airline increased its price, it could post a "suggested" price on a central computer and see whether the other airlines would increase their prices. By March 1994, eight of the nation's largest airlines (United Airlines, USAir Group, American Airlines, Delta Airlines, Northwest Airlines, Continental Airlines, Trans-World Airlines, and Alaska Air) had agreed to drop this practice. According to Ann Bingaman of the antitrust division of the Justice Department, advance price listing allowed airlines to fix prices at an artificially high level, costing consumers an extra $1.9 billion for airline tickets.[3]

6 *Steel beam pricing in Europe (1994).* The European Union Commission fined 16 steel companies a total of 104 million euros ($116 million) for conspiring to fix the price of steel beams.

7 *Carton board pricing in Europe (1994).* The European Union Commission fined 19 manufacturers of carton board a total of 132 million euros ($165 million) for operating a cartel that fixed prices at secret meetings in luxury Zurich hotels.

8 *Food additives (1996).* An employee of Archer Daniels Midland (ADM), a huge food company that likes to call itself "the supermarket to the world," provided audio and videotapes of ADM executives scheming to fix prices. ADM pleaded guilty to the charges of price fixing and was fined $100 million.

9   *Sugar in the United Kingdom (1998).* Four sugar producers that together controlled 90% of the market (British Sugar, Tate & Lyle, Napier Brown, and James Budgett) conspired to fix prices for industrial and retail markets and were fined a total of 50.2 million euros by the European Commission.

10   *Greek and Italian ferry services (1998).* Seven companies offering ferry service between Greece and Italy met regularly to coordinate prices for passengers and vehicles. The fine from the European Commission was relatively light (9.12 million euros) because the cartel had a "fairly limited impact on the market."

11   *Music distribution (2000).* In exchange for subsidies for advertising, music retailers agreed to adhere to the minimum advertised prices (MAP) specified by the distributors. Any retailer that advertised a CD for less than the MAP would lose all of its "cooperative advertising" funds from the distributor. In May 2000, the Federal Trade Commission reached an agreement with music distributors to end their MAP policy. The FTC estimated that the MAP policy imposed an annual cost of $160 million on U.S. music consumers.[4]

Alternative Models of Oligopoly Pricing

Price leadership

An implicit agreement under which firms in a market choose a price leader, observe that firm's price, and match it.

We will discuss two alternative models of oligopoly pricing. Under the model of **price leadership**, one of the oligopolists plays the role of price leader, setting a price with the expectation that the other firms will match the leader's price. Under the second model, firms in an oligopoly go along when one firm increases its price but don't follow a firm when it cuts its price.

Price Leadership

Because explicit price fixing is illegal, firms often rely on implicit pricing agreements to fix prices at the monopoly level. Under a price leadership arrangement, one firm becomes recognized as the price leader. The other firms in the market observe the price chosen by the leader, and then match it. Such an agreement allows firms to cooperate without actually discussing their pricing strategies.

The problem with an implicit pricing agreement is that it relies on indirect signals that are often garbled and misinterpreted. Suppose that two firms have cooperated for several years, both sticking to the cartel price. When one firm suddenly drops its price, the other firm could interpret the price cut in one of two ways:

▶ *A change in market conditions.* Perhaps the first firm has observed a change in demand or production cost and decides that both firms would benefit from a lower price.
▶ *Underpricing.* Perhaps the first firm is trying to increase its market share and profit at the expense of the second firm.

The first interpretation would probably cause the second firm to match the lower price of the first firm, and price fixing would continue at the lower price. In contrast, the second interpretation could trigger a price war, destroying the price-fixing agreement. Because firms often pull the grim trigger when a more moderate response would be appropriate, implicit pricing agreements are difficult to maintain.

The Kinked Demand Curve Model

The **kinked demand curve model** of oligopoly gets its name from its assumptions about how firms in an oligopoly respond when one firm changes its price. Figure 15.6 shows the demand curve facing Kirk, one of three firms in the oligopoly. Suppose each of the three firms starts out with a price of $6, and Kirk sells 30 units of output (point k).

- If Kirk increases his price, the other two firms will not change their prices. Kirk will have a higher price than the other firms, so his quantity will decrease by a large amount (from 30 to 10 units).
- If Kirk decreases his price, the other firms will decrease their prices. Kirk will have the same (lower) price as other firms, so his quantity will increase by a small amount (from 30 to 33 units).

These assumptions mean that the demand curve of the typical firm has a kink at the prevailing price: It is relatively flat (price-elastic) for higher prices because other firms won't match a higher price but relatively steep (price-inelastic) for lower prices because other firms will match a lower price. Once a price has been established, it will tend to persist because there is a large penalty for a firm that picks a higher price (a large decrease in the quantity sold) and a small benefit for a firm that picks a lower price (a small increase in the quantity sold).

The model of kinked demand is really a model of pessimism. Each firm assumes the worst about how its fellow oligopolists will respond to a change in price: The other firms will not go along with a higher price, but will match a lower price. Although this model may have some intuitive appeal, there is no evidence that firms really act this way. Starting in 1947, various studies of oligopolies have failed to find compelling evidence to support the kinked demand model of oligopoly.[5]

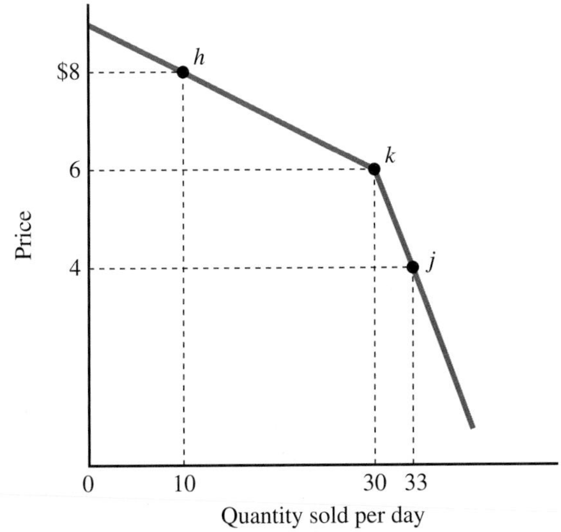

Kinked demand curve model

A model under which firms in an oligopoly match price reductions by other firms but do not match price increases by other firms.

FIGURE 15.6

The Kinked Demand Curve Model

Under the kinked demand model, when one firm increases its price, the other firms don't change their prices, so the quantity sold by the firm will decrease by a large amount. But when one firm decreases its price, the other firms cut their prices too, so the quantity sold by the firm will increase by a small amount.

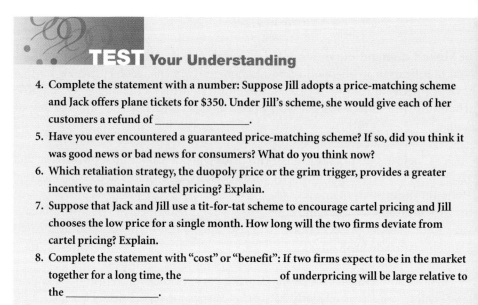

TEST Your Understanding

4. Complete the statement with a number: Suppose Jill adopts a price-matching scheme and Jack offers plane tickets for $350. Under Jill's scheme, she would give each of her customers a refund of _____.

5. Have you ever encountered a guaranteed price-matching scheme? If so, did you think it was good news or bad news for consumers? What do you think now?

6. Which retaliation strategy, the duopoly price or the grim trigger, provides a greater incentive to maintain cartel pricing? Explain.

7. Suppose that Jack and Jill use a tit-for-tat scheme to encourage cartel pricing and Jill chooses the low price for a single month. How long will the two firms deviate from cartel pricing? Explain.

8. Complete the statement with "cost" or "benefit": If two firms expect to be in the market together for a long time, the _____ of underpricing will be large relative to the _____.

The Insecure Monopolist and Entry Deterrence

We've seen what happens when two duopolists try to act as one, fixing the price at the monopoly level. Now let's think about how a monopolist might try to prevent a second firm from entering its market. To explain how a monopolist tries to protect its monopoly, we will use some of the numbers from our airline example, although we will look at a different city with a different cast of characters.

Suppose that Mona initially has a secure monopoly in the market for air travel between two cities. When there is no threat of entry, Mona uses the marginal principle (marginal revenue = marginal cost) to pick a quantity and a price. In Figure 15.7 we start at point *m*, with a quantity of 150 passengers per day and a price of $400 per passenger. Her profit per passenger is $100 ($400 minus the average cost per passenger of $300), so her daily profit is $15,000. If Mona discovers that Doug, the manager of a second airline, is thinking about entering the market, what will she do? Now that she has an insecure monopoly, she has two options: She can be passive and allow the second airline to enter the market, or she can try to prevent the second airline from entering.

The Passive Approach: Do Nothing to Deter Entry

The passive approach will lead to the duopoly outcome we saw earlier in the chapter. In Figure 15.7, the market will move downward along the demand curve from point *m* to point *d* (the duopoly outcome). In a duopoly, Mona will charge a price of $350 and serves 100 passengers (half the quantity demanded). Her daily profit will be $5,000, equal to the profit per passenger of $50 ($350 – the average cost per passenger of $300) multiplied by 100 passengers.

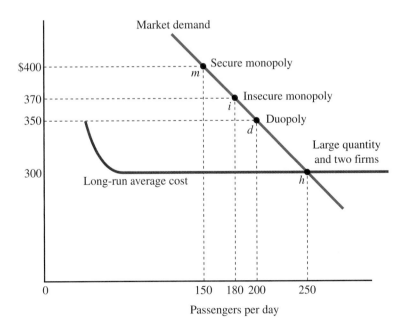

FIGURE 15.7

Deterring Entry with Limit Pricing
Moving downward along the demand curve, point *m* shows the secure monopoly, point *i* shows the insecure monopoly, and point *d* shows the duopoly. Point *h* shows what happens if the insecure monopolist produces a large quantity but a second firm enters anyway.

The Entry Deterrence Approach: Use Limit Pricing to Deter Entry

The second option is to take actions that prevent Doug from entering the market. In thinking about the alternative to the passive approach, Mona must answer two questions:

▶ What must she do to deter entry?
▶ Given what she must do to deter entry, is deterrence more profitable than being passive and sharing the market with a second firm?

To prevent Doug from entering the market, Mona must commit herself to serving a large number of passengers. If she commits to a large passenger load, there won't be enough passengers left for a potential entrant to make a profit. How many passengers must she commit to serve? In Figure 15.7, point *h* shows the point of zero economic profit in the market: If the two firms serve a total of 250 passengers per day, the price ($300) equals average cost, so each firm makes zero economic profit. Suppose that because of economies of scale in providing air travel, the minimum entry quantity is 70 passengers per day: That is, it would be impractical for a firm to serve fewer than 70 passengers. In Figure 15.7, the economies of scale are reflected in a long-run average cost curve is negatively sloped for relatively low levels of output. We can compute the entry-deterring quantity as follows:

entry-deterring quantity = zero economic profit quantity − minimum entry quantity
$$180 = 250 - 70$$

If Mona serves 180 passengers and Doug were to enter with the minimum quantity of 70 passengers, the price would drop to average cost, making entry unprofitable.

It's important to note that Mona can't simply announce that she will serve 180 passengers. She must take actions that ensure that 180 passengers—not the secure monopoly quantity of 150 passengers—is her most profitable quantity. In other words, she must commit to 180 passengers. She could commit to the larger passenger load by purchasing a large fleet of airplanes and signing labor contracts that require her to hire a large workforce. The daily cost of serving 180 passengers is $54,000 (the average cost of $300 times 180 passengers), so if she pays this amount up front, her profit-maximizing quantity will be 180 passengers.

Which is more profitable, entry deterrence or the passive duopoly outcome? The deterrence strategy, shown by point *i* in Figure 15.7, generates a price of $370 and a profit per passenger of $70. Total profit is $12,600 (equal to $70 times 180 passengers). This is larger than the $5,000 profit under the passive approach, so deterrence is the best strategy. Figure 15.8 summarizes this example of entry deterrence. Mona makes the first move, choosing either a small quantity (passive approach) or a large one. If she is passive, Doug would enter the market, and they would end up in profit rectangle 1, each earning $5,000. If Mona picks the large quantity, Doug's entry would drive economic profit to zero, so he won't enter. The path is square **X** to square **Z** to rectangle 4.

Limit Pricing

Mona's entry deterrence strategy generates a market price between the price charged by a secure monopolist ($400) and the price charged in a market with two firms ($350). Mona can avoid sharing the market by accepting the lower price associated with an insecure monopoly ($370). The strategy of picking a price that is lower than the normal monopoly price to deter entry is known as **limit pricing**.

For an example of limit pricing, consider the pricing of the Windows operating system by Microsoft Corporation. The Windows operating system runs about 90% of the world's personal computers, so it is natural to think that Microsoft has a monopoly in the market for operating systems. According to economist Richard Schmalensee, an

Limit pricing

A scheme under which a monopolist accepts a price below the normal monopoly price to deter other firms from entering the market.

FIGURE 15.8

Game Tree for Deterring Entry

Mona knows that if she picks the small quantity (the passive approach), Doug will enter, resulting in profit rectangle 1. By picking the large quantity, Mona can ensure that Doug's profit will be zero, so he will not enter, resulting in profit rectangle 4. For Mona, rectangle 4 is better than rectangle 1, so she picks the large quantity and deters entry. The path of the game is square **X** to square **Z** to rectangle 4: Mona earns a profit of $12,600, and Doug gets nothing.

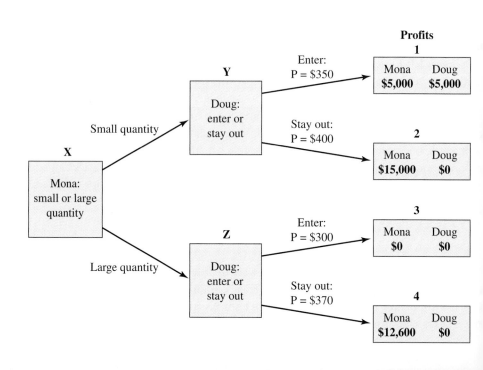

expert on oligopoly and monopoly, Microsoft's profit-maximizing monopoly price is between $900 and $2,000. That's the amount Microsoft would charge if it acted like a secure monopolist.[6] The fact that Microsoft charges only $99 for Windows suggests that Microsoft is an insecure monopolist and picks a low price to discourage entry and preserve its monopoly. If Microsoft charged $2,000 for its operating system, there would be an incentive for other firms to develop alternative operating systems.

Sometimes firms use other means to prevent the entry of other firms into a market. For some examples, read "A Closer Look: Crafty—and Illegal—Entry Deterrence in Europe."

When Is the Passive Approach Better?

Although our example shows that entry deterrence is the best strategy for Mona, it won't be the best strategy for all insecure monopolists. The key variable is the minimum entry quantity. Suppose that the scale economies in air travel were relatively small, so a second firm could enter the market by serving as few as 10 passengers. In this case, if Mona commits to serving only 180 passengers, that won't be enough to deter entry: A firm entering with say, 10, 20, or 30 passengers will still make a profit. If the minimum entry quantity is 10 passengers, the entry-deterring quantity rises to 240 passengers:

$$\text{entry-deterring quantity} = \text{zero economic-profit quantity} - \text{minimum entry quantity}$$
$$240 = 250 - 10$$

The limit price associated with this entry-deterring quantity is $310. Although Mona could deter entry by committing to 240 passengers at a $310 price per ticket, her profit would be only $2,400, compared to $5,000 if she is passive and shares the market with another firm.

The general lesson is that entry deterrence is not sensible when the minimum entry quantity is relatively low. In this case, the quantity required to deter entry is relatively large. As a result, the limit price required to deter entry is close to the average cost of production, and the profit from the insecure monopoly is less than the profit from sharing the market.

A CLOSER LOOK

Crafty—and Illegal—Entry Deterrence in Europe

In recent years, the European Commission has uncovered many examples of entry deterrence that are illegal under the rules of the European Union.[7]

As an example, Van den Bergh Foods, a subsidiary of Unilever, held a dominant position in the market for ice cream in Ireland in 1998. The company provided "free" freezer cabinets to retailers, under the condition that the cabinets were to be used exclusively for the storage of Unilever's products. Irish retailers were reluctant to replace Unilever cabinets, so 40% of retailers offered Unilever products only. The Commission concluded that this practice constituted an abuse of Unilever's dominant position. In 2003, the European Court of First Instance ordered Unilever to share the freezer cabinets with its competitors, including the Mars Company, which had argued that it was unable to sell its ice cream in many retail outlets in Ireland.

Applications: Aluminum, Plane Tickets, and Campus Bookstores

Between 1893 and 1940, the Aluminum Company of America (Alcoa) had a monopoly on aluminum production in the United States.[8] During this period, Alcoa kept other firms out of the market by producing a large quantity and keeping its price low. Although a higher price would have generated more profit in the short run, other firms would have entered the market, so Alcoa's profit would have been lower in the long run.

At the beginning of this chapter, we saw that Katrina paid more for her plane ticket than Brian paid for his, even though they both live in cities that are served by a single airline. If the monopolist in Katrina's city is secure, meaning that there is no threat that another airline will enter the market, the monopolist will charge the normal monopoly price of $400. In Brian's city, an insecure monopolist prevents a second airline from entering the market by committing itself to produce a large quantity and accepting a low price. Brian pays a lower price because he buys his ticket from an insecure monopolist.

We can apply the notion of entry deterrence to your favorite monopoly: your campus bookstore. On most college campuses, the campus bookstore has a monopoly on the sale of textbooks. Other organizations are prohibited, usually by the state government or the college, from selling textbooks on campus. The recent growth of Internet commerce has given students another option: Order textbooks over the Web and have them shipped by mail, UPS, Federal Express, or Airborne Express. Several Web booksellers charge less than the campus bookstore, and the growth of Web book sales threatens the campus bookstore monopoly. If your campus bookstore suddenly feels insecure about its monopoly position, it could cut its prices to prevent Web booksellers from capturing too many of its customers. If it does this, you will pay lower prices even if you don't patronize the Web seller.

Campus bookstores now compete with online booksellers.

Entry Deterrence and Contestable Markets

We've seen that an insecure monopolist may cut its price to prevent other firms from entering the market. The threat of entry moves the market price closer to the price that would occur in a market with two firms. The same logic applies to a monopolized market that could potentially have many firms: The threat of entry will force the monopolist to charge a price that could be close to the one that would occur in a market with many firms. The mere existence of a monopoly does not mean that it will necessarily charge high prices and earn large profits, however. To protect its monopoly, a monopolist may act like a firm in a market with many firms, picking a lower price and earning a smaller profit.

The threat of entry faced by an insecure monopolist like the airline underlies the theory of market contestability. Firms can enter or leave a **contestable market** without incurring large costs. The few firms in a contestable market will be threatened constantly by the entry of new firms, so prices and profits will be low. In the extreme case of perfect contestability, firms can enter and exit a market at zero cost. In this case, the price will be the same as the price that would occur in a perfectly competitive market, one with dozens of firms. Although few markets are perfectly contestable, many markets are contestable to a certain degree, and the threat of entry tends to decrease prices and profits.

Contestable market

A market in which the costs of entering and leaving are low, so the firms that are already in the market are constantly threatened by the entry of new firms.

Ballpoint Pens from R.I.P.

In 1945, Reynolds International Pen Corporation introduced a revolutionary product: the ballpoint pen. The new type of pen could be produced with a very simple production technology.[9] For three years, Reynolds earned enormous profits on this innovative product. In 1948, Reynolds stopped producing pens, dropping out of the market entirely. What happened?

Economic Puzzle

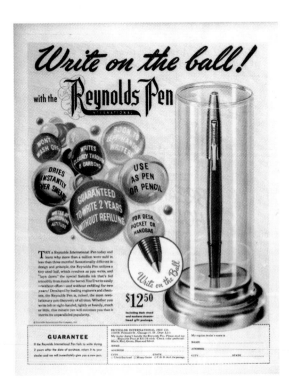

The key to solving this mystery is the fact that Reynolds earned enormous profits for a short time. The simple technology of the ballpoint pen could be easily copied by other producers, so the price required to deter entry was very low. The entry-deterring price was so low that it was better for Reynolds to charge a high price and squeeze out as much profit as possible from a short-lived monopoly. Reynolds sold its pens for $12.50, about 16 times the average production cost ($0.80). By 1948, a total of 100 firms had entered the ballpoint market, and the price had fallen close to the production cost. ■

The Advertisers' Dilemma

We have explored two sorts of strategic behavior of firms in an oligopoly—price fixing and entry deterrence. A third type of strategy concerns advertising. As we'll see, firms in an oligopoly may suffer from an advertisers' dilemma: Although both firms would be better off if neither spent money on advertising, each firm advertises.

Consider the producers of two brands of aspirin. Each firm must decide whether to spend $7 million on an advertising campaign for its product. In Table 15.4, the first two columns of numbers show what happens if neither firm advertises. Each earns $8 million in net revenue (revenue minus production cost) and spends no money on advertising, so the profit is $8 million for each firm. The third and fourth columns of numbers show what happens if each firm spends $7 million on advertising. Net revenue increases from $8 million to $13 million, a benefit of $5 million. This $5 million benefit of advertising is less than the $7 million cost, so the profit earned by each firm falls, from $8 million to $6 million.

What happens if one firm advertises and the other does not? The last two columns of numbers in Table 15.4 show that advertising is profitable for the advertising firm. If Adeline spends $7 million on advertising and Vern spends nothing, Adeline's net revenue increases to $17 million, so her profit increases to $10 million ($17 million – $7 million). Adeline's advertisements cause some of Vern's consumers to switch to Adeline, and Vern's net revenue (and profit) drops to $5 million.

We can use the data in Table 15.4 to construct a game tree for the advertising game. In Figure 15.9, Adeline makes her decision first, followed by Vern.

▶ If neither firm advertises, we go from square **X** to square **Z** to rectangle 4, and the payoff (profit) is $8 million for each firm.
▶ If both firms advertise, we go from square **X** to square **Y** to rectangle 1, and each firm earns a profit of $6 million.
▶ If Adeline advertises and Vern does not, we go from square **X** to square **Y** to rectangle 2, and Adeline earns $10 million, while Vern earns $5 million. If the roles are reversed, we end up in rectangle 3, with Vern, the advertiser, earning $10 million, while Adeline earns $5 million.

To determine the outcome of this advertising game, let's start with Vern's possible actions. If Adeline advertises (we move along the upper branches of the game tree from square **X** to square **Y**), Vern will earn $6 million if he advertises, too (rectangle 1), but only $5 million if he does not advertise (rectangle 2). Therefore, Vern's best response is

TABLE 15.4

Advertising and Profit

	Neither Advertises		Both Advertise		Adeline Advertises	
	Adeline	Vern	Adeline	Vern	Adeline	Vern
Net revenue from sales ($ million)	8	8	13	13	17	5
Cost of advertising ($ million)	0	0	7	7	7	0
Profit ($ million)	8	8	6	6	10	5

to match Adeline's campaign. If Adeline does not advertise (we move along the lower branches from square **X** to square **Z**), Vern will earn $10 million if he advertises but only $8 million if he does not. Therefore, if Adeline does not advertise, Vern's best response is to advertise. To summarize, advertising is Vern's dominant strategy (the best response no matter what Adeline does).

Consider next the options faced by Adeline. She can figure out that advertising is a dominant strategy for Vern. Knowing this, Adeline realizes that the only possible outcomes are shown by rectangles 1 and 3. From her perspective, rectangle 1 ($6 million) is better than rectangle 3 ($5 million), so her best response is to advertise. Both firms advertise, and each earns a profit of $6.

What is the advertisers' dilemma? Both Adeline and Vern would be better off if neither advertised: Each would get a profit of $8 million if neither advertised, compared to $6 million when both advertise. Each firm has an incentive to use advertising to increase its net revenue at the expense of the other. Knowing this, each firm spends

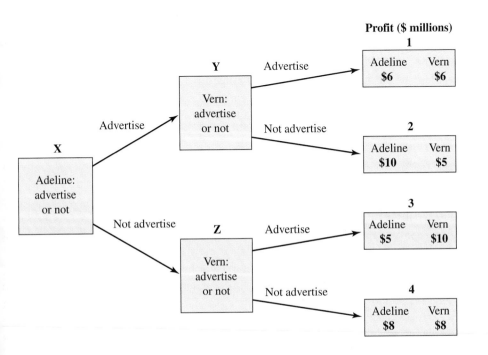

Profit ($ millions)

FIGURE 15.9

Game Tree for an Advertisers' Dilemma
Adeline moves first, choosing to advertise or not. Vern's best response is to advertise no matter what Adeline does. Knowing this, Adeline realizes that the only possible outcomes are shown by rectangles 1 and 3. From Adeline's perspective, rectangle 1 ($6 million) is better than rectangle 3 ($5 million), so her best response is to advertise. Both Adeline and Vern advertise, and each earns a profit of $6 million.

$7 million to counter the advertising campaign of the other firm. Stuck in the dilemma, each firm earns $2 million less than it would if neither advertised.

The advertisers' dilemma occurs when advertising causes a relatively small increase in the total sales of the industry but allows a firm that advertises to gain at the expense of firms that don't. In our example, a pair of advertising campaigns costing a total of $14 million increases the industry's net revenue by only $10 million—from $16 million ($8 million each) to $26 million ($13 million each). If the increase in industry net revenue were larger, advertising could benefit both firms. We'll see an example of that type of advertising in the Using the Tools exercise, "Got Milk?"

TEST Your Understanding

9. Complete the statement: Suppose that Mona picks a small quantity of output. In Figure 15.8, the path of the game would be square _____ to square _____ to rectangle _____.
10. In Figure 15.8, Mona would prefer rectangle 2 to rectangle 4. Why can't she get to rectangle 2?
11. Why does a secure monopolist charge a higher price than an insecure monopolist?

Game Theory and Nash Equilibrium

In this chapter, we explore three strategies used by oligopolies to generate profit, including price fixing, entry deterrence, and advertising. We can use game trees to find the equilibrium strategies for oligopolists. For example, in the equilibrium for the advertisers' game, both firms advertise, although it would be better for each firm if neither did. This is a **Nash equilibrium**, named after John Nash, the recipient of the 1994 Nobel Prize in economics. Nash developed his equilibrium concept as a 21-year-old graduate student at Princeton University. His life story, which includes a 25-year bout with schizophrenia and a dramatic recovery, is chronicled in the book *A Beautiful Mind*, later made into a movie starring Russell Crowe as John Nash.[10]

Nash equilibrium

An outcome of a game in which each player is doing the best he or she can, given the action of the other players.

Nash Equilibrium

Each player is doing the best he or she can, given the action of the other player.

In the advertising game, the equilibrium is for both Adeline and Vern to advertise. This is a Nash equilibrium:

▶ If Vern advertises, the best action for Adeline is to advertise.
▶ If Adeline advertises, the best action for Vern is to advertise.

John Nash developed his equilibrium concept as a 21-year-old graduate student at Princeton University.

There are three other possible outcomes in the advertising game, none of which is a Nash equilibrium.

1 *Neither advertises.* This is not a Nash equilibrium because if Vern does not advertise, Adeline' best action is to advertise. Similarly, if Adeline does not advertise, Vern's best action is to advertise.
2 *Only Adeline advertises.* This is not a Nash equilibrium because if Adeline advertises, Vern's best action is to advertise.
3 *Only Vern advertises.* This is not a Nash equilibrium because if Vern advertises, Adeline's best action is to advertise.

In all three cases, at least one of the players has an incentive to change his or her action given what the other player is doing, so we don't have a Nash equilibrium.

We can also apply the notion of Nash equilibrium to the price-fixing game discussed earlier in the chapter. The Nash equilibrium is for both firms to pick the low price.

▶ If Jill picks the low price, the best action for Jack is to pick the low price, too.
▶ If Jack picks the low price, the best action for Jill is to pick the low price, too.

The outcome with both picking the high price is not a Nash equilibrium because if Jill picks the high price, Jack's best action is to pick the low price.

The concept of the Nash equilibrium has been applied to a wide variety of decisions. In addition to strategic decisions for firms, it has been used to analyze the nuclear arms race, terrorism, evolutionary biology, art auctions, environmental policy, and urban development.

Economic Experiment

A Price-Fixing Game

Here is a price-fixing or cartel game for the classroom. You'll have an opportunity to conspire to fix prices in a hypothetical market with five firms. The instructor divides the class into five groups. Each group represents one of five firms that produce a particular good. Each group must develop a pricing strategy for its firm, recognizing that the other groups are choosing prices for their firms at the same time. There are only two choices: a high price (the cartel price) or a low price. The profit of a particular firm depends on the price chosen by the firm and the prices chosen by the four other firms. Here is the profit matrix:

Number of High-Price Firms	Number of Low-Price Firms	Profit for Each High-Price Firm	Profit for Each Low-Price Firm
0	5	—	$ 5
1	4	$2	7
2	3	4	9
3	2	6	11
4	1	8	13
5	0	10	—

From the second row, if one of the five firms chooses the high price, and the other four firms choose the low price, the high-price firm earns a profit of $2, and each low-price firm earns a profit of $7. The game is played for several rounds. In the first three rounds, the firms make their choices without talking to each other in advance. In the fourth and fifth rounds, the firms discuss their strategies, disperse, and then make their choices. The group's score equals the profit earned by the firm. ●

USING THE TOOLS

We've used one of the tools of economics—the game tree—to predict the outcomes of three types of strategic games played by oligopolists: price fixing, entry deterrence, and advertising. Here are some opportunities to use this tool to do your own economic analysis of markets.

1. Advertising and Price Fixing

Consider two sellers of CD players (Cecil and Dee) who suffer from the duopolists' dilemma. Although both Cecil and Dee would be better off if both chose the high price, they both choose the low price. Cecil recently discovered that Dee is planning a big advertising campaign, the purpose of which is to increase her sales at Cecil's expense (without changing her price). Suppose that Cecil has the opportunity to launch his own advertising campaign before Dee starts hers. What sort of advertising campaign should he launch?

2. Entry Deterrence

Your firm sells a popular children's toy. The manager of another firm is thinking about introducing a similar toy. Your average cost of production is constant at $2 per toy. At the current monopoly price of $5 per toy, you sell 120 toys per day. You could prevent the entry of the second firm by increasing your output to 150 toys per day and cutting your price to $4 per toy. If the second firm enters the market, your price would decrease to $3 per toy, and you would sell only 80 toys per day. Should you prevent entry of the second firm?

3. Advertising with Spillover Benefits: Got Milk?

Bessie and George are milk producers, and each must decide whether to spend $7 million on an advertising campaign. If neither advertises, each will earn $10 million in net revenue from sales (net revenue). If both advertise, each will earn $20 million in net revenue and $13 million in profit ($20 million − $7 million for advertising). If only one producer advertises, that firm will earn $16 million in net revenue, and the other firm will earn $15 million in net revenue. Prepare a game tree like Figure 15.9 (assume that Bessie decides first) and predict the outcome of this advertising game. If there is an advertisers' dilemma, how does it differ from the advertisers' dilemma discussed earlier in the chapter? How might the dairy industry solve this dilemma? (*Hint*: Think white mustaches.)

SUMMARY

In this chapter, we've seen that when a few firms share a market, they have an incentive to act strategically. Firms may use cartel pricing or price fixing to avoid competition and keep prices high. If another firm threatens to enter a monopolist's market, the monopolist may cut its price to discourage other firms from entering a market. Here are the main points of the chapter:

1 Each firm in an oligopoly has an incentive to underprice the other firms, so price fixing (also known as cartel pricing) will be unsuccessful unless firms have some way of enforcing a price-fixing agreement.

2 One way to maintain price fixing is a guaranteed price-matching scheme: One firm chooses the high price and promises to match a lower price offered by its competitor.

3 Price fixing is more likely to occur if firms choose prices repeatedly and can punish a firm that chooses a price below the cartel price.

4 To prevent a second firm from entering the market, an insecure monopolist may commit itself to producing a relatively large quantity and accepting a relatively low price.

KEY TERMS

1 Consider two firms, Speedy and Hustle, which provide land transportation from the downtown area to the airport. The practice of guaranteed price matching is illegal. If the two firms act independently (they do not engage in price fixing or any other collusive behavior), each firm will serve 100 passengers per day at a price of $20 per passenger and an average cost of $15 per passenger. Under a price-fixing or cartel arrangement, each firm would serve 75 passengers at a price of $28 and an average cost of $18 per passenger. If one firm charges $20 and the other firm charges $28, the low-price firm will earn a profit of $900, and the high-price firm will earn a profit of $400. Speedy chooses a price first, followed by Hustle. Draw a game tree for the price-fixing game and predict the outcome.

2 Recall the example of the repeated pricing game between Jack and Jill. Suppose that each firm uses the grim-trigger strategy to punish underpricing. Each person expects to go out of business in one month, meaning that each person is about to choose a price for the last time. Which price will each person choose?

3 Many firms have going-out-of-business sales with remarkable bargains. What insights does the material in this chapter provide about such sales?

4 Consider the example of entry deterrence shown in Figure 15.8. Suppose that just one number changes: If Mona chooses a large quantity and Doug stays out, Mona's profit would be $4,500. All the other numbers are the same as those shown in Figure 15.8. Draw a new game tree and predict the outcome: Will Mona choose a large or a small quantity, and will Doug enter or stay out?

5 On Wa-ki-ki beach, there are two hotels, Weird and Bizarre. The practice of guaranteed price matching is illegal. If the two firms act independently (they do not engage in price fixing or any other collusive behavior), each firm will rent 50 rooms per day at a price of $50 per room and an average cost of $45 per room. Under a price-fixing or cartel arrangement, each hotel would rent 30 rooms per day at a price of $60 and an average cost of $48. If one firm charges $50 and the other firm charges $60, the low-price firm will earn a profit of $500, and the

high-price firm will earn a profit of $150. Bizarre picks a price first, followed by Weird.
   a. Suppose each firm must pick a price and maintain its chosen price for the remaining lifetime of the firm. Draw a game tree and predict the outcome.
   b. Suppose the two firms can change their prices daily, and expect to be in business for three more days. Weird announces that he will start with the high price and maintain the price as long as Bizarre does too. If Bizarre undercuts Weird, however, Weird will pick the low price for the remainder of the game. Predict the outcome of the game.

6 Consider the market for air travel between Madison and Chicago. The long-run average cost is constant at $200 per passenger, and the demand curve is linear, with a slope of −$1 per passenger. A secure monopolist would charge a price of $280 and serve 70 passengers per day. The other possible prices are $260 for an insecure monopolist, $250 for the duopoly outcome, and $180 for the case in which one firm picks a large quantity and a low price but a second firm enters anyway.
   a. Use these numbers to draw two figures, one like Figure 15.7 and a second like Figure 15.8. Provide a complete set of numbers, and briefly explain how you got them. Label any curves you draw, and identify the relevant points on your graph.
   b. Use your second figure to predict the outcome of the entry deterrence game. What is the price of air travel?

7 In the state of Turnover, the typical car-stereo seller stays in business for one year. In the state of Longtime, the typical car-stereo seller stays in business for five years. Which state is likely to have higher prices for car stereos?

8 Consider the Jack and Jill repeated-price game described in the text. Suppose Jill uses the duopoly-pricing strategy, and the two firms expect to be in business for three periods.
   a. In the current period, what are Jack's costs and benefits of underpricing?
   b. Will Jack underprice in the final period? If Jill can predict Jack's behavior in the last period, what will she do? What are the implications for the second period?

9 Consider two automobile companies that are considering advertising campaigns. If neither firm advertises, each will earn net revenue of $5 million. If each spends $10 million on advertising, each firm's net revenue will be $12 million. If one advertises and the other does not, the firm that advertises will earn $17 million in net revenue, while the firm that does not will earn $1 million. Draw a game tree and predict the outcome. From the industry perspective, do the benefits of advertising exceed the costs?

MODEL ANSWERS TO QUESTIONS

Chapter-Opening Questions

1 It is likely to lead to higher prices because it eliminates the possibility of underpricing. The promise to issue refunds is an empty promise.

2 The price-fixing arrangement is more likely to persist if the airlines pick prices repeatedly over time, giving the airlines the opportunity to punish anyone who cheats on the agreement.

3 Entry deterrence is not sensible when the minimum entry quantity is relatively low and thus the limit price is relatively low.

4 The firms suffer from the advertisers' dilemma. There is a big payoff from being the only advertiser and a big penalty from not advertising if the other advertises, so both advertise.

Test Your Understanding

1 *c, d.*

2 X, Z, 4, $5,000.

3 He will choose the low price and gain at Jill's expense. Jack's promise is not credible because once Jill chooses the high price, he will earn more profit by choosing the low price. Jill should ignore the incredible promise and choose the low price.

4 $50 ($400 − $350).

5 They are common in appliance and electronics stores and in hardware stores. Many grocery stores honor the coupons of other stores. Although these schemes appear to be good news for consumers, they actually facilitate price fixing and lead to higher prices.

6 The grim-trigger strategy leads to zero economic profit, while the duopoly price leaves each firm with a positive profit. The costs of underpricing are higher with the grim trigger, so there is a greater incentive to charge the cartel price.

7 Two months. In the first month, Jill underprices Jack. In the second month, Jill chooses the high price but is underpriced by Jack, who is punishing her for underpricing him in the first month. In the third month, they both choose the high price.

8 Cost, benefit.

9 X, Y, 1.

10 If she chooses a small quantity, Doug will enter.

11 To prevent the entry of a second firm, an insecure monopolist commits itself to produce a large quantity of output and accepts a low price. A secure monopolist doesn't have to worry about other firms entering the market.

NOTES

1. Adam Smith, *The Wealth of Nations* (New York: Modern Library, 1994).
2. David Barboza, "Tearing Down the Facade of 'Vitamins Inc.'" *New York Times*, October 10, 1999, Section 3, p. 1; Department of Justice, "Four Foreign Executives Of Leading European Vitamin Firms Agree to Plead Guilty to Participating in International Vitamin Cartel," Press Release, April 6, 2000.
3. Sharon Walsh, "Six Airlines to Halt Advance Price Listing," *New York Times News Service*, printed in *The Oregonian*, March 18, 1994, p. B1.
4. Federal Trade Commission, "Record Companies Settle FTC Charges of Restraining Competition in CD Music Market," Press Release, May 10, 2000.
5. George Stigler, "The Kinked Oligopoly Demand Curve and Rigid Prices," *Journal of Political Economy*, vol. 55, 1947, pp. 432–449.
6. "Big Friendly Giant," *The Economist*, January 30, 1999, p. 72.
7. European Commission, *Report on Competition Policy 1998*, pp. 35–39.
8. Leonard W. Weiss, *Economics and American Industry* (New York: Wiley, 1963), pp. 189–204.
9. Thomas Whiteside, "Where Are They Now?" *New Yorker*, February 17, 1951, pp. 39–58.
10. Sylvia Nassar, *A Beautiful Mind* (New York: Simon & Schuster, 1998).

Market Structure and Public Policy

n 1997, a U.S. court blocked the proposed merger of Staples and Office Depot, the nation's two largest office-supply retailers. The judge in the case observed that the merger would eliminate Office Depot as a competitor and allow Staples to increase its prices by 13%. Where did the judge get that number?

When you buy groceries, hardware, or office supplies, a scanner at the checkout stand reads bar-code information, recording the price you pay and the quantity you purchase. The scanner system helps retailers keep track of their stock and allows them to instantly change prices without putting new price tags on their products. The scanner data can also be used to observe pricing patterns from firms like Staples. Economists with the Federal Trade Commission (FTC) found an interesting pattern: The prices charged by Staples were lower in cities where Office Depot also had a store. The competition generated by Office Depot led to prices that were, on average, 13% lower.[1]

his chapter looks at various public policies dealing with markets that are dominated by a small number of firms. We'll start with the case of natural monopoly, which occurs when the scale economies in production are so large that only a single large firm can survive. In this case, the government can intervene by regulating the price charged by the natural monopolist. Then we'll look at markets in which the government can affect the number of firms in the market, using various policies to promote competition. The government uses antitrust policies to break up monopolies into several smaller companies, prevent corporate mergers that would reduce competition, and regulate business practices that tend to reduce competition. Sometimes prior government regulations actually end up inhibiting competition, so the government later "de-regulates" an industry to promote more competition. In the last part of the chapter, we'll look at recent deregulation of three markets: air travel, telecommunications, and electricity. In these three markets, the government reversed a long history of regulation, deregulating the industries to promote competition. Here are some practical policy questions that we answer:

1 Two firms, XM Satellite Radio and Sirius Satellite Radio, each spent about $2 billion on satellites and ground stations to provide dozens of radio channels with fewer commercials (and pledge drives) than broadcast radio. Will both firms survive?
2 Why did the government prevent the proposed merger between Heinz and Beech-Nut, the second and third largest firms in the market for baby food?
3 How did the deregulation of air travel affect the price of air travel?

Natural Monopoly

In an earlier chapter, we considered monopolies that resulted from artificial barriers to entry such as patents and government licenses. In this chapter, we'll look at natural monopolies, which occur when the economies of scale for producing a product are so large that only a single firm can survive. Some examples are water systems, electricity transmission, and cable TV service. It is natural for a city to have a single supplier of water service because a second supplier would install a second set of water pipes when a single set of pipes would suffice. Similarly, it is sensible to have a single set of transmission lines for electricity and a single set of cables for TV service.

Picking an Output Level

Figure 16.1 shows the long-run average-cost curve for cable TV service in a particular city. The curve is negatively sloped and steep, reflecting the large economies of scale that occur because of the cost of building and maintaining the system of cables that deliver TV service to individual subscribers. The system of cables strung along power lines is an indivisible input in the sense that it is the same whether the cable firm has 70

FIGURE 16.1

A Natural Monopoly Uses the Marginal Principle to Pick Quantity and Price

Because of the indivisible input of cable service (the cable system), the long-run average-cost curve is negatively sloped. The monopolist chooses point *n* (where marginal revenue equals marginal cost), serving 70,000 subscribers at a price of $27 per unit (point *m*) and an average cost of $21 (point *c*). The profit per subscriber is $6 ($27 – $21).

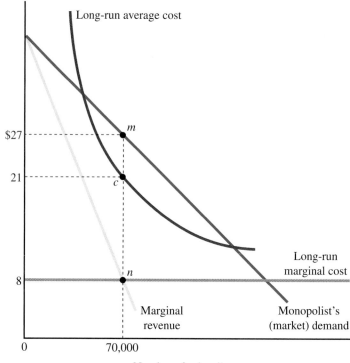

subscribers in the city or 70,000. As the number of subscribers increases, the average cost of cable service decreases because the cost of the indivisible cable system is spread over more people.

What about the long-run marginal cost—the cost to add one subscriber—once the system is built? For each additional subscriber, a cable company incurs the cost of hooking the house into the system and the administrative cost associated with billing the subscriber. To simplify matters, we'll assume that each additional subscriber increases cost by $8 per month, so the marginal-cost curve is horizontal at $8 per subscriber.

Figure 16.1 shows how to use the cost curves and revenue curves to pick the output level that maximizes profit. If a single firm—a monopolist—provides cable service, the monopolist's firm-specific demand curve is the same as the market demand curve: To determine how many subscribers the monopolist will have at a particular price, we look at the market demand curve. The demand curve is negatively sloped, and the marginal-revenue curve lies below the demand curve. The marginal principle is satisfied at point *n*, with 70,000 subscribers. The price associated with this quantity is $27 per subscriber (shown by point *m*) and the average cost is $21 per unit (shown by point *c*), so the profit per subscriber is $6. The price exceeds the average cost, so the cable company will earn a profit.

Will a Second Firm Enter?

If there are no artificial barriers to entry, a second firm could enter the cable TV market. What would happen if a second firm entered the market? In Figure 16.2, the entry of a second firm would shift the firm-specific demand curve of the first firm—the former monopolist—to the left, from D_1 to D_2: At each price, the first firm will have fewer subscribers because it now shares the market with another firm. For example, at a price of $27, there are 70,000 subscribers, or 35,000 for each firm (point t). In general, the larger the number of firms, the lower the firm-specific demand curve for the typical firm.

Will a second firm enter the market? Notice that the demand curve of the typical firm in a two-firm market lies entirely below the long-run average-cost curve, so there is no quantity at which the price exceeds the average cost of production. No matter what price the typical firm charges, it will lose money. The firm's demand curve lies below the average-cost curve because the average-cost curve is steep, reflecting the large economies of scale for cable service. A second firm—with half the market— would have a very high average cost and wouldn't be able to charge a price high enough to cover the cost of building the system in the first place. Therefore, the second firm will not enter the market, so there will be a single firm, a natural monopoly. For an example of a potential new natural monopoly, read "A Closer Look: Will Satellite Radio Be a Natural Monopoly?"

Price Controls for a Natural Monopoly

When a natural monopoly is inevitable, the government often sets a maximum price for the monopolist. There are many examples of natural monopolies that are subject to maximum prices. Local governments regulate utilities and firms that provide water,

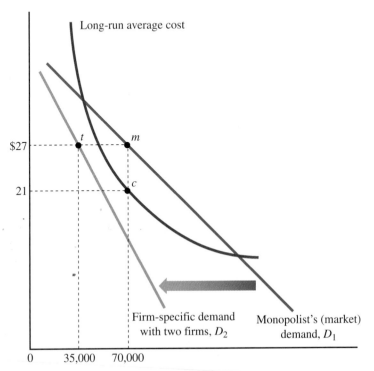

FIGURE 16.2

Will A Second Cable Firm Enter the Market?
The entry of a second cable firm would shift the firm-specific demand curve of the typical firm to the left. After entry, the firm's demand curve lies entirely below the long-run average cost curve. No matter what price the typical firm charges, it will lose money. Therefore, a second firm will not enter the market.

electricity, cable service, and local telephone service. Many state governments use public utility commissions (PUCs) to regulate the electric power industry.

We can use the cable TV market to explain the effects of government regulation on a natural monopoly. Suppose the government sets a maximum price for cable service and forces the cable company to serve all consumers who are willing to pay the maximum price. In other words, the government—not the firm—picks a point on the market demand curve. Under an **average-cost pricing policy**, the government picks the price at which the market demand curve intersects the monopolist's long-run average-cost curve. In Figure 16.3, the average-cost curve intersects the demand curve at point *r*, with a price of $12 per subscriber. This is much lower than the price the firm would choose to maximize its profit ($27). Notice that under the pricing policy, the monopolist has many more subscribers (120,000 versus 70,000), a result of the much lower price ($12 versus $27). The purpose of the average-cost pricing policy is to get the lowest feasible price. The cable company would lose money at any price less than $12, so a lower price isn't feasible.

How will this regulatory policy affect the monopolist's production costs? Under average-cost pricing, a change in the monopolist's production cost will have little effect on its profit because the government will soon adjust the regulated price to keep the price equal to the average cost. The government will increase the regulated price when the monopolist's cost increases, and decrease the price when its cost decreases. Because the monopolist has no incentive to cut costs and faces no penalty for higher costs, its costs are likely to creep upward. As average cost increases, the regulated price will too.

Average-cost pricing policy

A regulatory policy under which the government picks the point on the demand curve at which price equals average cost.

FIGURE 16.3

Regulators Use Average-Cost Pricing to Pick a Monopoly's Quantity and Price

Under an average-cost pricing policy, the government chooses the price at which the demand curve intersects the long-run average-cost curve, point *r* ($12 per subscriber). Compared to the outcome with an unregulated monopoly, the policy leads to a lower price ($12 versus $27) and a larger quantity (150,000 versus 70,000).

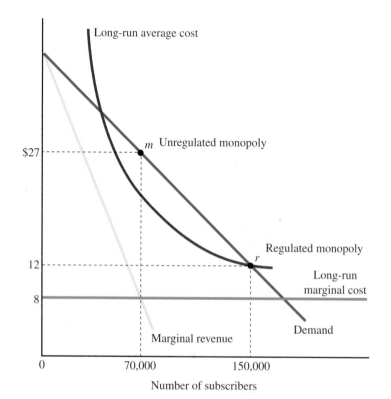

A Decrease in Demand Decreases the Price?

When the population of Fleeburg decreased, the demand for all sorts of goods—including housing and cable TV service—decreased. The decrease in the demand for housing decreased the price of housing, consistent with the laws of supply and demand. By contrast, the price of cable TV service, a regulated natural monopoly in Fleeburg, increased. The higher price for cable service seems to defy the laws of supply and demand. What explains the puzzling increase in price?

The key to solving this mystery is that cable TV is a regulated natural monopoly, with a price equal to the average cost of providing cable service. A decrease in the number of subscribers will cause the cable company to move upward along its negatively sloped average-cost curve to a higher average cost and a higher regulated price. In graphical terms, the demand curve for cable service shifts to the left, so it intersects the negatively sloped average-cost curve at a higher average cost. Intuitively, there are fewer subscribers to share the large fixed cost of the cable system, so each subscriber must pay more. ■

A CLOSER LOOK — Will Satellite Radio Become a Natural Monopoly?

The biggest development in radio since the emergence of the FM band is satellite radio. Two firms—Sirius Satellite Radio and XM Satellite Radio—provide dozens of national radio channels that can be accessed by special radio receivers for cars and homes.[2] The quality of the reception is on par with compact discs and is the same throughout the continental United States. Both firms provide dozens of channels, including music channels with rock and roll, punk, pop, country/western, R&B, and classical music. The information channels include the Bloomberg News Radio, CNBC, C-SPAN, BBC WorldService, NPR Talk, and Public Radio International.

The advantage of satellite radio is that most stations are free of annoying commercials that clutter most broadcast radio stations. The music channels on the Sirius system are commercial-free, and the information channels air just a few minutes of commercials every hour. About half the XM channels are commercial-free, and the others have no more than 6 minutes of commercials every hour (compared to 20 minutes at the typical broadcast radio station). The monthly charge for Sirius is $13. XM radio costs less—$10 per month—reflecting the larger number of commercials on that network.

How many satellite radio systems can the market support? The cost of setting up the system—with satellites and ground stations—is $2 billion, and the break-even point for each firm is about 3 million subscribers. In June 2003, XM radio had 500,000 subscribers, and Sirius had 68,000. The firms expect to reach break-even levels by 2005 or 2006. If their projection of a total market of 50 million subscribers is accurate, each firm could be profitable. Alternatively, if there are fewer than 6 million total subscribers (3 million for each firm), one or both of the firms will fail.

Antitrust Policy

The purpose of antitrust policy is to promote competition among firms. Antitrust policy is used to break up existing monopolies and to prevent existing firms from becoming monopolies. We'll explore three types of antitrust policies.

Breaking Up Monopolies

One form of antitrust policy is to break up a monopoly into several smaller firms. A **trust** is an arrangement under which the owners of several companies transfer their decision-making powers to a small group of trustees, who then make decisions for all the participating firms. Firms in a trust act as a single firm, so an industry that appears to have many firms may in fact be a virtual monopoly.

Trust
An arrangement under which the owners of several companies transfer their decision-making powers to a small group of trustees, who then make decisions for all the firms.

In 1911, the Supreme Court found that Rockefeller had used "unnatural methods" to maintain his monopoly power and drive his rivals out of business.

The label "antitrust" comes from the names of the early conglomerates that were broken up. The classic example is John D. Rockefeller's Standard Oil Trust, which was formed in 1882 when the owners of 40 oil companies empowered nine trustees to make the decisions for all 40 companies. The trust controlled over 90% of the market for refined petroleum products, and the trustees ran it like a monopoly. In 1911, the government ordered its breakup. The Supreme Court found that Rockefeller had used "unnatural methods" to maintain his monopoly power and drive his rivals out of business. In addition to forming the trust, he coerced railroads to give him special rates for shipping, and he spied on his competitors. The government broke up Standard Oil into 34 separate companies, including the corporate ancestors of Exxon, Mobil, Chevron, and Amoco.

After the American Tobacco Company bought 30 of its competitors, it controlled 95% of the U.S. cigarette market. The Supreme Court found that American Tobacco maintained its monopoly power by driving rivals out of business and agreeing to exclusive contracts with wholesalers that prevented them from purchasing cigarettes from other companies. The court-ordered breakup in 1911 led to several new companies, including several of today's big cigarette companies: Reynolds, Liggett and Meyers, and P. Lorillard.

In 1982, the government broke up American Telephone and Telegraph (AT&T) into seven regional phone companies. AT&T had used its legal monopoly in local telephone service to prevent competition in the markets for long-distance service and communications equipment. After an eight-year legal battle, AT&T agreed to form seven Regional Bell Operating Companies, transforming "Ma Bell" into seven "Baby Bells." The new AT&T was allowed to compete in the market for long-distance service, where it faced competition from newcomers MCI and Sprint. AT&T was also allowed to operate in the market for communications equipment, where it faced competition from newcomers Mitel and Northern Telecom.

Blocking Mergers

A **merger** occurs when two firms combine their operations. A second type of antitrust policy is to block corporate mergers that would reduce competition and lead to higher prices. We saw in Chapter 14 that as the number of firms in a market increases, competition among firms drives down prices. Because a merger decreases the number of firms in a market, it is likely to lead to higher prices. In 1994, Microsoft tried to purchase Intuit, the maker of Quicken, a personal-finance software package that was a substitute for a similar Microsoft product. The merger would have reduced competition in the personal-finance software market, so the government blocked it.

Of course, the government does not oppose all corporate mergers. One possible benefit from a merger is that the new firm could combine production, marketing, and administrative operations, producing products at a lower average cost. Consumers might reap the rewards in the form of lower prices. In 1997, the Justice Department and the Federal Trade Commission released new guidelines for proposed mergers. The new guidelines allow companies involved in a proposed merger to present evidence that the merger would reduce costs and lead to lower prices, better products, or better service. If the evidence for greater efficiency is convincing, the government might allow

Merger

A process in which two or more firms combine their operations.

a merger that reduces the number of firms in a market. FTC Chairman Robert Pitofsky assessed the effects of the new guidelines as follows[3]:

> There may be some deals that go through which otherwise would not have. But it won't change the result in a large number of cases [rather it will have] the greatest impact in a transaction where the potential anticompetitive problem is modest and efficiencies that would be created are great.

The new guidelines will bring the U.S. antitrust rules closer in line with those of Europe and Canada and could help U.S. companies compete in those markets.

In recent years, the analysis of proposed mergers has shifted from counting the number of firms in a market to predicting how a particular merger would affect price effects. The data generated by retail checkout scanners provides an enormous amount of information about prices and quantities sold. Using this data, economists can determine how one firm's pricing policies affect the sales of that firm and its competitors. Economists can use this information to predict whether a merger would lead to higher prices.

As we saw in the chapter opener, the FTC used pricing data to support its decision to block a proposed merger between Staples and Office Depot. The data showed that prices charged by Staples were lower in cities where Office Depot also had stores. Figure 16.4 shows Staples' revenue and cost curves for one specific product: file folders. Panel A shows what happens when Staples faces no competition from an Office Depot, and Panel B shows what happens when it does. The firm-specific demand curve of Staples is lower in the city where it faces competition with Office Depot because the two firms share the market. Using the marginal principle, Staples picks the quantity and price where its marginal revenue equals its marginal cost. The profit-maximizing price is $14 in a city without an Office Depot and $12 in a city with one.

The FTC used this logic to convince the court that the proposed merger of Staples and Office Depot would lead to higher prices. The judge in the case observed that, "direct evidence shows that by eliminating Staples' most significant, and in

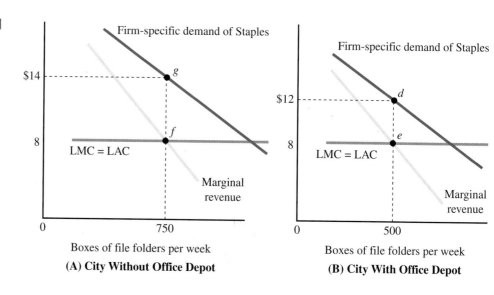

FIGURE 16.4

Pricing by Staples in Cities With and Without Competition
Using the marginal principle, Staples picks the quantity at which its marginal revenue equals its marginal cost. In a city without a competing firm, Staples picks the monopoly price of $14. In a city where Staples competes with Office Depot, the demand facing Staples is relatively low, so the profit-maximizing price is only $12.

(A) City Without Office Depot

(B) City With Office Depot

many markets, only, rival, the merger would allow Staples to increase prices or otherwise maintain prices at an anticompetitive level." Evidence from the companies' pricing data showed that the merger would have allowed Staples to increase its prices by about 13%. According to an FTC study, blocking the merger saved consumers an estimated $1.1 billion over five years. For another example of blocking a merger to promote competition and lower prices, read, "A Closer Look: Is Triopoly Better than Duopoly?"

Application: Merger Remedies for Xidex and Wonder Bread

In some cases, the government allows a merger to happen but imposes restrictions on the new company. In 1981, the Federal Trade Commission brought an antitrust suit against Xidex Corporation for its earlier acquisition of two rivals in the microfilm market.[5] By acquiring Scott Graphics, Inc. in 1976 and Kalvar Corporation in 1979, Xidex increased its market share of the U.S. microfilm market from 46% to 71%. As a result, the price of microfilm increased: The price of one type of microfilm (diazo) increased by 11%, and the price of a second type (vesicular) increased by 23%. These price hikes were large enough that Xidex recovered the cost of acquiring its two rivals ($4.2 million for Scott Graphics and $6 million for Kalvar) in less than two years. To settle the antitrust lawsuit, Xidex agreed to license its microfilm technology—at bargain prices—to other firms. The idea was that if other firms have access to the microfilm technology, the competition between Xidex and the competing firms would decrease the price of microfilm.

A CLOSER LOOK

Is Triopoly Better than Duopoly?

In 2001, H.J. Heinz Company announced plans to buy Milnot Holding Company's Beechnut for $185 million. The merger would combine the nation's second- and third-largest sellers of baby food, with a combined market share of 28%. The combined company would still be less than half the size of the market leader, Gerber, with its 70% market share. The Federal Trade Commission successfully blocked the merger, based on two observations:

▶ Most retailers stock only two brands of baby food, Gerber and either Heinz or Beech-Nut. The two smaller companies compete vigorously for shelf space, with discounts, coupons, and other programs that lead to lower prices for consumers. After the merger, the Heinz brand would disappear, leaving Beech-Nut as a secure second brand on the shelves next to Gerber. The elimination of competition for second place would lead to higher prices.

▶ The smaller the number of firms in an oligopoly, the easier it is to coordinate pricing. The FTC argued that "significant market concentration makes it easier for firms in the market to collude, expressly or tacitly, and thereby force price above or farther above the competitive level." In other words, in a market with two firms instead of three, it would be easier for the baby-food manufacturers to fix prices.[4]

In 1995, Interstate Bakeries (the nation's third-largest wholesale baker) tried to buy Continental Baking (the maker of Wonder Bread). Based on grocery store scanner data, the government concluded that Wonder Bread is a close substitute for Interstate's bread: The demand for Wonder Bread increases when the price of Interstate's bread increases, and vice versa.[6] The scanner data showed that when Interstate increased its price, many consumers switched to Wonder Bread, so their bread money went to Continental instead of Interstate. The substitutability of the two brands discouraged Interstate from increasing its prices.

Table 16.1 shows an example of a merger leading to higher prices and smaller quantities. Let's assume that the average cost per loaf of bread is $1.50, and this doesn't change with a merger. The situation before the merger is shown in columns 1 and 3: For each brand, the price per loaf of bread is $2.00, the quantity is 100 loaves, and the profit is $50 (the profit $0.50 per loaf times 100 loaves).

How would a merger affect the incentives to raise prices? After a merger, a single company would earn the profits from both brands (Wonder and Interstate) and pick both prices. Suppose the new company increased the price of Interstate bread to $2.20 but kept the price of Wonder Bread at $2.00. The price hike would bring bad news and good news for the new company:

▶ Bad news: Less profit on Interstate Bread. As shown in columns 3 and 4, the price hike decreases the quantity of Interstate bread from 100 to 70 loaves. Although the profit per loaf increases to $0.70 (the new price of $2.20 minus the average cost of $1.50), only 70 loaves are sold, so the profit from the brand drops to $49, down from $50. The bad news is the $1 loss of profit on Interstate Bread.

▶ Good news: More profit on Wonder Bread. As shown in columns 1 and 2, the increase in the price of Interstate Bread increases the quantity of Wonder Bread sold from 100 to 110 loaves. The profit per loaf is still $0.50 per bread, so the profit on Wonder Bread increases to $55, up from $50. The good news is the extra $5 of profit on Wonder Bread.

In this case, the good news ($5 more profit from Wonder) exceeds the bad news ($1 less profit from Interstate), so the price hike increases the total profit of the merged com-

TABLE 16.1 A Merger Increases Prices

	Wonder Brand		Interstate Brand		Total	
	Before Merger	After Merger	Before Merger	After Merger	Before Merger	After Merger
Average cost	$1.50	$1.50	$1.50	$1.50		
Price	$2.00	$2.00	$2.00	$2.20		
Quantity	100	110	100	70	200	180
Profit	$50	$55	$50	$49	$100	$104
Column	1	2	3	4	5	6

pany. This is shown in columns 5 and 6. Although the total quantity drops, total profit increases by $4. A merger means that this good news stays within the larger firm, encouraging that firm to increase prices.

The lesson from this example is that a merger of two firms selling close substitutes may lead to higher prices. That's what the Department of Justice concluded in the case of Interstate Bakeries and Continental Bakery. The government allowed the merger between the two companies but forced Interstate to sell some of its brands and bakeries. For example, Interstate sold the rights to sell its Weber brand bread to Four-S Baking Company. The idea was to ensure that other companies would be able to compete with the new merged company.

Check the Yellow Pages?

On Katrina's first day on the job as an economist with the Federal Trade Commission, she was put on a team examining a proposed merger between the country's second- and fourth-largest hardware store chains. Her job was to predict whether a merger would increase hardware prices. Her boss handed her some disks with checkout scanner data from the second-largest chain. Each disk contained scanner data from one small town, listing the prices and quantities of hammers, wrenches, nuts, bolts, rakes, glue, drills, and hundreds of other hardware products. Her boss also gave her the telephone Yellow Pages for each small town. What can she do with the disks and the Yellow Pages?

The key to solving this puzzle is to recognize the similarity to the case of Staples and Office Depot. A merger of the country's second- and fourth-largest hardware chains could reduce competition and lead to higher prices. If the scanner data showed that prices are lower in some towns, Katrina could look in the Yellow Pages to see which towns have hardware stores from both chains and which don't. If the towns that are served by both chains have lower prices, the proposed merger would probably decrease competition and increase prices. ■

Regulating Business Practices: Price Fixing, Tying, and Cooperative Agreements

The third type of antitrust policy involves the regulation of business practices. The government may intervene when a specific business practice increases market concentration in an already concentrated market. Among the practices that are subject to scrutiny are price fixing (discussed in Chapter 15) and **tie-in sales** (forcing a buyer of one product to purchase a second product). The FTC recently charged a pharmaceutical company with tying the sale of clozapine, an antipsychotic drug, to a blood testing and monitoring system. Another illegal business practice is a cooperative agreement to limit advertising. The FTC recently charged a group of auto dealers with restricting comparative and discount advertising.

The Robinson–Patman Act prohibits selling products at "unreasonably low prices" with the intent of reducing competition, a practice known as **predatory pricing**. A firm engages in predatory pricing when it sells a product at a price below its production costs, forcing its rivals to do the same or leave the market. Once the predator's

Tie-in-sales

A business practice under which a consumer of one product is required to purchase another product.

Predatory pricing

A pricing scheme under which a firm decreases its price to drive a rival out of business and increases the price when the other firm disappears.

rivals drop out of the market, the firm then charges a monopoly price, well above it production cost. This will be a profitable strategy if the firm can charge the monopoly price for a long enough period to offset the losses it experienced while driving its rival out of business.

But is predatory pricing really practical? Consider a market with two firms, one o which is determined to have the market to itself. By cutting its price below its cost, the firm can drive its competitor out of business, losing perhaps $10 million in the process. If it increases its price next year, there may be nothing to prevent a new firm from entering the market. If so, it would have to cut its price below its cost again to drive the new firm out. The problem with predatory pricing is that it never ends; the firm must repeatedly lose money to drive out an endless series of competitors.

Application: The Microsoft Case

In recent years, the most widely reported antitrust actions have involved Microsoft Corporation, the software giant. Microsoft receives royalties from computer makers that install the Microsoft operating software on their computers. The curious—and illegal—feature of the original arrangement was that Microsoft received a royalty for every computer made by the firm, even if the firm installed other operating systems on some of its computers. This scheme discouraged computer makers from using software from Microsoft's rivals, and the courts declared the practice illegal in 1994.

The case of *United States v. Microsoft Corporation* demonstrated that Microsoft stifled competition in the software industry. Under an initial ruling, the remedy was to break up the corporation into two companies, one producing the Windows operating system and a second producing application software. On appeal, this remedy was rejected, and instead Microsoft was directed to release more technical information about how its operating system works and to refrain from retaliating against computer-makers that install software from other companies.

A Brief History of U.S. Antitrust Policy

Table 16.2 provides a brief summary of the history of antitrust policy. The first legislation was the Sherman Antitrust Act of 1890, which made it illegal to monopolize a market or to engage in practices that result in a restraint of trade. Because the act did not specify which practices were illegal, it led to conflicting court rulings.

Many of the ambiguities of the Sherman Act were resolved by the Clayton Act of 1914. The Clayton Act outlawed specific practices that discourage competition, including tying contracts (requiring a consumer who buys one product to buy a second product) and price discrimination that reduces competition (discussed in Chapter 13). The act also outlawed mergers resulting from the purchase of a competitor's stock when such a merger would substantially reduce competition.

More recent legislation clarified and extended antitrust laws. The Robinson–Patman Act of 1936 prohibited predatory pricing. The Celler–Kefauver Act of 1950

TABLE 16.2

Brief History of Antitrust Legislation

1890	Sherman Act: Made it illegal to monopolize a market or to engage in practices that result in a restraint of trade.
1914	Clayton Act: Outlawed specific practices that discourage competition, including tying contracts, price discrimination for the purpose of reducing competition, and stock-purchase mergers that would substantially reduce competition.
1914	Federal Trade Commission Act: Established to enforce antitrust laws.
1936	Robinson-Patman Act: Prohibited selling products at "unreasonably low prices" with the intent of reducing competition.
1950	Celler-Kefauver Act: Outlawed asset-purchase mergers that would substantially reduce competition.
1980	Hart-Scott-Rodino Act: Extended antitrust legislation to proprietorships and partnerships.

closed a loophole in the Clayton Act by prohibiting one firm from purchasing another firm's physical assets (like buildings and equipment) when the acquisition would reduce competition substantially. The Hart–Scott–Rodino Act of 1980 extended antitrust legislation to proprietorships and partnerships. Before this act, antitrust legislation applied only to corporations.

Two government organizations, the Antitrust Division of the Department of Justice and the Federal Trade Commission, are responsible for initiating actions against individuals or firms that may be violating antitrust laws. The courts have the power to impose penalties on the executives found to be in violation of the laws, including fines and prison sentences. In some cases, the government seeks no penalties but directs the firm to discontinue illegal practices and take other measures to promote competition.

TEST Your Understanding

4. List three types of antitrust policies.
5. Why was the federal government concerned about the merger of Interstate Bakeries and Continental Baking?
6. What are the essential provisions of the new guidelines for corporate mergers?

Deregulation of Airlines and Telecommunications

Up to this point in the chapter, we have discussed government policies that address the problems that result from market concentration. When a monopoly is inevitable, the government can regulate a natural monopoly to prevent excessive prices. When the merger of two firms would increase concentration, the government can prevent the merger and thereby promote competition. In this part of the chapter, we shift the emphasis and look at situations in which government regulations inhibit competition rather than promote it. When a regulation inhibits competition, reversing the course—deregulation—can promote it. We explore the recent deregulation of two markets: air travel and telecommunications. The Airline Deregulation Act of 1978 eliminated entry restrictions and price controls in the market for air travel. The Telecommunications Act of 1996 eliminated most price controls for cable television and established a framework for entry into the markets for cable television service, local telephone service, and Internet service.

Deregulation of Airlines

Consider first the deregulation of airline service.[7] Before 1978, the Civil Aeronautics Board (CAB) regulated interstate air travel by limiting entry into the market and controlling prices. About 90% of the markets were monopolized, and studies indicated that prices were 30% to 50% higher than they would have been in a more competitive environment. The Airline Deregulation Act of 1978 eliminated most of the entry restrictions and price controls, and the CAB eventually disappeared.

Deregulation led to lower prices, which fell by about 28%, on average. By 1998, deregulation had generated $24 billion in savings for passengers. Several factors contributed to the lower prices: competition from incumbent carriers (18% of the savings), competition from Southwest Airlines (31%), competition from other entrants (10%), and improvements in carriers' operating efficiencies (41%). Although prices fell on most routes, about a quarter of routes actually experienced price increases. In general, prices were lower on long routes and higher on short routes. This is not surprising, because the CAB had a policy of setting long-haul fares above average cost and short-haul fares below average cost.

A continuing problem is that many airports are dominated by just one or two airlines. In 1998, there were 12 hub airports where the two largest carriers had at least 85% of the market. At these airports, fares were 23% higher than at other airports with more competition, including low-cost carriers like Southwest Airlines.

Deregulation of Telecommunication Services

Consider next the deregulation of telecommunication services.[8] The Telecommunications Act of 1996 established new rules for firms involved in the transmission of video, voice, and data in order to promote competition in those markets. Several provisions of the act affect the Regional Bell Operating Companies (the Baby Bells) that were formed as a result of the breakup of AT&T in 1982. Here are the most important provisions of the act:

▶ *Local telephone service.* The act opened local telephone service to competition. New firms will now compete with the Baby Bells for local-service customers. In addition, cable TV firms might eventually provide telephone service over their cables.

► *Cable TV service.* Price controls for cable TV services were eliminated, and telephone companies will now be allowed to enter the market for cable TV services.
► *Long-distance service.* Once there is sufficient competition for local telephone service, the Baby Bells will be allowed to enter the long-distance market.

The challenge in deregulating local telephone service is to develop a set of rules giving competitors access to the copper wires leading into residences. That access is currently controlled by the Baby Bells. After a slow start, there has been some progress in opening up local telephone service to competition, with most of the progress in large cities. As competition spreads, we can expect lower prices for local service, just as we saw with the deregulation of long-distance service in 1984.

Deregulation of Electricity

Consider next the deregulation of electricity. The electricity industry has been regulated as a natural monopoly since its early days. There are three stages of producing electricity: generation in power plants, transmission along high-voltage lines, and distribution to final users along low-voltage lines. The transmission stage is subject to economies of scale because a city can be served by one set of transmission lines from power plants. There are substantial fixed costs associated with laying the transmission lines, so it is sensible to lay one set of lines and regulate the single firm as a natural monopolist. The same economies of scale occur when it comes to the distribution of power to individual users.

Until recently, there were also substantial economics of scale in electricity generation. The minimum efficient scale for power plants was large relative to the size of the markets they served, meaning that a single firm could supply the market more efficiently than several small firms. Under traditional electricity regulation, public and private utilities were responsible for all three phases of electricity production: They generated electricity in their own power plants and then used their own transmission and distribution systems to deliver electricity to consumers. State and local governments granted each utility a monopoly over a particular geographical area and set the price of electricity at a level so the utility earned a reasonable or "fair" accounting profit, including a fair return on capital investment. This is the average-cost pricing we discussed earlier in the chapter. Because utilities were responsible for all three stages of production, there was just one price to control—the retail price charged to consumers.

In the 1990s, there was growing pressure to deregulate the electricity market. Technological innovations reduced the economies of scale in electricity generation, so generation was no longer a true natural monopoly. For example, the minimum efficient scale for combined cycle gas turbine technology (CCGT) is about one-fifth the scale of a traditional power plant. Instead of a single power source for a city, there could be many generators, with competition among alternative producers leading to lower prices. A second factor in the pressure for deregulation was the substantial variation in electricity prices across states. For example, the price was 10 cents per kilowatt hour (kWh) in some northeastern states (Massachusetts, Connecticut, and New York),

6 cents in some central states (Indiana and Wisconsin), and 5 cents in northwestern states (Oregon and Washington). In California, the price was 9.5 cents per kWh. Consumers in high-price states called for deregulation to allow electricity to be transmitted across state lines.

Electricity Deregulation in California

The state of California reformed its electricity regulation program in 1998. Although the plan is often labeled "California's Deregulation Plan," the label is inaccurate because although some regulations were eliminated, others remained in force. In an attempt to foster competition at the generation level, the state's utilities sold off their generating facilities to the highest bidders. The wholesale price of electricity (paid by utilities and other energy retailers to generators) was allowed to fluctuate with market forces. In contrast, the retail price was subject to strict controls: It was rolled back by 10% and was to be maintained at this level for several years.

Two years after the reform program was implemented, the California electricity market was in disarray. Because of growing demand and a delay in getting new generation facilities up and running, utilities did not have enough power to meet demand and were forced to implement rolling blackouts—cutting off the power supply for an hour in alternating areas. The wholesale price for electricity soared above $200 per megawatt hour (MWh) while the retail price remained at about $60 per MWh. Electric utilities lost money on each kilowatt they sold, totaling billions of dollars. By 2001, the retailer/utilities had lost $12 billion, and in early 2001 one of the state's largest utilities, Pacific Gas and Electric, filed for bankruptcy.

The higher wholesale price was caused by a combination of higher fuel costs for generators, a drought that decreased supply from hydroelectric generators in the

Electricity deregulation in California caused rolling power outages. Wholesale prices for electricity were allowed to fluctuate, but retail prices were not.

Pacific Northwest, and price manipulation by generating companies. The objective of the reform plan had been to promote competition in the generating market, but after the utilities sold their power plants to the highest bidders, just a few companies controlled most of the power generated in the state. As we saw earlier in the book, firms in oligopolies have the power to charge a price higher than the competitive price, and there is evidence that's what happened in California. One study suggests that the market price was almost twice the competitive price and that generating companies used a strategy of withholding supply (taking plants off line to create an artificial shortage) to manipulate prices.[9]

The California energy crisis is an example of the "perfect storm" explanation of disasters. Although no one factor that contributed to the problem—an increase in demand for electricity, stagnant supply, rising fuel costs, retail price controls, price manipulation, or the drought in the Pacific Northwest—by itself would have caused major problems, their convergence in 2001 led to an electricity crisis.

Electricity Deregulation in Other U.S. States

In the mid-1990s, Pennsylvania and New York restructured their electricity markets, with both moving toward deregulation. Consumers in both states can now choose from several electricity retailers. Some retailers also generate their own power, whereas others buy power from generating companies and transmit it to business and residential users. Consumers can get on the Internet and type in their zip codes to get a list of alternative suppliers. By April 2001, almost 800,000 Pennsylvanians had selected alternative electricity suppliers.

The early experience with electricity deregulation in the two states is mixed. Prices are lower in Pennsylvania but much higher in New York. Under the New York plan, utilities sold off their generating plants to the highest bidders. The plants were sold to a small number of firms, and the purchase prices were much higher than expected, reflecting the expectations that in the deregulated market with a small number of firms, each could charge a high price. Over a one-year period, the average bill from Con Ed, a generating company in New York, increased by about 38% as a result of higher fuel costs and perhaps some exercise of market power by Con Ed.

It is too early to determine the long-term effects on electricity deregulation. The energy debacle in California has provided some important lessons for policymakers in other states. Many other states are at earlier stages of the deregulation process and may modify their plans to avoid some of the problems generated by the perfect storm in California.

TEST Your Understanding

7. Did the deregulation of the airline industry lead to low prices in all cities?
8. Under what conditions will the Baby Bells be allowed to provide long-distance service?
9. List the factors that contributed to the California energy crisis.

In this chapter, we've explored some policy issues concerning firms in concentrated industries. We've looked at different government antitrust policies and examined the effects of deregulation on competition and prices. Here are some opportunities to do your own economic analysis.

1. Environmental Costs for Regulated Monopoly

The Bonneville Power Administration (BPA) is a regulated monopoly in the Northwest that uses dozens of hydroelectric dams to generate electricity. Unfortunately, the BPA's dams block the paths of migrating fish, contributing to the decline of several species. Suppose that BPA spends $100 million to make its hydroelectric dams less hazardous for migrating fish. Who will bear the cost of this program?

2. Cost Savings from a Merger

Consider the following statement from a firm that has proposed a merger between two companies: "The two companies could save about $50 million per year by combining our production, marketing, and administrative operations. In other words, we could realize substantial economies of scale. Therefore, the government should allow the merger." In light of the new guidelines concerning mergers, how would you react to this statement?

3. Willingness to Pay for New Airport Gates

Your city is considering an airport expansion project that would increase the number of airport gates and allow additional airlines to serve your city. According to a recent report, the additional competition made possible by the new gates would decrease the average airline fare from $220 to $200 and increase the number of passengers from 400 to 600 per day. The city would borrow money to finance the project, and the daily payment required to pay off the loan (over 20 years) would be $8,100. Is the project worthwhile from a social perspective?

SUMMARY

In this chapter, we've explored public policies for markets with a few dominant firms. In the case of natural monopoly, the government can regulate prices. In other industries, the government uses antitrust policies to affect the number of firms in the market, encouraging competition that leads to lower prices. Here are the main points of the chapter:

1 A natural monopoly occurs when there are large-scale economies in production, so the market can support only one firm.

2 Under an average-cost pricing policy, the regulated price for a natural monopoly is equal to the average cost of production.

3 The government uses antitrust policy to break up some dominant firms, prevent some corporate mergers, and regulate business practices that reduce competition.

4 The modern approach to merger policy uses price data to predict the effects of a merger.

5 In most circumstances, predatory pricing is unprofitable because the monopoly power is costly to acquire and hard to maintain.

6 The deregulation of the airline industry led to more competition and lower prices on average, but higher prices in some markets.

PROBLEMS AND DISCUSSION QUESTIONS

1 Consider a regulated natural monopoly with an initial price (equal to average cost) of $3 per unit. Suppose the demand for the monopolist's product increases. What will happen to the price? How does this differ from the effects of an increase in demand for a product produced in a perfectly competitive market?

2 Consider a natural monopolist. Here are some data on its prices and quantities:

Price per unit	$20	$19	$18	$17	$16
Quantity (units)	100	120	140	160	180
Marginal revenue	—	—	—	—	—

  a. Complete the table: For each quantity, use the formula for marginal revenue (from Chapter 13) to compute the marginal revenue.

  b. Draw the monopolist's demand curve and the monopolist's marginal-revenue curve.

  c. Suppose that the monopolist's long-run marginal cost is $9. How much output should the monopolist produce?

3 Consider a market that is initially served by two firms, each of which charges a price of $10 and sells 100 units of the good. The long-run average cost of production is constant at $9 per unit. Suppose a merger would increase the price to $14 and reduce the total quantity sold from 200 to 150. Compute the consumer loss associated with the merger. How does it compare to the increase in profit? What is the net loss from the merger?

4 Consider an allegation that a firm is engaging in predatory pricing. Why might you be skeptical about such a claim?

5 A construction project at your city's airport is nearing completion, and your job is to decide how to use the 10 new gates of the airport. The city is currently served by Gotcha Airlines, which has offered the city $20 million to help cover the cost of the airport construction project. In return, the new gates would be designated for the exclusive use of Gotcha. What trade-offs are associated with accepting Gotcha's offer?

6 As the recently appointed head of the Federal Communications Commission, your job is to develop a set of rules for the use of the cables laid by cable television companies. You must decide whether Internet Service Providers (ISPs) should be able to access the cable company's lines, and, if so, at what price.

MODEL ANSWERS TO QUESTIONS

Chapter-Opening Questions

1 For each firm, the break-even output is about three million subscribers. In 2003, neither firm had reached this level, but both expect to do so by 2005 or 2006.

2 The two firms compete vigorously for shelf space alongside the market leader, Gerber, so eliminating one brand would lead to less competition and higher prices.

3 Deregulation decreased prices on average, but increased concentration in some cities led to higher fares in those cities.

Test Your Understanding

1 Marginal revenue, marginal cost.

2 The firm's demand curve shifts to the left: At each price, the firm sells a smaller quantity.

3 Below.

4 Breaking up monopolies, blocking mergers, and regulating business practices (price fixing, tying, and price discrimination).

5 Scanner data showed that the white breads produced by the two firms were close substitutes. An unregulated merger would have reduced competition and led to higher prices.

6 Companies that are involved in a proposed merger can present evidence that the merger would reduce costs and lead to lower prices, better products, or better service for consumers. If the evidence for this is convincing, the government might allow a merger that reduces the number of firms in a market.

7 No. On average, prices decreased, but travelers to and from some cities that are served by only one or two airlines pay higher prices.

8 Sufficient competition in the market for local telephone service.

9 An increase in demand for electricity, stagnant supply, rising fuel costs, retail price controls, price manipulation, and drought in the Pacific Northwest.

NOTES

1. "The Economics of Antitrust: The Trustbuster's New Tools," *The Economist*, May 2, 1998, pp. 62–64.; *Federal Trade Commission v. Staples, Inc.*, 970 F. Supp. 1066 (D.D.C. 1997, Hogan, J); U.S. Federal Trade Commission, *Promoting Competition, Protecting Consumers: A Plain English Guide to Antitrust Laws* (*http://www.ftc.gov/bc/compguide/index.htm*).

2. Associated Press Wire News, "Satellite Radio Takes Off in U.S.," June 1, 2003.

3. John R. Wilke, "New Antitrust Rules May Ease Path to Mergers," *Wall Street Journal*, April 9, 1997, pp. A3–A4.

4. *Wall Street Journal*, "Baby-Food Makers Heinz, Beech-Nut Call Off Merger Following Court Ruling," April 27, 2001; United State District Court for the District of Columbia, "*Federal Trade Commission v. H. J. Heinz Company*: Memorandum in Support of Plaintiff's Motion for Preliminary Injunction," July 24, 2000.

5. David M. Barton and Roger Sherman, "The Price and Profit Effects of Horizontal Merger: A Case Study," *Journal of Industrial Economics*, vol. 33, December 1984, pp. 165–177.

6. "The Economics of Antitrust: The Trustbuster's New Tools," *The Economist*, May 2, 1998, pp. 62–64.

7. William G. Shepherd and James W. Brock, "Airlines," Chapter 10 in *The Structure of American Industry*, edited by Walter Adams and James W. Brock (Upper Saddle River, NJ: Prentice Hall, 1995); Clifford Winston, "U.S. Industry Adjustment to Economic Deregulation," *Journal of Economic Perspectives*," vol. 12, no. 3, Summer 1998, pp. 89–110; Paul MacAvoy, *Industry Regulation and the Performance of the American Economy* (New York: W. W. Norton, 1992); Alfred E. Kahn, "Airline Deregulation—A Mixed Bag But a Clear Success Nonetheless," *Transportation Law Journal*, vol. 16, 1988, pp. 229–252; Steven A. Morrison, "Airline Service: The Evolution of Competition Since Deregulation," Chapter 6 in *Industry Studies*, 3rd ed., edited by Larry Duetsch (New York: Sharpe, 2002).

8. Susan McMaster, "Telecommunications: Competition and Network Access," Chapter 14 in *Industry Studies*, 3rd ed. edited by Larry Duetsch (New York: Sharpe, 2002).

9. Paul Joskow and Edward Kahn, "A Quantitative Analysis of Pricing Behavior in California's Wholesale Electricity Market During Summer 2000," NBER Working Paper 8157, March 2001.

Part

5

The Labor Market and Income Distribution

The Labor Market and the Distribution of Income

ecent reports on the earnings of college graduates have made the jobs of college recruiters easier:[1]

▶ In 1972, the typical college graduate earned 43% more than a high-school graduate.

▶ In 2000, the typical college graduate earned 94% more than a high-school graduate.

These facts raise two questions: First, why do college graduates earn so much more than high-school graduates? Second, why did the earnings gap almost double during the last three decades?

U p to this point in the book, we have discussed the markets for final goods and services. In this chapter, we switch to the market for one of the factors of production, labor. Labor costs are responsible for about three-fourths of production costs, and for most people, labor income is by far the most important source of income. We'll use a model of supply and demand to see how wages are determined and why wages differ between college graduates and high-school graduates, men and women, and people in different occupations. Here are some of the practical questions we answer:

1 If the wage increases, will an individual work more hours or fewer hours?
2 If a worker switches from a relatively safe factory job to a job in a steel mill, by how much will his or her wage increase?
3 Why do women, on average, earn only about 75% as much as men?
4 Why has the distribution of income become more unequal in the last 30 years?

The Demand for Labor

We can use supply and demand curves to show how wages are determined and show how changes in the labor market affect wages and employment. We'll start with the demand side of the labor market, looking first at how an individual firm can use the key principles of economics to decide how many workers to hire.

The demand for labor and other productive inputs is different from the demand for consumer products such as stereos, books, haircuts, and pizza. Firms use workers to produce the products demanded by consumers, and so economists say that labor demand is a "derived demand." That is, it is determined by or derived from the demand for the products produced by workers. As we'll see in this chapter, the demand for labor is determined by the demand for consumer products and the price of those products.

Labor Demand by an Individual Firm in the Short Run

Consider a perfectly competitive firm that produces rubber balls. Because this firm is perfectly competitive, it takes the price of its output and the prices of its inputs as given. Because it hires a tiny fraction of the workers in the labor market, it takes the market wage as given and can hire as many workers as it wants at that wage. In addition, the firm produces a tiny fraction of the rubber balls sold in the market, so it takes the price of its output as given. Let's say the price of rubber balls is $0.50.

Consider the firm's hiring decision in the short run, defined as the period during which at least one input—for example, its factory—cannot be changed. We can use two of the key principles of economics to explain the firm's hiring decision. Recall the marginal principle:

MARGINAL *Principle*

Increase the level of an activity if its marginal benefit exceeds its marginal cost, but reduce the level if the marginal cost exceeds the marginal benefit. If possible, pick the level at which the marginal benefit equals the marginal cost.

The firm will pick the quantity of labor at which the marginal benefit of labor equals the marginal cost of labor. It can hire as many workers as it wants at the market wage, so the marginal cost of labor equals the hourly wage. If the wage is $8 per hour, the extra cost associated with one more hour of labor—the marginal cost—is $8, regardless of how many workers the firm hires.

What is the marginal benefit of labor? The firm hires labor to produce balls, so the marginal benefit equals the monetary value of the balls produced with an additional hour of labor. Table 17.1 shows how to compute the marginal benefit associated with different quantities of labor. The first two columns show the relationship between the number of workers and the quantity of balls produced. Recall the principle of diminishing returns:

Principle OF DIMINISHING RETURNS

Suppose that output is produced with two or more inputs and we increase one input while holding the other inputs fixed. Beyond some point—called the point of diminishing returns—output will increase at a decreasing rate.

TABLE 17.1 Using the Marginal Principle to Make a Labor Decision

Number of Workers	Balls per Hour	Marginal Product of Labor	Price per Ball	Marginal Revenue Product of Labor (*MRP*)	Marginal Cost when Wage = $8
1	26	26	$0.50	$13	$8
2	50	24	0.50	$12	$8
3	72	22	0.50	$11	$8
4	92	20	0.50	$10	$8
5	108	16	0.50	$ 8	$8
6	120	12	0.50	$ 6	$8
7	128	8	0.50	$ 4	$8
8	130	2	0.50	$ 1	$8

To simplify matters, we'll assume diminishing returns start to occur with the second worker, but as we saw earlier in the book, the **marginal product of labor**, the change in output from one additional unit of labor, typically rises for the first few workers and then eventually decreases. As shown in the third column of Table 17.1, marginal product of labor decreases as the number of workers increases, from 26 for the first worker, to 24 for the second worker, and so on.

Marginal product of labor
The change in output from one additional unit of labor

The marginal benefit of labor equals the **marginal-revenue product of labor (MRP)**, defined as the extra revenue generated by one additional worker. To compute the MRP, we multiply the marginal product of labor by the price of output ($0.50 per ball in this example):

$$MRP = \text{marginal product} \times \text{price of output}$$

Marginal-revenue product of labor (MRP)
The extra revenue generated from one more unit of labor; MRP is equal to the price of output times the marginal product of labor.

Figure 17.1 shows the marginal-revenue product curve. Because the marginal product drops as the number of workers increases, the MRP curve is negatively sloped, falling from $11 for the third worker (point n) to $8 for the fifth worker (point m), and so on.

A firm can use its MRP curve to decide how much labor to hire at a particular wage. In Figure 17.1, the marginal-cost curve is horizontal at the market wage ($8). The perfectly competitive firm takes the wage as given, so the marginal-cost curve is also the labor-supply curve faced by the firm. The marginal principle is satisfied at point m, where the marginal cost equals the marginal-revenue product. The firm will hire 5 workers because for the first 5 workers, the marginal benefit (the MRP) is greater than or equal to the marginal cost (the $8 wage). It would not be sensible to hire another worker because the additional revenue from the sixth worker ($6) would be less than the $8 additional cost of that worker. If the wage increases to $11, the firm will satisfy the marginal principle at point n, hiring only 3 workers.

Short-run demand curve for labor
A curve showing the relationship between the wage and the quantity of labor demanded over the short run, the period when the firm cannot change its production facility.

The MRP curve is also the firm's **short-run demand curve for labor**, which shows the relationship between the wage and the quantity of labor demanded in the

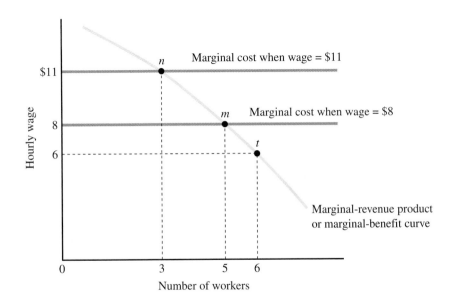

The Marginal Principle and the Firm's Demand for Labor
Using the marginal principle, the firm picks the quantity of workers at which the marginal benefit (the marginal revenue product of labor) equals the marginal cost (the wage). The firm's short-run demand curve for labor is the marginal revenue product curve.

short run, the period when the firm cannot change its production facility. The demand curve answers the following question: At each wage, how many hours of labor does the firm want to hire? We've already used the *MRP* curve to answer this question for two different wages ($11 and $8), and we can do the same for any other wage. Because the *MRP* curve is a marginal-benefit curve, and the firm uses the marginal principle to decide how much labor to hire, the *MRP* curve is the same as the firm's demand curve for labor. If you pick a wage, the *MRP* curve tells you exactly how much labor the firm will demand at that wage.

What sort of changes would cause the demand curve to shift? To draw the labor-demand curve, we fix the price of the output and the productivity of workers. Therefore, an increase in the price of the output will increase the *MRP* of workers, shifting the entire demand curve for labor to the right: At each wage, the firm will hire more workers. This is shown in Figure 17.2. An increase in the price of balls shifts the labor-demand curve to the right. At a wage of $8, the firm hires 7 workers instead of 5. Similarly, if workers become more productive, the increase in the marginal product of labor will increase the *MRP* and shift the demand curve to the right. Conversely, a decrease in price or labor productivity would shift the demand curve to the left.

Market Demand for Labor in the Short Run

To draw the short-run market demand curve for labor, we add the labor demands of all the firms that use a particular type of labor. In the simplest case, all firms are identical and we simply multiply the number of firms by the quantity of labor demanded by the typical firm. If there were 100 firms and each hired 5 workers at a wage of $8, the market demand for labor would be 500 workers. Similarly, if the typical firm hired 3 workers at a wage of $11, the market demand would be 300 workers.

FIGURE 17.2

An Increase in the Price of Output Shifts the Labor-Demand Curve

An increase in the price of the good produced by workers increases the marginal revenue product at each quantity of workers, shifting the demand curve to the right. At each wage, the firm will demand more workers. For example, at a wage of $8, the demand for labor increases from 5 workers (point *m*) to 7 workers (point *z*).

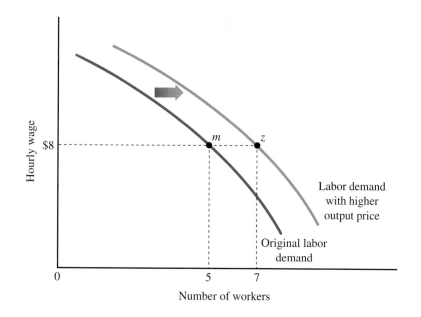

What About Labor Demand in the Long Run?

Recall that in the long run, firms can enter or leave the market and firms already in the market can change all of their inputs, including their production facilities. The **long-run demand curve for labor** shows the relationship between the wage and the quantity of labor demanded over the long run when the number of firms in the market can change and firms in the market can modify their production facilities.

Although there are no diminishing returns in the long run, the market demand curve is still negatively sloped. As the wage increases, the quantity of labor demanded decreases for two reasons:

- *The* **output effect**. An increase in the wage will increase the cost of producing balls, and firms will pass on at least part of the higher labor cost to their consumers: Prices will increase. According to the law of demand, firms will sell fewer balls at the higher price, so they will need less of all inputs, including labor.
- *The* **input-substitution effect**. An increase in the wage will cause the firm to substitute other inputs for labor. At a wage of $4, it may not be sensible to use much machinery in the ball factory, but at a wage of $20, it may be sensible to mechanize the factory, using more machinery and fewer workers.

The output effect reinforces the input-substitution effect, so the market demand curve is negatively sloped.

The notion of input substitution applies to other labor markets as well. For the most graphic examples of factor substitution, we can travel from a developed country such as the United States, Canada, France, Germany, or Japan to a less-developed country in South America, Africa, or Asia. Wages are much lower in the less-developed countries, so production tends to be more labor-intensive. In other words, labor is less costly relative to machinery and equipment, so labor is substituted for these other inputs. Here are some examples:

- Mining. U.S. firms use huge earth-moving equipment to mine for minerals, while many firms in less-developed countries use thousands of workers, digging by hand.
- Furniture. Firms in developed countries manufacture furniture with sophisticated machinery and equipment, while many firms in less-developed countries make furniture by hand.
- Accounting. Accountants in developed countries use computers and sophisticated software programs, while some accountants in less-developed countries use simple calculators and ledger paper.

Short-Run versus Long-Run Demand

How does the short-run demand curve for labor compare to the long-run demand curve? There is less flexibility in the short run because firms cannot enter or leave the market and they cannot modify their production facilities. As a result, the demand for labor is less elastic in the short run. That means the short-run demand curve is steeper than the long-run demand curve. You may recall that we used the same logic to explain

Long-run demand curve for labor
A curve showing the relationship between the wage and the quantity of labor demanded over the long run, when the number of firms in the market can change and firms can modify their production facilities.

Output effect
The change in the quantity of labor demanded resulting from a change in the quantity of output produced.

Input-substitution effect
The change in the quantity of labor demanded resulting from an increase in the price of labor relative to the price of other inputs.

why the short-run supply curve for a product (plain cotton T-shirts) was steeper than the long-run supply curve for the product.

TEST Your Understanding

1. The owner of a professional basketball team is considering hiring a new player for $3 million per year. Under what circumstances would it be sensible to hire the player?
2. Complete the statement with "increase" or "decrease": According to the output effect, a decrease in the wage will _____ production costs, so the price of output will _____. The quantity of output produced will _____, so the demand for labor will _____.
3. Explain the input-substitution effect associated with a decrease in the wage.

The Supply of Labor

The labor-supply curve answers the following question: How many hours of labor will be supplied at each wage? When we speak of a labor market, we are referring to the market for a specific occupation in a specific geographical area. Consider the supply for nurses in the city of Florence. The supply question is, How many hours of nursing services will be supplied at each wage? To answer that question, we must think about how many nurses are in the city and how many hours each nurse works.

The Individual Labor-Supply Decision: How Many Hours to Work?

Let's start with an individual's decision about how many hours to work. The decision to work is a decision to sacrifice some leisure time for money: Each hour of work reduces leisure time by one hour. Therefore, the demand for leisure is the flip side of the supply of labor. The price of leisure time is the income sacrificed for each hour of leisure, that is, the hourly wage.

We know from Chapter 4 that an increase in the price of a good has two effects: A substitution effect and an income effect. An increase in the wage—the price of leisure—has two effects on the demand for leisure: The **substitution effect** and the **income effect**.

Consider first the substitution effect. The worker faces a trade-off between leisure time and consumer goods such as music, books, food, and entertainment. For each hour of leisure time Leah takes, she loses one hour of work time, and her income drops by an amount equal to the wage. Therefore, she has less money to spend on consumer goods. For example, if the wage is $8 per hour, each hour of leisure decreases the amount of income available to spend on consumer goods by $8. When the wage increases to, say, $10, Leah will sacrifice more income—and consumer goods—for each hour of leisure she takes. Given the larger sacrifice of consumer goods per hour of leisure time, she will demand less leisure. That means that she will work more hours

Substitution effect for leisure demand

The change in leisure time resulting from a change in the wage (the price of leisure) relative to the price of other goods.

Income effect for leisure demand

The change in leisure time resulting from a change in real income caused by a change in the wage.

nd earn more money for consumer goods. In other words, as the wage increases, she will substitute income—and the consumer goods it buys—for leisure time.

Consider next the income effect of an increase in the wage. For most people, leisure is a normal good in the sense that the demand for leisure increases as real income increases. An increase in the wage increases Leah's real income in the sense that she can afford more of all goods, including leisure time. Suppose Leah has a total of 100 hours per week to divide between leisure and work. At a wage of $10, she works 36 hours and has 64 hours of leisure. She also earns $360 ($10 per hour times 36 hours of work) and spends that amount on consumer goods. If her wage increases to $15, her real income increases because she can have more consumer goods and more leisure time. For example, if she worked only 30 hours, she could buy $450 worth of consumer goods ($15 per hour × 30 hours) and have 70 hours of leisure (100 hours per week – 30 hours of work). The increase in real income causes Leah to consume more of all normal goods, including leisure time. The increase in real income causes her to demand more leisure and supply less labor.

As you can see, in the labor market the income and substitution effects of an increase in wages have opposite results: The substitution effect decreases the desired leisure time, while the income effect increases the desired leisure time. Therefore, we can't predict whether an increase in the wage will cause Leah to demand more leisure time (supply less labor) or less leisure (supply more labor).

A simple example will show why we can't predict a worker's response to an increase in the wage. Suppose each nurse initially works 36 hours per week at an hourly wage of $10 and the wage increases to $12. Here are three reasonable responses to the higher wage:

1 Lester works fewer hours. If Lester works 30 hours instead of 36 hours, he gets 6 hours of extra leisure time and still earns the same income per week ($360 = 30 hours × $12 per hour).
2 Sam works the same number of hours. If Sam continues to work 36 hours per week, he gets an additional $72 of income ($2 per hour × 36 hours) and the same amount of leisure time.
3 Maureen works more hours. If Maureen works 43 hours instead of 36 hours, she sacrifices 7 hours of leisure time but earns a total of $516, compared to only $360 at a wage of $10 per hour.

Empirical studies of the labor market confirm that each of these responses is reasonable. When the wage increases, some people work more, others work less, and others work about the same amount.[2] In most labor markets, the average number of hours per worker doesn't change very much as the wage changes because the increases in work hours from people like Maureen are nearly offset by decreases in work hours from people like Lester.

The Market Supply Curve for Labor

Now that we know how individual workers respond to changes in wages, we're ready to consider the supply side of the labor market. The **market supply curve for labor** shows the relationship between the wage and the quantity of labor

Market supply curve for labor

A curve showing the relationship between the wage and the quantity of labor supplied.

FIGURE 17.3

Supply, Demand, and Labor Market Equilibrium

At the market equilibrium (point *e*, with wage = $15 per hour and quantity = 16,000 hours), the quantity supplied equals the quantity demanded, so there is neither excess demand for labor nor excess supply of labor.

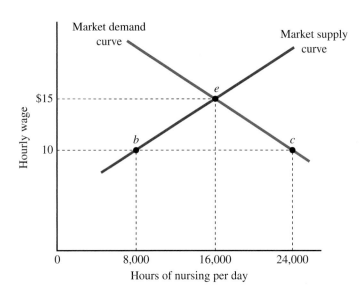

supplied. In Figure 17.3, the market supply curve for labor is positively sloped, consistent with the law of supply: The higher the wage (the price of labor), the larger the quantity of labor supplied. An increase in the wage affects the quantity of nursing supplied in three ways:

1 **Hours worked per employee.** When the wage increases, some nurses will work more hours, while others will work fewer hours, and others will work the same number of hours. We don't know for certain whether the average number of work hours will increase, decrease, or stay the same, but the change in the average number of hours worked is likely to be relatively small.

2 **Occupational choice.** An increase in the nursing wage will cause some workers to switch from other occupations to nursing and motivate more new workers to pick nursing over other occupations.

3 **Migration.** Some nurses in other cities will move to Florence to earn the higher wages offered there.

The second and third effects reinforce one another, so an increase in the wage causes movement upward along the market supply curve. If the wage of Florence nurses increases from $10 to $15 per hour, the quantity of nurses supplied increases from 8,000 hours per day (point *b*) to 16,000 hours per day (point *e*). Although individual workers may not work more hours as the wage increases, the supply curve is positively sloped because an increase in the wage changes workers' occupational choices and causes migration.

Another decision relevant for labor supply is whether a person will be in the work force at all. Some people choose alternative pursuits, including education, leisure, and raising families. For a discussion of workers' retirement decisions and the impact of early retirement on European societies, read, "A Closer Look: The Economics of Not Working."

A CLOSER LOOK

The Economics of Not Working

In the last 30 years, the amount of time spent in retirement has increased dramatically.[3] People are retiring at earlier ages and living longer. In Britain, only about a quarter of people aged 60–64 work, down from about three-quarters 30 years ago. Over the same period, the life expectancy at age 60 increased from 15 years to 20 years. In the European Union, only 39% of people aged 55–64 are working, compared to about three-fourths of people aged 25–54.

This is great news for older folks, but it is causing a strain in systems that support retirees. If current trends continue, the share of national income spent by developed countries to support their retirees will increase from about 15% to 22%, and people in the workforce will pay higher taxes. One simple solution would be to increase the retirement age, matching longer life spans with more time in the workforce. Compared to 30 years ago, the typical person today works 5 fewer years because of earlier retirement but earns 10 more years of retirement income (5 years from earlier retirement and 5 years from a longer life span). The Prime Minister of France suggests that to prevent a growing financial burden, the French must (a) extend working life by 6 years, (b) raise contributions to retirement accounts by half, or (c) reduce benefits by a third. Another solution would be to encourage workers to save for their own retirement years, which would eventually reduce the tax burden on the general public.

Response to a Wage Cut?

Elise is the absentee owner of a sweater factory that employs 50 workers. After hearing that changes in wages cause nearly offsetting changes in the number of hours that people work—leaving total hours unchanged—she decides to cut wages in her sweater factory by 10%. She expected that the total hours worked and total output would remain about the same. Much to her surprise, the total output of her factory dropped by 90%. What happened?

The key to solving this puzzle is that workers respond to a wage cut in two ways. First, they can work more or fewer hours, and we know that, on average, they will work about the same number of hours. Second, they can quit and go to work for another firm. In a labor market with many potential employers, a firm that cuts its wage below the market wage will lose most if not all of its workers. ■

Labor Market Equilibrium

We're ready to put supply and demand together to think about equilibrium in the labor market. A market equilibrium is a situation in which there is no pressure to change the price of a good or service. Figure 17.3 shows the equilibrium in the market for nurses. The supply curve intersects the demand curve at point *e*, so the equilibrium wage is $15 per hour and the equilibrium quantity is 16,000 hours of nursing per day. At this wage, there is neither an excess demand for labor nor an excess supply of labor, so the market has reached an equilibrium.

Changes in Demand and Supply for Labor

How would a change in the demand for nurses affect the equilibrium wage of nurses? We know from Chapter 4 that a change in demand causes the equilibrium price and the equilibrium quantity to move in the same direction: An increase in demand increases the equilibrium price and quantity, whereas a decrease in demand decreases the equilibrium price and quantity. For example, suppose that the demand for medical care increases. Nurses help provide medical care, so an increase in the quantity of medical care demanded will shift the demand curve for nurses to the right: At each wage, firms will demand more hours of nursing services. As shown in Figure 17.4, an increase in demand increases the equilibrium wage and the equilibrium quantity of nursing services.

How would a change in supply of nurses affect the equilibrium wage of nurses? We know from Chapter 4 that a change in supply causes price and quantity to move in opposite directions: An increase in supply decreases the equilibrium price but increases the equilibrium quantity, whereas a decrease in supply increases the equilibrium price but decreases the equilibrium quantity. Suppose a new television program makes nursing look like an attractive occupation, causing a large number of youngsters to become nurses rather than accountants, lawyers, or doctors. The supply curve for nurses will shift to the right: At each wage, more nursing hours will be supplied. The equilibrium wage will decrease, and the equilibrium quantity will increase.

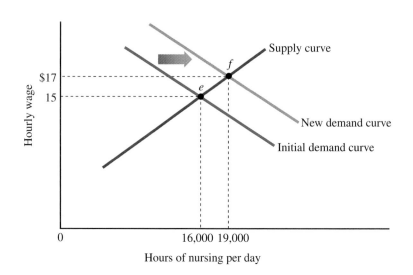

FIGURE 17.4

The Market Effects of an Increase in Demand for Labor

An increase in the demand for nursing services shifts the demand curve to the right, moving the equilibrium from point *e* to point *f*. The equilibrium wage increases from $15 to $17 per hour, and the equilibrium quantity increases from 16,000 hours to 19,000 hours.

The Market Effects of the Minimum Wage Laws

We can use the model of the labor market to show how various public policies like the federally mandated minimum wage affect total employment. In 2001, the federal minimum wage was $5.15 per hour. Figure 17.5 shows the effects of a minimum wage on the market for restaurant workers. The market equilibrium is shown by point *e*: The supply of restaurant workers equals demand at a wage of $4.70 and a quantity of 50,000 worker hours per day. Suppose a minimum wage is established at $5.15 per hour. At this wage, the quantity of labor demanded is only 49,000 hours (point *d* on the demand curve). In other words, the minimum wage decreases the quantity of labor used by restaurants by 1,000 hours per day.

What are the trade-offs associated with the minimum wage? From the perspectives of restaurant workers and restaurant diners, there is good news and bad news:

- Good news for some restaurant workers. Some workers keep their jobs and receive a higher wage ($5.15 per hour instead of $4.70 per hour).
- Bad news for some restaurant workers. Some workers lose their jobs. If the typical workday for restaurant workers is five hours, the loss of 1,000 hours of restaurant work per day translates into a loss of 200 jobs.
- Bad news for diners. The increase in the wage increases the cost of producing restaurant meals, increasing the price of meals.

There are winners and losers from the minimum wage: Workers who keep their jobs gain at the expense of other workers and at the expense of diners. A recent study suggests that a 10% increase in the minimum wage decreases the number of minimum-wage jobs by about 1%.[4]

In recent years, there has been growing concern in the United States about poor working conditions and low wages for foreign workers who produce products for U.S. consumers. For a discussion of this issue, read "A Closer Look: Foreign Sweatshops and Industry Codes of Conduct."

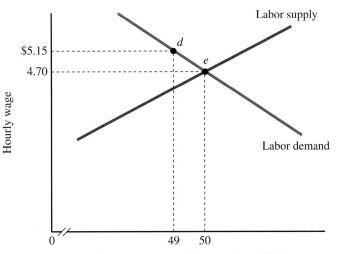

Hours of restaurant labor per day (1,000)

FIGURE 17.5

The Market Effects of a Minimum Wage

The market equilibrium is shown by point *e*. The wage is $4.70 per hour, and the quantity of labor is 50,000 labor hours per day. A minimum wage of $5.15 per hour decreases the quantity of labor demanded to 49,000 hours per day. Although some workers receive a higher wage, others lose their jobs or work fewer hours.

A CLOSER LOOK

Foreign Sweatshops and Industry Codes of Conduct

Several widely publicized reports have documented poor working conditions and low wages in foreign factories that produce shoes, clothing, and toys for U.S. corporations.[6] In 1996, a report revealed that part of Wal-Mart's Kathie Lee Collection was produced in Honduras by people working 20 hours per day for $0.31 per hour. Similar reports suggested that goods sold by Nike, Disney, and Mattel were produced in overseas sweatshops. Some human-rights activists have organized protests to publicize what they consider unethical business practices and have organized consumer boycotts.

The corporations have responded to the uproar by monitoring the firms that produce their goods and establishing codes of conduct for foreign suppliers. The Council on Economic Priorities, an interest group in New York, inspects workplaces and awards the "Social Accountability 8000" to businesses that meet its criteria for wages and working conditions. The Apparel Industry Partnership, a group that includes social activists and apparel firms, is developing a code of conduct for apparel producers. The group was pleased to see the results of a survey suggesting that three-fourths of America's shoppers would be willing to pay higher prices for clothes and shoes bearing a "No Sweat" label. Some companies have hired accounting firms such as PriceWaterhouseCoopers to audit their foreign suppliers. On campus, the United Students Against Sweatshops is developing a code of conduct for companies that produce products bearing university logos. The efforts to monitor the labor practices of foreign suppliers raise several questions:

▶ The improvement of working conditions and higher wages will increase the cost of producing the products. By how much will prices increase?

Corporations with overseas production facilities responded to the uproar over sweatshops by monitoring the foreign firms that produce the goods for the corporations and establishing codes of conduct for foreign suppliers.

▶ How much are consumers really willing to pay for "No Sweat" products?
▶ How many customers will firms selling "No Sweat" products lose to firms that don't meet the codes of conduct?
▶ How many apparel workers will lose their jobs?

The Trade-offs from Immigration

Since about 1850, international migration has played an important role in labor markets. In the first wave of immigration, from 1850 to 1913, over one million people migrated to the Americas each year. Most of the immigrants were from European countries. After several decades of war and economic depressions, massive immigration resumed in 1945. This time, most of the immigrants were from less-developed countries.

Immigration creates winners and losers within the economy. The increase in the supply of labor decreases wages for the native workers who have the same skill level as the immigrants. Because the average U.S. immigrant has less education and earns less income than the average native, immigrants compete with low-skill natives, decreasing their wages. On the benefit side, the decrease in the wages of low-skill labor decreases production costs and product prices, so consumers benefit. In general, we expect low-skill workers to lose as a result of immigration because the lower wages will dominate the benefits of lower consumer prices. In contrast, we expect high-skill workers to benefit from lower prices.

In 1994, economist George Borjas found that the net effect of immigration to the United States was positive, consistent with the idea that exchange increases efficiency and the size of the overall economic pie.[5] Immigration decreases the wages of low-skilled natives by $133 billion, but it generates benefits for consumers and firms totaling $140 billion. The net gain to the economy is $7 billion per year, about one tenth of 1% of total income. Immigration also changes how the economic pie is sliced, with high-skill workers gaining at the expense of low-skill workers. These conflicting effects lead to spirited debates over immigration policy.

TEST Your Understanding

4. Your objective is to earn exactly $120 per week. If your wage decreases from $6 to $4 per hour, how will you respond?
5. Each worker in a certain occupation works exactly 40 hours per week, regardless of the wage. Does this mean that the market supply curve for the occupation is vertical (a fixed quantity, regardless of the wages)?
6. Complete the following: A decrease in the supply of nurses will _____ the equilibrium wage and _____ the equilibrium quantity of nursing services.

Explaining Differences in Wages and Income

Now that we know how the equilibrium wage for a particular occupation is determined, we're ready to explain why wages vary from one job to another. Let's think about why some occupations pay more than others, why women earn less than men, and why college graduates earn more than high-school graduates.

Why Do Wages Differ Across Occupations?

There is substantial variation in wages across occupations. Most professional athletes earn more than medical doctors, who earn more than college professors, who earn more than janitors. We'll see that the wage for a particular occupation will be high if the supply of workers in that occupation is small relative to the demand for those workers.

This is shown in Figure 17.6, where the supply curve intersects the demand curve at a high wage. The supply of workers in a particular occupation could be small for four reasons:

1 *Few people with the required skills.* To play professional baseball, people must be able to hit balls thrown at them at about 90 miles per hour. The few people who have this skill are paid a lot of money because baseball owners compete with one another for skillful players, bidding up the wage. The same logic applies to other professional athletes, musicians, and actors. The few people who have the skills required for these occupations are paid high wages.

2 *High training costs.* The skills required for some occupations can only be acquired through education and training. For example, the skills that are required of a medical doctor can only be acquired in medical school, and legal skills can only be acquired in law school. If it is costly to acquire these skills, a relatively small number of people will become skilled, and they will receive high wages. The higher wage compensates workers for their training costs.

3 *Undesirable job features.* Some occupations are dangerous, and only a relatively small number of people are willing to work under these conditions. The workers with the greatest risk of losing their lives on the job are lumberjacks, boilermakers, taxicab drivers, and mine workers. The workers who choose dangerous occupations receive high wages, so they are compensated for the danger associated with their jobs. Each year one in 10,000 steelworkers is killed on the job. To compensate for the higher risk of getting killed on the job, steelworkers receive a wage premium of 3.7%, or about $700 more per year than they would in another occupation, given their skills and education.[7] The same logic applies to other undesirable job features. For example, wages are higher for jobs that are stressful or dirty or that force people to work at odd hours.

4 *Artificial barriers to entry.* As we'll see in the next chapter, government and professional licensing boards restrict the number of people in certain occupations, and labor unions restrict their membership. These supply restrictions increase wages.

The Equilibrium Wage when Labor Supply Is Low Relative to Demand

If supply is low relative to demand—because few people have the skills, training costs are high, or the job is undesirable—the equilibrium wage will be high.

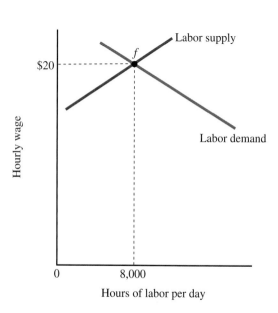

The Gender Pay Gap

Why do women, on average, earn less than men? In the United States, the typical woman earns about 75% as much as the typical man. The gender gap is smaller in European nations but much larger in Japan. An important factor in the gender gap is the concentration of women in occupations that have low wages. Given the distribution of men and women in different occupations, about half of female workers would have to change occupations to achieve equal gender representation in all occupations.[8]

A recent study explored several factors that contribute to the gender pay gap.[9] The study observed a gap of about 20% among workers aged 26–34. The study identified four factors that contribute to the gender gap.

▶ *Difference in worker skills and productivity.* More productive workers receive higher wages. On average, women have less education and work experience, so they receive lower wages. The study concluded that lower productivity is the most important factor in the gender gap.
▶ *Differences in occupational preferences.* Wages vary across occupations: Clerical and service occupations receive lower wages than craft and professional occupations. Compared to men, women express stronger preferences for low-wage occupations such as clerical and service occupations, and weaker preferences for some high-wage occupations such as craft and operator occupations. In contrast, women have slightly stronger preferences for high-wage professional and technical occupations. On balance, the general orientation of women toward low-wage occupations contributes to the gender gap.
▶ *Occupational discrimination.* Given the variation in wages across occupations, if employers have a bias against hiring women for high-paying occupations, women will receive lower wages. The study shows that on average, women are less successful than men in attaining their desired occupations, and this occupational discrimination by employers explains between 7% and 25% of the gender gap.
▶ *Wage discrimination.* If employers pay women less than their equally productive male counterparts, women's wages will be lower. The results of the study on this issue are mixed, with some evidence that wage discrimination is a significant factor in the gender pay gap.

The general conclusion of the study is that differences in productivity and occupational status are the most important factors in the gender pay gap. The relatively large number of women in low-paying occupations results both from the occupational preferences of women and employer discrimination that inhibits occupational attainment for women.

Racial Discrimination

What about differences in earnings by race? In 1995, African American males who worked full time earned 73% as much as their white counterparts earned, while African American females earned 86% as much as their white counterparts. Hispanic males earned 62% as much as white males, while Hispanic females earned 73% as much as white females.[10] For both males and females, part of the earnings gap is caused by differences in productivity: On average, whites have more education and work experience, so they are paid higher wages. Part of the wage gap is caused by racial discrimination. Some African American and Hispanic workers are paid lower wages for similar jobs, and others are denied opportunities to work in some high-paying jobs.

How much of the earnings gap is caused by discrimination? A recent study suggests that racial discrimination decreases the wages of African American men by about 13%.[11] Another study[12] shows that these earnings differences have decreased over the last few decades and that the differences are now small enough that "most of the disparity in earnings between blacks and whites in the labor market of the 1990s is due to the differences in skills they bring to the market, and not to discrimination within the labor market." The differences in skills brought to the labor market are caused by a number of factors, including past discrimination that has inhibited the acquisition of job skills and differences in educational opportunities. For example, in urban areas, about one-third of African American high-school students have above-

A CLOSER LOOK

Racial Discrimination in Hiring

Imagine that two recent high-school graduates apply for low-skill jobs advertised in the newspaper. The jobs include waiting tables, dishwashing, and working in warehouses. One man is white and admits to serving 18 months in prison for selling cocaine. The other applicant is an African American man without a criminal record. Which applicant has a greater chance of being called back for a second interview? In a carefully designed experiment with college students posing as job applicants, the white applicant with a criminal record was called back 17% of the time, while the crime-free African American applicant was called back only 14% of the time. In other words, the disadvantage of being African American is roughly equivalent to the disadvantage of spending 18 months in prison.[13]

This experiment in Milwaukee revealed substantial racial discrimination in hiring for low-skill jobs. According to Devah Pager, the researcher who conducted the experiment,

In these low-wage, entry-level markets, race remains a huge barrier. Affirmative-action pressures aren't operating here. Employers don't spend a lot of time screening applicants. They want a quick signal whether the applicant seems suitable. Stereotypes among young black men remain so prevalent and so strong that race continues to serve as a major signal of characteristics of which employers are wary.

In another experiment, economists responded in writing to help-wanted ads in Chicago and in Boston, using hypothetical names that were likely to be identified by employers as either white or African American. Applicants named Greg Kelly or Emily Walsh were 50% more likely to be called for interviews than those named Jamal Jackson or Lakisha Washington. Having a white-sounding name on an application was equivalent to about eight additional years of work experience. The researchers experimented with different resumes for both types of applicants. Adding work experience and computer skills increased the likelihood of interviews by 30% for white-sounding applicants but only 9% for those whose names suggested an African American background.

verage scores on reading and math exams, compared to about two-thirds of white
students.

Some recent experiments have demonstrated that for participants in the market
or low-skill jobs, race matters. Specifically, job applicants who are African American
are treated less favorably than whites. For a discussion of two experiments, read "A
Closer Look: Racial Discrimination in Hiring."

Why Do College Graduates Earn Higher Wages?

In 1999, the typical college graduate earned 80% more than the typical high-school
graduate. There are two explanations for the college premium.

The first explanation is based on supply and demand analysis. A college education
provides the skills necessary to enter certain occupations, so a college graduate has
more job options than a high-school graduate. Both high-school grads and college
grads can fill jobs that require only a high-school education, so the supply of workers
for these low-skill jobs is plentiful, and the equilibrium wage for these jobs is low. In
contrast, there is a smaller supply of workers for jobs that require a college education,
so the wages in these high-skill jobs are higher than the wages for low-skill jobs. This is
the **learning effect** of a college education: College students learn the skills required
for certain occupations, increasing their human capital.

The second explanation of the college premium requires a different perspective on
college and its role in the labor market. Suppose certain skills are required for a particular job, but an employer cannot determine whether a prospective employee has these
skills. For example, most managerial jobs require the employee to manage time efficiently, but it is impossible for an employer to determine whether a prospective
employee is a good manager of time. Suppose that these skills are also required to complete a college degree. For example, to get passing grades in all your classes, you must
be able to use your time efficiently. When you get your college degree, firms will con-
clude that you have some of the skills they require, so they may hire you instead of an
equally skilled high-school graduate. This is the **signaling effect** of a college education: People who complete college provide a signal to employers about their skills. This
second explanation suggests that colleges simply provide a testing ground where students can reveal their skills to potential employers.

Over the last three decades, this wage gap, or "college premium," has almost doubled. The most important factor in doubling the college premium is technological
change. Changes in technology have increased the demand for college graduates relative to the demand for other workers. In all sectors of the economy, firms are switching
to sophisticated machinery and equipment that require highly skilled workers.
Consequently, the share of jobs that require a college education has increased steadily,
increasing the demand for college graduates. Of course, the supply of college graduates
has increased too, but not by as much as demand. Because the increase in demand is
large relative to the increase in supply, the wages of college graduates have increased.
Another factor in the growing college premium is the pace of technological change.
Workers with more education can more easily learn new skills and new jobs, so firms
are willing to pay more for college graduates.

Learning effect
The increase in a person's
wage resulting from the
learning of skills required for
certain occupations.

Signaling effect
The increase in a person's
wage resulting from the signal
of productivity provided by
completing college.

7. Complete the statement with "demand" or "supply": The wage for a particular occupation will be low if _____ is small relative to _____.
8. The wages of police officers vary from city to city. What could explain the wage differences?
9. In some countries, it is customary to tip restaurant waiters. What are the implications for the wages paid to waiters?

The Distribution of Income

In 2001, the median household income in the United States was $42,228, but this simple average tells only part of the income story. Some households earn much more income, and others earn much less. In this part of the chapter, we'll discuss the extent of income inequality in the United States and explore some of the reasons why the households with the highest income are receiving a larger and larger share of total income.

Income Distribution Facts

Table 17.2 shows the distribution of income without considering the effects of taxes or noncash transfers such as food stamps, public housing, or medical care. To compute the numbers in the table, we take four steps.

1 Rank the nation's households according to income: The household with the highest income is at the top of the list, and the household with the lowest income is at the bottom of the list.
2 Divide the households into five groups, or "quintiles": The lowest fifth includes the poorest 20% of households (the lowest 20% of the list), the second fifth is the next poorest 20%, and so on. The second column of the table shows the income ranges for each of the five groups: The lowest fifth includes households with income up to $17,970, the second fifth includes households with income between $17,971 and $33,314, and so on.

TABLE 17.2

Shares of Income Earned by Different U.S. Groups, 2001

Income Group	Income Range	Percent of Total Income
Lowest fifth	0 to $17,970	3.5%
Second fifth	$17,971 to $33,314	8.7
Middle fifth	$33,315 to $53,000	14.6
Fourth fifth	$53,001 to $83,500	23.0
Highest fifth	$83,501 and greater	50.1

Source: *Money Income in the United States: 2001*, Table A-2.

3 Compute each group's income by adding up the income received by all the households in the group.
4 Compute each group's percentage of total income (the number in the third column of the table) by dividing the group's income by the nation's total income.

What explains the differences in the incomes of U.S. households? There are five key factors:

1 Differences in labor skills and effort. Some people have better labor skills than others, so they earn higher wages. Labor skills are determined by innate ability and education. In addition, some people work longer hours or at more demanding jobs, so they earn more income.
2 Inheritances. Some people inherit large sums of money and earn income by investing this money.
3 Luck and misfortune. Some people are luckier than others in investing their money, starting a business, or picking an occupation. Among the unlucky people are those who develop health problems that make it difficult to earn income.
4 Discrimination. Some people are paid lower wages or have limited opportunities for education and work because of their race or gender.
5 Redistribution programs. The government uses various redistribution programs like welfare and Social Security to give money to individual households. These cash transfers are included in the computations of income in Table 17.2.

How does government policy affect the distribution of income? In the absence of government cash transfers, the share of the lowest quintile would be 0.90 %, while the share of the highest quintile would be 55.6 %. Adding cash transfers increases the share of the lowest quintile to 3.5%. Adding in taxes (higher for the rich) and the value of noncash transfers (higher for the poor) increases the share of the lowest quintile to 4.7%, while the share of the highest quintile drops to 46.5%. In other words, government transfer and tax policies reduce income inequality.

Recent Changes in the Distribution of Income

Table 17.3 shows the changes in the distribution of income between 1970 and 2001. The share of the top fifth rose from 43.3% to 50.1%, while the share of every other group dropped. By historical standards, these changes in the distribution of income were very rapid. What caused these changes in the distribution in income?

It appears that the most important reason for growing inequality is what labor economists call an increase in the demand for skill.[14] In the labor market, the demand for highly skilled (highly educated) workers has increased relative to the demand for less-skilled (less-educated) workers. As a result, the wage gap between the two groups has widened. As we saw at the beginning of the chapter, in the last three decades, the college premium has increased significantly. At the same time, the premium for advanced degrees increased. Finally, the dropout penalty (the wage gap between high-school graduates and dropouts) has nearly doubled.

TABLE 17.3

Changes in U.S. Income Shares, 1970–2001

Year	Lowest Fifth	Second Fifth	Third Fifth	Fourth Fifth	Highest Fifth
2001	3.5	8.7	14.6	23.0	50.1
2000	3.6	8.9	14.8	23.0	49.8
1995	3.7	9.1	15.2	23.3	48.7
1990	3.9	9.6	15.9	24.0	46.6
1985	4.0	9.7	16.3	24.6	45.3
1980	4.3	10.3	16.9	24.9	43.7
1975	4.4	10.5	17.1	24.8	43.2
1970	4.1	10.8	17.4	24.5	43.3

Why did the demand for skill increase over the last three decades? There are two main reasons.

▶ *Technological change.* Advances in technology have simultaneously decreased the demand for less-educated workers and increased the demand for college graduates and people with advanced degrees. While the new technology has made it possible to replace many low-skilled workers with "smart" machines and computers, it has increased the demand for workers who have the education and skills required to produce the new technology and use it.

▶ *Increased international trade.* An increase in international trade means more exports and imports. Trade allows developed countries like the United States to easily export goods produced with high-skilled labor and import goods produced with low-skilled labor. As a result, the expansion of international trade in the last three decades has increased the demand for high-skilled workers and decreased the demand for low-skilled workers in the United States.

Economists have not yet reached a consensus on the relative importance of these two factors.

Changes in the Top End of Income Distribution: 1920–1998

Figure 17.7 shows the trends in the income shares of the several groups at the top of the income distribution. The upper line shows the share for the top decile (top 10%) of income earners. The income share was just over 40% in 1917 and just under 45% at the start of World War II. The share plunged during the war and leveled out in the postwar period at about 33%. The share started increasing in 1970, rising from 32% to 42% by 1998. The middle line shows the income share for the top 5% of earners. It follows a similar pattern, with lower shares after the war, a long period of relative stability, and then increases starting in 1970. The lower line, showing the income share for the top 1% of the distribution, shows a similar pattern.

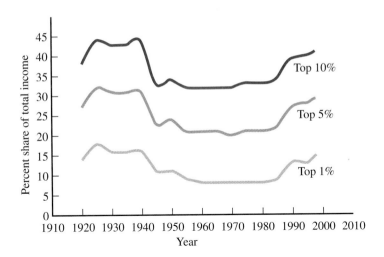

FIGURE 17.7

Top Income Distribution Shares, 1920–1998

Source: Thomas Piketty and Emmanuel Saez, "Income Inequality in the United States, 1913–1998," Working Paper 8467, National Bureau of Economic Research, 2001.

What caused these patterns? Recent studies of the trends for the top decile generated the following observations:[15]

1 During World War II, the income share of the top decile decreased because government wage controls compressed wages. In addition, the government increased tax rates on invested money (stock dividends, interest earnings, and entrepreneurial income) to support the war effort, and these rates remained relatively high until the 1980s. The higher tax rates decreased the return that could be earned on investments and slowed the rate at which fortunes were amassed.

2 The stability of the income share in the period 1945–1970 is puzzling because one would expect wages to rebound after wage controls ended following World War II. During this time period, there *was* a postwar rebound in top-decile wages in France and other countries, just not in the United States.

3 Between 1920 and 1998, the share of income from wages increased at the expense of income from investments. For the top decile, the share of income from wages rose from 58% to 84%. For the top 1%, the wage share rose from 42% to 70%.

4 The increase in the income shares since 1970 has been caused by rapid increases in the compensation of the highest-wage workers—the executives of large corporations and other organizations. Most of the action in the top decile is in the top 1% of earners, and most of the action at the top is in rising wages, not increases in investment income. After adjusting for inflation, the salaries of top executives increased by about 6% per year in the 1990s, much more rapidly than average salaries.

5 The chief executives in the United States are paid much more than their counterparts in other developed nations. For example, U.S. executives receive 3 to 4 times more than their counterparts in Britain, Germany, and France. In the United States, the average pay for a chief executive is 24 times the pay of the average production worker. In Germany, the average executive is paid only 8 times as much as the average production worker.

6 The U.S. experience in the last 30 years contrasts sharply with that of France where the income share of the top decile actually decreased between 1970 and 1998, from 33% to 32%.

USING THE TOOLS

We've seen how to use supply and demand curves to explain differences in wages and to predict the effects of changes in the labor market on the equilibrium wage and employment. Here are some opportunities to do your own economic analysis.

1. Market Effects of Immigration

In the initial equilibrium, the wage for farm workers is $5 per hour. The elasticity of supply of farm workers is 2.0, and the elasticity of demand for farm workers is 1.0. Suppose that immigration increases the supply of farm workers by 12%: The supply curve shifts to the right by 12%.
a. Predict the effect of immigration on the wage paid to farm workers: By how much will the wage increase or decrease?
b. How will immigration affect the cost of producing food and the equilibrium price of food?

2. Demand for Newskids

Consider the market for newspaper delivery kids in Kidsville. Each newskid receives a piece rate of $2 per subscriber per month and has a fixed territory that initially has 100 subscribers. The price elasticity of demand for subscriptions is 2.0. Suppose the new city council of Kidsville passes a law that establishes a minimum piece rate of $3 per subscriber per month. As a result, the publisher increases the monthly price of a subscription by 20%. How will the new law affect the monthly income of the typical newskid?

SUMMARY

We've seen how wages are determined in perfectly competitive labor markets and why wages differ from one occupation to another. We've also looked at the distribution of income in the United States and explored possible reasons for growing inequality. Here are the main points of the chapter:

1 The wage in a particular occupation will be relatively high if supply is small relative to demand. This will occur if (a) few people have the skills required for the occupation, (b) training costs are high, or (c) the job is dangerous or stressful.

2 College graduates earn more than high-school graduates because a college education provides new skills and allows people to reveal their skills to employers.

3 There are trade-offs with a minimum wage: Some workers earn higher income, but others lose their jobs.

4 The wealthiest 20% of families in the United States earn about half of total income, while the wealthiest 10% earn 42% of total income. At the other end of the income distribution, the poorest 20% earn only 3.5% of total income.

KEY TERMS

ncome effect for leisure
   demand, 384
nput-substitution effect, 383
earning effect, 395
ong-run demand curve
   for labor, 383

marginal product of labor, 381
marginal-revenue product of labor
   (*MRP*), 381
market supply curve
   for labor, 385
output effect, 383

short-run demand curve
   for labor, 381
signaling effect, 395
substitution effect for leisure
   demand, 384

PROBLEMS AND DISCUSSION QUESTIONS

1 You are an economic consultant to a city that just imposed a payroll tax of $1 per hour of work. This payroll tax is paid by workers through a payroll deduction: For each hour of work, the employer deducts $1 and sends the money to the city government. The initial wage (before the tax) is $10, and total employment is 20,000 hours per day. Use a graph to show the effect of the tax on the equilibrium wage and employment.

2 We discussed the response of Lester, Sam, and Maureen to an increase in the wage. Which person's response is closest to your own? If your wage increased, would you work more hours, fewer hours, or about the same number of hours?

3 Critically appraise the following statement from Mr. Chuckles: "The law of supply says that an increase in price increases the quantity supplied. A decrease in the income tax rate will increase the worker's net wage, so each worker will work more hours. As a result, the revenue from the income tax will increase."

4 Consider two markets for carpenters: the city of Portland and the United States. Draw two supply curves for carpenters: one for the city of Portland and one for the United States. In which market would you expect a more elastic supply of carpenters?

5 The advocates of higher salaries for teachers point out that most teachers have college degrees and that teaching children is an important job.

a. Why aren't teachers' salaries higher, given the importance of the job and the education required?

b. Suppose a new law requires that teachers are paid the same hourly wage as college graduates who work in business. Predict the effects of this law on the market for teachers.

6 Comment on the following: "There is no substitute for an airline pilot: Someone has to fly the plane. Therefore, an increase in the wage of airline pilots will not change the number of pilots used by the airlines."

7 Suppose a new government program improves worker safety in coal mines. Use a graph to predict the effect of the program on the equilibrium wage for coal workers.

8 Under some occupational licensing laws, licensed members of an occupation write licensing exams. An example is the bar exam for licensing lawyers. How might this practice limit entry into an occupation?

9 One response to the gap in wages between men and women is a policy called comparable worth, under which the government specifies a minimum wage for some occupations, typically the occupations with a disproportionate number of women. Evaluate the merits of such a policy. What are the trade-offs?

MODEL ANSWERS TO QUESTIONS

Chapter-Opening Questions

1 When the wage increases, some people work more, others work less, and others work about the same amount.

2 As we saw in the section on wages for different occupations, the worker's income would increase by about 3.7%.

3 The gender gap results from differences in productivity and occupational status.

4 Two of the factors contributing to greater inequality are (a) technological change that increases the demand for high-skilled labor and decreases the demand for low-skilled labor, and (b) increased international trade, which decreases the demand for low-skilled labor.

Test Your Understanding

1 If the marginal-revenue product of the new player exceeds $3 million. For example, if the player increased the revenue from ticket sales by $4 million, it would be sensible to hire the player.

2 Decrease, decrease, increase, increase.

3 As the wage decreases, labor will become less expensive relative to other inputs, so the firm will substitute labor for other inputs.

4 You will work 30 hours per week instead of 20 hours.

5 No. An increase in the wage will increase the number of workers because of changes in occupational choices and migration.

6 Increase, decrease.

7 Demand, supply.

8 Wages are higher in cities where police officers face a greater chance of being killed on the job.

9 Waiters in tipping countries will have lower wages than waiters in nontipping countries.

NOTES

1. W. Michael Fox and Beverly J. Fox, "What's Happening to Americans' Income?" The *Southwest Economy, Federal Reserve Bank of Dallas,* Issue 2, 1995, pp. 3–6; *U.S. Bureau of the Census, Statistical Abstract of the United States 2002,* Table 654 (Washington, DC: U.S. Government Printing Office, 2002).

2. Mark Killingsworth, *Labor Supply* (New York: Cambridge University Press, 1983).

3. "Early Retirement? Don't Even Think about It," *The Economist,* March 23, 2002, p. 53; "French Pensions: Work Now, Enjoy Later," *The Economist,* February 8, 2003, p 54.

4. Victor R. Fuchs, Alan B. Krueger, and James M. Poterba, "Why Do Economists Disagree About Policy? The Role of Beliefs about Parameters and Values," *Journal of Economic Literature,* vol. 36, no. 3, 1998, pp. 1387–426.

5. George Borjas, "The New Economics of Immigration," *Atlantic Monthly,* November 1996, pp. 73–78; George Borjas, "The Economics of Immigration," *Journal of Economic Literature,* vol. 32, 1994, pp. 1667–717.

6. "Stamping Out the Sweatshops: Dress Code," *The Economist,* April 19, 1997; "Sweatshop Wars," *The Economist,* February 27, 1999.

7. Craig Olson, "An Analysis of Wage Differentials Received by Workers on Dangerous Jobs," *Journal of Human Resources,* vol. 16, Spring 1981, pp. 167–185.

8. Suzanne Bianchi and Daphne Spain, "Women, Work, and Family in America," *Population Bulletin,* vol. 51, no. 3, 1998, pp. 2–48.

9. Eric J. Solberg, "Occupational Assignment, Hiring Discrimination, and the Gender Pay Gap," *Atlantic Economic Journal* 32 (2004), pp. 11–27.

10. U.S. Department of Labor, *Employment and Earnings* (Washington, DC: U.S. Government Printing Office, 1996).

11. William Darity and Patrick Mason, "Evidence on Discrimination in Employment: Codes of Color, Codes of Gender," *Journal of Economic Perspectives,* vol. 12, no. 2, 1998, pp. 63–90.

12. James Heckman, "Detecting Discrimination," *Journal of Economic Perspectives*, vol. 12, no. 2, 1998, pp. 101–116.

13. David Wessel, "Racial Discrimination Is Still at Work in U.S," *Wall Street Journal*, September 4, 2003, p. A2.

14. Finis Welch, "In Defense of Inequality," *American Economic Review*, vol. 89, no. 2 (1999), pp. 1–17.

15. Thomas Piketty and Emmanuel Saez, "Income Inequality in the United States, 1913–1998," Working Paper 8467, National Bureau of Economic Research, 2001; Alan Krueger, "Attempting to Explain Income Inequality," *New York Times*, April 4, 2002, page C2.

Beyond Perfect Competition: Union Monopsony, and Imperfect Information

n the early days of the automobile industry, the prevailing wage for autoworkers was $3 per day. Assembly-line jobs were repetitive and tedious, and the turnover rate of workers was very high. When Henry Ford decided to increase the daily wage for his workers from $3 to $5, most observers were baffled. They figured that Ford's labor costs would be almost twice as high as those of his rivals, so he would lose a lot of money and quickly go out of business. The wage hike appeared to be a great act of generosity but very bad business. You can imagine their surprise when Ford's profit doubled from $30 million to $60 million. How was this possible? How can higher wages lead to higher profits?

This chapter continues our discussion of labor markets, exploring three topics that take us beyond the simple model of perfect competition discussed in the previous chapter. One of the assumptions of perfect competition in the labor market is that each worker acts independently of other workers, taking the market wage as given. We start the chapter with a discussion of labor unions, which enable workers to act collectively, controlling the supply of labor and negotiating wages. A second assumption for perfect competition is that each firm takes the wage as given, meaning that it can hire an unlimited number of workers at the prevailing market wage. In the second part of the chapter, we see what happens when a single firm dominates the demand for labor, giving it the opportunity to determine the market wage. A third assumption of perfect competition is perfect information: Each firm knows the productivity level of each worker. In the third part of this chapter, we see what happens when firms cannot distinguish between workers with different productivities. We'll use the notion of imperfect information in the labor market to explain Henry Ford's puzzling wage hike.

Moving beyond the model of perfect competition provides some important insights into real labor markets. Here are some of the practical questions that we address:

1 How do unions affect wages and worker productivity?
2 If a city has a single hospital, how would that affect the wages and total employment of nurses?
3 Could a minimum wage actually increase total employment?

Labor Unions

A **labor union** is an organized group of workers that can influence wages. Acting as a group, union members have some control over the wages and fringe benefits they receive. There are two types of labor unions:

▶ A **craft union** includes workers from a particular occupation, such as plumbers, bakers, or electricians.
▶ An **industrial union** includes all types of workers from a single industry, such as steelworkers or autoworkers.

There are also umbrella organizations that include many individual unions. The largest of these "unions of unions" is the AFL-CIO (the American Federation of Labor–Congress of Industrial Organizations). Unions use **collective bargaining** to negotiate contracts covering wages, fringe benefits, job security and working conditions.

Labor union
An organized group of workers. Unions try to increase job security, improve working conditions, and increase wages and fringe benefits for their members.

Craft union
A labor organization that includes workers from a particular occupation, for example, plumbers, bakers, or electricians.

Industrial union
A labor organization that includes all types of workers from a single industry, for example, steelworkers or autoworkers.

Collective bargaining
Negotiations between a union and a firm over wages, working conditions, and job security.

A Brief History of Labor Unions in the United States

As shown in Panel A of Figure 18.1, about one-sixth of all workers in the United States belong to a union, down from about one-third of workers 40 years ago. Among private-sector workers, the unionization rate is 8.5% whereas 37.5% of public-sector workers belong to unions. As shown in Panel B, unionization rates are higher in most other industrial countries. For a description of the working conditions that led to the formation of the first unions, read "A Closer Look: Working Conditions and Unions."

Let's take a brief look at the history of labor organizations in the United States. In the nineteenth century, there were all sorts of craft unions, and the main umbrella organizations were the Knights of Labor (founded in 1869) and the AFL (founded in 1881). The CIO (formed in 1931) was a collection of industrial unions that represented semiskilled workers in mass production, including workers in the automobile, rubber, and steel industries. The CIO merged with the AFL in 1955. In the last 30 years, the fraction of the workforce in unions has decreased, but the number of government workers in unions and employee associations has more than doubled.

Labor unions have been empowered by the states and the federal government. The most important labor legislation gave workers the right to form unions, but limited their power:

▶ The Wagner Act (1935) guaranteed workers the right to join unions and required each firm to bargain with a union formed by a majority of its workers. The National Labor Relations Board (NLRB) was established to enforce the provisions of the Wagner Act.

▶ The Taft–Hartley Act (1947) gave government the power to stop strikes that "imperiled the national health or safety" and allowed states to pass **right-to-work laws**. These laws, which are currently in force in 21 states, outlaw union shops, defined as workplaces where union membership is required as a condition of employment.

▶ The Landrum–Griffin Act (1959) was a response to allegations of corruption and misconduct by union officials. This act guaranteed union members the right to fair elections, made it easier for them to monitor union finances, and made the theft of union funds a federal offense.

> **Right-to-work laws**
>
> Laws that prohibit union shops, where union membership is required as a condition of employment

Labor Unions and Wages

There is evidence that unions raise the wages of union workers. For the U.S., the consensus is that union workers earn about 15% more than nonunion workers doing the same work.[1] Most other industrialized countries have a smaller union "markup." The markup is about 10% in the United Kingdom, about 12% in Canada, and about 5% in both Japan and Germany. The markup is relatively small for unionized firms that operate in a competitive product market, but larger for firms with little competition in the product market. In other words, unions have their largest effects on the wages paid by monopolists and oligopolists. The higher wages decrease the profits of these firms, so union workers gain at the expense of the owners of the firms.

Unions try to increase the wages of their members in three ways. First, unions organize workers and negotiate a higher wage. Suppose workers in a particular industry form an industrial union and agree on a union wage that exceeds the equilibrium wage. Like a minimum wage imposed by a government, a wage negotiated by a union

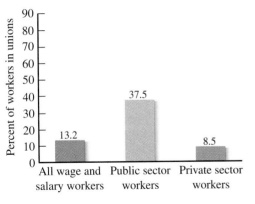

(A) Unionization Rates in the United States, 2002

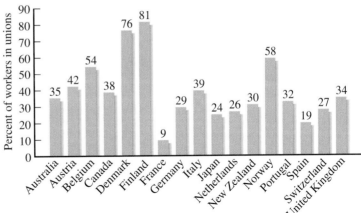

(B) Unionization Rates in OECD Countries, 1994

FIGURE 18.1 **Unionization Rates in the United States and OECD Countries**

Sources: U.S. Bureau of Labor Statistics; OECD Statistics

means that some workers will earn higher wages but other workers who are willing to work will not have the opportunity to do so. To deal with this problem, the union can reduce the number of workers by restricting membership or can share the smaller number of jobs among union members.

Another way to increase the union wage is to promote the products produced by union workers. You've probably seen advertisements encouraging people to buy products with the "union label." As we learned in Chapter 17, the demand for labor is a

A CLOSER LOOK

Working Conditions and Unions

Labor unions arose in the late 1800s and early 1900s largely in response to awful working conditions in factories. In garment factories, iron plants, and textile mills, laborers worked 14-7—about 14 hours per day, seven days a week. The long workweek was not new to those who had worked on farms, but the working conditions were. Men, women, and children as young as age 5 operated clattering machinery so dangerous that many workers lost their sight, hearing, and limbs. For the early union organizers, the key demands were higher wages, shorter hours, and safer work environments. One reason for the decline of unions since the 1940s is the passage of legislation that limits work hours and improved the safety of workplaces.

derived demand, so an increase in the demand for a final good will increase the demand for labor used to produce that good, increasing the equilibrium wage. This approach can be used together with a negotiated union wage to prevent an excess supply of labor at the union wage.

A third approach—which may or may not increase wages—is to impose work rules that increase the amount of labor required to produce a given quantity of output. This is called **featherbedding**. One example of featherbedding is requiring a minimum crew size, which forces a firm to hire more workers than it needs to perform a particular task. For example, the typical unionized airline hires three workers to guide an airplane into the gate, whereas nonunion airlines use only two workers. In the past, railroad unions forced railroads to use firemen (whose job was to shovel coal) on diesel-powered engines, which don't use coal.

Featherbedding

Work rules that increase the amount of labor required to produce a given quantity of output.

Featherbedding may or may not increase the demand for labor. Although it forces the firm to use more labor per unit of output, it also decreases the quantity of output. A firm that is forced to hire workers it doesn't need will have higher production costs, resulting in higher prices for its products. Consumers respond to higher prices by purchasing less output, so although the firm may use more labor per unit of output, it sells less output. If output falls by a large amount, the quantity of labor demanded by the firm will actually decrease, decreasing the wage and total employment.

A different approach to managing union employment comes from Volkswagen A.G., Europe's largest automaker. In 1993, Volkswagen got its labor unions to switch to a four-day, 28-hour workweek, down from a five-day, 36-hour workweek. If workers hadn't accepted the shorter workweek and lower pay, Volkswagen would have eliminated 30,000 of its 100,000 jobs in Germany. In other words, the switch to the shorter workweek preserved 30,000 union jobs in the automobile industry.[2] Some analysts suggest that shorter workweeks for union workers will become more common as European unions grapple with lower demand for their workers.

Effects of Unions on Worker Productivity and Turnover

We've seen that unions lead to higher wages, meaning that unions increase production costs. What are the possible benefits of unions? First, unions may increase worker productivity by facilitating communication between workers and managers. The evidence on worker productivity is mixed. Some studies show higher productivity in unionized firms, and others show lower productivity. Union workers are more productive when the union facilitates smooth relations between labor and management.

A second possible benefit of unions is lower turnover among workers. If a worker is unhappy with a job, one option is to quit. From the firm's perspective, this is costly because the firm loses an experienced worker and must train a new one. A dissatisfied worker who belongs to a union has a second option: The worker can use the union as an intermediary to discuss job issues with managers. This sort of communication can solve problems before they become so severe that the worker quits. There is evidence that firms whose workers are in unions have lower turnover rates, in part because they facilitate communication between workers and managers.[3] These lower turnover rates lead to lower training costs and a more experienced workforce. The savings for unionized firms is equivalent to a 1 to 2% reduction in costs.

Monopsony Power

In the previous chapter, we assumed that each employer is such a small part of the labor market that the employer takes the market wage as given. In graphical terms, the labor-supply curve faced by the firm is horizontal at the market wage. In contrast, some labor markets have a single employer, so the lack of competition for workers gives the firm some control over wages. Of course, the lower the wage, the smaller the quantity of labor supplied. For example, if your city has a single hospital, there will be a single employer of surgical nurses. This is the case of **monopsony**: There is a single buyer of a particular input. The classic example of a pure monopsony is a company town, where most or all the workers are employed by a single firm.

Monopsony
A market in which there is a single buyer of an input.

Picking a Workforce and a Wage

A monopsonist faces a positively sloped market supply curve of labor. If the monopsonist hires more workers, it must pay a higher wage to attract them away from other activities. In Figure 18.2, the firm can hire 7 workers at a wage of $10 (point *c*) and 8 workers at a wage of $12 (point *d*). The firm's **marginal labor cost** (also known as marginal factor cost) is defined as the increase in total labor cost from one more unit of labor. When the firm decides to hire 8 workers instead of 7, its total labor cost increases from $70 per hour ($10 per worker per hour times 7 workers) to $96 per hour ($12 per worker per hour times 8 workers), an increase of $26. Therefore, the firm's marginal labor cost for the eighth worker is $26 (shown by point *e* in Figure 18.2).

Marginal labor cost
The increase in total labor cost resulting from one more unit of labor.

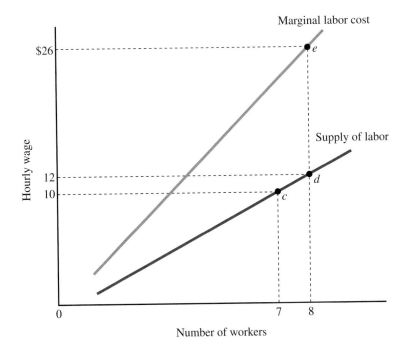

FIGURE 18.2

The Supply of Labor and Marginal Labor Cost for a Monopsonist
To hire more workers, the monopsonist must pay a higher wage, so the marginal labor cost exceeds the wage. To hire the eighth worker, the firm increases the wage from $10 to $12. The marginal labor cost for the eighth worker is $26, equal to $12 paid to the eighth worker plus $14 extra money paid to the 7 original workers, each of whom receives $2 more per hour.

As shown in Figure 18.2, the marginal labor cost exceeds the hourly wage. The reason is that when the firm increases the wage to hire one more worker, it must increase the wage for all of its workers. To hire the eighth worker, the firm pays $12 to the new worker, but it also pays an extra $2 for each of the 7 workers who were willing to work at the $10 wage. We compute the marginal labor cost as follows:

$$\text{marginal labor cost} = \text{wage paid to new worker}$$
$$+ (\text{change in wage} \times \text{quantity of original workers})$$
$$\$26 = \$12 + (\$2 \times 7)$$

In this case, the marginal labor cost is $26, including $12 for the new worker and $14 for the original workers.

Figure 18.3 shows the hiring decision of the monopsonist. The firm can use the marginal principle to determine how many workers to hire.

 MARGINAL *Principle*

Increase the level of an activity if its marginal benefit exceeds its marginal cost, but reduce the level if the marginal cost exceeds the marginal benefit. If possible, pick the level at which the marginal benefit equals the marginal cost.

The firm chooses the quantity of labor at which the marginal benefit of labor equals the marginal cost. As we saw in the previous chapter, the marginal benefit of labor equals the marginal-revenue product of labor—that is, the increase in revenue generated by an

FIGURE 18.3

The Hiring Decision of a Monopsonist
The monopsonist chooses point *m*, where the marginal benefit of labor (the marginal-revenue product) equals the marginal labor cost, hiring 40 workers. The labor-supply curve indicates that to hire 40 workers, the monopsonist must pay a wage of $4 (point *w*).

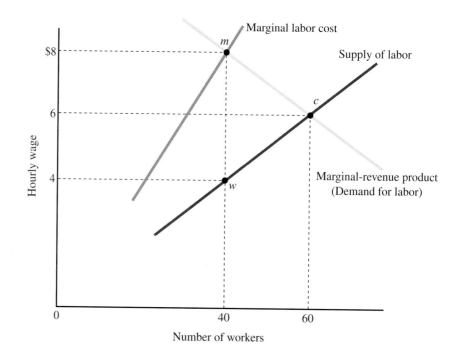

additional worker. The marginal-revenue product curve is also the demand curve for labor. In Figure 18.3, the marginal-labor cost curve intersects the marginal-revenue product curve at point *m*, so the monopsonist hires 40 workers. As shown by the labor-supply curve, to hire 40 workers, the firm must pay a wage of $4 (shown by point *w*).

Why does the monopsonist stop at 40 workers when it could hire an additional worker for just over $4, and that worker would have a marginal-revenue product of just under $8? To hire one more worker, the monopsonist must increase the wage to $4.10. The marginal-labor cost of the 41st worker incorporates the higher wages that must be paid to the first 40 workers:

marginal labor cost = wage paid to new worker
+ (change in wage × quantity of original workers)
$8.10 = $4.10 + ($0.10 × 40)

Because a higher wage must be paid to the 40 original workers, the marginal-labor cost ($8.10) exceeds the marginal-revenue product (less than $8.00), so the firm stops at 40 workers.

Monopsony versus Perfect Competition

How does the monopsony outcome compare to the perfectly competitive outcome? Any firm that hires workers—either a monopsonist or perfect competitor—will continue to hire more workers until the marginal cost equals the marginal benefit (the marginal revenue product). For a perfectly competitive firm, the marginal cost is simply the wage. For a monopsonist, the marginal cost is the marginal labor cost, which exceeds the wage because the monopsonist must increase its wage to hire more workers. The monopsonist will hire fewer workers because its higher marginal cost equals the marginal benefit at a smaller quantity of labor. Compared to a collection of perfectly competitive firms, each of which takes the price as given, a monopsonist will hire fewer workers. In Figure 18.3, the perfectly competitive equilibrium is shown by the intersection of the demand curve (marginal-revenue product curve) and the supply curve. The equilibrium wage is $6 and the equilibrium quantity is 60 workers.

You may have noticed the similarity between a monopsonist and a monopolist. A monopolist (a single seller) uses its market power to increase the price of output; a monopsonist (a single buyer) uses its market power to decrease the wage. The monopolist produces an artificially small quantity of output; the monopsonist hires an artificially small quantity of a particular input, such as labor. Table 18.1 summarizes the key features of a monopolist and a monopsonist.

What is the role of a labor union in a labor market with a single buyer? Monopsony leads to an artificially low wage, and a union may lead to an artificially high wage. A market with both a union and a monopsonist will have a wage somewhere between the two extremes, depending on the bargaining power of the two sides. In such a market, the market powers on the two sides of the market counteract each other, leading to a wage between the artificially low monopsony wage and the articially high union wage.

TABLE 18.1		
Monopoly versus Monopsony	**Monopoly**	**Monopsony**
	Single seller of output High price of output Small quantity of output	Single buyer of input Low price of input Small quantity of input

Monopsony and a Minimum Wage

In the previous chapter, we showed that a minimum wage decreases the quantity of labor demanded below the equilibrium level. In this case, there is a trade-off between higher wages and total employment. How does this analysis change when a monopsonist has market power on the demand side of the market?

Figure 18.4 shows the effects of a minimum wage of $7. This wage exceeds the monopsony wage of $4 as well as the perfectly competitive wage of $6. The minimum wage rules out wages below $7, so the supply curve facing the firm is horizontal up to 70 workers. The first through the 70th workers are willing to work at the minimum wage, so to get an additional worker (say the 41st), the firm doesn't have to pay any more than it did for the first 40 workers. The marginal labor cost is the minimum wage of $7, the same amount for the first worker, the 10th worker, and so on, up to 70 workers. If the firm wants to hire more than 70 workers, it must pay a wage higher

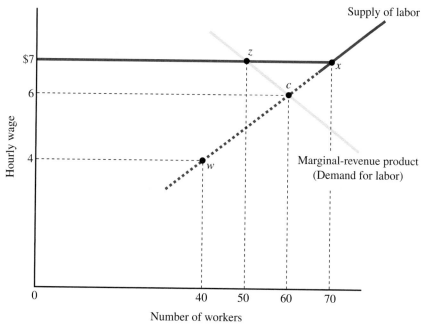

FIGURE 18.4 **A Minimum Wage Increases Employment by a Monopsonist**
With a minimum wage, the labor-supply curve is horizontal at the minimum wage ($7) up to the point where the minimum-wage line intersects the original supply curve. Beyond that point, the supply curve is the same as the original curve. As long as the supply curve is horizontal, the marginal labor cost for the monopsonist equals the minimum wage. The monopsonist chooses point z, where the marginal benefit of labor (the marginal-revenue product) equals the marginal labor cost. The minimum wage increases the quantity of labor from 40 workers to 50.

than the minimum. The wage that would be required is shown by the market supply curve beyond point *x*. But for fewer than 70 workers, the supply curve facing the firm is horizontal, so the marginal labor cost is constant at the minimum wage of $7.

To maximize its profit, the firm will pick the quantity of labor at which the marginal benefit equals the marginal cost. At point *z*, the marginal labor cost (shown by the horizontal portion of the new supply curve) equals the marginal benefit (shown by the marginal-revenue product curve), so the monopsonist will hire 50 workers, up from 40 workers before the minimum wage. In other words, the minimum wage increases the quantity of labor demanded.

How does this analysis compare to the analysis of the minimum wage in the previous chapter? You may recall that in a perfectly competitive market, the minimum wage decreases the quantity of labor. In Figure 18.4, competitive outcome is shown by point *c*, with 60 workers. So a minimum wage of $7 generates less than the competitive quantity but more than the monopsony quantity (40 workers). Starting from the monopsony outcome, a minimum wage of $7 moves the market closer to the perfectly competitive outcome. In fact, if the minimum wage were set at $6 (the competitive level), the market would reach the competitive quantity of 60 workers. The minimum wage essentially makes the monopsonist into a price-taking firm. With a minimum-wage law in place, the monopsonist acts like a perfectly competitive firm, taking the minimum wage as given. That's why the minimum wage increases the quantity of labor demanded by the monopsonist.

Monopsony and the Real World

Although a pure monopsony like a company town is rare, the insights from the monopsony model are relevant for actual labor markets. The essential feature of the model is that if an individual firm wants to hire additional workers, it must increase its wage to attract more workers. In other words, the firm faces a positively sloped supply curve for workers, not a horizontal curve. We saw that a positively sloped supply curve generates a marginal labor cost curve above the supply curve, and the profit-maximizing quantity of labor is less than the perfectly competitive quantity (where the supply curve intersects the demand curve).

A firm could face a positively sloped labor-supply curve for several reasons. British economist Joan Robinson (1903–1983), a leader in the modeling of imperfect competition, listed the reasons:[4]

> There may be a certain number of workers in the immediate neighbourhood and to attract those from farther afield it may be necessary to pay a wage equal to what they can earn near home plus their fares to and fro; or there could be workers attached to the firm by preference or custom and to attract others it may be necessary to pay a higher wage. Or ignorance may prevent workers from moving from one to another in response to differences in the wages offered by the different firms.

In other words, there are frictions in the labor market that require a firm to pay a higher wage to get more workers, meaning the supply curve is positively sloped. With a positively sloped supply curve, the marginal labor cost exceeds the wage, and the firm will hire fewer workers than would be hired in a perfectly competitive market. For some evidence of labor frictions, read "A Closer Look: Pubs and the Labor-Supply Curve."

A CLOSER LOOK

Pubs and the Labor-Supply Curve

In his book, *Monopsony in Motion: Imperfect Competition in Labor Markets*, labor economist Alan Manning provides some unconventional evidence of positively sloped labor-supply curves.[5] He notes that "people go to the pub to celebrate when they get a job, rather than greeting the news with a shrug of the shoulders. . . . " In other words, a new job is a big deal.

If a pub celebration seems like the obvious response to a new job, consider what happens when each firm faces a horizontal supply curve for labor, with a single market wage. A firm has no incentive to pay a higher wage because it can hire as many workers as it wants at the market wage. And if the firm paid a lower wage, all of its workers would instantly switch to other firms paying the market wage. In this perfectly competitive environment, a worker won't celebrate a new job because the new job pays the same as any other job.

Suppose instead that the supply curve facing a firm is positively sloped. To hire more workers, the firm must pay a higher wage. For most workers, the market wage will be greater than the opportunity cost, meaning that they are willing to work for less than they ultimately get. In other words, each worker gets a producer surplus. People celebrate a new job because they switch jobs to get a bigger producer surplus.

Manning also notes that people also "go to the pub to drown their sorrows when they lose their jobs." This wouldn't be sensible with a horizontal supply curve because someone who loses a job could instantly get another one at the same wage. But with a positively sloped supply curve, losing a job means losing a producer surplus.

TEST Your Understanding

1. Suppose a union's objective is to maximize total employment in a particular occupation, but it cannot affect the demand for labor. Employers are perfectly competitive, taking the market wage as given. What should the union do?
2. Complete the statement with "high" or "low": A monopolist sells its output at a relatively _____ price, while a monopsonist buys its inputs at a relatively _____ price.
3. Fill the blanks: A monopsonist hires workers to the quantity at which _____ equals _____.

Imperfect Information and Efficiency Wages

Up to this point, our discussion of labor markets has been based on the assumption of perfect information. Each employer knows the productivity level of each worker and only hires a worker if the marginal benefit (the marginal-revenue product) exceeds the marginal cost. In some markets, workers differ in their skill levels and the amount of effort they exert on the job. At the time of hiring, employers cannot always distinguish between skillful and unskillful workers or between hard workers and lazy workers. In other words, there is asymmetric information in the labor market. What happens when there is asymmetric information?

We know from our discussion of the market for used cars in Chapter 8 that asymmetric information causes high-quality and low-quality goods to be sold in a mixed market at a single price. Suppose there are two types of workers:

▶ Low-skill workers, whose marginal revenue product = $100 per day
▶ High-skill workers, whose marginal revenue product = $200 per day

The employer cannot distinguish between these two types of workers before hiring them, and offers a single wage to all, realizing that it will probably hire some workers of each type.

What is the appropriate wage in this case? Suppose the opportunity cost of high-skill workers is $130 and a firm offers a wage of $110. Because the wage is less than the opportunity cost of high-skill workers, only low-skill workers will apply for jobs. The firm will lose money because the $110 wage exceeds the $100 marginal-revenue product of the low-skill workers. To get some high-skill workers, the employer must pick a wage that exceeds the $130 opportunity cost of high-skill workers. If the firm increases its wage, it will attract more high-skill workers and the average productivity of its workforce will increase. Depending on the responses of the two types of workers to the higher wage, a firm could make more profit by offering a higher wage. This is known as **paying efficiency wages**: The firm pays a higher wage to increase the average productivity of its workforce.

Another reason for paying relatively high wages is to encourage employees to work hard. Firms realize that their employees can vary their work efforts, from working hard to hardly working (shirking). To encourage their employees to work hard, employers fire workers who are caught shirking. The penalty associated with being fired will be much greater if the firm pays a wage above the worker's opportunity cost. For example, suppose a worker could earn $80 per day in another job. If the firm pays its workers $100 per day, a worker who is fired—and then immediately gets a job with another firm—would take a pay cut of $20 per day. This is another example of paying efficiency wages: By increasing the wage, the firm increases the work effort of its employees and increases the average productivity of its workforce.

Another reason for paying efficiency wages is to reduce turnover in the workforce. If one firm pays a higher wage than its competitors, that discourages workers from switching employers. The firm paying the higher wage will have lower turnover and thus incur smaller costs in hiring and training workers.

Paying efficiency wages
The practice of a firm paying a higher wage to increase the average productivity of its workforce.

Higher Wages at Ford Motor Company

Recall the chapter opener about Henry Ford's puzzling wage hike. Ford increased the daily wage for his workers from $3 to $5, and his profit doubled from $30 million to $60 million. Why did higher wages lead to more profit?

The key to solving this puzzle is the concept of efficiency wages. When Ford raised the wage, the average productivity of Ford workers increased by about 50%, a result of several changes in the workforce:[6]

- The pool of job applicants improved, so Ford could choose better workers.
- Fewer workers were fired for shirking.
- Fewer workers quit voluntarily.
- The rate of absenteeism was cut in half.

In the words of Henry Ford, "There was no charity in any way involved. . . . The payment of five dollars a day for an eight-hour day was one of the finest cost cutting moves we ever made." ∎

Economic Puzzle

TEST Your Understanding

4. Explain how an increase in the wage can increase the average productivity of a firm's workforce.
5. Why is the marginal labor cost always greater than the wage?

USING THE TOOLS

We've seen the effects of market power on both sides of the labor market and the effects of asymmetric information on wages. Here are some opportunities to do your own economic analysis.

1. Effects of a Nurses Union

Suppose that the nurses in the city of Florence form a union and that to work as a nurse you must belong to the union. The nurses do not allow new members to join the union, so the supply of nurses decreases by 3% per year as older union members retire. Before the union was formed, the equilibrium wage was $15 and the equilibrium quantity was 16,000 hours per day.
a. Depict graphically the effect of the union on the nursing market.
b. If the price elasticity of demand for nursing is 1.5, by what percentage would the wage of nurses increase each year?

2. Effects of a Higher Minimum Wage

Using Figure 18.3 as a starting point, suppose the minimum wage is set at $9. Depict graphically the

effects of the minimum wage on total employment. Predict the new quantity of labor. Does the quantity of labor increase or decrease?

3. Equilibrium with Efficiency Wages

Consider a labor market with asymmetric information: Each worker knows his or her marginal-revenue product, but firms cannot distinguish between low-skill and high-skill workers. Each low-skill worker has an opportunity cost of $80 and a marginal revenue product of $100, and each high-skill worker has an opportunity cost of $130 and a marginal-revenue product of $200. The workforce is divided equally between the two types of workers. Your job is to predict the equilibrium wage in the market given that each firm takes the price as given and earns zero economic profit. Try the following wages: (a) $90, (b) $100, (c) $140, (d) $150, (e) $170.

SUMMARY

In this chapter, we extended our discussion of labor markets beyond the simple world of perfectly competitive markets, with each side of the labor market taking the market wage as given. Unions achieve market power on the supply side of the market, and a monopsonist achieves market power on the demand side of the market. When there is imperfect information, with workers

knowing more about their productivity than employers, this asymmetric information provides an incentive for firms to increase wages in order to attract better workers. Here are the main points of the chapter:

1 There are trade-offs with union wage: Some workers earn higher wages, but others lose their jobs.

2 A monopsonist hires fewer workers than a perfectly competitive firm and pays a lower wage

3 In a monopsonistic market, a minimum wage may increase total employment.

4 A firm that pays efficiency wages may increase the average productivity of its workers and increase its profit.

KEY TERMS

collective bargaining, 405
craft union, 405
featherbedding, 408

industrial union, 405
labor union, 405
marginal labor cost, 409

monopsony, 409
paying efficiency wages, 415
right-to-work laws, 406

PROBLEMS AND DISCUSSION QUESTIONS

1 Suppose a union's objective is to maximize the total income of nurses (total money spent by firms on nurses). At the current wage, the price elasticity of demand for nurses is 1.5. Should the union increase or decrease the union wage? Explain.

2 Suppose that featherbedding increases the labor time per unit of output from 5 hours to 6 and increases the firm's production cost and its price by 15%. The firm initially produces and sells 100 units of output. If the price elasticity of demand for the firm's product is 2.0, how will featherbedding affect the firm's total demand for labor?

3 Consider the following data on the number of workers, wages, marginal labor cost, and marginal-revenue product. The first three rows show the supply side of the market, and the last two rows show the demand side.

a. How many workers will a monopsonist hire?
b. Pick a minimum wage that would generate the perfectly competitive outcome.

4 Suppose that half of the workers have low productivity, with marginal-revenue product of $50 and an opportunity cost of $60, and the other half have high productivity, with marginal-revenue product of $100 and an opportunity cost of $80.

a. If the firm offers a wage equal to the average productivity of workers, will the firm be profitable?
b. If the firm pays a wage of $90, will it be profitable?

Wage		$5	$6	$7	$8	$9	$10	$11
Quantity of workers supplied		1	2	3	4	5	6	7
Marginal labor cost		$5	$7	$9	$11	$13	$15	$17
Quantity of workers demanded	1	2	3	4	5	6	7	
Marginal-revenue product		$20	$18	$16	$14	$12	$10	$8

MODEL ANSWERS TO QUESTIONS

Chapter-Opening Questions

1 Unions increase wages and may increase productivity by facilitating communication between workers and managers.

2 A monopsonist pays lower wages and hires fewer workers.

3 In a labor market with a monopsonist, a minimum wage may increase total employment.

Test Your Understanding

1 Set the wage at the competitive level. Total employment is maximized at the intersection of supply and demand, so the union should do nothing. It should let the market reach equilibrium on its own.

2 High, low.

3 Marginal-revenue product, marginal labor cost.

4 The firm will attract better applicants, and workers are less likely to shirk.

5 To attract one more worker, the firm must increase the wage. The marginal labor cost equals the wage paid to the new worker plus the extra income that must be paid to the original workers who were working at the old wage.

NOTES

1. Toke Aidt and Zafiris Tzannatos, *Unions and Collective Bargaining: Economic Effects in a Global Environment* (Washington DC: World Bank, 2002).

2. Ferdinand Protzman, "VW Plan for 4-Day Workweek Is Adopted," *New York Times*, November 26, 1993, p. D11; Tyler Marshall, "VW, Unions, OK 20% Reduction in Work Week," *Los Angeles Times*, November 26, 1993, p. A1: "Worldwire," *Wall Street Journal*, July 8, 1994, p. A5.

3. Richard B. Freeman and James Medoff, *What Do Unions Do?* (New York: Basic Books, 1985).

4. Joan Robinson, *The Economics of Imperfect Competition* (London: Macmillan,1933), p. 296.

5. Alan Manning, *Monopsony in Motion: Imperfect Competition in Labor* Markets (Princeton NJ: Princeton University Press, 2003).

6. J. R. Lee, "So-Called Profit Sharing System in the Ford Plant," *Annals of the American Academy of Political and Social Science*, May 1915, pp. 297–310; David Halberstam, *The Reckoning* (New York: William Morrow, 1986), pp. 91–92; Daniel M. G. Graff and Lawrence H. Summers, "Did Henry Ford Pay Efficiency Wages?" *Journal of Labor Economics*, vol. 5, 1987, pp. 557–586.

Part

6

The Basic Concepts in Macroeconomics

Measuring a Nation's Production and Income

n December 7, 1999, the United States Department of Commerce announced its "achievement of the century." What sort of achievement could rival other great U.S. accomplishments such as providing electricity to homes and businesses throughout the country, completing the interstate highway system, or landing a man on the moon? The Department of Commerce chose, as its great achievement, the development of the National Income and Product Accounts.

How could a mere system of accounting compare to the other great feats of the century, you might wonder? When the Department of Commerce made its announcement, it noted that the National Income and Product Accounts actually played a role in winning World War II by helping the government understand the development of our economy and allowing policymakers to stabilize it to promote economic growth. As odd as it may sound, an accounting system can indeed be powerful.

Macroeconomics

The branch of economics that looks at a nation's economy as a whole.

This chapter begins your study of **macroeconomics**: the branch of economics that deals with a nation's economy as a whole. Macroeconomics focuses on the economic issues—unemployment, inflation, growth, trade, and the gross domestic product—that are most often discussed in newspapers, on the radio, and on television. Macroeconomic issues lie at the heart of political debates. All presidential candidates must first learn a quick lesson in macroeconomics. Once elected, a president learns that the prospects for reelection will depend on how well the economy performs during the term in office. If the voters believe that the economy has performed well, the president will be reelected. Otherwise, the president will not likely be reelected. On the one hand, Democrats such as Jimmy Carter as well as Republicans like George H. W. Bush failed in their bids for reelection because of the voters' macroeconomic concerns. On the other hand, Bill Clinton survived a personal scandal in part because the U.S. economy performed superbly while he was in office.

Macroeconomic events profoundly affect our everyday lives. For example, if the economy fails to create enough jobs, workers will become unemployed throughout the country, and millions of lives will be disrupted. Similarly, slow economic growth means that living standards will not increase rapidly. If prices for goods begin rising rapidly, some people will find it difficult to maintain their lifestyles.

This chapter and the next will introduce you to the concepts you need to understand what macroeconomics is all about. In this chapter, we'll focus on a nation's production and income. We'll learn how economists measure the income and production for an entire country and what these measures are used for. In the next chapter, we'll look carefully at unemployment and inflation. Both chapters will explain the terms that are often used when economics is reported in the media.

After reading this chapter, you will be able to answer the following questions:

1 What does the term "gross domestic product" really mean?
2 Since prices change, how can we measure real income over long periods of time?
3 What are recessions and how frequently have they occurred?
4 Do increases in gross domestic product necessarily translate into improvements in the welfare of citizens?

As we learn the answers to these questions, we will build the necessary foundation for studying macroeconomics.

Macroeconomics focuses on two basic issues. One focus is on long-run economic growth. We need to understand what happens during the long run to understand what factors are behind the rise in living standards in modern economies. Today, in the United States, living standards are much higher than they were for our grandparents. They are also much higher than those of millions of people throughout the globe.

The other focus of macroeconomics is fluctuations in economic performance. Although living standards have improved over time, the economy has not always grown smoothly. There are periods when the economy appears to malfunction. During these periods, not enough jobs are created, and large numbers of workers become unemployed. These episodes are commonly known as recessions. An economy is considered to be in a **recession** when it fails to grow for at least six consecutive months.

At other times, unemployment may not be a problem, but we become concerned that the prices of everything that we buy seem to increase rapidly. Sustained increase in prices are called **inflation**. We'll explore inflation in the next chapter.

Recession

Commonly defined as six consecutive months of negative economic growth.

Inflation

Sustained increases in prices.

The "Flip" Sides of Macroeconomic Activity: Production and Income

Before we can study growth and fluctuations, we need to have a basic vocabulary and understanding of some key concepts. We begin with the terms *production* and *income* because these are the "flip" sides of the macroeconomic "coin," so to speak. Every day men and women go off to work, where they "produce" or sell merchandise or provide services. At the end of the week or month they return home with their paychecks or "income." They then spend some of that money on other products and services, produced by other people. In other words, production leads to income, and income leads to production.

But this chapter really isn't about production and income of individuals in markets. That's what a microeconomist studies. On the contrary, this chapter is about the production and income of the economy as a whole. From a "big picture" perspective, we will look at certain measures that will tell us how much the economy is producing and how well it is growing. We will also be able to measure the total income generated in the economy and how this income flows back to workers and investors. These two measures—a country's production and income—are critical to a nation's economic health. They help us to understand how many people will find jobs and whether their living standards are rising or falling. This is what macroeconomists do.

The Circular Flow of Production and Income

Let's begin with a simple diagram known as the circular flow. Let's start with a very simple economy that does not have a government or a foreign sector. In this economy, depicted in Figure 19.1, there are only households and firms, which make transactions

FIGURE 19.1

The Circular Flow of Production and Income
The circular flow shows how the production of goods and services generates income for households and how households purchase goods and services by firms.

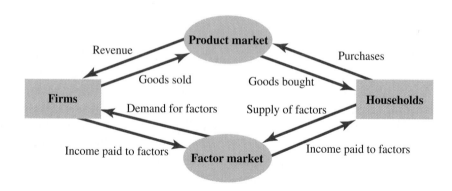

n two markets known as **factor markets** and **product markets**. In factor, or input, markets, households supply labor to firms and also capital for land, buildings, machines, and equipment used to produce output. Product or output markets are markets in which goods and services are sold to consumers.

The point of the circular flow diagram is simple but fundamental. Production generates income. In factor markets, when households supply labor and capital to firms, they are compensated by the firms. They earn wages for the work they do and they earn interest, dividends, and rents on the capital that they supply to the firms. The households then take their income and purchase goods and services in the product markets. The revenues the firm receives from the sale of its products are then used to pay for the factors of production. The important part of this diagram is that production generates income. When goods and service are produced, income flows throughout the economy.

For example, consider a manufacturer of computers. At the same time the computer manufacturer produces and sells new computers, it also generates income through its production. The computer manufacturer pays wages to workers, perhaps pays rent on offices and factory buildings, and pays interest on borrowed money. Whatever is left over after paying for the cost of production is the firm's profit, which is income to the owners of the firm. Wages, rents, interest, and profits are all different forms of income.

In another example, your taxes pay for a school district to hire principals, teachers, and other staff to provide educational services to the students in your community. These educational services are considered production in the modern economy. At the same time, the principals, teachers, and staff all earn income through their employment with the school district. The school district may also rent buildings where classes are held and pay interest on borrowed funds.

Our goal is to understand both sides of this macroeconomic "coin"—the production in the economy and the generation of income in the economy. In the United States, the National Income and Product Accounts, published by the Department of Commerce, are the source for the key data on production and income in the economy. In this chapter, we will study how these accounts work in practice. Let's begin by learning how to measure the production for the entire economy.

The Production Approach: Measuring a Nation's Macroeconomic Activity Using Gross Domestic Product

To measure the production of the entire economy, we need to combine an enormous array of goods and services—everything from new computers to NBA basketball games. We can actually add computers to basketball games, as we could add apples and oranges if we were trying to determine the total monetary value of a fruit harvest. Our goal is to summarize the total production of an entire economy into a single number, which we call the **gross domestic product (GDP)**. Gross domestic product is the total market value of all the final goods and services produced within an economy in a given year. It is also the most common measure of an economy's total output. All the words in the GDP definition are important, so let's analyze them.

Factor markets
The markets in which labor and capital are traded.

Product markets
The markets in which goods and services are traded.

Gross domestic product (GDP)
The total market value of all the final goods and services produced within an economy in a given year.

"Total market value" means that we take the quantity of goods produced and multiply them by their respective prices and then add up the totals. If an economy produced 2 cars at $15,000 per car and 3 computers at $3,000 per computer, the total value of these goods and services would be

$$(2 \text{ cars} \times \$15,000/\text{car}) + (3 \text{ computers} \times \$3,000/\text{computer}) = \$39,000$$

The reason we multiply the goods by their prices is that we cannot simply add together the number of cars and the number of computers. Using prices allows us to express the value of everything in a common unit of measurement—in this case, dollars. (In countries other than the United States, we would express the value in terms of the local currency.) This is how we add apples and oranges together: by finding out what is the value of both the apples and the oranges (as measured by what you would pay for them) and adding them up in terms of their prices.

"Final goods and services" in the definition of GDP means those goods and services that are sold to ultimate, or final, purchasers. For example, the 2 cars that were produced would be final goods if they were sold to households or to a business. However, to produce the cars, the automobile manufacturer bought steel that went into the body of the cars. This steel would not be counted as a final good or service in GDP. It is an example of an **intermediate good**, a good that is used in the production process. It is not considered a final good or service.

Intermediate goods

Goods used in the production process that are not final goods or services.

The reason we do not count intermediate goods as final goods is to avoid double-counting. The price of the car already reflects the price of the steel that is contained in it. We do not want to count the steel twice. Similarly, the large volumes of paper used by an accounting firm are also intermediate goods because they become part of the final product delivered by the accounting firm to its clients.

The final words in our definition of GDP are "in a given year." GDP is expressed as a rate of production, that is, as "X" amount of dollars per year. In 2002, for example, GDP in the United States was $10,480 billion. Goods produced in prior years, like cars or houses that one consumer later sells to another, are not included in GDP. Only newly produced products are included in GDP.

Because we measure GDP using the current prices for goods and services, GDP will increase if prices increase, even if the physical amount of goods that are produced remains the same. Suppose that next year the economy again produces 2 cars and 3 computers, but in the following year, all the prices in the economy have doubled: The price of cars is $30,000, and the price of computers is $6,000. GDP in the following

Neither used cars nor steel used to make cars (or other goods) are "currently produced goods and services" counted directly in GDP.

year will also be twice as high, or $78,000 [(2 cars × $30,000/car) + (3 computers × $6,000/computer)] even though the quantity produced is the same as during the prior year. But to say that GDP has doubled, would be misleading. To avoid this problem, let's apply the real-nominal principle, one of our five basic principles of economics:

 REAL-NOMINAL *Principle*

What matters to people is the real value of money or income— its purchasing power—not the face value of money or income.

What we need is another measure of total output that doesn't increase just because prices increase. For this reason, economists have developed the concept of **real GDP**, a measure of GDP that takes into account price changes. Later in this chapter, we explain how real GDP is calculated. The basic idea is simple. When we use current prices to measure GDP, that is what we call **nominal GDP**. Nominal GDP can increase for one of two reasons: Either the production of goods and services has increased or the prices of those goods and services have increased.

To explain real GDP, we need first to look at a simple example. Suppose an economy produces a single good: computers. In year 1, 10 computers were produced, and each sold for $1,000. In year 2, 12 computers were produced, and each sold for $1,100. Nominal GDP would be $10,000 in year 1 and $13,200 in year 2. Nominal GDP would have increased by a factor of 1.32. We can measure real GDP by calculating GDP using year 1 prices as a measure of what was produced in year 1 and also what was produced in year 2. In year 1, real GDP would be 10 computers × $1,000/computer = $10,000; and in year 2, it would be 12 computers × $1,000/computer = $12,000. Real GDP in year 2 is greater than real GDP in year 1 by a factor of 1.2. The key idea is that we construct a measure using the same prices for both years and thereby take price changes into account.

Figure 19.2 plots real GDP for the U.S. economy for the years 1930–2003. The graph shows that real GDP has grown substantially over this period. This is what economists call **economic growth**—sustained increases in the real production of an economy over a long time. In Chapter 22, we'll study economic growth in detail. Later in this chapter, we'll look carefully at the behavior of real GDP over shorter periods, during which time it can rise and fall. Decreases in real GDP disrupt the economy greatly and lead to unemployment.

Real GDP
A measure of GDP that controls for changes in prices.

Nominal GDP
The value of GDP in current dollars

Economic growth
Sustained increases in the real production of an economy over a period of time.

The Components of GDP

Economists divide GDP into four broad categories, each corresponding to different types of purchasers represented in GDP:

1 Consumption expenditures: purchases by consumers.
2 Private investment expenditures: purchases by firms.
3 Government purchases: purchases by federal, state, and local governments.
4 Net exports: net purchases by the foreign sector (domestic exports minus domestic imports).

FIGURE 19.2

U.S. Real GDP, 1930–2003

During the Great Depression in the 1930s, GDP initially fell and then was relatively flat. The economy was not growing much. However, the economy began growing rapidly in the 1940s during World War II and has grown substantially since then.

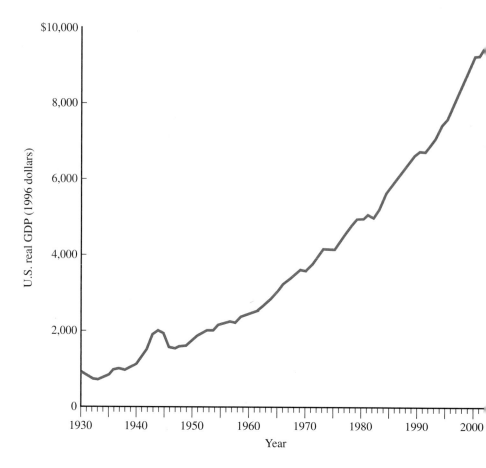

Before discussing these categories, let's look at some data for the U.S. economy to get a sense of the size of each of these four components. Table 19.1 shows the figures for GDP for the third quarter of 2003. (A quarter is a three-month period; the first quarter runs from January through March, and the third quarter runs from July through September.) In the third quarter of 2003, GDP was $11,107 billion, or approximately $11.1 trillion. To get a sense of the magnitude, consider that the U.S. population is approximately 290 million people, making GDP per person approximately $38,300. (This does not mean that every man, woman, and child actually spends $38,300, but it is a useful indicator of the productive strength of the economy.)

TABLE 19.1

Composition of U.S. GDP, Third Quarter 2003 (Billions of Dollars Expressed at Annual Rates)

GDP	Consumption Expenditures	Private Investment Expenditures	Government Purchases	Net Exports
11,107	7,836	1,689	2,072	−490

Source: U.S. Department of Commerce.

Consumption Expenditures

Consumption expenditures are purchases by consumers of currently produced goods and services, either domestic or foreign. These purchases include TV sets, VCRs, automobiles, clothing, hair-styling services, jewelry, movie or basketball tickets, food, and all other consumer items. We can break down consumption into durable goods, nondurable goods, and services. **Durable goods**, such as automobiles or refrigerators, last for a long time. **Nondurable goods**, such as food, last for a short time. **Services** reflect work done in which people play a prominent role in delivery (such as a dentist filling a cavity); they range from haircutting to health care. Services are the fastest-growing component of consumption in the United States. Overall, consumption spending is the most important component of GDP, constituting about 71% of total purchases.

Private Investment Expenditures

Private investment expenditures in GDP consist of three components:

1 First, there is spending on new plants and equipment during the year. If a firm builds a new factory or purchases a new machine, it is included in the year's GDP. Purchasing an existing building or buying a used machine does not count in GDP because the goods were not produced during the current year.
2 Second, newly produced housing is included in investment spending. The sale of an existing home to a new owner is not counted because the house was not built in the current year.
3 Finally, if firms add to their stock of inventories, the increase in inventories during the current year is included in GDP. If a hardware store had $1,000 worth of nuts and bolts on its shelves at the beginning of the year and $1,100 at the year's end, its inventory investment would be $100 ($1,100 − $1,000). This $100 increase in inventory investment is included in GDP.

We call the total of new investment expenditures **gross investment**. During the year, some of the existing plant, equipment, and housing will deteriorate or wear out. This wear and tear is called **depreciation**. If we subtract depreciation from gross investment, we obtain net investment. **Net investment** is the true addition to the stock of plant, equipment, and housing in a given year.

Make sure you understand this distinction between gross investment and net investment. Consider the $1,689 billion in total investment spending for the third quarter of 2003, a period in which there was $1,090 billion in depreciation. That means that there was only (1,689 − 1,090) = $599 billion in net investment by firms in that year; 64% of gross investment went to make up for depreciation of existing capital.

Warning: When we discuss measuring production in the GDP accounts, we use *investment* in a different way than when we use the word in the sense we have come to understand it. For an economist, investment in the GDP accounts means purchases of new final goods and services by firms. In everyday conversation, we may talk about investing in the stock market or investing in gold. Buying stock for $1,800 on the stock market is a purchase of an existing financial asset; it is not the purchase of new goods and services by firms. That $1,800 does not appear anywhere in GDP. The same is true

Consumption expenditures
Purchases of newly produced goods and services by households

Durable goods
Goods that last for a long period of time, such as household appliances.

Nondurable goods
Goods that last for short periods of time, such as food.

Services
Reflect work done in which people play a prominent role in delivery, ranging from haircutting to health care.

Private investment expenditures
Purchases of newly produced goods and services by firms.

Gross investment
Actual investment purchases.

Depreciation
The wear and tear of capital as it is used in production.

Net investment
Gross investment minus depreciation.

of purchasing a gold bar. In GDP accounting, *investment* denotes the purchase of new capital. Be careful not to confuse the common usage of *investment* with the definition of *investment* as we use it in the GDP accounts.

Government Purchases

Government purchases

Purchases of newly produced goods and services by all levels of government.

Government purchases are the purchases of newly produced goods and services by federal, state, and local governments. They include any goods that the government purchases plus the wages and benefits of all government workers (paid when the government purchases their services as employees). The majority of spending in this category actually comes from state and local governments: $1,302 billion of the total $2,072 billion in 2003. Government purchases affect our lives very directly. For example, all salaries of public school teachers are counted as government purchases.

Transfer payments

Payments to individuals from governments that do not correspond to the production of goods and services.

This category does not include all the spending by governments. It excludes **transfer payments**; these are funds paid to individuals but are not associated with the production of goods and services. For example, payments for Social Security, welfare, and interest on government debt are all considered transfer payments and are not included in government purchases in GDP. The reason they are excluded is that nothing is being produced by the recipients in return for money being paid or "transferred" to them. But wage payments to the police, postal workers, and the staff of the Internal Revenue Service are all included because they do correspond to services that are currently being produced.

Because transfer payments are excluded from GDP, a vast portion of the budget of the federal government is not part of GDP. In 2003, the federal government spent approximately $2,157 billion, of which only $770 billion (about one-third) was counted as federal government purchases. Transfer payments are important, however. They affect both the income of individuals and their consumption and savings behavior. They also affect the size of the federal budget deficit, which we will study in a later chapter. At this point, keep in mind the distinction between government purchases—which are included in GDP—and total government spending or expenditure—which may not be included.

Net Exports

Imports

A good produced in a foreign country and purchased by residents of the home country (for example, the United States).

To understand the role of the foreign sector, we first need to define three terms. **Imports** are goods we buy from other countries. **Exports** are goods made here and sold to other countries. **Net exports** are total exports minus total imports. In Table 19.1, we see that net exports in the third quarter of 2003 were −$490 billion. Net exports were negative because our imports exceeded our exports.

Consumption, investment, and government purchases include all purchases by consumers, firms, and the government, whether or not the goods were produced in the United States. However, GDP is supposed to measure the goods produced in the United States. Consequently, purchases of foreign goods by consumers, firms, or the government should be subtracted when we calculate GDP because these goods were not produced in the United States. At the same time, we must add to GDP any goods produced here and sold abroad. For example, supercomputers made in the United States and sold in Europe should be added to GDP. By including net exports as a component of GDP, we correctly measure U.S. production by adding exports and subtracting imports.

Exports

Goods produced in the home country (for example, the United States) and sold in another country.

Net exports

Exports minus imports.

For example, suppose someone in the United States buys a $25,000 car made in Japan. If we look at final purchases, we will see that consumption spending rose by $25,000 because a consumer made a purchase of a consumption good. Net exports fell

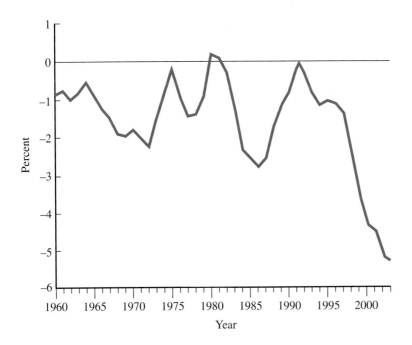

FIGURE 19.3
U.S. Trade Balance as a Share of GDP
In the 1980s and the 1990s the United States briefly ran a trade surplus. (When the line on the graph is at zero or above, this indicates a surplus.) However, trade deficits in excess of 2% of GDP (lower than −2 on the graph) have often been run. In recent years, they have become the norm.

by $25,000, however, because the value of the import (the car) was subtracted from total exports. Notice that total GDP did not change with the purchase of the car. This is exactly what we want in this case, because the car wasn't U.S produced.

Now suppose that the United States sells a car for $18,000 to a resident of Spain. In this case, net exports would increase by $18,000 because the car was a U.S. export. GDP would also be a corresponding $18,000 higher because this sale represents U.S. production.

Recall that for the United States in the third quarter of 2003, net exports were −$490 billion dollars. In other words, in that quarter, the United States bought $490 billion more goods from abroad than it sold abroad. When we buy more goods from abroad than we sell, we have a **trade deficit**. A **trade surplus** occurs when our exports exceed our imports. Figure 19.3 shows the U.S. trade surplus as a share of GDP from 1960 to 2003. Although at times the United States had a trade surplus, in the 1980s and the period beginning in the late 1990s, the United States ran a trade deficit that often exceeded 2% of GDP. Trade deficits affect the economy in a number of different ways. In later chapters, we study how trade deficits can directly affect the level of GDP in a country.

Trade deficit
The excess of imports over exports.

Trade surplus
The excess of exports over imports.

Putting It All Together: The GDP Equation

We can summarize our discussion of who purchases GDP with a simple equation. Letting the symbol "Y" stand for GDP and the symbols C, I, G, NX stand for consumption, investment, government purchases and net exports, respectively, we can write:

$$Y = C + I + G + NX$$

or, in words,

GDP = consumption + investment + government purchases + net exports

This equation is an "identity," which means that is always true. That is because in an economy, GDP consists of the sum of its four components. This equation can help you remember the components that constitute GDP.

TEST Your Understanding

1. What are the four components of GDP?
2. The circular flow describes the process by which GDP generates _____, which is spent on goods.
3. What part of government spending is excluded from GDP because it does not correspond to goods or services being produced currently?
4. What is the difference between gross investment and net investment?
5. Define net exports.

The Income Approach: Measuring a Nation's Macroeconomic Activity Using National Income

Recall from the circular flow that when GDP is produced, income is created. One person's production ends up being another person's income. This is the flip side of our macroeconomic "coin." As a result, in addition to measuring a nation's activity by measuring production, we can also gauge it by measuring a nation's income. The income that flows to the private sector is called **national income**. It is the income that all the individuals and firms earn from their production.

National income

Net national product less indirect taxes.

Measuring National Income

To measure national income, economists first make three adjustments to GDP.

First, we add to GDP the net income earned by U.S. firms and residents abroad. To make this calculation, we add to GDP any income earned abroad by U.S. firms or residents and subtract any income earned in the United States by foreign firms or residents. For example, we add the profits earned by U.S. multinational corporations that are sent back to the United States but subtract the profits from multinational corporations operating in the United States that are sent back to their home countries. The result of these adjustments is the total income earned worldwide by U.S. firms and residents. This is called the **gross national product (GNP)**.

Gross national product (GNP)

GDP plus net income earned abroad.

For most countries, the distinction between what they produce within their borders, GDP, and what their citizens earn, GNP, is not that important. For the United States, the difference between GDP and GNP is typically just 0.2%. In some countries, however, the differences are much larger. The country of Kuwait, for example, earned vast amounts of income from its oil riches, which it invested abroad. Earnings from these investments are included in Kuwait's GNP; in 2002, those earnings comprised approximately 8.8% of the total income of Kuwait—in other years, it reached as high as 19%. Australia has traditionally borrowed from foreign countries to finance its investments. Consequently, its net income from abroad was negative in 2002 and Australian GDP in that year exceeded Australian GNP by 3.1%.

The second adjustment that we make on the way to calculating national income is to subtract depreciation from GNP. Recall that depreciation is the wear and tear on plant and equipment that occurred during the year. In a sense, our income is reduced because our buildings and machines are wearing out. When we subtract depreciation from GNP, we reach **net national product (NNP)**, where "net" means after depreciation.

The third and last adjustment we make to reach national income is to subtract **indirect taxes**, which are sales taxes or excise taxes on products. If a store sells you a product for $1.00 and the sales tax is $0.08, your total bill is $1.08. However, only $1.00 of that purchase goes to the store to pay wages, rent, interest, and maybe even some profit to the owners. The remainder, $0.08, goes to the government; it is not part of private-sector income and therefore not a part of national income.

After making all three adjustments, we reach national income. Table 19.2 shows these adjustments (ignoring a few minor items) for the third quarter of 2003.

In turn, national income is divided among six basic categories: Compensation of employees (wages and benefits), corporate profits, rental income, proprietor's income (income of unincorporated business), net interest (interest payments received by households from business and from abroad) and other items. Figure 19.4 presents U.S. data for the second quarter of 2003. Approximately 63% of all national income goes to workers in the form of wages and benefits. For most of the countries in the world, wages and benefits are the largest part of national income.

In addition to national income, which measures the income earned in a given year by the entire private sector, we are sometimes interested in determining the total payments that flow directly into households, a concept known as **personal income**. To calculate personal income, we begin with national income and subtract any corporate profits that are retained by the corporation and not paid out as dividends to households. We also subtract all social insurance taxes, which are payments for Social Security and Medicare. We then add any personal interest income received from the government and consumers and all transfer payments. The result is the total income available to households, or personal income. The amount of personal income that households keep after paying income taxes is called **personal disposable income**.

Net national product (NNP)
GNP less depreciation.

Indirect taxes
Sales and excise taxes.

Personal income
Income (including transfer payments) received by households.

Personal disposable income
Personal income after taxes.

TABLE 19.2

From GDP to National Income, Third Quarter 2003 (billions of dollars)

Gross domestic product	11,107
plus net income from abroad =	
Gross national product	11,144
minus depreciation =	
Net national product	9,836
minus indirect taxes (and other adjustments) =	
National income	9,782

Source: U.S. Department of Commerce.

FIGURE 19.4

Composition of U.S. National Income, Third Quarter of 2003 (billions of dollars)
The chart shows that compensation for employees is the largest component of national income.

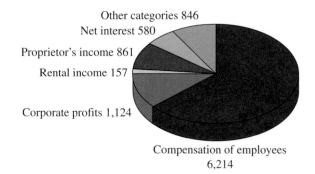

Other categories 846
Net interest 580
Proprietor's income 861
Rental income 157
Corporate profits 1,124
Compensation of employees 6,214

Measuring National Income Through Value Added

Value added

The sum of all the income (wages, interest, profits, rent) generated by an organization.

Another way to measure national income is to look at the **value added** of each firm in the economy. Economists define the value added of a firm as the sum of all the income—wages, profits, rents, and interest—that it generates. By adding up the value added for all the firms in the economy (plus nonprofit and governmental organizations), we can calculate national income. Consider a simple example.

Suppose an economy consists of two firms: an automobile firm that sells its cars to consumers and a steel firm that sells only to the automobile firm. If the automobile company sells a car for $16,000 to consumers and purchases $6,000 worth of steel from the steel firm, the auto firm has $10,000 remaining—its value added—which can then be distributed as wages, rents, interest, and profits. If the steel firm sells $6,000 worth of steel but does not purchase any inputs from other firms, its value added is $6,000, which is paid out in the form of wages, rents, interest, and profits. Total value added in the economy from both firms is $16,000 ($10,000 + $6,000), which is the sum of wages, rents, interest, and profits for the entire economy (consisting of these two firms).

As this example illustrates, we measure the value added for a typical firm by starting with the value of its total sales and subtracting the value of any inputs it purchases from other firms. The amount of income that remains is the firm's value added, which is then distributed as wages, rents, interest, and profits. In calculating national income, it is important to include all the firms in the economy, even the firms that produce intermediate goods.

An Expanded Circular Flow

Now that we have examined both production and income, including both the government and the foreign sector, let's take another look at a slightly more realistic circular flow. Figure 19.5 depicts a circular flow that includes both the government and the foreign sector. Both households and firms pay taxes to the government. The government, in turn, supplies goods and services in the product market and also purchases inputs (labor and capital) in the factor markets just like private-sector firms do. Net exports (which can be positive or negative) are shown interacting with the product market.

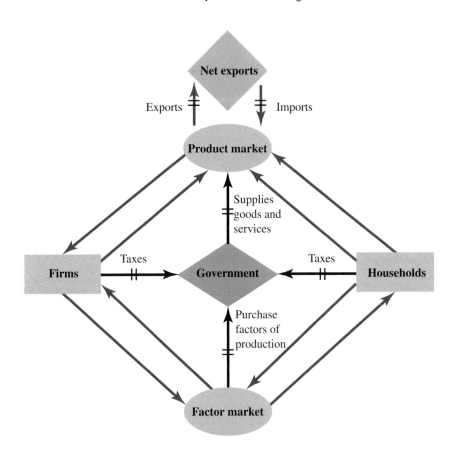

FIGURE 19.5

The Circular Flow with Government and the Foreign Sector
The new linkages demonstrate the roles that the government and the foreign sector play in the circular flow.

In summary, we can look at GDP from two sides: We can ask who buys the output that is produced, or we can ask how the income that is created through the production process is divided between workers and investors. From the spending side, we see that nearly 71% of GDP consists of consumer expenditures. From the income side, we see that nearly 63% of national income is paid in wages and benefits. Depending on the precise question at hand, macroeconomists may use data based either on the production that occurs in the economy or on its flip side, the income that is generated.

TEST Your Understanding

6. What do we add to GDP to reach GNP?
7. What is the largest component of national income?
8. Complete the statement with "households" or "firms": Personal income and personal disposable income refer to payments ultimately flowing to _____.

A Closer Examination of GDP

Of all the measures we discussed, GDP is the most important and is used the most. For that reason, let's take a little closer look at it.

Measuring Real versus Nominal GDP

Output in the economy can increase from one year to the next. And prices can rise from one year to the next. Recall that we defined nominal GDP as GDP measured in current prices, and we defined real GDP as GDP adjusted for price changes.

Now we take a closer look at how real GDP is measured in modern economies. Let's start with a simple economy in which there are only two goods, cars and computers, produced in the years 2006 and 2007. The data for this economy, the prices and quantities produced for each year, are shown in Table 19.3. The production of cars and the production of computers increased, but the production of computers increased more rapidly. The price of cars rose, while the price of computers remained the same.

Let's first calculate nominal GDP for this economy in each year. Nominal GDP is the total value of goods and services produced in each year. Using the data in the table, we can see that nominal GDP for the year 2006 is

$$(4 \text{ cars} \times \$10,000/\text{car}) + (1 \text{ computer} \times \$5,000 \text{ computer}) = \$45,000$$

Similarly, nominal GDP for 2007 is $75,000.

Now we'll find real GDP. To compute real GDP, we calculate GDP using constant prices. What prices should we use? For the moment, let's use the prices for the year 2006. Because we are using 2006 prices, real GDP and nominal GDP for 2006 are both equal to $45,000. But for 2007, they are different. In 2007, real GDP is

$$(5 \text{ cars} \times \$10,000/\text{car}) + (3 \text{ computers} \times \$5,000 \text{ computer}) = \$65,000$$

Note that real GDP for 2007, which is $65,000, is less than nominal GDP for 2007, which is equal to $75,000. The reason real GDP is less than nominal GDP here is because prices of cars rose between 2006 and 2007, and we are measuring GDP using 2006 prices. We can measure real GDP for any other year simply by calculating GDP using constant prices.

We now calculate the growth in real GDP for this economy between 2006 and 2007. Because real GDP was $45,000 in 2006 and $65,000 in 2007, real GDP grew by

$$(\$65,000 - \$45,000)/\$45,000 = 0.444$$

which equals 44.4%. This is an average of the growth rates for both goods, cars and computers.

TABLE 19.3

GDP Data for a Simple Economy

| Year | Quantity Produced | | Price | |
	Cars	Computers	Cars	Computers
2006	4	1	$10,000	$5,000
2007	5	3	12,000	5,000

How to Use the GDP Deflator

We can also use the data in Table 19.3 to measure the changes in prices for this economy. The basic idea is that the differences between nominal GDP and real GDP for any year arise only because of changes in prices. Thus, by comparing real GDP and nominal GDP, we can measure the changes in prices for the economy. In practice, we do this by creating an index, called the **GDP deflator**, which measures how prices change over time. Because we are calculating real GDP using year 2006 prices, we will set the value of this index equal to 100 in the year 2006, which we call the base year. To find the value of the GDP deflator for the year 2007 (or other years), we use the following formula:

GDP deflator
An index that measures how the price of goods included in GDP changes over time.

value of GDP deflator in 2007 = $100 \times [$ (nominal GDP in 2007)/(real GDP in 2007)$]$

Using this formula, we find that the value of the GDP deflator for 2007 is

$$100 \times (\$75,000/\$65,000) = 100 \times 1.15 = 115$$

Since the value of the GDP deflator is 115 in 2007 and was 100 in the base year of 2006, this means that prices rose by 15% ($[(115 - 100)/100] = 0.15$) between the two years. Note that this 15% is an average of the price changes for the two goods, cars and computers.

Up until 1996, the Commerce Department, which produces the GDP figures, used these methods to calculate real GDP and measure changes in prices. It chose a base year and measured real GDP by using the prices in that base year, and it also calculated the GDP deflator, just as we did, by taking the ratio of nominal GDP to real GDP. Today, the Commerce Department calculates real GDP and the price index for real GDP using a more complicated method. In our example, we measured real GDP using 2006 prices. But we could have also measured real GDP using prices from 2007. If we did, we would have come up with slightly different numbers both for the increase in prices between the two years and for the increase in real GDP. To avoid this problem, the Commerce Department today uses a **chain index**, a method for calculating price changes based on taking an average of price changes using base years from neighboring years (that is, 2006 and 2007 in our example). If you look in the newspapers today or at the data produced by the Commerce Department, you will see real GDP measured in chained-dollars and a chain-type price index for GDP.

Chain index
A method for calculating changes in prices that uses base years from neighboring years.

Fluctuations in GDP

As we discussed, real GDP does not always grow smoothly—sometimes it collapses suddenly and the result is an economic downturn. Let's look at an example from the late 1980s and early 1990s. Figure 19.6 plots real GDP for the United States from 1988 to 1992. Notice that in mid-1990, real GDP begins to fall. As we discussed earlier, a recession is a period when real GDP falls for six or more consecutive months. Economists talk more in terms of quarters of the year—consecutive three-month periods—than in terms of months. So they would say that when real GDP falls for two

The 1990 Recession
Recessions can be illustrated by peaks and troughs. The date at which the recession starts and output begins to fall is called the peak. The date at which the recession begins to end and output begins to rise is called the trough.

Source: U.S. Department of Commerce.

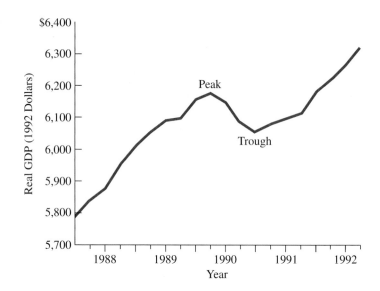

Peak

The time at which a recession begins.

Trough

The time at which output stops falling in a recession.

Expansion

The period after a trough in the business cycle during which the economy recovers

consecutive quarters, that's a recession. The date at which the recession starts—that is, when output starts to decline—is called the **peak**; the date at which the recession begins to end—that is, when output starts to increase again—is called the **trough**. In Figure 19.6, we see the peak and trough of the recession. After a trough, the economy enters a recovery period, or period of **expansion**.

From World War II through 2001, the United States experienced ten recessions. Table 19.4 contains the dates of the peaks and troughs of each recession as well as the percent decline in real GDP from each peak to each trough. The sharpest decline in output occurred during the recession from 1973 to 1975, which started as a result of a sharp rise in world oil prices. In the last three decades, there have been three recessions starting near the beginning of each of the decades: 1981, 1990, and 2001. In the most recent recession, employment began to fall in March of 2001, before the advent of the terrorist attack on the United States on September 11, 2001. The attack further dis-

Ten Postwar Recessions

Peak	Trough	Percent Decline in Real GDP
November 1948	October 1949	−1.5
July 1953	May 1954	−3.2
August 1957	April 1958	−3.3
April 1960	February 1961	−1.2
December 1969	November 1970	−1.0
November 1973	March 1975	−4.9
January 1980	July 1980	−2.5
July 1981	November 1982	−3.0
July 1990	March 1991	−1.4
March 2001	November 2001	−0.6

upted economic activity, damaged producer and consumer confidence, and plunged the economy into a recession.

Throughout the broader sweep of U.S. history, there have been other periods of downturns—20 of them from 1860 up to World War II. Not all of these were particularly severe, and in some, unemployment hardly changed. However, there were economic downturns, such as those in 1893 and 1929, that were severe.

Although we used the common definition of a recession as a period when real GDP falls for six months, in practice, a committee of economists at the National Bureau of Economics Research (a private organization of primarily academic economists known as the NBER) officially proclaims the beginning and end of recessions in the United States using a broader set of criteria. "A Closer Look: The NBER and the 2001 Recession" describes this process.

Depression is the common term for a severe recession. In the United States, the Great Depression refers to 1929–1933, the period when real GDP fell by over 33%. It created the most severe disruptions to ordinary economic life in the United States during the twentieth century. Throughout the country and in much of the world, banks closed, businesses failed, and many people lost their jobs and their life savings. Unemployment rose sharply. In 1933, over 25% of people who were looking for work failed to find jobs.

Although the United States has not experienced a depression since that time, other countries have. In the last 20 years, several Asian countries (for example, Thailand) and Latin American countries (for example, Argentina) suffered severe economic disruptions that were true depressions.

Depression
The common name for a severe recession.

A CLOSER LOOK

The NBER and the 2001 Recession

On November 26, 2001, a committee of economists from the National Bureau of Economic Research announced that the peak of the 2001 recession occurred in March 2001. Nearly two years later, on July 17, 2003, they dated the trough as occurring in November of 2001. In deciding on the timing of the recession, the committee followed its past practices of looking at a full range of economic data. Although the level of GDP is an extremely important indicator, the NBER committee also examined a full range of other data, including data on retail and wholesale trade, personal income, and measures of employment.

Although the common definition of a recession is a six-month consecutive period of negative economic growth, the NBER defines a recession as a "significant decline in activity spread across the economy, lasting more than a few months, visible in industrial production, employment, real income, and wholesale-retail trade." When the NBER first dated the peak of the recession, the quarterly GDP data from the U.S. Department of Commerce did *not* show a six-month fall in GDP. This created some confusion in the popular press, which was accustomed to the common definition. However, this is a useful reminder that the NBER looks carefully at a wide range of data on a monthly basis, not just quarterly data for GDP.

GDP as a Measure of Welfare

GDP is our best measure of the value of output produced by an economy. As we have seen, we can use GDP and related indicators to measure economic growth within a country. In a later chapter, we will use GDP to compare the value of output across countries as well. Economists use GDP and related measures to determine if an economy has fallen into a recession or has entered into a depression. And when GDP performs poorly, presidents are punished. But while GDP is a very valuable measure of the health of an economy, it is not a perfect measure.

Shortcomings of GDP as a Measure of Welfare

There are several recognized flaws in the construction of GDP that you need to be wary of. Because of these flaws, we should be cautious if we want to interpret GDP as a measure of our economic well-being. First, GDP ignores transactions that do not take place in organized markets. The most important example is services, such as cleaning, cooking, and providing free child care, that people do for themselves in their own homes. Because these services are not transferred through markets, GDP statisticians cannot measure them. This has probably led us to overestimate GDP growth in recent years. For example, in the last three decades, there has been a big increase in the percentage of women in the labor force. Since more women are now working outside the home, there is naturally a demand for more meals in restaurants, more cleaning services, and more paid child care. All this new demand shows up in GDP, but the services that were provided earlier—when they were provided free—did not show up in earlier GDP. This naturally overstates the true growth in GDP.

Second, leisure time is not included in GDP, since GDP is designed to be a measure of the production that occurs in the economy. Leisure time, along with other nonmarket activities, is ignored in GDP accounting. To the extent that leisure is valued by households, increases in leisure time will lead to higher social welfare, but not higher GDP.

Third, GDP ignores the underground economy, where transactions are not reported to official authorities. These transactions can be legal, but people don't report

The growth in GDP is exaggerated because the cost of restaurant meals includes cooking services that were previously performed at home and not counted in GDP.

he income they have generated because they want to evade paying taxes on that income. For example, waiters and waitresses may not report all their tips, and owners of flea markets may make under-the-table cash transactions with their customers. There are also illegal transactions that result in unreported income, such as profits from the illegal drug trade.

In the United States, the Internal Revenue Service estimated that in 2001 about $310 billion in federal income taxes from the underground economy were not collected each year. If the average federal income tax rate was about 20%, this means that approximately $1.5 trillion ($310 billion ÷ 0.20) in income escaped the GDP accountants from the underground economy that year, about 15% of GDP at the time.

Fourth, GDP does not value changes in the environment that occur in the production of output. Suppose a factory produces $1,000 of output but pollutes a river and lowers the river's value by $2,000. Instead of recording a loss to society of $1,000, GDP will show a $1,000 increase. This is an important limitation of GDP accounting as a measure of our economic well-being because changes in the environment are important.

In principle, we can make adjustments to try to correct for this deficiency. In the early 1990s, the U.S. Department of Commerce, which collects the GDP data, undertook a study to account for environmental changes. In 1994, it released a report on the first phase of the study, which focused on the value of mineral resources (oil, gas, coal, and so forth.) in the United States. The government first measured "proven" reserves of minerals from 1958 to 1991. Proven reserves are those that can be extracted, given current technology and current economic conditions. Proven reserves decrease when minerals are extracted and increase when new investments (such as oil wells or mines) are made.

The Commerce Department was trying to determine whether the stock of proven reserves had been depleted—that is, depreciated—over time. The stock of proven reserves had depreciated, but by only a very small amount—less than $1 billion per year. It is important to note that this calculation focuses only on proven reserves, not the total stock of minerals in the earth. The reason the Commerce Department counts only proven reserves is that some mineral deposits are simply too expensive to extract under current economic conditions. Changes in proven reserves alone correspond most closely to changes in our current economic well-being.

Because the depreciation of proven reserves turned out to be very small, the Commerce Department found that these adjustments had very little effect on measures of national income. However, mineral stocks comprise only part of our environment. The same GDP adjustment methods could forseeably be extended to include renewable resources, such as forests and fish, although the data may not be as accurate as the data for minerals. A much more challenging task would be to value changes in clean air and clean water. Has our environment improved or deteriorated as we experienced economic growth? Finding the answer to this question will pose a real challenge for the next generation of economic statisticians.

Finally, most of us would prefer to live in a country with a high standard of living and few of us would want to experience poverty up close. But does a higher level of GDP really lead to more satisfaction? As "A Closer Look: Does Money Buy Happiness?" explores, higher income does not necessarily lead to higher levels of perceived happiness.

A CLOSER LOOK

Does Money Buy Happiness?

Two economists, David Blanchflower of Dartmouth College and Andrew Oswald of Warwick University in the United Kingdom, have systematically analyzed surveys over nearly a 30-year period that ask individuals to describe themselves as "happy, pretty happy, or not too happy." The results of their work are provocative. Over the last 30 years, reported levels of happiness have actually declined in the United States and remained relatively flat in the United Kingdom, despite very large increases in per capita income in both countries. Could it be the increased stress of everyday life has taken its toll on our happiness despite the increase in income?

At any point in time, however, money does appear to buy happiness. Holding other factors constant, individuals with higher incomes do report higher levels of personal satisfaction. But these "other factors" are quite important. Unemployment and divorce lead to sharply lower levels of satisfaction. Blanchflower and Oswald calculate that a stable marriage is worth $100,000 in terms of equivalent reported satisfaction.

Perhaps most interesting are their findings about trends in the relative happiness of different groups in our society. While whites report higher levels of happiness than African Americans,

Does money really buy happiness?

the gap has decreased over the last 30 years as the happiness of African Americans has risen faster than whites. Men's happiness has risen relative to that of women over the last 30 years. Finally, reported happiness appears to peak at age 40. What economic and social factors do you think account for these trends?

Source: David G. Blanchflower and Andrew J. Oswald, National Bureau of Economic Research Working Paper 7847, January 2000.

USING THE TOOLS

In this chapter, we looked closely at how we measure a nation's production and how we measure its income. Here's an opportunity to test your understanding of some of the key concepts.

1. Crime, Police, and Measured GDP

Suppose a community spends $1 million on salaries and equipment for its police department. Because it believes that citizens are now more law abiding, the community decides to cut back on the number of police it employs. As a result, the community now spends only $800,000 on the police. The crime rate remains the same.

1. What happens to measured GDP?
2. Does GDP accurately reflect welfare in this case? Explain the underlying issue that this example poses.

2. Fish and National Income

Suppose you were worried that national income does not adequately take into account the depletion of the stock of fish in the economy. Describe how you would advise the Commerce Department to take this into account in their calculations.

3. Transfer Payments Versus Government Employment

In Economy A, the government puts workers on the payroll who cannot find jobs for long periods, but these "employees" do no work. In Economy B, the government does not hire any long-term

unemployed workers; instead, it just gives them cash grants. How do the GDP statistics compare between the two otherwise identical economies?

4 Counting Recessions

Consider the data for the fictitious economy of Euronet:

Year and Quarter	2003:1	2003:2	2003:3	2003:4	2004:1	2004:2	2004:3
Real GDP	195	193	195	196	195	194	198

How many recessions occurred in the economy over the time indicated?

SUMMARY

In this chapter, we learned how economists and government statisticians measure the income and production for an entire country and what these measures are used for. Developing meaningful statistics for an entire economy is difficult. As we have seen, statistics can convey useful information—if they are used with care. Here are some of the main points to remember in this chapter:

1 The circular flow shows how the production of goods and services generates income for households and how households purchase goods and services by firms.
2 GDP is the market value of all final goods and services produced in a given year.
3 GDP consists of four components: consumption, investment, government purchases, and net exports.

4 National income is obtained from GDP by adding net income U.S. individuals and firms earn from abroad, then subtracting depreciation and indirect taxes.
5 Real GDP is calculated by using constant prices. The Commerce Department now uses methods that take an average using base years from neighboring years.
6 A recession is commonly defined as a six-month consecutive period of negative growth. However, in the United States, the National Bureau of Economic Research uses a broader definition.
7 GDP does not include nonmarket transactions, leisure time, the underground economy, or changes to the environment.

KEY TERMS

chain index, 435
consumption expenditures, 427
depreciation, 427
depression, 437
durable goods, 427
economic growth, 425
expansion, 436
exports, 428

factor markets, 423
GDP deflator, 435
government purchases, 428
gross domestic product (GDP), 423
gross investment, 427
gross national product (GNP), 430
imports, 428
indirect taxes, 431

inflation, 422
intermediate goods, 424
macroeconomics, 421
national income, 430
net exports, 428
net investment, 427
net national product (NNP), 431
nominal GDP, 425

PROBLEMS AND DISCUSSION QUESTIONS

1 Should we care more about the growth of nominal GDP or real GDP?

For Problems 2–4, use the following data:

	Quantities Produced		Prices	
	CDs	**Tennis Rackets**	**$/CD**	**$/Tennis Rackets**
Year 2006	100	200	20	110
Year 2007	120	210	22	120

2 Calculate real GDP using prices from 2006. By what percent did real GDP grow?

3 Calculate the value of the price index for GDP for 2007 using 2006 as the base year. By what percent did prices increase?

4 Repeat Problem 2 but use prices from 2007.

5 Suppose someone told you that the value of a price index in a country was 115. Is this information, by itself, useful?

6 A student once said, "Trade deficits are good because we are buying more goods than we are producing." What is the downside to trade deficits?

7 Consumer durables depreciate over time. In your household, which consumer goods have substantial depreciation? Can you estimate the value of depreciation in a given year for consumer goods in your household?

8 A publisher buys paper, ink, and computers to produce textbooks. Which of these purchases is included in investment spending?

9 Air quality in Los Angeles deteriorated in the 1950s through the 1970s and then improved in the 1980s and 1990s. How could a change in air quality like this be incorporated into our measures of national income?

10 When we calculate value added, we add up the value created in all organizations, even those producing intermediate goods. Can you explain why this does not cause double-counting?

11 In the 1980s and 1990s, computers were rapidly introduced into the economy. The prices of computers fell rapidly over time during this period. Suppose that in calculating real GDP, the Commerce Department used a single base year, one in which computer prices were still at their earlier, high levels. What distortions would using this base year cause to measures of real GDP and to changes in prices?

12 To compare how deeply recessions affected the economies of two different countries, we might use the following measures:

   a. The number of recessions
   b. The proportion of time each economy was in a recession
   c. The magnitude of the worst recession

Draw several diagrams that show economies experiencing recessions. Use these diagrams to illustrate how these measures convey different features of recessions.

13 *Web Exercise.* Go to the Website for the Federal Reserve Bank of St. Louis (***http://research.stlouisfed.org/fred2/***). Find the data for nominal GDP, real GDP in chained dollars, and the chain price index for GDP.

   a. Calculate the percentage growth for nominal GDP since 1990 until the most recent year.
   b. Calculate the percentage growth in real GDP since 1990 until the most recent year.
   c. Finally, calculate the percentage growth in the chain price index for GDP over this same period and compare it to the difference between your answers to (a) and (b).

14 *Web Exercise.* Search the Web for articles on the underground economy. You might want to start with the topic "IRS and Underground Economy" on *www.yahoo.com.* What are some of the different ways in which economists try to measure the size of the underground economy?

MODEL ANSWERS TO QUESTIONS

Chapter Opening Questions

1 Gross domestic product is the total value of all final goods and services produced in a given year.

2 We use constant prices to measure real income.

3 Recessions are periods when real GDP falls for at least six months. There have been 10 recessions in the United States since World War II.

4 GDP is not a perfect measure of economic welfare.

Test Your Understanding

1 The four components of GDP are consumption, investment, government spending, and net exports.

2 Income

3 Transfer payments are excluded.

4 The difference is depreciation.

5 Net exports are exports minus imports.

6 We add net income earned abroad.

7 The largest component is compensation of employees.

8 Households.

Unemployment and Inflation

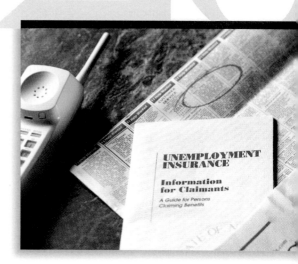

n early December, the Bureau of Labor Statistics announced that the unemployment rate for November 2003 was 5.9%. That meant that of all the people who had jobs or were actively looking for work, 5.9% did not have jobs.

But the official unemployment statistics did not include the following individuals:

▶ A steelworker in Ohio who was laid off two years ago. He stopped looking for work because there were no steel mills remaining in his town and he believed no jobs were available.

▶ A young woman, living in the far suburbs of a city. She wanted to work, and had worked in the past, but she had no transportation to the places where jobs were available.

▶ A young man who was working 25 hours a week. He wanted to work 40 hours a week, but his employer did not have enough work for him. Nor could he easily find another job.

The Bureau of Labor Statistics now publishes alternative statistics that reflect these circumstances. How big a difference does it make to include these cases in the BLS statistics?

I n this chapter, we look at unemployment and inflation, two key phenomena in macroeconomics. Losing a job is one of the most stressful experiences a person can suffer. For the elderly, the fear that the purchasing power of their wealth will evaporate with inflation is also a source of deep concern.

In this chapter, we will examine how economists define unemployment and inflation and the problems in measuring them. We also will explore the various costs that unemployment and inflation impose on society. Once we have a basic understanding of what unemployment is and what inflation is, we will be able to investigate their causes further.

After studying this chapter, you will be able to answer the following questions:

1 What is unemployment?
2 Do the official unemployment statistics fully measure the extent of unemployment in society?
3 What are the costs of unemployment?
4 What is the Consumer Price Index and how is it related to the cost of living?
5 How accurately can we measure inflation in the economy? If we don't do a good job, what impact does our inaccuracy have?
6 Why does inflation impose costs on society?

Examining Unemployment

One of the reasons we want the economy to avoid performing poorly is that it imposes costs on individuals and society. Recall from Chapter 19 that one of the key issues for macroeconomics is understanding fluctuations—the ups and downs of the economy. During periods of poor economic performance and slow economic growth, unemployment rises sharply and becomes a cause of public concern. During times of good economic performance and rapid economic growth, unemployment falls but does not disappear. Our first task is to understand how economists and government statisticians measure unemployment and then learn to interpret what they measure.

How is Unemployment Defined and Measured?

Unemployed

People who are looking for work but do not have jobs.

Employed

People who have jobs.

Labor force

The employed plus the unemployed.

Let's begin with some definitions.

The **unemployed** are those individuals who do not currently have a job but who are actively looking for work. The phrase "actively looking" is critical. Individuals who looked for work in the past but are not looking currently are not counted as unemployed. The **employed** are individuals who currently have jobs. Together, the unemployed and employed comprise the **labor force**.

$$\text{labor force} = \text{employed} + \text{unemployed}$$

Unemployment rate

The fraction of the labor force that is unemployed.

The **unemployment rate** is the number of unemployed divided by the total labor force; it represents the percentage of the labor force unemployed and looking for work.

$$\text{unemployment rate} = \text{unemployed/labor force}$$

Labor force participation rate

The fraction of the population over 16 years of age that is in the labor force.

Finally, we need to understand what is meant by the **labor force participation rate**, defined as the labor force divided by the population 16 years of age and older. It represents the fraction of the population 16 years of age and older that is in the labor force.

$$\text{labor force participation rate} = \text{labor force/population 16 and over}$$

To illustrate these concepts, suppose that an economy consists of 200,000 individuals 16 years of age and older. Of all these people, 122,000 are employed and 8,000 are unemployed. This means that 130,000 (122,000 + 8,000) people are in the labor force. The labor force participation rate is 0.65, or 65% (130,000/200,000) and the unemployment rate is 0.0615, or 6.15% (8,000/130,000).

Figure 20.1 helps to put these definitions into perspective for the U.S. economy. The large box is the total population 16 years of age and older, which in 2004 was comprised of 222,357,000 individuals. This population is divided into two groups: those in the labor force and those outside the labor force. For this year, the labor force participation rate was 65.9%. As you can see, just over three-fifths of the U.S. population participates in the labor force. Within the labor force, there were 146,771,000 employed and 8,170,000 unemployed.

Figure 20.2 contains some international data on unemployment for 2004. Notice the sharp differences among countries; for example, Belgium had a 12.8% unemployment rate, while Japan had an unemployment rate of 5%.

People who are retired are not considered unemployed.

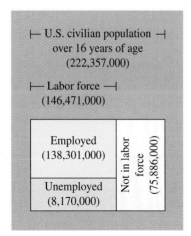

FIGURE 20.1

Unemployment Data, February 2004

Approximately 65.9% of the civilian population is in the labor force. 94.4% of those are employed.

Source: Bureau of Labor Statistics, U.S. Department of Labor, 2004.

Alternative Measures of Unemployment and Why They're Important

We defined the unemployed as those people who are looking for work but do not currently have jobs. With that in mind, let's take a closer look at our measures of unemployment.

It is relatively straightforward in principle to determine who is employed: Just count the people who are working. What is more difficult is to distinguish between those who are unemployed and those who are not in the labor force. How are these two groups distinguished? Each month, the Bureau of Labor Statistics directs its staff to interview a large sample of households. It asks about the employment situation of all members of households 16 years of age and older. If someone in a household is not working, the interviewer asks whether the person is actively looking for work. If the answer is "yes," he or she is classified as unemployed; but if the answer is "no,"— he or she is not actively looking for work—that person is classified as not being in the labor force.

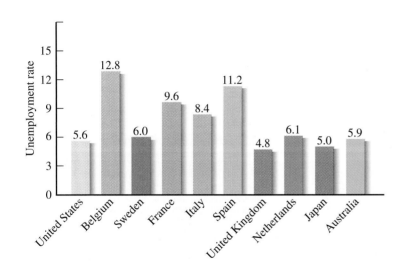

FIGURE 20.2

Unemployment Rates Around the World

There are substantial variations in unemployment around the world.

Source: The Economist, March 20, 2004.

The traditional measure of unemployment does not capture all the employment experiences individuals face, however. In the chapter-opening story, we highlighted the cases of three individuals who wanted full-time jobs but did not have them: a steelworker who stopped looking for work because he felt there were no jobs, a young woman who did not seek work because she had no transportation, and a young man who worked only part-time but sought full-time employment. None of them would be counted as unemployed in the official statistics—the first two were not in the labor force and the third was employed. Because of these limitations, in 1994, the Bureau of Labor Statistics began to publish alternative statistics that reflect these circumstances.

Individuals who want to work, have searched for work in the prior year, but are not currently looking for work because they believe they won't be able to find a job are called **discouraged workers**. Note that these individuals are not included in the official statistics because they are not currently looking for work.

Second, there are other individuals who would like to work, have searched for work in the recent past, but have stopped looking for work for a variety of reasons. These individuals are known as **marginally attached workers**. Discouraged workers—who point to a lack of jobs as the reason they stopped looking for work—are included among the marginally attached, but so are workers who are not looking for jobs not because they believe they don't exist but for other reasons, including lack of transportation or child care.

Finally, there are those workers who would like to be employed full-time but hold part-time jobs. These individuals are counted as employed in the official statistics, because they have a job; however, they would like to be working more hours. They are known as **individuals working part time for economic reasons**. We do not include in this category individuals who prefer part-time employment.

How important are these alternative measures? Figure 20.3 puts these measures into perspective. In 2002, there were 8.26 million individuals who were officially classified as unemployed. The number of discouraged workers was relatively small—only 0.15 million. However, including the discouraged workers, there were 1.07 million marginally attached workers. If we add the marginally attached individuals to those who were involuntarily working part-time, the total is 5.23 million. Thus,

Discouraged workers

Workers who left the labor force because they could not find jobs.

Marginally attached workers

Individuals who have worked in the past but stopped working for a variety of reasons.

Individuals working part-time for economic reasons

Individuals who would like to work full time but are forced to take part-time jobs.

FIGURE 20.3

Alternative Measures of Unemploment, 2002

Including discouraged workers, marginally attached workers, and individuals working part-time for economic reasons, substantially increases measured unemployment in 2002 from 8.26 million to 13.49 million.

Source: Bureau of Labor Statistics, Department of Labor.

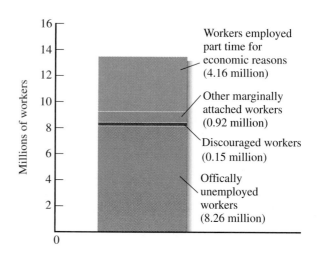

depending on the statistic you want to emphasize, there were anywhere between 8.26 million unemployed (the official number) or 13.49 million unemployed (the official number plus all those seeking full-time employment who did not have it). If we count those 13.49 million as unemployed, the unemployment rate in 2002 would be 9.4%—substantially higher than the 5.8% official rate. As we have seen, the official statistics for unemployment do not include the full range of individuals who would like to participate fully in the labor market.

Suspicious Unemployment Statistics

Suppose that after a long period of high unemployment, government statisticians noticed that the labor force was smaller than it was before the spell of unemployment. Is there any reason you might be suspicious of these numbers?

If you are suspicious, you may have good reasons to be. During the period of high unemployment, some workers may have become discouraged and dropped out of the labor force. It's possible they may return to the labor force when economic conditions improve. ■

Who Are the Unemployed?

Another fact about unemployment is that different groups of people suffer more unemployment than other groups. Figure 20.4 contains some unemployment statistics for selected groups for February 2004. Adults have substantially lower unemployment rates than teenagers. Minorities have higher unemployment rates; African-American teenagers have extremely high unemployment rates. On average, men and women have

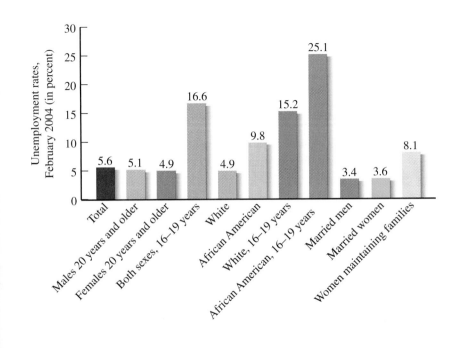

FIGURE 20.4

Selected U.S. Unemployment Statistics, Unemployment Rates for February 2004

The incidence of unemployment differs sharply among demographic groups.

Source: Bureau of Labor Statistics, U.S. Department of Labor, 2004.

roughly the same unemployment rates, but the unemployment rates for married men and married women are lower than unemployment rates of women who maintain families alone.

These relative differentials among unemployment rates do vary somewhat as GDP rises and falls. Teenage and minority unemployment rates often rise very sharply during poor economic times. In better times, there is typically a reduction of unemployment for all groups. Nonetheless, teenage and minority unemployment remains relatively high at all times.

Many economic time series, including employment and unemployment, are substantially influenced by seasonal factors. These are recurring calendar-related effects caused by, for example, the weather, holidays, the opening and closing of schools, and related factors. Unemployment due to recurring calendar effects is called **seasonal unemployment**. Examples of seasonal unemployment include higher rates of unemployment for farm workers and construction workers in the winter and higher unemployment rates for teenagers in the early summer as they look for summer jobs.

Seasonal unemployment

The component of unemployment attributed to seasonal factors.

The Bureau of Labor Statistics uses statistical procedures to remove these seasonal factors—that is, it seasonally adjusts the statistics—so that users of the data can more accurately interpret underlying trends in the economy. The seasonally adjusted unemployment rates control for these predictable patterns, so those patterns aren't reflected in the overall unemployment numbers.

The Three Types of Unemployment: Cyclical, Frictional, and Structural

Once we have seasonally adjusted the unemployment statistics, we can divide unemployment into three other basic types. By studying each type separately, we can gain insight into some of the causes of each type of unemployment.

The unemployment rate is closely tied to the overall fortunes of the economy. Unemployment rises sharply during periods when real GDP falls and decreases when real GDP grows rapidly. During periods of falling GDP, firms will not want to employ as many workers as they do in good times because they are not producing as many goods and services. Firms will lay off or fire some current workers and will be more reluctant to add new workers to their payrolls. The result will be fewer workers with jobs and rising unemployment. Economists call the unemployment that accompanies fluctuations in real GDP **cyclical unemployment**. Cyclical unemployment rises during periods when real GDP falls or grows at a slower-than-normal rate and decreases when the economy improves.

Cyclical unemployment

The component of unemployment that accompanies fluctuations in real GDP.

However, unemployment still exists even when the economy is growing. For example, the unemployment rate in the United States has not fallen below 3.9% of the labor force since 1970. Unemployment that is not associated with economic fluctuations is either frictional unemployment or structural unemployment.

Frictional unemployment is the unemployment that occurs naturally during the normal workings of an economy. It occurs because it simply takes time for people to find the right jobs and for employers to find the right people to hire. This happens

Frictional unemployment

The part of unemployment associated with the normal workings of the economy, such as searching for jobs.

The internet can help match employers with job seekers and reduce frictional unemployment.

when people change jobs, move across the country, get laid off from their current jobs and search for new opportunities, or take their time after they enter the labor force to find an appropriate job. Suppose that when you graduate from college, you take six months to find a job that you like. During the six months in which you are looking for a good job, you are among those unemployed who make up frictional unemployment. Searching for a job, however, makes good sense. It would not be wise to take the first job you were offered if it had low wages, poor benefits, and no future. Likewise, employers are wise to interview multiple applicants for jobs to find the best employees, even if it takes some time.

Could we eliminate unemployment by posting all job vacancies on the Internet along with the resumes of job seekers and automatically match them up with one another? It's possible that such an automated system could shorten the duration of frictional unemployment, but it wouldn't eliminate it entirely. Some workers, for example, would prefer to continue searching for jobs in their own area rather than moving across country to take the jobs they had been automatically matched with. Firms would also still want to scrutinize employees very carefully because hiring and training a worker is costly.

Structural unemployment occurs when the economy evolves. It occurs when different sectors give way to other sectors or certain jobs are eliminated while new types of jobs are created. For example, when the vinyl record industry gave way to the CD music industry in the 1980s, some workers found themselves "structurally unemployed." Structural unemployment is more of a "permanent condition." These workers will require retraining. Frictional unemployment is more of a situation where workers are "between jobs."

Structural unemployment

The component of unemployment reflecting a mismatch of skills and jobs.

The line between frictional unemployment and structural unemployment is sometimes hard to draw. Suppose a highly skilled steelworker is laid off because his company shuts down its plant in his area and moves it overseas. The worker would like to find a comparable job, but only low-wage, unskilled work is available in his town. Jobs are available but not his kind of job, and the steel company will never return. Is this person's unemployment frictional or structural? There really is no correct answer. You might think of the steelworker as experiencing either frictional or structural unemployment. For all practical purposes, however, it does not matter which it is. The former steelworker is still unemployed.

The Natural Rate of Unemployment

Natural rate of unemployment

The level of unemployment at which there is no cyclical unemployment.

Full employment

The level of employment that occurs when the unemployment rate is at the natural rate.

Total unemployment in an economy is composed of all three types of unemployment: cyclical, frictional, and structural. The level of unemployment at which there is no cyclical unemployment is called the **natural rate of unemployment**. The natural rate of unemployment consists of only frictional unemployment and structural unemployment. The natural rate of unemployment is the economist's notion of the rate unemployment should be, when there is **full employment**. It may seem strange to think that workers can be unemployed when the economy is at full employment. However, the economy actually needs some frictional unemployment to operate efficiently: Frictional unemployment exists so that workers and firms find the right employment matches. An economy that lacks frictional unemployment will become stagnant.

In the United States today, economists estimate that the natural rate of unemployment is between 5.0% and 6.5%. The natural rate of unemployment varies over time and differs across countries. In Europe, for example, estimates of the natural rate of unemployment place it between 7% and 10%. In a later chapter, we explore why the natural rate of unemployment is higher in Europe than in the United States and why the natural rate of unemployment can vary over time in the same country.

The actual unemployment rate can be higher or lower than the natural rate of unemployment. During a period in which the real GDP fails to grow at its normal rate, there will be positive cyclical unemployment, and actual unemployment can far exceed the natural rate of unemployment. For example, in the United States in 1983, unemployment exceeded 10% of the labor force. As we pointed out earlier, a more extreme example occurred in 1933 during the Great Depression, when the unemployment rate reached 25%. On the other hand, when the economy grows very rapidly for a long period, actual unemployment can fall below the natural rate of unemployment. With sustained rapid economic growth, employers will be aggressive in hiring workers. During the late 1960s, unemployment rates fell below 4%; the natural rate of unemployment was estimated to be over 5% at that time. In this case, cyclical unemployment was negative.

Unemployment also fell to 4.0% in 2000, the last year of the Clinton administration. In this case, many economists believed that the natural rate of unemployment had fallen to close to 5%, so that cyclical unemployment in that year was negative.

Just as a car will overheat if the engine is overworked, so the economy will overheat f economic growth is too rapid. At low unemployment rates, firms will find it difficult o recruit workers, and competition among firms will lead to increases in wages. As wages increase, increases in prices soon follow. The sign of this overheating will be a general rise in prices for the entire economy, which we commonly call inflation. As we discuss in later chapters, when the actual unemployment rate falls below the natural rate of unemployment, inflation will increase.

The Costs of Unemployment

When there is excess unemployment—actual unemployment above the natural rate of unemployment—both society and individuals suffer economic loss. From a social point of view, excess unemployment means that the economy is no longer producing at its potential. The resulting loss of resources can be very large. For example, in 1983, when the unemployment rate averaged 9.6%, typical estimates of the shortfall of GDP from potential were near 6%. Simply put, this meant that society was wasting 6% of the total resources at its disposal.

To families with fixed obligations such as mortgage payments, the loss in income can bring immediate hardships. **Unemployment insurance**, payments received from the government upon becoming unemployed, can cushion the blow to some degree, but unemployment insurance is typically only temporary and does not replace a worker's full earnings.

Unemployment insurance
Payments received from the government upon becoming unemployed.

The effects of unemployment can also linger into the future. As we noted, workers who suffer from a prolonged period of unemployment are likely to lose some of their skills. For example, an unemployed stockbroker might be unaware of the latest developments and trends in financial markets. This will make it more difficult for that person to find a job in the future. Economists who have studied the high rates of unemployment among young people in Europe point to the loss of both skills and good work habits (such as coming to work on time) as key factors leading to long-term unemployment.

The costs of unemployment are not simply financial. In our society, a person's status and position are largely associated with the type of job the person holds. Losing a job can impose severe psychological costs. Some studies have found, for example, that increased crime, divorce, and suicide rates are associated with increased unemployment.

While unemployment insurance can temporarily offset some of the financial costs of inflation, the presence of unemployment insurance also tends to increase the length of time that unemployed workers remain unemployed. The extra financial cushion that unemployment insurance provides allows workers to remain unemployed a bit longer before obtaining another job. In other words, unemployment insurance actually leads to additional time spent unemployed. "A Closer Look: Optimal Unemployment Insurance" takes a look at the economic factors that we need to account for to develop an efficient system of unemployment insurance.

A CLOSER LOOK

Optimal Unemployment Insurance

Suppose that the government provided all unemployed workers a payment that was equal to their previous salary as long as they remained unemployed. While this would prevent unemployed workers from suffering any financial hardship, very few workers would return to work if the government were paying them their full salaries. This, of course, would lead to excessive unemployment. States recognize this and replace only a fraction of a worker's prior salary—typically about 40%.

Economist Jonathan Gruber of MIT explored both the benefits and costs of unemployment insurance and attempted to calculate the optimal amount of unemployment insurance. To measure the benefits, he used survey data to determine how much workers decreased their consumption after becoming unemployed. For example, without unemployment insurance, he estimated that food consumption would fall nearly 22%. Unemployment insurance can offset part of this sharp decrease in consumption. Looking at both the costs and the benefits of unemployment insurance, Gruber found that the optimal level of insurance was probably somewhat lower than the current amount provided by the states.

Source: Jonathan Gruber, "The Consumption Smoothing Benefits of Unemployment Insurance," *American Economic Review*, March 1997, pp. 192–205.

TEST Your Understanding

1. What is the labor force?
2. True or false and why? Individuals who have stopped looking for work because they did not believe jobs were available are not counted as unemployed in the traditional unemployment statistics.
3. In addition to seasonal unemployment, the other types of unemployment are cyclical, frictional, and _____.
4. The natural rate of unemployment consists solely of _____ and _____ unemployment.

The Consumer Price Index and the Cost of Living

Suppose you moved to France and began to work. You received your first paycheck, which was in euros, the European currency. The actual number of euros written on the check would not mean much to you initially. What you would like to know is what goods and services your paycheck could buy. Was this a fat paycheck or a thin one? Should you celebrate your first paycheck with a five-course gourmet dinner or head for the nearest inexpensive café?

Although the price of a new Mustang today has certainly increased sharply, economists need to adjust for quality changes when they develop their price indexes.

Even in our own country, where we feel we have a reasonable sense of what a dollar can buy, we do know that the value of a dollar—what it purchases—varies over time. In 1976, a new starting professor of economics was paid $15,000. In 2003, a new starting professor at the same university was paid $75,000. Prices, of course, had risen in those 27 years. Which starting professor had the best deal?

These examples are illustrations of one of our five principles of economics, the real-nominal principle:

REAL-NOMINAL *Principle*

What matters to people is the real value of money or income—its purchasing power—not the face value of money or income.

Economists have developed a number of different measures to track the cost of living over time. The best known of these measures is the **Consumer Price Index (CPI)**. The CPI is widely used by both government and the private sector to measure changes in prices facing consumers. It measures changes in prices in a fixed *basket of goods*—a collection of items chosen to represent the purchasing pattern of a typical consumer. We first find out how much this basket of goods costs in a given year. This is called the base year (it serves a similar purpose as the base year we designated for the GDP deflator). We then ask how much it costs in other years and measure changes in the cost of living relative to this base year. The CPI index for a given year, say year K, is defined as

CPI in year K = (cost of basket in year K/cost of basket in base year) × 100

Suppose a basket of goods costs $200 in 1992, which we'll define as the base year. In 2004, the same basket of goods is $250. First, the value for the CPI in 1992 (the base year) is

CPI in 1992 = (200/200) × 100 = 100

That is, the CPI for 1992 is 100. Note that the base year for the CPI will always equal 100. Now let's calculate the value of the CPI for 2004:

CPI in 2004 = (250/200) × 100 = 125

Consumer price index (CPI)

A price index that measures the cost of a fixed basket of goods chosen to represent the consumption pattern of individuals.

The CPI in 2004 is 125. The CPI rose from 100 in 1992 to 125 in 2004 in this example, a 25% increase in average prices over this 12-year period.

Here is how you would use this information. Suppose you had $300 in 1992. How much would you need to be able to have the same standard of living in 2004? The answer is given by multiplying the $300 by the ratio of the CPI in 2004 to the CPI in 1992:

$$\$300 \times (125/100) = \$375$$

You need $375 in 2004 just to maintain what was your standard of living in 1992. This is the type of calculation that economists do to evaluate changes in living standards over time.

How do we actually calculate the CPI in practice? Each month, the Bureau of Labor Statistics sends its employees out to sample prices for over 90,000 specific items around the entire country. Figure 20.5 shows the broad categories that are used in the CPI and the importance of each category in household budgets. Rent and food and beverages account for 44% of total spending by households.

The CPI Versus the Chain Index for GDP

In Chapter 19, we discussed measuring nominal GDP and real GDP. We also mentioned that since 1996, the Commerce Department has used a chain index (replacing the GDP deflator) to measure changes in prices for goods and services included in GDP. The chain index for GDP and the CPI are both measures of average prices for the economy, yet they differ in several ways.

First, the CPI measures the costs of a typical basket of goods for consumers. It includes goods produced in prior years (such as older cars) as well as imported goods. The chain price index for GDP does not measure price changes from either used goods or imports. The reason that the chain index for GDP does not include used or imported goods is that it is based on the calculation of GDP, which measures only goods and services produced in the United States in the current year.

Second, unlike the chain price index for GDP, the CPI asks how much a fixed basket of goods costs in the current year compared to the cost of those same goods in a

FIGURE 20.5

Components of CPI
Rent and food and beverages make up 46% of the CPI basket. The remainder consists of other goods and services.

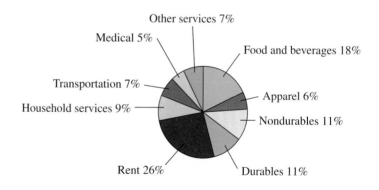

ase year. Because consumers will tend to buy less of goods if their prices rise, the CPI will tend to overstate true changes in the cost of living. For example, if the price of steak rises, consumers may switch to chicken and spend less on steak. But if the current basket of goods and services in the CPI includes steak, the CPI thinks the share of higher-priced steak in the basket is the same as the share of steak before its price increase; the CPI does not allow the share of steak in the index to decrease. Another measurement problem occurs when new products are introduced into the marketplace. Again, this is because the CPI measures a fixed basket of goods. The Bureau of Labor Statistics will eventually adjust its "basket" to account for successful new products, but this will take some time.

Problems in Measuring Changes in Prices

Most economists believe that in reality all the indexes—the chain index for GDP and the CPI—overstate actual changes in prices. In other words, the increase in prices is probably less than the reported indexes tell us. The principal reason for this overstatement is that we have a difficult time measuring quality improvements. Suppose that the new computers sold to consumers become more powerful and more efficient each year. Further, suppose that the dollar price of a new computer remains the same each year. Even though the prices remain the same, the computers in later years are of much higher quality. If we looked simply at the prices of computers and did not take into account the change in quality, we would say there was no price change for computers. But in later years we are getting more computer power for the same price. If we failed to take the quality change into account, we would not see that the price of computer power has fallen.

Government statisticians do try to adjust for quality when they can. But quality changes are so common in our economy and products evolve so rapidly that it is impossible to keep up with all that is occurring. As a result, most economists believe that we overestimate the inflation rate by between 0.5% and 1.5% each year. This overstatement has important consequences. Some government programs, such as Social Security, automatically increase payments when the CPI goes up. Some union contracts also have **cost-of-living adjustments (COLAs)** or automatic wage changes based on the CPI. If the CPI overstates increases in the cost of living, the government and employers might be overpaying Social Security recipients and workers for changes in the cost of living, as "A Closer Look: The CPI and Social Security" explains.

Cost-of-living adjustments (COLAs)

Automatic increases in wages or other payments that are tied to a price index.

Inflation

We have now looked at two different price indexes: the chain price index used for calculating real GDP and the Consumer Price Index. Using either price index, we can calculate the percentage rate of change of the index. The percentage rate of change of a price index is the **inflation rate**:

Inflation rate

The percentage rate of change in the price level.

$$\text{inflation rate} = \text{percentage rate of change of a price index}$$

A CLOSER LOOK

The CPI and Social Security

Each year, the federal government increases Social Security payments to the elderly by the rate of increase of prices as measured by the Consumer Price Index. The reason for this adjustment is to make sure that the elderly, whose other income tends to be fixed, do not suffer from cost-of-living increases. But as we have seen, the CPI does not fully account for quality changes, so that the true increase in prices is less than the increase as measured by the CPI. Because Social Security payments are increased by the CPI, we actually overcompensate the elderly for price changes and actually increase their benefits in real terms.

How much extra are we paying the elderly because of the bias in the CPI? Economists believe that the CPI overstates actual price increases by between 0.5% and 1.5% a year. Assume that the figure is 1%. According to the Congressional Budget Office, if we reduced this adjustment for Social Security by 1%, it would save $42 billion dollars over a five-year period! As you can tell, not accounting for technical change is a costly bias in our price indexes.

Defenders of the elderly claim this is a misleading argument. Although the CPI may overstate price increases in general, it probably understates the rate of price increases facing the elderly. The elderly consume more medical care than do average citizens in the United States and prices for medical care have increased faster than other prices in the economy. Regardless of which side of the debate we favor, it is evident that many tax dollars depend on precise calculation of the CPI.

Here is an example. Suppose that a price index in a country was 200 in 1998 and 210 in 1999. Then the inflation rate between 1998 and 1999 was

$$\text{inflation rate} = (210 - 200)/200 = 0.05 = 5\%$$

The country experienced a 5% inflation rate, in other words.

It is important to distinguish between the price level and the inflation rate. In everyday language, people sometimes confuse the level of prices with inflation. You might hear someone say that inflation is high in San Francisco because rents for apartments are high, but this is not a correct use of the term *inflation*. Inflation refers not to the level of prices, whether they are high or low, but to their percentage change. If rents were high in San Francisco but remained constant between two years, there would be no inflation in rents there during that time.

Historical U.S. Inflation Rates

To gain some historical perspective, Figure 20.6 plots a price index for GDP from 1875 to 2000 for the United States. As you can see from the figure, from 1875 to the period just before World War I, there was virtually no change in the price level. The price level rose during World War I, fell after the war ended, and also fell sharply during the early 1930s. However, the most pronounced feature of the figure is the sustained rise in

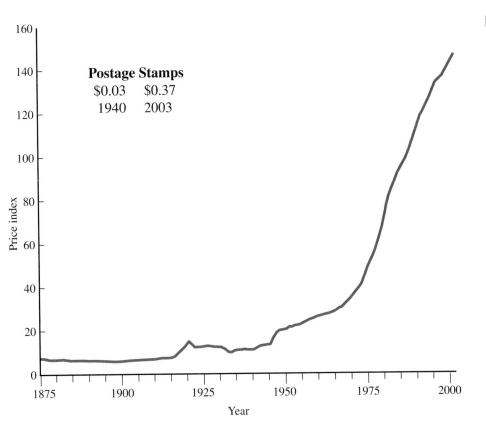

FIGURE 20.6

Price Index for U.S. GDP, 1875–2003

After remaining relatively flat for 60 years, the price level began to steadily increase after World War II.

Sources: R. J. Gordon, *Macroeconomics* (New York: HarperCollins, 1993); U.S. Department of Commerce.

prices beginning around the 1940s. Unlike the earlier periods, in which the price level did not have a trend, after 1940 the price level increased sharply. By 2000, the price level had increased by a factor of 14 over its value in 1940. Table 20.1 contains the prices of a few selected goods from the 1940s. Wouldn't you like to buy a postage stamp today for $0.03?

Taking a closer look at the period following World War II, Figure 20.7 plots the inflation rate, the percentage change in the price index, from 1950–2003. In the 1950s

Gallon of gasoline	$0.18
Loaf of bread	0.08
Gallon of milk	0.34
Postage stamps	0.03
House	6,550
Car	800
Haircut in New York City	0.50
Movie tickets in New York City	0.25
Men's tweed sports jacket in New York City	15
Snake tattoo on arm	0.25

TABLE 20.1

Prices of Selected Goods, 1940

Sources: The Value of a Dollar 1860–1989; and *http://www.tvhistory.tv*

FIGURE 20.7

U.S. Inflation Rate, 1950–2003 Based on Chain Price Index

Inflation reached its highest peak in the postwar era during the mid-1970s, when the economy was hit with several increases in oil prices. In recent years, the inflation rate has been relatively low.

Source: U.S. Department of Commerce.

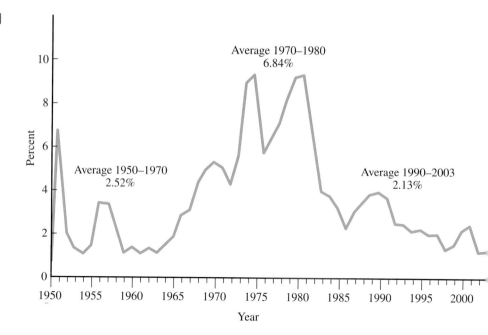

and 1960s, the inflation rate was frequently less than 2% a year. The inflation rate was a lot higher in the 1970s, reaching nearly 12% per year. In those years, the economy suffered from several increases in the world price of oil. In recent years, the inflation rate has subsided and has been between 1% and 2% in recent years.

The Perils of Deflation

Deflation

Negative inflation or falling prices.

Prices rarely fall today but they have actually fallen at times in world history. You might think it would be great if prices fell and we had what economists term a **deflation**. It may surprise you that we think you should hope that this never occurs.

During the Great Depression, the United States underwent a severe deflation. Prices fell on average 33% and wages fell along with prices. The biggest problem caused by a deflation is that people cannot repay their debts. Imagine that you owe $40,000 for your education and expect to be able to pay it off over several years if you earn $27,000 a year. If a massive deflation caused your wages to fall to $18,000, you might not be able to pay your $40,000 debt, which does not fall with deflation. You would be forced to default on your loan, as millions of people did during the Great Depression.

In recent years, Japan experienced a deflation, although much milder than the Great Depression in the United States—only about 1% per year. Nonetheless, banks in Japan faced rocky economic times as borrowers, including large corporations, defaulted on their loans. With their banks in difficult shape, Japan's economy has suffered. Japan's experience today mirrors the experience of other countries throughout the world in the 1930s during the period of deflation.

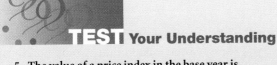

Your Understanding

5. The value of a price index in the base year is _____.
6. Economists believe that the CPI tends to underestimate the increase in the cost of living over time. True or false? Explain.
7. Unlike the CPI, the chain price index for GDP does not include used goods or _____ goods.
8. If a price index is 50 in 1998 and 60 in 1999, the rate of inflation between the two years is _____.

The Costs of Inflation

Economists typically separate the costs of inflation into two categories. One includes costs associated with fully expected or **anticipated inflation**. The other includes the costs associated with unexpected or **unanticipated inflation**. Although inflation causes both types of costs, it is convenient to discuss each case separately.

Anticipated Inflation

Let's consider the costs of anticipated inflation first. Suppose the economy had been experiencing 4% annual inflation for many years and everyone was fully adjusted to it.

Even in this case, inflation still has some costs. First, there are the actual physical costs of changing prices, which economists call **menu costs**. Restaurant owners, catalog producers, and any other business that must post prices will have to incur costs to physically change their prices because of inflation. For example, they will need to pay to reprint their menus or billboards. Economists believe that these costs are relatively small for the economy.

Second, people will want to hold less cash when there is inflation. Inflation will erode the value of the cash people hold. They will respond by holding less cash at any one time. If they hold less cash, they must visit the bank or their ATM more frequently because they will run out of cash sooner. Economists use the term **shoe-leather costs** to refer to the additional wear and tear necessary to hold less cash. Economists who have estimated these costs find that they can be large, as much as 1% of GDP.

In practice, our tax system and financial system do not fully adjust even to fully anticipated inflation. It is difficult for the government and businesses to change their normal rules of operation every time inflation changes. As an example, consider the tax system. Our tax system is typically based on nominal income, not real income. Suppose you own a stock in a corporation that increases by 5% during the year. If the inflation rate is also 5% a year, your stock did not increase in real terms—it just kept up with inflation. Nonetheless, if you sold your stock at the end of the year, you would be taxed on the full 5% gain, despite the fact that the real value of your stock did not increase. Inflation distorts the operation of our tax and financial system.

Anticipated inflation
Inflation that is expected.

Unanticipated inflation
Inflation that is not expected.

Menu costs
Costs of inflation that arise from actually changing prices.

Shoe-leather costs
Costs of inflation that arise from trying to reduce holdings of cash.

Unanticipated Inflation

What about if inflation is unexpected? The cost of unexpected inflation is arbitrary redistributions of income. Suppose you expected the inflation rate would be 5% and that you negotiated a salary based on that expectation. The problem is, if you miscalculate and the inflation rate turns out to be higher, the purchasing power of your wages would be less than you anticipated. The firm would have gained at your expense. On the other hand, if the inflation rate turned out to be less than 5%, the purchasing power of your wage would be higher than you had anticipated. In this case, you would gain at the expense of the company. As long as the inflation rate differs from what is expected, there will be winners and losers.

These redistributions eventually impose real costs on the economy. Consider an analogy. Suppose you live in a very safe neighborhood where no one locks the doors. If a rash of burglaries (transfers between you and the crooks) starts to occur, people will invest in locks, alarms, and more police. You and your community will incur real costs to prevent these arbitrary redistributions.

The same is true for unanticipated inflation. If a society experiences unanticipated inflation, individuals and institutions will change their behavior. For example, potential homeowners will not be able to borrow from banks at fixed rates of interest, but will be required to accept loans whose rates can be adjusted as inflation rates change. Banks do not want to lend money at a fixed interest rate if there is a strong likelihood that inflation will erode the real value of the income stream they expected. However, if banks become reluctant to make loans with fixed interest rates, this imposes more risk on homeowners.

What about the loans made prior to the unanticipated inflation? In this case, debtors will gain at the expense of creditors. Creditors will lose because inflation will erode the amount of money they planned to earn on the loans. But since the loans have already been made, there's nothing they can do about it. Debtors, on the other hand, will get a deal. It will be easier for them to repay their loans with inflated dollars.

If unanticipated inflation becomes extreme, individuals will spend more of their time trying to profit from inflation rather than working at productive jobs. As inflation became more volatile in the late 1970s in the United States, many people devoted their time to speculation in real estate and commodity markets to try to beat inflation, and the economy became less efficient. Latin American countries that have experienced high and variable inflation rates know all too well these costs from inflation. Indeed, when inflation rates exceed 50% per month, we have what is called **hyperinflation**. Think about what an inflation rate of 50% a month means: If a can of soda costs $1.25 at the beginning of the year, it would cost $162 at the end of year! In a later chapter, we'll study the causes of hyperinflation, but you can readily see that inflation of this magnitude would seriously disrupt normal commerce.

Even in less extreme cases, the costs of inflation are compounded as inflation rises. At high inflation rates, these costs grow rapidly, and at some point, policymakers are forced to take actions to reduce inflation. As we mentioned earlier, when unemployment falls below the natural rate, inflation increases. Similarly, in later chapters we'll see that stopping inflation may require unemployment to exceed its natural rate and even plunge an economy into a recession. Although unemployment and recessions are quite costly to society, they sometimes become necessary in the face of high inflation.

Hyperinflation

An inflation rate exceeding 50% per month.

USING THE TOOLS

1. Government Employment and the Unemployment Rate

Suppose the government hires workers who are currently unemployed but does not give them any work to do. What will happen to the measured unemployment rate? Is this an accurate reflection of the underlying economic situation?

2. Starting Salaries for Young Professors

The starting salary for a new assistant economics professor was $15,000 in 1976 and $75,000 in 2003. The value of the CPI for 2003 was 184.0 compared to 56.9 in 1976. In which year did a newly hired professor earn more in real terms?

3. Interpreting World Unemployment Statistics

A student looking at Figure 20.2 argues that Belgium must have very high cyclical unemployment compared to Japan because the Belgian unemployment rate is so high. Explain why the student may not be correct.

4. Apartment Vacancies and Unemployment

In a major city, the vacancy rate for apartments was approximately 5%, yet substantial numbers of individuals were searching for new apartments. Can you explain why this occurs and relate it to unemployment?

SUMMARY

In this chapter, we continued our introduction to the basic concepts of economics and explored the nature of both unemployment and inflation. We also looked at the complex issues involved in measuring unemployment and inflation as well as the costs of both to society. Here are the key points to remember:

1 The unemployed are individuals who do not have jobs but are actively seeking employment.
2 Seasonal, cyclical, frictional, and structural are all different types of unemployment.
3 Unemployment rates vary across groups. Alternative measures of unemployment take into account individuals who would like to work full-time, but who are no longer in the labor force or are holding part-time jobs.
4 Economists measure changes in the cost of living through the Consumer Price Index, which is based on the cost of purchasing a standard basket of goods and services.
5 We measure inflation as the percentage change in the price level.
6 Economists believe that most price indices overstate true inflation because they fail to capture quality improvements.
7 Unemployment imposes both financial and psychological costs on workers.
8 Both anticipated and unanticipated inflation impose costs on society.

KEY TERMS

anticipated inflation, 461
consumer price index (CPI), 455
cost-of-living adjustments
(COLAs), 457
cyclical unemployment, 450
deflation, 460
discouraged workers, 448
employed, 445
frictional unemployment, 450

full employment, 452
hyperinflation, 462
individuals working part-time
for economic reasons, 448
inflation rate, 457
labor force, 445
labor force participation rate, 446
marginally attached workers, 448
menu costs, 461

natural rate of unemployment, 452
seasonal unemployment, 450
shoe-leather costs, 461
structural unemployment, 451
unanticipated inflation, 461
unemployed, 445
unemployment insurance, 453
unemployment rate, 446

PROBLEMS AND DISCUSSION QUESTIONS

1 Here are some data for an economy:
  ▶ 10 million individuals 16 years of age and older
  ▶ 5.5 million employed
  ▶ 0.5 million unemployed
  Calculate the labor force, the labor force participation rate, and the unemployment rate for this economy.

2 Sometimes at the beginning of an economic boom, total employment increases sharply but the unemployment rate does not fall. Why might this occur?

3 In inner cities, minority youths have high unemployment rates. Many economists believe that the unemployment picture is worse than the statistics portray. What could be the basis for this belief?

4 Suppose the government decided that housewives and househusbands should be counted as employed because they perform important services. How do you think this change would affect our measure of the labor force, the labor force participation rate, and the unemployment rate? (You may want to construct a numerical example.)

5 Why is the natural rate of unemployment always positive?

6 When oil prices increased sharply in the 1970s, some businesses were affected more adversely than others. Explain why some economists believe that the oil price increase led to higher frictional unemployment.

7 A country reports a price index of 55 in 2005 and 60 in 2006. What is the inflation rate between 2005 and 2006?

8 A job paid $3,000 in 1960. The CPI in 1960 was 29.6 compared to 179.9 in 2002. In 2002, what salary would be comparable to 1960's $3,000 in real terms?

9 An economy has 100,000,000 people employed, 8,000,000 unemployed, and 4,000,000 discouraged workers. What is the conventional measure of the unemployment rate? What would be the best alternative measure that takes into account discouraged workers?

10 Critically evaluate the following statement: "Tokyo is an expensive place to live. They must have a high inflation rate in Japan."

11 How do you think the Internet and online shopping would affect the menu costs from inflation?

12 *Web Exercise.* Go to the data section of the Website for the Bureau of Labor Statistics (*http://stats.bls.gov*). Contrast the change in the price indexes from 1960 to the present for the overall CPI with the change in some of its components such as food and beverage and medical care services. What are some of your findings?

13 Web Exercise. Use the Web to find articles about the difficulties in precisely measuring changes in prices in the economy. You might want to start with The Boskin Commission report, which can be found on the history page of the Social Security Administration (*http://www.ssa.gov/history/reports/boskinrpt.html*). On the basis of your reading, what do you consider to be the most important problem?

MODEL ANSWERS TO QUESTIONS

Chapter Opening Questions

1 Unemployment is defined as ratio of the unemployed to the labor force.

2 No, the official unemployment rate does not measure the full extent of unemployment because it does not include those individuals who have stopped looking for work for a variety of reasons or are working part time but would prefer full-time work.

3 The costs of unemployment include both financial costs and psychological costs.

4 The Consumer Price Index is a price index that is used to measure changes in the cost of living.

5 Because of changes in the quality of goods and other factors, we cannot measure inflation perfectly and probably tend to overestimate the true inflation rate. This will have financial implications if payments are linked to changes in measured prices.

6 Inflation imposes several costs: it can redistribute income unfairly, use resources to change posted prices, and also use resources to avoid holding cash balances.

Test Your Understanding

1 The labor force is the total of the unemployed and the employed.

2 False.

3 Structural.

4 Frictional and structural.

5 100

6 False. The CPI overestimates the increase in the cost of living over time because it does not fully take into account technological change and assumes that the quantity of goods consumed do not decrease as prices increase.

7 Imported.

8 20%.

Part

7

The Economy in the Long Run

The Economy at Full Employment

he Statue of Liberty is an enduring symbol in the United States. In the late nineteenth and early twentieth century, immigrants arriving primarily from Europe and Eastern Europe, got a glimpse of the famous statue as they entered New York harbor. However, in the last 20 years, immigrants to the United States now frequently come from Mexico, Latin America, and many parts of Asia. Most U.S. history books stress how the character of our country has been influenced and enriched by immigration.

Yet today, immigration is a hotly contested political issue. Employers, ranging from large farm owners seeking field hands to tech firms looking for computer programmers, support programs that bring foreign workers into the country. These firms contend that without the workers, their industries could not profit. Union representatives, on the other hand, contend that bringing in foreign workers displaces existing U.S. workers and lowers wages. How does increased immigration affect output and wages in the economy?

I n this chapter, we will explain how the amount of capital and labor help determine GDP when the economy is operating at full employment. Although the economy does experience booms and busts, in the long run it returns to full employment. This makes full employment an important benchmark, or barometer, of GDP.

In this chapter, we see how full employment is determined at any point in time when wages and prices adjust freely and quickly to changes in demand and supply. It is this flexibility in wages and prices that allows the economy to operate at full employment. In the next chapter, we will study economic growth when the amount of capital and technology evolve over time.

There are some very important macroeconomic issues and debates that are best examined by the models and tools developed in this chapter. Among those debates are the extent to which taxes may potentially depress economic activity and lower the level of GDP. We will also learn about real business cycle theory, a relatively new school of thought that can help us understand why booms and busts occur.

Here are some of the questions we can address with the tools we will develop in this chapter:

1 How does increased immigration affect wages and the level of output in the economy?
2 If the government increases spending for several years to fight a war, what effects will this have on the level of consumption and investment in the economy?
3 What are the benefits of increased investment?
4 What happens to wages, employment, and GDP if employers must pay higher taxes for hiring labor?
5 If we are concerned about low wages in the economy, what policy actions can be taken to raise the level of wages in the long run?

Wage and Price Flexibility and Full Employment

The models we develop in this chapter assume that wages and prices adjust freely and quickly to changes in demand and supply. This is a powerful assumption and will allow us to develop very important models to study how the economy operates at full employment. Models that assume that wages and prices adjust freely to changes in demand and supply are called **classical models**. The term *classical* refers to a school of economics that believed that over a relatively short period of time, wages and prices will adjust quickly and naturally to bring the economy back to full employment. The classical school of thought dominated economics until about the mid-1930s.

Classical model

Models that assume wages and prices adjust freely to changes in demand and supply.

Following the Great Depression in the 1930s, though, economists began to change their minds about this. During the Great Depression, unemployment was rampant and long. Nearly 25% of the labor force was unemployed. Economists subsequently began to develop models that explained persistent unemployment. In these models, wages and prices don't always adjust quickly to changes in demand and supply. Booms and busts occur precisely because they don't. In later chapters in the book on economic fluctuations, we will study models in which wages and prices are slow to adjust, and booms and busts occur.

Economists today, however, believe that even though wages and prices may be slow to adjust in the short run, they will eventually respond and restore the economy to full employment. That's why it is important to study the full-employment model. Many long-term issues we address in this chapter—for example, the role that taxes play in determining the level of GDP or the effects that immigration has on wages and GDP— are best addressed with models that use full employment and flexible wages and prices in the long run.

Understanding Full Employment

When the economy is at full employment, that doesn't mean there are no unemployed workers. Recall the distinction among frictional, structural, and cyclical unemployment. Frictional unemployment occurs naturally in the labor market as workers search for jobs. Structural unemployment arises from a mismatch of skills and jobs. Cyclical unemployment is the part of unemployment that rises and falls with economic fluctuations. Cyclical unemployment can be positive, when unemployment exceeds the natural rate during a recession, or negative, when unemployment is less than the natural rate during a boom. Full employment corresponds to zero cyclical unemployment; that means that when the economy is at full employment, the only unemployment is frictional and structural. In other words, at full employment the economy is experiencing neither a boom nor a bust.

The Production Function

Production function

The relationship between the level of output and the factors of production.

Stock of capital

The total of all the machines, equipment, and buildings in the entire economy.

Labor

Human effort, including both physical and mental effort, used to produce goods and services.

As you recall, a critical part of the circular flow of economic activity is the production of total goods and services from the factors of production. The factors of production include capital, labor, and land that are the inputs to a technologically-based production process. We'll discuss more of these aspects in the next chapter. However, in order to study how this production actually occurs, in this chapter, we develop the idea of a **production function**. The production function explains how the total level of output or GDP in the economy is generated from the factors of production.

To simplify our discussion of the economy's production function, let's first assume there are only two factors of production: capital and labor. The **stock of capital** comprises all the machines, equipment, and buildings in the entire economy. **Labor** consists of the efforts of all the workers in the economy. The production function is written as follows:

$$Y = F(K,L)$$

here Y is total output, or GDP, K is the stock of capital, and L is the labor force. (F represents the relationship between the factors of production and output.) What the math says in words is that total output is produced from both capital and labor. The production function $F(K,L)$ tells us how much output is produced from the inputs to production, K and L. This simplified model tells us that more inputs of either capital or labor in an economy lead to increased output.

The stock of capital that a society has at any point in time is determined by investments that have been made in new plants and equipment in the past. Investments made today will have no, or little, immediate effect on the total stock of machines, equipment, and buildings used in production today, because today's level of investment is typically just a small fraction of all past investments. Therefore, it takes time for investment to change the stock of capital. In this chapter, we will assume for most of our discussion that the stock of capital is fixed at a constant level, which we call K^*. But there will be a few places where we will stray from that assumption to consider what happens when the stock of capital changes. (We promise to let you know where we are straying from the assumption of fixed capital.)

With the stock of capital fixed at the constant level K^*, only variations in the amount of labor can change the level of output in the economy. Figure 21.1 plots the relationship between the amount of labor used in an economy and the total level of output with a fixed stock of capital. Although the stock of capital is fixed, we do vary the amount of labor employed in production.

Figure 21.1 shows that as we increase labor from L_1 to L_2, output increases sharply from Y_1 to Y_2. However, as more labor is put into production to get us to L_3 and Y_3, output does not rise as sharply. With capital fixed, the relationship between output and labor shown here reflects the principle of diminishing returns.

The capital equipment in this modern plant allows workers to produce high levels of output.

FIGURE 21.1

**The Relationship
Between Labor and
Output with Fixed
Capital**
With capital fixed, output
increases with labor input
but at a decreasing rate.

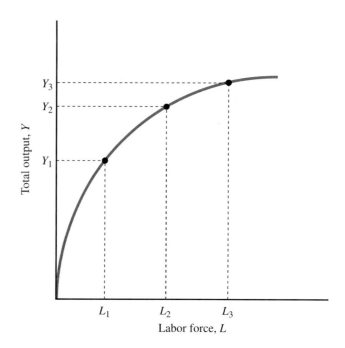

Principle OF DIMINISHING RETURNS

Suppose that output is produced with two or more inputs and
that we increase one input while holding the other inputs fixed.
Beyond some point—called the point of diminishing returns—output will
increase at a decreasing rate.

To explain what diminishing marginal returns means, look at the data in Table 21.1
from a typical production function. The table shows the amount of output that can be
produced from different amounts of labor inputs while the stock of capital is held constant at some amount. (We don't care what amount, as long as it is constant.) First
notice that as the amount of labor increases, so does the amount of output produced.
Second, as output increases, it increases at a diminishing rate. For example, as labor
input increases from 300 to 400 labor units, output increases by 500 output units—
from 1,000 to 1,500 output units. But as labor input increases from 400 to 500 labor
units, output only increases by 400 output units—from 1,500 to 1,900 output units. The

TABLE 21.1

Output and Labor Output

Y (Output)	L (Labor Input)
1,000	300
1,500	400
1,900	500
2,200	600

ate of output dropped from 500 output units per additional unit of labor to 400 output units per additional unit of labor input. That's diminishing returns at work.

What happens if the stock of capital increases, say, from K^* to K^{**}? Figure 21.2 shows that when the stock of capital increases, the entire short-run production function shifts upward. At any level of labor input, more output can be produced than before the stock of capital was increased. As we add more capital, workers become more productive and can produce more output. That's why the production function curve is higher for more capital. For example, an office has five staff members who must share one copier. They will inevitably waste some time waiting to use it. Adding a copier will enable the staff to be more productive.

The benefit of additional capital is a higher level of output from any level of labor input. Capital inputs have helped many Asian countries dramatically expand their output despite the fact that their labor forces haven't grown much. As we discuss in the next chapter, much of Singapore's dramatic growth in recent years has been brought about by increased capital.

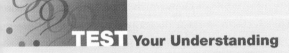 **TEST Your Understanding**

1. What does the production function illustrate?
2. Complete the statement with "increases" or "decreases." With the stock of capital fixed, output increases with labor input but at a rate that _____.
3. Complete the statement with "upward" or "downward." An increase in the stock of capital shifts the production function _____.

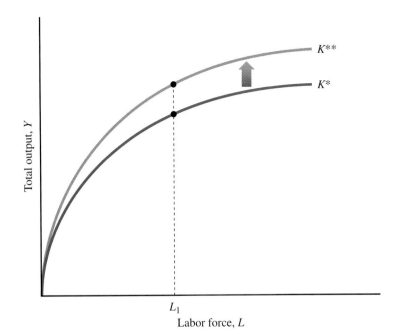

FIGURE 21.2

An Increase in the Stock of Capital
When the capital increases from K^* to K^{**} the production function shifts up. At any level of labor input, the level of output increases.

Wages and the Demand and Supply for Labor

We've just learned from the production function that with the amount of capital fixed the level of output in the economy will be determined exclusively by the amount of labor employed. Now we'll see how the amount of employment in an economy is determined by the demand and supply for labor.

On the basis of what you already know about supply and demand from Chapter 4, you should be able to see what Figure 21.3 represents when it comes to wages and the demand and supply for labor for the entire economy. The amount of labor firms in the economy will hire depends on the **real wage**: the wage rate paid to employees adjusted for changes in the price level.

Real wage
The wage paid to workers adjusted for changes in prices.

As the real wage rate falls, firms will hire more labor. That is, consistent with the law of demand, the labor demand curve in Figure 21.3 is downward sloping. In panel A, we see that as the real wage falls from $20 to $10 per hour, the firm will increase the amount of its labor from 5,000 to 10,000 workers.

The labor-supply curve, on the other hand, is based on the decisions of workers. They must decide how many hours they want to work and how much leisure they want to enjoy. Changes in wages have two different effects on workers' decisions about those wants.

First, an increase in the real wage will make working more attractive and raise the opportunity cost of not working. Real wage increases lead workers to supply more hours of labor. This is called the **substitution effect** because workers want to substitute work for leisure. Second, a higher wage raises workers' income for the amount of hours that they are currently working. As income rises, workers may choose to enjoy more leisure hours and work fewer hours. This is known as the **income effect** because as workers have more income, they can afford to have more leisure time.

Substitution effect
An increase in the wage will raise the opportunity cost of leisure and lead to an increase in hours worked.

Income effect
As income rises, a worker may choose to work fewer hours and enjoy more leisure.

The substitution effect and the income effect work in opposite directions. In principle, a higher wage could lead workers to supply either more or fewer hours of work. In our analysis, we will assume that the substitution effect dominates, so a higher wage rate will lead to increases in the supply of labor. In Panel B of Figure 21.3 we see that 5,000 people would like to work at $10 per hour, but $20 per hour motivates 10,000 people to want to work.

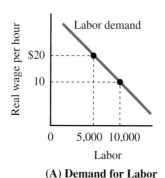
(A) Demand for Labor

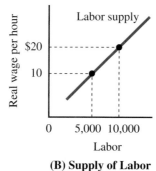
(B) Supply of Labor

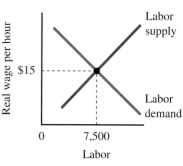
(C) Demand and Supply

FIGURE 21.3 **The Demand and Supply of Labor**
Together the demand and supply for labor determine the level of employment and the real wage.

Higher wages can, in principle, lead to either increased work effort or simply an increase in leisure.

Labor Market Equilibrium

Panel C puts the demand and supply curves together. At a wage of $15 per hour, the amount of labor that firms want to hire—7,500 workers—will be equal to the number who want to work—7,500 workers. This is the labor market equilibrium: The quantity demanded for labor equals the quantity supplied. Together, the demand and supply curves determine the level of employment in the economy and the level of real wages.

When firms increase their capital stock they find that each worker becomes more productive with the additional capital. For example, suppose that the marginal benefit of an additional hour of work to the firm is initially $15 and an increase in the supply of capital raises it to $20. Firms will want to hire additional workers at the existing wage until the marginal benefit again equals the marginal cost.

Because the demand for labor increases at any real wage, the labor-demand curve shifts to the right. Panel A of Figure 21.4 shows the effects of an increase in labor demand. The new market equilibrium moves from *e* to *e′*. Real wages increase, and the amount of labor employed in the economy increases as well. Having more capital in the economy is beneficial for workers.

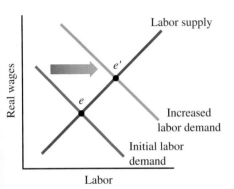

(A) If the demand for labor increases, real wages rise and the amount of labor employed increases.

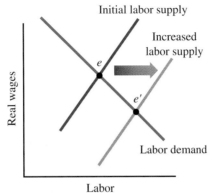

(B) If the supply of labor increases, real wages fall and labor employed increases.

FIGURE 21.4

Shifts in Labor Demand and Supply
Shifts to demand and supply will change both real wages and employment.

Changes in Supply and Demand

We also can analyze the effect of an increase in the supply of labor that might come, for example, from immigration. If the population increases, we would expect that more people would want to work at any given wage. This means that the labor-supply curve would shift to the right. Panel B of Figure 21.4 shows that with an increase in the supply of labor, the labor market equilibrium moves from e to e'. Real wages have fallen and the amount of labor employed has increased. Workers who were employed before the increase in labor supply suffer because real wages have fallen—all wages, including theirs.

We can now see why currently employed workers might be reluctant to favor increased immigration. However, there's a flip side to this. Lower wages (lower input prices) eventually lead to lower prices for the products workers buy. In other words, there are trade-offs from immigration for society. Our model also explains why workers would like to see increases in the supply of machines and equipment as long as full employment can be maintained. The increased supply of capital increases labor demand and leads to higher real wages.

Wages and Employment in a Small European Country

Suppose you were told that in a small European country both wages and employment increased substantially over a five-year period. As you begin to unravel this puzzle, would you look primarily at factors that increased labor demand or increased labor supply?

To solve this puzzle, we would want to examine some factors like the increase in the stock of capital, which would increase both wages and employment. This, therefore, could be the reason wages and employment increased in our small country. However, increases in the supply of labor (more people in the workforce) would account for the increase in employment, but not for the increase in wages. Obviously, then, this could not have been what happened in our country. ■

TEST Your Understanding

4. Labor market equilibrium occurs at a real wage at which the quantity demanded for labor equals the quantity _____ of labor.
5. Explain why the demand curve for labor is negatively sloped and the supply curve for labor is positively sloped.
6. Complete the statement with "right" or "left." An increase in the amount of capital in the economy will shift the demand for labor curve to the _____, leading to higher real wages and employment.
7. Complete the statement with "right" or "left." Increased immigration is likely to lead to a shift in the labor-supply curve to the _____.
8. If wages and employment both fall, this is likely caused by a decrease in the demand for labor. True or false? Explain.

Labor Market
Equilibrium and Full Employment

We now show exactly how much output the economy can produce when it is operating at full employment—a big objective of this chapter. We'll put the production function in a context with the demand and supply for labor. Together, they will give us a model that will help us to achieve our objective as well as help us to understand how taxes on employers affect the level of output.

Figure 21.5 brings the model of the labor market together with the short-run production function. Panel B depicts equilibrium in the labor market, which we saw in Figure 21.3. The demand and supply for labor determine the real wage rate W^* and identify the level of employment L^*. Panel A plots the short-run production function. With the level of employment determined at L^* in Panel B, we move upward to Panel A and use that level of employment to determine that the level of production is Y^*. **full-employment output** is the level of output that is produced when the labor market is in equilibrium. It is also known as potential output.

Full-employment output
The level of output that results when the economy is producing at full employment.

FIGURE 21.5
Determining Full Employment Output
Panel B determines the equilibrium level of employment at L^* and the real wage rate at W^*. Full employment output in panel A is Y^*.

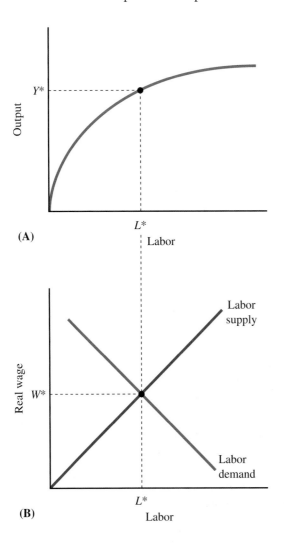

It is important to note that full-employment output is based on the idea that the labor market is in equilibrium, with the supply of labor equal to the demand for labor at the equilibrium wage. Potential output is not the absolute maximum level of output that an economy can produce—an economy could produce more with higher levels of labor input—but potential output reflects the level of labor input that workers wish to supply.

Measuring an Economy's Output at Full Employment

How do economists typically measure the level of full-employment output, or potential output? They start with an estimate of what the unemployment rate would be if cyclical unemployment were zero—that is, if the only unemployment were due to frictional or structural factors. In the United States, estimates of the natural rate in recent years have varied between 5.0% to 6.5%. Economists then estimate how many workers will be employed and use the production function to determine potential output.

Let's look at some real numbers. In 1996, the unemployment rate was 5.6%, very close to the natural rate of unemployment. The labor force in that year was approximately 133.9 million, and 126.7 million individuals were employed. Real GDP in that year was $7.8 billion, measured in 1996 dollars. This level of GDP was produced with the labor of the 126.7 million employed workers and the existing stock of capital and technology. Since the unemployment rate in 1996 was close to the natural rate, the level of real GDP was also very close to the level of potential output in that year.

The level of potential output in an economy increases as the supply of labor increases or the stock of capital increases. An increase in the supply of labor, perhaps from more liberal immigration, would shift the labor supply curve to the right and lead to a higher level of employment in the economy. With a higher level of employment, the level of full employment output will increase. An increase in the stock of capital will increase the demand for labor. As labor demand increases, the result will be higher wages and increased employment. Higher employment will again raise the level of full employment output.

Potential output depends on both capital and labor. Consequently, differences in the quantity of labor supplied to the market will affect the level of potential output in a country. As "A Closer Look: Labor Supply Across Countries and Time" shows, the supply of labor by workers does vary over time and across countries.

Using the Full-Employment Model

The full-employment model is used extensively in macroeconomics to analyze a wide range of issues. For example, many politicians and economists have argued that high tax rates have hurt the U.S. economy and reduced the level of output and production. We can use the full-employment model to explore the logic of these claims. We will also see how the model can be used to explain booms and recessions—fluctuations in output. This will allow us to understand the fundamental idea of an influential school of economic thought known as real business cycle theory.

Labor Supply Across Countries and Time

Although work may be universal, the amount of work done varies substantially, and consequently affects output. Let's start with vacation time. Apart from national holidays, a typical worker in the United States has 12 days of vacation. This pales in comparison to 28 vacation days in the United Kingdom, 35 days in Germany, and a whopping 42 days (over 8 weeks) in Italy. Vacations are serious business in Europe.

These differences in hours worked are important. Per capita output is higher in the United States than in Germany. But if Germans worked as many hours as their U.S. counterparts, per capita output would be similar in both countries.

Within the United States, the amount of work we do has changed substantially over time. In the last 50 years, the labor force participation rate (the fraction of the population over 16 years of age in the labor force) has increased from 59% to 67%. However, this relatively modest overall change masks sharp differences in the labor force participation of women and men. In the last 50 years, the labor force participation of women increased dramatically, from 34% to nearly 60%. At the same time, the labor force participation of men fell from 86% to 75%. Without the rise in the labor force participation of women, potential output would be substantially less in the United States than it is today.

Application: Taxes and Potential Output

We use the full-employment model in Figure 21.6 to study the effects of a tax paid by employers for hiring labor, such as the taxes they pay for their portion of workers' Social Security. (Economists use similar arguments to study a variety of taxes, including personal and corporate income taxes.) A tax on labor will make labor more expensive and raise the marginal cost of hiring workers. For example, let's say that there is no tax on labor and suddenly a 10% tax is imposed. An employer who had been paying $10 an hour for workers will now find that labor costs $11 an hour. Since the marginal cost of hiring workers has gone up but the marginal benefit to the firm has not changed, employers will respond by hiring fewer workers at any given wage. In Panel A of Figure 21.6, the labor-demand curve shifts to the left, reflecting the change in demand due to the tax. As the demand curve shifts to the left, the market equilibrium moves from e to e_1. The result is lower real wages and lower employment.

As we have just seen, higher taxes lead to less employment. With reduced employment, potential output in the economy will be reduced as the economy moves to a lower level of output on the short-run production function. Higher taxes therefore lead to lower output. The size of the reduction in output depends critically on the slope of the labor-supply curve. The slope of the labor-supply curve indicates how sensitive labor supply is to changes in real wages. Panel B in Figure 21.6 shows the effect of the same tax with a vertical labor-supply curve. A vertical labor-supply curve means that workers will supply the same amount of labor regardless of the wage. For example, a single parent might work a full 40 hours a week regardless of the wage so the supply curve will be vertical. If, say, other workers in the economy also put in the same hours regardless of the wage, the supply curve for labor in the

FIGURE 21.6

How Employment Taxes Affect Labor Demand and Supply

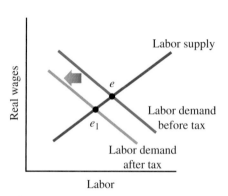

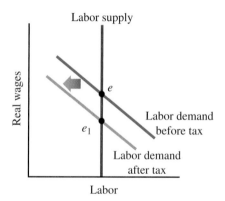

(A) **A tax on labor shifts the labor demand curve to the left and leads to lower wages and reduced employment.**

(B) **If the supply curve for labor is vertical, wages fall but employment does not change.**

entire economy will be vertical. In Panel B, we see that with a vertical supply curve the tax will reduce wages but have no effect on employment and therefore no effect on output.

This example illustrates that taxes can affect wages and output. In both cases either output or wages were lowered when the tax was imposed. However, the extent of the decline in output depends on the slope of the labor-supply curve. To understand the effects of taxes on output, we need information about the slope of the labor-supply curve.

There have been many studies of labor supply. There is strong evidence that part-time workers or second earners in a family are very sensitive to changes in wages and do vary their labor supply when wages change. There is less consensus about the behavior of primary earners in the family. For many years, economists believed that their labor supply was not very sensitive to changes in compensation. However, recent research has shown that taxes do matter even for primary earners, as "A Closer Look: Why Europeans Now Work Less than Americans" explains.

The entire area of taxation and economics is an active branch of economics research. Economists such as Martin Feldstein of Harvard University have studied how many different types of taxes affect employment, saving, and production. Economists use models to try to measure these effects, just as we did for the employment tax.

Real Business Cycle Theory

Fluctuations in economic activity can result from a variety of causes. Here are some examples: A developing country that is highly dependent on agriculture can lose its cash crop because of a prolonged drought. According to economic historian Stanley Lebergott, the nineteenth-century U.S. agricultural-based economy was devastated by grasshopper invasions in North Dakota from 1874 to 1876 and by the boll weevil

A CLOSER LOOK

Why Europeans Now Work Less than Americans

On average today, the French (and other Europeans) work one-third fewer hours than do Americans. You might be tempted to attribute this difference to the Europeans' taste for leisure or vacations. However, in the early 1970s, Europeans actually worked slightly more hours than did Americans. What explains this dramatic turnaround in the space of just 20 years?

Nobel-laureate Edward Prescott of the Federal Reserve Bank of Minneapolis and Arizona State University has compared the experiences of United States and Europe. Prescott attributes the decreases in hours of work in Europe to increases in the tax burden that ultimately falls on workers. Government spending and transfers play a larger role in European economies than in the United States. For example, workers in these countries pay higher taxes but also receive more benefits, such as health care. Transfers in European countries increased from the 1970s to the 1990s along with tax burdens during this period. Taking into account all taxes, Prescott calculated that the effective rate of tax on labor was 40% in the United States, 59% in Germany and France, and 64% in Italy. Japan's tax burden was similar to the United States and its hours of work were also similar.

Prescott notes that as our society ages and the burdens of Social Security and Medicare increase, the United States may be tempted to increase its tax rates to European levels. Indeed, to maintain the current benefits promised by these programs, we will need to increase our tax rates substantially. If we do not make changes in the underlying programs and allow tax rates to increase, Prescott warns that we will also see sharp declines in labor supply—and potential output—in the United States in the future. Living standards would fall as a result.

Source: Edward Prescott, "Why Do Americans Work So Much More Than Europeans," Federal Reserve Bank of Minneapolis Research Department, Staff Report 321, November 2003.

migration from Mexico to Texas in 1892. Sharp increases in the price of oil can hurt economies that use oil in production, as was the case throughout the world in both 1973 and 1979. Wars can devastate entire regions of the world, and natural disasters, such as earthquakes or floods, can cause sharp reductions in GDP.

Major shifts in technology, which we'll discuss more in the next chapter, can also cause economic fluctuations. Consider some economic developments, starting with the early nineteenth century. There were large investments in textile mills and steam power. The birth of the steel industry and railroads dominated the last half of the century. At the end of the nineteenth century, new industries arose that were based on chemical manufacturing, electricity, and the automobile. It is inconceivable that the vast change in technology that led to the creation of these new industries would not have profound effects on the economy. For example, the invention of the automobile sounded the death knell for makers of horse-drawn buggies, buggy whips, and a host of other industries.

Economic fluctuations can also occur because a number of small shocks all hit the economy at the same time. For example, a case of mad cow disease could cause consumer preferences to change from beef to pork. Or a series of small improvements in breeding technology could cause output to rise among worldwide producers of cattle.

One school of economic thought, known as **real business cycle theory**, emphasizes that shocks to technology can have a big part in causing economic fluctuations.

Real business cycle theory

The economic theory that emphasizes how shocks to technology can cause fluctuations in economic activity.

Led by Nobel-laureate economist Edward Prescott, real business cycle economists have developed newer models that integrate shocks to technology into the full-employment model we have been discussing.

The idea behind real business cycle theory is simple: Changes in technology will usually change the level of full employment or potential output. For example, if there is a significant technological improvement, it will enable the economy to increase the level of both actual and potential output. Similarly, if there are adverse technological developments (such as would occur if the Internet were to crash, for example) or adverse shocks to the economy, output and potential output will fall.

Figure 21.7 gives a simple example of how the real business cycle theory works. Suppose an adverse technological shock occurred, decreasing the demand for labor. The demand curve for labor would shift to the left, and the labor market equilibrium would move from e to e_1. The result would be a lower level of employment and lower real wages. Total GDP would fall both because employment would be low and because the economy would be less productive than before from the adverse technological shock.

Conversely, a positive technological shock would increase labor demand and result in both higher wages and employment. Total GDP would rise because employment would be high and because the economy was more productive than before.

An economy buffeted by positive and negative economic shocks would experience economic fluctuations even though the economy would always be at full-employment output. The key lesson from real business cycle theory is that potential output itself will vary over time.

The real business cycle school of thought has been influential with some academic economists but, in its most extreme form, has been viewed as controversial. Critics of the real business cycle theory find it difficult to understand how many of the post-World War II recessions could be explained by adverse changes in technology. In

FIGURE 21.7

How an Adverse Technology Shock Affects Labor Demand and Supply

The decrease in labor demand from the shock to technology lowers both real wages and employment.

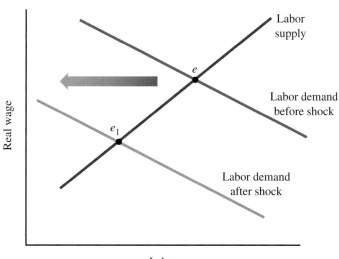

ddition, it does not provide an explanation of unemployment. In the real business ycle model, the labor market is in equilibrium and the quantity demanded for labor quals the quantity supplied. At the equilibrium wage, the quantity of labor emanded equals the quantity of labor supplied, and everyone who seeks employ- 1ent finds employment.

Proponents of the real business cycle model counter that other types of economic 1odels can be used to explain unemployment and that the real business cycle can still xplain fluctuations in employment. Real business cycle theory is an active area of esearch, and both its methods and approach, grounded in firm economic reasoning, ave had a major influence on professional research today.

Dividing Output Among Competing Demands

Dur model of full employment is based entirely on the supply of factors of production. The demand for and supply of labor determine the real wage and total employment in he economy. Together, labor and the supply of capital determine the level of output hrough the production function. And that means that in a full-employment economy, otal GDP is determined by the supply of factors of production.

Full-employment GDP must be divided among competing demands in the econ- omy. From the previous two chapters, you know that economists think of GDP as eing composed of consumption, investment, government purchases, and net exports, which we denote as $C + I + G + NX$. In this section, we first discuss how the GDP of different societies' total GDP is composed. Because governments, for many different easons, increase their level of spending, we would like to know how increased govern- ment spending affects private spending. We will see how increases in government pending must reduce other types of expenditures when the economy is operating at ull employment.

Some Comparative Data

Countries divide GDP among its competing demands in very different ways. Table 21.2 presents data on the percent of GDP in alternative uses for five countries in 2002. Recall that consumption (C), investment (I), and government purchases (G) refer to

	C	I	G	NX
Japan	57%	24%	18%	1%
United States	70	18	16	−4
France	54	20	24	2
Singapore	42	24	12	22
Germany	59	18	20	3

TABLE 21.2

Percentage of GDP Composition, Assorted Countries, 2002

Source: *International Financial Statistics*, International Monetary Fund, 2003.

total spending by residents of that country. Net exports (*NX*) is the difference between exports (sales of goods to foreign residents) and imports (purchases of goods abroad). If a country has positive net exports (like Japan, France, Singapore, and Germany), it is selling more goods in other countries than it is buying from other countries. If a country has negative net exports (like the United States), it is buying more goods than it is selling to other countries.

Let's make one more point: These data are from the *International Financial Statistics*, which is published by the International Monetary Fund. In these statistics, government purchases include only government consumption (such as military spending or wages for government employees). Government investment (such as spending on bridges or roads) is included in the investment category (*I*).

Table 21.2 reveals considerable diversity among countries. The United States consumes 70% of its GDP, a higher fraction than all the other countries. As far as investment goes, the United States and Germany invest a smaller share of GDP than the other countries in the table. Japan and Singapore invest the most—24%. Countries also differ greatly when it comes to government consumption. France has the highest rate of government consumption, while Singapore has the lowest. Finally, the countries differ sharply in the size of net exports relative to GDP.

This wide diversity challenges economists to explain these differences. Some economists have suggested that Japan has a high saving rate, that is, a relatively low percent of GDP devoted to consumption, because it has a relatively fast-growing population and young adults tend to be a high-saving part of the population. Other economists have suggested that high payroll taxes in Singapore reduce workers' incomes and their ability to consume. But not all economists accept these explanations, and there are no obvious, purely economic reasons why the United States, France, and Germany should exhibit such different behavior.

Crowding Out in a Closed Economy

Crowding out
The reduction in investment (or other component of GDP) in the long run caused by an increase in government spending.

We know that government spending is part of GDP. Let's say that GDP is fixed and the government increases its spending. What happens in a country that increases its government purchases within a fixed GDP? Because the level of full-employment output is given by the supply of factors in the economy, an increase in government spending must come at the expense of other uses of GDP. Another way of looking at this: Increased government spending crowds out other demands for GDP. This is called **crowding out**. Crowding out illustrates the principle of opportunity cost:

Principle OF OPPORTUNITY COST

The opportunity cost of something is what you sacrifice to get it.

t full employment, the opportunity cost of increased government spending is some ther component of GDP.

To understand crowding out, let's first consider what will happen when government spending increases in an economy without international trade. An economy ithout international trade is called a **closed economy**. In a closed economy, full mployment output is divided among just three different demands: consumption, vestment, and government purchases. We can write this as

$$\text{output} = \text{consumption} + \text{investment} + \text{government purchases}$$
$$Y = C + I + G$$

ecause we are considering an economy at full employment, the supply of output (Y) fixed. Increases in government spending must reduce—that is, crowd out—either onsumption or investment. In general, both are affected. On the investment side, the overnment will be in increased competition with businesses trying to borrow funds om the public to finance their investment plans. This increased competition from the overnment will make it more difficult and costly for them to do that. As a result, vestment spending on their part will decrease. They will get crowded out, by the government, in other words.

Crowding out occurred in the United States during World War II as the share of overnment spending as a part of GDP rose sharply. Figure 21.8 and Figure 21.9 show hat at the same time the share of government spending increased, the shares of consumption and investment spending in GDP decreased.

Closed economy
An economy without international trade.

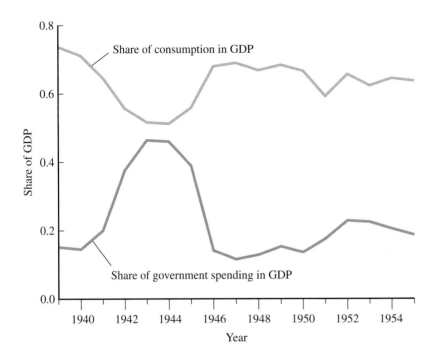

FIGURE 21.8

U.S. Consumption and Government Spending During WWII
Increased government spending crowds out consumption by consumers.

Source: U.S. Department of Commerce.

U.S. Investment and Government Spending During WWII
Increased government spending also crowds out private investment spending.

Source: U.S. Department of Commerce.

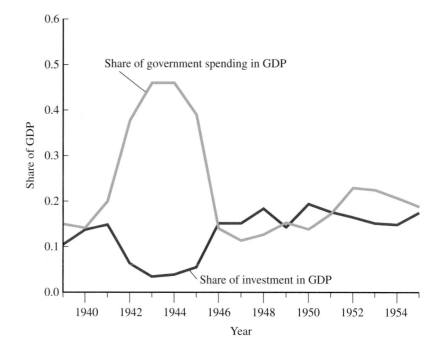

Crowding Out in an Open Economy

Open economy

An economy with international trade.

In an **open economy**, an economy with international trade, full-employment output is divided among four uses: consumption, investment, government purchases, and net exports (exports − imports):

$$Y = C + I + G + NX$$

In an open economy, increases in government spending need not crowd out either consumption or investment. Increased government spending could lead to reduced exports and increased imports. Therefore, what could instead get crowded out is net exports.

Here is how this might happen: Suppose the U.S. government began buying domestic goods to use for some governmental purpose. Let's say these are goods that consumers would have purchased but now cannot. If consumers want to maintain their consumption level despite the goods no longer being available because the government's got them, they could purchase goods previously sold abroad (exports) and purchase goods sold by foreign countries (imports). The result would be a decrease in the amount of goods exported and an increase in imports, that is, a decrease in net exports. In practice, increases in government spending in an open economy would crowd out consumption, investment, and net exports.

Crowding in

The increase of investment (or other component of GDP) in the long run caused by a decrease in government spending.

Crowding In

Governments do not always increase spending. Sometimes, they decrease it. When the government cuts spending and the level of output is fixed, some other type of spending will increase. We call this **crowding in**. In a closed economy, consumption or invest ment or both could increase. In an open economy, net exports could increase as well. As an example, after a war, we might see increases in consumption, investment spending, or net exports as they replace military spending.

The nature of changes in government spending will have some effect on the type of spending that is crowded in (or crowded out). If the government spent less on mail service—leading to longer delays in the mail—businesses and households would most likely want to spend more on private mail or delivery services. If the government built more public swimming pools, households would most likely cut back on their own spending on backyard pools.

TEST Your Understanding

9. When the economy operates at full employment, an increase in government spending must crowd out consumption. True or false? Explain.
10. In an open economy, increases in government spending can crowd out consumption, investment, or _____.
11. Compared to other countries, does the United States have a relatively high or low share of consumption spending in GDP?

USING THE TOOLS

In this chapter, we developed several tools, including labor demand, labor supply, and the production function. Using these tools, we developed a model of potential output. Here are four problems that test and extend your understanding of the tools developed in this chapter:

1. Payroll Tax for a Health Program

To finance a health care program, the government places a 10% payroll tax on all labor that is hired.
a. Show how this shifts the demand for labor.
b. If the labor-supply function is vertical, what are the effects on real wages, output, and employment? Explain why economists say that labor bears the full burden of the tax in this case.
c. If the labor supply were horizontal, what would be the effects on wages, output, and employment?

2. Migration and Wages

Between 1870 and 1910, 60 million Europeans left Europe to go to the United States, Canada, Australia, and Argentina. This sharply increased the labor force in these countries but decreased it Europe. Draw demand and supply diagrams to show what happened to wages in both Europe and the other countries.

3. Taxes and Labor Supply for High-Income Married Women

The Tax Reform Act of 1986 cut the tax rates sharply for high-income earners. Consider the families in the top 1% of all families ranked in terms of income. Before the law was passed, a woman in this group faced a marginal tax rate (the tax rate applied to the first dollar she earned) of an average of 52%. After the law was passed, the rate fell to 38%. The decreases in tax rates, however, were much less for families with lower levels of income. According to study by Professor Nada Eissa, after the decrease in taxes took effect, the labor supply of women in the highest income group increased more than for the other income groups.

Use a labor demand and supply model to illustrate the differences between the high-income group and other groups.

4. Would a Subsidy for Wages Necessarily Increase Employment?

Suppose the government paid a subsidy to firms for hiring workers; that is, it paid them an amount for every worker they hired. Using supply and demand diagrams, show how this could possibly lead to higher wages but no increase in employment. Under what circumstances would employment increase the most?

SUMMARY

In this chapter, we studied the economy at full employment. In the model we developed in this chapter, the level of GDP is determined by the supply of factors of production, labor, and capital. We focused on how the economy operates when it is at full employment; in later chapters, we consider economic fluctuations. Here are the main points from this chapter:

1 Full employment or potential output is the level of GDP produced from a given supply of capital when the labor market is in equilibrium. Potential output is fully determined by the supply of factors of production in the economy.

2 Increases in the stock of capital raise the level of full-employment output and real wages.

3 Increases in the supply of labor will raise the level of full-employment output but lower the level of real wages.

4 The full-employment model has many applications. Many economists use it to study the effects of taxes on potential output. Others have found it useful in understanding economic fluctuations.

5 At full employment, increases in government spending must come at the expense of other components of GDP. In a closed economy, either consumption or investment must be crowded out. In an open economy, net exports can be crowded out as well. Decreases in government spending will crowd in other types of spending.

KEY TERMS

classical model, 469
closed economy, 485
crowding in, 486
crowding out, 484
full-employment output, 477

income effect, 474
labor, 470
open economy, 486
production function, 470
real business cycle theory, 481

real wage, 474
stock of capital, 470
substitution effect, 474

PROBLEMS AND DISCUSSION QUESTIONS

1 Economists who are interested in the damage that taxation can do to the economy often discuss the labor market in Europe, where there are high payroll taxes and employment growth has been low. Why are they interested in this case?

2 Suppose economist A claims that the natural rate of unemployment is 4%, while economist B claims that it's 5%. Which economist will estimate a higher value for potential output?

3 Explain why labor unions might be interested in limiting the employment of young workers.

4 Some economists have argued that while immigration does not have a major impact on the overall level of wages, it does increase the wage gap between high-school graduates and college graduates. Can you explain the wage gap?

5 Studies have shown that U.S. towns near the border with Mexico have lower wages than towns farther away. Can you explain why?

6 Let's say the labor-supply curve is close to vertical. Explain why raising payroll tax rates will increase the total revenue the government receives from the payroll tax.

7 Draw a graph to show how a real business cycle economist would explain an economic boom. According to real business cycle theory, how do real wages behave during recessions and booms?

8 Some Japanese economists have argued that we should limit the use of our credit cards in the United States to increase our rate of investment. Explain why they say this.

9 At one time, labor economists found that married women had relatively flat labor-supply curves, which are very sensitive to real wages. Do you believe that married women still have relatively flat labor curves today?

10 In some societies, it is a custom for the bride's family to give a gift having very large monetary value to the family of the groom. How might this affect the saving rate in those societies?

11 Suppose that a country has very limited opportunities for successful investment projects but that the population has a high savings rate. Explain why this country is likely to have a large trade surplus.

12 Web Exercise. Go to the Website for the Congressional Budget Office (*http://www.cbo.gov*) and find a study that explores the effects of taxation on economic behavior and on total tax revenue.

13 Web Exercise. Edward Prescott is one of the leaders of the real business cycle school. Several of his influential papers are on the Website of The Federal Reserve Bank of Minneapolis (*http://research. mpls.frb.fed.us/research/economists/ecp.html*). Read his article "Theory Ahead of Business Cycle Measurement." What is the key message he is trying to convey?

MODEL ANSWERS TO QUESTIONS

Chapter-Opening Questions

1 Increased immigration will typically lower real wages while increasing the level of output in the economy.

2 In a closed economy (not open to trade) operating at full employment, increased government spending must lead to reduced spending on either consumption or investment. In an open economy (which allows for trade), higher government spending could lead to a reduction in net exports.

3 Increased investment will mean a higher capital stock in the future. The higher stock of capital will allow a higher standard of living.

4 If employers are required to pay higher taxes for hiring labor, wages will fall; typically, employment and GDP will fall as well. As the chapter explains, the amount that employment and GDP fall depends on how sensitive labor supply is to real wages.

5 Increased investment, which will lead to a higher stock of capital, will raise wages in the long run.

Test Your Understanding

1 A production function shows the relationships between inputs and outputs in the economy.

2 Decreases.

3 Upward.

4 Supplied.

5 The demand curve slopes downward because when wages are lower, the firm will want to hire more labor. The supply curve slopes upward because at higher wages, more people will seek employment.

6 Right.

7 Right.

8 True. The demand curve shifts to the left, lowering both wages and employment.

9 False. Investment could also be crowded out.

10 Net exports.

11 It is high.

Why Do Economies Grow?

o understand what economic gro
means, consider how the typical
American lived in 1783, seven years after
Declaration of Independence was written.
According to economic historian Stanley Leberg
an average U.S. home at that time had no central he
one fireplace, no plumbing, no hot water, and toilets th
were outdoor shacks surrounding a hole in the ground.

Now move ahead well into the nineteenth century. Then, a typical farmer took a bath once a week. Houses had no
electricity or gas; a solitary candle provided light at night. There were no refrigerators, no toasters, or any appliances.
Bedrooms contained no furniture other than a bed (with no springs); two people slept in what we now consider a singl
bed. For women, things were particularly hard. They were expected to bake over half a ton of bread a year, kill chicke
and butcher hogs, as well as prepare all vegetables. Canned foods were not readily available until a century later. And
really don't want to hear about medical "science" in those days.[1]

And, just think, only 50 years ago children in the United States still were afflicted with polio. Most households did
have television sets, and even those were black and white. What changes will occur in the next 50 years?

Our living standards are dramatically different today because there has been a remarkable growth in GDP per person. Growth in GDP is perhaps the most critical aspect of a country's economic performance. Over long periods, there is no other way to raise the standard of living in an economy.

With the tools developed in this chapter, here are some questions we can answer:

1   What countries have the highest living standards today?
2   Do countries with high savings rates have faster rates of GDP growth?
3   Do trade deficits help or hinder economic growth?
4   What factors determine technological progress?

The chapter begins by looking at some data from both rich and poor countries over the last 30 years. We will see how GDP per capita (meaning per person—every man, woman, and child) compare over this period.

We'll then look at how growth occurs. Economists believe that there are two basic mechanisms that increase GDP per capita over the long term. One is **capital deepening**, or increases in an economy's stock of capital (like plants and equipment) relative to its workforce. **Technological progress** is the other mechanism by which economies can grow. To economists, technological progress specifically means that an economy operates more efficiently, producing more output, but without using any more inputs like capital or labor. We'll examine different theories of the origins of technological progress and discuss how to measure its overall importance for the economy. Finally, we'll discuss in detail the role of education and investments in human beings in fostering economic development, which is called **human capital**.

The appendix to this chapter contains a simple model of capital deepening known as the Solow model. It shows how increases in capital per worker lead to economic growth. It will also allow us to better understand the role of technological progress in sustaining economic growth.

Capital deepening
increases in the stock of capital per worker.

Technological progress
an increase in output without increasing inputs.

Human capital
the knowledge and skills acquired by a worker through education and experience and used to produce goods and services.

Economic Growth Rates

Throughout the world, there are vast differences in standards of living and in rates of economic growth. To understand these differences, we first need to look at the concepts and the tools economists use to study economic growth. With these concepts and tools, we will be equipped to understand the data that measure economic growth.

But before we learn how to measure growth, let's take a broad overview of what we mean by economic growth. We can understand economic growth by using one of the tools we developed in Chapter 2: the production possibilities frontier, or PPF. The production possibility frontier shows the set of feasible production options for an economy at a given point of time. In Figure 22.1 we show an economy's trade-off when it

FIGURE 22.1

What Is Economic Growth?
Economic growth means an expanded production possibility frontier.

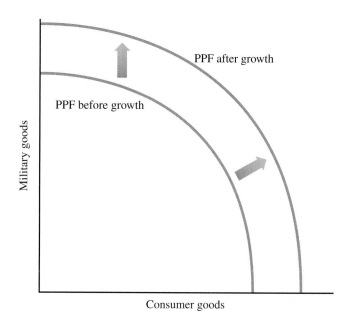

comes to producing consumer goods versus military goods. As the economy grows, th entire PPF shifts outward. This means that the economy can produce more of bot] goods—that is what we mean by economic growth. Growth also expands the amoun of goods available for people to consume. Just think about your own family. A typica family 40 years ago had only one car; today many families have two or three. And, a our chapter-opening story highlights, for many people in history and in the worle today, economic growth means a qualitative transformation of their lifestyles.

Measuring Economic Growth

Real GDP per capita
Gross domestic product per person adjusted for changes in prices. It is the usual measure of living standards across time and between countries.

Growth rate
The percentage rate of change of a variable.

From earlier chapters, we know that real GDP measures in constant prices the tota value of final goods and services in a country. Since countries differ in the size of thei populations, we want to know what a country's real GDP per person, or its **real GDF per capita**, is.

Real GDP per capita typically grows over time. A convenient way to describe the changes in real GDP per capita is growth rates. The **growth rate** of a variable is the percentage change in that variable from one period to another. For example, to calcu- late the growth rate of real GDP from year 1 to year 2, suppose real GDP was 100 ir year 1 and 104 in year 2. In this case, the growth rate of real GDP would be

$$\text{growth rate} = [(\text{GDP in year 2} - \text{GDP in year 1})/(\text{GDP in year 1})] \times 100$$
$$= [(104 - 100)/100] \times 100$$
$$= [4/100] \times 100$$
$$= [.04] \times 100 = 4\% \text{ per year}$$

Real GDP grew by 4% from year 1 to year 2, in other words.

Economies can grow at different rates from one year to the next. But it often is useful to consider what happens when an economy grows at a constant rate, say g, for a number of years. Suppose that real GDP for an economy was 100 and that the economy grew at a rate g for n years. How large would the real GDP be after n years? The answer is given by a simple formula:

$$\text{GDP } [n \text{ years later}] = (1 + g)^n(100)$$

Example: If the economy starts at 100 and grows at a rate of 4% a year for 10 years, output (after 10 years) will be

$$\text{GDP } [10 \text{ years later}] = (1 + .04)^{10}(100) = (1.48)(100) = 148$$

which is nearly 50% higher than in the first year.

Here's a rule of thumb to help you understand the power of growth rates. Suppose you know the growth rate of real GDP and it is constant, but you want to know how many years it will take until the level of real GDP doubles. The answer is given by the **rule of 70**:

$$\text{years to double} = 70/(\text{percentage growth rate})$$

Example: For an economy that grew at 5% a year, it would take

$$70/5 = 14 \text{ years}$$

for real GDP to double. (In case you were curious, the rule of 70 is derived by using the mathematics of logarithms.)

Rule of 70
A rule of thumb that says that output will double in 70/x years where x is the percentage rate of growth.

Comparing the Growth Rates of Various Countries

Making comparisons of real GDP or GNP across countries is difficult. Not only do countries have their own currencies but patterns of consumption and prices can differ sharply between countries. Two examples can illustrate this point. First, because land is scarce in Japan, people live in smaller spaces than do residents of the United States, so the price of housing is higher (relative to other goods) than in the United States. Second, developing countries (such as India or Pakistan) have very different price structures than developed countries. In particular, in developing countries the prices of goods that are not traded—such as household services or land—are relatively cheaper than goods that are traded in world markets. In other words, while all residents of the world may pay the same price for gold jewelry, hiring a cook or household helper is considerably less expensive in India or Pakistan than in the United States.

It is important to take these differences into account. Fortunately, a team of economists led by Robert Summers and Alan Heston of the University of Pennsylvania has devoted decades to developing methods for measuring real GNP across countries. Their procedures are based on gathering extensive data on prices of comparable goods in each country and making adjustments for differences in relative prices and consumption patterns. These methods are now officially used by the World Bank and the International Monetary Fund, two prominent international organizations.

According to these methods, the country with the highest level of income in 2001 was Luxembourg; its real income per capita was $48,560. The United States was second at $34,280 and Switzerland was third at $30,970.

Table 22.1 lists real GNP per capita for 2001 and average annual growth rate of GNP per capita between 1960 and 2001 for 11 countries. (GNP is most commonly used in international comparisons.) Japan, with a GNP per capita of $25,550, follows the United States. Not far behind are Italy, the United Kingdom, and France. More representative of typical countries were Costa Rica and Mexico, with GNPs per capita in 2001 of $9,260 and $8,240, respectively. This is less than 30% of per capita GNP in the United States. Very poor countries have extremely low GNP per capita. Pakistan, for example, had a GNP per capita of $1,860—just 6% of the GNP per capita of the United States.

In the third column of Table 22.1, notice the differences in growth rates. Consider Japan. In 1960, Japan had a GDP per capita that was only one-half that of France and one-fourth that of the U.S. GDP per capita. But notice from column three that Japan's GDP per capita grew on average at 4.16% per year during the period, compared to 2.18% for the United States and 2.70% for France. To place Japan's growth rate for this period into perspective, recall the rule of 70. If an economy grows at an average annual rate of x percent a year, it takes $70/x$ years for output to double. In Japan's case, per capita output was doubling every 70/4.16 years, or approximately every 16 years. At this rate, from the time someone was born to the time he or she reached the age of 32, living standards would have increased by a factor of four—an extraordinary rate of growth. The rule of 70 reinforces how important are small differences in economic growth rates. A per capita GDP growth rate of 5% a year means that the living standard doubles in 14 years. With only 1% growth, doubling would take 70 years.

TABLE 22.1

GNP Per Capita and Economic Growth
The table shows the level of GNP per capita and the growth rates for 11 countries in different stages of development.

Country	GNP Per Capita in 2001 dollars	Per Capital Growth Rate 1960–2001
United Sates	$34,280	2.18%
Japan	25,550	4.16
Italy	24,530	3.07
United Kingdom	24,340	2.17
France	24,080	2.70
Costa Rica	9,260	2.50
Mexico	8,240	2.27
India	2,820	2.43
Zimbabwe	2,220	.82
Pakistan	1,860	.98
Zambia	750	−1.15

Source: World Bank Development Indicators, 2001, and Penn World Tables.

Luxembourg and Pakistan represent some of the extremes in per capita income today.

Are Poor Countries Catching Up?

One question economists ask is whether poorer countries can close the gap between their level of GDP per capita and the GDP per capita of richer countries. Closing this gap is called **convergence**. To converge, poorer countries have to grow at more rapid rates than richer countries are growing. Since 1960, Japan, Italy, and France all have grown more rapidly than the United States and have narrowed the gap in per capita incomes.

Let's look at the evidence, Figure 22.2 plots the average growth rate for 16 currently developed countries from 1870 to 1979 versus the level of per capita income in 1870. Each point represents a different country. Notice that the countries with the lowest initial per capita incomes are plotted higher on the graph. That is, they had higher growth rates than the countries with more income per capita. The downward-sloping line plotted through the points indicates that the countries with higher levels of per capita income in 1870 grew more slowly than countries with lower levels of per capita

Convergence

The process by which poorer countries "catch up" with richer countries in terms of real GDP per capita.

FIGURE 22.2

Growth Rates versus Per Capita Income, 1870–1979

Each point on the graph represents a different currently developed country. Notice that the countries with the lowest per capita incomes in 1870 (shown along the horizontal axis) are plotted higher on the graph. In other words, there was a tendency for countries with lower levels of initial income to grow faster.

Source: M. Obstfeld and K. Rogoff, *Foundation of International Macroeconomics* (Cambridge, MA: MIT Press, 1996), Table 7.1.

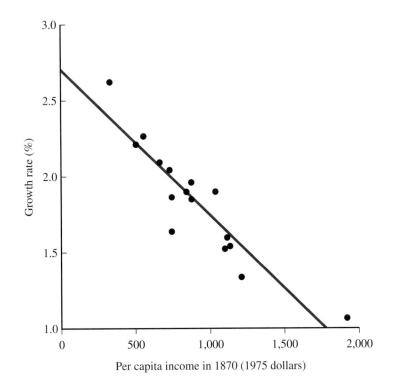

income. In other words, there was a tendency for countries with lower levels of initial income to grow faster and catch up. The graph shows that among the currently developed countries—for example, the United States, France, and the United Kingdom—there was a tendency for convergence over the last century.

Now let's compare the countries that are currently less developed to the advanced industrial countries. Here, the picture is not so clear in recent times. While Costa Rica grew at a faster rate than the United States, Pakistan grew only 0.98% per year and fell farther behind advanced economies. In Africa, GDP per capita fell substantially in Zambia while in Zimbabwe GDP per capita grew less than 1%. In general, economists who have studied the process of economic growth in detail find weak evidence that poorer countries are currently closing the gap in per capita income with richer countries.

Indeed, in the last 20 years, there has been little convergence. Economist Stanley Fischer, formerly with the IMF and the Massachusetts Institute of Technology, found that on average, countries with higher GDP per capita in 1980 grew slightly faster from 1980 to 2000 as compared to countries with lower GDP per capita.[2] African countries, which were among the poorest countries, grew the slowest. However, there were some important exceptions: The two most populous countries, China and India, grew very rapidly. Since they contain a large fraction of the world's population, the good news is that living conditions for many people around the globe have improved substantially in the last 20 years.

It was commonly thought that as countries developed, inequality would increase among their populations. But recent research challenges this finding, as "A Closer Look: Growth and Inequality," explains.

A CLOSER LOOK   Growth and Inequality

For many years, economists believed, following the work of Nobel laureate Simon Kuznets, that as a country develops, inequality within a country followed an inverted "U" pattern—it initially increased as a country developed and then narrowed over time. However, recent research by economists Emmanuel Saez, of Harvard, and Thomas Piketty, a French economist, casts doubt that this phenomenon is solely the result of growth.

Piketty and Saez looked carefully at data in the United States over the twentieth century. Inequality—as measured by the income share of the top 10% of families—increased from 40% at the beginning of the 1920s to 45% through the end of the Great Depression, consistent with Kuznet's theory. But things changed during World War II. During that time, the share fell to 32% by 1944 and remained at that level until the early 1970s, at which time inequality began to again increase.

Piketty and Saez suggest that wage and price controls during World War II reduced differentials in wages and salaries and thereby reduced inequality. Moreover, even after the war, these patterns persisted until the 1970s because society perceived them to be fair. After the 1970s, salaries at the top of the income distribution increased sharply. (Think of the vast sums paid to some major league baseball players or corporate executives.) These findings, as well as related results from other countries, suggest that inequality does not naturally accompany economic development. Social norms and other factors, such as perceived fairness of compensation and the nature of the tax system, also play a role. Moreover, the U.S. experience suggests that these norms can change over time, even within the same country, regardless of growth rates.

Source: Thomas Piketty and Emmanuel Saez, "Income Inequality in the United States, 1913–1998," NBER Working Paper, No. 8467, September 2001.

TEST Your Understanding

1. What measure of output do we use to gauge living standards across countries with populations of different sizes?
2. How do the relative prices for nontraded goods (such as household services) and traded goods (such as jewelry) compare between poor countries and rich countries?
3. Economists who have studied economic growth find only weak evidence for convergence. True or false? Explain.
4. At a 2% annual growth rate in GDP per capita, how many years would it take for GDP per capita to double?

Capital Deepening

One of the most important mechanisms of economic growth economists have identified is increases in the amount of capital per worker due to capital deepening.

In Chapter 21, we studied the effects of an increase in capital in a full-employment economy. Figure 22.3 shows the effects on output and real wages. For simplicity, the supply of labor is assumed not to be affected by real wages and is drawn as a vertical line (see Panel B). In Panel A, an increase in capital shifts the production function upward because more output can be produced from the same amount of labor. In addition, firms increase their demand for labor because the marginal benefit from employing labor will increase. Panel B shows how the increase in capital raises the demand for labor and increases real wages. That is, as firms increase their demand and compete for a fixed supply of labor, they will bid up real wages in the economy.

An economy is better off with an increase in the stock of capital. With additions to the stock of capital, workers will enjoy higher wages and total GDP in the economy will increase. Workers are more productive because each worker has more capital at his or her disposal. But how does an economy increase its stock of capital per worker? The answer is with saving and investment, which we'll discuss next.

Saving and Investment

Let's begin with the simplest case: an economy with a constant population, producing at full employment. This particular economy has no government or foreign sector. Output can be purchased only by consumers or by firms. In other words, output consists solely of consumption (C) and investment (I). At the same time, this output generates an amount of income that is equivalent to the amount of output. That is, output (Y) equals income. Any income that is not consumed we call **saving**.

In this economy, saving must equal investment. Here's why: By definition, consumption plus saving equals income:

$$C + S = Y$$

Saving

Total income minus consumption.

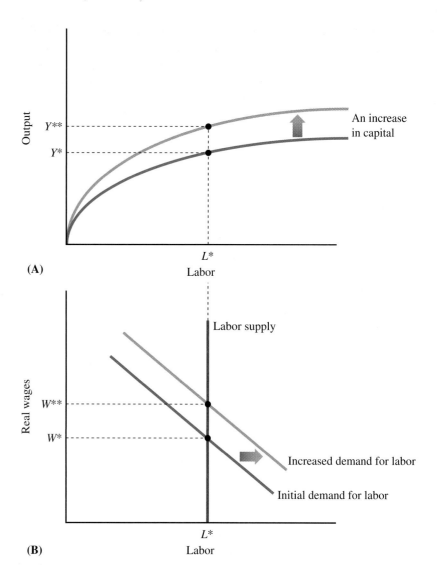

FIGURE 22.3
Increase in the Supply of Capital
An increase in the supply of capital will shift the production function upward and increase the demand for labor. Real wages will increase from $W*$ to $W**$, and potential output will increase from $Y*$ to $Y**$.

but at the same time income—which is equivalent to output—also equals consumption plus investment:

$$C + I = Y$$

Thus, saving must equal investment:

$$S = I$$

This means that whatever consumers decide to save goes directly into investment. Whatever income individuals do not spend is savings. In turn, those savings go directly into investment.

Next, we need to link the level of investment in the economy to the stock of capital in the economy. The stock of capital depends on two factors: investment and depreciation. The stock of capital increases with any gross investment spending but decreases with depreciation. Why does depreciation decrease the stock of capital? The answer is simple: As capital stock items like buildings and equipment get older (depreciate) they wear out and become less productive. New investment is needed to replace the buildings and equipment that become obsolete.

Suppose, for example, the stock of capital at the beginning of the year is $10,000. During the year, if there were $1,000 in gross investment and $400 in depreciation, the capital stock at the end of the year would be $10,600 (= $10,000 + $1000 − $400).

It may be helpful to picture this as being like a bathtub. The level of water in a bathtub (the stock of capital) depends on the flow of water into the bathtub through the input faucet (gross investment) minus the flow of water out of the bathtub down the drain (depreciation). As long as the flow in exceeds the flow out, the water level in the bathtub (the stock of capital) will increase.

Higher saving, which leads to higher gross investment, will therefore tend to increase the stock of capital available for production. As the stock of capital grows, however, there typically will be more depreciation, because there is more capital (building and equipment) to depreciate. It is the difference between gross investment and depreciation—net investment—that ultimately determines the change in the stock of capital for the economy, the level of real wages, and output. In our example, net investment is $1,000 − $400 = $600.

How Do Population Growth, Government, and Trade Affect Capital Deepening?

So far, we've considered the simplest economy. Let's consider a more realistic economy that includes population growth, a government, and trade.

First, consider the effects of population growth: A larger labor force will allow the economy to produce more total output. However, with a fixed amount of capital and an increasing labor force, the amount of capital per worker will be less. With less capital per worker, output per worker will also tend to be less because each worker has fewer machines to use. This is an illustration of the principle of diminishing returns.

Principle OF DIMINISHING RETURNS

Suppose that output is produced with two or more inputs and that we increase one input while holding the other inputs fixed. Beyond some point—called the point of diminishing returns—output will increase at a decreasing rate.

Consider India, with over a billion people and the world's second-largest population. Although India has a large labor force, the amount of capital per worker is low. With sharp diminishing returns to labor, per capita output in India will tend to be low.

The government can affect the process of capital deepening in several ways through its policies of spending and taxation. Suppose the government taxed its citizens so that it could fight a war, pay its legislators higher salaries, or give foreign aid to needy countries. The higher taxes will reduce total income. If consumers save a fixed fraction of their income, total private saving (savings from the nongovernmental sector) will fall. In these cases, the government is not investing the funds it collects and putting those funds into capital formation. It is taxing the private sector to engage in consumption spending. This drains the private sector of saving that would have been used for capital deepening.

Now suppose the government took all the extra tax revenues and invested them in valuable infrastructure such as roads, buildings, and airports. These infrastructure investments add to the capital stock. If consumers were saving 20% of their income and the government collected a dollar in taxes from each taxpayer, private saving would fall by 20 cents per taxpayer, but government investment in the infrastructure would increase by a full $1 per taxpayer. In other words, the government "forces" consumers (by taxing them) to invest an additional 80 cents in infrastructure that they otherwise wouldn't have. The net result is an increase in total social saving (private plus government) of 80 cents per taxpayer.

Finally, the foreign sector can affect capital deepening. An economy can run a trade deficit and import investment goods, such as precision machine tools, to aid capital deepening. The United States, Canada, and Australia built their vast railroad systems in the nineteenth century by running trade deficits (selling less goods and services to the rest of the world than they were buying—and financing this gap by borrowing). This enabled them to purchase the large amount of capital needed to build their rail networks and grow at more rapid rates by deepening capital. Eventually these economies had to pay back the funds that were borrowed from abroad by running trade surpluses (selling more goods and services to the rest of the world than they were buying from abroad). But since economic growth had increased GDP and wealth, the three countries were able to afford to pay back the borrowed funds. Therefore, this was a reasonable strategy for them to pursue.

Not all trade deficits promote capital deepening, however. Suppose a country runs a trade deficit because it wants to buy more consumer goods. The country would be borrowing from abroad, but there would be no additional capital deepening—just additional consumption spending. When the country is forced to pay back the funds, there will be no additional GDP to help foot the bill. In order to fund current consumption, the country will be poorer in the future.

Limits to Capital Deepening

There are natural limits to growth through capital deepening. Capital is subject to diminishing returns just as labor is. With a given labor force, increases in capital will lead to increases in output but at a diminishing rate. Eventually, growth through capital deepening will cease.

To more fully understand these limits, let's recall that the stock of capital increases only when there is positive net investment. Remember that net investment equals gross investment minus depreciation. Gross investment depends on the rate of saving in the economy. Depreciation depends on the total stock of capital that the economy has in place.

As the stock of capital increases, as we have explained, output increases but at a decreasing rate, due to diminishing returns. With a given saving rate, gross investment will also increase along with output, but at a decreasing rate. Depreciation, however, increases directly with the stock of capital. Eventually, the economy reaches a point where gross investment equals depreciation. In other words, just as much water is being drained from the bathtub as is flowing in. At this point, net investment becomes zero.

Therefore, there is a limit to growth through capital deepening because even though a higher rate of saving can increase the level of real GDP, eventually the process comes to a halt. However, it takes time—decades—for this point to be reached. Capital deepening can be an important source of economic growth for a long time.

TEST Your Understanding

5. Explain why saving must equal investment if we are not taking into account the government sector or the foreign sector.

6. If everything else is held equal, how does an increase in the size of the population affect total and per capita output?

7. If the private sector saves 10% of its income and the government raises taxes by $200 to finance public investments, by how much will total investment—private and public investment—increase?

8. If a country runs a trade deficit to finance increased current consumption, it will have to reduce consumption in the future to pay back its borrowings. True or false? Explain.

The Key Role of Technological Progress

The other mechanism affecting economic growth is technological progress. Economists use the term *technological progress* in a very specific way: It means that an economy operates more efficiently by producing more output without using any more inputs.

In practice, technological progress can take many forms. The invention of the lightbulb made it possible to read and work indoors at night, the invention of the thermometer assisted doctors and nurses in their diagnoses, and the invention of disposable diapers made life easier at home. All these examples—and you could provide many more—enable society to produce more output without more labor or more capital. With higher output per person, we enjoy a higher standard of living.

Technological progress can be thought of as the birth of new ideas. These new ideas enable us to rearrange our economic affairs and make us more productive. Not all technological innovations are necessarily major scientific breakthroughs; some are much more basic. An employee of a soft-drink company who discovers a new and popular flavor for a soft drink is engaged in technological progress, just as scientists and engineers are. Even simple, commonsense ideas from workers or managers can help a business use its capital and labor more efficiently to deliver a better product to consumers at a lower price. This is also technological progress. As long as there are new ideas, inventions, and new ways of doing things, the economy can become more productive and per capita output can increase.

How Do We Measure Technological Progress?

If someone asked you how much of the increase in your standard of living was due to technological progress, how would you answer? Robert Solow, a Nobel laureate in economics from the Massachusetts Institute of Technology, developed a method for measuring technological progress in an economy. As is usual with good ideas, his theory was simple. It was based on the idea of a production function.

You know from Chapter 21 that the production function links inputs to outputs:

$$Y = F(K,L)$$

where output (Y) is produced from capital (K) and labor (L), which are linked through the production function F. What Solow did was include in the production function some measure of technological progress, A:

$$Y = F(K,L,A)$$

Increases in A represent technological progress. Higher values of A mean that more output is produced from the same level of inputs K and L. If we could find some way to measure A, we could estimate how much technological progress affects output.

Solow noted that over any period, we can observe increases in capital, labor, and output. Using these, we can measure technological progress indirectly. We first ask how much of the change in output can be explained by contributions from the changes in the amount of capital and labor that are used. Whatever growth we cannot explain by increases in capital and labor must therefore be caused by increases in technological progress. The method Solow developed to measure the contributions to economic growth from capital, labor, and technological progress is called **growth accounting**.

Table 22.2 and Figure 22.4 illustrate the relative contributions of these growth sources for the U.S. economy from 1929 to 1982 using growth accounting, based on a classic study by the economist Edward Denison. During this period, total output grew at a rate of nearly 3%. Because capital and labor growth are measured at 0.56% and

Growth accounting
A method to determine the contribution to economic growth from increased capital, labor, and technological progress.

TABLE 22.2

Sources of Real GDP Growth, 1929–1982 (average annual percentage rates)

Growth due to capital growth	0.56%
Growth due to labor growth	1.34
+ technological progress	1.02
Total output growth	2.92

Source: Edward F. Denison, *Trends in Economic Growth 1929–82* (Washington, DC: The Brookings Institution, 1985).

1.34%, respectively, the remaining portion of output growth, 1.02%, must be due to technological progress. That means that approximately 35% of output growth came directly from technological progress.

Examples of Growth Accounting

Growth accounting is a useful tool for understanding different aspects of economic growth. Here are three examples of how economists use growth accounting.

Application: Input Differences in Singapore Versus Hong Kong

Singapore and Hong Kong have both had phenomenal post-World War II economic growth. From 1980 to 1985, each grew at a rate of approximately 6% a year. But a closer examination, by Alwyn Young of the University of Chicago, revealed that the sources of growth in each were very different.[3] In Singapore, nearly all the growth was accounted for by increases in labor and capital. Investment levels were extremely high in Singapore, reaching 43% as a share of GDP in 1983.

Hong Kong had a much lower investment rate—approximately a 20% share of GDP—and technological progress made an important contribution. This meant that the residents of Hong Kong could enjoy the same level of GDP but consume, not save, a higher fraction of GDP. Residents of Hong Kong were enjoying higher consumption than residents of Singapore were, despite the similarity in growth rates.

The difference in the sources of economic growth between Singapore and Hong Kong may also have important implications for future growth. As we explained a moment ago, there are natural limits to growth through capital deepening. Singapore increased its GDP by increasing its labor inputs and stock of capital. Singapore realized it would eventually find it difficult to keep increasing inputs to production. Economic leaders became concerned that unless they managed to increase their rate of technological progress, their long-term growth prospects would not be good.

In Hong Kong, there is currently a different concern. Technological progress has been the driving force for growth in Hong Kong. Now that it has become part of China, Hong Kong's residents hope its economy will remain free and open to sustain the system that produced technological innovation.

Application: What Caused Lower U.S. Labor Productivity?

One of the common statistics reported about the U.S. economy is **labor productivity**. Defined as output per hour of work, labor productivity is a simple measure of how much a typical worker can produce given the amount of capital in the economy and the state of technological progress. Since 1973, there has been a slowdown in the growth of labor productivity in the United States and other countries in the world. Table 22.3 shows U.S. productivity growth for different periods since 1959.

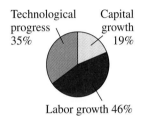

FIGURE 22.4

Growth Sources of the U.S. Economy
From 1929 to 1982 total output in the United States grew at a rate of nearly 3%. Approximately 35% of the growth came directly from technological progress.

Source: Data from Edward F. Denison, *Trends in Economic Growth 1929–82* (Washington, DC: The Brookings Institution, 1985).

Labor productivity
Output produced per hour of work.

TABLE 22.3

U.S. Annual Productivity Growth, 1959–2002

Years	Annual Growth Rate
1959–1968	3.5%
1968–1973	2.5
1973–1980	1.2
1980–1986	2.1
1986–1994	1.4
1994–2002	2.6

Source: *Economic Report of the President* (Washington, DC: U.S. Government Printing Office, 2000) and Bureau of Labor Statistics.

The table shows that productivity growth was extremely high during the 1960s. It slowed a bit in the late 1960s and then slowed dramatically after the oil shocks in the 1970s. In recent years there has been a resurgence in productivity growth, which reached 2.6% from 1994 to 2002. Nonetheless, the rate of productivity growth was very low from the late 1960s to the mid-1990s.

The slowdown in productivity growth has also meant slower growth in real wages and in GDP in the United States since 1973. Figure 22.5 plots real hourly earnings for U.S. workers; it shows that real hourly earnings have fallen since 1973. Total compensation, which includes employee benefits such as health insurance, did continue to rise through the 1980s and 1990s as employees received lower wages but higher benefits. But the rate of growth of total compensation was less than the growth of real hourly earnings in the pre-1973 period.

The decrease in the growth of labor productivity was the primary factor behind this pattern of real wages, because wages can rise with a growing labor force only if output per worker continues to increase. What can explain this decrease in the growth rate? Economists are not short of possible answers. Among the factors, they say, are declines in the education and skills of the workforce, lower levels of investment and thus a lower level of capital, less spending on infrastructure (such as highways and bridges), and the belief that managers are more concerned with producing short-term profits than long-term profits, among lots of other economic and sociological factors as well.

Growth accounting has been used to narrow the range of plausible explanations. Using growth accounting methods, economists typically find that the slowdown in labor productivity, in the United States and abroad, cannot be explained by reduced rates of capital deepening. Nor can they be explained by changes in the quality or experience of the labor force. Either a slowdown in technological progress or other factors that are not directly included in the analysis, such as higher worldwide energy prices, must be responsible for the slowdown. Moreover, since the slowdown has been worldwide, it's possible that factors that affect all countries (such as higher energy prices) are responsible rather than factors specific to a single country. Dale Jorgenson, a Harvard economist, has conducted extensive research attempting to link higher energy prices to the slowdown in productivity growth. Not all economists accept this view, however, and so the productivity slowdown remains a bit of a mystery despite the use of growth accounting methods to try to explain it.

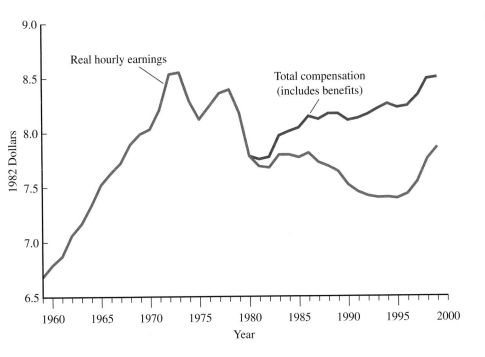

FIGURE 22.5

Real Hourly Earnings and Total Compensation for U.S. Employees
Real hourly earnings have fallen since 1973. Total compensation, which includes employee benefits, continued to rise through the 1980s and 1990s because even though employees' wages were lower, they received higher benefits.

Application: How Have the Internet and Information Technology Affected GDP?

As Table 22.3 shows, U.S. productivity growth did climb in the last half of the 1990s. "New economy" proponents believe the computer and Internet revolution are responsible for the increase in productivity growth. Skeptics wonder, however, whether this increase in productivity growth is truly permanent or just temporary. Higher investment in computer technology began in the mid-1980s, but until recently there was little sign of increased productivity growth. Had the investment in information technology finally paid off?

Robert J. Gordon of Northwestern University used growth accounting methods to shed light on this issue. After making adjustments for the low unemployment rate and high GDP growth rate in the late 1990s, he found that there had been increases in technological progress. In earlier work, he found that these increases were largely confined to the durable goods manufacturing industry, including the production of computers itself. Since the increase in technological progress was confined to a relatively small portion of the economy, Gordon was originally skeptical that we were now operating in a "new economy" with permanently higher productivity growth. However, in subsequent studies he found that productivity growth had spread to other sectors of the economy, such as retail sales and financial institutions.

Other economists as well, also using growth accounting methods, found that technological progress was more widespread throughout the economy, suggesting that the increase was likely to be permanent. Productivity growth continued to be rapid, even during the recessionary period at the beginning of this century, when most economists believed it would slow down. One possible explanation is that it took a substantial

The growth in information technology has enhanced productivity in the United States and throughout the world.

period of time before businesses began to harness the use of modern computer technology and the Internet. If productivity growth does continue at its current high rate, we will enjoy more rapid economic growth in the United States and across the globe.

What Causes Technological Progress?

Because technological progress is an important source of growth, we want to know how it occurs and what government policies can do to promote it. Economists have identified a variety of factors that may influence the pace of technological progress in an economy.

Research and Development Funding

One way to induce more technological progress in an economy is to pay for it. If the government or large firms employ workers and scientists to advance the frontiers in physics, chemistry, and biology, their work can lead to technological progress in the long run. Figure 22.6 presents data on the spending on research and development as a percent of GDP for seven major countries for 1999. The United States has the highest percentage of scientists and engineers in the world. However, although the United States spends the most money overall, as a percent of GDP, it spends less than Japan. Moreover, a big part of U.S. spending on research and development is in defense-related areas, unlike in Japan. Many economists believe that defense-related research and development is less likely to lead to long-run technological change than nondefense spending.

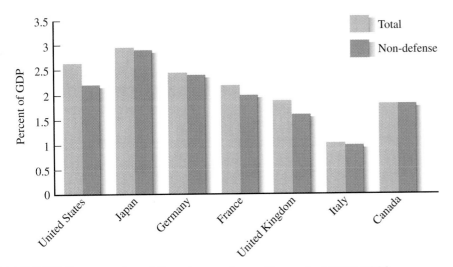

FIGURE 22.6 **Research and Development as a Percent of GDP, 1999**
The United States spends more total money than any other country on research and development. However, when the spending is measured as a percentage of each nation's GDP, Japan spends more. A big part of U.S. spending on research and development is in defense-related areas.
Source: National Patterns of R&D Resources, 2002, Washington, DC.

Monopolies That Spur Innovation

The radical notion that monopolies spur innovation was put forth by economist Joseph Schumpeter. In his view, a firm will try to come up with new products and more efficient ways to produce products only if it reaps a reward. The reward a firm seeks is high profit from its innovations. And high profit can be obtained only if the firm is the sole seller or monopolist for the product. Other firms will try to break its monopoly through more innovation, a process Schumpeter called **creative destruction**. Schumpeter believed that by allowing firms to compete to become monopolies, society benefits from increased innovation.

Creative destruction
The process by which competition for monopoly profits leads to technological progress.

Governments do allow temporary monopolies for new ideas by issuing patents. A patent allows the inventor of a product to have a monopoly until the term of the patent expires, which in the United States is now 20 years. With a patent, we tolerate some monopoly power (the power to raise prices that comes with limited competition) in the hope of spurring innovation.

A related idea, which is becoming increasingly important, is the need to protect intellectual property rights. Information technology has made the free flow of products and ideas ubiquitous. Publishers of both books and computer software face problems of unauthorized copying, particularly in some developing countries. While the residents of those countries clearly benefit from inexpensive copied software or books, the producers of the software and books in the developed countries will face reduced incentives to enter the market. Even in the United States pirated music posed a threat to the viability of the entertainment industry. Large and profitable firms may continue to produce despite unauthorized copying, but other firms may be discouraged. The United States has put piracy and unauthorized reproduction among its top agenda items in recent trade talks with several countries.

The Scale of the Market

Adam Smith stressed that the size of a market was important for economic development. In larger markets there are more incentives for firms to come up with new products and new methods of production. Just as Schumpeter suggested, the lure of profits guides the activities of firms, and larger markets provide firms the opportunity to make larger profits. This supplies another rationale for free trade. With free trade, markets are larger, and there is more incentive to engage in technological progress.

Induced Innovations

Some economists have emphasized that innovations come about through inventive activity designed specifically to reduce costs. This is known as induced innovation. For example, during the nineteenth century in the United States, the largest single cost in agriculture was wages. Ingenious farmers and inventors came up with many different machines and methods to cut back on the amount of labor required.

Education and the Accumulation of Knowledge

Education can contribute to economic growth in two ways. First, the increased knowledge and skills of people complement our current investments in physical capital. Second, education can enable the workforce in an economy to use its skills to develop new ideas or to copy ideas or import them from abroad. Consider a developing country today. In principle, it has at its disposal the vast accumulated knowledge of the developed economies. But this probably requires a skilled workforce—one reason why many developing countries send their best students to educational institutions in developed countries.

A Key Governmental Role: Getting the Incentives Right

As we discussed in Chapter 3, governments play a critical role in a market economy. Governments must enforce the rules of the market economy, using its police powers to ensure that contracts are upheld, and individual property rights are enforced and firms can enter safely into economic transactions. But governments also have a broader role in designing the institutions in a society in which individuals and firms work, save, and invest. Economists have increasingly recognized the importance of these institutions in determining economic growth. For example, as we discussed, the residents of Hong Kong link their rapid economic growth to free and open institutions that provide the right incentives for technological innovations.

But, for many countries, growth has been more elusive. For many years, international organizations such as the World Bank—a consortium of countries created to promote development—have tried a variety of diverse methods to assist developing countries. These have included increases in foreign aid, infusions of new machinery, promotion of universal education, and efforts to stem population growth. Despite these efforts, some areas of the world, such as Sub-Saharan Africa, have failed to grow at all.

The rate of return on human capital investment through elementary education in Africa is extremely high.

A former World Bank economist, William Easterly, believes that the World Bank and other international organizations have failed to take into account one of the basic laws of economics: individuals and firms respond to incentives. According to Easterly, governments in developing countries have failed to provide the proper economic environment that would motivate individuals and firms to take actions that promote economic development. As an example, providing free schooling is not enough—individuals need to know that their investments in education will pay off in the future in terms of higher incomes or better jobs. Without the prospect that education will lead to an improvement in their lives, individuals will not make the effort to obtain an education.

What else can go wrong? Governments in developing countries often adopt policies that effectively tax exports, pursue policies that lead to rampant inflation, and enforce laws that inhibit the growth of the banking and financial sectors. The results are predictable: fewer exports, an uncertain financial environment, and reduced savings and investment. All of these outcomes can cripple an economy's growth prospects. Sometimes these actions are simply based on bad economic advice. Other times, racial or ethnic groups in polarized societies use the economic system to take advantage of their rivals.

What can be done? In Easterly's view, the World Bank and other international organizations need to stop searching for the magic bullet for development. Instead, they should hold governments responsible for creating the proper economic environment. With the right incentives, Easterly believes that individuals and firms in developing countries will take actions that promote economic growth.[4]

Human Capital

Increasing knowledge and skills are part of human capital—an investment in human beings. Human capital is as important, even more important, than physical capital. Many economists, including Nobel laureate Gary Becker of the University of Chicago, have studied this in detail.

A classic example of human capital is the investment a student makes to attend college. The costs of attending college consist of the direct out-of-pocket costs (tuition and fees) plus the opportunity costs of forgone earnings. The benefits of attending college are the higher wages and more interesting jobs offered to college graduates as compared to high-school graduates. Individuals decide to attend college because these benefits exceed the costs, and it is a rational economic decision. A similar calculation faces a newly graduated doctor who must decide whether to pursue a specialty. Will the forgone earnings of a general physician (which are quite substantial) be worth the time spent learning a specialty that will eventually result in extra income? Investments in health and nutrition can be analyzed within the same framework.

Human capital theory has two implications for understanding economic growth. First, not all labor is equal. When economists measure the labor input in a country, they must adjust for differing levels of education. These levels of education reflect past investments in education and skills; individuals with higher educational levels will, on average, be more productive. Second, health and fitness also affect productivity. In developing countries, economists have found that there is a strong correlation between the height of individuals (reflecting their health) and the wages that they can earn in the farming sector. At the same time, increases in income through economic growth have led to sharp increases in height and weight, as "A Closer Look: Our Tiny Ancestors" explains.

Human capital theory can also serve as a basis for important public policy decisions. Should a developing country invest in capital (either public or private) or in education? The poorest developing countries lack many things: good sanitation systems, effective transportation systems, and capital investment for agriculture and industry. However, the best use of investment funds may not be for bridges, sewer systems, and roads, but for human capital and education. Studies demonstrate that the returns from investing in education are extremely high in developing countries. The

A CLOSER LOOK   Our Tiny Ancestors

As you may have seen in a museum, men and women have grown taller and heavier in the last 300 years As an example, an average American male adult today stands at approximately 5 feet 10 inches tall, which is nearly 4.5 inches taller than the typical Englishman in the late eighteenth century. Body weights are also substantially higher today. According to Nobel laureate Robert Fogel of the University of Chicago, the average weight of English males in their thirties was about 134 pounds in 1790—20% below today's average. A typical Frenchman in his thirties at that time weighed only 110 pounds!

Fogel has argued that these lower weights and heights reflected inadequate food supplies and chronic malnutrition. Not only did lower food supplies lead to smaller physical stature, they also led to a higher incidence of chronic disease. Fogel estimated that the chronic malnutrition caused by limited food supplies at those times limited labor productivity. In France, 20% of the labor force lacked enough physical energy to put in more than three hours of light work a day. A high percentage of workers in the society were too frail and ill to contribute much to national output.

Economic growth produced a "virtuous" circle. It increased food supplies, enabling workers to become more productive and increase GDP even more.

gains from elementary and secondary education, in particular, often exceed the gains from more conventional investments. In developing countries, people having an extra year in school can often raise their wages by 15% to 20% a year.

Interestingly, the return from educating women in developing countries is often higher than the return for men. This is particularly true in the poorest countries, where female literacy rates are often less than 10%. Women's health in developing countries is closely tied to their education, too. Education promotes not only their productivity but their overall development as well. For these reasons, the World Bank has focused attention on the crucial role that increased female education can play in promoting economic development.

As you see, human capital analysis is a valuable tool for understanding economic growth.

New Growth Theory

For many years, economists who studied technological progress typically did so independently of economists who studied models of economic growth. But starting in the mid-1980s, several economists, including Nobel laureate Robert E. Lucas of the University of Chicago and Paul Romer, now of Stanford University, began to develop models of growth that contained technological progress as essential features. Their work helped to initiate what is known as **new growth theory**, which accounts for technological progress within a model of economic growth.

In this field, economists study, for example, how incentives for research and development, new product development, or international trade interact with the accumulation of physical capital. It enables economists to address policy issues, such as whether subsidies for research and development are socially justified and whether policies that place fewer taxes on income earned from investment will spur economic growth or increase economic welfare. Current research in economic growth now takes place within a broad framework that includes explanation of technological progress. As an example, new growth theory suggests that investment in comprehensive education in a developing country will lead to permanent increases in the rate of technological progress as the workforce will be better able to incorporate new ideas and technologies into the workplace.

All growth theory today is "new growth theory."

New growth theory
Modern theories of growth that try to explain the origins of technological progress.

TEST Your Understanding

9. Technological progress means that we produce more output without using any additional inputs. True or false? Explain.
10. Explain how economists estimate the contribution of technological change to the growth of output.
11. Who invented the theory of creative destruction?
12. Define human capital.

USING THE TOOLS

In this chapter, we studied what affects economic growth. Here are some opportunities to do your own economic analysis.

1. Shorten the Length of Patents?

A group of consumer activists claim that drug companies earn excessive profits because of the patents they have on drugs. The activists advocate cutting to five years the length of time that a drug company can hold a patent. They argue this will lead to lower prices for drugs because competitors will enter the market after the five-year period. Do you see any drawbacks to this proposal?

2. Capital Deepening

Which of the following will promote economic growth through capital deepening?
a. Higher taxes used to finance universal health care

b. Increased imports to purchase new VCRs for consumers
c. Increased imports to purchase supercomputers for industry

3. Future Generations

Some economists say that economic growth involves a trade-off between current generations and future generations. If a current generation raises its saving rate, what does it sacrifice? What will be gained for future generations?

4. Will the Poorer Country Catch Up?

Suppose one country has a GDP that is one-eighth the GDP of its richer neighbor. But the poorer country grows at 10% a year, while the richer country grows at 2% a year. In 35 years, which country will have a higher GDP? (*Hint:* Use the rule of 70.)

SUMMARY

In this chapter, we explored the mechanisms of economic growth. Although economists do not have a complete understanding of what leads to growth, they regard increases in capital per worker, technological progress, human capital, and governmental institutions as key factors. In this chapter, we discussed these factors in detail. Here are the main points to remember:

1 There are vast differences in per capita GDP throughout the world. There is debate about whether poorer countries in the world are converging in per capita incomes to richer countries.

2 Economies grow through two basic mechanisms: capital deepening and technological progress. Capital deepening is an increase in capital per worker. Technological progress is an increase in output with no additional increases in inputs.

3 Ongoing technological progress will lead to sustained economic growth.

4 A variety of theories try to explain the origins of technological progress and determine how we can promote it. They include spending on research and development, creative destruction, the scale of the market, induced inventions, and education and the accumulation of knowledge.

5 Governments can play a key role in designing institutions that promote economic growth.

6 Investments in human capital are a key component of economic growth.

KEY TERMS

capital deepening, 491
convergence, 495
creative destruction, 507
growth accounting, 502

growth rate, 492
human capital, 491
labor productivity, 503
new growth theory, 511

real GDP per capita, 492
rule of 70, 493
saving, 497
technological progress, 491

PROBLEMS AND DISCUSSION QUESTIONS

1 If a country's GDP grows at 3% per year, how many years will it take for GDP to increase by a factor of four?

2 The growth rate of real GDP per capita equals the growth rate of real GDP minus the growth rate of the population. If the growth rate of the population is 1% per year, how fast must real GDP grow for real GDP per capita to double in 14 years?

3 Does economic growth automatically lead to increased inequality?

4 Explain why the expansion of markets from free trade can lead to increased technological innovation.

5 If we cannot measure every invention or new idea, how can we possibly measure the contribution to growth of technological progress?

6 Even with a high saving rate, there is a natural limit to capital deepening. Why is there a limit?

7 Suppose a government places a 10% tax on incomes and spends half of the money from taxes on investment and half on a public consumption good such as military parades. Individuals save 20% of their income and consume the rest. Does total investment (public and private) increase or decrease in this case?

8 The United States ran large trade deficits during the 1980s and 1990s. How would you determine whether these trade deficits led to increased or decreased capital deepening?

9 Economic historians have found that the average height of individuals in both the United States and the United Kingdom fell during the mid-nineteenth century before rising again. This was a period of rapid industrialization as well as migration into urban areas and foreign immigration. Incomes appeared to continue to rise. What factors do you think might account for this fall in height and how would it affect your evaluation of economic welfare during the period?

10 Most law students tend to be in their twenties and thirties, rather than in their forties. Explain this phenomenon, using the idea of investment in human capital.

11 Web Exercise. The Website for the National Bureau of Economic Research (*http://www.nber.org*) contains links to online data, including the Penn World Tables. Using these links, compare the relative growth performance for real GDP of Italy, Great Britain, and France (or other countries) over a period of your choice.

12 Web Exercise. Using the Website for the World Bank (*http://www.worldbank.org*), prepare a short paper on prospects and barriers for economic growth in Africa.

MODEL ANSWERS TO QUESTIONS

Chapter-Opening Questions

1 Countries with the highest standard of living today include the United States, Luxembourg, Japan, and Germany.

2 Countries with higher saving rates can grow faster for some period of time, although the growth of per capita income in the long run is determined by the rate of technological progress.

3 A trade deficit that is used to finance investment can lead to higher growth; however, a trade deficit that is used to finance consumption will allow higher consumption now but will reduce consumption in the future.

4 Technological progress depends on a number of factors, including research and development, the process of creative destruction, the scale of the market, induced innovations, and education and the accumulation of knowledge.

Test Your Understanding

1 We use per capita real GDP.

2 Nontraded goods are relatively cheaper in poor countries.

3 True. Developing countries have not caught up to developed countries.

4 It would take 35 years (70/2).

5 Output is divided into consumption and investment. Output also equals income. Income is either consumed or saved. Therefore, saving must equal investment.

6 Total output increases, while per capita output falls.

7 $180. Government investment is $200, but with a saving rate of 10%, the $200 in taxes reduces private saving (and private investment) by $20.

8 True. Without using the trade deficit to increase investment, consumption must fall in the future.

9 True. Technological progress means more output without additional inputs.

10 The contribution from technological progress is estimated by determining how much of the growth in output cannot be explained by the growth in inputs.

11 Joseph Schumpeter.

12 Human capital includes investments in education and skills.

NOTES

1. Stanley Lebergott, *The Americans* (New York: W.W. Norton, 1984), pp. 65–68.
2. Stanley Fischer, "Globalization and Its Challenges," *American Economic Review Papers and Proceedings*, vol. 93, no.2, May 2003.
3. Alwyn Young, "A Tale of Two Cities: Factor Accumulation and Technical Change in Hong Kong and Singapore," in

NBER Macroeconomic Annual 1992, edited by Olivier Blanchard and Stanley Fischer (Cambridge, MA: MIT Press, 1992), pp. 1–53.
4. William Easterly, *The Elusive Quest for Growth: Economists Adventures and Misadventures in the Tropics* (Cambridge, MA: MIT Press, 2002).

APPENDIX

A Model of Capital Deepening

Here's a simple model showing the links among saving, depreciation, and capital deepening. Developed by Nobel laureate Robert Solow of the Massachusetts Institute of Technology, the Solow model will help us understand more fully the critical role technological progress must play in economic growth. In using it, we rely on one of our basic principles of economics to help explain the model as well as make a few simplifying assumptions. We assume constant population and no government or foreign sector. In the chapter we discussed the qualitative effects of population growth, government, and the foreign sector on capital deepening. Here we focus solely on the relationships among saving, depreciation, and capital deepening.

Figure 22A.1 plots the relationship in the economy between output and the stock of capital, holding the labor force constant. Notice that output increases as the stock of capital increases but at a decreasing rate. This is an illustration of the principle of diminishing returns.

Principle OF DIMINISHING RETURNS

Suppose output is produced with two or more inputs and we increase one input while holding the other inputs fixed. Beyond some point—called the point of diminishing returns—output will increase at a decreasing rate.

Increasing the stock of capital while holding the labor force constant will increase output, but at a decreasing rate.

As Figure 22A.1 indicates, output increases with the stock of capital. But what causes the stock of capital to increase? The capital stock will increase as long as gross investment exceeds depreciation. Therefore, we need to determine the level of gross investment and the level of depreciation to see how the capital stock changes over time.

Recall that without government or a foreign sector, saving equals gross investment. Thus, to determine the level of investment, we need to specify how much of output is saved and how much is consumed. We will assume that a fraction s of total

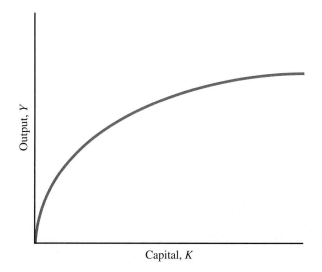

FIGURE 22A.1

Diminishing Returns to Capital
Holding labor constant, increases in the stock of capital increases output but at a decreasing rate.

output (Y) is saved. For example, if $s = 0.20$, then 20% of GDP would be saved and 80% would be consumed. Total saving will be sY, the product of the saving rate and total output.

In Panel A of Figure 22A.2, the top curve is total output as a function of the stock of capital. The curve below it represents saving as a function of the stock of capital. Because saving is a fixed fraction of total output, the saving curve is a constant fraction of the output curve. If the saving rate is 0.2, saving will always be 20% of output for any level of the capital stock. Total saving increases in the economy with the stock of capital, but at a decreasing rate.

To complete our model, we need to determine depreciation. Let's say the capital stock depreciates at a constant rate of d per year. If $d = 0.03$, the capital stock would depreciate at 3% a year. If the capital stock were 100 at the beginning of the year, depreciation would equal 3. Total depreciation can be written as dK, where K is the stock of capital.

Panel B of Figure 22A.2 plots total depreciation as a function of the stock of capital. The larger the stock of capital, the more total depreciation there will be. Because the depreciation rate is assumed to be constant, total depreciation as a function of the stock of capital will be a straight line through the origin. Then if there is no capital, there will be no depreciation, no matter what the depreciation rate.

If the depreciation rate is 3% and the stock of capital is 100, depreciation will be 3; if the stock of capital is 200, the depreciation rate will be 6. Plotting these points will give a straight line through the origin.

We are now ready to see how the stock of capital changes:

$$\text{change in the stock of capital} = \text{savings} - \text{depreciation}$$
$$= sY - dK$$

The stock of capital will increase—the change will be positive—as long as total saving in the economy exceeds depreciation.

Figure 22A.3 shows how the Solow model works by plotting output, saving, and depreciation all on one graph. Suppose the economy starts with a capital stock K_0. Then total saving will be given by point a on the saving schedule. Depreciation at the

---

FIGURE 22A.2

**Saving and
Depreciation as
Functions of the Stock
of Capital**

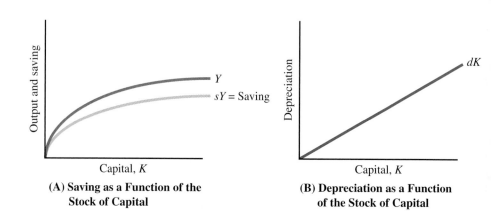

**(A) Saving as a Function of the
Stock of Capital**

**(B) Depreciation as a Function
of the Stock of Capital**

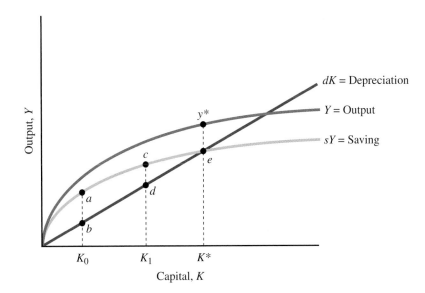

FIGURE 22A.3
Basic Growth Model
Starting at K_0, saving
exceeds depreciation. The
stock of capital increases.
This process continues until
the stock of capital reaches
its long-run equilibrium
at K^*.

capital stock K_0 is given by point b. Because a lies above b, total saving exceeds depreciation and the capital stock will increase. As the capital stock increases, there will be economic growth through capital deepening. With more capital per worker in the economy, output is higher and real wages increase. The economy benefits from the additional stock of capital.

Using the diagram, we can trace the future for this economy. As the stock of capital increases, we move to the right. When the economy reaches K_1, total saving is at point c and total depreciation is at point d. Because c is still higher than d, saving exceeds depreciation and the capital stock continues to increase. Economic growth continues. Eventually, after many years, the economy reaches capital stock K^*. The level of output in the economy now is Y^*, and the saving and depreciation schedules intersect at point e. Because total saving equals depreciation, the stock of capital no longer increases. The process of economic growth through capital deepening has stopped.

In this simple model, the process of capital deepening must eventually come to an end. As the stock of capital increases, output increases but at a decreasing rate because of diminishing returns. Because saving is a fixed fraction of output, it will also increase but also at a diminishing rate. On the other hand, total depreciation is proportional to the stock of capital. As the stock of capital increases, depreciation will always catch up with total saving in the economy. It may take decades for the process of capital deepening to come to an end. But as long as total saving exceeds depreciation, the process of economic growth through capital deepening will continue.

What would happen if a society saved a higher fraction of its output? Figure 22A.4 shows the consequences of a higher saving rate. Suppose the economy were originally saving at a rate s_1. Eventually, the economy would reach e_1, where saving and depreciation meet. If the economy had started to save at the higher rate s_2, saving would exceed depreciation at K_1 and the capital stock would increase until the economy reached K_2. At K_2 the saving line again crosses the line representing depreciation.

FIGURE 22A.4

Increase in the Saving Rate

A higher saving rate will lead to a higher stock of capital in the long run. Starting from an initial capital stock of K_1, the increase in the saving rate leads the economy to K_2.

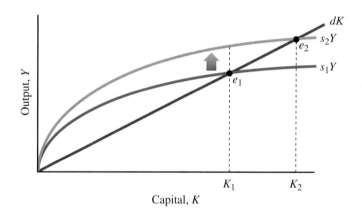

Output is higher than it was initially, but the process of capital deepening stops at this higher level of output.

If there is ongoing technological progress, economic growth can continue. If technological progress raises GDP, saving will increase as well, because saving increases with GDP. This will lead to a higher stock of capital. In Figure 22A.5 technological progress is depicted as an upward shift of the saving function. The saving function shifts up because saving is a fixed fraction of output and we have assumed that technological progress has raised the level of output.

With a higher level of saving, the stock of capital will increase. If the stock of capital were originally at K_0, the upward shift in the saving schedule will lead to increases in the stock of capital to K_1. If there are further gains in technological process, capital deepening will continue.

FIGURE 22A.5

Techonological Progress and Growth

Technological progress shifts up the saving schedule and promotes capital deepening.

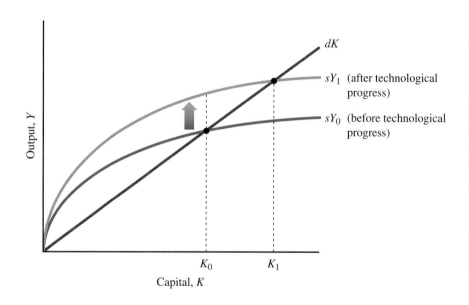

Technological progress conveys a double benefit to a society. Not only does the increased efficiency directly raise per capita output, it also leads to additional capital deepening. Therefore, output increases for two reasons.

Let's summarize the basic points of the Solow model:

1 Capital deepening, an increase in the stock of capital per worker, will occur as long as total saving exceeds depreciation. As capital deepening occurs, there will be economic growth and increased real wages.

2 Eventually, the process of capital deepening will come to a halt as depreciation catches up with total saving.

3 A higher saving rate will promote capital deepening. If a country saves more, it will have a higher output. But eventually, the process of economic growth through capital deepening alone comes to an end, even though this may take decades to occur.

4 Technological progress not only directly raises output but allows capital deepening to continue.

It is possible to relax our assumptions and allow for population growth, government taxes and spending, and the foreign sector. In more advanced courses, these issues are treated in detail, but the underlying message is the same. There is a natural limit to economic growth through capital deepening. Technological progress is required to ensure that per capita incomes grow over time.

TEST Your Understanding

1. What two factors determine how the stock of capital changes over time?
2. Why does capital deepening come to an end?
3. Does a higher saving rate lead to a permanently higher rate of growth?

USING THE TOOLS

1. Germany and Japan After World War II

Much of the stock of capital in the economies of Japan and Germany was destroyed during World War II. Both economies had high saving rates after the war ended. Use the Solow model to explain why after the war growth in the economies was higher than that in the United States.

2. Faster Depreciation

Suppose a society switches to equipment that depreciates rapidly. Use the Solow model to show what will happen to the stock of capital and output if the rate of depreciation increases.

MODEL ANSWERS FOR THE APPENDIX

Test Your Understanding

1 The factors are gross investment and depreciation.

2 Depreciation eventually catches up with saving.

3 No. A higher saving rate will raise the level of output, but eventually, capital deepening and economic growth comes to an end.

Part

8

Economic Fluctuations and Fiscal Policy

Aggregate Demand and Aggregate Supply

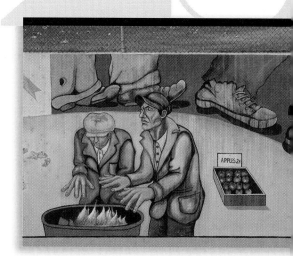

s we explained in previous chapters, recessions occur when output fails to grow and unemployment rises. But *why* do they occur?

In a sense, recessions are massive failures in social coordination. For example, during the Great Depression in the 1930s, nearly one-fourth of the U.S. labor force was unemployed. Unemployed workers could not afford to buy goods and services. Factories had to be shut down because there was little or no demand. As these factories closed, even more workers became unemployed, fueling additional factory shutdowns. This vicious cycle caused the U.S. economy to spiral downward. Similar failures in coordination were happening throughout the world. The worldwide depression continued through the 1930s. How could this destructive chain of events have been halted?

conomies do not always operate at full employment, nor do they always grow smoothly. At times, real GDP grows below its potential or falls steeply, as it did in the Great Depression. Recessions and excess unemployment occur when real GDP falls. At other times, GDP grows too rapidly, and unemployment falls below its natural rate.

"Too slow" or "too fast" real GDP growth are examples of **economic fluctuations**—movements of GDP away from potential output. Economic fluctuations, also called business cycles, are the subject of this part of the book.

After studying this chapter, you will be able to answer the following questions:

1 Why doesn't the economy always operate at full employment?
2 Why can a sharp decrease in government spending cause a recession?
3 Why can a sharp increase in oil prices plunge an economy into a recession?
4 How do changes in the demand for goods and services affect prices and output in the short run and in the long run?

During the Great Depression, there was a failure in coordination. Factories would have produced more output and hired more workers if there had been more demand for their products. Insufficient demand for goods and services was a key problem of the Great Depression, identified by British economist John Maynard Keynes in the 1930s. Following Keynes's work, economists began to distinguish between real GDP in the long run, when prices have time to fully adjust to changes in demand, and real GDP in the short run, when prices don't yet have time to fully adjust to changes in demand. It is during the short run that economic coordination problems are most pronounced. In the long run, however, economists believe the economy will return to full employment, although economic policy may assist it in getting there more quickly.

In the last two chapters, we analyzed the economy at full employment and studied economic growth. Those chapters provided the framework for analyzing the behavior of the economy in the long run, but not in the short run when there can be sharp fluctuations in output. We therefore need to develop an additional set of tools to analyze both.

Sticky Prices and Their Macroeconomic Consequences

Why do recessions occur? In Chapter 21, we discussed how real, adverse shocks to the economy could cause economic downturns. We also outlined the theory of real business cycles, which focuses on how shocks to technology cause economic fluctuations. Now we examine another approach to understanding economic fluctuations.

Economic fluctuation
Movements of GDP above or below normal trends.

Led by Keynes, many economists since his time have focused attention on economic coordination problems. Normally, the price system efficiently coordinates what goes on in an economy—even in a complex economy. The price system provides signals as to who buys what, how much to produce, what resources to use, from whom to buy and so on. For example, if consumers decide to consume fresh fruit in lieu of chocolate, the price of fresh fruit will rise and the price of chocolate will fall. More fresh fruit and less chocolate will be produced on the basis of these price signals. On a day-to-day basis, the price system works silently in the background, matching the desires of consumers with the output from producers.

But the price system does not always work instantaneously. If prices are slow to adjust, then the proper signals are not given quickly enough to producers and consumers to bring them together. Demands and supplies will not be brought immediately into equilibrium, and coordination can break down.

In modern economies, some prices are very flexible, whereas others are not. In the 1970s, U.S. economist Arthur Okun distinguished between *auction prices*, prices that adjust on a nearly daily basis, and *custom prices*, prices that adjust slowly. Prices for fresh fish, vegetables, and other food products are examples of auction prices—they typically are very flexible and adjust rapidly. Prices for industrial commodities such as steel rods or machine tools are custom prices and tend to adjust slowly to changes in demand. As shorthand, economists often refer to slowly adjusting prices as "sticky prices" (just like a door that won't open immediately but sometimes gets stuck).

Steel rods and machine tools are input prices. Like other input prices, the price of labor also adjusts very slowly. Workers often have long-term contracts that do not allow employers to change wages at all during a given year. Union workers, university professors, high-school teachers, and employees of state and local governments are all groups whose wages adjust very slowly. As a general rule, there are very few workers in the economy whose wages change quickly. Perhaps movie stars, athletes, and rock stars are the exceptions; their wages rise and fall with their popularity. But they are far from the typical worker in the economy. Even unskilled, low-wage workers are often protected from a decrease in their wages by minimum-wage laws.

For most firms, the biggest cost of doing business is wages. If wages are sticky, firms' overall costs will be sticky as well. This means that firms' product prices will remain sticky, too. Sticky wages cause sticky prices and hamper the economy's ability to bring demand and supply into balance in the short run.

Prices of some commodities, like oranges, adjust quickly, but wages adjust more slowly to economic conditions.

Typically, firms that supply intermediate goods such as steel rods or other inputs et demand—not price—determine the level of output in the short run. To understand his idea, consider an automobile firm that buys material from a steelmaker on a regular basis. Because the auto firm and the steel producer have been in business with one nother for a long time and have an ongoing relationship, they have negotiated a contract that keeps steel prices fixed in the short run.

But suppose that the automobile company's cars suddenly become very popular. The firm needs to expand production, so it needs more steel. Under the agreement made earlier by the two firms, the steel company would meet this higher demand and ell more steel—without raising its price—to the automobile company. As a result, the production of steel is totally determined in the short run by the demand from automobile producers, not by price.

But, what if the firm discovered that it had produced an unpopular car and needed to cut back on its planned production? The firm would require less steel. Under the greement, the steelmaker would supply less steel but not reduce its price. Again, demand, not price, determines steel production in the short run.

Similar agreements between firms, both formal and informal, exist throughout the economy. Typically, in the short run, firms will meet changes in the demand for their products by adjusting production with only small changes in the prices they charge their customers.

What we have just illustrated for an input such as steel applies in the same way to workers, who are also "inputs" to production. Suppose that the automobile firm hires union workers under a contract that fixes their wages for a specific period. If the economy suddenly thrives at some point during that period, the automobile company will employ all the workers and perhaps require some to work overtime. If the economy stagnates at some point during that period, the firm will lay off some workers, using only part of the union labor force. In either case, wages will not change during the period of the contract.

Over longer periods of time, prices do change. Suppose the automobile company's car remains popular for a long time. The steel company and the automobile company will adjust the price of steel on their contract to reflect this increased demand. These price adjustments only occur over long periods; in the short run, demand, not prices, determines output, and prices are slow to adjust.

To summarize, the **short run in macroeconomics** is the period in which prices don't change or don't change very much. In the macroeconomic short run, both formal and informal contracts between firms mean that changes in demand will be reflected primarily in changes in output, not prices.

Short run in macroeconomics
The period of time that prices do not change very much.

Understanding Aggregate Demand

In this section, we develop a graphical tool known as the aggregate demand curve. Later in the chapter we will develop the aggregate supply curve. Together the aggregate demand and aggregate supply curves will enable us to study how output and prices are determined in both the short run and in the long run. They will also provide a framework in which we can study the role the government can play in stabilizing th economy through its spending, tax, and money creation policies.

What Is the Aggregate Demand Curve?

Aggregate demand is the total demand for goods and services in an entire economy. I other words, it is the demand for currently produced GDP by consumers, firms, th government, and the foreign sector. It is a macroeconomic concept, because it refers t the economy as a whole, not individual goods or markets.

Aggregate demand curve
The relationship between the level of prices and the quantity of real GDP demanded.

The **aggregate demand curve** plots the total demand for GDP as a function o the price level. (Recall that the price level is the average level of prices in the economy as measured by a price index.) An aggregate demand curve is show in Figure 23.1. A each price level, shown on the y axis, we ask what the total quantity demanded will b for all goods and services in the economy, shown on the x axis. In Figure 23.1, th aggregate demand curve is downward sloping. As the price level falls, the total quantit demanded for goods and services increases. To understand what the aggregate demand curve represents, we must first learn the components of aggregate demand, why th curve for it slopes downward, and the factors that can shift it.

The Components of Aggregate Demand

In our study of GDP accounting, we divided GDP into four components: consumption spending (C), investment spending (I), government purchases (G), and net export (NX). These four components are also the four parts of aggregate demand because th aggregate demand curve really just describes the demand for total GDP at differen price levels. As we will see, changes in demand coming from any of these four sources C, I, G, or NX will shift the aggregate demand curve.

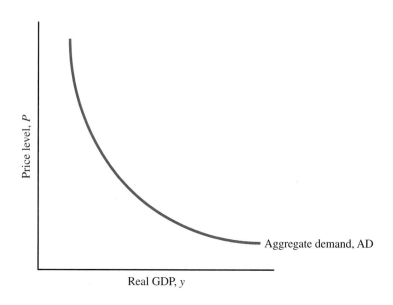

FIGURE 23.1

Aggregate Demand
The aggregate demand curve plots the total demand for real GDP as a function of the price level. The aggregate demand curve slopes downward, indicating that aggregate demand increases as the price level in the economy falls.

Why the Aggregate Demand Curve Slopes Downward

To understand the slope of the aggregate demand curve, we need to consider the effects of a change in the overall price level in the economy. First, let's consider the supply of money in the economy. We discuss the supply of money in detail in later chapters, but for now, just think of the supply of money as being the total amount of currency (cash plus coins) held by the public and the value of all deposits in savings and checking accounts. As the price level or average level of prices in the economy changes, so does the purchasing power of your money. This is an example of the real-nominal principle:

REAL-NOMINAL *Principle*

What matters to people is the real value or purchasing power of money or income, not the face value of money or income.

The change in the purchasing power of money will affect aggregate demand—the total demand for all goods and all services in the economy. As the price level falls, the purchasing power of money increases. When this happens, people holding money find they are better off, or wealthier, and are more willing to spend money on additional goods and services than they had before.

The increase in spending that occurs because the real value of money increases when the price level falls is known as the **wealth effect**. This is one reason the aggregate demand curve slopes downward. Lower prices lead to higher levels of wealth, and higher levels of wealth increase spending on total goods and services. Conversely, when the price level rises, the real value of money decreases, reducing people's wealth and their total demand for goods and services in the economy. When this happens, consumers can't simply substitute one good for another that's cheaper because at a higher price level, *everything* is more expensive.

In addition to the wealth effect, there are two other reasons why the aggregate demand curve is downward sloping: One has to do with interest rates, and the other has to do with international trade.

First, consider the interest rate effect. With a given supply of money in the economy, a lower price level will lead to lower interest rates. With lower interest rates, both consumers and firms will find it cheaper to borrow money in order to make purchases. As a consequence, the demand for goods in the economy (consumer durables purchased by households and investment goods purchased by firms) will increase. (We'll explain the effects of interest rates in more detail in later chapters.)

Second, consider the effects from international trade. In an open economy, a lower price level will mean that domestic goods (goods produced in the home country) become cheaper relative to foreign goods, so the demand for domestic goods will increase. For example, if the price level in the United States falls, it will make U.S. goods cheaper relative to foreign goods. If U.S. goods become cheaper than foreign goods, exports from the United States will increase and imports will decrease. Thus, net exports—a component of demand—will increase.

Wealth effect

The increase in spending that occurs because the real value of money increases when the price level falls.

The wealth effect, the interest rate effect, and the effects from international trade reinforce one another, leading to the downward-sloping aggregate demand curve in Figure 23.1.

Shifts in the Aggregate Demand Curve

Different factors can shift the aggregate demand curve. An increase in aggregate demand means that total demand for all the goods and services contained in real GDP has increased—even though the price level hasn't changed. In other words, increases in aggregate demand shift the curve to the right. Conversely, factors that decrease aggregate demand shift the curve to the left—even though the price level hasn't changed.

Let's look at the key factors that cause these shifts:

1. Changes in the Supply of Money

An increase in the supply of money in the economy will increase aggregate demand and shift the aggregate demand curve to the right. We know that an increase in the supply of money will lead to higher demand by both consumers and firms. At any given price level, a higher supply of money will mean more consumer wealth and an increased demand for goods and services. A decrease in the supply of money will decrease aggregate demand and shift the aggregate demand curve to the left. (We will discuss the money supply and aggregate demand further in later chapters.)

2. Changes in Taxes

A decrease in taxes will increase aggregate demand and shift the aggregate demand curve to the right. Lower taxes will increase the income available to households and increase their spending on goods and services—even though the price level in the economy hasn't changed. For opposite reasons, increases in taxes will decrease aggregate demand and shift the aggregate demand curve to the left. (We will discuss taxes and aggregate demand further in the next chapter.)

3. Changes in Government Spending

At any given price level, an increase in government spending will increase aggregate demand and shift the aggregate demand curve to the right. Because the government is a source of demand for goods and services, higher government spending naturally leads to an increase in total demand for goods and services. Similarly, decreases in government spending will decrease aggregate demand and shift the curve to the left. (We will discuss government spending and aggregate demand further in the next chapter.)

4. Other Factors

Any change in demand from households, firms, or the foreign sector will also change aggregate demand. For example, if the Japanese economy expands very rapidly, and Japanese citizens buy more U.S. goods, U.S. aggregate demand will increase. Or, if households decide they want to spend more, consumption will increase and aggregate demand will increase. Expectations about the future also matter. For example, if firms become optimistic about the future and increase their investment spending, aggregate demand will also increase. On the other hand, if they become pessimistic, they will cut their investment spending and aggregate demand will fall.

When we discuss factors that shift aggregate demand, we must not include any changes in the demand for goods and services that arise from movements in the price

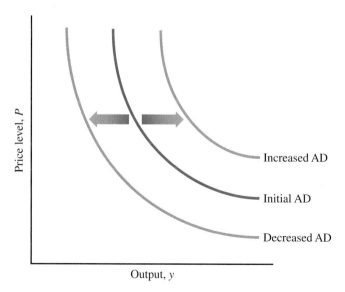

FIGURE 23.2

Shifting Aggregate Demand
Decreases in taxes, increases in government spending, and an increase in the supply of money all shift the aggregate demand curve to the right. Higher taxes, lower government spending, and a lower supply of money shift the curve to the left.

evel. Changes in aggregate demand that accompany changes in the price level are already included in the curve and do not shift the curve. The increase in consumer spending that occurs when the price level falls from the wealth effect, the interest rate effect, and international trade effect are in the curve and do not shift the curve.

Both Figure 23.2 and Table 23.1 summarize our discussion. Decreases in taxes, increases in government spending, and increases in the supply of money all shift the aggregate demand curve to the right. Increases in taxes, decreases in government spending, and decreases in the supply of money shift it to the left. In general, any increase in demand (not brought about by a change in the price level) will shift the curve to the right. Decreases in demand shift it to the left.

How the Multiplier Makes the Shift Bigger

Let's take a closer look at the shift in the aggregate demand curve and see how far changes really make it shift. Suppose that the government increases its spending on goods and services by $10 billion. You might think that the aggregate demand curve would shift to the right by $10 billion, reflecting the increase in demand for these goods and services. Initially, the shift will be precisely $10 billion. In Figure 23.3, this is depicted by the shift (at a given price level) from *a* to *b*. But after a brief period of time, total aggregate demand will increase by *more* than $10 billion. In Figure 23.3, the total shift in the aggregate demand curve is shown by the larger movement from *a* to *c*. The ratio of the total shift in aggregate demand to the initial shift in aggregate demand is known as the **multiplier**.

Multiplier
The ratio of the total shift in aggregate demand to the initial shift in aggregate demand.

Factors That Increase Aggregate Demand	Factors That Decrease Aggregate Demand
Decrease in taxes	Increase in taxes
Increase in government spending	Decrease in government spending
Increase in money supply	Decrease in money supply

TABLE 23.1

Factors That Shift Demand

FIGURE 23.3

The Multiplier
Initially, an increase in desired spending will shift the aggregate demand curve horizontally to the right from *a* to *b*. The total shift from *a* to *c* will be larger. The ratio of the total shift to the initial shift is known as the multiplier.

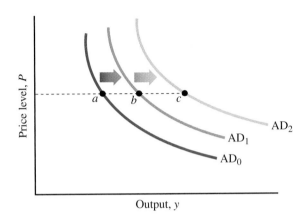

Why does the aggregate demand curve shift more than the initial increase in desired spending? The logic goes back to the ideas of economist John Maynard Keynes. Here's how it works: Keynes believed that as government spending increases and the aggregate demand curves shifts to the right, output will subsequently increase too. As we saw with the circular flow, increased output also means increased income for households, as firms pay households for their labor and for supplying other factors of production. Typically, households will wish to spend, or consume, part of that income, which will further increase aggregate demand. It is this additional spending by consumers, over and above what the government has already spent, that causes the further shift in the aggregate demand curve.

The basic idea of how the multiplier works in an economy is simple. Let's say that the government invests $10 million to construct a new plant. Initially, total spending in the economy increases by this $10 million paid to a private construction firm. The construction workers and owners of the firm then spend part of this $10 million in income they are paid. Suppose the owners and workers spend $6 million of it on new cars. To meet the increased demand for new cars, automobile producers will expand their production and earn an additional $6 million in wages and profits. They, in turn, will spend part of this additional income—let's say, $3.6 million—on televisions. The workers and owners who produce televisions will then spend part of the $3.6 million they earn, and so on, and so on.

To take a closer look at this process, we first need to look more carefully at the behavior of consumers and how their behavior helps to determine the level of aggregate demand. Economists have found that consumer spending depends on the level of income in the economy. When consumers have more income, they want to purchase more goods and services. The relationship between consumer spending and income is known as the **consumption function**:

Consumption function
The relationship between the level of income and consumption spending.

$$C = C_a + by$$

where consumption spending C has two parts. The first part, C_a, is a constant and is independent of income. Economists call this **autonomous consumption spending**

Autonomous consumption spending
The part of consumption that does not depend on income.

Autonomous spending is spending that does not depend on the level of income. For example, all consumers, regardless of their current income, will have to purchase some food. The second part, *by*, represents the part of consumption that is dependent on income. It is the product of a fraction *b*, called the **marginal propensity to consume (MPC)**, and the level of income, or *y*, in the economy. The MPC (or *b* in our formula) tells us how much consumption spending will increase for every dollar that income increases. For example, if *b* = 0.6, then for every $1 that income increases, consumption increases by $0.60.

Here is another way to think of the MPC: If a household receives some additional income, it will increase its consumption by some additional amount. The MPC is defined as the ratio of additional consumption to additional income, or

$$\text{MPC} = \text{additional consumption/additional income}$$

For example, if the household receives an additional $100 and consumes an additional $70, the MPC will be $70/$100, or 0.7.

Now we are in a better position to understand the multiplier. Suppose the government increases its purchases of goods and services by $10 million. This will initially raise aggregate demand and income by $10 million. But since income has risen by $10 million, consumers will now wish to increase their spending by an amount equal to the marginal propensity to consume multiplied by the $10 million. (Remember: the MPC tells us how much consumption spending will increase for every dollar that income increases.) If the MPC were 0.6, then consumer spending would increase by $6 million when the government spends $10 million. Thus, the aggregate demand curve would continue to shift to the right by another $6 million in addition to the original $10 million, for a total of $16 million.

But the process does not end here. As aggregate demand increases by $6 million, income will also increase by $6 million. Consumers will then wish to increase their spending by the MPC × $6 million or, in our example, by $3.6 million (0.6 × $6 million). The aggregate demand curve will continue to shift to the right, now by *another* $3.6 million. Adding $3.6 million to $16 million gives us a new aggregate demand total of $19.6 million. As you can see, this process will continue, as consumers now have an additional $3.6 million in income, part of which they will spend again. Where will it end?

Table 23.2 shows how the multiplier works in detail. In the first round, there is an initial increase in government spending of $10 million. This additional demand leads to an initial increase in GDP and income of $10 million. Assuming that the MPC is 0.6, the $10 million of additional income will increase consumer spending by $6 million.

Marginal propensity to consume (MPC)

The fraction of additional income that is spent.

Round of Spending	Increase in Aggregate Demand	Increase in GDP and Income	Increase in Consumption
1	$10	$10	$6
2	6	6	3.6
3	3.6	3.6	2.16
4	2.16	2.16	1.296
.	.	.	.
.	.	.	.
.	.	.	.
Total	$25	$25	$15

TABLE 23.2

The Multiplier in Action
The initial $10 million increase in aggregate demand, will, through all the rounds of spending, eventually lead to a $25 million increase.

Round 2 begins with this $6 million increase in consumer spending. Because of this increase in demand, GDP and income increase by $6 million. At the end of round 2, consumers will have an additional $6 million; with a MPC of 0.6, consumer spending will therefore increase by 0.6 × $6 million, or $3.6 million. The process continues in round 3 with an increase in consumer spending of $2.16 million. It continues, in diminishing amounts, through subsequent rounds. If we add up the spending in all the (infinite) rounds, we will find that the initial $10 million of spending leads to a $25 million increase in GDP and income. That's 2.5 times what the government initially spent. So in this case, the multiplier is 2.5.

Instead of calculating spending round by round, we can use a simple formula to figure out what the multiplier is. It is as follows:

$$\text{multiplier} = 1/(1 - \text{MPC})$$

Thus, in the preceding example, when the MPC is 0.6, the multiplier would be $1/(1 - 0.6)$, or 2.5.

Now you should clearly understand why the total shift in the aggregate demand curve from *a* to *c* in Figure 23.3 is greater than the initial shift in the curve from *a* to *b*. This is the multiplier in action. The multiplier is important because it means that relatively small changes in spending could lead to relatively large changes in output. For example, if firms cut back on their investment spending, the effects on output would be "multiplied" and this decrease in spending could have a large, adverse impact on the economy.

In practice, once we take into account other realistic factors such as taxes and indirect effects through financial markets, the multipliers are smaller than our previous examples, typically, near 1.5 for the U.S economy. This means that a $10 million increase in one component of spending will shift the U.S. aggregate demand curve by approximately $15 million. Knowing the value of the multiplier is important for two reasons. First, it tells us how much shocks to aggregate demand are "amplified." Second, to design effective economic policies to shift the aggregate demand curve, we need to know the value of the multiplier to measure the proper "dose" for policy. In the next chapter, we present a more detailed model of aggregate demand and explain the role for economic policy.

TEST Your Understanding

1. What are the four components of aggregate demand?
2. A decrease in the price level will increase aggregate demand through three channels: the _____ effect, the interest rate effect, and the effects through international trade.
3. A decrease in taxes will shift the aggregate demand curve to the _____.
4. If the MPC is 0.6, the simple multiplier will be _____.
5. Because of other economic factors like taxes, the multiplier in the United States is _____ (larger/smaller) than 2.5.

Understanding Aggregate Supply

Now we turn to the supply side of our model. The **aggregate supply curve** depicts the relationship between the level of prices and the total quantity of final goods and services that firms are willing and able to supply. The aggregate supply curve will complete our macroeconomic picture, uniting the economy's demand for real output with the firm's willingness to supply output. To determine both the price level and real GDP, we need to combine *both* aggregate demand and aggregate supply. One slight complication is that since prices are "sticky" in the short run, we need to develop two different aggregate supply curves, one corresponding to the long run and one to the short run.

Aggregate supply curve

The relationship between the level of prices and the quantity of output supplied.

The Long-Run Aggregate Supply Curve

First we'll consider the aggregate supply curve for the long run, that is, when the economy is at full employment; it is also called the **long-run** aggregate supply curve. In previous chapters, we saw that the level of full-employment output, y^*, depends solely on the supply of factors—capital, labor—and the state of technology. These are the fundamental factors that determine output in the long run, that is, when the economy operates at full employment.

In the long run, the economy operates at full employment and changes in the price level do not affect this. To illustrate why this is so, imagine that the price level in the economy increases by 50%. That means firms' prices, on average, will also increase by

Long-run aggregate supply curve

A vertical aggregate supply curve. It reflects the idea that in the long run, output is determined solely by the factors of production.

The long-run supply of output is determined by the state of technology and the factors of production, labor and capital.

50%. However, so will their input costs. Their profits will still be the same, consequently, so will their output. Because the level of full-employment output does not depend on the price level, we can plot the long-run aggregate supply curve as a vertical line (unaffected by the price level), as in Figure 23.4.

Determining Output and the Price Level

We combine the aggregate demand curve and the long-run aggregate supply curve in Figure 23.5. Together, they show us the price level and output in the long run when the economy returns to full employment. This will allow us to understand how changes in aggregate demand affect prices in the long run.

Given an aggregate demand curve and an aggregate supply curve, their intersection determines the price level and equilibrium level of output. At that intersection point, the total amount of output demanded will just equal the total amount supplied by producers—the economy will be in macroeconomic equilibrium. The exact position of the aggregate demand curve will depend on the level of taxes, government spending, and the supply of money, although it will always slope downward. The level of full-employment output determines the long-run aggregate supply curve.

An increase in aggregate demand (perhaps brought about by a tax cut or an increase in the supply of money) will shift the aggregate demand curve to the right, as shown in Figure 23.5. In the long run, the increase in aggregate demand will raise prices but leave the level of output unchanged. In general, shifts in the aggregate demand curve in the long run do not change the level of output in the economy, but only change the level of prices. Here is an important example to illustrate this idea: If the money supply is increased by 5% a year, the aggregate demand curve will also shift by 5% a year. In the long run, this means that prices will increase by 5% a year—that is there will be 5% inflation.

FIGURE 23.4

Long-Run Aggregate Supply

In the long run, the level of output, y^*, is independent of the price level.

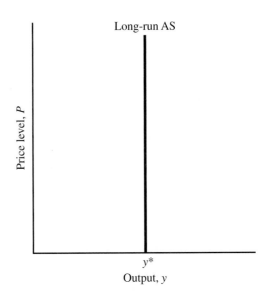

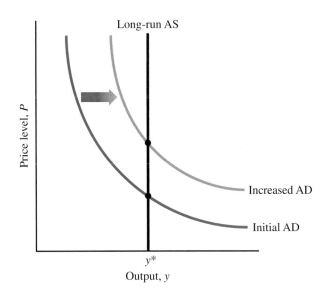

FIGURE 23.5

Aggregate Demand and the Long-Run Aggregate Supply
Output and prices are determined at the intersection of AD and AS. An increase in aggregate demand leads to a higher price level.

This is the key point about the long run: In the long run, output is determined solely by the supply of capital and the supply of labor, not the price level. As our model of the aggregate demand curve with the long-run aggregate supply curve indicates, changes in demand will affect only prices, not the level of output.

Short-run aggregate supply curve
A relatively flat horizontal supply curve. It reflects the idea that prices do not change very much in the short run and that firms adjust production to meet demand

The Short-Run Aggregate Supply Curve

In the short run, prices are sticky (slow to adjust), and output is determined primarily by demand. This is what Keynes thought happened during the Great Depression. We can use the aggregate demand curve combined with a **short-run aggregate supply curve** to illustrate this idea. Figure 23.6 shows a relatively flat short-run aggregate

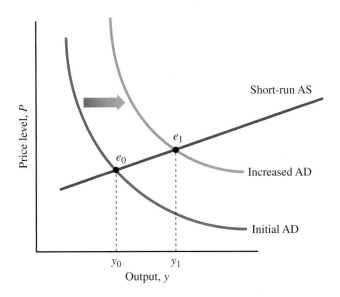

FIGURE 23.6

Aggregate Demand and Short-Run Aggregate Supply
With a short-run aggregate supply curve, shifts in aggregate demand lead to large changes in output but small changes in prices.

supply curve (AS). The short-run aggregate supply curve is relatively flat because in the short run, firms are assumed to supply all the output demanded, with small changes in prices. We previously discussed that with formal and informal contracts, firms will supply all the output that is demanded with only relatively small changes in prices. The short-run aggregate supply curve has a small upward slope. As firms supply more output, they may have to increase prices somewhat if, for example, they have to pay higher wages to obtain more overtime from workers or pay a premium to obtain some raw materials.

As we just explained, the short-run supply curve is relatively flat because at any point in time, firms are assumed to supply all the output demanded with relatively small changes in prices. However, the entire short-run supply curve can shift upward or downward as prices adjust to their long-run levels, as we shall see later in this chapter. Our description of the aggregate supply curve is consistent with evidence about the behavior of prices in the economy. Most studies find that changes in demand have relatively little effect on prices within a few quarters. Thus, the aggregate supply curve can be viewed as relatively flat within a limited time. However, changes in aggregate demand will ultimately have an effect on prices.

The intersection of the AD and AS curves at point e_0 determines the price level and the level of output. Because the aggregate supply curve is flat, aggregate demand primarily determines the level of output. In Figure 23.6, as aggregate demand increases, the new equilibrium will be at a slightly higher price, and output will increase from y_0 to y_1.

If the aggregate demand curve moved to the left, output would decrease. If the leftward shift in aggregate demand were sufficiently large, it could push the economy into a recession. Sudden decreases in aggregate demand have been important causes of recessions in the United States. However, the precise factors that shift the aggregate demand curve in each recession will typically differ. "A Closer Look: What Caused the 2001 Recession?" looks at the factors that shifted aggregate demand in the last recession.

It is important to realize and understand that the level of output where the aggregate demand curve intersects the short-run aggregate supply curve need not correspond to full-employment output. Firms will produce whatever is demanded. If demand is very high and the economy is "overheated," output may exceed full-employment output; if demand is very low and the economy is in a slump, output will fall short of full-employment output. Because prices do not adjust fully over short periods of time, the economy need not always remain at full employment or potential output. With sticky prices, changes in demand in the short run will lead to economic fluctuations and over- and underemployment. Only in the long run, when prices fully adjust, will the economy operate at full employment.

Supply Shocks

Up to this point, we have been exploring how changes in aggregate demand affect output and prices in the short run and in the long run. However, even in the short run, it is possible for external disturbances to hit the economy and cause the short-run aggregate supply curve to move. **Supply shocks** are external events that shift the aggregate supply curve.

Supply shocks
External events that shift the aggregate supply curve.

What Caused the 2001 Recession?

Following the November 2000 presidential election, in 2001, the U.S. economy entered into a recession. To determine what caused the 2001 recession and how it differed from past recessions, economist Kevin Kliesen of the Federal Reserve Bank of St. Louis compared data for recessions over time. Kliesen found that during earlier recessions spending on consumer durables (like automobiles or refrigerators) decreased, as did new residential housing production. Since both these types of spending are very sensitive to interest rate levels, the data suggested that financial factors and the government's monetary policies were to blame.

However, during the 2001 recession, spending on consumer durables and new housing production *both* grew throughout the recession. Instead, business investment and net exports dropped. Prior to the recession, there had been large increases in business investment. But following the sharp fall in the stock market in 2000, both investors and firms realized that the economic boom times of the late 1990s were over. As expectations were dashed, firms cut back sharply on their planned investment spending. Net exports fell during the recession for two reasons: World economic growth slowed down, decreasing the demand for U.S. goods; the value of the dollar also increased relative to foreign currencies, making U.S. goods more expensive.

Most forecasters didn't anticipate the drops in business investment and net exports that caused the recession. Indeed, that is the pattern in most recessions: Shocks to aggregate demand are largely unanticipated. That is, after all, whey they are called "shocks."

Source: Kevin Kliesen, "The 2001 Recession: How Was It Different and What Developments May Have Caused It?" *Federal Reserve Bank of St. Louis Review*, September/October 2003, pp. 23–37.

The most notable supply shocks for the world economy occurred in 1973 and again in 1979 when oil prices increased sharply. Oil is a vital input for many companies, used for even basic transportation for their products. The higher oil prices raised firms' costs and squeezed their profits. To maintain their profit levels, firms raised their product prices.

Figure 23.7 illustrates a supply shock that raises prices. The short-run aggregate supply curve shifts up with the supply shock because firms will supply their output

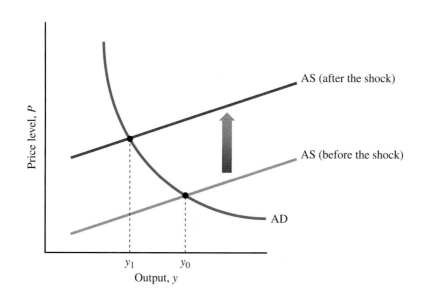

FIGURE 23.7

Supply Shock
An adverse supply shock, such as an increase in the price of oil, will shift up the AS curve. The result will be higher prices and a lower level of output.

Favorable Supply Shocks

During the 1970s, the world economy was hit with a series of unfavorable supply shocks that raised prices and lowered output, including spikes in oil prices and the prices of many agricultural commodities from weather disasters and climatic changes. In the 1990s, things were different—pleasantly different. Between 1997 and 1998, the price of oil on the world market fell from $22 a barrel to less than $13 a barrel. The result was that gasoline prices, adjusted for inflation, were lower than they had ever been in our lifetimes. This not only meant cheaper vacations and commuting, it also had positive macroeconomic effects. Favorable supply shocks allowed output to rise and prices to fall simultaneously—the best of all worlds. These favorable shocks allowed the U.S. economy to grow rapidly and to reduce unemployment.

Stagflation

A decrease in real output with increasing prices.

only at a higher price. The AS curve shifts upward, raising the price level and lowering the level of output from y_0 to y_1. Adverse supply shocks can therefore cause a recession (a fall in output) with increasing prices. This phenomenon is known as **stagflation**, and it is precisely what happened in 1973 and 1979. The U.S. economy suffered on two grounds: rising prices and falling output.

Favorable supply shocks, such as falling prices, are also possible. In this case, the short-run aggregate supply curve will shift down. As "A Closer Look: Favorable Supply Shocks" indicates, this happened in the United States in the 1990s.

Economic Puzzle

Did Higher Taxes Cause the Recession?

The economy went into a recession. The political party that was in power blamed it on an increase in the price of world oil and food. Opposing politicians blamed a tax increase that the party in power had enacted. On the basis of aggregate demand and aggregate supply analysis, what evidence should you look at to try to determine what, or who, caused the recession?

To determine whether increases in world prices for oil and food or tax increases caused the recession, you need to look at what happened to domestic prices in the economy. If prices rose sharply while output fell, then supply shocks (like increases in world oil and food prices) caused the recession. However, if both prices and output fell, tax increases probably were the culprit. ■

From the Short Run to the Long Run

Up to this point, we have examined how aggregate demand and aggregate supply determine output and prices both in the short run and in the long run. You may be wondering how long is the short run and how short is the long run. Here is a preview of how the short run and the long run are connected.

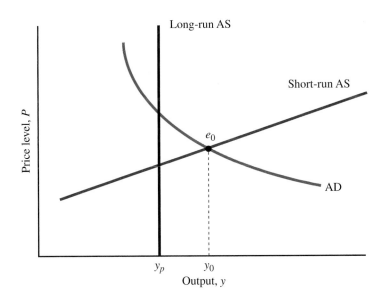

FIGURE 23.8
The Economy in the Short Run
In the short run, the economy produces at y_0, which exceeds potential output y_p.

In Figure 23.8, we show the aggregate demand curve intersecting the short-run aggregate supply curve at e_0 at an output level y_0. We also depict the long-run aggregate supply curve in this figure. The level of output in the economy, y_0, exceeds the level of potential output, y_p. In other words, this is a boom economy: Output exceeds potential.

What happens during a boom? Because the economy is producing at a level beyond its long-run potential, the level of unemployment will be very low. This will make it difficult for firms to recruit and retain workers. They will also find it more difficult to purchase needed raw materials and other inputs for production. As firms compete for labor and raw materials, there will be a tendency for both wages and prices to increase over time.

Increasing wages and prices will shift the short-run aggregate supply curve upward. Figure 23.9 illustrates this graphically, showing how the short-run aggregate

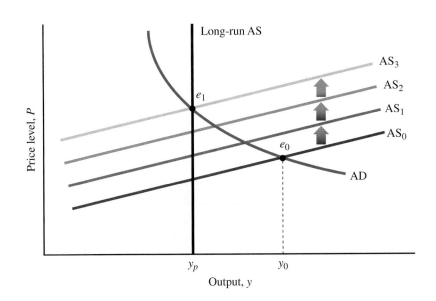

FIGURE 23.9
Adjusting to the Long Run
With output exceeding potential, the AS curve shifts upward over time. The economy adjusts to the long-run equilibrium at e_1.

supply curve shifts upward over time. As long as the economy is producing at a level of output that exceeds potential output, there will be continuing competition for labor and raw materials that will lead to continuing increases in wages and prices. In the long run, the short-run aggregate supply curve will keep rising until it intersects the aggregate demand curve at e_1. At this point, the economy reaches the long-run equilibrium—precisely the point where the aggregate demand curve intersects the long-run aggregate supply curve.

When the economy is producing below full employment or potential output, the process works in reverse. Unemployment will exceed the natural rate, and there will be excess unemployment. Firms will find it easy to hire and retain workers and they will offer them less. As firms cut wages, the average wage level in the economy falls. Because wages are the largest component of costs, prices start to fall as well. In this case, the process works in reverse.

The lesson here is that adjustments in wages and prices take the economy from the short-run equilibrium to the long-run equilibrium. In later chapters, we will explain in detail how this adjustment occurs and we will show how changes in wages and prices can steer the economy back to full employment in the long run.

TEST Your Understanding

6. Complete the statement with "vertical" or "horizontal": The long-run aggregate supply curve is _____.
7. True or false? "A sharp decrease in aggregate demand will cause a boom in the short run." Explain your answer.
8. What does a positive supply shock do to output and prices in the short run?
9. Suppose the supply of money increases. How do prices and real GDP change in both the short run and the long run?

Looking Ahead

The aggregate demand and aggregate supply models in this chapter provide an overview of how demand affects output and prices in both the short run and the long run. The next several chapters explore more closely how aggregate demand determines output in the short run. We expand our discussion of aggregate demand to see in detail how such realistic and important factors as spending by consumers and firms, government policies on taxation and spending, and foreign trade affect the demand for goods and services. We will also study the critical role that the financial system and monetary policy play in determining demand. Finally, in later chapters we will study in more depth how the aggregate supply curve shifts over time, enabling the economy to recover both from recessions and the inflationary pressures generated by economic booms.

USING THE TOOLS

In this chapter we explored the nature of economic fluctuations and developed the tools of aggregate demand and aggregate supply. Take this opportunity to test your skills using the tools we developed in this chapter.

1. The Internet and Sticky Prices

The Internet enables us to search for the lowest prices for goods such as books, music CDs, and airline tickets. Prices for these goods are likely to become more flexible as consumers shop around quickly and easily on the Internet. What types of goods and services do you think may not become more flexible because of the Internet?

2. Frugal Consumers

Suppose households become nervous about the future and decide to increase their saving and decrease their consumption spending. How will this shift the aggregate demand curve? Use the short-run aggregate supply curve to figure out what will happen to prices and output in the short run. Use the long-run aggregate supply curve to determine what will happen to prices and output in the long run.

3. Stagflation

Suppose oil prices suddenly increase and the economy is hit by an adverse supply shock. What will happen to the price level and real GDP? Why is this sometimes called stagflation?

4. A Recession Abroad

Suppose the rest of the world falls into a recession. How do you think this would shift the aggregate demand curve in the United States? What would be the short-run effect on output and prices? (*Hint:* If a country falls into a recession, its consumption spending—including its imports—will fall.)

SUMMARY

In this chapter, we discussed how sticky prices—or lack of full wage and price flexibility—cause output to be determined by demand in the short run. We developed a model of aggregate demand and supply to help us analyze what is happening or has happened in the economy. Here are main points in this chapter:

1 Economists think of GDP as being determined primarily by demand factors in the short run.

2 The aggregate demand curve depicts the relationship between the price level and total demand for real output in the economy. The aggregate demand curve is downward sloping because of the wealth effect, an interest rate effect, and an international trade effect.

3 Decreases in taxes, increases in government spending, and increases in the supply of money all increase aggregate demand and shift the aggregate demand curve to the right. Increases in taxes, decreases in government spending, and decreases in the supply of money all decrease aggregate demand and shift the aggregate demand curve to the left. In general, anything (other than price movements) that increases the demand for total goods and services will increase aggregate demand.

4 The total shift in the aggregate demand curve is greater than the initial shift. Their ratio known as the multiplier.

5 The aggregate supply curve depicts the relationship between the price level and the level of output firms supply in the economy. Output and prices are determined at the intersection of the aggregate demand and aggregate supply curves.

6 The long-run aggregate supply curve is vertical because, in the long run, output is determined by the supply of factors of production. The short-run aggregate supply curve is fairly flat because, in the short run, prices are largely fixed, and output is determined by demand.

7 Supply shocks can shift the short-run aggregate supply curve.

8 The short-run aggregate supply curve shifts in the long run, restoring the economy to the full employment equilibrium.

KEY TERMS

aggregate demand curve, 526

aggregate supply curve, 533

autonomous consumption spending, 530

consumption function, 530

economic fluctuation, 523

long-run aggregate supply curve, 533

marginal propensity to consume, 531

multiplier, 529

short-run aggregate supply curve, 535

short run in macroeconomics, 525

stagflation, 538

supply shocks, 536

wealth effect, 527

PROBLEMS AND DISCUSSION QUESTIONS

1 Explain why the aggregate demand curve is downward sloping.

2 In one year, a consumer's income increases by $200 and her consumption increases by $160. What is her marginal propensity to consume?

3 Explain why an increase in the marginal propensity to consume will increase the multiplier.

4 Does a decrease in the price level shift the aggregate demand curve? Explain.

5 Give an example of a good or service whose price is sticky. What factors tend to make its price sticky?

6 Explain why the long-run aggregate supply curve is vertical and why the short-run aggregate supply curve is relatively flat.

7 Suppose that in the long run there was a new higher level of full-employment output. What would happen to the level of prices in the economy?

8 In the short run, what happens to the unemployment rate if aggregate demand suddenly falls?

9 Suppose the economy is at full employment and aggregate demand falls. Show the effects on output and prices in the short run. Also show how the short-run aggregate supply curve adjusts over time to bring the economy to the long-run equilibrium.

10 Use aggregate demand and aggregate supply diagrams to show the effects of "favorable" supply shocks.

11 Web Exercise. Are increases in government purchases associated with increases in real GDP? A good place to start to find out might be the Website of the Federal Reserve Bank of St. Louis (*http://research.stlouisfed.org/fred2/*). You might also want to explore this issue for other countries.

12 Web Exercise. Are increases in exports associated with increases in real GDP? Use the Website in Problem 11 or your own source to answer this question.

MODEL ANSWERS TO QUESTIONS

Chapter-Opening Questions

1 Since wages and prices are slow to adjust, the economy may not always operate at full employment.

2 In the short run, output is largely determined by demand. Therefore, a sharp decrease in government spending could cause a recession.

3 Higher oil prices decrease aggregate supply, raising prices and reducing output.

4 In the short run, changes in the demand for goods and services primarily affect output. In the long run, changes in demand for goods and services primarily affect prices.

Test Your Understanding

1 Consumption, investment, government spending, and net exports.

2 Wealth.

3 Right.

4 2.5

5 Smaller.

6 Vertical.

7 False, it will cause a recession.

8 It raises output and lowers prices.

9 In the short run, output increases and prices increase somewhat. In the long run, only prices increase.

Fiscal Policy

During the decade of the 1990s, the Japanese economy was in a prolonged recession. Economists and journalists put forward many different ideas to try to jump-start the economy. One suggestion was that the Japanese government should issue everyone a certificate entitling each person to the equivalent, in yen, of $200. However, these yen certificates would only be valid for purchases for one month; after that time, the certificates would be worthless.

The logic behind issuing these time-dated certificates was straightforward. Individuals would feel compelled to rush out and use the certificates within the month. They would therefore immediately purchase goods and services and stimulate demand. Firms would increase production to meet the increased demand, thereby creating more jobs and lifting the economy out of the recession. This is an example, although an unusual one, of government fiscal policy.

When the U.S. economy entered a recession in 2001, it was not long before journalists, policymakers, and politicians of all parties were calling for government action to combat the downturn. Common prescriptions included increasing government spending or reducing taxes, although specific recommendations differed sharply among those making them.

Fiscal policy

Changes in taxes and spending that affect the level of GDP.

This chapter studies how governments can use **fiscal policy**—changes in taxes and spending that affect the level of GDP—to stabilize the economy. It explores the logic of fiscal policy and explains why changes in government spending and taxation can, in principle, stabilize the economy. However, stabilizing the economy in theory is much easier than in actual practice, as we will see.

The chapter also provides an overview of federal government spending and taxation. These are essentially the "tools" that the government uses to implement its fiscal policies. We will also examine the federal deficit and begin to explore the controversies surrounding "deficit spending."

One of the best ways to really understand fiscal policy is to see it in action. In the last part of the chapter, we trace the history of U.S. fiscal policy from the Great Depression in the 1930s to the present time. As you will see, the public's attitude toward government fiscal policy has not been constant, but has changed sharply over time.

After reading this chapter, you should be able to answer the following questions:

1 Why do governments increase spending or decrease taxes to increase economic growth?
2 What are some limitations of using fiscal policy to stabilize the economy?
3 Why do governments deliberately spend more than they collect in taxes, in order to stimulate their economies?
4 How do our attitudes towards the use of active fiscal policy today differ from our attitudes during the Great Depression?

The Role of Fiscal Policy

In the last chapter, we discussed how output and prices are determined where the aggregate demand curve intersects the short-run aggregate supply curve. Over time, we also saw that the aggregate supply curve will shift to bring the economy back to full employment. In this section, we will explore how the government can shift the aggregate demand curve.

Fiscal Policy and Aggregate Demand

As we discussed in the last chapter, government spending and taxes can affect the level of aggregate demand. Increases in government spending or decreases in taxes will increase aggregate demand and shift the aggregate demand curve to the right. Decreases in government spending or increases in taxes will decrease aggregate demand and shift the aggregate demand curve to the left.

Why do changes in government spending or taxes shift the aggregate demand curve? Recall from our discussion in the last chapter that aggregate demand consists of four components: consumption spending, investment spending, government purchases, and net exports. These four components are the four parts of aggregate demand. Thus, increases in government purchases directly increase aggregate demand because they are a component of aggregate demand. Decreases in government purchases directly decrease aggregate demand.

Changes in taxes affect aggregate demand indirectly. For example, if the government lowers taxes on consumers, they will have more income at their disposal and will increase their consumption spending. Since consumption spending is a component of aggregate demand, aggregate demand will increase as well. Increases in taxes will have the opposite affect. Consumers will have less income at their disposal and decrease their consumption spending. As a result, aggregate demand will decrease. Changes in taxes can also affect businesses and lead to changes in investment spending. Suppose, for example, that the government cuts taxes in such a way as to provide incentives for new investment spending by businesses. Since investment spending is a component of aggregate demand, the increase in investment spending will increase aggregate demand.

In Panel A of Figure 24.1, we show a simple example of fiscal policy in action. The economy is initially operating at a level of GDP, y_0, where the aggregate demand curve AD^0 intersects the short-run aggregate supply curve AS. This level of output is below the level of full employment or potential output, y_p. In order to increase the level of output, the government can increase government spending—say, on military goods— which will shift the aggregate demand curve to the right, to AD^1. Now the new aggregate demand curve intersects the aggregate supply curve at the full-employment level of output. Alternatively, instead of increasing its spending, the government could reduce taxes on consumers and businesses. This would also shift the aggregate demand curve to the right. Government policies that increase aggregate demand are called **expansionary policies**. Increasing government spending and cutting taxes are examples of expansionary policy.

Expansionary policies
Government policy actions that lead to increases in output.

Fiscal policy can also be used to decrease GDP if the economy is operating at too high a level of output, which would lead to the economy overheating and rising prices. In Panel B of Figure 24.1, the economy is initially operating at a level of output, y_0, that exceeds full-employment output, y_p. An increase in taxes can shift the aggregate demand curve from AD^0 to AD^1. This will bring the economy back to full employment. Alternatively, the government could cut its spending to move the aggregate demand curve to the left. Government policies that decrease aggregate demand are called **contractionary policies**. Decreasing government spending and increasing taxes are examples of contractionary policy.

Contractionary policy
Government policy actions that lead to decreases in output.

Both these examples illustrate the use of fiscal policy to stabilize the economy. In these two simple examples, fiscal policy seems very straightforward for policymakers to use. But as we will soon see, in practice, it is more difficult to implement effective policy.

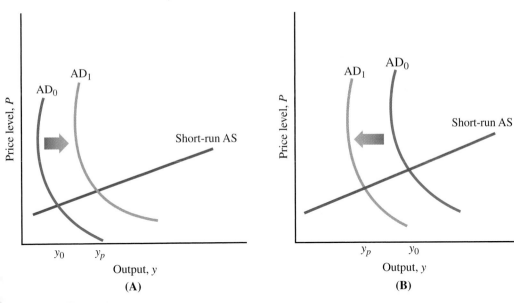

FIGURE 24.1 **Fiscal Policy in Action**

Panel A: An increase in government spending shifts the aggregate demand curve from AD_0 to AD_1, restoring the economy to full employment. This is an example of expansionary policy. Panel B: An increase in taxes shifts the aggregate demand curve to the left, from AD_0 to AD_1, restoring the economy to full employment. This is an example of contractionary policy.

The Fiscal Multiplier

Let's recall the idea of the multiplier that we developed in the last chapter. The basic idea of the multiplier is that the final shift in the aggregate demand curve will be larger than the initial increase. For example, if government purchases increased by $10 billion, that would initially shift the aggregate demand curve to the right by $10 billion. However, the total shift in the aggregate demand curve will be larger, say, $15 billion. Conversely, a decrease in purchases by $10 billion may cause a total shift of the aggregate demand curve to the left by $15 billion.

This multiplier effect occurs because an initial change in output will affect the income of households and thus change consumer spending. For example, an increase in government spending of $10 billion will initially raise household incomes by $10 billion and lead to increases in consumer spending. As we discussed in the last chapter, the precise amount of the increase will depend on the marginal propensity to consume. In turn, the increase in consumer spending will raise output and income further, leading to further increases in consumer spending. The multiplier takes all these effects into account.

As the government develops policies to stabilize the economy, it needs to take the multiplier into account. The total shift in aggregate demand will be larger than the initial shift. As we will see later in this chapter, U.S. policymakers have taken the multiplier into account as they developed policies for the economy.

The Limits to Stabilization Policy

As we have seen, the government can use fiscal policy—changes in the level of taxes or government spending—to alter the level of GDP. If the current level of GDP is below full employment or potential output, the government can use expansionary policies such as tax cuts, and increased spending, to raise the level of GDP and reduce unemployment.

Both expansionary policies and contractionary policies are examples of **stabilization policies**, actions to move the economy closer to full employment or potential output.

On paper, this sounds simple. In practice, it is difficult—very difficult—for two big reasons. First, there are lags, or delays, in stabilization policy. Lags arise because decision-makers are often slow to recognize and respond to changes in the economy, and fiscal policies and other stabilization policies take time to operate. The other reason is that economists simply do not know enough about all aspects of the economy to be completely accurate in all their forecasts. Although economists have made great progress in understanding the economy, the difficulties of forecasting the precise behavior of human beings (who can change their minds or sometimes act irrationally) places limits on our forecasting ability.

Lags

Poorly timed policies can magnify economic fluctuations. Suppose that (1) GDP is currently below full employment but will return to full employment on its own within one year and that (2) stabilization policies take a full year to become effective. If policymakers tried to expand the economy today, their actions would not take effect until a year from now. One year from now, the economy would normally, by itself, be back at full employment. But one year from now, if stabilization policies were enacted, the economy would be stimulated unnecessarily, and output would exceed full employment.

Figure 24.2 illustrates the problem caused by lags. Panel A shows an example of successful stabilization policy. The solid line represents the behavior of GDP in the absence of policies. Successful stabilization policies can dampen (reduce in magnitude) economic fluctuations, lowering output when it exceeds full employment and raising output when it falls below full employment. This would be easy to accomplish if there were no lags in policy. The dashed curve shows how successful policies can reduce economic fluctuations.

Panel B shows the consequences of ill-timed policies. Again, assume that policies take a year before they are effective. At the start of Year 1, the economy is below potential. If policymakers engaged in expansionary policies at the start of Year 1, the change would not take effect until the end of Year 1. This would raise output even higher above full employment. Ill-timed stabilization policies can magnify economic fluctuations.

Where do the lags in policy come from? Economists recognize two broad classes of lags: **inside lags** and **outside lags**. Inside lags refer to the time it takes to formulate a policy; outside lags refer to the time it takes for the policy to actually work. To help you understand inside and outside lags, imagine that you are steering a large ocean liner and you are looking out for possible collisions with hidden icebergs. The time it takes

Stabilization policies
Policy actions taken to bring the economy closer to full employment or potential output.

Inside lags
Lags in implementing policy.

Outside lags
The time it takes for policies to work.

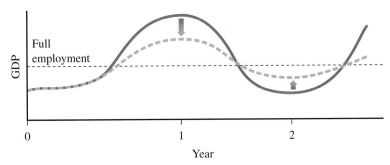

(A) Ideal stabilization policy can dampen fluctuations.

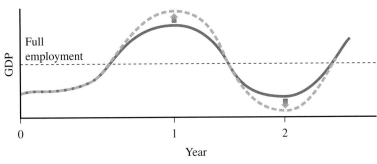

(B) Ill-timed policies can magnify fluctuations.

FIGURE 24.2

Possible Pitfalls in Stabilization Policy
Panel A shows an example of successful stabilization policy. The solid line represents the behavior of GDP in the absence of policies. The dashed line shows the behavior of GDP when policies are in place. Successfully timed policies help smooth out economic fluctuations. Panel B shows the consequences of ill-timed policies. Again, the solid line represents the behavior of GDP in the absence of policies, and the dashed line, GDP with policies in place. Notice how ill-timed policies make economic fluctuations greater.

you to spot an iceberg, communicate this information to the crew, and initiate the process of changing course is the inside lag. Because ocean liners are large and have lots of momentum, it will take a long time before your ocean liner begins to turn; this is the outside lag.

Inside lags occur for two basic reasons. One reason is that it takes time to identify and recognize a problem. For example, the data available to policymakers may be poor and conflicting. Some indicators of the economy may look fine; others may appear worrisome. It often takes from several months to a year before it is clear that there is a serious problem with the economy.

A good example of an inside lag occurred at the beginning of the Great Depression. Although the stock market crashed in October 1929, we know from newspaper and magazine accounts that business leaders were not particularly worried about the economy for some time. Not until late in 1930 did the public begin to recognize the severity of the depression.

The other reason for inside lags is that once a problem has been diagnosed, it still takes time before any actions can be taken. This problem is most severe for fiscal policy in the United States. Any changes in taxes or spending must be approved by both houses of Congress and by the president. In recent years, political opponents have been preoccupied with fights about the size of the government and the role it should play in the economy, making it is difficult to reach a consensus in a timely manner.

For example, soon after he was elected, President Bill Clinton proposed an expansionary stimulus package as part of his overall budget plan. The package contained a variety of spending programs that were designed to increase the level of GDP and avert a recession. However, the plan was attacked as wasteful and unnecessary, and it did not survive. As it turned out, the stimulus package was not necessary—the economy grew rapidly in the next several years. Nonetheless, this episode illustrates how difficult it is to develop expansionary fiscal policies in time to have the effect we want them to.

Policies are also subject to outside lags—the time it takes for them to become effective. For example, if taxes are cut, it takes time for individuals and businesses to change their spending plans to take advantage of the tax cuts. Therefore, it will take some time before increases in spending will raise GDP. Outside lags in fiscal policy are relatively short, however, as the multiplier effects tend to work though the economy rather quickly.

Economists use **econometric models** to replicate the behavior of the economy mathematically and statistically and to assist in developing economic forecasts. They can also be used to estimate the length of outside lags. One such model predicts that an increase in government spending will increase GDP by its maximum effect after just six months.

Econometric models
Mathematical computer-based models that economists build to capture the actual dynamics of the economy.

Forecasting Uncertainties

What makes the problem of lags even worse is that economists are not very accurate in forecasting what will happen in the economy. For example, a classic problem that policymakers face when the economy appears to be slowing down is knowing whether the slowdown is temporary or will persist. Unfortunately, stabilization policy cannot be effective without accurate forecasting. If economic forecasters predict an overheated economy and the government adopts a contractionary policy, the result could be disastrous if the economy weakened before the policy took effect. Today, most economic policymakers understand these limitations and are cautious in using activist policies.

TEST Your Understanding

1. To increase aggregate demand, a government can either increase spending or _____ taxes.
2. Contractionary policies include _____ government spending or increasing taxes.
3. If the multiplier for government spending is 1.5, then a $15 million increase in government spending will ultimately shift the aggregate demand curve by _____.
4. _____ lags refer to the time it takes for policymakers to recognize an economic problem and take appropriate action.

The Federal Budget

The federal budget—the actual document that describes what the federal government spends and how it pays for it—provides the framework for fiscal policy. In this section, we will take a closer look at federal spending and taxation and what happens when one exceeds the other. The federal budget is extremely large and the programs that the federal government supports are very complex. To give you a sense of the magnitude of the budget, in 2003, total federal spending approximately was 19.9% of GDP in 2003, or $2.15 trillion. Federal taxes were 16.5% of GDP. With a U.S. population of 290 million, total federal spending amounted to approximately $7,400 per person.

Probably the best way to begin to grasp the scope and complexities of the U.S. federal budget is to look at recent data and to see where we spend money and how we raise it. As we explore the budgetary data, keep in mind that the government runs its budget on a **fiscal year** basis, not a calendar year basis. Fiscal year 2003, for example, began on October 1, 2002 and ended on September 30, 2003.

States and local governments also provide government services and collect taxes. Some important services, for example, education, are primarily funded by state and local governments, and others, such as welfare and health care for the poor, are funded jointly by the federal government and state governments. However, since our focus in this chapter is on federal fiscal policy, we will concentrate our discussion on federal spending and taxation.

Fiscal year

The calendar on which the federal government conducts its business, which runs from October 1 to September 30.

Federal Spending

Federal spending, spending by the U.S. government, consists of two broad components: federal government expenditures and transfer payments. As you should recall from our discussion of GDP accounting, only federal government expenditures are included in GDP. Transfer payments, although an important part of the federal budget, are not a component of GDP because they do not represent any currently produced goods or services.

To study the components of federal spending, we will look at the final data from fiscal year 2003 provided by the Congressional Budget Office, a nonpartisan agency of the Congress that provides both budgetary forecasts and historical data on the budget. Table 24.1 provides key data on federal expenditures for fiscal year 2003, both in absolute dollar terms and as a percent of GDP.

Let's begin with the broad categories of the budget. Total spending, or outlays, in fiscal year 2003 were $2,158 billion or approximately 19.9% of GDP. Three components of the budget add up to this total: discretionary spending, entitlements and mandatory spending, and net interest.

Category	Outlays (billions)	Percent of GDP
Total outlays	$2,158	19.9%
Discretionary spending	825	7.6
Defense	405	3.7
Nondefense	420	3.9
Entitlements and mandatory spending	1,179	10.9
Social Security	470	4.3
Medicare and Medicaid	535	4.9
Other programs	174	1.7
Net interest	153	1.4

TABLE 24.1

Federal Spending for Fiscal Year 2003

Discretionary spending

The spending programs that Congress authorizes on an annual basis.

Discretionary spending constitutes all the programs that Congress authorizes on an annual basis, which are not automatically funded by prior laws passed by Congress. It includes defense spending, and all nondefense domestic spending. When people commonly discuss federal spending, they often focus on this category, which includes the Defense Department, the Environmental Protection Agency, the State Department, the Interior Department, and other agencies. However, discretionary spending is less than 40% of total federal spending. Total nondefense spending is less than 4% of GDP.

Congress and the president can use discretionary spending funds directly for activist fiscal policy. To stimulate the economy, they can authorize additional spending by government agencies, or they can urge agencies to accelerate their current spending plans. However, it does take time for bureaucracies to act, and just because new spending is authorized by Congress does not mean that agencies will spend the funds immediately.

Entitlement and mandatory spending

Spending that Congress has authorized by prior law.

Entitlement and mandatory spending constitutes all spending that Congress authorized by prior laws. These expenditures must be made by the federal government unless Congress changes the laws. The terms *entitlement* and *mandatory* spending are not totally accurate, however. Individuals are only "entitled" to benefits to the extent that they meet the requirements passed by Congress to collect them. Congress can always change the rules. Similarly, this category of spending is only "mandatory" to the extent that Congress maintains the current programs in place.

Social Security

A federal government program to provide retirement support and a host of other benefits.

Entitlements and mandatory spending are the single largest component of the federal budget. One of the most familiar programs is **Social Security**, which provides retirement payments to retirees as well as a host of other benefits to widows and families of disabled workers. **Medicare** provides health care to all individuals once they reach the age of 65. **Medicaid** provides health care to the poor, in conjunction with the

Medicare

A federal government health program for the elderly.

Medicaid

A federal government health program for the poor.

During the Great Depression, the government sponsored public works projects to stimulate the economy and provide employment for those out of work.

states. The government provides a range of other programs as well; examples include additional retirement and disability programs (aside from Social Security) and farm price supports to provide income to farmers. Some of these programs are **means-tested**. That is, they are partly based on the income of the recipient. Medicaid, for example, is an example of a means-tested program.

Net interest is the interest that the government pays the public on the government debt held by the public, for example, U.S. Treasury bonds, bills, and other debt such as U.S. savings bonds. We will discuss more about how the government borrows money later in the chapter. In fiscal year 2003, total net interest payments to the public were $153 billion, or approximately 1.4% of GDP. Total expenditures on net interest are directly related to the total government debt held by the public and the level of interest rates. Increased government debt and higher interest rates will lead to higher net interest payments by the government.

As the population ages, entitlements and net interest are the fastest-growing component of the federal budget, as "A Closer Look: The Budgetary Challenge of an Aging Society" explains.

Means-tested

Based on the income of individuals or families.

A CLOSER LOOK

The Budgetary Challenges of an Aging Society

As life expectancies increase, the population ages, and new medical technologies become available, economists and budget analysts predict that spending on federal retirement and health programs will grow extremely rapidly. Today, Social Security, Medicare, and Medicaid constitute approximately 9% of GDP. Experts estimate that in 2075—when youth born today are in the early part of their retirement years—spending on these programs will be approximately 21% of GDP. This is a larger share of GDP than *all* government spending today! How will our society cope with these increased demands for these services?

One possibility is to leave the existing programs in place and just raise taxes to pay for these programs. This would have two implications: First, if we maintained the federal share of GDP of all other programs, it would mean a large expansion of the federal government, from 20% of GDP to 32% of GDP. Second, it would mean a very large increase in our tax burden. That would impose burdens on future workers and businesses.

Some economists suggest that the government should save and invest now to increase GDP in the future in order to reduce the burden on future generations. The saving and investment would indeed increase GDP, but entitlement payments would also grow right along with it. As a result, the relative burden of taking care of the elderly would not change dramatically.

Another strategy would be to try to reform the entitlement systems, placing more responsibility on individuals and families for their retirement and well-being. For example, we could increase the age at which retirement benefits begin to be paid and thereby require individuals to spend more years in the labor force. Or we could try to reform the health care system to encourage more competition in order to reduce health care expenditures.

All of these changes would be very difficult to make, however. Other countries, including Japan and many in Europe, which have even older populations, will face even more severe challenges and face them earlier than the United States will. Perhaps we can learn from them. Nonetheless, pressures on the federal budget will begin to escalate in the next decade and some steps will need to be taken soon to cope with the challenge.

Federal Revenues

The federal government receives its revenue from taxes levied on both individuals and businesses. Table 24.2 shows the revenues the federal government received in fiscal year 2003 in both dollar terms and as a percent of GDP. Figure 24.3 presents a pie chart showing the relative importance of the components of federal revenue.

Let's review the categories that comprise total federal revenue. The single largest component of federal revenue is the **individual income tax**. Most everyone is familiar with the federal income tax. Tax returns calculating the tax due by individuals or couples during the prior year must be filed by April 15 of every year. During the year, the federal government collects in advance some of the taxes due by **withholding** a portion of workers' paychecks. Taxpayers not subject to withholding or who earn income through investments must make estimated tax payments so that the tax due to the federal government is paid evenly over the year in which it is earned.

The second-largest component of federal revenue is **social insurance taxes**, which are taxes levied on earnings to pay for Social Security and Medicare. Today, social insurance taxes are almost as large as individual income taxes and together they comprise nearly 84% percent of total federal revenue. Unlike individual income taxes, social insurance taxes are only paid on wages and not on income from investments.

Other taxes paid directly by individuals and families are **estate and gift taxes**. Sometimes known as the "death tax," these taxes are levied on the estates and previous gifts of individual when they pass away. In 2004, estates are taxed only if they exceed $1.5 million—so small estates do not pay this tax—and that threshold is scheduled to increase during this decade. The estate and gift tax raised only $22 billion in fiscal year 2003 but it generates a great deal of controversy. Opponents of the tax argue that it destroys family-held businesses (like family farms passed down from one generation to the next), while proponents claim it is necessary to prevent unfair accumulation of wealth across generations.

The **corporate tax** is a tax levied on the earnings of corporations. This tax raised less than 7.5% of total federal revenues during fiscal year 2003. The tax was a more important source of revenue in past decades but has declined to today's relatively low level. This decline has been attributed to many factors, including falling corporate profits as a share of GDP, the growth of opportunities for tax shelters, tax

---

Individual income taxes
Taxes levied on the income earned by individuals.

Withholding
Taxes collected directly from the paychecks of workers.

Social insurance taxes
Taxes levied on earnings to pay for Social Security and Medicare.

Estate and gift taxes
Taxes levied on the estates and gifts of individuals.

Corporate tax
A tax levied on the earnings of a corporation.

TABLE 24.2

Sources of Federal Government Revenue, Fiscal Year 2003

Category	Receipts (billions)	Percent of GDP
Total revenue	$1,782	16.5%
Individual income taxes	794	7.3
Social insurance taxes	713	6.6
Estate and gift taxes	22	0.2
Corporate income taxes	132	1.2
Excise taxes and customs duties	87	0.8
Miscellaneous receipts	34	0.3

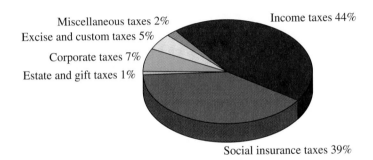

Miscellaneous taxes 2%
Excise and custom taxes 5%
Corporate taxes 7%
Estate and gift taxes 1%
Income taxes 44%
Social insurance taxes 39%

FIGURE 24.3

Components of Federal Revenue, 2003
Individual income taxes and social insurance taxes make up the bulk of the U.S. government's revenue.

incentives provided by Congress to stimulate investment and research and development, and complex rules for taxing multinational corporations that operate on a global basis.

The other sources of government revenue are relatively minor. **Federal excise taxes** are taxes levied on the sale of some products, for example, gasoline, tires, firearms, alcohol, and tobacco. **Custom duties** are taxes levied on goods imported to the United States, such as foreign cars or wines.

Supply-Side Economics and the Laffer Curve

Is it possible for a government to cut tax rates yet still raise more revenue? That's a politician's dream. People would face lower tax rates yet there would be more money for politicians to spend. Economist Arthur Laffer argued in the late 1970s that there was a strong possibility that we could do this in the U.S. economy. Laffer's views influenced many politicians at the time and became the basis for **supply-side economics**. Supply-side economics is a school of thought that emphasizes the role taxes play in the supply of output in the economy. Supply-side economists look not just at the effects of taxes on aggregate demand (as we did earlier in this chapter) but also on aggregate supply. As we saw in Chapter 21, a decrease in tax rates will typically tend to increase labor supply and output. Thus, changes in taxes can also shift the aggregate supply curve.

Laffer also developed a model known today as the **Laffer curve**. Suppose a government imposed extremely high tariffs (taxes) on imported goods—tariffs so high that no one could afford to import any goods whatsoever. If this were the case, the government would not collect any revenue from the tariffs. But, if the government cut the rates and individuals began to buy imported goods, the government would start to collect at least some tariff revenue. This was Laffer's point: Lower taxes (tariffs) could actually lead to higher government revenues.

Virtually all economists today believe Laffer's tax revenue idea won't work when it comes to broad-based income taxes or payroll taxes. For these types of taxes, cutting rates would simply reduce the revenues that the government collects, because most economists believe that the supply of labor is not as sensitive to changes in tax rates as Laffer believed. But there are some taxes, such as tariffs or taxes on the gains investors' earn by holding stocks and bonds, for which this claim is plausible.

Federal excise taxes
Taxes levied directly on the sale of selected products by the federal government.

Custom duties
Taxes levied on goods imported to the United States

Supply-side economics
A school of thought that emphasizes the role that taxes play in the supply of output in the economy.

Laffer curve
A relationship between tax rates and tax revenues that illustrates that high tax rates do not always lead to high tax revenues if they discourage economic activity.

The Federal Deficit and Fiscal Policy

Budget deficit

The difference between spending and revenues for a government.

The federal government runs a **budget deficit** when it spends more than it receives in tax revenues. Here is how it works. Suppose a government wishes to spend $100 billion but only receives $95 billion in tax revenue. To actually spend the $100 billion, it must obtain funds from some source. Facing a $5 billion shortfall, the government will borrow that money from the public by selling government bonds. The public then transfers $5 billion to the government, and in return, these lenders receive $5 billion in government bonds that pay interest.

Budget surplus

The difference between revenues and spending for a government—the opposite of a budget deficit.

If the government collects more in taxes than it wishes to spend, it is running a **budget surplus**. In this case, the government has excess funds and can buy back bonds previously sold to the public.

Both government spending and tax revenues are very sensitive to the state of the economy. Since tax collections are largely based on individual and corporate income, tax revenues will fall sharply during a recession as national income falls. At the same time, government transfer payments for things like unemployment insurance and food stamps will also tend to increase during a recession. The result is higher government spending and lower tax collections and the increased likelihood that the government will run a budget deficit. Similarly, when the economy grows rapidly, tax collections increase and government expenditures on transfer payments decrease, and the likelihood of the federal government running a surplus is greater.

Automatic Stabilizers

Suppose an economy had a balanced federal budget—neither deficit nor surplus. An external shock then plunged the economy into a recession. Tax revenues fall and expenditures on transfer payments increase, resulting in a budget deficit. Believe it or

In the 1970s, increases in the world price of oil created difficulties for motorists. The price of oil affected not only gasoline but the prices of many other commodities, too. Automatic stabilizers can help dampen, but not eliminate, the effects of shocks like these.

not, the increased budget deficit actually serves a valuable role in stabilizing the economy. The increased federal budget deficit works through three channels:

1 Increased transfer payments such as unemployment insurance, food stamps, and other welfare payments increase the income of some households, partly offsetting the fall in household income.
2 Other households whose incomes are falling pay less in taxes; this also partly offsets the decline in their household income. Since incomes do not fall as much as they would have in the absence of the deficit, consumption spending does not decline as much.
3 Since the corporation tax depends on corporate profits and profits fall in a recession, taxes also fall on businesses. Lower corporate taxes help to prevent them from cutting their spending as much as they would otherwise during a recession.

The government deficit itself, in effect, offsets part of the adverse effect of the recession and thus helps stabilize the economy.

Similarly, during an economic boom, transfer payments fall and taxes increase. This dampens the increase in household income and also the increase in consumption and investment spending that would accompany higher household income and higher corporate profits. Taxes and transfer payments that stabilize GDP without requiring explicit actions by policymakers are called **automatic stabilizers**.

The great virtue of automatic stabilizers is that they do not require explicit action from the president and Congress to change the law. Given the long inside lags caused by ideological battles in Washington, D.C. over spending, taxes, and the deficit, it is fortunate to have mechanisms in place that dampen economic fluctuations without requiring explicit and deliberative action.

Automatic stabilizers
Taxes and transfer payments that stabilize GDP without requiring policymakers to take explicit action.

Concerns About Deficits

Let's take a closer look at fiscal policy designed to stabilize the economy. If the budget were initially balanced and the economy plunged into a recession, a budget deficit would emerge as tax revenues fell and expenditures increased. To combat the recession, policymakers could then either increase government spending or cut taxes. Both actions, however, would increase the deficit—an important point to remember.

Despite concerns about increasing the deficit, this is precisely the right policy. If policymakers tried to avoid running a deficit by raising taxes or cutting spending, that would actually make the recession worse. The key lesson here is that during a recession, we should focus on what our fiscal policy actions do to the economy, not what they do to the deficit.

Does that mean that concerns about the federal budget deficit are misplaced? No, in the long run, large budget deficits can have an adverse effect on the economy. We explore these issues in more detail in a later chapter, but we can easily understand the basic problem. We have seen that when an economy is operating at full employment, then output must be divided between consumption, investment, government spending, and net exports. Suppose, then, that the government cuts taxes for households and runs a deficit. The reduced taxes will tend to increase consumer spending. (Consumers may save some

Crowded out

The reduction in a component of GDP that results when government spending is increased or taxes are decreased.

of the tax cut, but will consume the rest.) However, since output is fixed at full employment, some other component of output must be reduced, or **crowded out**, which we first discussed in Chapter 21. Crowding out is an example of the principle of opportunity cost.

 Principle OF OPPORTUNITY COST

The opportunity cost of something is what you sacrifice to get it.

In this case, we normally expect that the increased consumption spending will come at the sacrifice of reduced investment spending. As we have seen, with reduced investment spending, the economy will grow more slowly in the future. Thus, the budget deficit will increase current consumption but slow the growth of the economy in the future. This is the real concern with prolonged budget deficits.

Another way to understand the concern about long-run deficits is to think of what happens in the financial markets when the government runs large deficits. As the government runs large deficits, it will have to borrow increasing amounts of money from the public by selling U.S. government securities. In the financial markets, the government will be in increased competition with businesses that are trying to raise funds from the public to finance their investment plans, too. This increased competition from the government will make it more difficult and costly for businesses to raise funds and, as a result, investment spending will decrease.

 **TEST Your Understanding**

5. Fiscal year 2005 begins on October 1, _____.
6. Discretionary spending is the largest component of federal spending. True or false? Explain.
7. What are two examples of entitlement spending?
8. "Corporate taxes are the main source of federal government revenue." True or false? Explain.

Fiscal Policy in U.S. History

The Depression Era

The basic mechanisms of fiscal policy—using government spending and taxation to stabilize the economy—have been known for many years and, indeed, were discussed in the 1920s. However, it took a long time before economic-policy decisions were based on these principles. Many people associate active fiscal policy in the United States with actions taken by President Franklin Roosevelt during the 1930s. But this is a misleading view, according to E. Cary Brown, a former economics professor at the Massachusetts Institute of Technology.

During the 1930s, politicians did not believe in modern fiscal policy, largely because they feared the consequences of government budget deficits. According to Brown, fiscal policy was expansionary only during two years of the Great Depression, 1931 and 1936. In those years, Congress voted for substantial payments to veterans, over objections of Presidents Herbert Hoover and Franklin Roosevelt. Although government spending increased during the 1930s, taxes increased sufficiently during that same period, with the result that there was no net fiscal expansion.

The Kennedy Administration

Although modern fiscal policy was not deliberately used during the 1930s, the growth in military spending at the onset of World War II increased total demand in the economy and helped to pull the economy out of its long decade of poor performance. But to see fiscal policy in action, we need to turn to the 1960s. It was not until the presidency of John F. Kennedy during the early 1960s that modern fiscal policy came to be accepted.

Walter Heller, the chairman of the president's Council of Economic Advisers under John F. Kennedy, was a forceful advocate of active fiscal policy. From his perspective, the economy was operating far below its potential, and a tax cut was the perfect medicine to bring the economy back to full employment. When Kennedy entered office, the unemployment rate was 6.7%. Heller believed that the unemployment rate at full employment—the "natural rate" of unemployment, that is—was really only about 4%. He convinced Kennedy of the need for a tax program to stimulate the economy, and Kennedy put forth an economic program that was based largely on modern fiscal policy principles.

Two other factors led the Kennedy administration to support the tax cut: First, tax rates were extremely high at the time. The top individual tax rate was 91%, compared to about 40% today. The corporate tax rate was 52%, compared to 35% today. Second, Heller convinced Kennedy that even if a tax cut led to a federal budget deficit, it was not a problem. In 1961, the federal deficit was less than 1% of GDP, and future projections indicated that the deficit would disappear as the economy grew because of higher tax revenues.

The tax cuts were enacted in February 1964, after Lyndon Johnson became president following Kennedy's assassination. The tax cuts included permanent cuts in rates for both individuals and corporations. Estimating the actual effects that the tax cuts had on the economy is difficult; however, in order to make a valid comparison, we need to estimate how the economy would have behaved without the tax cuts. What we do know is that the economy grew at a rapid rate following the tax cuts. From 1963 to 1966, both real GDP and consumption grew at rates exceeding 4%. We cannot rule out the possibility that the economy could have grown just as rapidly without the tax cuts. Nonetheless, the rapid growth during this period suggests that the tax cuts had the effect, predicted by Heller's theory, of stimulating economic growth.

The Vietnam War Era

The next major use of modern fiscal policy occurred in 1968. As the Vietnam War began and military spending increased, unemployment fell to very low levels. From 1966 to 1969, the overall unemployment rate fell below 4%. Policymakers became concerned that the economy was overheating and that this would lead to a higher inflation rate. In 1968, a temporary tax surcharge of 10% was enacted to reduce total demand for goods and services. The 10% surcharge was a "tax on a tax," so it raised the taxes paid by households by 10%. Essentially, the surcharge was specifically designed to be temporary and expired within a year.

The surcharge did not decrease consumer spending as much as economists had initially estimated, however. Part of the reason was that the tax increase was temporary. Economists who have studied consumption behavior have noticed that consumers often base their spending on an estimate of their long-run average income or **permanent income**, not on their current income.

Permanent income

An estimate of a household's long-run average level of income.

For example, consider a salesperson who usually earns $50,000 a year, although her income in any single year might be slightly higher or lower. Knowing that her permanent income is $50,000, she consumes $45,000. If her income in one year is higher than average, say $55,000, she is still likely to consume $45,000 (as if she earned just her normal $50,000) and save the rest.

The temporary, one-year tax surcharge during the Vietnam War had a similar effect. Because consumers knew the surcharge was not permanent, they didn't alter their spending habits very much. The surtax reduced households' savings, not their consumption. The result was a smaller decrease in demand for goods and services than economists anticipated.

During the 1970s, there were many changes in taxes and spending but no major changes in overall fiscal policy. A recession in 1973 led to a tax rebate and other incentives in 1975, but, by and large, changes to fiscal policy were mild.

The Reagan Administration

The tax cuts enacted during 1981 at the beginning of the first term of President Ronald Reagan were significant. However, they were not proposed to increase aggregate demand. Instead, the tax cuts were justified on the basis of improving economic incentives and increasing the supply of output. In other words, they were supply-side movtivated. Taxes can have important effects on the supply of labor, saving, and economic growth. Proponents of the 1981 tax cuts emphasized these particular effects and not increases in aggregate demand. Nonetheless, the tax cuts did appear to increase consumer demand and helped the economy recover from the back-to-back recessions in the early 1980s.

By the mid-1980s, large government budget deficits began to emerge and policymakers became concerned by them. As the deficits grew and became the focus of attention, interest in using fiscal policy to manage the economy waned. Although there were government spending and tax changes in the 1980s and 1990s, few of them were justified solely as policies to change aggregate demand.

The Clinton and George W. Bush Administrations

At the beginning of his administration, President Bill Clinton proposed a "stimulus package" that would increase aggregate demand, but it was defeated in Congress. Clinton later successfully passed a major tax increase that brought the budget into balance. By the year 2000, the federal budget actually began to show surpluses rather than deficits, setting the stage for tax cuts. During his first year in office, President George W. Bush passed a 10-year tax cut plan that decreased tax rates. The first year of the tax cut featured tax rebates or refunds of up to $600 per married couple. The refunds were intended to increase aggregate demand. Did they? According to Professors Matthew Shapiro and Joel Slemrod of the University of Michigan, consumers by and large saved, not spent, the rebates, as "A Closer Look: Exploring the 2001 Tax Rebates," explains.

After the September 11, 2001 terrorist attack on the World Trade Center in New York City, President Bush and Congress became less concerned with balancing the federal budget and authorized new spending programs to provide relief to victims and to stimulate the economy, which had fallen into a recession.

In May of 2003, President Bush signed another tax bill to stimulate the sluggish economy and, in particular, to increase investment spending. This bill had many distinct features, including moving up some of the previously scheduled cuts in tax rates

A CLOSER LOOK

Exploring the 2001 Tax Rebates

In 2001, approximately 90 million U.S. households received tax rebate checks from the government. These checks were up to $300 for a single taxpayer or $600 for joint, or married, filers. The tax rebate was just the first installment of a multiyear tax reduction for households stemming from a new tax bill passed that year.

According to conventional economic theory, a permanent cut in taxes should largely be spent by households because it represents a new permanent source of income for them. To discover whether in practice households actually spent the tax cuts, Professors Matthew Shapiro and Joel Slemrod surveyed households using the University of Michigan Survey Research Center Monthly Survey. They asked a nationally representative set of households whether they were more likely to spend the rebate, save it, or pay down existing debts (another form of saving). Shapiro and Slemrod surveyed households both when the rebate checks were being mailed and following their arrival.

They found that less than 25% of households were likely to spend the rebate—which defied conventional economic wisdom. Moreover, to their surprise, low-income households were no more likely to spend the rebate than higher-income households. According to their results, the tax rebates had only limited success in stimulating aggregate demand.

In analyzing the survey results, Shapiro and Slemrod noted that many households surveyed did not believe that they would receive future rebates of a similar size, despite the change in the tax law. They also speculated that the large fall in the stock market in the two previous years may have made households more financially tentative and inclined to save the tax cut. These results suggest that policymakers need to be cautious in their use of fiscal policy.

Source: Matthew Shapiro and Joel Slemrod, "Consumer Response to Tax Rebates," *American Economic Review*, March 2003, vol. 93, no. 1, pp. 381–396.

FIGURE 24.4

Federal Taxes, Spending, and Deficits, 1992–2003

Budget deficits might sharply limit the ability of the U.S. government to conduct expansionary fiscal policy in the near future.

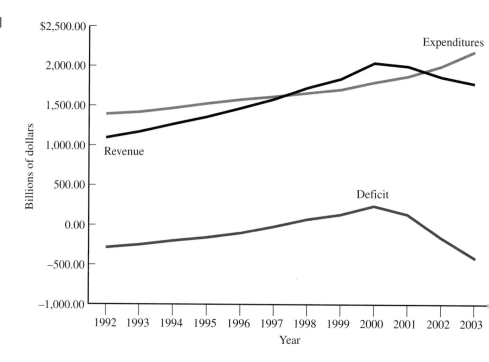

that were part of the 2001 tax bill, increasing the child tax credit, and lowering taxes on dividends and capital gains.

The combination of the recession, tax cuts, and the increased expenses associated with the war in Iraq in 2003 sharply changed the fiscal landscape again. For fiscal year 2003, the deficit was approximately $400 billion. Figure 24.4 plots the course of spending, taxes, and the deficit over the last 10 years and shows the recent reemergence of deficits. The prospect of future deficits sharply limits the ability of the U.S. government to conduct expansionary fiscal policy in the near future and will set the background for the political debates in Washington, D.C. for many years to come.

USING THE TOOLS

In this chapter, we explored the role that fiscal policy can play in stabilizing the economy, the nature of the federal budget, and the U.S. experience with active fiscal policy. Take this opportunity to use the tools developed in this chapter.

1. The States and Balanced Budgets

Unlike the federal government, virtually all states have requirements that they must either plan for or maintain a balanced budget.

a. Suppose the national economy experiences a recession. How will this affect the budgets of the states?

b. What actions must the states then take to balance the budget?

c. Explain why these actions, taken together, may destabilize the national economy.

2. A Chinese Experiment

In order to stimulate consumer spending, in 2000 the Chinese government mandated three, one-week holidays throughout the year. The idea was that these extended vacations would induce the Chinese to spend more of their earnings while on vacation.
a. Using the AD-AS framework, show the mechanism through which the Chinese government believed that the mandated holidays would stimulate the economy.
b. Although consumption spending rose during the vacation period, the data show that consumption fell before and after the vacation. Did the policy work?

3. Tax Refunds and Consumer Spending

In 1999, the Internal Revenue Service began to mail out refund checks because of changes in the tax law in 1998. Economic forecasters predicted that consumption and GDP would increase because of higher refunds on income taxes. Evaluate the reasoning of these forecasters under the following different assumptions:
a. Taxpayers were not aware that they would receive refunds until they had completed their income tax statements.

b. Taxpayers did know that they would receive refunds but, as consumers, based their spending decisions solely on their current levels of income.
c. Taxpayers did know that they would receive refunds and, as consumers, based their consumption decisions on their permanent incomes.

4. Time-Dated Certificates

The chapter-opening story presented a discussion of a proposal made in Japan to issue time-dated certificates to each person that had to be spent on goods and services within a fixed period or it became worthless. Suppose the government was considering whether to issue $400 in time-dated certificates to each household or give each household $400 in cash instead.
a. What plan would lead to the greatest economic stimulus? How would that depend on the marginal propensity to consume and the fact that this was a one-time program?
b. Which plan do you think the government would find easier to administer?
c. Suppose a household had large credit card debt, which it wished to reduce. How would that household view the two plans?

SUMMARY

This chapter explored the role of government fiscal policy. Using the AD-AS model, we showed how fiscal policy can stabilize the economy. We also discussed the multiplier and the limits to stabilization policy. In addition, the chapter gave us an overview of the federal budget, including spending, revenues, deficits, and surpluses. Finally, we explored how fiscal policy in the United States has changed over time. Here are the key points:

1 Increases in government spending or decreases in taxes will increase aggregate demand.
2 Decreases in government spending or increases in taxes will decrease aggregate demand.

3 Because of the multiplier, the total shift in the aggregate demand curve will be larger than the initial shift. Policymakers need to take the multiplier into account as they formulate policy.
4 Both inside lags (the time it takes to formulate policy) and outside lags (the time it takes the policy to work) limit the effectiveness of active fiscal policy.
5 The largest component of federal spending is entitlements and mandatory programs.
6 The largest components of federal revenues are income taxes and social insurance contributions collected from individuals.

7 Government deficits act as an automatic stabilizer that help to stabilize the economy in the short run.

8 In the short run, fiscal policy actions taken to combat a recession will increase the deficit; in the long run, deficits are a concern because they may lead to crowding out of investment spending.

9 Active fiscal policy has been periodically used in the United States to stimulate the economy; at other times, concerns about deficits have limited the use of fiscal policy.

KEY TERMS

automatic stabilizers, 557
budget deficit, 556
budget surplus, 556
contractionary policy, 546
corporate tax, 554
crowded out, 558
custom duties, 555
discretionary spending, 552
econometric models, 550
entitlement and mandatory
   spending, 552

estate and gift taxes, 554
expansionary policies, 546
federal excise taxes, 555
fiscal policy, 545
fiscal year, 551
individual income taxes, 554
inside lags, 548
Laffer curve, 555
means-tested, 553

Medicaid, 552
Medicare, 552
outside lags, 548
Permanent income, 560
stabilization policies, 548
social insurance taxes, 554
Social Security, 552
supply-side economics, 555
withholding, 554

PROBLEMS AND DISCUSSION QUESTIONS

1 Why is it important for policymakers to take into account the multiplier as they design fiscal policies?

2 Describe the mechanisms through which increases in government spending and decreases in taxes affect aggregate demand. How are they different?

3 Using the idea of automatic stabilizers, explain why states with more generous unemployment insurance programs will experience smaller fluctuations in output.

4 What factors led the United States from federal surpluses at the end of the 1990s to deficits in the first decade of 2000?

5 Why does fiscal policy exhibit long inside lags?

6 If interest rates rise, what component of federal spending will automatically increase?

7 At one point in the business cycle should we become concerned about federal deficits?

8 Contrast the attitudes about fiscal policy of the Kennedy administration in the 1960s and the Roosevelt administration during the Great Depression.

9 If a college student received a tax rebate, do you think she would be more likely to save it or spend it? How about a middle-aged married man? Explain your reasoning.

10 Web Exercise. Go to the Website for the Congressional Budget Office (*www.cbo.gov*) and find historical data on government revenues. Show how the importance of corporate taxes has changed over time.

11 Web Exercise. The Congressional Budget Office also makes long-run deficit budget projections, extending far into the twenty-first century. What are the main causes of the long-run deficits projected by the CBO?

MODEL ANSWERS TO QUESTIONS

Chapter-Opening Questions

1 Governments increase or decrease spending to affect aggregate demand, which helps to determine real GDP in the short run.

2 Fiscal policy is subject to both inside lags and outside lags. Moreover, policymakers also need to have accurate forecasts of the economy to design effective fiscal policies.

3 Deficit financing increases aggregate demand. This is a useful policy when an economy is in a recession.

4 During the Great Depression, active fiscal policy was not used. Today it is used to stimulate the economy although concerns about deficits limit its use.

Test Your Understanding

1 Decrease.

2 Decreasing.

3 $22.5 billion

4 Inside.

5 2004.

6 False, mandatory spending is larger.

7 Social Security and Medicare.

8 False. They are much less important than individual income taxes and social insurance taxes.

The Income-Expenditure Model

n 1996, the recession in Japan appeared to be over. Policymakers then became more concerned with the growing gap between spending and taxes—a fiscal deficit. The Japanese politicians and economists, accustomed to budget surpluses in the 1980s and mindful of growing demands on the public sector, became very concerned. To offset the budget deficit, they enacted a very large tax increase on consumption, scheduled to begin on July 1, 1997. At first, policymakers did not perceive any problems with their tax plan. Anticipating that the increased taxes on consumption would raise prices, consumers increased their purchases of new goods before July 1. However, after July 1, the increase in taxes had its predictable, negative effect on aggregate demand. The economy began to slow rapidly, precisely at the time another financial crisis was to strike the whole of Asia. Japan was now about to enter another prolonged, recessionary period. Policymakers should not have been surprised by this outcome. According to one study of the macroeconomics of Japan, "the Japanese economy behaved much as the textbooks would have predicted."

Source: Kenneth K. Kuttner and Adam S. Posen, "The Great Recession: Lessons for Macroeconomic Policy from Japan," *Brookings Papers on Economic Activity*, 2001, vol. 2, p. 95.

Newspaper and television stories about the economy tend to focus on what causes the changes in short-term real GDP. For example, it is common to read about how changes in economic conditions in Europe or Asia or changes in government spending or taxation will affect near-term economic growth. To understand these stories, we need to understand the behavior of the economy in the short run.

As we have seen, in the short run, changes in aggregate demand play the key role in determining the level of output. In the short run, prices are slow to change and therefore fluctuations in aggregate demand translate directly into fluctuations in GDP and income. In this chapter, we take a more detailed look at short run fluctuations in GDP.

The model we develop in this chapter is called the "income-expenditure" model. It was originally developed by the economist John Maynard Keynes in the 1930s and later extended and refined by many economists. When Keynes developed his theories, the world economy was in the midst of severe depression. Unlike many other economists at the time, Keynes did not believe that the economy would return to full employment by itself. An economy could get "trapped" in a depression and not recover.

But Keynes provided both a diagnosis of the problem and a cure. He argued that the fundamental problem causing the world depression was an insufficient demand for goods and services. Here was the problem: Firms would not increase their production and put the unemployed back to work unless there was sufficient demand for the goods and services they produced. But consumers and firms would not demand enough goods and services unless the economy improved and their incomes were higher. Keynes argued that active fiscal policy—increasing government spending or cutting taxes—could increase total demand for goods and services and bring the economy back to full employment. The income-expenditure model is based on the idea that higher *expenditures* were necessary to generate higher levels of *income* in the economy.

The income-expenditure model focuses on change in the level of output or GDP (we will use these terms interchangeably in this chapter). However, it does not take into account changes in prices. The income-expenditure model is very useful for understanding economic fluctuations in the very short run when prices do not change very much—and that will be the focus of this chapter. It is less useful in the intermediate or longer run, when prices do adjust to economic conditions. For intermediate or longer-run analysis, we need to use the aggregate demand and aggregate supply curves in order to understand movements in both output and prices.

Today, we also recognize that Keynes's model also provides a foundation for our model for aggregate demand. In the last part of this chapter, we show how Keynes's income-expenditure model provides an important building block for our model of aggregate demand. In later chapters, we will also incorporate financial markets into our discussion of aggregate demand.

This chapter will primarily use graphical tools to explain the income-expenditure model. An appendix to this chapter provides an algebraic treatment of the model and shows how some of the key formulas are derived.

With the tools in this chapter, you will be able to answer the following questions:

1 Why do increases in government spending have larger effects on the economy than decreases in taxes by the same amount?
2 Can an increase in the value of the stock market lead to increased spending by consumers?
3 If consumers become more confident about the future of the economy, can that confidence lead to faster economic growth in the short run?
4 If foreign countries stop buying goods produced in the United States, could that lead to a recession?

A Simple Income-Expenditure Model

In this section, we will develop a very simple income-expenditure model to illustrate the ideas of Keynes. Later in the chapter, we will expand the income-expenditure model to make it more realistic.

Equilibrium Output

Let's begin with the simplest income-expenditure model. The simplest model uses a graph with total expenditures for goods and services represented on the vertical axis, output (y) represented on the horizontal axis, and a 45° line, as shown in Figure 25.1. A 45° line marks all the points on the graph at which the value of the variable measured on the horizontal axis (output) equals the value of the variable measured on the vertical axis (total expenditures).

In our most basic model, we temporarily omit the government and the foreign sector. Only consumers and firms can demand output: Consumers demand consumption goods, and firms demand investment goods. We make things even simpler, assuming that consumers and firms each demand a fixed amount of goods. Let consumption

FIGURE 25.1

The 45° Line
At any point on the 45° line, the distance to the horizontal axis is the same as the distance to the vertical axis.

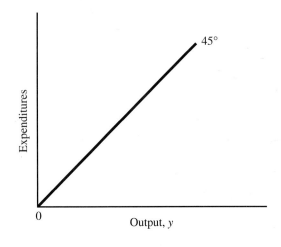

emand be an amount C and let investment demand be an amount I. Total demand ill be $C + I$. Total demand is also called **planned expenditures**. Thus, planned xpenditures in this simple economy are equal to $C + I$.

In the income-expenditure model, firms are assumed to supply all the output that demanded. This assumes that the short-run aggregate supply curve is flat, so that rms will produce whatever is demanded without changing their prices. This is a reaonable assumption in the short run.

Since firms are willing to supply whatever is demanded, demand is the key factor determining the level of output, or GDP. Here is how output or GDP is determined the income-expenditure model:

Determining Output

In the income-expenditure model, the level of output in the economy will adjust to equal the level of planned expenditures. This level of output is called equilibrium output.

Let's denote the level of **equilibrium output** as y^*. Then the level of equilibrium utput will be

$$\text{equilibrium output} = y^* = C + I = \text{planned expenditures}$$

quilibrium output is the level of output or GDP at which planned expenditures for oods and services equals the level of output.

Figure 25.2 can help us to understand how the level of equilibrium output or GDP the economy is determined. On the expenditure-output diagram, we superimpose ne line representing planned expenditures, $C + I$, which is a horizontal line because oth C and I are fixed amounts. Because planned expenditures are fixed at $C + I$, they o not depend on the level of output. The height of the horizontal line represents the evel of planned expenditures.

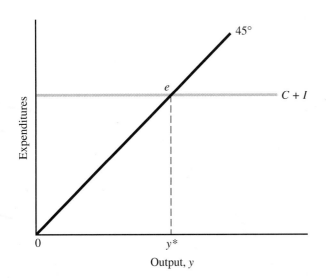

Equilibrium output is at y^*, the level of output at which the planned expenditure line crosses the 45° line. They cross at point e, where output measured on the horizontal axis equals planned expenditures by consumers and firms measured on the vertical axis. Recall that on a 45° line, the value on the horizontal axis equals the value on the vertical axis.

Adjusting to Equilibrium Output

What would happen if the economy were producing at a higher level of output, such as y_1 in Figure 25.3? At that level of output, more goods and services are being produced than consumers and firms are wanting and buying. Goods that are produced but not purchased will pile up on the shelves of stores. Firms will react to this by cutting back on production. The level of output will fall until the economy reaches y^*, as indicated by the leftward arrow in Figure 25.3.

If the economy were producing at a lower level of output, y_2, planned expenditures would exceed total output. When planned expenditures exceed output, firms find that the demand for consumption and investment goods is greater than their current production. Inventories disappear from the shelves of stores, and firms face increasing backlogs of orders for their products. Firms respond by stepping up production, so GDP increases back to y^*, as indicated by the rightward arrow in Figure 25.3.

Table 25.1 also helps to illustrate the process that determines equilibrium output. The table shows, with a numerical example, what happens to production when planned expenditures do not equal output. Planned expenditures (consumption plus investment) equal 100 billion dollars. In the first row, we see that if current production is only 80 billion, stocks of inventories will be depleted by 20 billion, so firms will increase output to restore their inventory levels. In the third row, production is at 120 billion, creating an excess of inventories of 20 billion, and firms will cut back production. In the second row, planned expenditures equal output: Neither inventories nor production changes.

FIGURE 25.3

Equilibrium Output
Equilibrium output (y^*) is determined at e, where demand intersects the 45° line. If output were higher (y_1), it would exceed demand and production would fall. If output were lower (y_2), it would fall short of demand and production would rise.

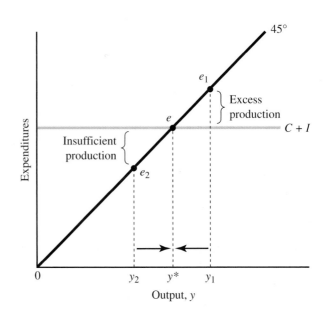

C + I	Production	Inventories	Direction of Output
100	80	Depletion of inventories of 20	Output increases
100	100	No Change	Output stays constant
100	120	Excess of inventories of 20	Output decreases

TABLE 25.1

Adjustments to Equilibrium Output

Be sure you remember that the equilibrium level of output occurs where planned expenditures equal production. If the economy were not producing at that level, we would find either that the demand for goods was too great relative to production or that there was insufficient demand relative to production. In either case, the economy would rapidly adjust to reach the equilibrium level of output.

The Consumption Function

To make the income-expenditure model more realistic, we will need to introduce other components of demand, including the government and the foreign sector. But the first step we need to take is to recognize that planned expenditures by consumers will depend on the level of income that they have.

Consumer Spending and Income

Let's begin by reviewing the **consumption function** that we first introduced in the last chapter. The consumption function describes the relationship between desired spending by consumers and the level of income. When consumers have more income, they will want to purchase more goods and services.

As we have seen, a simple consumption function can be described by the equation

$$C = C_a + by$$

in which total consumption spending, C, has two parts. The first part, C_a, is called **autonomous consumption** and does not directly depend on the level of income. The second part, by, represents the part of consumption that does depend on income. It is the product of the fraction b, called the **marginal propensity to consume (MPC)**, and level of income in the economy, y. The MPC (which has a value of b in our formula) tells us how much consumption spending will increase for every dollar that income increases. If $b = 0.7$, then for every \$1 that income increases, consumption would increase by \$0.70.

In our simple income-expenditure model, *output is also equal to the income that flows to the households*. As firms produce output, it is paid to the households as income in the form of wages, interest, profits, and rents. We can therefore use the symbol y to represent both output and income.

We plot a consumption function in Figure 25.4. The consumption function is a line that intersects the vertical axis at C_a, the level of autonomous consumption spending,

Consumption function

The relationship between the level of income and consumption spending.

Autonomous consumption

The part of consumption that does not depend on income.

Marginal propensity to consume

The fraction of additional income that is spent.

FIGURE 25.4

Consumption Function
The consumption function relates desired consumer spending to the level of income.

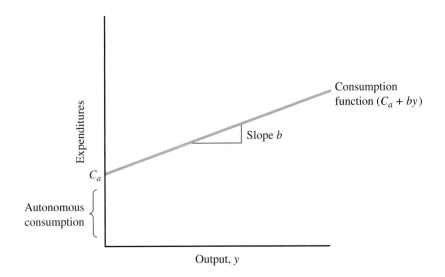

which is typically greater than zero so it has a positive intercept. Its slope equals b, the marginal propensity to consume. Although output is plotted on the horizontal axis, remember that it is also equal to income, so income rises dollar for dollar with output. That is why we can plot the consumption function (which depends on income) on the same graph that determines output.

Changes in the Consumption Function

The consumption function is determined by the level of autonomous consumption and by the MPC. The level of autonomous consumption can change, and so can the MPC. Changes in either shift the consumption function to another position on the graph. A higher level of autonomous consumption but no change in MPC will shift the entire consumption function upward and parallel to its original position. More consumption occurs at every level of income. We show an increase in autonomous consumption in Panel A of Figure 25.5.

A number of factors can cause autonomous consumption to change. Here are two:

▶ Increases in consumer wealth will cause an increase in autonomous consumption. Wealth consists of the value of stocks, bonds, and consumer durables (consumer goods that last a long time, such as automobiles and refrigerators). Note that wealth is not the same as income. Income is the amount of money earned during a period, such as in a given year, whereas wealth represents total net worth. Nobel laureate Franco Modigliani found that increases in stock prices, which raise consumer wealth, will lead to increases in autonomous consumption. Conversely, a sharp fall in stock prices will lead to a decrease in autonomous consumption.

▶ Increases in consumer confidence will increase autonomous consumption. Forecasters pay attention to consumer confidence, based on household surveys; consumer confidence is reported regularly in the financial press.

Despite the sharp decline in stock market wealth beginning in 2000 and the drop in consumer confidence as the economy entered a recession in 2001, consumer

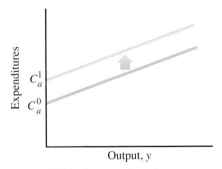

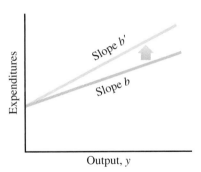

FIGURE 25.5

Movements of the Consumption Function

(A) An increase in autonomous consumption from C_a^0 to C_a^1 shifts up the entire consumption function.

(B) An increase in the MPC from b to b' increases the slope of the consumption function.

demand nonetheless remained relatively strong. Some economists have argued that increases in the value of residential homes have stimulated consumer spending. "A Closer Look: Home Equity and the Wealth Effect," examines this argument.

A change in the marginal propensity to consume will cause a change in the slope of the consumption function. We show an increase in the MPC in Panel B of Figure 25.5,

A CLOSER LOOK

Home Equity and the Wealth Effect

From 2000 to 2003, the value of home equity—the difference between the value of homes and the amount of mortgage debt on the property—increased by approximately $2 trillion. Home equity is the single largest component of net wealth for most families in the United States. Compared to wealth holdings in the stock market, which tend to be concentrated in the highest income brackets, home equity wealth is more widely dispersed across the income spectrum.

A study by the International Monetary Fund found that increases in home equity have larger effects on consumption than increases in the stock market. In particular, it found that a dollar increase in home equity increased consumption by approximately 7 cents, whereas increases in stock market wealth led to an increase of only 4.5 cents. Why the difference? First, households may believe that increases in home equity are more likely to be permanent than increases in stock market values. Second, since stock holdings are concentrated at the

higher end of the income distribution, those households may be more likely to save—not spend—the increase in wealth.

Source: Frank Nothaft, "Home Equity 'Wealth Effect' Fuels Consumer Spending," Freddie Mac, *Economic & Housing Research*, Special Commentary, August 22, 2003.

where we assume that autonomous consumption is fixed. As the MPC increases, th
consumption function rotates upward, counterclockwise; that means that the con
sumption function line gets steeper.

TEST Your Understanding

1. True or false, and explain why. "The income-expenditure model is most appropriate for long-run analysis."
2. Explain why equilibrium output occurs where the planned expenditure line crosses the 45° line.
3. What is the slope of the consumption function called?
4. Complete the statement with "upward" or "downward." An increase in autonomous consumption will shift the consumption function _____.

Equilibrium Output and the Consumption Function

Using the consumption function, we can now begin to look at more complex version
of the income-expenditure model. We continue to assume that investment spending, *I*
does not depend on the level of income. The only difference between what we did in
the preceding section and what we are about to do here is that we now recognize tha
consumption increases with the level of income.

Figure 25.6 shows how GDP is determined. We first plot the consumption func
tion, *C*, as before: a sloping line graphically representing that consumption spending i

FIGURE 25.6

Equilibrium Output and the Consumption Function

Equilibrium output is determined where the *C* + *I* line intersects the 45° line. At that level of output, y^*, desired spending equals output.

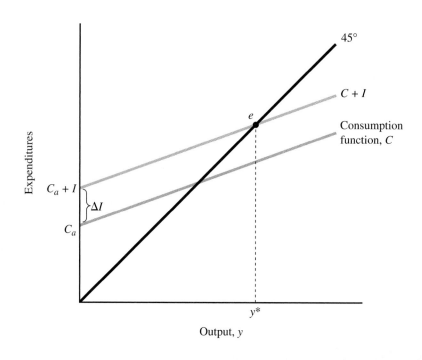

function of income. Because we are assuming that investment is constant at all levels f income, to graphically get the $C + I$ line, we can simply add vertically the constant vel of investment I to the consumption function. Doing this gives us the $C + I$ line, presenting total planned expenditures in the economy. This line is upward sloping ecause consumption spending increases with income. At any level of income, we now now the level of total planned expenditures, $C + I$.

The level of equilibrium output, y^*, occurs where the planned expenditure line $+ I$ crosses the 45° line. At this level of output, planned expenditures equal output. At ny other level of production, planned expenditures will not equal output and the conomy will adjust back to y^*, for the same reasons and in the same way as in the cor- esponding example in the preceding section.

In the appendix to this chapter, we show that the equilibrium output in this simple conomy is

equilibrium output = (autonomous consumption + investment)/(1 – MPC)

or, in the mathematical terms representing those words,

$$y^* = (C_a + I)/(1 - b)$$

From this relationship and the numerical values for C_a, b, and I, we can calculate quilibrium output. Suppose that

$$C_a = 100$$
$$b = 0.6$$
$$I = 40$$

This means that the consumption function is $C = 100 + 0.6y$.) Then, using our for- nula for equilibrium output, we have:

$$y^* = (100 + 40)/(1 - 0.6)$$
$$= (140)/0.4$$
$$= 350$$

Savings and Investment

quilibrium output can be determined in another way, which highlights the relation- hip between savings and investment. To understand this relationship, recall that in an conomy without taxation or government, the value of output, or production (y), quals the value of income. Households receive this income and either consume it (C), ave it (S), or some of both. Realizing that, we can say that savings equals output minus onsumption or, in mathematical terms,

$$S = y - C$$

In our simple economy, output is determined by planned expenditures, $C + I$, or

$$y = C + I$$

If we subtract consumption from both sides of this equation, we have

$$y - C = I$$

But we just saw that the left side, $y - C$, equals savings, S, so we have

$$S = I$$

Thus, equilibrium output is determined at the level of income where savings equal investment.

The level of savings in the economy is not fixed; it changes, and how it changes depends on the real GDP. To illustrate this, let's return to the previous example in which the consumption function is $C = 100 + 0.6y$. Because $S = y - C$, savings is

$$S = y - (100 + 0.6y)$$
$$S = -100 + 0.4y$$

Savings function

The relationship between the level of income and the level of savings.

This is the savings function for this example. A **savings function** describes the relationship between savings and income. In this example's savings function, the marginal propensity to save (MPS) is 0.4. That means that for every dollar y increases, savings increase by $0.40.

In our previous example, investment $I = 40$ and equilibrium output was 350. Let's check that savings does equal that level of investment. Plugging in the value of equilibrium output (or income) into the savings function, we get

$$S = -100 + 0.4(350)$$
$$S = -100 + 140$$
$$S = 40$$

So savings equals investment at the level of equilibrium output.

Understanding the Multiplier

In all economies, investment spending fluctuates. We can use the model we developed that determines output in the short run to see what happens if there are changes in investment spending. In all economies, investment spending fluctuates. We can use the model we developed that determines output in the short run to see what happens if there are changes in investment spending. Suppose investment spending originally was I_0 and increased to I_1—an increase that we will call ΔI (the symbol Δ, the Greek capital letter delta, is universally used to represent change). What happens to equilibrium output?

Figure 25.7 shows how equilibrium output is determined at the original level of investment and at the new level of investment. The increase in investment spending shifts the $C + I$ curve upward by ΔI. The intersection of the $C + I$ curve with the 45° line shifts from e_0 to e_1. GDP increases from y_0 to y_1 by the amount Δy. The figure shows that the increase in GDP—that is, the amount Δy— is greater than the increase

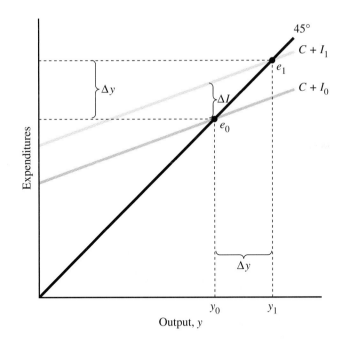

FIGURE 25.7

Multiplier
When investment increases by ΔI from I_0 to I_1, equilibrium output increases by Δy from y_0 to y_1. The change in output (Δy) is greater than the change in investment (ΔI).

n investment—the amount ΔI—or $\Delta y > \Delta I$. This is a general result; the increase in output always exceeds the increase in investment because of the multiplier effect we discussed in the last chapter.

Let's review the logic of the multiplier that we discussed in the last chapter. Suppose that there is an initial increase of investment spending by $20 million. This additional demand will initially increase output, income, and aggregate demand by $20 million. Assuming the MPC is 0.8, the $20 million in additional income will lead to $16 million in increased consumer spending (the MPC of 0.8 × $20 million). With an increase in consumer demand of $16 million, output, income, an aggregate demand will therefore increase by another $16 million. In turn, this will increase consumer spending by another $12.8 million (the MPC of 0.8 × $16 million). This increased demand will therefore increase output, income, and aggregate demand by $12.8 million, generating further increases in consumer spending of $10.24 million. As this process continues over time, total spending will continue to increase, but in diminishing amounts. If we add up all the spending in the (infinite) rounds, we find that the initial increase in investment spending will generate a total increase in equilibrium income of $100 million, far more than the initial $20 million we began with. In this case, the multiplier is 5 (5 × $20 million = $100 million).

We show how to derive the formula for a simple multiplier in the appendix to this chapter:

$$\text{multiplier} = 1/(1 - \text{MPC})$$

Suppose the MPC = 0.8; then the multiplier would be $1/(1 - 0.8)$, or 5.

Notice that the multiplier increases as the MPC increases. If MPC = 0.4, the multiplier = 1.67; if the MPC = 0.6, the multiplier = 2.5. To see why the multiplier increases

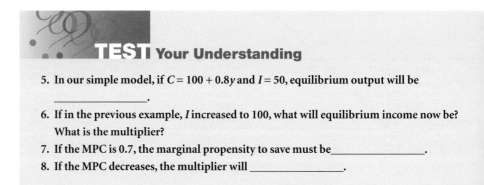

as the marginal propensity to consume MPC increases, think back to our examples of the multiplier. The multiplier occurs because the initial increase in investment spending increases income, which leads to higher consumer spending. With a higher MPC, the increase in consumer spending will be greater, since consumers will spend a higher fraction of the additional income they receive as the multiplier increases. (For example, if the MPC is 0.8 they will spend an additional $0.80, whereas if the multiplier was 0.6 they would spend only an additional $0.60.) With a higher MPC, the eventual increase in output will be greater, and therefore so will the multiplier.

TEST Your Understanding

5. In our simple model, if $C = 100 + 0.8y$ and $I = 50$, equilibrium output will be
   _____.

6. If in the previous example, I increased to 100, what will equilibrium income now be?
   What is the multiplier?

7. If the MPC is 0.7, the marginal propensity to save must be_____.

8. If the MPC decreases, the multiplier will _____.

Government Spending and Taxation

We now make our model more realistic by bringing in government spending and taxation, which makes the model useful for understanding economic policy debates. In those debates, we often hear recommendations for increasing government spending to increase GDP or cutting taxes to increase GDP. As we will explain, both the level of government spending and the level of taxation, through their influence on the demand for goods and services, affect the level of GDP in the short run.

Using taxes and spending to influence the level of GDP in the short run is known as Keynesian fiscal policy. As we discussed in Chapter 21, changes in taxes can also affect the supply of output in the long run through the way taxes can change incentives to work or invest. However, in this chapter, we concentrate on the role of taxes and spending in determining demand for goods and services and, hence, output, in the short run.

Fiscal Multipliers

Let's look first at the role government spending plays in determining GDP. Government purchases of goods and services are a component of total spending:

$$\text{planned expenditures including government} = C + I + G$$

Increases in government purchases, G, shift the $C + I + G$ line upward, just as increases in investment, I, or autonomous consumption do. If government spending increases by $1, the $C + I + G$ line will shift upward by $1.

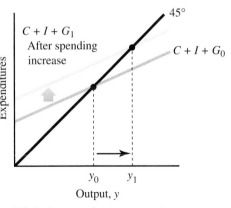

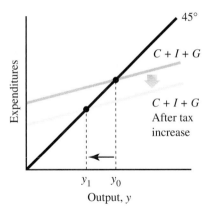

FIGURE 25.8

Government Spending, Taxes, and GDP

(A) An increase in government spending leads to an increase in output.

(B) An increase in taxes leads to a decrease in output.

Panel A of Figure 25.8 shows how increases in government spending affect GDP. The increase in government spending from G_0 to G_1 shifts the $C + I + G$ line upward and increases the level of GDP from y_0 to y_1.

As you can see, changes in government purchases have exactly the same effects as changes in investment or changes in autonomous consumption. The multiplier for government spending is also the same as for changes in investment or autonomous consumption:

$$\text{multiplier for government spending} = 1/(1 - \text{MPC})$$

For example, if the MPC were 0.6 and the multiplier were 2.5 $[1/(1 - 0.6) = 2.5]$, a $10 billion increase in government spending would therefore increase GDP by $25 billion. The multiplier for government spending works just like the multiplier for investment or consumption. An initial increase in government spending raises GDP and income. The increase in income, however, generates further increases in demand as consumers increase their spending.

Now let's consider taxes. We need to take into account that government programs affect households' disposable personal income—income that ultimately flows back to households and to consumers after subtraction from their income of any taxes paid and after addition to their income of any transfer payments they receive (such as Social Security, unemployment insurance, or welfare). If the government takes $10 net out of every $100 you make, your income after taxes and transfer payments is only $90.

Here's how we include taxes and transfers into the model: We make consumption spending depend on income after taxes and transfers, or $y - T$, where T is net taxes (taxes paid to government minus transfers received by households). For simplicity, we'll just refer to T as taxes, but remember that it is taxes less transfer payments. The consumption function with taxes is

$$C = C_a + b(y - T)$$

If taxes increase by $1, after-tax income will decrease by $1. Since the marginal propensity to consume is b, this means that consumption will fall by $b \times \$1$, and the $C + I + G$ line will shift downward by $b \times \$1$. For example, if b is 0.6, a $1 increase in taxes will mean that consumers will have a dollar less of income and will therefore decrease consumption spending by $0.60.

Panel B of Figure 25.8 shows how an increase in taxes will decrease the level of GDP. As the level of taxes increases, the demand line will shift downward by b (the increase in taxes). Equilibrium income will fall from y_0 to y_1.

The multiplier for taxes is slightly different than the multiplier for government spending. If we cut government spending by $1, the $C + I + G$ line will shift downward by $1. However, if we increase taxes by $1, consumers will cut back their consumption by only $b \times \$1$. Thus, the $C + I + G$ line will shift downward by slightly less than $1, or $b \times \$1$. For example, if $b = 0.6$, the demand line would shift down vertically by $0.60.

Since the demand line does not shift by the same amount with taxes as it does with government spending, the formula for the tax multiplier is slightly different. Here's the formula for the tax multiplier; in the appendix, we show how to derive it:

$$\text{tax multiplier} = -\text{MPC}/(1 - \text{MPC})$$

The tax multiplier is negative because increases in taxes decrease disposable personal income and lead to a reduction in consumption spending. If the MPC = 0.6, the tax multiplier will be $-0.6/(1 - 0.6) = -1.5$.

Notice that the tax multiplier is smaller (in absolute value) than the government spending multiplier, which for the same MPC is 2.5. The reason the tax multiplier is smaller is that an increase in taxes first reduces income of households by the amount of the tax. However, because the MPC is less than 1 (0.6), the decrease in consumer spending is less than the increase in taxes.

Finally, you may wonder what would happen if we increased both government spending and taxes by an equal amount at the same time. Because the multiplier for government spending is larger than the multiplier for taxes, equal increases in both government spending and taxes will increase GDP. Economists call the multiplier for equal increases in government spending and taxes the *balanced-budget multiplier* because equal changes in government spending and taxes will not unbalance the budget. In the appendix, we show that the balanced-budget multiplier in our simple model is always equal to 1. For example, if spending and taxes are both increased by $10 billion, then GDP will also increase by $10 billion.

Using Fiscal Multipliers

Let's look at several examples of how we can use fiscal policy, altering taxes and government spending to affect GDP. In all these examples, suppose that GDP is $6,000 billion, the marginal propensity to consume is 0.6, the government-spending multiplier is $1/(1 - 0.6) = 2.5$, and the tax multiplier is $-0.6/(1 - 0.6) = -1.5$.

1. Suppose policymakers want to increase GDP by 1%, or $60 billion. By how much do policymakers have to increase government spending to meet this target?

ince the multiplier for government spending is 2.5, we need to increase government spending by only $24 billion. With a multiplier of 2.5, the $24 billion increase
 government spending leads to an increase in GDP of $60 billion ($24 billion ×
 5 = $60 billion).

2. Suppose policymakers wanted to use tax cuts rather than government spending
ncreases to increase GDP by $60 billion. How large a tax cut would be necessary? Since
he tax multiplier is −1.5, we need to cut taxes by $40 billion. The $40 billion tax cut
mes the multiplier will lead to the objective, a $60 billion increase in GDP (−$40 bil-
on × −1.5 = $60 billion).

3. Finally, if policymakers wanted to change taxes and government spending by
qual amounts, so as to not affect the federal budget, how large a change would be
eeded to increase GDP by $60 billion? Since the balanced-budget multiplier is 1, both
overnment spending and taxes must be increased by $60 billion.

The models that we are using are very simple and leave out important factors.
onetheless, the same basic principles apply in real situations. Here are five examples
f activist Keynesian fiscal policy from recent times.

1. In 1993, the three members of the President's Council of Economic Advisers
rote a letter to President Clinton stating that they thought the cuts in government
pending being proposed at the time were $20 billion too large. The economic model
he council members used had a multiplier for government spending of approxi-
nately 1.5. With this multiplier, the decrease in GDP from the $20 billion spending
ut would be ($20 billion × 1.5) = $30 billion. This was approximately 0.5% of GDP.
, in the absence of these cuts, GDP was expected to grow at 3% a year, the president's
dvisers estimated that with these cuts, GDP would grow at only 2.5% a year.
lowever, the advice of the council members came too late to influence the policy
ecisions.

2. During 1994, the U.S. government urged the Japanese to increase Japanese pub-
c spending and cut taxes to stimulate their economy. The Japanese then came up with
 plan and presented it to U.S. policymakers, who then evaluated it using multiplier
nalysis. These policymakers thought that this plan did not provide enough fiscal stim-
lus and urged the Japanese to take more aggressive actions. Several years later, the
apanese did adopt a more aggressive plan. Unfortunately, as our chapter-opening
tory describes, the Japanese government raised taxes in 1997, actually sending the
ountry further into a slump.

3. During the late 1990s, the Chinese economy came under pressure from the eco-
omic downturn in Asia and its own attempts to reform and restructure its economy.
o prevent a severe economic slowdown, the Chinese successively engaged in active fis-
al policy, increasing spending on domestic infrastructure, including roads, rails, and
rban facilities.

4. In 2001, President George W. Bush led the effort for a tax cut that would be
hased in over 10 years. In the first year, taxpayers received a one-time cut of up to a
naximum of $600. This was designed to provide direct stimulus to a sluggish economy.

5. After the September 11, 2001 terrorist attack on the United States, the gov-
rnment increased spending for disaster relief in New York and provided subsidies
nd loan guarantees to the airlines. In addition, Bush and Congress immediately
egan to work on additional spending programs and tax-relief programs to stimu-
te the economy.

A CLOSER LOOK

John Maynard Keynes

John Maynard Keynes was born into an academic family in Cambridge, England in 1883. His father, John Neville Keynes, was an economist and later an academic administrator at the King's College in Cambridge. His mother was one of the first female graduates of the same university, which Keynes entered in 1902. At King's College, Keynes began a lifetime association with an important group of writers and artists, the Bloomsbury group, which included the well-regarded writer Virginia Woolf. Members of the group were known both for their progressive views and their controversial lifestyles. In 1925, Keynes married the Russian ballerina Lydia Lopolova and was very active in promoting the arts.

After earning his degrees, Keynes became a civil servant, taking a job with the India Office in Whitehall, England. He then returned to Cambridge, where he taught economics. With the onset of World War I, Keynes returned to government employment, this time in the Treasury. After World War I, he attended the Versailles Peace Conference and wrote a book, *The Economic Consequences of the Peace*, which condemned the peace treaty and its negotiators for what he believed were the unfair and devastating burdens of the reparations (payments for causing the war) that Germany was required to pay to the allies. This book established Keynes as both a first-rate economic analyst and a brilliant writer, with a keen wit and shrewd political insights. Indeed, the reparation burdens on Germany partly led to its disastrous postwar economy and the rise of Nazism and Hitler.

Between the wars, Keynes wrote his most famous work, *The General Theory of Employment, Interest and Money*, which challenged the conventional wisdom that economies would automatically recover from economic downturns. It was a bold and controversial work, probably the most famous economics book written in the twentieth century. Because he believed economies would not necessarily recover by themselves and

monetary policies could also be ineffective during deep recessions, Keynes argued that governments needed to adopt activ policies, such as increased public works, in order to stimula the economy. His work influenced an entire generation of economists, especially in the United States and Great Britain, an provided the rationale for activist fiscal policy today.

The *General Theory* was Keynes's last major written work After World War II, he played a prominent role at the Bretto Woods Conference in 1944, which established the postwar worl monetary system and led to the creation of the Internationa Monetary Fund and the World Bank. His last major public servic was his negotiation in 1945 of a multibillion-dollar loan grante by the United States to Britain. Keynes died in 1946.

Although our income-expenditure model with government is very simple an leaves out many factors, like all models, it illustrates some important lessons.

▶ An increase in government spending will increase total planned expenditures fo goods and services.

▶ Cutting taxes will increase the after-tax income of consumers and will also lead t an increase in planned expenditures for goods and services.

▶ Policymakers need to take into account the multipliers for government spending and taxes as they develop their policies.

The idea that governments should use active fiscal policy to combat recessions was argued forcibly by John Maynard Keynes in the 1930s. His book *The General Theory of Employment, Interest, and Money* provided the intellectual foundation for the income-expenditure model in this chapter and explained why economies could become mired in recessions and fail to recover by themselves. As a consequence, he strongly advocated aggressive fiscal policymaking as the best option policymakers have for bringing economies out of recessions. Keynes was a very public figure and took a major role in policy debates throughout his life. "A Closer Look: John Maynard Keynes" discusses some aspects of his varied career.

One of Keynes' controversial ideas was that governments could stimulate the economy even if they spent money on wasteful projects. In the *General Theory*, he even remarked (tongue-in-cheek) how lucky the Egyptians were, because the death of the pharaohs would lead to new pyramids being built. Pyramids do not add to the stock of capital to produce regular goods and services. But Keynes's point was that building pyramids (or cruise missiles today) does add to planned expenditures and stimulates GDP in the short run.

In the long run, of course, we are better off if government spends the money wisely, such as on needed infrastructure like roads and bridges. But even here, we can carry things too far. Japan is notorious for its excessive public spending on infrastructure, driven in part by the central government doing favors for local politicians by creating jobs in their districts. Economists have even compared spending on bridges and roads in Japan to Keynes's famous pyramids.

Understanding Automatic Stabilizers

With a slight addition to our basic model, we can explain one of the important facts in U.S. economic history. Figure 25.9 plots the rate of growth of U.S. real GDP from 1871 to 2003. It is apparent from the graph that the U.S. economy has been much more stable after World War II than before. The reason is that government taxes and transfer payments (such as unemployment insurance and welfare payments) grew sharply after the war. These taxes and transfer payments can automatically reduce fluctuations in real GDP and thereby stabilize the economy. As we saw in the last chapter, taxes and transfers act as automatic stabilizers for the economy.

Again, here is how the automatic stabilizers work. When income is high, the government collects more taxes and pays out less in transfer payments. Because the government is taking funds out of the hands of consumers, there will be reduced consumer spending. On the other hand, when output is low (such as during recessions), the government collects less taxes and pays out more in transfer payments, increasing consumer spending because the government is putting funds into the hands of consumers. The automatic stabilizers prevent consumption from falling as much in bad times and from rising as much in good times. This stabilizes the economy without any need for decisions from Congress or the White House.

To see how automatic stabilizers work in our model, we must take into account that the government levies income taxes by applying a tax rate to the level of income.

FIGURE 25.9

**Growth Rate of U.S.
GDP, 1871–2003**

After World War II,
fluctuations in GDP growth
became considerably
smaller.

Source: Angus Maddison,
*Dynamic Forces in Capitalist
Development* (New York: Oxford
University Press, 1991); Bureau
of Economic Analysis,
Department of Commerce.

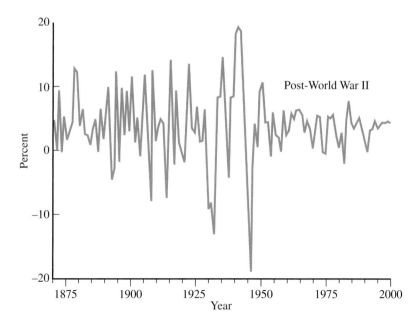

To simplify, suppose there is a single tax rate of 0.2 (in percent, 20%) and income is
$100. The government would then collect $0.2 \times \$100 = \$20$ in taxes.

If consumption depends on after-tax income, we have the following consumption
function:

$$C = C_a + b(1 - t)y$$

This is the consumption function with income taxes. The only difference between
the consumption function with income taxes and the consumption function without
income taxes is that the marginal propensity to consume is adjusted for taxes, and so

$$\text{adjusted MPC} = b(1 - t)$$

The reason for this adjustment is that consumers keep only a fraction $(1 - t)$ of their
income; the rest, t, goes to the government. When income increases by $1, consumers'
after-tax incomes increase by only $1 \times (1 - t)$, and of that $\$(1 - t)$, they spend a
fraction, b.

Raising the tax rate therefore lowers the MPC adjusted for taxes. Figure 25.10
shows the consequences of raising tax rates. With a higher tax rate, the government
takes a higher fraction of income, and less is left over for consumers. Recall that the
slope of the $C + I + G$ line is the marginal propensity to consume. Raising the tax rate
lowers the adjusted MPC and reduces the slope of this line. The $C + I + G$ line with
taxes intersects the 45° line at a lower level of income. Output falls from y_0 to y_1.

Note that as we raise tax rates, the $C + I + G$ schedule rotates and does not just
move down vertically as in our previous examples. The reason for this difference is that
as we change the tax rate, we change the adjusted MPC and thus the slope of the line.

Remember that a smaller marginal propensity to consume also leads to a lower
value for the multiplier. As tax rates increase and the adjusted MPC falls, the multiplier

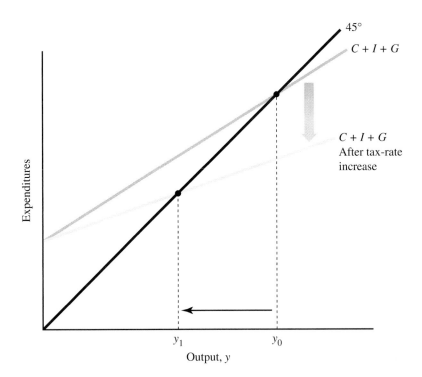

FIGURE 25.10

Increase in Tax Rates
An increase in tax rates
decreases the slope of the
$C + I + G$ line. This lowers
output and reduces the
multiplier.

will decrease. A smaller multiplier means that any shocks, such as shocks to investment, will have less of an impact on the economy.

Now that we have introduced income taxes into our model, we can see how automatic stabilizers work. Since World War II, taxes and transfer payments in the United States have increased sharply. As we have seen, higher tax rates will lower the multiplier and make the economy less susceptible to shocks. With higher taxes and transfer payments, there is a much looser link between fluctuations in disposable personal income and fluctuations in GDP. Because disposable personal income is more stable, consumption spending is also more stable. Thus, there is a smaller multiplier, and the economy is more stable.

As we have said, automatic stabilizers work silently in the background, doing their job without requiring explicit action by policymakers. Total tax collections rise and fall with GDP without requiring that policymakers change tax rates. The fact that the automatic stabilizers work without any laws being enacted is particularly important at times when it is difficult to obtain a political consensus for taking any action and policymakers are reluctant to use Keynesian fiscal policy as a deliberate policy tool.

Other factors contribute to the stability of the economy as depicted in Figure 25.9. As we explained in the last chapter, many consumers base their spending decisions in part on their long-run average income or permanent income, not just their current level of income. If households base their consumption on their long-run income, they will not be very sensitive to changes in their current income. For example, if their income temporarily rises, they are likely to save, not spend the additional income. Similarly, if their income temporarily falls, they are likely to maintain their consumption and reduce their current savings. In effect, when consumers base their consumption on their long-run average income, their MPC out of current income (which could be higher or lower than their long-run income) will be small. And since the MPC out of current income is small, the multiplier will be small as well.

Another important factor in promoting the stability of the economy is the knowledge by firms that the federal government will often be taking actions to stabilize the economy. Firms are less likely to decrease their investment spending in the face of a possible recession if they believe that government is likely to intervene to offset the severity of the recessions. Since investment spending tends to be a very volatile component of spending, any factor that helps stabilize investment spending will also stabilize the economy. The same logic also applies to consumers. If they believe the government will offset the severity of economic fluctuations, they are less likely to change their consumption spending in the face of shocks to their income.

Finally, in recent decades changes in inventory management practices by firms have also contributed to the stability of the economy. In the past, manufacturing firms often kept large inventories at their factories. If an unexpected shock slowed the economy down, the demand for firms' products would decrease and inventories would pile up. Firms would be forced to cut production even further to reduce their stock of inventories, adding additional downward pressure on the economy. This additional decrease in demand was known as the **inventory cycle** and was a significant component of earlier recessions. In recent times, U.S. firms have paid more attention to forecasting changes in the demand for their products and have adopted sophisticated computer management techniques to reduce the inventories that they normally hold. With less inventory on hand, firms do not have to change their production as much to adjust their inventories. The result is that the inventory cycle has become a less important factor for economic instability.

Inventory cycle

The process by which an increase in demand would lead firms to produce more for their inventories, thereby increasing demand further.

Exports and Imports

With international trade becoming increasingly important economically and politically, it is critical to understand how exports and imports affect the level of GDP. Two simple modifications of our model will allow us to understand how exports and imports affect GDP in the short run.

Exports affect GDP through their influence on how the world beyond the United States demands goods and services produced in the United States. An increase in exports means that there's an increase in the demand for goods produced in the United States. On the other hand, an increase in imports means that there's an increase in foreign goods purchased by U.S. residents. Importing goods rather than purchasing them from our domestic producers reduces the demand for U.S. goods. For example, if we in the United States spend a total of $10 billion on all automobiles but we imported $3 billion of them, then only $7 billion is spent on U.S. automobiles.

To get a clearer picture of the effects on GDP from exports and imports, let's for the moment ignore government spending and taxes. In the appendix, we present a complete model with both a domestic government and foreign countries to whom we sell our exports and from whom we buy our imports. To modify our model to include

e effects of world spending on exports and U.S. spending on imports, we need to take
vo steps:

1 Add exports, X, as another source of demand for U.S. goods and services.
2 Subtract imports, M, from total spending by U.S. residents. We will assume that
   imports, like consumption, increase with the level of income.

onsumers will import more goods as income rises. We can write this as

$$M = my$$

here m is a fraction known as the **marginal propensity to import**. We subtract this
action from b, the overall marginal propensity to consume, to obtain the MPC for
ending on domestic goods, $b - m$. For example, if $b = 0.8$ and $m = 0.2$, then for every
1 that GDP increases, total consumption increases by $0.80 but spending on domes-
c goods increases by only $0.60 because $0.20 is spent on imports. The MPC in this
xample, adjusted for imports is $(0.8 - 0.2) = 0.6$.

Figure 25.11 shows how equilibrium output is determined in an open economy,
nat is, an economy that engages in trade with the rest of the world. We plot planned
xpenditures for U.S. goods and services on our graph and find the level of equilibrium
ncome where it intersects the 45° line. The planned expenditure line has an intercept
n the vertical axis of $C_a + I + X$, which is the sum of autonomous consumption,
nvestment, and exports. The slope of the line is $b - m$, which is the MPC adjusted for
mports. Equilibrium output is the value of output where planned expenditures for
J.S. goods cross the 45° line.

Let's examine an application of the model that we just developed. Suppose Japan
ecides to buy another $5 billion worth of goods from the United States. What will

**Marginal propensity
to import**

The fraction of additional
income that is spent on
imports.

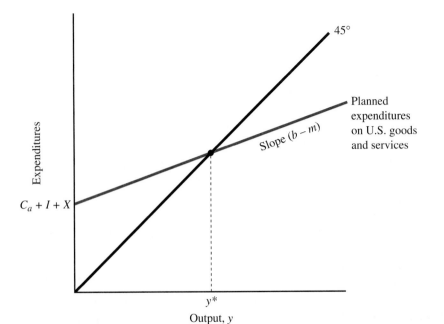

**U.S. Equilibrium Output
in an Open Economy**
Output is determined when
the demand for domestic
goods equals output.

happen to U.S. domestic output? Panel A of Figure 25.12 shows the effect of an increase in exports. The demand line will shift vertically upward by the increase in exports (ΔX). This will increase equilibrium income from y_0 to y_1.

The increase in income will be larger than the increase in exports because of the multiplier effect. This multiplier is based on the MPC adjusted for trade. For example, if $b = 0.8$ and $m = 0.2$, the adjusted MPC ($b - m$) is 0.6 and the multiplier will be $1/(1 - 0.6) = 2.5$. Therefore, a $5 billion increase in exports will lead to a $12.5 billion increase in GDP.

Now, suppose that U.S. residents become more attracted to foreign goods, and as a result, our marginal propensity to import increases. What happens to GDP? Panel B of Figure 25.12 depicts the effect of an increase in imported foreign goods. The adjusted MPC ($b - m$) will fall as the marginal propensity to import increases. This reduces the slope of the planned expenditure line, and output will fall from y_0 to y_1. The reason that the line rotates rather than shifting down vertically is because an increase in the propensity to import changes the *slope* of the planned expenditure line.

We can now understand why our domestic political leaders are eager to sell our goods abroad. Whether it is electronics or weapons, increased U.S. exports will increase U.S. GDP and reduce unemployment in the short run. At the same time, we can also understand why politicians will find "buy American" policies attractive in the short run. To the extent that U.S. residents buy U.S. goods rather than imports, output will be higher.

Belgium's Multiplier

Some economists have argued that the multiplier for government spending in Belgium is smaller than the multiplier for government spending in the United States. As an economic detective, can you explain this difference? (*Hint*: Imports and exports are a higher fraction of GDP in Belgium.)

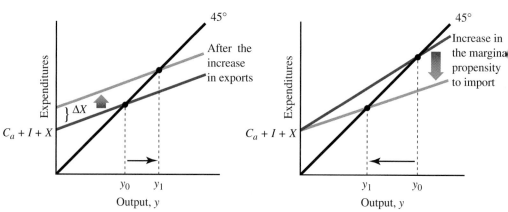

(A) An increase in exports will increase the level of GDP.

(B) An increase in the marginal propensity to import will decrease the level of GDP.

FIGURE 25.12 **How Increases in Exports and Imports Affect U.S. GDP**

Belgium is a small country and highly dependent on foreign trade. It has a high marginal propensity to import, which makes its adjusted MPC $(b - m)$ low. A low adjusted MPC will make the multiplier low as well. Thus, the multiplier for fiscal policy in Belgium is less than the fiscal policy multiplier for the United States because Belgium has a higher marginal propensity to import. ■

The Income-Expenditure Model and the Aggregate Demand Curve

We used the income-expenditure model in this chapter to understand more fully short-term economic fluctuations. The income-expenditure model is based on the assumption that prices do not change. However, the model can also be used to provide a foundation for the aggregate demand curve, which will enable us to analyze both changes in output and prices.

Figure 25.13 shows how the income-expenditure model provides the foundation for the aggregate demand curve. Suppose the price level in the economy is P_0 and, at that level of prices, planned expenditures are $C_0 + I_0$. At the top of the figure, we show how equilibrium output is determined at level of output, y_0. In the bottom part of the figure,

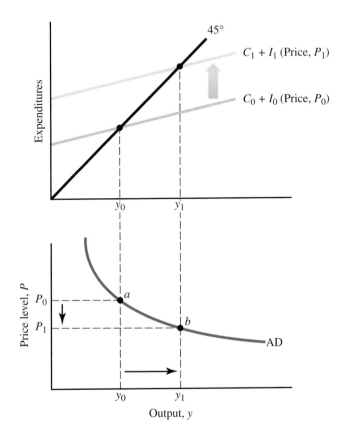

FIGURE 25.13

Deriving the Aggregate Demand Curve

As the price level falls from P_0 to P_1, planned expenditures increase, which increases the level of output from y_0 to y_1. The aggregate demand curve shows the combination of prices and equilibrium output.

we plot the price level, P_0, and corresponding level of output, y_0. In the graph, this point a.

Now let's lower the price level to P_1. Recall from our discussion in Chapter 23 th. a lower price level will increase the demand for goods and services through wealt effects, the interest rate effect, and effects from international trade. (You may want t go back and review this discussion.) As a consequence of the increased demand fo goods and services arising from a lower price level, we show a higher level of planne expenditure, $C_1 + I_1$, and a higher level of equilibrium output, y_1, in the top part of th figure. In the bottom part, we again plot the price level, P_1, and the corresponding lev of output, y_1. In the graph, this is point b.

Both point a and point b are on the aggregate demand curve. By the same logic, w can create all the other points on the aggregate demand curve, by either raising or low ering the aggregate price level. For any price level, the income-expenditure model ca be used to determine the level of output and the corresponding point on the aggregat demand curve. Thus, the income-expenditure model provides the basic foundation fo the aggregate demand curve.

At any price level, the income-expenditure model determines the level of equi librium output and the corresponding point on the aggregate demand curve. Wha

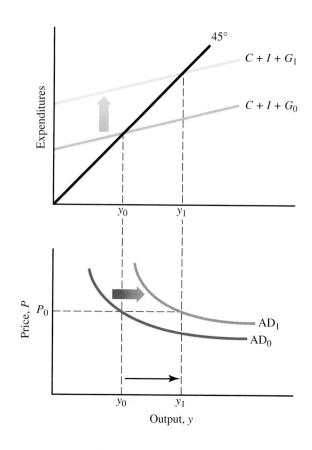

FIGURE 25.14

Shifts in Aggregate Demand

As government spending increases from G_0 to G_1, planned expenditures increase, which raises output from y_0 to y_1. At the price level P_0, this shifts the aggregate demand curve to the right, from AD_0 to AD_1.

would happen if we kept the price level at P_0 but increased planned expenditures, let's say through an increase in government expenditures from G_0 to G_1? We depict this case in Figure 25.14. The increase in government expenditure will raise the equilibrium output, from y_0 to y_1. Since the price level has not changed, we have a higher level of output at the same level of price. This means that the aggregate demand curve would shift to the right, from AD_0 to AD_1. In general, increases in planned expenditures that are not directly caused by changes in prices will shift the aggregate demand curve to the right; decreases in planned expenditures will shift the curve to the left.

In the remaining chapters, we will use the aggregate demand and supply curves to analyze economic fluctuations. This will enable us to understand movements in both prices and output in the intermediate and longer runs. But, as we have seen, the income-expenditure model developed in this chapter provides the underlying foundation for the aggregate demand curve.

Economic Experiment

Estimating the Marginal Propensity to Consume

For this experiment, each class member is asked to fill out the following table. Given a certain monthly income, how would you spend it and how much would you save? The top row of each column gives you the monthly disposable income. How would you allocate it each month among the various categories of spending in the table and savings? Complete each column in the table. The sum of your entries should equal your disposable income at the top of each column.

Monthly Disposable Income	$1,250	$1,500	$1,750	$2,000
Expenditures and Savings				
Food				
Housing				
Transportation				
Medical				
Entertainment				
Other expenses				
Savings				

After you have filled out the chart, compute the changes in your savings and total consumption as your income goes up. What is your marginal propensity to save (MPS)? What is your marginal propensity to consume (MPC) over your total expenditures? Graph your consumption function. ●

USING THE TOOLS

In this chapter, we developed the graphical and algebraic tools to use the income-expenditure model. Here is an opportunity to do your own economic analysis.

1. Estimating Changes in Aggregate Demand

a. Suppose $C = C_a + 0.6y$; a shock decreases C_a by $10 billion. By how much will equilibrium income decrease?

b. An economy has MPC = 0.6. By how much will a $10 billion increase in government purchases increase equilibrium income? By how much will a $10 billion increase in taxes decrease equilibrium income?

2. The Paradox of Thrift

One implication of the income-expenditure model is that an increase in the desire of consumers to save more will not necessarily lead to higher savings. In fact, total savings will either remain the same or perhaps fall. Let's see why this is true with an example.

a. Suppose that $I = 40$ and the savings function is $S = -100 + 0.4y$. Equilibrium income, y, in the economy is 350. Now suppose consumers wish to increase their savings; the new savings function becomes $S = -80 + 0.4y$. Calculate the new level of equilibrium output and savings after the change in the savings function.

b. Explain why equilibrium output is unchanged.

c. Now suppose that with a decline in equilibrium income, investment also falls. What would be the effect on equilibrium output and total savings if households now wished to increase their desired savings?

3. Using Multipliers

a. Suppose the MPC is equal to 0.8. Government spending increases by $20 billion. By how far does the aggregate demand curve shift to the right?

b. Now suppose that the MPC is 0.8 and the marginal propensity to import is 0.2. How far to the right will the $20 billion in government spending now shift the aggregate demand curve?

4. Trade Wars

During the 1930s, many countries in the world—including the United States—tried to help their own economies by restricting imported goods. But since one country's imports are another country's exports, there will be international repercussions. Let's look at the worldwide consequences of such policies using the income-expenditure model.

a. Suppose the United States adopted policies to reduce imports from Europe. Since this means that European exports to the United States would be reduced, what would happen to equilibrium income in Europe?

b. Suppose in response to our policies, the Europeans decide to restrict imports from the United States. What then happens to U.S equilibrium income?

c. What do you think happened to the volume of world trade during the 1930s?

SUMMARY

This chapter developed the income-expenditure model, which is useful for understanding short-run fluctuations. The chapter developed the graphical and algebraic tools to study the effects of consumer behavior, govern-ment spending and taxation, and exports and imports in determining GDP in the short run. Here are the chapter's main points:

1 In the income-expenditure model, the level of output in the economy will adjust to equal the level of planned expenditures. This level of output is called equilibrium output.

2 Consumption spending consists of two parts. One part is independent of income, but can be influenced by changes in wealth or consumer sentiment. The other part depends on the level of income.

3 Increases in planned expenditures by households, the government, or the foreign sector lead to increases in equilibrium output.

4 Because of the multiplier, the final increase in equilibrium output is larger than the initial increase.

5 Policymakers can use multipliers to calculate the appropriate size of economic policies.

6 Higher tax rates, by reducing the multiplier, can reduce fluctuations in GDP.

7 Increases in exports lead to increases in equilibrium output; increases in imports lead to decreases in equilibrium output.

8 The income-expenditure model can be used to derive the aggregate demand curve.

KEY TERMS

autonomous consumption, 571
consumption function, 571
equilibrium output, 569

inventory cycle, 586
marginal propensity to consume, 571

marginal propensity to import, 587
planned expenditures, 569
savings function, 576

PROBLEM AND DISCUSSION QUESTIONS

1 Consider an economy in which $C = 200 + 0.5y$ and $I = 200$.
   a. Find equilibrium income.
   b. What is the multiplier for investment spending for this economy?
   c. What is the savings function?
   d. What is the level of savings at the level of equilibrium income?

2 A country wishes to increase its GDP by 100. The marginal propensity to consume is 0.8.
   a. Using the government spending multiplier, by how much should government spending be increased?
   b. Using the tax multiplier, by how much should taxes be decreased?

3 A country has a marginal propensity to consume of 0.6 and a tax rate of 0.15. How much of an increase in investment would be needed to raise GDP by 150?

4 In an open economy, the marginal propensity to consume is 0.9, and the marginal propensity to import is 0.3. How much of an increase in exports would be necessary to raise GDP by 200?

5 Explain why in the model in this chapter, a higher tax rate leads to a lower multiplier for the economy. Does that mean that raising the tax rate is good for the economy in the model in this chapter?

6 Why do you think the model in this chapter is called the "income-expenditure model"?

7 a. Suppose clothing stores anticipate a good season and add substantially to inventories in their stores. What will happen to GDP?
   b. Suppose economists see inventories suddenly increasing. Does this necessarily mean that there are increases in demand?

8 Sometimes the newspapers state that if the economies of Europe and Japan grow rapidly, this will increase the growth of real GDP in the United States. Using our model with exports and imports, explain the logic of this argument.

9 During the 1970s, President Gerald Ford proposed that taxes be decreased but, to avoid increasing the government budget deficit, government spending should be decreased by the same amount. What happens to GDP if taxes and government spending are both decreased by the same amount?

10 Why could a collapse of the stock market lead to reduced consumer spending?

11 What are some of the important reasons that the economy may be more stable today than in the past?

12 Web Exercise. As we have seen in this chapter, changes in consumer spending can have powerful effects on the economy. While many factors, including income and wealth, affect consumer spending, general consumer confidence may also be a factor. For many years, the University of Michigan has published an index of consumer sentiment. Using the business/fiscal data on the Website for the Federal Reserve Bank of St. Louis (*http://research.stlouisfed.org/fred2*) explore the relationships between changes in consumer sentiment and consumer spending for the periods preceding several postwar recessions.

13 Web Exercise. Although John Maynard Keynes is best known today for his book *The General Theory of Employment, Interest and Money*, he wrote several other books as well. Use the Web to find information about some of Keynes's other well-known books. You may want to start with the Website from *Time* magazine's list of the most important people in the twentieth century (*http://www.pathfinder.com/time/time100*) or search for Keynes on a useful Website on schools of economic thought (*http://cepa.newschool.edu/het/thought.htm*). What were his other writings about?

MODEL ANSWERS TO QUESTIONS

Chapter-Opening Questions

1 Increased government spending directly increases aggregate demand. Cutting taxes increases aggregate demand through increasing consumption spending; however, some of the tax cut is saved.

2 Yes, an increase in the stock market can stimulate consumption spending through the wealth effect.

3 Yes, it will lead to increased consumption spending and an increase in GDP.

4 Yes, a sharp drop in exports could precipitate a recession.

Test Your Understanding

1 False; it is a short-run model.

2 At the point where the planned expenditure line crosses the 45° line, planned spending equals output.

3 The marginal propensity to consume.

4 Upward.

5 750

6 1000; the multiplier is 5.

7 0.3

8 The multiplier will decrease.

APPENDIX

Formulas for Equilibrium Income and the Multiplier

In this appendix, we do three things:

▶ Derive a simple formula for calculating equilibrium output for the simplest economy in which there is no government spending nor taxes.

➤ Derive the multipliers for the economy with the government.
➤ Derive equilibrium output with both government and the foreign sector.

To derive the formula for equilibrium output, we use simple algebra in the following steps:

1 We know that equilibrium output occurs where output equals planned expenditures, and we know that planned expenditures $= C + I$, therefore,

$$\text{output} = \text{planned expenditures} = C + I$$
$$\text{output} = C + I$$

2 Next, we substitute the symbol y for output; more important, we substitute for the consumption function, $C = (C_a + by)$:

$$y = (C_a + by) + I$$

3 Collect all terms in y on the left side of the equation:

$$y - by = C_a + I$$

4 Factor the left side:

$$y(1 - b) = C_a + I$$

5 Divide both sides by $(1 - b)$:

$$y^* = (C_a + I)/(1 - b)$$

where y^* means the equilibrium level of output.

This is the formula for equilibrium output in the text.

Now let's find the multiplier for investment in this simple economy. To do that, we use the formula we just derived and calculate the equilibrium income at one level of investment, which we call the original level, and then calculate the equilibrium income at some other level of investment, which we call the new level. (We will "calculate" in general terms, not in specific numerical quantities.) What we will get is a formula for the change in output that results from the changes in investment.

For the original level of investment at I_0, we have

$$y_0 = (C_a + I_0)/(1 - b)$$

For a new level of investment at I_1, we have

$$y_1 = (C_a + I_1)/1 - b)$$

The change in output, Δy, is the difference between the two levels of output that occur at each level of investment:

$$\Delta y = y_1 - y_0$$

Substituting for the levels of output, we have

$$\Delta y = (C_a + I_1)/(1 - b) - (C_a + I_0)/(1 - b)$$

Because the denominator in both expressions is the same $(1 - b)$, we can put the numerators over that common denominator:

$$\Delta y = [(C_a + I_1) - (C_a + I_0)]/(1 - b)$$
$$\Delta y = (I_1 - I_0)/(1 - b)$$

Finally, because $(I_1 - I_0)$ is the change in investment, ΔI, we can write

$$\Delta y = \Delta I/(1 - b)$$

or

$$\Delta y/\Delta I = 1/(1 - b)$$

Therefore, because the multiplier is the ratio of the change in income to the change in investment spending, we have

$$\text{the multiplier} = \Delta y/\Delta I = 1/(1 - b)$$

Here is another way to derive the formula for the multiplier. This way helps to illustrate its underlying logic. Suppose investment spending increases by $1. Because spending determines output, output will rise by $1. However, because consumption depends on income, consumption will increase by the marginal propensity to consume times the change in income. This means that as output rises by $1, consumption will increase by $(b \times \$1)$. Because spending determines output, this additional increase in consumer demand will cause output to rise further $(b \times \$1)$. But again, as output and income increase, consumption will increase by MPC times the change in income, which in this case will be $b \times (b \times \$1)$ or $b^2 \times \$1$. As we allow this process to continue, the total change in output will be

$$\Delta y = \$1 \times (\$1 \times b) \times (\$1 \times b^2) \times (\$1 \times b^3) \ldots$$

or

$$\Delta y = \$1 \times (1 + b + b^2 + b^3 + \cdots)$$

The term in parentheses is an infinite series whose value is equal to $1/(1 - b)$. Substituting this value for the infinite series, we have the expression for the multiplier:

$$\Delta y = \$1 \times 1/(1 - b)$$

Now we introduce government spending and taxes. Government spending is another determinant of planned expenditures, and consumption spending depends on after-tax income, so consumption equals $C_a + b(y - T)$. Following the same steps we used for equilibrium output without government, we do the same, but now with government:

$$\text{output} = \text{planned expenditures} = (C + I + G)$$
$$y = C_a + b(y - T) + I + G$$

We first collect all terms in y on the left and leave the other terms on the right:

$$y - by = C_a - bT + I + G$$

We then factor the left side:

$$y(1 - b) = C_a - bT + I + G$$

We then divide both sides by $(1 - b)$:

$$y^* = (C_a - bT + I + G)/(1 - b)$$

Using this formula and the method just outlined, we can find the multiplier for changes in government spending, taxes, and the multiplier for changes in taxes:

$$\text{government spending multiplier} = 1/(1 - b)$$
$$\text{tax multiplier} = -b/(1 - b)$$

The multiplier for an increase in government spending is larger than the tax multiplier for a reduction in taxes in the same amount as an increase in government spending. Government spending increases total demand directly. Reductions in taxes first affect consumer's incomes. Because consumers will save a part of their income increase from the tax cut, not all of the tax cut is spent. Therefore, the tax multiplier is smaller (in absolute value) than the government spending multiplier.

As we explained in the text, because government spending has a larger multiplier than taxes, equal increases in government spending and taxes, called balanced-budget increases, will increase total output. For equal dollar increases in both taxes and government spending, the positive effects from the spending increase will outweigh the

negative effects from the tax increase. To find the balanced-budget multiplier, just add
the government spending and tax multipliers:

$$\text{balanced-budget multiplier} = \text{government spending multiplier} + \text{tax multiplier}$$
$$= 1/(1-b) = -b/(1-b)$$
$$= (1-b)/(1-b)$$
$$= 1$$

The balanced-budget multiplier equals 1; a $10 billion increase in both taxes and gov-
ernment spending will increase GDP by $10 billion.

Finally, we derive equilibrium output with government spending, taxes, and the
foreign sector. First, recall that equilibrium output occurs where output equals
demand. We now must include planned expenditures from both the government sector and the foreign sector. Planned expenditures from the foreign sector are exports
minus imports:

$$\text{output} = \text{planned expenditures} = (C + I + G + X - M)$$

Consumption depends on disposable income:

$$C = C_a + b(y - T)$$

and imports depend on the level of output:

$$M = my$$

Substitute the equations for consumption and imports into the equation where output
equals demand:

$$y = C_a + b(y - T) + I + G + X - my$$

Collect all terms in y on the left and leave the other terms on the right:

$$y - (b - m)y = C_a - bT + I + G + X$$

Factor the left side:

$$y[1 - (b - m)] = C_a - bT + I + G + X$$

Divide both sides by $[1 - (b - m)]$:

$$y^* = (C_a - bT + I + G + X)/[1 - (b - m)]$$

This is the expression for equilibrium income with government in an open economy. It can be used, following the method we outlined, to calculate multipliers in the
open economy.

USING THE TOOLS

1. Find the Multiplier

An economy has a marginal propensity to consume $b = 0.6$ and a marginal propensity to import $m = 0.2$. What is the multiplier for government spending for this economy?

2. The Effects of Taxes and Spending

Suppose the economy has a marginal propensity to consume $b = 0.4$. The government increases its spending by \$2 billion and raises taxes by \$1 billion. What happens to equilibrium income?

3. Savings and Taxes

When there are taxes, savings is defined as disposable income minus consumption, or $S = (y - T) - C$. In an economy with government but no foreign sector —a closed economy—equilibrium income is determined where output equals demand,

or $y = C + I + G$. Show that we can also determine equilibrium income using the relationship $S + T = I + G$.

3. Working with a Model

An economy has

$$C = 100 + 0.5(y - T)$$
$$I = 50$$
$$G = 50$$
$$T = 20$$

a. Find equilibrium income.
b. What is the multiplier for government spending?
c. Find the savings function.
d. What is the level of savings when the economy is in equilibrium?
e. Show that at equilibrium, $S + T = I + G$

Investment and Financial Intermediation

At the peak of the high-tech boom in the late 1990s, firms and investors were extremely optimistic about the future of the technology industry. This was especially true in Northern California, home to Silicon Valley. Any new idea, even if it was wacky, seemed plausible to investors as long as it involved technology. As the stock market soared and venture capitalists funded new, start-up companies, other entrepreneurs—anticipating a shortage of office space for new, high-tech firms—erected huge numbers of new office buildings.

Unfortunately, when the stock market fell and the high-tech boom ended abruptly in 2001, the demand for office space dried up. Rents fell sharply, and instead of a shortage of office space in Silicon Valley, there was a glut of office buildings. Many of them stood vacant along vast stretches of highways, and drivers passing by the empty buildings could actually see right through them. They were the "ghosts" of the 2001 recession.

I nvestment spending plays a number of critical roles in the economy. As we have seen, economic growth depends critically on whether the stock of capital—plant and equipment—increases in the economy. Moreover, investment is also a key component of aggregate demand, so fluctuations in investment spending can cause recessions and booms. In this chapter, we will study the factors that determine investment spending by firms. We also will examine the role that institutions such as banks, savings and loans, and other financial institutions play in facilitating that investment.

After reading this chapter, you will be able to answer these kinds of questions:

1 Why does investment spending depend on interest rates? Does it also depend on other factors?

2 What are the links between the stock market and investment?

3 Why do businesses and homeowners want to borrow in inflationary times, when interest rates are high?

4 How can banks and other financial institutions make risk seem to vanish?

5 Why do runs on healthy and profitable banks, which occur when depositors all try to withdraw their money at the same time, rarely happen today?

An investment, broadly defined, is an action that creates a cost today but provides benefits in the future. A firm builds a new plant today to earn more revenue in the future. College students pay money to attend school now so they can earn higher salaries later. A government spends money today to constructs a dam that will provide hydroelectric power for years to come. These are examples of investments. Notice that we're using the term *investment* in a broader sense than we did in Chapter 19 when we discussed GDP. In that chapter when we talked about investment, we were talking about expenditures by firms on currently produced goods and services. In this chapter we broaden the definition to include actions taken by anyone—individuals firms, and governments—to improve one's well-being later.

An Investment: A Plunge into the Unknown

When people, firms, or governments make an investment, they incur costs today in the hope of future gains. The phrase "hope of" is an important aspect of investment decisions. That simply means that payoffs occurring in the future cannot be known with certainty. Investments are a plunge into the "unknown."

Firms and individuals frequently revise their outlook on the future precisely because it is uncertain. These changes can occur suddenly and lead to sharp swings in investment spending. Sometimes investors are optimistic and decide to increase their investment spending; at other times, they may quickly become pessimistic and cut back on their investment spending. To estimate future events, firms pay careful attention to the current pace of the economy. If economic growth is sluggish, they are likely to forecast it will be sluggish in the future and cut back on investment spending. If economic growth is strong, they are likely to forecast it will remain so and increase their investment spending. In other words, investment spending tends to be closely related to the current pace of economic growth.

This latter phenomenon is known as the **accelerator theory** of investment spending. The accelerator theory postulates that when real GDP growth is expected to be high, firms anticipate that investing in plants and equipment will pay off later, so they increase their total investment spending. However, John Maynard Keynes had another theory. Keynes said the sharp swings in optimism and pessimism related to investment spending were often irrational, reflecting, perhaps, our most basic, primal instincts. He often referred to them as "the animal spirits" of investors.

It is likely that *both* projections for the future *and* Keynes's animal spirits are closely associated with current economic growth. If this is the case, we would expect investment spending to be a very volatile component of GDP. As Figure 26.1 indicates, this is indeed the case.

Figure 26.1 plots total investment spending as a share of U.S. GDP from 1970 to 2002. There are two things you need to notice about Figure 26.1:

▶ From 1970 to 2002, the share of investment as a component of GDP ranged from a low of about 11% in 1975 to a high of nearly 20% in 2000—a dramatic nine-percentage-point difference.
▶ Swings in investment spending often occurred over short periods of time. For example, during recessions (noted by the shaded areas in the figure), investment

Accelerator theory

The theory of investment that says current investment spending depends positively on the expected future growth of real GDP.

FIGURE 26.1

Investment Spending as a Share of U.S. GDP, 1970–2002

The shaded areas represent U.S. recessions.

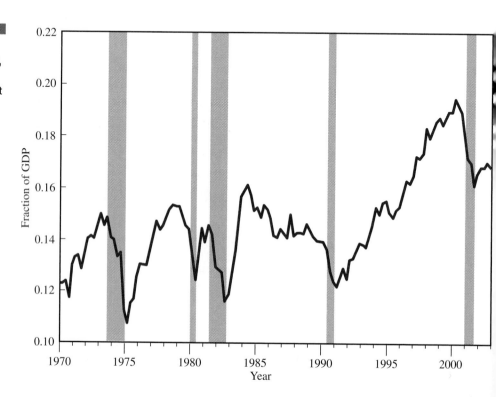

spending fell sharply. During booms, investment spending rose sharply. Investment spending is highly **procyclical**, in other words. It increases during booms and falls during recessions.

Procyclical

Moving in same direction as real GDP.

Although investment spending is a much smaller component of GDP than consumption, it is much more volatile than consumption. Recall that changes in the components of GDP—C, I, G, or NX—are amplified by the multiplier. For example, if the multiplier is 1.5, and investment spending initially falls by 1% of GDP, then GDP will fall by 1.5%. However, if the fall in GDP makes firms more pessimistic, they may cut investment even further. This further cut in investment will decrease GDP even more. That is, a small initial fall in investment can trigger a much larger fall in GDP. Nobel laureate Paul Samuelson described this phenomenon of investment volatility by developing the **multiplier-accelerator model**. The multiplier-accelerator model showed that a downturn in real GDP leads to an even sharper fall in investment, which further reduces GDP via the multiplier.

Multiplier-accelerator model

A model in which a downturn in real GDP leads to a sharp fall in investment, which triggers further reductions in GDP through the multiplier.

Investment spending is not only affected by psychology or expectations about real GDP growth in the future. Because investments are really trade-offs—something in the present traded for something in the future—the "terms" affecting the trade-off are also important. These terms are interest rates, which we discuss next.

Evaluating the Future

A dollar paid today is not the same as a dollar paid next year. Since investments involve future payoffs, we need to be able to compare costs and benefits at different points in time. As we will see, we can use interest rates to compare the different payoffs over time.

Understanding Present Value

Suppose that a good friend comes to you and says, "I need some cash, badly. If you give me $100 today, I can give you back $105 next year. Do we have a deal?" How would you decide whether to accept this deal? Somehow, you need a tool to be able to compare dollars today versus dollars received in the future. That tool is present value.

The **present value** of a payment to be received in the future is the maximum amount a person is willing to pay today to get that payment later. Recall the principle of opportunity cost.

Present value

The maximum amount a person is willing to pay today to receive a payment in the future.

 Principle OF OPPORTUNITY COST
The opportunity cost of something is what you sacrifice to get it.

Let's think about how much you are willing to pay for the right to receive $105 in one year. Suppose that you can earn 5% per year in a savings account or money market account.

A moment of thought will show you that you would be willing to lend your friend $100. Here is why: If you kept your $100 in the bank at 5% interest, you would have $105 at the end of the year—just the amount that your friend would repay you. While you would have sacrificed $5 in interest, you would have earned $5 on the loan ($105 – $100).

On the other hand, you would not want to lend your friend more than $100. If you lent your friend more—say $102—then your loss in interest $5.10 (5% of $102) would be greater than your $3 gain on the loan ($105–$102). In this case, the amount you would sacrifice would be greater than what you would get in return.

Of course, you would like to lend your friend less than $100 and make even more profit. But the *maximum amount* you would be willing to pay today to receive $105 next year, when the interest rate is 5%, is $100. Thus, the present value of $105 in this example is $100.

Present Value and Interest Rates

Here is another useful way to think of present value. Suppose you want to know how much you would need to have in your bank account today so that after a certain number of years, the total sum amounted to what you wanted? (Assume there was something you wanted to buy with that money, and you planned to earn interest on it to accumulate the money you needed for the purchase.) A simple formula shows the present value of a future payment. Let's say that K is the amount of money you would get at some point in the future, that t is the amount of time, or years, in the future you're going to get the money, and that i is the interest rate you're going to earn. If you receive K dollars in t years and the interest rate is i, the present value (PV) of the future payment is

$$\text{present value} = K/(1 + i)^t$$

In the example that involved your friend, her payment (K) is $105, the interval of time (t) in which she's going to pay it is one year, and the interest rate (i) is 0.05. Using the present value formula, the present value of $105 in one year is $100:

$$\text{present value} = \$105/(1 + 0.05)^1 = \$100$$

This is the maximum amount you are willing to lend her today to receive $105 from her in one year.

Let's consider another example. Suppose the interest rate was 10% and you were offered $1,000 to be paid to you in 20 years. How much would that $1,000 be worth today? That is, how much of your money today would you be willing to "tie up" (loan out) to get $1,000 in 20 years? At an interest rate of 10%, this is how much:

$$\text{present value} = \$1,000/(1 + 0.10)^{20} = \$148.64$$

You would be willing to pay only $148.64 today to receive $1,000 in 20 years from now. The reason that you would be willing to pay so much less than $1,000 is that money earning interest grows over time. At a 10% interest rate, after 20 years you would have earned exactly $1,000 by initially investing just $148.64.

Returning to our original example with our friend, what happens if the interest rate is 10% instead of 5%? If your friend still promises you $105 after one year, but the interest rate is double, how much would you be willing to loan her today? Using the formula, you would loan your friend only $95.45 today:

$$\text{present value} = \$105/(1 + 0.10)^1 = \$95.45$$

What this means is that if the interest rate is higher, you will be willing to pay *less* for the same payment in the future. This is an important result. *The present value of a given payment in the future decreases as the interest rate increases.* Here is why: With a higher interest rate, the opportunity cost of lending out your money is higher. Since you can earn more on your money with a higher rate, you will not be willing to pay as much now to get the same $105 dollars in the future. Similarly, *when interest rates fall, the present value of a given payment in the future increases.* For example, if interest rates fell to 2%, the present value (the value today) of $105 in one year would be more—$102.94:

$$\text{present value} = \$105/(1 + 0.02)^1 = \$102.94$$

With a lower interest rate, the opportunity cost of keeping your money in the bank or loaning it to a friend is less. That means you will be willing to pay more money now for the same $105 payment in the future.

Let's summarize our discussion of present value:

1 The present value (the value today) of a given payment in the future is the maximum amount a person is willing to pay today for that payment.
2 As the interest rate increases, the opportunity cost of your funds also increases, so the present value of a given payment in the future falls. (You need *less* money today to get to your future "money goal," in other words.)
3 As the interest rate decreases, the opportunity cost of your funds also decreases, so the present value of a given payment in the future rises. (You need *more* money today to get to your money goal, in other words.)

Individuals, firms, and the government all use interest rates to make decisions that involve the future. For example, individuals take interest rates into account when they decide how much to save for the future or even when to retire. And, as we will see, firms and the government use interest rates to decide whether to undertake important investments.

Options for a Lottery Winner

The lucky winner of a lottery was given an option. She could either receive $1 million a year for 20 years, for a total of $20 million, or simply receive $10 million today. Why would anyone take the $10 million today?

To solve the puzzle, we need to use the concept of present value. A dollar paid today is not the same as a dollar paid next year. Depending on the interest rate, the $10 million today might be more valuable than the $20 million paid over 20 years. Indeed, if interest rates were 10%, you could take the $10 million today, put it in the bank, and earn $1 million in interest (10% of $1 million) forever—not just for 20 years! To determine which payment option is best, our lottery winner would first need to calculate the present value of $1 million for each of the 20 years, add up the result, and compare it to the $10 million being offered to her today. With an 8% interest rate, the present value of an annual payment of $1 million every year for 20 years is $9.8 million. So if interest rates exceed 8%, it is better to take the $10 million dollars. (The actual calculation—adding up the present value at an 8% interest rate for all 20 years—is a bit tedious. In the problems at the end of the chapter, we show you how to make this calculation using an Excel spreadsheet.) ∎

Real and Nominal Interest Rates

Even if you deposit $100 in a bank account and get $105 at the end of the year, if the economy's annual rate of inflation amounts to 5% or more, your purchasing power would not have increased at all. The 5% inflation will "eat up" all of your 5% earnings, in other words. This is an example of the real-nominal principle:

REAL-NOMINAL *Principle*

What matters to people is the real value of money or income—its purchasing power—not the face value of money or income.

Nominal interest rates
Interest rates quoted in the market.

Real interest rate
The nominal interest rate minus the inflation rate.

When there is inflation, economists make a distinction between the interest rates quoted in the market, which is called the **nominal interest rate**, and the **real interest rate**, which is what you actually earn after inflation has taken its toll. The real interest rate is defined as the nominal interest rate minus the inflation rate:

$$\text{real rate} = \text{nominal rate} - \text{inflation rate}$$

If the nominal rate of interest is 6% per year and the inflation rate is 4% during the year, the real rate of interest is 2% $(6 - 4)$.

To understand what the real rate of interest means, suppose you have $100 and there is 4% annual inflation. It's not hard to figure out that next year you will need $104 to have the same purchasing power you do today. Let's say you deposit today $100 at a 6% annual interest rate. At the end of the year, you will have $106 ($100 × 1.06).

Now let's calculate your real gain. After one year, you will have increased your holdings by $6, but taking into account the $4 you needed to keep up with inflation, your gain is only $2. The real rate of interest you earned, the nominal rate adjusted for inflation, is 2%, or $2.

Let's see what happens when you borrow money. Suppose you borrow $100 at a 10% annual interest rate, but there is 6% inflation during the year. At the end of the year, you must pay back $110 ($100 × 1.10). But with 6% inflation, the lender would need six of the ten dollars you paid in interest just to keep up with inflation. That means the lender would effectively get just a $4 gain ($10 − $6), instead of the full $10 gain. Thus, when corrected for the effects of inflation, the real rate of interest you will have to pay is just 4%, or $4 on the original $100 loan.

As an example, in 2002 if seniors invested their money in three-month U.S. government Treasury bills, they would have earned an average interest rate of 1.6%. However, inflation as measured by the Consumer Price Index, was 2.4%. In real terms, these seniors would have actually lost money during the year, earning a negative real rate of interest of −0.8%.

We defined the real interest rate as the nominal interest rate minus the actual inflation rate. When firms or individuals borrow or lend money, they do not know what the rate of inflation will actually be in the future. Instead, they must form an expectation—an estimate—of what they believe the inflation rate will be in the future. For a given nominal interest rate, we can define the **expected real interest rate** as the nominal rate minus the expected inflation rate. The expected real interest rate is the rate at which borrowers or lenders *expect* to make transactions.

Expected real interest rate
The nominal interest rate minus the expected inflation rate.

It is difficult to precisely determine expected real rates of interest because we never know exactly what inflation rates people really anticipate. One approach is to rely on the judgments of professional forecasters. Table 26.1 presents the expected real rates of interest in 2004 for the five developed countries in column one based on economic forecasts. The second column shows the nominal interest rates on three-month loans; the third column shows the inflation rate forecasts for 2004. The last column shows estimates of the expected real rate of interest in each country by subtracting the inflation forecast from the interest rate. As you can see, both nominal and expected real interest rates differ among developed countries. The fact that real interest rates differ across the countries means that investors in those countries are expecting to earn different real returns on their investments. In order to determine real returns, we need to know both the nominal rate of interest and forecasts for inflation.

At any point in time, there are many different interest rates, as "A Closer Look: The Variety of Interest Rates" illustrates.

Country	3-Month Interest Rate	Inflation Rate Forecast for 2004	Expected Real Rate of Interest
Australia	5.5%	2.3%	2.2%
Canada	2.6	1.7	0.9
Denmark	2.3	1.6	0.7
Switzerland	0.3	0.6	−0.3
United States	1.1	1.5	−0.4

TABLE 26.1

Expected Real Rates of Interest for Five Countries

Source: The Economist, Jan. 3, 2004.

A CLOSER LOOK

The Variety of Interest Rates

There are many different interest rates in the economy. Loans vary by their riskiness and by their maturity (the length of the loan). Riskier loans and loans for longer maturities typically have higher interest rates.

Figure 26.2 depicts movements in three interest rates during 2002 for three types of investments: Corporate AAA bonds (loans to corporations that are good credit risks), 10-year U.S. Treasury bonds (loans to the government for 10 years), and 6-month Treasuries (loans to the U.S. government for 6 months).

Notice that rates for corporate bonds are higher than the rates for 10-year Treasury bonds. That's because corporations are less likely to pay back their loans than the U.S. government. Notice, too, that the U.S. government typically pays lower rates when it borrows for shorter periods of time (6 months) than for longer periods of time (10 years).

FIGURE 26.2

Interest Rates on Corporate and Government Investments, 2002

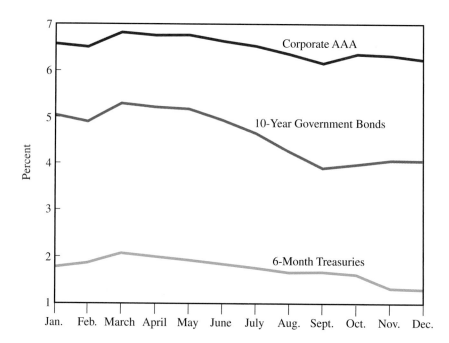

TEST Your Understanding

1. Investment is a smaller component of GDP than consumption, but it is a more stable component. True or false?
2. Investment spending is very procyclical, moving in conjunction with GDP. True or false? Explain.
3. If the interest rate is 10%, what is the present value of $200 paid one year from now?
4. If interest rates increase, the present value of a fixed payment in the future
   _____.
5. With 6% annual inflation, a nominal rate of interest of 10% per year means a real rate of interest of _____ % per year.

Understanding Investment Decisions

Now that we understand the concept of present value and interest rates, we can use these tools to understand investment decisions. Consider a project we have to pay for today to benefit from in the future. Here is the simple investment rule for such a project.

■ Investment Rule

Invest in a project if the cost you incur today is less than or equal to the present value of the future payments from the project.

In our first present value example, the "project" (the loan to your friend) pays $105 in one year, and the present value (with an interest rate of 5%) is $100. Since the cost of the project is also $100, the project is worthwhile.

Consider a more complicated project that pays $110 in year 1 and in year 2. The interest rate is 10%. The present value of the benefits from this project are

$$\text{present value} = \$110/(1 + 0.10) + \$110/(1.10)^2 = \$191$$

As long as the cost of the project today is less than $191, it pays to do it.

We can use our theory to develop the relationship between investment spending and the real rate of interest in the economy. In the economy as a whole, there are millions of investment projects that can be undertaken, nearly all providing different returns from any other. Consider the array of investments A through E in Table 26.2. Each project costs $100 in the current period and provides a return one period later. The returns are expressed in real terms; that is, they have been adjusted for inflation.

Let's look at the present value of these investments at various interest rates. At an interest rate of 2% per year, only investment A is unprofitable. All the other investments have a positive present value. If the interest rate in the market increases to 4%,

Project	Cost	Return
A	$100	$101
B	100	103
C	100	105
D	100	107
E	100	109

both A and B will be unprofitable. At an interest rate of 6%, A, B, and C will be unprof itable; D will be unprofitable as well, if the market interest rate increases to 8%. If the interest rate exceeds 9%, all the investments will be unprofitable.

As interest rates rise, there will be fewer profitable investments that firms will be willing to invest in and the total level of investment spending in the economy will decline. Figure 26.3 depicts the negative relationship, graphically represented as the downward-sloping line, between real interest rates and investment. As the graph indi cates, high real interest rates will deter investment spending. As an example, during the early 1980s, when real interest rates rose, there was a sharp drop in business investment

In practice, firms need to take into account other factors besides interest rates in making their investment decisions. In the **neoclassical theory of investment**, pio neered by Dale Jorgenson of Harvard University, taxes along with the real interest rate play a key role in determining investment spending. Jorgenson used his theory to analyze how investors respond to a variety of tax incentives, including investment tax credits.

Should we use a real or nominal interest rate to determine whether or not to invest? The answer is, it doesn't really matter, as long as we are consistent. If the future benefits of the project are not adjusted for inflation, then we should use the nominal interest rate because the nominal interest rate takes into account overall inflation— inflation is "built-into" the nominal rate, so to speak. But if we first express the future benefits of the investment in current dollars—that is, we reduce their nominal value by

Neoclassical theory of investment

A theory of investment that says both real interest rates and taxes are important determinants of investment.

As the real interest rate declines, investment spending in the economy increases.

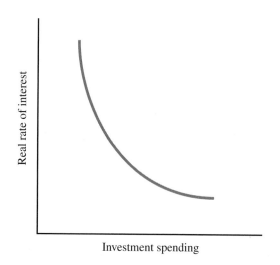

Real rate of interest

Investment spending

the amount that prices in the economy are expected to increase—then we should use the real rate of interest in our calculations.

It is important to keep this distinction between real and nominal interest rates in mind. If nominal interest rates are 10% but inflation is 9%, the real rate of interest is only 1%. A firm makes its investment decisions by comparing its expected real net return from investment projects to the real rate of interest. Just because nominal interest rates are high does not mean that the real interest rate is also high.

During the 1970s, homeowners in California understood this. They purchased homes in record numbers, even though it meant borrowing money at interest rates exceeding 10%. They were willing to borrow at such high rates because housing prices in California had been rising by more than 10% annually and they believed the trend would continue. They realized for example, if housing prices rose by 12% per year, they were essentially earning a 2% annual return because their mortgage loans were just 10% (They would earn the returns only when they sold their homes.) That would mean the real interest rate of the money borrowed would be –2%. This caused a housing boom in California that lasted until housing prices stopped rising at such high rates.

Investment and the Stock Market

Economists have long noticed a correlation between the stock market and investment spending. All other things being equal, when the level of the stock market is high, investment spending also tends to be high. It makes sense that the two are related. Consider a firm's options when it wants to finance a new project. The firm really has three choices: First, it can rely on its **retained earnings**—the earnings the firm hasn't paid out in dividends to its owners. Second, it can borrow funds from a bank or sell **corporate bonds** to the public. Third it can issue and sell new shares, or stock. When a firm's stock price is high, it can issue shares at a premium and use the proceeds from their sale to finance new investments. The higher the share price is, the fewer number of shares it needs to sell to raise capital. This means, essentially, that the cost of the project the firm wants to undertake falls as the company's stock price climbs. High stock prices lead to high investment, in other words. This is known as the **Q-theory of investment**, and it was originally developed by Nobel laureate James Tobin of Yale University. In the boom of the late 1990s when the level of the stock market was high along with share prices, many firms financed large investments by selling their shares.

During roughly this same time period, the stock market and investment spending appeared to be even more tightly linked than in the past. Figure 26.4 plots the Standard and Poor's index of stock prices on the same graph as the share of investment spending as a component of GDP from 1997 to 2003. As you can see, both the stock market and investment spending rose sharply from 1997, peaking in mid-2000. They then both fell sharply—the stock market plunged, investment spending fell, and the economy entered a recession.

The reason the two were so tightly linked was because investors were overly optimistic about the future. They believed that driven by new technology, the new found

Retained earnings
Corporate earnings that are not paid out as dividends.

Corporate bond
A bond sold by a corporation to the public in order to borrow money.

Q-theory of investment
The theory of investment that links investment spending to stock prices.

FIGURE 26.4

**The Stock Market and
Investment Levels,
1997–2003**

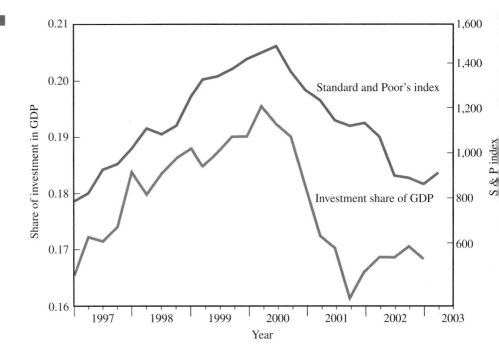

economic prosperity would last forever (or at least certainly longer than it did). With optimistic expectation about the future, stock prices should have been high because stock prices are based on the present value of the dividends people expect firms to pay in the future:

$$\text{price of a stock} = \text{present value of expected future dividend payments}$$

Because investors' expectations about future dividends were high, stock prices were high. Firms, like individual investors, rushed to make massive, long-term investments, particularly in the fiber-optics and telecommunications industries. Some observers questioned whether the expectations were rational. Still, there were enough optimistic investors to sufficiently drive up prices.

As we saw in Figure 26.1, investment spending during this period in the United States reached new highs. In many cases, stock prices for companies that had never turned a profit nonetheless soared to astronomical heights. Alas, both investors and firms were subject to what Yale economist Robert Shiller famously dubbed "irrational exuberance"—something similar to Keynes's, "animal spirits." Although the economy had performed very well in the late 1990s, it could not grow at those rates forever. Many investors and firms believed it could, though. When they began to realize it couldn't, the stock market plunged and investment plans were curtailed. What linked the stock market and investment on both their rise and fall were first optimistic and then pessimistic expectations about the economy. Rather than causing the rise and fall of investment spending, the stock market mirrored expectations about the economy held by firms and individual investors.

TEST Your Understanding

6. If a project costs $100 and pays $107 next year, what is the maximum interest rate at which the present value of the investment exceeds its cost?

7. As real interest rates rise, investment spending in the economy _____.

8. Does a high nominal rate of interest necessarily deter investment?

9. The Q-theory of investment links the level of investment with _____.

How Financial Intermediaries Facilitate Investment

Households, or people save and invest their funds for different reasons than firms do. A typical couple might be saving money for their retirement or for their children's education, and they generally won't like the idea of their savings being subject to risk. They do, however, want their savings to be readily accessible—what economists call **liquid**—in case they have a financial emergency. Funds deposited in a bank account, for example, provide a source of liquidity for households because they can be withdrawn at any time.

Unlike households, firms and business managers are typically risk-takers. They are gambling that their vision of the future will come true and make them vast profits. These investors need funds that can be tied up for long periods of time. For example, an entrepreneur who wants to build a skyscraper or casinos may need financing for several years before beginning construction and for years afterward until the business begins to produce profits.

Suppose that individual entrepreneurs had to obtain funds directly from individual savers. First, they would have to negotiate with thousands of savers to obtain sufficient funds. This would take a lot of time and be costly. Second, the savers would face extraordinarily high risks if they loaned all of their money to a single entrepreneur who had a risky project to undertake. Not only would all of their funds be tied up in a single project, it would not be easy to monitor the investor's decisions. How could they be certain the entrepreneur wouldn't run off with their money? Nor would their investments be liquid. To compensate these investors for the risk they would be taking and the lack of liquidity they would face, investors would have to pay them extremely high interest rates But higher interest rates would make it harder, perhaps impossible, for the entrepreneur to make a profit. No prospect of profits would mean no one would invest in the project in the first place. Society would not be able to turn its savings into profitable investment projects, in other words. Figure 26.5 depicts this dilemma. How can the problem be solved?

The answer is through **financial intermediaries**, of course. Financial intermediaries include banks, savings and loans, insurance companies, brokerage firms, companies that run mutual funds, and other types of financial institutions. These institutions accept funds from savers and make loans to businesses and individuals. For example, a local bank accepts deposits from savers and uses the funds to make loans to local

Liquid

Easily convertible to money on short notice.

Financial intermediaries

Organizations that receive funds from savers and channel them to investors.

FIGURE 26.5

Savers and Investors

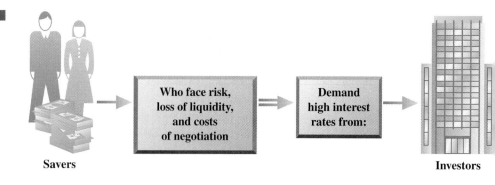

businesses. Savings and loan institutions will accept deposits in savings accounts and use these funds to make loans, often for housing. Insurance companies accept premium payments from individuals in exchange for the protection provided by the insurance payments. Then insurance companies lend the premiums received to earn returns from investments so that they can pay off the insurance claims of individuals. Figure 26.6 shows how financial intermediaries create a valuable link between savers and investors. Pooling the funds of savers to make loans to individual borrowers reduces the costs of negotiation. Financial institutions also have more expertise to evaluate and monitor investments than most individual investors.

To some degree, these financial intermediaries also provide liquidity. In normal circumstances, not all households withdraw their money at the same time, so financial intermediaries can lend out most of the money and still have enough money on hand to meet the withdrawals by depositors.

But how do financial intermediaries reduce risk? They do that by diversifying investors' assets—by not putting "all the eggs in one basket," so to speak. Risk can be reduced by investing in a large number of projects whose returns, although uncertain, are independent of one another. By independent, we mean that the return from one investment is unrelated to the return on another investment. Consider a bank investing

FIGURE 26.6

Financial Intermediaries

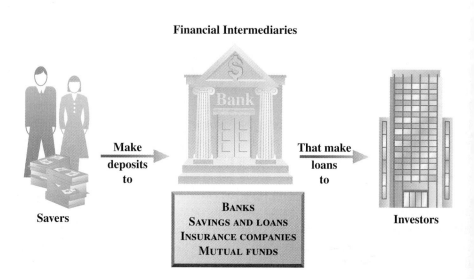

n a large number of projects that all together produce an average return of 8% annually. Each project alone is risky and could pay either a return higher or a lower than 8%.
However, as long as the returns on these projects are independent of one another, the
number of projects with higher returns will likely offset the number of projects with
lower returns. By investing in a large number of projects, the odds are better that as a
group they will earn 8%.

Other financial intermediaries reduce risks in related ways. A fire insurance company accepts premiums from many individuals and uses the funds to make investments. Since not all houses will burn down in the same year, the insurance company
knows that it will have a stable source of funds for its investments. Insurance diversification works well only when companies insure events that are independent of one
another. Some situations are not independent, however, and therefore can't easily be
insured by the same company. For example, an insurance company would be unwise to
provide earthquake insurance for just the Los Angeles area. If an earthquake did occur,
the firm would be faced with making many payments to its clients who suffered loss
without anyone else's payments to offset them. In somewhat the same way, even bank
loans are not fully independent. During a recession, many more firms will experience
financial difficulties and have trouble meeting their loan obligations to their banks.

When Financial Intermediaries Malfunction

Financial intermediation can sometimes go wrong. When it does, the economy suffers.
Important examples of the failure of financial intermediation include commercial
bank failures during the Great Depression, the U.S. savings and loans crisis of the
1980s, and a similar crisis in Japan in the 1990s.

Depositors gathered
anxiously outside as banks
closed during the Great
Depression.

In the early days of the Great Depression, many banks in the United States, particularly in rural areas, provided farmers or local businesses loans that turned out to be unprofitable. This worried depositors, and rumors circulated the banks would fail. Depositors panicked and tried to withdraw their money simultaneously. This is called a **bank run**. During the Great Depression, bank runs occurred throughout the world. In 1931, a panic broke out after the collapse of Creditanstalt, Austria's largest bank. Banking panics occurred throughout other countries in Europe, including Belgium, France, Germany, Italy, and Poland.

Bank run
Panicky investors trying to withdraw their funds from a bank they believe may fail.

No bank, profitable or unprofitable, can survive a run because not all deposits are kept on hand. The result was that thousands of healthy U.S. banks shut down, leaving large parts of the United States without a banking system. Many farms and businesses could no longer find a source of loans, and the severity of the Great Depression worsened. Studies have shown that the countries with the most severe banking panics were hardest hit by the Depression.

To prevent this from happening again, in 1933 the U.S. government began providing **deposit insurance** on money placed in banks and savings and loans. Deposit insurance guarantees the government will reimburse depositors for amounts up to $100,000 should their banks fail. Since everyone knows their deposits are secure, banks runs no longer occur. Today, most countries have some form of deposit insurance intended to prevent panics.

Deposit insurance
Federal government insurance on deposits in banks and savings and loans.

Ironically, deposit insurance indirectly led to the U.S. savings and loan crisis, which occurred during the 1980s. In the early 1970s, savings and loan institutions made mortgage loans to households at low interest rates. However, later in the decade, nominal interest rates rose sharply as inflation increased. The savings and loans were in trouble: They had to pay high interest rates to attract deposits, but they were earning interest at low rates from the money they had loaned out previously. Many of them failed.

The government tried to assist the saving and loan industry by broadening the range of investments the industry could make. S&Ls soon began aggressively investing in speculative real estate and other risky projects to earn higher returns. Depositors weren't worried, though, because they knew their savings were insured by the government. Unfortunately, many of these risky projects failed, and the government was forced to bail out the S&Ls at a cost of nearly $100 billion to taxpayers. Because depositors' savings were insured, most people didn't suffer directly from the collapse of their savings and loan institutions. Taxpayers suffered, though, as they had to foot the bill.

Japan suffered from similar problems in the 1990s. By 1995, seven of the eight largest Japanese mortgage lenders had gone bankrupt following a crash in real estate prices. Like the U.S. government, the Japanese government also used taxpayers' funds to bail these lenders out.

From these examples, you can see that there are reasons why financial intermediation does not always work. There is a continual debate on the role government should play in investment decisions for the economy and its role in regulating financial intermediaries. Today, some economists worry about the financial risks in the U.S. mortgage market, as we discuss in "A Closer Look: Are Fannie Mae and Freddie Mac Too Risky?"

A CLOSER LOOK

Are Fannie Mae and Freddie Mac Too Risky?

Fannie Mae and Freddie Mac are two very large and important government-sponsored financial intermediaries that facilitate home ownership in the United States. Here is how they operate: First, they purchase home mortgages from savings and loans and banks that have made loans to homeowners. This frees up money and allows the S&Ls and banks to make additional home loans to other borrowers. Second, Fannie Mae and Freddie Mac package together the mortgages they purchase and then sell guaranteed, mortgage-backed securities to investors who want to hold a diversified portfolio of home mortgages. Finally, in order to obtain funds to buy the mortgages from banks and S&Ls, they borrow money from other investors in the market. Fannie Mae and Freddie Mac are a huge presence in the U.S. financial market. Together they

account for just under 50% of the mortgage business in the United States.

In recent years, economists and investors have begun to worry whether Fannie Mae and Freddie Mac are fully safe. The mortgage business is very risky. Interest rates can rise and fall sharply, and homeowners can refinance or pay off their mortgages when rates fall. Although both institutions try to manage their risks through extensive use of complex financial strategies, their underlying business is very risky. Like many other financial intermediaries, they hold relatively small amounts of capital or reserves. The financial community became even more concerned in 2003 when Freddie Mac revealed that its accounting practices needed to be changed because they were not fully reflecting their complex financial transactions. Today, the Congress and many agencies in Washington, D.C. are subjecting both organizations to increased scrutiny.

Economic Experiment

Diversification

This classroom exercise illustrates the power of diversification. Your instructor will describe the game and how to participate. To take part in this exercise, you need to recall a simple lesson from basic statistics: If you flip a coin many times, the fraction of heads that results approaches 1/2 as you increase the number of flips.

You are offered a chance to play this game in which you receive a payoff according to the following formula.

payoff = $10 + $100 (number of heads/number of tosses − 0.5)

In this game, you first get $10, but you either win or lose additional funds, depending on whether the fraction of heads that comes up exceeds 1/2.

To help you understand what's going on in this game, suppose you toss the coin only once. Here, the outcome depends only on whether the coin comes up either heads or tails:

Heads: $10 + $100(1/1 − 0.5) = $60
Tails: $10 + $100(0/1 − 0.5) = −$40

The game does have a positive expected payoff or return. The expected or average payoff for this game is the probability of getting a head (1/2) times $60 plus the probability of getting a tail (1/2) times −$40. That is,

expected payoff = (0.5)$60 + (0.5)(−$40) = $10

On average, if you toss the coin many times, this game would pay $10. But this game is risky if you are
(continued)

allowed to toss the coin only once. Now that you understand the game, answer the following question:

● Would you play this game if limited to only one toss?

Now suppose you were free to toss the coin 1,000 times and received 450 heads. If that happened, your payoff would be

$$\$10 + \$100(450/1000 - 0.5) = \$5$$

● Would you play if you could toss the coin 1,000 times?

Questions for Discussion

a. Did a higher percentage of the class agree to play the game with 1,000 tosses? How does this illustrate the principle of diversification?
b. If you toss the coin 1,000 times, what is the expected payoff?
c. If you toss the coin 1,000 times and receive heads fewer than 400 times, you will lose money. What do you think is the probability of this occurring? ●

USING THE TOOLS

1. Animal Spirits

Use an aggregate demand and supply diagram to show the effects on GDP of an "animal spirits" burst that leads to higher investment in the economy.

2. Brazilian Economics

During the early 1990s, interest rates in Brazil were typically at double-digit levels, but firms were investing in a large number of projects. Does this make economic sense? If so, in what way?

3. Investments in Solar Energy

Proponents of solar energy point to the vast savings that come in the long run from using a free source of energy (the sun) rather than paying high prices for electricity. Unfortunately, solar energy systems typically have large up-front expenses to install the system. Use the concept of present value to show that solar energy systems are more likely to be profitable when interest rates are low.

4. Understanding Banks

How can a bank invest in illiquid loans (say, lend depositors' savings to home buyers over 25 years) and still provide liquid deposits (provide depositors with their savings when they ask for them)?

SUMMARY

In this chapter, we discussed investment spending, present value, interest rates, and financial intermediaries. We saw that investment spending is volatile, rising and falling sharply with real GDP, and depends on expectations about the future. By developing the concept of present value, we saw how firms can make investment decisions when the costs and benefits of an investment occur at different times. We also explained why investment spending also depends inversely on real interest rates. Finally, we examined how financial intermediaries channel funds from savers to investors, reduce interest rates, and promote investment. Here are the main points of this chapter to keep in mind:

1 Investments result in costs today but provide benefits in the future.
2 Investment spending is a volatile component of GDP because expectations about the future are uncertain and ever-changing.

3 We use the concept of present value to compare the costs and benefits of investments that occur at different points in time.

4 Investment spending depends inversely on real interest rates.

5 Financial intermediaries reduce the risk and costs of making investments by pooling the funds of savers and monitoring the projects of borrowers.

KEY TERMS

accelerator theory, 602
bank run, 616
corporate bond, 611
deposit insurance, 616
expected real interest rate, 607
financial intermediaries, 613

liquid, 613
multiplier-accelerator model, 603
neoclassical theory of investment, 610
nominal interest rates, 606
present value, 603

procyclical, 603
retained earnings, 611
Q-theory of investment, 611
real interest rate, 606

PROBLEM AND DISCUSSION QUESTIONS

1 The components of investment spending in the national income accounts include plant and equipment, housing, and inventories. Give a reason why spending in each of these categories is likely to be volatile.

2 "When real interest rates are high, so is the opportunity cost of funds." What does this statement mean?

3 "If the real interest rate were zero, it would be a financially sound decision to level the Rocky Mountains so that automobiles and cars would save on gas mileage." Putting aside ecological concerns, why is this statement true?

4 A solar water heating system costs more to install than a conventional water heater but saves money each year on operating costs because it does not use fuel. Using the concept of present value, explain why solar water heating systems are more likely to be adopted when interest rates are low.

5 A lottery pays a winner $1 million a year for 20 years (starting in year 1). What is the present value of this sum at an 8% interest rate? You can do this by hand (not recommended) or in an Excel spreadsheet. Here is how: Enter "1" in cells A1 through A20. In cell C3, enter @NPV(.08, A1:A20) and press enter. This will give you the result. What happens to

the present value of the lottery if the interest rate falls to 5%?

6 Traditionally, savings and loan institutions made loans only for housing. At one point, this was viewed as a safe way of doing business. Explain why making loans only for housing may be very risky.

7 If the inflation rate is 10% over the year and annual interest rates are 9%, would you invest in a project that only paid an annual real return of 1%?

8 Explain why some insurance companies have been interested in national programs for insurance for floods, earthquakes, and hurricanes.

9 Why does it make sense for individual investors to invest in mutual funds (which invest in a wide range of stocks) rather than in just a few individual companies?

10 Why do many investors put their funds in investments in countries throughout the world, not just investments in the United States?

11 While deposit insurance protects depositors' savings and prevents runs on banks, it can motivate banks to take excessive risks in the loans they make. Explain why.

12 Web Exercise. Search the Web to find the current values for interest rates on short-term and long-term government bonds, the prime rate, and long-term corporate bonds. You may want to start with the data Website for the Federal Reserve Bank of St. Louis (*http://research.stlouisfed.org/fred2*). Try to account for the differences in these rates.

13 Web Exercise. Use the same Website to find out how investment in residential housing behaved over the 1990–91 recession. Compare it to other types of investment.

MODEL ANSWERS TO QUESTIONS

Chapter-Opening Questions

1 Interest rates represent the opportunity cost of an investment. The higher the opportunity cost, the less the investment. Investment also depends on other factors such as expectations, taxes, and the expected growth of the economy.

2 As the value of a stock rises, a firm will find it cheaper to raise new funds for investment.

3 While the nominal interest rate may be high, the real rate of interest may be low.

4 Diversification reduces risk.

5 Today, deposit insurance makes runs on profitable banks a rare occurrence.

Test Your Understanding

1 False, it is more volatile than consumption.

2 True, investment is procyclical.

3 The present value is $200/1.10 = $181.81

4 Decreases.

5 4

6 7%

7 Falls.

8 No, what matters is the real rate.

9 The stock market.

Part 9

Money, Banking, and Monetary Policy

Money and the Banking System

s long as there has been paper money, there have been counterfeiters. In 1023, China formed a government agency to print paper money; by 1107, it had begun to print money in three colors to thwart counterfeiters. Over the years, the U.S. Treasury has introduced one cutting-edge printing technique after another to make life difficult for counterfeiters—many of whom now just use high-quality photocopiers to recreate money. For example, if you hold up a real $5 dollar bill to the light, you'll notice a faint hologram of Lincoln directly to the right of the printed image of Lincoln. The hologram can't be reproduced easily with photocopiers, but they are easily visible to cashiers and bank personnel (and anyone else willing to look). The new printing techniques seem like ingenious technological marvels. But the institution of money is really even a greater marvel.

T he term *money* has a special meaning for economists, so in this chapter we'll look carefully at how money is defined and the role that it plays in the economy. The overall level of money in the economy is very important to its performance. In Chapter 23, we learned that increases in the money supply increase aggregate demand. In the short run, when prices are largely fixed, this will raise total demand and output. But in the long run, continuing money growth leads to inflation.

Our nation's central bank, the Federal Reserve, is responsible for controlling the money supply. In this chapter, we'll see how the Federal Reserve is structured, how it operates, and why it's so powerful.

After reading this chapter, you should be able to answer the following questions:

1 Why do all societies have some form of money?
2 What role do banks play in our economy?
3 Can banks really create money through computer entries?
4 What role does the Federal Reserve play in financial crises?

What *Is* Money?

Money
anything that is regularly used
in exchange.

Economists define **money** as anything that is regularly used in economic transactions or exchanges. Let's consider some examples of money used in that way.

We use money regularly every day. In an ice-cream store, we hand the person behind the counter some dollar bills and coins, and we receive an ice-cream cone. This is an example of an economic exchange: One party hands over currency—the dollar bills and the coins—and the other party hands over goods and services (the ice-cream cones). Why do the owners of ice-cream stores accept the dollar bills and coins in payment for the ice cream? The reason is that they will be making other economic exchanges with the dollar bills and coins they accept. Suppose ice-cream cones cost $1.50 each and 100 ice-cream cones are sold in a day. The seller then has $150 in currency. If the ice cream costs the seller $100, the seller pays $100 of the currency received and keeps $50 for other expenses and profits. Money makes that possible.

In the real world, transactions are somewhat more complicated. The ice-cream store owners take the currency they receive each day, deposit it in bank accounts, and then pay suppliers with checks drawn on those accounts. Clearly, currency is money because it is used to purchase ice cream. Checks also function as money because they are used to pay suppliers. In some ancient cultures, precious stones were used in exchanges. In more recent times, gold bars have served as money. During World War II, prisoners of war did not have currency, but they did have rations of cigarettes, so they used them like money, trading them for what they wanted.

Three Properties of Money

Regardless of what money is used in a particular society, it serves several functions, a related to making economic exchanges easier. Here we discuss three key properties money.

1. Money Serves as a Medium of Exchange.

As our examples illustrate, money is accepted in economic exchanges so it is therefor a **medium of exchange**. Suppose money did not exist and you had a car you wante to sell to buy a boat. You could look for a person who had a boat and wanted to buy car and then trade your car directly for a boat. This would be an example of **barte** trading goods directly for goods.

But there are obvious problems with barter. Suppose local boat builders were inte ested in selling boats but not interested in buying your car. Unless there were a **doubl coincidence of wants**—that is, unless you wanted to trade a car for a boat, and th boat owner wanted to trade a boat for your car—this economic exchange wouldn't occu The probability of a double coincidence of wants occurring is very, very tiny. Even if boat owner wanted a car, he or she might want a different type of car than yours.

By serving as a medium of exchange, money solves this problem. The car own can sell the car to anyone who wants it and receive money in return. With that mone the car owner can then find someone who owns a boat and purchase the boat fo money. The boat owner can use the money in any way he or she pleases. With mone there is no need for a double coincidence of wants. This is why money exists in all soc eties: It makes economic transactions much easier.

2. Money Serves as a Unit of Account.

Money also provides a convenient measuring rod when prices for all goods are quote in money terms. A boat may be listed for sale at $5,000, a car at $10,000, and a movi ticket at $5.00. All these prices are quoted in money. We could, in principle, quot everything in terms of movie tickets. The boat would be worth 1,000 tickets, and th car would be worth 2,000 tickets. But since we are using money (and not movie tickets as a medium of exchange, it is much easier if all prices are expressed in terms of mone When we say that money is used as a **unit of account** all we mean is that prices ar quoted in terms of money. This also makes it easier to conduct economic transaction since there is a standard unit—whether that unit is movie tickets or money.

3. Money Serves as a Store of Value.

If you sell your car to purchase a boat, you may not be able to purchase the boat imme diately. In the meantime, you will be holding the money you received from the sal Ideally, during that period, the value of the money should not change. What we ar referring to here is the function of money as a **store of value**.

Money is actually a somewhat imperfect store of value because of inflation Suppose inflation is 10% a year, which means that all prices rise 10% each year. Let say you sold a tennis racket for $100 to buy 10 CDs worth $100 but that you waited year to buy them. Unfortunately, at the end of the year, the 10 CDs now cost $11 ($100 × 1.10), or $11 each. With your $100, you can now buy only 9 CDs and get $1 i change. Your money has lost some of its stored value.

As long as inflation is low and you do not hold the money for a long time, the los in its purchasing power won't be a big problem. But as inflation rates increase, mone becomes less useful as a store of value.

Medium of exchange

The property of money that exchanges are made through the use of money.

Barter

Trading goods directly for goods.

Double coincidence of wants

The problem in a system of barter that one person may not have what the other desires.

Unit of account

The property of money that prices are quoted in terms of money.

Store of value

The property of money that it preserves value until it is used in an exchange.

Different Types of Monetary Systems

Historically, the world has witnessed different types of monetary systems. The first system is one in which a commodity, such as gold or silver, is used as money, either in the form of bars or coins. This is an example of **commodity money** in which an actual commodity (gold or silver) serves as money. At some point, governments began issuing paper money. However, the paper money was backed by an underlying commodity, for example, so many ounces of gold. Under a traditional **gold standard**, an individual could present paper money to the government and receive its stated value in gold. Paper money could be exchanged for gold, in other words. Prior to 1933 in the United States, individuals could exchange their dollars for gold. President Franklin Roosevelt, however, banned private possession of gold in 1933, although foreign governments could still exchange dollars for gold until 1971. The next step in the evolution of monetary systems was to break the tie between paper money and gold and create a system of **fiat money**. Fiat money has no intrinsic value—it is simply created by a government decree. A government will issue paper money and make this money the official legal tender of the society. In the United States today, if you take a $100 bill to the government you will not receive any gold or silver—just another $100 bill in return.

You may wonder what gives money value under a fiat system if it has no intrinsic backing? The answer is that the government controls the value of fiat money by controlling its supply in the economy. In the next chapter, we will see precisely how the government controls the supply of money.

Commodity money
A monetary system in which the actual money is a commodity, such as gold or silver.

Gold standard
A monetary system in which gold backs up paper money

Fiat money
A monetary system in which money has no intrinsic backing.

TEST Your Understanding

1. Money solves the problem of double coincidences of wants that would regularly occur under a system of _____.
2. Why is money an imperfect store of value?
3. What is the problem associated with the double coincidence of wants?
4. Because we measure all prices in monetary units, money serves as a unit of account. True or false? Explain.
5. Why are checks included in the definition of money?

Measuring Money in the U.S. Economy

In the United States and other modern economies, there are typically several different ways in which economic transactions can be carried out. In practice, this leads to different measures of money. The most basic measure of money in the United States is called **M1**. It totaled $1,287 billion in January 2004. Table 27.1 contains the components of M1 and their size, and Figure 27.1 shows their relative percentages.

The first part of M1 is currency that is held by the public, that is, all currency held outside of bank vaults. The next two components are deposits in checking accounts, called demand deposits. Until the 1980s, checking accounts did not pay interest. A

M1
The sum of currency in the hands of the public, demand deposits, other checkable deposits, and travelers' checks.

TABLE 27.1

**Components of M1,
January 2004**

Currency held by the public	$665 billion
Demand deposits	301 billion
Other checkable deposits	313 billion
Travelers' checks	8 billion
Total of M1	1,287 billion

Source: Federal Reserve Bank of St. Louis.

different kind of account, called other checkable deposits, introduced in the early 1980s, did pay interest, however. Today, the distinction between the two types of accounts is not as meaningful because many checking accounts earn interest if the balances are sufficiently high. Finally, travelers' checks are included in M1 because they are regularly used in economic exchanges.

Let's take a closer look at the amount of currency in the economy. Since there are approximately 290 million people in the United States, the $665 billion of currency amounts to over $2,293 in currency for every man, woman, and child in the United States. Do you and your friends each have $2,293 of currency?

Most of the currency in the official statistics is not used in ordinary commerce in the United States. Much of it is held abroad by wealthy people who want U.S. currency in case of emergencies or who use it to keep their wealth out of sight of their own governments and tax authorities. Some of it circulates in other countries along with their local currencies. Currency is also used in illegal transactions such as the drug trade. Few dealers of illegal drugs open bank accounts that could be inspected by international law authorities.

M1 does not include all the assets that are used to make economic exchanges. Economists also use a somewhat broader definition of money known as **M2**. M2 also includes deposits in saving accounts, deposits in money market mutual funds, and small time deposits (those less than $100,000). These assets often can't readily be used for exchanges without first being converted to M1. M2 consists of all these investment-like assets plus M1. In January 2004, M2 totaled $6,075 billion. That's about 4.7 times the total of M1.

Economists use different definitions of money because it is not always clear which assets are used primarily as money—that is, which assets are used for economic exchanges and which are used primarily for saving and investing. Money market mutual funds came into existence only in the late 1970s. Some people temporarily "park" their assets in these funds anticipating they will move the funds into riskier, higher-earning stock market investments later. Others may use them to earn interest while avoiding the risks of the stock market or bond market. Sometimes, money mar

M2

M1 plus other assets, including deposits in savings and loans and money market mutual funds.

FIGURE 27.1

**Components of M1
for the United States**
Currency is the largest
component of M1, the most
basic measure of money.
Demand and other
checkable deposits are the
next largest components.

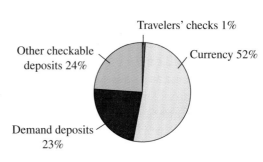

Currency held by the public is part of the official money supply.

...et mutual funds are used like regular checking accounts; other times, they are used like savings accounts. If they are used like checking accounts, they should be considered part of M1; but if they are used like savings accounts, they should be part of M2. Economists keep an eye on both M1 and M2 because they don't know precisely how all of these money market accounts are being used.

While credit cards are commonly used in our economy to make transactions, they are not part of the money supply. Here's why: Suppose you have a credit card from the First Union Bank and purchase a new television set from an electronics store. As you use your credit card, you are effectively borrowing the amount for the purchase of the television set from the First Union Bank, which, in turn, will pay the electronics store. When you receive your credit card bill, you must begin to pay off the loan from the bank. Credit cards enable you to purchase goods now but use money at a later date to pay for them. The credit card is—unlike money—not a medium of exchange, a unit of account, or a store of value. Credit cards do make it easier to conduct business, but they are not an official part of the money supply.

TEST Your Understanding

6. About one-half of M1 consists of _____.
7. Complete the statement with "M1" or "M2": Economists use _____ to measure the amount of money that is regularly used in transactions
8. Which is greater, M1 or M2?
9. How do you explain the fact that the total amount of currency divided by the U.S. population is approximately $2,293?
10. Why are money market mutual funds hard to classify?

A Bank's Balance Sheet: Where the Money Comes From and Where It Goes

Balance sheet

An account for a bank that shows the sources of its funds (liabilities) as well as the uses for the funds (assets).

Liabilities

The sources of funds for a bank, including deposits of a financial intermediary.

Assets

The uses of the funds of a bank, including loans and reserves.

Owners' equity

The funds provided to a bank by its owners.

Reserves

The fraction of banks' deposits set aside in either vault cash or as deposits at the Federal Reserve.

Required reserves

The fraction of banks' deposits that banks are legally required to hold in their vaults or as deposits at the Fed.

Excess reserves

Any additional reserves that a bank holds above required reserves.

In Chapter 26, we learned that a typical commercial bank accepts funds from savers in the form of deposits, for example, in checking accounts. The bank does not leave all these funds idle; if it did, it would never make a profit. Instead, the bank turns the money around and loans it out to borrowers. It will be easier to understand how banks create money if we first look at a simplified **balance sheet** for a commercial bank. The balance sheet will show us how the bank raises the money and where it goes after it's been raised.

Balance sheets have two sides: one for assets and one for liabilities. **Liabilities** are the source of funds for the bank. If you open a checking account and deposit your funds in it, the bank is liable for returning the funds to you when you want them. The bank must also pay you interest on the account, if you keep enough money it. Your deposits are therefore the bank's liabilities. **Assets**, on the hand, generate income for the bank. Loans made by the bank are examples of its assets because borrowers must pay interest on the loans the bank collects.

When a bank is initially opened, its owners must place their own funds into the bank so it has some start-up funds. We call these funds **owners' equity**. If the bank subsequently makes a profit, owners' equity increases; if it loses money, owners' equity decreases.

In Figure 27.2, we show the assets and liabilities of a hypothetical bank. On the liability side, the bank has $2,000 of deposits and owners' equity is $200. Owners' equity is entered on the liability side of the balance sheet because it is a source of the bank's funds. The total source of funds is therefore $2,200—the deposits in the bank plus owners' equity.

On the asset side, the bank holds $200 in **reserves**; these are assets that are not lent out. Banks are required by law to hold a specific fraction of their deposits as reserves, called **required reserves**. If a bank chooses to hold additional reserves beyond what is required, these are called **excess reserves**. A bank's reserves are the sum of its required and excess reserves. Reserves can be either cash kept in a bank's vaults or deposits in the nation's central bank, the Federal Reserve. Banks do not earn any interest on these reserves. Hence, they try to keep as little excess reserves on hand as possible and loan out as much as they can.

Assets	Liabilities
$ 200 Reserves	$2,000 Deposits
$2,000 Loans	$ 200 Owners' equity
Total: $2,200	Total: $2,200

FIGURE 27.2 **A Balance Sheet for a Bank**
The figure shows a hypothetical balance sheet for a bank holding 10% in required reserves ($200). Banks don't earn interest on their reserves, so they will want to loan out any in excess of the amounts they are required to hold. This bank has loaned out all of its excess reserves ($2,000).

In our example, the bank is holding 10% of its deposits, or $200, as reserves. The remainder of the bank's assets, $2,000 consists of the loans it's made. By construction, total assets will always equal liabilities, including owners' equity. Balance sheets must therefore always balance.

How Banks Create Money

To understand the role that banks play in determining the supply of money, let's suppose that someone walks into the First Bank of Hollywood and deposits $1,000 in cash to open a checking account. Because currency held by the public and checking deposits are both included in the supply of money, the total money supply has not changed with this transaction. The cash deposit into the checking account reduced the currency held by the public by precisely the amount the deposit in the checking account increased.

Now let's assume that banks are required to keep 10% of their deposits as reserves. That means that the **reserve ratio**—the ratio of reserves to deposits—will be 0.1. The First Bank of Hollywood will keep $100 in reserves and make loans totaling $900. The top panel in Figure 27.3 shows the change in First Hollywood's balance sheet after it has made its loan.

Reserve ratio

The ratio of reserves to deposits.

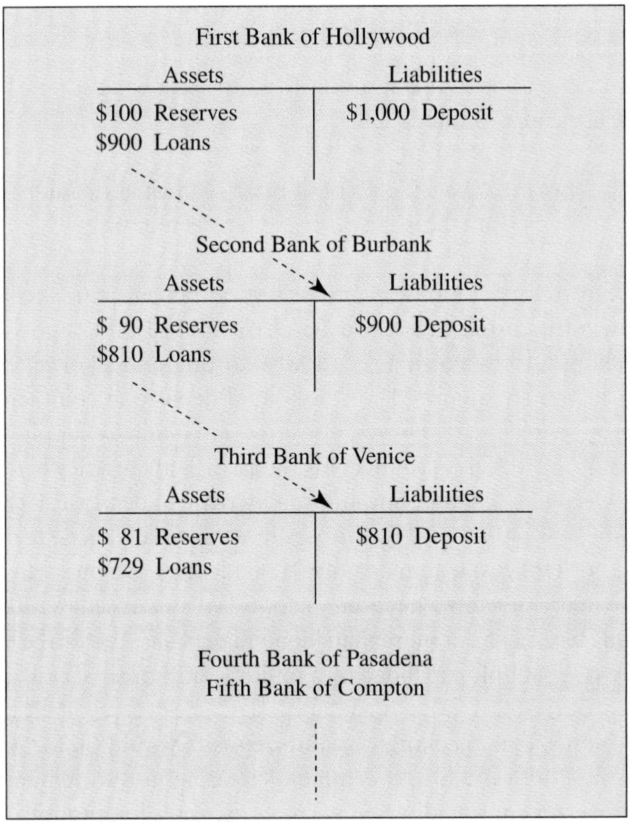

FIGURE 27.3

Process of Deposit Creation: Changes in Balance Sheets
The figure shows how an initial deposit of $1,000 can expand the money supply. The first three banks in the figure loaned out all of their excess reserves and the borrowers deposited the full sum of their loans. In the real world, though, people hold part of their loans as cash and banks don't necessarily loan out every last dime of their reserves. Consequently, a smaller amount of money will be created than what's shown here.

First Bank of Hollywood

Assets	Liabilities
$100 Reserves	$1,000 Deposit
$900 Loans	

Second Bank of Burbank

Assets	Liabilities
$ 90 Reserves	$900 Deposit
$810 Loans	

Third Bank of Venice

Assets	Liabilities
$ 81 Reserves	$810 Deposit
$729 Loans	

Fourth Bank of Pasadena
Fifth Bank of Compton

Suppose the First Bank of Hollywood loans the funds to an aspiring movie produce The producer opens a checking account at First Hollywood with the $900 he borrowe He then buys film equipment from a supplier, who accepts his $900 check and deposits in the Second Bank of Burbank. The next panel in Figure 27.3 shows what happens to th balance sheet of the Second Bank of Burbank. Liabilities increase by the deposit of $90 The bank must hold $90 in reserves (10% of the $900 deposit) and can lend out $810.

Suppose that the Second Bank of Burbank lends the $810 to the owner of a coffe house and opens a checking account for her with a balance of $810. She then purchase $810 worth of coffee with a check made out to a coffee supplier, who deposits it int the Third Bank of Venice.

The Third Bank of Venice receives a deposit of $810. It must keep $81 in reserve and can lend out $729. This process continues throughout the Los Angeles area wit new loans and deposits. The Fourth Bank of Pasadena will receive a deposit of $72 hold $72.90 in reserves, and lend out $656.10. The Fifth Bank of Compton will receiv a deposit of $656.10, and the process goes on.

How the Money Multiplier Works

The original $1,000 cash deposit has created checking account balances throughou Los Angeles. What's the total amount? Adding up the new accounts in all the bank (even the ones we have not named), we have

$$\$1,000 + \$900 + \$810 + \$729 + \$656.10 + \ldots = \$10,000$$

How did we come up with this sum? It's from the following simple formula, whic we derive in the appendix to this chapter:

total increase in checking account balance throughout all banks
= (initial cash deposit) × (1/reserve ratio)

In our example, the reserve ratio is 0.1, so the increase in checking account balances 1/0.1, or 10 times the initial cash deposit. The initial $1,000 deposit led to a tota increase in checking account balances of $10,000 throughout all of the banks.

Recall that the money supply, M1, is the sum of deposits at commercial banks plu currency held by the public. Therefore, the change in the money supply, M1, will be th change in deposits in checking accounts plus the change in currency held by the publi Notice that we referred to "change," meaning an increase or decrease. Here's why: In ou example, the public (as represented by the person who initially made the $1,000 depos at the First Bank of Hollywood) holds only $1,000 less in currency. However, deposit increased by $10,000. Therefore, the money supply, M1, increased by $9,000 ($10,000 $1,000). No single bank lent out more than it had in deposits. Yet for the banking syste as a whole, the money supply expanded by a multiple of the initial cash deposit.

The term 1/reserve ratio in the formula is called the **money multiplier**. It tells u what the total increase in checking account deposits would be for any initial cas deposit. Recall the multiplier for government spending in our demand-side model An increase in government spending led to larger increases in output through the mul

Money multiplier
An initial deposit leads to a multiple expansion of deposits. In the simplified case increase in deposits = (initial deposit) × (1/reserve ratio).

plier. The government spending multiplier arose because additional rounds of consumption spending were triggered by an initial increase in government spending. In the banking system, an initial cash deposit triggers additional rounds of deposits and lending by banks. This leads to a multiple expansion of deposits.

As of 2004 in the United States, banks were required to hold 3% reserves against checkable deposits between $6.6 million and $45.4 million and 10% on all checkable deposits exceeding $45.4 million. Since large banks would face a 10% reserve requirement on any new deposits, you might think, on the basis of our formula, that the money multiplier would be approximately 10.

However, the money multiplier for the United States is between only 2 and 3—much smaller than the value of 10 implied by our simple formula. The primary reason is that our formula assumed that all loans made their way directly into checking accounts. In reality, people hold part of their loans as cash. The cash that people hold is not available for the banking system to lend out. The more money people hold in cash, the lower the amount they have on deposit that can be loaned out again. This decreases the money multiplier. The money multiplier would also be less if banks held excess reserves. We can represent these factors in a money multiplier ratio, but it will not be as simple as the one we introduced here.

How the Money Multiplier Works in Reverse

The money creation process also works in reverse. Suppose you go to your bank and ask for $1,000 in cash from your checking account. The bank must pay you the $1,000. Its liabilities fall by $1,000, but its assets must also fall by $1,000. Withdrawing your $1,000 means two things at the bank: First, if the reserve ratio is 0.1, the bank will reduce its reserves by $100. Second, your $1,000 withdrawal minus the $100 reduction in reserves means that the bank has $900 less to lend out; hence, it will reduce its loans by $900. With fewer loans, there will be fewer deposits in other banks. The money multiplier working in reverse decreases the money supply.

You may wonder how a bank goes about reducing its outstanding loans. If you had borrowed from a bank to invest in a project for your business, you would not want the bank phoning you, asking for its funds, which are not lying idle but are invested in your business. Banks do not typically call in outstanding loans from borrowers. Instead, if banks cannot tap into their excess reserves when their customers want to withdraw cash, they have to make fewer new loans. In these circumstances, a new potential borrower would find it harder to obtain a loan from the bank.

Up to this point, our examples have always started with an initial cash deposit. However, suppose that Paul receives a check from Freda and deposits it into his bank. Paul's bank will eventually receive payment from Freda's bank. When it does, it will initially have an increase in both deposits and reserves—just as if a cash deposit were made. Because Paul's bank has to hold only a fraction of the deposits as reserves, it will be able to make loans with the remainder.

However, there is one crucial difference between this example, in which one individual writes a check to another, and our earlier example, in which an individual makes a cash deposit: When Paul receives the check from Freda, the money supply will not be changed in the long run. Here's why it won't: When Freda's check is deposited in Paul's bank, the money supply will begin to expand, but when Freda's bank loses its deposit, the money supply will start to contract. The expansions and contractions offset each other when private citizens and firms write checks to one another.

In the next chapter, we will see how the Federal Reserve (commonly called the "Fed") can *change* the money supply to stabilize the economy. In the remainder of this chapter, we'll look at the structure of the Federal Reserve and the critical role that it plays as a central bank stabilizing the financial system.

TEST Your Understanding

11. Banks are required by law to keep a fraction of their deposits as _____.
12. Define owners' equity.
13. Why does a bank prefer to make loans rather than keep reserves?
14. If the reserve ratio is 0.2 and a deposit of $100 is made into a bank, the bank will lend out _____.
15. If the reserve ratio is 0.2, the simplified money multiplier will be _____.
16. Why is the actual money multiplier much smaller than in our simple formula?

A Banker's Bank: The Federal Reserve

The Federal Reserve System was created in 1913 after a series of financial panics in the United States. Financial panics can occur when there is bad news about the economy or the vitality of financial institutions. During these panics, numerous bank runs occurred, depleting the funds on hand that could be loaned out. Severe economic downturns followed.

Congress created the Federal Reserve System to be a **central bank**, or "a banker's bank." When it was created, one of the Fed's primary jobs was to serve as a **lender of last resort**. When banks need to borrow money during a financial crisis, they can turn to the central bank as "a last resort" for these funds. As an example, if a bank experienced a run, the Federal Reserve would lend it the funds it needed.

All countries have central banks. The Indian central bank is known as the Reserve Bank of India. In the United Kingdom, the central bank is the Bank of England. Central banks serve as lenders of last resort to the banks in their countries and also help to control the level of economic activity. If the economy is operating at a level that's "too hot" or "too cold," they can manipulate the money supply to fend off economic problems.

Central bank

A banker's bank; an official bank that controls the supply of money in a country.

Lender of last resort

A central bank is the lender of last resort, the last place, all others having failed, from which banks in emergency situations can obtain loans.

The Structure of the Federal Reserve

When members of Congress created the Federal Reserve System, they were aware the institution would be very powerful. Consequently, they deliberately created a structure that attempted to disperse the power, moving it away from major U.S. financial centers like New York) to other parts of the country. They divided the United States into 12 Federal Reserve districts, each of which has a **Federal Reserve Bank**. These district banks provide advice on monetary policy, take part in decision-making on monetary policy, and provide a liaison between the Fed and the banks in their districts.

Figure 27.4 shows where each of the 12 Federal Reserve Banks are located. At the time the Fed was created, economic and financial power in this country was concentrated in the East and the Midwest. This is no longer true. What major Western city does not have a Federal Reserve Bank? It is, of course, Los Angeles. While financial power is no longer concentrated in the East and Midwest, the locations of the Federal Reserve Banks still reflect the Fed's historical roots.

There are two other subgroups of the Fed in addition to the Federal Reserve Banks. The **Board of Governors of the Federal Reserve** is the second subgroup. It is the true seat of power in the Federal Reserve System. Headquartered in Washington, D.C., the seven members of the board are appointed for staggered, 14-year terms by the president. The chairperson of the Board of Governors serves a 4-year term. As the principal spokesperson for monetary policy in the United States, what the chairperson says, or might say, is carefully observed or anticipated by financial markets throughout the world. The chairperson and the seven members must also be confirmed by the Senate.

The third subgroup of the Fed is the **Federal Open Market Committee (FOMC)**, which makes decisions about monetary policy The FOMC is a 12-person board consisting of the 7 members of the Board of Governors, the president of the New York Federal Reserve bank, plus the presidents of four other regional Federal Reserve Banks. (Presidents of the regional banks other than New York serve on a rotating basis; the 7 nonvoting bank presidents attend the meetings and offer their opinions). The chairperson of the Board of Governors also serves as the chairperson of the FOMC. The FOMC makes the actual decisions on changes in the money supply. Its members are assisted by vast teams of professionals at the Board of Governors and at the regional Federal Reserve Banks. The structure of the Federal Reserve System is depicted in Figure 27.5.

Federal Reserve Banks

One of 12 regional banks that are an official part of the Federal Reserve System.

Board of Governors of the Federal Reserve

The seven-person governing body of the Federal Reserve system in Washington, DC.

Federal Open Market Committee (FOMC)

The group that decides on monetary policy; it consists of the 7 members of the Board of Governors plus 5 of 12 regional bank presidents on a rotating basis.

FIGURE 27.4

Where the 12 Federal Reserve Banks Are Located

There are 12 Federal Reserve banks scattered across the United States. These district banks serve as a liaison between the Fed and the banks in their districts.

Decisions about monetary policy are made at meetings of the Federal Open Market Committee.

On paper, monetary policy-making power appears to be spread throughout the government and the country. In practice, however, the Board of Governors and espe cially the chairperson have the real control. The Board of Governors operates with considerable independence. Presidents and members of Congress can bring politica pressures on the Board of Governors, but 14-year terms tend to insulate the member. from external pressures.

Countries differ in the degree to which their central banks are independent o political authorities. In the United States, the chairperson of the Board of Governors i required to report to Congress on a regular basis, but in practice, the Fed makes its own

FIGURE 27.5

The Structure of the Federal Reserve

The Federal Reserve System in the United States consists of the Federal Reserve Banks, the Board of Governors, and the Federal Open Market Committee (FOMC). The Federal Open Market Committee (FOMC) is responsible for making money policy decisions.

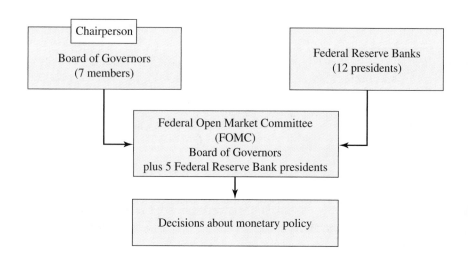

ecisions and later informs Congress what it did. The chairperson of the Federal Reserve also often meets with members of the executive branch to discuss economic affairs. The central banks in both the United States and the United Kingdom operate with considerable independence of elected officials. In other countries, the central bank is part of the treasury department of the government and potentially subject to more direct political control. There is a lively debate among economists and political scientists as to whether countries with more independent central banks (banks with less external political pressure) experience less inflation. Central banks that are not independent will always be under pressure to help finance their country's government deficits by creating money. We'll see in a later chapter that when central banks succumb to this pressure, the result is inflation. Independence, on the other hand, typically means less inflation.

What the Federal Reserve Does During a Financial Crisis

As the lender of last resort, the Fed can quell disturbances in the financial markets. Let's look at two historical examples.

Application: Black Monday, 1987

On October 19, 1987, known as "Black Monday" the Dow Jones index of the stock market fell a dramatic 22.6% in one day. Similar declines were felt in other indices and stock markets around the world. This shocked both businesses and investors. In just 24 hours, many people and firms found themselves much less wealthy. The public began to worry that banks and other financial institutions—to protect their own loans and investments—would call in borrowers' existing loans and stop making new ones. A sharp drop in available credit could, conceivably, plunge the economy into a deep recession.

Alan Greenspan had just become chairman of the Federal Reserve that year. As a sophisticated economist with historical knowledge of prior financial crises, he recognized the seriousness of the situation. He quickly issued a public statement in which he said that the Federal Reserve stood ready to provide liquidity to the economy and the financial system. Banks were told that the Fed would let them borrow liberally. In fact, the Fed provided liquidity to such an extent that interest rates even fell. As a result of Greenspan's action, "Black Monday" did not cause a recession in the United States.

Application: September 11, 2001

The Fed was tested again September 11, 2001, following the terrorist attacks against the United States. Many financial firms keep little cash on hand and expect to borrow on a daily basis to pay their ongoing bills and obligations. When the financial markets closed after September 11, many of these firms were in trouble. Unless some action were taken quickly, these firms would default on their debts, leading to payment problems for other firms and further defaults. To prevent a default avalanche, the Federal Reserve immediately took a number of steps to provide additional funds to the financial system.

The first tool that the Federal Reserve used was to allow banks to borrow more. In regular times, the volume of these direct loans from the Federal Reserve is not very large. On Wednesday, September 12, total lending to banks rose to $45.5 billion, up from just $99 million the week before.

In normal times, the Federal Reserve System serves as a clearinghouse for checks. A bank will bring checks it receives from customers to the Federal Reserve and receive immediate credit on its accounts. The Federal Reserve then debits the account of the bank upon which the check was written. The difference between the credits and the debits extended by the Federal Reserve is called the "Federal Reserve float." Immediately following September 11, the Federal Reserve allowed this float to increase sharply from $2.9 billion to $22.9 billion. These actions effectively put an additional $20 billion into the banking system.

The Federal Reserve also purchased government securities in the marketplace and, as a result, put $30 million into the hands of private citizens and their banks. It also arranged to provide dollars to foreign central banks that needed them to meet their

A CLOSER LOOK   Two Decades, Two Chairmen

Since 1979, the Federal Reserve Board has had only two chairmen: Paul Volcker, who served from 1979 to 1987, and Alan Greenspan, who served from 1987, until the present time. In their day, each was the country's major figure in monetary policy.

Paul Volcker was appointed by President Jimmy Carter, who sought an established banker to help combat inflation. Volcker, who served as the president of the New York Federal Reserve Bank, took a pay cut to come to Washington to fight inflation. A tall, imposing figure who smoked cigars, Volcker was relentless in his fight against inflation. Under his regime, the Federal Reserve drove interest rates up to 18% and precipitated a recession in order to bring down inflation. By the time Volcker left office, inflation was fully under control.

Alan Greenspan was appointed by President Ronald Reagan. As we described earlier, Greenspan was first tested by the 1987 stock market crash and steered the economy away from a recession. Over the following years, he successfully guided monetary policy. Except for the recessions in the early 1990s and in 2001, the economy grew smoothly and inflation remained under control. During the mid-1990s, the Federal Reserve allowed the economy to grow at a faster rate than most economists believed possible, but the gamble paid off and there was no resurgence of inflation. In 1999 and 2000, the Federal Reserve may have tightened monetary policy prematurely, contributing to the subsequent economic contraction. Nonetheless, Greenspan's performance has earned universal praise, and one author deemed him the "maestro."

wn needs and the needs of their banks in this crisis. Taken together, all these actions ncreased the credit extended by the Federal Reserve by over $90 billion. This massive esponse by the Federal Reserve prevented a financial panic that could have had devastat-ng effects on the world economy.

In recent years, the United States has been fortunate to have strong and talented hairmen of the Federal Reserve, as "A Closer Look: Two Decades, Two Chairmen" ecounts.

Economic Experiment

Money Creation

This experiment demonstrates the money-creation process. Students act like bankers and investors. Bankers loan money to investors, who then buy machines that produce output. The experiment is divided into several separate days. On each day, all loans are executed in the morning, all deposits happen over the lunch hour, and all machines are purchased in the afternoon. Each bank can receive only one deposit and issue only one loan. The interest rate paid to depositors and the interest rate paid by borrowers are negotiable. The experiment starts when the instructor deposits $625 from the sale of a government bond into a bank.

Bank Actions

The sequence of possible bank actions on a given day are as follows:

1 Early morning: Count money. Check for excess reserves, including deposits from the previous noon.
2 Middle morning: Loan out any excess reserves in a single loan to a borrower and negotiate an interest rate for the loan. The loan is executed by writing a bank check to the borrower.
3 Noon: Receive a deposit (bank check deposited into a checking account).
4 Afternoon: Relax, golf.

Rules for Banks

1 For each $1 deposited, you must hold $0.20 in reserve.
2 If you don't issue a loan, you can earn 3% by investing overseas.

Investor Actions

The sequence of possible investor actions on a given day are as follows:

1 Early morning: Sleep-in while bankers count their money.
2 Middle morning: Borrow money from a bank and negotiate an interest rate for the loan.
3 Noon: Deposit the loan at the bank of your choice and negotiate an interest rate for the deposit.
4 Afternoon: Buy machines from Machine Inc., pay-ing with a personal check.

Investor Payoffs

Each machine costs $1, generates $1.10 worth of out-put, and then expires.

As the students play, the instructor keeps track of the model economy on a tally sheet, which shows the money creation process in action, round-by-round.

What role do the return on overseas investment (3%) and the return from owning a machine ($1.10 on a $1.00 investment) play in this experiment?

(continued)

Money Creation Experiment: Tally Sheet

Bank Receiving Deposit	Amount Deposited	Interest Rate on Deposit	Amount Loaned	Interest Rate on Loan	Amount Added to Reserves	Change in Money Supply

USING THE TOOLS

1. Bad Loans to South America

During the 1980s, U.S. banks made loans to South American countries. Many of these loans turned out to be worthless. How did this affect the assets, liabilities, and owners' equity of these banks?

2. Reserve Requirements as a Tax

Left on their own, most banks would reduce their reserve requirements far below 10%. Consequently, banks view reserve requirements as a "tax" on their holdings of deposits. Explain how a 10% reserve requirement could be viewed as a 10% tax.

3. Required Reserves and the Great Depression

During the Great Depression, banks held excess reserves because they were concerned that depositors might be more inclined to withdraw funds from their accounts. At one point, the Fed became concerned about the "excess" reserves and raised the reserve requirements for banks.

a. Assuming that banks were holding excess reserves for precautionary purposes, do you think they would continue to want to hold excess reserves even after reserve requirements were raised? Explain.

b. What do you think happened to the money supply after the Fed raised reserve requirements?

4. Debit Cards

In recent years, debit cards have become popular. Debit cards allow the holder of the card to pay a merchant for goods and services directly from a checking account. How do you think the introduction of debit cards affected the amount of currency in the economy? How about the amount of checking account deposits?

SUMMARY

We began this chapter by examining the role money plays in the economy and how economists define money. We then looked at the flow of money in and out of banks and saw how banks can create money with deposits and loans. Finally, we examined the structure of the Federal Reserve and the key roles that central banks can play during financial crises. Here are the main points you should remember from this chapter:

1 Money consists of anything that is regularly used to make exchanges. In modern economies, money consists primarily of currency and deposits in checking accounts.

2 Banks are financial intermediaries that earn profits by accepting deposits and making loans. Deposits, which are liabilities of banks, are included in the money supply.

3 Banks are required by law to hold a fraction of their deposits as reserves, either in cash or in deposits with the Federal Reserve. Total reserves consist of required reserves plus excess reserves.

4 If there is an increase in reserves in the banking system, the supply of money will expand by a multiple of the initial deposit. This multiple is known as the money multiplier.

5 Decisions about the supply of money are made at the Federal Open Market Committee (FOMC), which includes the seven members on the Board of Governors and the president of the New York Federal Reserve Bank, as well as four of the 11 other regional bank presidents, who serve on a rotating basis.

6 In a financial crisis like those that occurred in 1997 and 2001, the Fed can help stabilize the economy. Recent Fed Chairmen Paul Volcker and Alan Greenspan have been powerful and important figures in the national economy.

KEY TERMS

assets, 628
balance sheet, 628
barter, 624
Board of Governors of the Federal
   Reserve, 633
central bank, 632
commodity money, 625
double coincidence of wants, 624
excess reserves, 628

Federal Open Market Committee
   (FOMC), 633
Federal Reserve Banks, 633
fiat money, 625
gold standard, 625
lender of last resort, 632
liabilities, 628
M1, 625
M2, 626

medium of exchange, 624
money, 623
money multiplier, 630
owners' equity, 628
required reserves, 628
reserve ratio, 629
reserves, 628
store of value, 624
unit of account, 624

PROBLEMS AND DISCUSSION QUESTIONS

1 Why are travelers' checks classified as money?

2 Both insurance companies and banks are financial intermediaries. Why do macroeconomists study banks more intensively than insurance companies?

3 If you write a check from your checking account to your money market account, what happens to M1 and M2?

4 If a customer took $2,000 in cash from a bank and the reserve ratio was 0.2, by how much would the supply of money eventually be reduced?

5 In 1992, the state of California ran out of funds and could not pay its bills. It issued IOUs, called warrants, to its workers and suppliers. Only large banks and credit unions accepted the warrants. Should these warrants be viewed as money?

6 Occasionally, some economists or politicians suggest that the Secretary of the Treasury become a member of the Federal Open Market Committee. How do you think this would affect the independence of the Federal Reserve?

7 Why aren't credit cards part of the money supply? How do debit cards differ from credit cards?

8 Some societies have used gold as money. What are the advantages and disadvantages of using gold coins?

9 If no single bank can lend out more than it has, how does multiple expansion of deposits actually occur?

10 What are key actions that central bankers can take to stem financial crises?

11 Web Exercise. Go to the data Website of the Federal Reserve Bank of St. Louis (*http://research.stlouisfed. org/fred*). Look carefully at the components of M1 and M2 over the last 10 years. What trends do you see?

12 Web Exercise. Search the Web for articles on the "currency and the underground economy." See how various authors have used estimates of currency to measure the underground economy.

MODEL ANSWERS TO QUESTIONS

Chapter-Opening Questions

1 Money is needed for transactions and to avoid the problems of barter.

2 Banks play a special role in our economy because the liabilities of banks are part of the supply of money.

3 The banking system as a whole can create money through the process of multiple expansion. However, this depends on the actions of the Federal Reserve.

4 The Fed can supply extra funds in financial crises to prevent financial panics from spreading.

Test Your Understanding

1 Barter.

2 Inflation erodes its value.

3 Two individuals each have to want what the other has.

4 True. This is the definition of a unit of account.

5 They are readily accepted in exchange.

6 Currency.

7 M1.

8 M2.

9 Currency is held abroad and used in illegal or unreported transactions.

10 They are used both to make transactions and to save.

11 Reserves.

12 The funds invested by the owner of a bank.

13 It does not earn interest on reserves.

14 $80

15 5

16 Not all currency is redeposited in banks.

APPENDIX

Formula for Deposit Creation

To show how to derive the formula for deposit creation, let's use the example in the text. We showed that with 10% held as reserves, a $1,000 deposit led to total deposits of

$$\$1,000 + \$900 + \$810 + \$729 + \$656.10 + \ldots$$

Let's find the total sum of all these deposits. Because each bank successively had to hold 10% in its reserves, that means that each successive bank received only 0.9 of the deposits of the prior bank. Therefore, we can write the total for the deposits in all the banks as

$$\$1,000 \times (1 + 0.9 + 0.9^2 + 0.9^3 + 0.9^4 + \ldots)$$

We need to find the sum of the terms in parentheses. Using a formula for an infinite sum,

$$1 + b + b^2 + b^3 + b^4 + \ldots = 1/(1 - b)$$

the expression becomes

$$1 + 0.9 + 0.9^2 + 0.9^3 + 0.9^4 + \ldots = 1/(1 - 0.9) = 1/0.1 = 10$$

Therefore, the total increase in deposits will be

$$\$1,000 \times 10 = \$10,000$$

To derive the general formula, note that if the reserve ratio is r, the bank will lend out $(1 - r)$ per dollar of deposits. Following the steps we just outlined, we find the infinite sum will be $1/[1 - (1 - r)] = 1/r$ or 1/reserve ratio. Therefore, in general, we have the formula

increase in checking account balances = (initial deposit) × (1/reserve ratio)

The Federal Reserve
and Monetary Policy

difficult part of the job of the Federal Reserve is to gauge the reaction of the financial markets to its actions. Consider the Fed's deliberations during their Open Market Committee meeting on June 24–25, 2003. The economy had still not recovered from the recession, and the public knew that the Fed was planning to reduce the federal funds rate. But the Fed was divided—some members thought that only a small ¼ percentage point adjustment was needed, while others felt that a larger, ½ percentage point decrease was more appropriate. Eventually, the Fed, led by Chairman Alan Greenspan pictured above, settled for the smaller ¼ point decrease.

But in prior weeks, the financial markets had come to believe that the Fed was planning a major decrease in the federal funds rate—at least ½ point or more. Long-term interest rates fell in anticipation of the Fed's action. When the Fed cut the funds rate by only ¼ percentage point, the market was disappointed and uncertain about the Fed's future intentions. As a result, interest rates on long-term bonds, a benchmark for monetary policy, rose sharply by 1.5 percentage points. This was contrary to what usually happens when the Fed lowers rates and also what the Fed wanted to happen. Usually when it lowers the federal funds rate, the rates on long-term bonds drop as well. The Fed's decision on monetary policy had clearly backfired.

I n this chapter, we will learn why everyone is so interested in what the Federal Reserve is about to do. In the short run (when prices don't have enough time to change and we consider them temporarily fixed), the Federal Reserve can influence interest-rate levels in the economy. When the Federal Reserve lowers interest rates, investment spending and GDP increase because the cost of funds is cheaper. Conversely, when the Fed increases interest rates, investment spending and GDP decrease because the cost of funds is higher. It is this power of the Fed to affect interest rates in the short run that will influence firms' decisions to invest. It also explains why everyone wants to know what the Fed will do about interest rates in the near future. After reading this chapter, you will be able to answer the following questions:

1 Why do short-term interest rates rise after the Federal Reserve makes open market sales?

2 Why do the prices of bonds usually fall when the Federal Reserve raises interest rates?

3 How does the housing and construction industry respond after the Federal Reserve decides to increase the money supply?

4 How does monetary policy affect international trade?

5 Why is the Fed concerned about the financial markets' expectations of its policies?

The Money Market

Money market
The market for money in which the amount supplied and the amount demanded meet to determine the nominal interest.

The **money market** is the market for money where the amount supplied and the amount demanded meet to determine the nominal interest (the stated or quoted interest rate before inflation reduces it to its "real" rate). We begin by learning the factors that determine the public's demand for money. Once we understand what affects the demand for money, we can see how actions taken by the Federal Reserve determine the supply of money. Then we'll see how the two of them together determine interest rates.

The Demand for Money

Let's think of money as simply one part of wealth. Suppose your total wealth is valued at $1,000. In what form will you hold your wealth? Should you put all your wealth into the stock market? Or perhaps into the bond market? Or should you hold some of your wealth in money, that is, currency and deposits in checking accounts?

Interest Rates Affect Money Demand

If you invest in assets such as stocks or bonds, you will generally earn income on them. Stocks pay dividends and increase in value; bonds pay interest. If you hold your wealth in currency or in a checking account, however, you will receive either no interest or very low interest. And if inflation rises sharply, you might even lose money. Holding your wealth as money (in currency or a checking account) means that you sacrific some potential income.

Money does, however, provide a valuable service. It facilitates transactions. If you go to a grocery store to purchase some cereal, the store will accept currency or a check but you won't be able to pay for your cereal with your stocks and bonds. People hold money primarily for this basic reason: Money makes it easier to conduct everyday transactions. Economists call this reason for holding money the **transactions demand for money**.

Transactions demand for money

The demand for money based on the desire to facilitate transactions.

To understand the demand for money, we rely on the principle of opportunity cost

Principle OF OPPORTUNITY COST

The opportunity cost of something is what you sacrifice to get it.

The opportunity cost of holding money is the return that you could have earned by holding your wealth in other assets. We measure the opportunity cost of holding money by the interest rate. Suppose that the interest rate available to you on a long-term bond is 6% per year. If you hold $100 of your wealth in the form of this bond, you'll earn $6 a year. If you hold currency instead, you'll earn no interest. So the opportunity cost of holding $100 in currency is $6 per year, or 6% per year.

As interest rates increase in the economy, the opportunity cost of holding money also increases. Economists have found that as the opportunity cost of holding money increases, the public demands less money. The quantity demanded of money will decrease with an increase in interest rates.

In Figure 28.1, we draw a demand for money curve, M^d, as a function of the interest rate. At higher interest rates, individuals will want to hold less money than they will at lower interest rates because the opportunity cost of holding money is higher. As interest rates rise from r_0 to r_1, the quantity demanded of money falls from M_0 to M_1.

The Price Level and GDP Affect Money Demand

The demand for money also depends on two other factors. One is the overall price level in the economy. The demand for money will increase as the level of prices increases. If prices for your groceries are twice as high, you will need twice as much money to purchase them. The amount of money people typically hold during any time period will be closely related to the dollar value of the transactions that they make. This is an example of the real-nominal principle in action:

REAL-NOMINAL *Principle*

What matters to people is the real value of money or income— its purchasing power—not the face value of money or income.

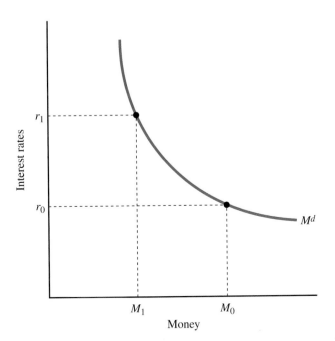

FIGURE 28.1

Demand for Money
As interest rates increase
from r_0 to r_1, the quantity
of money demanded falls
from M_0 to M_1.

The other factor that influences the demand for money is the level of real GDP or real income. It seems obvious that as income increases, individuals and businesses will make more purchases. Similarly, as real GDP increases, individuals and businesses will make more transactions. To facilitate these transactions, they will want to hold more money.

Figure 28.2 shows how changes in prices and GDP affect the demand for money. Panel A shows how the demand for money shifts to the right as the price level increases. At any interest rate, people will want to hold more money as prices increase. Panel B shows how the demand for money shifts to the right as real GDP increases. At any interest rate, people will want to hold more money as real GDP increases. These graphs both show the same result. An increase in prices or an increase in real GDP will increase money demand.

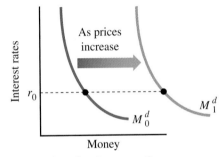

(A) **As prices increase, the demand for money shifts to the right.**

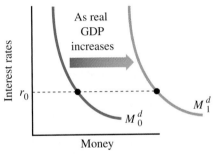

(B) **As real GDP increases, the demand for money shifts to the right.**

FIGURE 28.2

Shifting the Demand for Money
Changes in prices and real GDP shift the demand for money.

Other Components of Money Demand

Traditionally, economists have identified other motives besides transactions for individuals or firms to hold money. If you hold your wealth in the form of property, such as a house or a boat, it is costly to sell the house or boat on short notice if you need to obtain funds. These forms of wealth are **illiquid**, meaning that they are not easily transferable into money. If you hold your wealth in currency or checking accounts, you do not have this problem. Economists recognize that individuals have a **liquidity demand for money**: People want to hold money to be able to make transactions on quick notice.

During periods of economic volatility, investors might not want to hold stocks and bonds because their prices might fall. Instead, they might convert them into holdings that fall into the M2 category—like savings accounts and money market funds. These investments earn lower interest rates but are less risky than stocks and bonds, whose prices can fluctuate. This demand for "safer" assets is called the **speculative demand for money**. For example, after the stock market began to fall in 2000, individuals became very uncertain about the future and shifted their funds from the stock market to money market mutual funds. This temporarily increased M2. When the market started to recover, some investors shifted funds back into the stock market, decreasing M2 in the economy.

In summary, individuals hold money for three motives: to facilitate transactions, to provide liquidity, and to reduce risk. The amount of money they want to hold will depend on interest rates, the level of real GDP, and the price level.

How the Federal Reserve Can Change the Money Supply

As we discussed in the last chapter, the banking system as a whole can expand the money supply only if new reserves come into the system. As we saw, when private citizens and firms write checks to one another, there will be no net change in the supply of money. Because the total amount of reserves in the system is unchanged, the money supply cannot expand. There is one organization, however, that has the power to change the total amount of reserves in the banking system: the Federal Reserve.

Open Market Operations

The Fed can increase or decrease the total amount of reserves in the banking system through either of the following operations:

▶ In **open market purchases**, the Federal Reserve buys government bonds from the private sector.
▶ In **open market sales**, the Fed sells government bonds to the private sector.

To understand how the Fed can increase the supply of money, let's trace what happens after an open market purchase. Suppose the Federal Reserve purchases $1 million

---

Illiquid
Not easily transferable to money.

Liquidity demand for money
The demand for money that represents the needs and desires individuals or firms can fill on short notice without incurring excessive costs.

Speculative demand for money
The demand for money that reflects holding money over short periods is less risky than holding stocks or bonds.

Open market purchase
The Fed's purchase of government bonds, which increases the money supply.

Open market sale
The Fed's sales of government bonds to the public, which decreases the money supply.

worth of government bonds currently owned by the private sector. The Fed writes a check for $1 million and presents it to the party who sold the bonds. The Federal Reserve now owns those bonds. The party who sold the bonds then deposits the $1 million in its bank.

Here is the key to how that increases the supply of money: As we explained in the last chapter, each bank must keep an account with the Fed containing both its required and excess reserves The check written against the Federal Reserve increases the bank's total reserves, essentially giving it more money to loan out. In this case, the bank's account balance increases by $1 million. If the reserve requirement is 10%, the bank must keep $100,000 of it in reserves, but it can now loan out $900,000 of it from its excess reserves. Basically, when the Fed buys bonds, the proceeds go out into the economy. Open market purchases of bonds therefore increase the money supply.

The Federal Reserve has powers that ordinary citizens and even banks do not have. The Fed can write checks against itself to purchase government bonds without having any explicit "funds" in its account for the purchase. Banks accept these checks because they count as part of their total reserves.

As you might expect, open market sales will, conversely, decrease the supply of money. Suppose the Federal Reserve sells $1 million worth of government bonds to a Wall Street firm. The firm will pay for the bonds with a check for $1 million drawn on its bank and give this check to the Federal Reserve. The bank must either hand over $1 million in cash or, more likely, reduce its total reserves with the Federal Reserve by $1 million. When the Fed sells bonds, it is basically taking the money exchanged for them out of the hands of the public. Open market sales therefore decrease the money freely available in the economy.

In summary, if the Federal Reserve wishes to increase the money supply to stimulate the economy (perhaps it is operating too sluggishly), it buys government bonds from the private sector in open market purchases. If the Fed wishes to decrease the money supply to slow the economy down (perhaps it is growing too quickly and inflation is occurring), it sells government bonds to the private sector in open market sales.

Other Tools of the Fed

Open market operations are by far the most important way in which the Federal Reserve changes the supply of money. There are two other ways in which the Fed can change the supply of money, which we'll discuss next.

Changing Reserve Requirements

Another way the Fed can change the money supply is by changing the reserve requirements for banks. If the Fed wishes to increase the supply of money, it can reduce banks' reserve requirements so they have more money to loan out. This would expand the money supply. To decrease the supply of money, the Federal Reserve can raise reserve requirements.

Changing reserve requirements is a powerful tool, but it's not one the Federal Reserve uses very often because it disrupts the banking system. Suppose a bank is required to hold exactly 10% of its deposits as reserves and that it has loaned the other 90% out. If the Federal Reserve suddenly increases its reserve requirement to 20%, the bank would be forced to call in or cancel many of its loans. Its customers would not like this! Today, the Fed doesn't make sharp changes in reserve requirements. It has, however, in the past, including during the Great Depression.

Changing the Discount Rate

Discount rate
The interest rate at which banks can borrow from the Fed.

Another way the Fed can change the money supply is by changing the **discount rate**. The discount rate is the interest rate at which banks can borrow directly from the Fed. Suppose a major customer comes to the bank and asks for a loan. Unless the bank could find an additional source of funds, it would have to refuse to make the loan. Banks are reluctant to turn away major customers. They first try to borrow reserves from other banks through the **federal funds market**, a market in which banks borrow or lend reserves to each other. If the rate—called the **federal funds rate**—seemed too high to the bank, it could borrow directly from the Federal Reserve at the discount rate. By changing the discount rate, the Federal Reserve can influence the amount of borrowing by banks. If the Fed raises the discount rate, banks will be discouraged from borrowing reserves because it has become more costly. Lowering the discount rate will induce banks to borrow additional reserves.

Federal funds market
The market in which banks borrow and lend reserves to and from one another.

Federal funds rate
The interest rate on reserves that banks lend each other.

In principle, the Federal Reserve could use the discount rate as a tool independent of monetary policy. That is, it could lower the discount rate to expand the money supply and raise the discount rate to reduce the money supply. In practice, the Fed keeps the discount rate close to the federal funds rate to avoid large swings in borrowed reserves by banks. Changes in the discount rate, however, are quite visible to financial markets. Participants in the financial markets often interpret these changes as revealing clues about the Fed's intentions for future monetary policy.

How Interest Rates are Determined: Combining the Demand for Money with Its Supply

Combining the supply of money, determined by the Fed, with the demand for money, determined by the public, we can see how interest rates are determined in the short run in a demand-and-supply model of the money market.

Figure 28.3 depicts a model of the money market. The supply of money is determined by the Federal Reserve, and we assume for simplicity that it is independent of interest rates. We represent this independence by a vertical supply curve for money, M^s. In the same graph, we draw the demand for money M^d. Market equilibrium occurs where the demand for money equals the supply of money, at an interest rate of r^*.

At this equilibrium interest rate r^*, the quantity of money demanded by the private sector equals the quantity of money supplied by the Federal Reserve. What happens if the interest rate is higher than r^*? At a higher interest rate, the quantity of money demanded would be less than the fixed quantity supplied, so there would be an excess supply of money. In other markets, excess supplies cause the price to fall. It's the same here. The "price of money" in the market for money is the interest rate. If the interest rate were below r^*, the demand for money would exceed the fixed supply:

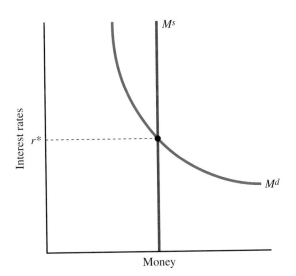

FIGURE 28.3

**Equilibrium in
the Money Market**
Equilibrium in the money
market occurs at an interest
rate of r^*, at which the
quantity of money
demanded equals the
quantity of money supplied.

There would be an excess demand for money. As in other markets when there are excess demands, the price rises. Here, the "price of money," or the interest rate, would rise until it reached r^*. As you see, money market equilibrium follows the same logic as any other economic equilibrium.

We can use this simple model of the money market to understand the power of the Federal Reserve. Suppose the Federal Reserve increases the money supply through an open market purchase of bonds. In Panel A of Figure 28.4, an increase in the supply of money shifts the money supply curve to the right, leading to lower interest rates. A decrease in the money supply through the Fed's open market sale of bonds, as depicted in Panel B of Figure 28.4, decreases the supply of money, shifting the money supply curve to the left and increasing interest rates.

We can also think of the process from the perspective of banks. Recall our discussion of money creation through the banking system. After the Fed's open market purchase of bonds, some of the money the Fed paid for the bonds gets deposited into

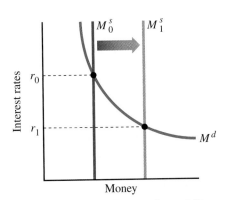

**(A) An open market purchase shifts
the supply of money to the right
and leads to lower interest rates.**

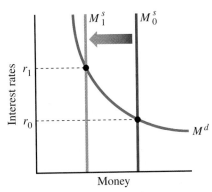

**(B) An open market sale shifts the
supply of money to the left and
leads to higher interest rates.**

FIGURE 28.4

**Federal Reserve
and Interest Rates**
Changes in the supply of
money will change interest
rates.

banks. Banks will want to make loans to consumers and businesses with that money because holding it in their reserves with the Fed earns them no interest. To entice people to borrow, they will lower the interest rates they charge on their loans. After an open market purchase of bonds by the Fed, interest rates will fall throughout the entire economy.

Now we understand why potential new homeowners—as well as businesspeople and politicians—want to know what the Federal Reserve is likely to do in the near future. The Fed exerts direct control over interest rates in the short run. If the Fed decides interest rates should be lower, it buys bonds in the open market to increase the supply of money. If it wants higher interest rates, it sells bonds in the open market to decrease the money supply.

Rising Interest Rates During an Economic Recovery

Economists have often noticed that as an economy recovers from a recession, interest rates start to rise. Some observers think this is puzzling because it seems to them that higher interest rates are associated with lower output. Using the demand-and-supply diagram for money helps explain why interest rates can, however, rise during an economic recovery.

The key to understanding this puzzle is that the extra income being generated by firms and individuals during the recovery will increase the demand for money. Because the demand for money increases while the supply of it remains fixed, interest rates rise. Thus, rising interest rates during a period of economic recovery are to be expected. ■

Interest Rates and Bond Prices

Sometimes you see in the financial section of the newspaper a statement like, "Today, interest rates rose as bond prices fell." You may wonder if these two things are connected. Indeed they are. When the Fed raises interest rates, bond prices fall.

To see why, recall that bonds represent a promise to pay money in the future. If you own a bond, you are entitled to receive payments on it at a later time. But why do the prices of bonds move in the opposite direction of interest rates?

Since a bond payment occurs in the future, we need to place a value on this payment today. Chapter 26 showed us how to do this using the concept of present value. The price of a bond is simply the present value of its future payments. Consider a bond that makes a payment one period in the future. The price of the bond (the present value of the payment) is equal to

$$\text{price of bond} = \text{promised payment}/(1 + \text{interest rate})$$

That is, the price of a bond is the payment promised divided by 1 plus the interest rate.

Suppose the promised payment next year were $106 and the interest rate were 6% per year. The price of the bond would be

$$\text{price of bond} = \$1.06/1.06 = \$100$$

In this case, the bond would cost $100 if it were issued today. But what happens if interest rates in the economy change later? What if rates rise higher than 6% or fall lower than 6%? What will the bond you are holding be worth then, if you decided, for example, you needed the money and had to sell it to someone else? This is important because most of the bonds for sale on the market are not newly issued bonds—they are bonds that have already been issued with specific promised payments that the people are buying and selling from one another.

Let's consider two examples:

▶ Suppose that the promised payment is still $106 but the interest rate falls from 6% to 4% per year. Using the formula, the price of the bond will rise to $106/1.04, or $101.92—$1.92 more than it was with an interest rate of 6%. The price of the bond rose because, at the lower interest rate of 4%, a buyer would need more money— $101.92 versus $100 to get the same $106 the bond will pay next year. At a lower interest rate, the value today of a future payment (the present value) is higher, in other words.

▶ Now suppose that interest rates rise from 6% to 8% per year. In this case, the price you could sell your bond for would fall to $106/1.08, or $98.15. The reason the price of the bond fell is that a buyer would need only $98.15 to get the $106 next year. As interest rates rose, the price of the bond fell. At a higher interest rate, the value today of a future payment (the present value) is lower, in other words.

In financial markets, there are many types of complex bonds that pay different sums of money at different times in the future. However, all bonds, no matter how complex or simple, promise to pay some money in the future. The same logic that applies to simple one-period bonds, like the one just described, applies to more complex bonds. As interest rates rise, investors need less money for the promised payments in the future, so the price of all these bonds falls. As interest rates fall, investors need more money for the promised payments. Therefore, as the Fed changes interest rates, bond prices will move in the opposite direction of interest rates.

How Open Market Operations Directly Affect Bond Prices

There is another way to understand why when bond prices change in one direction, interest rates will change in opposite directions. We know that when the Federal Reserve buys bonds in the open market, interest rates fall. But think about what the Federal Reserve is doing when it conducts the open market purchase. The Federal Reserve is buying bonds from the public. As it buys bonds, it increases the demand for bonds and raises their price. This is another reason bond prices rise as interest rates fall.

Similarly, interest rates rise following an open market sale of bonds by the Fed. When the Fed conducts an open market sale, it is selling bonds, increasing the supply of bonds in the market. With an increase in the supply of bonds, the price of bonds will fall.

Because the Federal Reserve can change interest rates with open market purchases and sales and thereby affect the price of bonds, you can now see why Wall Street firms typically hire Fed watchers (often former officials of the Federal Reserve) to try to predict what the Fed will do. If a Wall Street firm correctly predicts that the Fed will surprise the market and lower interest rates, the firm could buy millions of dollars of bonds for itself or its clients prior to the Fed's announcement and make vast profits as the prices on the bonds inevitably rise.

Good News for the Economy/Bad News for Bond Prices

You may have heard on television or read in the newspaper that prices in the bond market often fall in the face of good economic news, such as an increase in real output. Are the markets perverse? Why is good news for the economy bad news for the bond market?

We can understand the behavior of the bond market by thinking about the demand for money. When real GDP increases, the demand for money will increase. As the demand for money increases, the money demand curve will shift to the right. From our model of the money market, we know that increased money demand will increase interest rates. Bond prices move in the opposite direction from interest rates. Therefore, good news for the economy is bad for the bond market.

TEST Your Understanding

1. How do we measure the opportunity cost of holding money?
2. Complete the statement with "increase" or "decrease." The quantity of money demanded will _____ as interest rates increase.
3. Complete the statement with "increase" or "decrease": Both increases in the price level and increases in real GDP will _____ the demand for money.
4. To increase the supply of money, should the Fed buy or sell bonds?
5. What will happen to interest rates if the Fed sells bonds on the open market?
6. If interest rates are 3% per year, what will be the price of a bond that promises to pay $109 next year?

Interest Rates and How They Change Investment and Output (GDP)

Higher or lower interest rates are just a means to an end, though, for the Fed. The Fed's ultimate goal is to change output—either slow the economy down or speed the economy up by influencing aggregate demand.

To show how the Fed's affects the interest rate, which in turn affects investment (a component of GDP), and finally, GDP itself, we combine our supply and demand for money with the curve that shows how investment spending is related to interest rates. This is shown in Figure 28.5. The graph on the left in Figure 28.5 shows how interest rates are determined by the demand and supply for money. It is identical to Figure 28.3, which we studied earlier. It shows us the equilibrium interest rate for

Lower interest rates will stimulate new production of housing and other durable goods.

money. Now let's move to the graph on the right. We can see from the graph on the right that at the equilibrium interest rate r^* the level of investment in the economy will be given by I^*.

We should note that consumption as well as investment can depend on interest rates. That is, spending on consumer durables, such as automobiles and refrigerators, will also depend negatively on the rate of interest. Consumer durables are really investment goods for the household: If you buy an automobile, you incur the cost today and receive benefits (the ability to use the car) in the future. As interest rates rise, the opportunity costs of investing in the automobile will rise. Consumers will respond to the increase in the opportunity cost by purchasing fewer cars. In this chapter, we discuss how changes in interest rates affect investment, but keep in mind that the purchases of consumer durables are affected too.

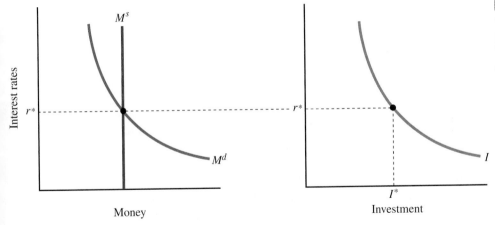

FIGURE 28.5

The Money Market and Investment Spending
The equilibrium interest rate r^* is determined in the money market. At that interest rate, investment spending is given by I^*.

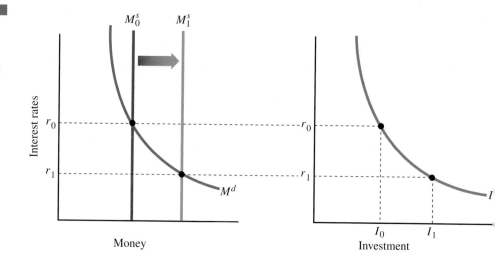

FIGURE 28.6

Monetary Policy and Interest Rates

As the money supply increases, interest rates fall from r_0 to r_1. Investment spending increases from I_0 to I_1.

In Figure 28.6, we show the effects of an increase in the money supply using our money market and investment graphs. As the supply of money increases, interest rates fall from r_0 to r_1. With lower interest rates, investment spending will increase from I_0 to I_1. This increase in investment spending will then increase aggregate demand—the total demand for goods and services in the economy—and shift the aggregate demand curve to the right.

We show the shift of the aggregate demand curve in Figure 28.7. With the increase in aggregate demand, both output (y) and the price level (P) in the economy as a whole will increase in the short run. Thus, by reducing interest rates, the Fed affects output and prices in the economy.

In summary, when the Fed increases the money supply, it leads to lower interest rates and increased investment spending. In turn, a higher level of investment spending will ultimately lead to a higher level of GDP.

| open market bond purchases | → | increase in money supply | → | fall in interest rates | → | rise in investment spending | → | increase in GDP |

FIGURE 28.7

When the money supply is increased, investment spending increases, shifting the *AD* curve to the right. Output increases in the short run.

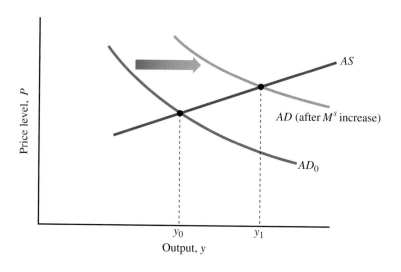

The Fed can also use its influence to increase interest rates, which will have the exact opposite effect. Investment spending will fall, along with aggregate demand. The aggregate demand curve will shift to the left, and the price level and output in the economy will fall, too. We can again represent this entire sequence of events:

open market bond sale	→	decrease in money supply	→	rise in interest rates	→	fall in investment spending	→	decrease in GDP

How Monetary Policy Affects International Trade

We have been discussing monetary policy without taking into account international trade or international movements of financial funds across countries. Once we bring in these considerations, we will see that monetary policy operates through an additional route.

Suppose the Federal Reserve lowers U.S. interest rates through an open market purchase of bonds. As a result, investors in the United States will be earning lower interest rates and will seek to invest some of their funds abroad. To invest abroad, they will need to sell their U.S. dollars and buy the foreign currency of the country where they intend to invest. This will affect the **exchange rate**—the rate at which one currency trades for another currency. As many investors sell their dollars to buy foreign currency, the exchange rate will fall. A fall in the exchange rate or a decrease in the value of a currency is called **depreciation of a currency**. Lower U.S. interest rates brought on by the Fed will cause the dollar to depreciate. This will ultimately change the demand and supply of goods and services around the globe because it will make U.S. goods cheaper than foreign goods. Let's see why.

In this case, the lower value of the dollar will mean that U.S. goods become relatively cheaper on world markets. Suppose that the exchange rate were two Swiss francs to the dollar, meaning you would receive two Swiss francs for every dollar you exchanged. If a U.S. machine sells for $100,000, it will cost 200,000 Swiss francs. Now suppose the value of the dollar depreciates so that one dollar now buys only one Swiss franc. The same U.S. machine will now cost Swiss residents half of what they used to pay for it—just 100,000 francs instead of 200,000. In other words, the lower value of the dollar makes U.S. goods cheaper for foreigners. As a result, foreign residents will want to buy more U.S. goods, and U.S. companies will want to export more goods to meet the higher foreign demand.

That's the good news about the lower value of the U.S. dollar. The bad news is that the lower value of the dollar will make it more expensive for U.S. residents to buy foreign goods. If the exchange rate were still two Swiss francs to the dollar as it originally was at the outset of our example, Swiss chemicals with a price tag of 60,000 francs would cost a U.S. resident $30,000. If the exchange rate of the dollar depreciates to one franc per dollar, however, the same chemicals will cost twice as much—$60,000. As the

Exchange rate
The rate at which currencies trade for one another in the market.

Depreciation of a currency
A decrease in the value of a currency.

dollar depreciates, imports become more expensive, and U.S. residents tend to import fewer of them.

Let's recap this: As the exchange rate for the U.S. dollar falls, U.S. goods become cheaper and foreign goods become more expensive. The United States then export more goods and imports fewer goods. *Net* exports increase, in other words. This increase in net exports increases the demand for U.S. goods and increases GDP.

Remember that this all began with an open market purchase of bonds by the Fed that increased the money supply. Here is the sequence of events:

open market bond purchase $\rightarrow$ increase in money supply $\rightarrow$ fall in interest rates $\rightarrow$ fall in exchange rate $\rightarrow$ increase in net exports $\rightarrow$ increase in GDP

The three new links in the sequence are from interest rates to exchange rates, from exchange rates to net exports, and from net exports to GDP.

This sequence also works in reverse. If the Fed conducts an open market sale of bonds, U.S. interest rates rise. As a result, foreign investors earning lower interest rates elsewhere will want to move their money to the United States where they can earn a higher return. As they buy more U.S. dollars, the exchange rate for the dollar will increase, and the dollar will increase in value. An increase in the value of a currency is called **appreciation of the currency**. The appreciation of the dollar will make U.S. goods more expensive for foreigners and imports cheaper for U.S. residents. Suppose the exchange rate for the U.S. dollar appreciates, and each dollar can now be exchanged for three francs instead of two. The same machine the Swiss had to pay 200,000 francs for when the exchange rate was one dollar to two francs now costs 300,000 francs. The Swiss chemicals U.S. residents bought for $30,000 will now cost them less—just $20,000.

When U.S. interest rates rise as a result of an open market sale by the Fed, we expect exports to decrease and imports to increase, decreasing net exports. The decrease in net exports will reduce the demand for U.S. goods and lead to a fall in output. Here is the sequence of events:

open market bond sale $\rightarrow$ decrease in money supply $\rightarrow$ rise in interest rates $\rightarrow$ rise in exchange rate $\rightarrow$ decrease in net exports $\rightarrow$ decrease in GDP

To summarize, an increase in interest rates will reduce both investment spending (including consumer durables) and net exports. A decrease in interest rates will increase investment spending and net exports. As you can see, monetary policy in an open economy is even more powerful than monetary policy used in a closed economy.

The Fed and other central banks are well aware of the power they have to influence exchange rates and international trade. Indeed, for countries that depend critically on international trade—like the Netherlands and Belgium—the effects of monetary policy on exchange rates are critical to their economic well-being. We'll study these issues in more depth in the last chapter in the book.

Appreciation of a currency
An increase in the value of a currency.

TEST Your Understanding

7. Complete the statement with "higher" or "lower": When the Federal Reserve sells bonds on the open market, it leads to _____ levels of investment and output in the economy.

8. Complete the statement with "sale" or "purchase": To increase the level of output, the Fed should conduct an open market _____ of bonds.

9. What are all the events in a closed economy in the sequence from an open market purchase to a change in output?

10. Complete the statement with "appreciate" or "depreciate": An increase in the supply of money will _____ a country's currency.

11. Explain how monetary policy works in an economy that is open to trade.

Monetary Policy Challenges for the Fed

Now that we have seen how changes in the money supply affect aggregate demand, we can see that the government has two different types of tools to change the level of GDP in the short run: The government can use either fiscal policy—changes in the level of taxes or government spending—or **monetary policy**—changes in the supply of money and interest rates—to alter the level of GDP.

Monetary policy
The range of actions taken by the Federal Reserve to influence the level of GDP or the rate of inflation.

If the current level of GDP is below full employment or potential output, the government can use expansionary policies such as tax cuts, increased spending, or increases in the money supply to raise the level of GDP and reduce unemployment. If the current level of GDP exceeds full employment or potential output, the economy will overheat, and the rate of inflation will increase. To avoid this, the government can use contractionary policies to reduce the level of GDP back to full employment or potential output.

In Chapter 24, we explored some of the limitations of stabilization policy. We saw that fiscal policy is subject to lags and fraught with complications because political parties have different ideas about what the government should or should not do, and it takes them time to reach agreement. Monetary policy also has its complications.

Lags in Monetary Policy

Recall that there are two types of lags in policy. Inside lags are the time it takes for policymakers to recognize and implement policy changes. Outside lags are the time it takes for policy to actually work.

The inside lags for monetary policy are relatively short as compared to those for fiscal policy. The FOMC meets eight times a year and can decide on major policy changes at any time and very quickly. It can even give the chairperson of the Board of Governors some discretion to make changes between meetings.

Of course, it does take time for the people working at the Fed to recognize that problems are beginning to occur in the economy. A good example is the 1990 recession. In 1990, Iraq invaded Kuwait. After the invasion, there was some concern that higher oil prices and the uncertainty of the political situation in Kuwait would trigger a recession in the United States, which, of course, is heavily dependent on oil. However, Alan Greenspan, the chairman of the Federal Reserve, testified before Congress as late as October 1990 that the economy had not yet slipped into a recession. Not until that December did Greenspan declare that the economy had entered into a recession. Yet looking back, we now know that the recession had actually started five months earlier in July.

Decisions about monetary policy are made by a committee. Judging from your own experience, do you think committees are efficient decision-makers? The results of experiments described in "A Closer Look: Do Committees Make Better or Worse Decisions?" may surprise you.

The outside lags related to monetary policy, however, are quite long. Most econometric models predict that an interest rate cut will take at least two years for most of its effects to be felt. This means that for the Fed to conduct successful monetary policy, it must be able to forecast accurately two years in the future! A study by two economists, David and Christina Romer, of the University of California, Berkeley, suggests that the Federal Reserve actually makes more accurate inflation forecasts than the private sector does, and that it is somewhat better at forecasting output as well. They attribute the Fed's success to its large staff and its access to more extensive information than private-sector forecasters have.

A CLOSER LOOK

Do Committees Make Better or Worse Decisions?

When Professor Alan Blinder returned to teaching after serving as vice-chairman of the Federal Reserve from 1994 to 1996, he was convinced that committees were not effective for making decisions about monetary policy. However, there had been no research done on this topic. With another researcher, Blinder developed an experiment to see whether individuals or groups make better decisions and who makes them more rapidly.

The type of experiment Blinder and his colleague developed was designed to explore how quickly individuals or groups could distinguish changes in underlying trends from random events. For example, if unemployment were to rise in one month, such a rise could be a temporary aberration or it could

be the beginning of a recession. Changing monetary p[...] would be a mistake if the rise were temporary, but waitin[...] long to change policy would be costly if the change were [...] manent. Who is better at making these sorts of determinati[...]

The results of the experiment showed that committees [...] form better than individuals. They make decisions as quickl[...] are more accurate than individuals making decisions by t[...] selves. Moreover, committee decisions were not simply relat[...] the average performance of the individuals who compose[...] committee—the actual *process* of having meetings and dis[...] sions appears to have improved the group's overall performa[...]

Source: Alan Krueger, "Economic Scene: A Study Shows Comm[...] Can Be More Than the Sum of Their Members," *New York T[...] December 7, 2000, p. C2.

On the other hand, it is notoriously difficult to predict when recessions are about to occur. As an example, in May of 2000, the Fed—fearing a rise in inflation—raised the federal funds rate from 6.00% to 6.50%. Yet, on January 3, 2001, the Fed reversed itself and restored the rate to 6.00%, as it now feared a recession. It was too little—and too late—to prevent the 2001 recession.

Because of the long outside lags for monetary policy and difficulties in forecasting the economy, many economists believe that the Fed should not take a very active role in trying to stabilize the economy. Instead, they recommend that the Fed concentrate on keeping the inflation rate low and stable.

Influencing Market Expectations: From the Federal Funds Rate to Interest Rates on Long-Term Bonds

It is important to recognize that the Fed only directly controls very short-term interest rates in the economy, not long-term interest rates. In fact, when the Fed makes its decisions on monetary policy, it really decides on what the rate should be in the federal funds market—the market in which banks trade reserves overnight. Once the Fed decides on what rate it wants in the market, it conducts open market operations—buying and selling short-term government bonds—to achieve this rate. Thus, when the Federal Reserve decides the course of monetary policy, it is really just setting a very short-term interest rate for the economy.

However, when a firm is deciding on a long-term investment or a household is deciding whether to purchase a new home, they will base their decisions on the interest rate at which they can borrow money, and these will typically be long-term interest rates—not short-term rates (For example, a household might take out a 30-year mortgage to purchase a home.) If the rate is too high, they might not take out the loan. So for the Fed to control investment spending, it must also somehow influence long-term rates. It can do this indirectly by influencing short-term rates. Here's how.

Long term interest rates are averages of current and expected future short-term interest rates. To see why future short-term interest rates are important, consider putting $100 of your money in the bank for two years. If the interest rate is 5% for the first year, you would have $105 at the end of that year. If the interest rate for the following year were 10%, you would then have $115.50 ($105 × 1.10) at the end of the second year. The value of your bank account would reflect *both* the current short-term interest rate (5%) and next year's short-term interest rate (10%). Similarly, the present value of payments in the future on a bond or loan will reflect both the current short-term interest rate as well as future short-term rates. Long-term interest rates are an average of the current short-term interest rate and expected future short-term rates.

The Fed can directly control the federal funds rate and other short-term interest rates. Its actions also provide information to the market about the likely course for future short-term rates. If the Fed wishes to stimulate long-term investment by cutting the short-term interest rate, it must also convince the public that it will keep future short-term rates low as well in order to reduce long-term interest rates. Influencing expectations of the financial markets is an important part of the Fed's job.

A CLOSER LOOK

What Should the Fed Say or *Not* Say?

In recent years, the Fed has gradually become more open in its deliberations. For many years, the Fed would not even say if it had changed interest rates. These policies began to change slowly in the 1990s. Starting in 2000, after each FOMC meeting it announces its target for the federal funds rate and makes a brief statement explaining its actions. But should the Fed go further in describing its intended future policies?

There was enough interest on this very topic for the FOMC to hold a special meeting—the first since 1979—to discuss the issue. Some members of the FOMC, including Ben Bernanke from Princeton University, believed that the financial markets needed more information so that they would have a clearer idea of what future Fed policy—and short term interest rates—were likely to be. Other members including William Poole, the president of the St. Louis Federal Reserve Bank, disagreed. Poole felt that the financial markets understood the implicit rules that the Fed followed and that issuing a more complex public statement would just confuse matters.

The special meeting did not lead to any dramatic change in the Fed's communication policies. But Chairman Greenspan now polls the members of the FOMC before issuing any statement. The Fed clearly recognizes that its statements may be just as important as its actions.

Source: Grep Ip, "Fed's Big Question: Not What to Do, But What to Say," *Wall Street Journal*, October 27, 2003, p. 1.

The Fed does try to communicate its general intentions for future policy actions to the public in order to be more effective. However, the public ultimately must form its own expectations of what the Fed is going to do. As we saw in our chapter-opening story, the public does not always anticipate the Fed's actions fully. Coping with financial market expectations complicates the Fed's task in developing monetary policy. The Fed itself has debated how best to communicate with the financial markets, as "A Closer Look: What Should the Fed Say or *Not* Say?" explains.

Looking Ahead: From the Short Run to The Long Run

The model for monetary policy that we developed in this chapter can be used to understand the behavior of the economy only in the short run, when prices do not change very much. Monetary policy can affect output in the short run when prices are largely fixed, but in the long run, changes in the money supply only affect the price level and inflation. In the long run the Federal Reserve can only indirectly control nominal interest rates. It can't control *real* interest rates—the rate after inflation is figured in. In the next part of the book, we will explain how output and prices change over time, and how the economy makes the transition by itself from the short to the long run regardless of what the Fed does.

USING THE TOOLS

Take this opportunity to use the tools that we developed in this chapter.

1. Interest Rates on Checking Accounts

During the 1980s, banks started to pay interest (at low rates) on checking accounts for the first time. Given what you know about opportunity costs, how would interest paid on checking affect the demand for money?

2. Pegging Interest Rates

Suppose the Federal Reserve wanted to fix, or "peg," the level of interest rates at 6% per year. Using a simple supply-and-demand diagram, show how increases in money demand would change the supply of money if the Federal Reserve pursued the policy of this fixed interest rate. Use your answer to explain this statement: "If the Federal Reserve pegs interest rates, it loses control of the money supply."

3. Nominal Interest Rates and the Demand for Money

We know that investment spending depends on real interest rates. Yet the demand for money will depend on nominal interest rates, not on real interest rates. Can you explain why money demand should depend on nominal rates?

4. The Presidential Praise and Blame Game

Because of lags, a president may get credit or blame from actions by his predecessor. Also, presidents may only have limited control over the Fed and thus can take credit or be blamed by decisions of the Fed that the president had little role in. Nonetheless, the public does want to hold someone responsible and it is usually the president.

SUMMARY

This chapter showed how monetary policy affects aggregate demand and the economy in the short run. Together, the demand for money by the public and the supply of money determined by the Federal Reserve determine interest rates. Changes in interest rates will in turn affect investment and output. In the international economy, exchange rates and net exports are also affected by interest rates. Still, there are limits to what effective monetary policies can do. Here are the main points of the chapter:

1 The demand for money depends negatively on the interest rate and positively on the level of prices and real GDP.

2 The Fed can determine the supply of money through open market purchases and sales, changing reserve requirements, or changing the discount rate. Open market operations are the primary tool of the Fed.

3 The level of interest rates is determined in the money market by the demand for money and the supply of money.

4 To increase the level of GDP, the Federal Reserve buys bonds on the open market. To decrease the level of GDP, the Federal Reserve sells bonds on the open market.

5 An increase in the money supply will decrease interest rates, increase investment spending, and increase output. A decrease in the money supply will increase interest rates, decrease investment spending, and decrease output.

6 In an open economy, a decrease in interest rates will depreciate the local currency and lead to an increase in net exports. Conversely, an increase in interest rates will appreciate the local currency and lead to a decrease in net exports.

7 Both lags in economic policies and the need to influence market expectations make successful monetary policy difficult in practice.

KEY TERMS

appreciation of a currency, 656
depreciation of a currency, 655
discount rate, 648
exchange rate, 655
federal funds market, 648

federal funds rate, 648
illiquid, 646
liquidity demand for money, 646
monetary policy, 657
money market, 643

open market purchase, 646
open market sale, 646
speculative demand for money, 646
transactions demand for money,
   644

PROBLEMS AND DISCUSSION QUESTIONS

1 Give another example from your own experience of the liquidity demand for money.

2 If a bond promised to pay $110 next year and the interest rate was 5% per year, what would be the price of the bond?

3 If you strongly believed that the Federal Reserve was going to surprise the markets and raise interest rates, would you want to buy bonds or sell bonds?

4 Explain why interest rates are sometimes called the price of holding money.

5 What would happen to the supply of money if the Fed purchased foreign currency held by the public?

6 Refrigerators and clothing are to some extent durable. Explain why the decision to purchase a refrigerator is likely to be more sensitive to interest rates than the decision to buy clothing.

7 In an open economy, changes in monetary policy affect both interest rates and exchange rates. Comparing the United States and the Netherlands, in which country would monetary policy have a more significant effect on GDP through changes in exchange rates?

8 Explain why interest rates usually fall in a recession.

9 Explain why the outside lag for monetary policy may be long. (Hint: Think of the channels through which monetary policy operates.)

10 Some central bankers have looked at asset prices such as prices of stocks, to guide monetary policy The idea is that if stock prices begin to rise, it migh signal future inflation or an overheated economy Are there any dangers to using the stock market as guide to monetary policy?

11 Web Exercise. The Federal Reserve uses both econometric models as well as other, more genera information about the economy to make decision about monetary policy. To see what some of thi general information looks like, go to the Website for the Federal Reserve Open Market Committee (*http://www.federalreserve.gov/fomc*) and read the report of the Beige Book (a briefing book named for the color of its cover). What type of information is provided in the Beige Book?

12 Web Exercise. As international trade becomes more important, monetary policy becomes more heavily influenced by developments in the foreign exchange markets. Go to the Web page of the Federal Reserve (*http://www.federalreserve.gov*) and read some recent speeches given by Fed officials. Do international considerations seem to affect policymakers in the United States today?

MODEL ANSWERS TO QUESTIONS

Chapter-Opening Questions

1 The supply of money has decreased.

2 The price of a bond is the present value of its promised payment and thus moves in the opposite direction of interest rates.

3 Both industries expand when interest rates fall.

4 Lower interest rates depreciate the dollar and stimulate net exports.

5 The Fed can only control short-term interest rates directly and thus must influence long-term rates through expectations about its future policies.

est Your Understanding

1 The interest rate.
2 Decrease.
3 Increase.
4 Buy bonds.
5 Interest rates will rise.
6 $109/1.03 = $105.82
7 Lower.
8 Purchase.
9 Interest rates fall, investment increases, output increases.
10 Depreciate.
11 Monetary policy affects interest rates, which, in turn, affect the exchange rate and net exports.

Part 10

Inflation, Unemployment, and Economic Policy

From the Short Run to the Long R

hey could not have differed more sharply on economic theory and policy:

John Maynard Keynes (1883–1946) was skeptical that an economy in a deep slump would ever return on its own to full employment and that even if it did, he believed it would be an extremely slow process. Moreover, Keynes didn't believe the public had to endure the economic hardships of a recession. In his opinion, swift and sensible action by the government could lift the economy out of a slump.

Economist Milton Friedman (1912–   ), who won a Nobel prize in 1976 thought otherwise. Friedman believed that, left to its own devices, an economy was very resilient and could quickly restore itself to full employment after a shock or disturbance. His greatest fear was that the government would actually make things worse by attempting to stabilize the economy. Friedman's prime example was the Great Depression. He believed the Great Depression would have been just another routine recession if disastrous monetary policy hadn't worsened it.

Both Keynes and Friedman are renowned for their contributions to economic thought. So who is right and who is wrong, and how can we come to terms with the differences the two men had?

One of the great debates surrounding macroeconomic policy-making centers on the short run versus the long run. Keynes and Friedman embody this debate. Up to this point in the book, we have discussed the short run and the long run separately. Now, however, we'll explain how the economy evolves *from* the short run *to* the long run. The relationship between the short run and the long run is one of the most important dimensions of "modern" macroeconomics, or macroeconomics as we understand it today, which carefully distinguishes between the short run and long run.

In this chapter, here some of the questions we will answer about modern macroeconomics:

1 When do wages in all sectors of the economy rise or fall together?
2 Why does expanding the money supply raise output in the short run but only lead to higher prices in the long run?
3 Why does the Federal Reserve "remove the punch bowl from the party," and what does this mean?
4 Why might tax cuts made today benefit the economy now but be harmful in the future?

The Difference Between the Short and Long Run

To begin to understand how the short run and the long run are related, let's return to what we mean by the long run and short run in macroeconomics.

In Chapter 23, we explained how in the short run, wages and prices are sticky and do not change immediately in response to changes in demand. Over time though, wages and prices adjust, and the economy reaches its long-run equilibrium. Short-run analysis applies to the period when wages and prices do not change—at least not substantially. Long-run, full-employment economics applies after wages and prices have largely adjusted to changes in demand.

In the short run, GDP is determined by the current demand for goods and services in the economy, so fiscal policy (like tax cuts or increased government spending) and monetary policy (like adjusting the money supply) can impact demand and GDP. However, in the long run, GDP is determined by the supply of labor, the stock of capital, and technological progress—in other words, the willingness of people to work and the overall "material" the economy has to work with. Full employment is another characteristic of the long run. Because the economy is operating at full employment in the long run, output can't be increased by changes in demand. So, for example, an increase in government spending won't increase GDP in the long run because spending on one good or service has to come at the expense of another good or service. Similarly,

At full employment, the economy is operating at the natural rate of unemployment and experiencing neither a boom nor bust.

increasing the supply of money won't increase GDP in the long run either. It will only cause the price level in the economy to rise.

Should economic policy be guided by what is expected to happen in the short run (as Keynes thought), or what is expected to happen in the long run (as Friedman thought)? To answer this question, we need to know two things:

1 How does what happens in the short run determine what happens in the long run?
2 How long is the short run?

Wages and Prices and Their Adjustment Over Time

Wages and prices change every day. If the demand for scooters rises at the same time as there's a fall in the demand for tennis rackets, we would expect to see a rise in the price of scooters and a fall in the price of tennis rackets. Wages in the scooter industry would tend to increase; wages in the tennis racket industry would tend to fall.

Sometimes, we see wages and prices in all industries rising or falling together. For example, prices for steel, automobiles, food, and fuel may all rise together. Why? Wages and prices will all tend to increase together during booms when GDP exceeds its full-employment level or potential output. Wages and prices will fall together during periods of recessions when GDP falls below full employment or potential output.

If the economy is producing at a level above full employment, firms will find it increasingly difficult to hire and retain workers, and unemployment will be below its atural rate. Workers, on the other hand, will find it easy to get and change jobs. To attract workers and prevent them from leaving, firms will raise their wages. As one firm raises its wage, other firms will have to raise their wages even higher to attract the workers that remain.

It just so happens that wages are the largest cost of production for most firms. Consequently, as their labor costs increase, they have no choice but to increase the prices of their products. However, as prices rise, workers need higher nominal wages to maintain their real wages. This is an illustration of the real-nominal principle:

REAL-NOMINAL *Principle*

What matters to people is the real value of money or income— its purchasing power—not the face value of money or income.

This process by which rising wages cause higher prices and higher prices feed higher wages is known as a **wage–price spiral**. It occurs when the economy is producing at a level of output that exceeds its potential.

When the economy is producing below full employment or potential output, the process works in reverse. Unemployment will exceed the natural rate. Firms will find it easy to hire and retain workers and they can offer them less. As all firms cut wages, the average level of wages in the economy falls. As we have said, wages are the largest component of firms' costs. So, when wages fall, prices start to fall, too. In this case, the wage–price spiral works in reverse.

Table 29.1 summarizes our discussion of unemployment, output, and changes in wages. It is important, however, to emphasize one point: In addition, to the changes in wages and prices that occur when the economy is producing at more or less than full employment, there is also typically ongoing inflation in the economy. For example, suppose an economy that has been operating at full employment has been experiencing 4% annual inflation. If output later exceeds full employment, prices will begin to rise at a rate faster than 4%. Conversely, if output falls to a level less than full employment, prices will then rise at a slower rate than 4%.

In summary, when output exceeds potential output, wages and prices throughout the economy will rise above previous inflation rates. If output is less than potential output, wages and prices will fall relative to previous inflation rates. (We will explore ongoing inflation more in the next chapter.)

Wage–price spiral

Changes in wages and prices causing more changes in wages and prices.

TABLE 29.1

Unemployment, Output, and Wage and Price Changes

When unemployment is below the natural rate . . .	When unemployment is above the natural rate . . .
Output is above potential. Wages and prices rise.	Output is below potential. Wages and prices fall.

How Wage and Price Changes Move the Economy Naturally Back to Full Employment

The transition between the short run and the long run is easy to understand. If GDP is higher than potential output, the economy starts to overheat and wages and prices increase. This increase in wages and prices will then push the economy back to full employment.

Using aggregate demand and aggregate supply, we can illustrate graphically how changing prices and wages help move the economy from the short to the long run. First, let's review the graphical representations of aggregate demand and aggregate supply.

1 *Aggregate demand.* Recall that the **aggregate demand curve** represents the total demand for all currently produced goods and services at different price levels.

2 *Aggregate supply.* Also recall from Chapter 23 that there are two aggregate supply curves—one for the short run and one for the long run. The **short-run aggregate supply curve** is represented as a relatively flat curve. It reflects the idea that prices do not change very much in the short run and that firms adjust production to meet demand. The **long-run aggregate supply curve**, however, is represented by a perfectly vertical line. The vertical line means that at any given price level, firms in the long run are producing all that they can, given the amount of labor, capital, and technology available to them in the economy. It represents what firms can supply in the long run at a state of full employment or potential output.

In Chapter 23, we looked at the adjustment process for an economy producing at a level of output exceeding full employment or potential output. Now let's look at what happens if the economy is in a slump, producing below full employment or potential output. Panel A of Figure 29.1 shows an aggregate demand curve and the two aggregate supply curves. In the short run, output and prices are determined where the aggregate demand curve intersects the short-run aggregate supply curve—point *a*. This corre

Aggregate demand curve
The relationship between the level of prices and the quantity of real GDP demanded.

Short-run aggregate supply curve
A relatively flat horizontal supply curve. It reflects the idea that prices do not change very much in the short run and that firms adjust production to meet demand.

Long-run aggregate supply curve
A vertical aggregate supply curve. It reflects the idea that in the long run, output is determined solely by the factors of production.

How the Economy Recovers from a Downturn

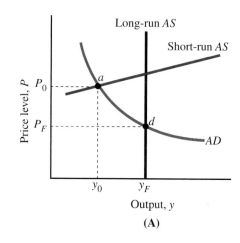

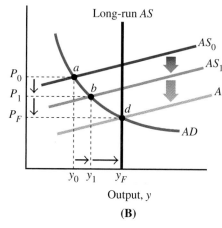

(A)   (B)

ponds to the level of output y_0 and a price level P_0. Notice that y_0 is a level less than full employment, or potential output, y_F. In the long run, the level of prices and output is given by the intersection of the aggregate demand curve and the long-run aggregate supply curve—point d. Output is at full employment y_F and prices are at P_F. How does the economy move from point a in the short run to point d in the long run? Panel B shows us how.

At point a, the current level of output y_0 falls short of the full-employment level of output y_F. With output less than full employment, the unemployment rate is above the natural rate. Firms find it relatively easy to hire and retain workers, and wages and then prices begin to fall. As the level of prices decreases, the short-run aggregate supply curve shifts downward over time, as shown in Panel B. The short-run aggregate supply curve shifts downward because decreases in wages lower costs for firms. Competition between firms will lead to lower prices for their products.

As shown in Panel B, this shift in the short-run aggregate supply curve will bring the economy to long-run equilibrium. The economy initially starts at point a, where output falls short of full employment. As prices fall from P_0 to P_1, the aggregate supply curve shifts downward from AS_0 to AS_1. The aggregate demand curve and the new aggregate supply curve intersect at point b. This corresponds to a lower level of prices and a higher level of real output. But that higher level of output still is less than full employment. Wages and prices will continue to fall, shifting the short-run aggregate supply curve downward.

Eventually, the aggregate supply curve will shift to AS_2, and the economy will reach point d, the intersection of the aggregate demand curve and the long-run aggregate supply curve. At this point, the adjustment stops; the economy is at full employment, and the unemployment rate is at the natural rate. With unemployment at the natural rate, the downward wage–price spiral ends. The economy has made the transition to the long run. Prices are lower and output returns to full employment. This is how an economy recovers from a recession or a downturn.

But what if the economy is "too hot" instead of sluggish? What will then happen is the process we just described, only in reverse, as we show in Figure 29.2. When output exceeds potential, unemployment will exceed the natural rate. As firms bid for labor,

FIGURE 29.2

How the Economy Returns from a Boom

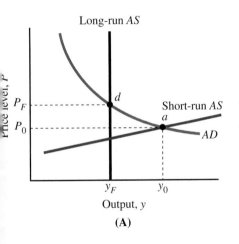

(A)

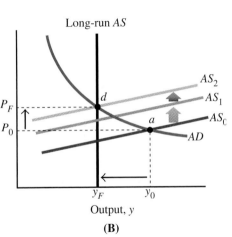

(B)

the wage–price spiral will begin, but this time in an upward direction instead of downward as in Panel B. The short-run aggregate supply curve will shift upward until the economy returns to full employment. That is, wages and prices will rise to return the economy to its long-run equilibrium at full employment.

In summary:

▶ If output is less than full employment, prices will fall as the economy returns to full employment, as in Figure 29.1.
▶ If output exceeds full employment, prices will rise and output will fall back to full employment, as in Figure 29.2.

TEST Your Understanding

1. **Wages and prices will increase when unemployment exceeds the natural rate. True or false? Explain.**
2. **In what direction does the short-run aggregate supply curve move if the economy's actual output is below full-employment output?**

How Economic Policy Can Hasten the Speed of Adjustment

How long does it take to move from the short run to the long run? Economists disagree on the answer. Some estimate that it takes the U.S. economy two years or less, some say six years, and others say somewhere in between. Because the adjustment process is slow, there is room, in principle, for policymakers to step in and guide the economy back to full employment.

Suppose the economy were operating below full employment at point *a* in Figure 29.3. One alternative for policymakers would be to do nothing, allowing the economy to adjust itself, with falling wages and prices, until it returns by itself to full employment, point *d*. This may take several years. During that time, the economy will experience excess unemployment and a level of real output below potential.

Another alternative would be to use expansionary policies (open market purchases by the Fed or increases in government spending and tax cuts) to shift the aggregate demand curve to the right. In Figure 29.3, we show how expansionary policies could shift the aggregate demand curve from AD_0 to AD_1 and move the economy to full employment, point *e*. Notice here that the price level is higher at point *e* than it would be at point *d*.

Demand policies can also be used to prevent a wage–price spiral from emerging if the economy is producing at a level of output above full employment. Rather than letting an increase in wages and prices bring the economy back to full employment, we can reduce aggregate demand. Either contractionary monetary policy (open market sales) or contractionary fiscal policy (cuts in government spending or tax

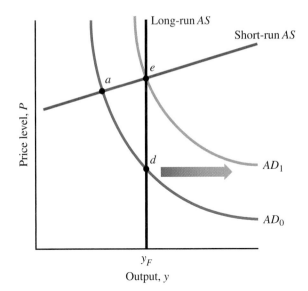

FIGURE 29.3

Using Economic Policy to Fight a Recession
Rather than letting the economy naturally return to full employment at point *d*, economic policies could be implemented to increase aggregate demand from AD_0 to AD_1 to bring the economy to full employment at point *e*. The price level within the economy would be higher though.

ncreases) can be used to reduce aggregate demand and the level of GDP until it eaches potential output.

Expansionary policies and demand policies are stabilization policies, which look imple on paper or on graphs. In practice, the lags and uncertainties that we discussed or both fiscal and monetary policy make the task difficult. For example, suppose we re in a recession and decide to increase aggregate demand using expansionary monetary policy. There will be a lag in the time it takes for the aggregate demand curve to hift to the right. In the meantime, the adjustment that occurs during a recession falling wages and prices) has begun to shift the short-run aggregate supply curve ownward. It is conceivable that if the adjustment were fast enough, the economy vould be restored to full employment before the effects of the expansionary monetary oolicy were actually felt. When the expansionary monetary policy actually kicks in and he aggregate demand curve finally shifts to the right, the additional aggregate demand vould increase the level of output so that it exceeded the full-employment level, leading to a wage–price spiral. In this case, monetary policy would have destabilized the conomy.

Active economic policies are more likely to destabilize the economy if the adjustment is quick enough. Economists like Friedman believe that the economy adjusts apidly to full employment and generally oppose using monetary or fiscal policy to try o stabilize the economy. Economists like Keynes believe that the economy adjusts lowly and are more sympathetic to using monetary or fiscal policy to stabilize the conomy.

It is possible that the speed of adjustment can vary over time, making decisions bout policy even more difficult. As an example, economic advisers for President George H.W. Bush had to decide whether the economy needed any additional stimulus fter the recession of 1990. Based on the view that the economy would recover on its wn, only some minor steps were taken. The economy recovered completely at the very nd of the Bush administration but too late for his reelection prospects.

OneKey is
all you need

Liquidity Traps

Up to this point, we have assumed that the economy could always recover from a recession without active policy, although it may take a long time. As our chapter-opening story mentioned, Keynes expressed doubts about whether a country could recover from a major recession without active policy. He had two distinct reasons. First, as we will discuss later in the chapter, the adjustment process requires interest rates to fall and thereby increase investment spending. But suppose that nominal interest rates become so low that they cannot fall any further. Keynes called this situation a **liquidity trap**. When the economy is experiencing a liquidity trap, the adjustment process no longer works. Second, Keynes also feared that falling prices could hurt businesses. Japan seems to have suffered from both of these problems in recent years, as "A Closer Look: Japan's Lost Decade" explains.

Liquidity trap
A situation in which interest rates are so low, they can no longer fall.

Political Business Cycles

Up to now, we have assumed that policymakers are motivated to use policy to try to improve the economy. But suppose that they are more interested in promoting their own personal well-being and the fortunes of their own political parties? Using monetary policy and fiscal policy in the short run to improve a politician's reelection prospects may generate what is known as a **political business cycle**.

Political business cycle
The effects on the economy of using monetary or fiscal policy to stimulate the economy before an election to improve reelection prospects.

A CLOSER LOOK   Japan's Lost Decade

Following World War II, Japan's economy grew rapidly. However, around 1992 it ground to a halt, and by 1993–1994, the country was literally suffering from a recession. Inflation started to fall, and by 1995, it had nearly disappeared from the economy altogether.

Falling inflation might sound like a good thing, but it actually caused a lot of problems for Japan. Wholesale prices fell for several years. Beginning in 1990, real-estate prices fell nearly 50%, and banks lost vast sums of money on real-estate-related loans. They also became reluctant to make new loans. For Japanese borrowers, falling inflation rates raised the *real* rate of interest they were paying on their preexisting loans, essentially increasing their burden of debt. This made them reluctant to purchase additional goods and services. With fewer loans being made in Japan and fewer goods and services being purchased, aggregate demand was weak.

For a number of years, the United States urged Japan to increase public spending to end its recession. Eventually, Japan did try this approach, but policymakers were cautious because government budget deficits were very large. Nominal interest rates were also very close to zero, making it difficult to use monetary policy to stimulate the economy. Some observers claimed that Japan was suffering from a Keynesian liquidity trap. Restoring the health of the banking system was a major priority. Toward the beginning of the first decade of 2000, things began to improve somewhat. In 2003, the Japanese economy grew by 2.3%. It was a modest gain, but a gain nonetheless, and economists predicted gains would continue. In retrospect, it now appears that Japan suffered from a 10-year extended slump.

Here is how a political business cycle might work. About a year or so before an election, a politician might use expansionary monetary policy or fiscal policy to stimulate the economy and lower unemployment. If voters respond favorably to lower unemployment, the incumbent politician may be reelected. After reelection, the politician faces the prospect of higher prices or crowding out. To avoid this, the politician may engage in contractionary policies. The result is a classic political business cycle: because of actions taken by politicians for reelection, the economy booms before an election but then contracts after the election. Good news comes before the election, and bad news comes later.

The evidence is not clear that the classic political business cycle always occurs. There are episodes that fit what we just described, such as President Nixon's reelection campaign in 1972. However, there are also counterexamples, such as President Carter's deliberate attempt to reduce inflation with contractionary policies just before his reelection bid in the late 1970s. Although the evidence on the classic political business cycle is mixed, there may be links between elections and economic outcomes. More recent research has investigated the systematic differences that may exist between political parties and economic outcomes. All this research takes into account both the short- and long-run effects of economic policies.

Behind the Adjustment Process: How Changes in Money Demand, Interest Rates, and Investment Help Return the Economy to Full Employment

Earlier in the chapter we explained that changes in wages and prices restore the economy to full employment in the long run and that the government and the Fed can "get there" more quickly with fiscal and monetary policy. But what is happening behind the scenes? What do changes in wages and the price level mean for the economy in terms of money demand, interest rates, and investment spending? Let's go back and take a closer look at the adjustment process in terms of these factors so that we can better understand how the adjustment process actually works.

First, recall that when an economy is producing below full employment, there will be a tendency for wages and prices to fall. Similarly, when an economy is producing at a level exceeding full employment or potential output, there will be a tendency for wages and prices to rise.

The adjustment process first begins to work as changes in prices affect the demand for money. Recall the real-nominal principle:

REAL-NOMINAL *Principle*

What matters to people is the real value of money or income— its purchasing power—not the face value of money or income.

According to this principle, the amount of money that people want to hold depends on the price level in the economy. If prices are cut in half, you need to hold only half as much money to purchase the same goods and services. Decreases in the price level will cause the money demand curve to shift to the left; increases in the price level will shift it to the right. Now let's put this idea to use.

Suppose the economy is initially in a recession. With output below full employment, actual unemployment will exceed the natural rate of unemployment, so there will be excess unemployment. Wages and prices will start to fall. Figure 29.4 shows how the fall in the price level can restore the economy to full employment via money demand, interest rates, and investment without active fiscal or monetary policy. First, we show with the AD–AS diagram in Panel A how prices fall when the economy is operating below full employment. Second, in Panel B, the fall in the price level decreases the demand for holding money. As the price level decreases from P_0 to P_1, the demand for money shifts to the left from M_0^d to M_1^d. Interest rates fall from r_0 to r_1, and the falling interest rates increase investment spending from I_0 to I_1. As the level of investment spending in the economy increases, total demand for goods and services also increases and the economy moves down along the aggregate demand curve as it returns to full employment.

Now you can also understand why the aggregate demand curve is downward sloping through the interest rate effect. As we move down the aggregate demand curve, lower prices lead to lower interest rates, higher investment spending, and a higher level of aggregate demand. Thus, aggregate demand increases as the price level falls, which explains why the curve slopes downward.

What we have just described continues until the economy reaches full employment. As long as actual output is below the economy's full-employment level, prices will continue to fall. A fall in the price level reduces money demand and interest rates

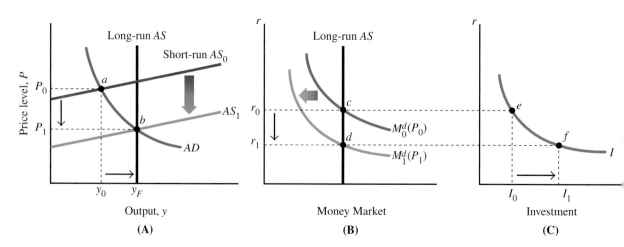

FIGURE 29.4 **How the Changing Price Level Restores the Economy to Full Employment**
With the economy initially below full employment, the price level falls as shown in Panel A, stimulating output. In Panel B, the lower price level decreases the demand for money and leads to lower interest rates at point d. In Panel C, lower interest rates lead to higher investment spending at point f. As the economy moves down the aggregate demand cure from point a toward full employment at point b in Panel A, spending increases along the aggregate demand curve.

lower interest rates stimulate investment spending and push the economy back toward full employment. All of this works in reverse if output exceeds the economy's potential output. In this case, the economy is overheating and wages and prices rise. A higher price level will increase the demand for money and raise interest rates. Higher interest rates will decrease investment spending and reduce the level of output. All this continues until the economy "cools off" and returns to full employment.

Now you should understand why changes in wages and prices restore the economy to full employment. The key is that (1) changes in wages and prices change the demand for money; (2) this changes interest rates, which then affect aggregate demand for goods and services and ultimately GDP.

We can also use the model that we just developed to understand the liquidity trap. If an economy is in a recession, interest rates will fall, restoring the economy to full employment. But it may be possible that at some point, interest rates may become so low that they become zero. Nominal interest rates cannot go far below zero, because investors would rather hold money (which pays a zero rate) than hold a bond that promises a negative return. Suppose, however, that as interest rates approach zero, the economy is still in a slump. The adjustment process then has nowhere to go. As we mentioned previously, this appears to be what happened in Japan in the 1990s. Interest rates on government bonds were zero, but prices continued to fall. At this point, the fall in prices, by itself, could not restore the economy to full employment.

What can be done if an economy is in a recession but nominal rates become so close to zero that the natural adjustment process ceases to work? Economists have suggested two solutions to this problem. First, expansionary fiscal policy—cutting taxes or raising government spending—still remains a viable option to increase aggregate demand. Second, the Fed could become extremely aggressive and try to expand the money supply so rapidly that the public begins to anticipate future inflation. If the pubic expects inflation, the expected real rate of interest (the nominal rate minus the expected inflation rate) can become negative even if the nominal rate cannot fall below zero. A negative expected real interest rate will tempt firms to invest, and this will increase aggregate demand. In other words, even though a liquidity trap may make it more difficult for an economy to recover on its own, there still is room for proper economic policy to have an impact.

The Long-Run Neutrality of Money

An increase in the money supply has a different effect on the economy in the short run than it does in the long run. In Figure 29.5, we show the effects of expansionary monetary policy in both the short run and the long run. In the short run, as the supply of money increases, the economy moves from the original equilibrium at point *e* to point *a*, with output above potential. But in the long run, the economy returns to point *b* at full employment but at a higher price level than at *e*. How is it that the Federal Reserve can change the level of output in the short run but affect prices only in the long run? Why is the short run different from the long run? We can use our model of the demand for money and investment to understand this issue.

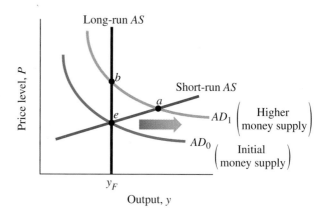

Figure 29.6 can help us understand some answers to these questions. Assume the economy starts at full employment. Interest rates are at r_F, and investment spending is at I_F. Now, suppose the Federal Reserve increases the money supply from M_0^s to M_1^s. We show this as a rightward movement in the money supply curve. In the short run, the increase in the supply of money will reduce interest rates to r_0, and the level of investment spending will increase to I_0. Increased investment will stimulate the economy and increase output above full employment. All this occurs in the short run. The red arrows show the movements in interest rates and investment in the short run.

However, once output exceeds full employment, wages and prices will start to increase. As the price level increases, the demand for money will increase. This will shift up the money demand curve and will start to increase interest rates. Investment will start to fall as interest rates increase, leading to a fall in output. The blue arrows in Figure 29.6 show the transition as prices increase. As long as output exceeds full employment, prices will continue to rise, money demand will continue to increase, and

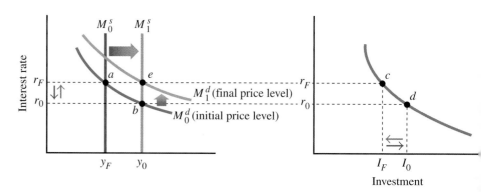

FIGURE 29.6 **Neutrality of Money**

Starting at full employment, an increase in the supply of money from M_0^s to M_1^s will initially reduce interest rates from r_F to r_0 (from point a to point b) and raise investment spending from I_F to I_0 (point c to point d). We show these changes with the red arrows. The blue arrows show that as the price level increases, the demand for money increases, restoring interest rates and investment to their prior levels—I_F and r_F, respectively. Both money supplied and money demanded will remain at a higher level, though, at point e.

interest rates will continue to rise. Where does this process end? It ends only when interest rates return to their original level of r_F. At an interest rate of r_F, investment spending will have returned to I_F. This is the level of investment that meets the total level of demand for goods and services and keeps the economy at full employment.

Notice that when the economy returns to full employment, the levels of real interest rates, investment, and output are precisely the same as they were before the Fed increased the supply of money. The increase in the supply of money had no effect on real interest rates, investment, and output. Economists call this the **long-run neutrality of money**. In other words, in the long run, changes in the supply of money are neutral with respect to "real" variables in the economy. For example, if the price of everything in the economy doubles, including your paycheck, you are no better or worse off than you were before. In the long run, increases in the supply of money have no effect on real variables, only on prices.

This example points out how, in the long run, it really does not matter how much money is in circulation because prices will adjust to the amount of nominal money available. Money is not neutral in the short run, however. In the short run, changes in the supply of money do affect interest rates, investment spending, and output. The Fed does have strong powers over real GDP, but those powers are ultimately temporary. In the long run, all the Fed can do is to determine the level of prices in the economy.

Now we can understand why the job of the Federal Reserve has been described by William McChesney Martin, Jr., a former Federal Reserve chairman, as "taking the punch bowl away at the party." The punch bowl at the party is money: If the Fed sets out the punch bowl of money, this will temporarily increase output or give the economy a brief high. But if the Federal Reserve is worried about increases in prices in the long run, it must take the punch bowl away and everyone must sober up. If the Fed doesn't take the punch bowl away, the result will be continuing increases in prices, or inflation.

> **Long-run neutrality of money**
> An increase in the supply of money has no effect on real interest rates, investment, or output in the long run.

TEST Your Understanding

3. What happens to the demand for money and interest rates as the price level increases in the economy?
4. If output is below full employment, we expect wages and prices to fall, money demand to decrease, and interest rates to fall. True or false? Explain.
5. An increase in the money supply will have no effect on the real rate of interest in the long run. True or false? Explain.

Crowding Out in the Long Run

Some economists are strong proponents of increasing government spending on defense or other programs to stimulate the economy. Critics, however, say increases in spending provide only temporary relief and ultimately harm the economy because government spending "crowds out" investment spending. In Chapter 21, we discussed the idea of **crowding out**. We can now understand it in more detail.

> **Crowding out**
> The reduction in investment (or other component of GDP) in the long run caused by an increase in government spending.

Suppose the economy starts out at full employment and then the government increases its spending. This will shift the aggregate demand curve to the right, causing output to increase beyond full employment. As we have seen, the result of this boom will be that wages and prices increase.

Now let's turn to our model of money demand and investment. Figure 29.7 shows that as prices increase, the demand for money shifts upward, raising interest rates from r_0 to r_1 and reducing investment from I_0 to I_1. Higher interest rates are the mechanism through which crowding out of public investment occurs As investment spending by the public then falls (gets crowded out), we know that aggregate demand decreases. This process will continue until the economy returns to full employment. Once the economy returns to full employment, the decrease in investment spending by the public will exactly match the increase in government spending. However, when the economy does return to full employment, it will be at a higher interest rate level and lower level of investment spending by the public.

Thus, the increase in government spending has no long-run effect on the level of output—just the interest rate. Instead, the increase in government spending displaced, or crowded out, private investment spending. If the government spending went toward government investment projects—such as bridges or roads—then the increased government investment will have just replaced an equivalent amount of private investment.

On the other hand, if the increased government spending did not go toward providing investment (but, for example, went for military spending), then the reduction in private investment will have reduced total investment in the economy, private and public. This decrease in total investment would have further negative effects on the economy.

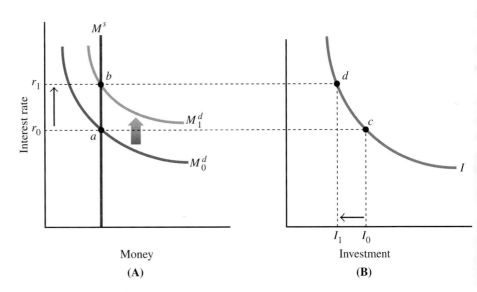

FIGURE 29.7 **Crowding Out in the Long Run**

Starting at full employment, an increase in government spending raises output above full employment. As wages and prices increase, the demand for money increases, as shown in Panel A, raising interest rates from r_0 to r_1 (point a to point b) and reducing investment from I_0 to I_1 (point c to point d). The economy returns to full employment but with a higher level of interest rates and a lower level of investment spending.

At full employment, higher spending on military goods will crowd out investment and consumption.

over time. As we saw in earlier chapters, a reduction in investment spending reduces capital deepening and leads to lower levels of real income and wages in the future.

Economists make similar arguments when it comes to tax cuts. Tax cuts initially will increase consumer spending and lead to a higher level of GDP. In the long run, however, adjustments in wages and prices restore the economy to full employment. However, interest rates will rise during the adjustment process and this increase in interest rates will crowd out private investment. In the long run, the increase in consumption spending will come at the expense of lower investment spending, less capital deepening, and lower levels of real income and wages in the future.

Decreases in government spending (such as a cut in military spending) will lead to increases in investment in the long run, which we call crowding in. Initially, a decrease in government spending will cause a decrease in real GDP. But as prices fall, the demand for money will decrease, and interest rates will fall. Lower interest rates will crowd in investment as the economy returns to full employment. In the longer run, the higher investment spending will raise living standards through capital deepening.

"Classical Economics" in Historical Perspective

The ideas developed in this chapter can shed some light on an historical debate in economics about the role of full-employment or "classical" economics. Classical economics refers to a body of work developed over time, starting with Adam Smith. Other classical economists—Jean Baptiste Say, David Ricardo, John Stuart Mill, Thomas Malthus, and others—developed their work from approximately the late eighteenth and nineteenth centuries. The term "classical model" was actually first used by Keynes

in the 1930s to contrast his "Keynesian" or activist model with the conventional eco
nomic wisdom of the time that didn't emphasize the difficulties that the econom
could face in the short run.

Say's Law

Classical economics is often associated with Say's law, the doctrine that "supply create
its own demand." To understand Say's law, recall from our discussion of GDP account
ing in Chapter 19 that production in an economy creates an equivalent amount o
income. For example, if GDP is $10 trillion, then production is $10 trillion and gener
ates $10 trillion in income. The classical economists argued that the $10 trillion of pro
duction also created $10 trillion in demand for current goods and services. This mean
that there could never be a shortage of demand for total goods and services in the
economy nor any excess.

But suppose that consumers, who earned the income, decided to save their income
rather than spend it. Wouldn't this increase in savings lead to a shortfall in the tota
demand for goods and services? Wouldn't, say, inventories of goods pile up in warehouses
Classical economists argued that the increase in savings would *eventually* find its way to an
equivalent increase in investment spending by firms because the savings by household
would eventually get channeled to firms via financial markets. The result would be that
spending on consumption and investment together would be sufficient enough so that all
the goods and services produced in the economy would be purchased.

Keynes argued that there could be situations in which total demand fell short o
total production in the economy—at least for extended periods of time. In particular
if consumers increased their savings, there was no guarantee that there would be a rise
in investment spending to offset the decrease in consumption. And, if total spending
did fall short of total demand, goods and services would go unsold. When producers
could not sell their goods, they would cut back on production, and output in the econ
omy would consequently fall, leading to a recession or depression.

Keynesian and Classical Debates

The debates between Keynesian and classical economists continued for several decades
after Keynes developed his theories. In the 1940s, Professors Don Patinkin and Nobel
laureate Franco Modigliani clarified the conditions for which the classical model
would hold true. In particular, they studied the conditions under which there would be
sufficient demand for goods and services when the economy was at full employment.
Both economists emphasized that one of the necessary conditions for the classical
model to work right was that wages and prices be fully flexible—that is, that they
adjust rapidly to changes in demand and supply.

If wages and prices are not fully flexible, then Keynes's view that demand could fall
short of production is more likely to hold true. As we have discussed, over short periods of time, wages and prices, indeed, are not fully flexible, so the insights of Keynes are
important. However, over longer periods of time, wages and prices do adjust and the
insights of the classical model are restored.

To help clarify the conditions under which the economy will return to full employment in the long run on its own, Patinkin and Modigliani developed the adjustment process model we used in this chapter. They highlighted many of the key points we emphasized, including the speed of the adjustment process and possible pitfalls, such as liquidity traps.

In the chapter-opening story, we contrasted Keynes with Milton Friedman. Where does he fit into this story? Contrary to Keynes, Friedman believed that the wage–price adjustment mechanism that restored the economy to full employment was reasonably effective. Moreover, he felt that activist government policies often made things worse, not better. For that reason, he preferred that the government not engage in activist stabilization policies.

USING THE TOOLS

1. Economic Policies and Supply Shocks

a. In Chapter 23, we discussed supply shocks, sudden increases in the prices of commodities such as oil or food. These shocks shift the short-run aggregate supply curve. For example, an increase in oil prices will shift the short-run aggregate supply curve upward because firms' costs have risen and firms must charge higher prices to avoid losing money. Suppose that the economy is operating at full employment and foreign countries raised the world price of oil. Assuming that policymakers do not take any action, describe what will happen to prices and output in the short run and in the long run.

b. Suppose the Federal Reserve decided that it wanted to offset any adverse effects on output due to a supply shock. What actions could it take? What would happen to the price level if the Fed used monetary policy to fight unemployment?

c. Economists say that supply shocks create a dilemma for the Federal Reserve that shocks to demand (for example, from sudden increases in investment spending by optimistic firms) do not create. Explain why economists say this, using your answer to part (b) and the aggregate demand and supply diagram.

2. Understanding Japanese Fiscal Policy

Japan's finance ministry agreed to income tax cuts to combat a decade-long recession in the 1990s—

but only if national sales taxes were increased several years later to offset the decrease in government revenue. Explain the logic of the finance ministry, using your understanding of the short-run effects and the long-run effects of fiscal policy. What was the finance ministry trying to prevent?

3. Optimistic Firms in the Long Run

Suppose the economy was operating at full employment and firms became increasingly optimistic about the future. They increase their investment spending; graphically, that means that their investment schedule shifts to the right. What happens to real GDP in the short run? Describe what happens to interest rates, investment, and real GDP in the long run. How is the investment boom self-correcting?

4. No Room to Maneuver?

When the recession of 2001 began, the Fed started to reduce the federal funds rate, and by 2003 it had reached 1.00%. Some observers were concerned that if the economy failed to recover from the recession, the Fed might not be able to stimulate the economy any further. Can you explain these concerns?

SUMMARY

This chapter explained how the economy makes the transition from the short run to the long run. It also highlighted why monetary and fiscal policies have effects different in the short run than in the long run. Understanding the distinction between the short run and the long run is critical to evaluating economic policy. Here are the main points to remember from this chapter:

1 When output exceeds full employment, wages and prices rise faster than their past trends. If output is less than full employment, wages and prices fall relative to past trends.

2 The price changes that occur when the economy is away from full employment push the economy back to full employment. Economists disagree on the length of time that this adjustment process takes; estimates range from less than two years to six years.

3 Economic policies are most effective when the adjustment process is slow. However, to improve their chances of being reelected, politicians can potentially take advantage of the difference between the short-run effects and the long-run effects of economic policies.

4 If the economy is operating below full employment, falling wages and prices will reduce money demand and lower interest rates. The fall in interest rates will stimulate investment and lead the economy back to full employment.

5 The reverse occurs when output exceeds full employment. Increases in wages and prices will increase money demand and interest rates. As investment spending falls, the economy returns to full employment.

6 In the long run, increases in the supply of money are neutral; that is, increases in the money supply do not affect real interest rates, investment, or output.

7 Increases in government spending will raise real interest rates and crowd out investment in the long run. Decreases in government spending will lower real interest rates and crowd in investment in the long run.

8 The adjustment model in this chapter helps us to understand the debate between Keynes and the "classical economists."

KEY TERMS

aggregate demand curve, 670
crowding out, 679
liquidity trap, 674

long run aggregate supply curve, 670
long-run neutrality of money, 679
political business cycle, 674

short run aggregate supply curve, 670
wage-price spiral, 669

PROBLEMS AND DISCUSSION QUESTIONS

1 When the unemployment rate fell to 4% in 1998, some economists became concerned that inflation would increase. Explain their concern.

2 Economists who believe that the transition from the short run to the long run occurs rapidly do not generally favor using active stabilization policy. Use the aggregate demand and aggregate supply graphs to illustrate how active policy, with a rapid adjustment process, could destabilize the economy.

3 During an economic boom, interest rates rise. Investment spending typically increases in the beginning of the boom and then declines. Can you explain why this pattern of economic activity occurs?

4 Suppose households decide to increase their desired savings. What will be the effect on GDP in the short run, the intermediate run, and the very long run?

5 Countries that have high money growth for long periods do not grow more rapidly than countries with low money growth. Why?

6 Explain why advocates for the housing industry (an industry very sensitive to interest rates) might want to advocate lower government spending for the long term.

7 Use the model in this chapter to explain how tax cuts for consumers will eventually lead to higher interest rates and crowd out investment spending in the long run.

8 The adjustment process can run into problems during a liquidity trap when interest rates are driven close to zero and the economy remains below full employment. Draw a money demand curve and an investment schedule to illustrate this possibility.

9 At one time in 1998, nominal interest rates on short-term Japanese government debt were slightly negative. Some foreign-owned banks also paid negative rates on yen deposits. Daniel L. Thornton, an economist at the St. Louis Federal Reserve Bank, argued that even though cash paid a zero rate of interest, banks could still attract funds with nega-

tive rates because there were costs to holding cash. What are some of these costs? How negative do you think interest rates could actually go?

10 Some economists estimate that the adjustment process takes up to six years to restore an economy back to full employment. What do you think makes the process so slow? (*Hint:* Think of the factors that cause lags in monetary policy.)

11 Web Exercise. During the Great Depression in the United States, some interest rates became close to zero. Search the historical database at the Website of the National Bureau of Economic Research (*http://www.nber.org*) to find out how low interest rates actually became and when they were at their lowest.

12 Web Exercise. Use the Website for the Federal Reserve Bank of St. Louis (*http://research.stlouisfed.org/fred2*) to find historical data on unemployment rates. Use these data to explore whether unemployment behaves differently in the first two years of a presidential term compared to the final two years. Are there any systematic differences in unemployment between Democratic and Republican presidencies?

MODEL ANSWERS TO QUESTIONS

Chapter-Opening Questions

1 Wages and prices will rise together when the economy is operating at a level of output that exceeds full employment. Conversely, they will fall (relative to trend) when the output level of the economy is below full employment.

2 In the short run, lower interest rates will stimulate investment and lead to higher output. But because prices rise when output exceeds full employment, the only long-run effect is higher prices.

3 The Federal Reserve is responsible for preventing inflation from emerging or increasing. This may require high interest rates to reduce output at a time when the economy is producing at too high a level.

4 Tax cuts stimulate consumer demand and lead to higher output in the short run. In the long run, increased consumer spending will crowd out investment spending. Lower investment means a lower capital stock in the future and reduced future output.

Test Your Understanding

1 False, they will fall.
2 It shifts down.
3 As prices rise, the demand for money increases and interest rates rise.
4 True, this is the adjustment process.
5 True, money is neutral in the long run.

The Dynamics of Inflation and Unemployment

onetary affairs were truly a mess in Russia during the 1990s. Inflation was so severe that the central bank tried many attempts at monetary reform. As a result of these reforms, the central bank issued not one, not two, but *three* different sets of currency. But that posed a problem: what to do with all the old Russian rubles?

The emerging private sector found a solution for this problem. It turned out that old Russian rubles could be converted into roofing material. After soaking them in water and mixing them with paper scraps and shredded cloth, the rubles became part of a roofing material called ruberoid that prevents roofs from leaking.

Certainly this is a clever use for useless rubles, but the purpose of the central bank is not to provide inexpensive roofing material. How did Russia find itself in this odd predicament to begin with?

Source: Andrew Higgins, "Worthless Rubles Have Their Uses in Keeping Roofs From Leaking," *Wall Street Journal*, July 26, 2000, p. A1.

wo themes that we've been stressing separately will now be integrated:

▶ In the short run, changes in money growth affect real output and real GDP.
▶ In the long run, the rate of money growth determines the rate of inflation and not real GDP.

This chapter brings these two themes together.

Economic policy debates often concern inflation and unemployment because they affect us all so directly. We will look at the relationships between inflation and unemployment, examining macroeconomic developments in the United States in the last several decades. We also explore why heads of central banks typically appear to be strong enemies of inflation.

Although the United States had serious difficulties fighting inflation in the 1970s and 1980s, other countries have, at times, had much more severe problems with inflation. In this chapter, we'll study the origins of extremely high inflationary periods and their links to government budget deficits. We'll also address these questions:

1 Why do countries with lower rates of money growth have lower interest-rate levels than countries with higher rates of money growth?
2 Why is the relationship between lower unemployment and higher inflation only temporary?
3 Why are the heads of central banks (such as the chairman of the Federal Reserve) typically very conservative, preferring to risk increasing unemployment rather than risk increasing the inflation rate?
4 Why does money "turn over" faster when inflation is higher?
5 Why do countries with large budget deficits often suffer from massive inflation?

Money Growth, Inflation, and Interest Rates

An economy can, in principle, produce at full employment with any inflation rate. There is no "magic" inflation rate that is necessary to sustain full employment. To understand this point, consider the long run when the economy operates at full employment. As we have seen, in the long run, money is neutral. If the Federal Reserve increases the money supply at 5% a year, there will be 5% annual inflation; that is, prices in the economy will rise by 5% a year.

Nominal wages
Wages expressed in current dollars.

Inflation in a Steady State

Real wages
Nominal or dollar wages adjusted for changes in purchasing power.

Let's think about how this economy looks in this "steady state" of constant inflation. The **nominal wages**—wages in dollars—of workers are all rising at 5% a year. However, because prices are also rising at 5% a year, **real wages**—wages adjusted for changes in purchasing power—remain constant.

Some workers may feel cheated by the inflation. They might believe that without it they would experience real-wage increases because their nominal wages are rising 5% a year. Unfortunately, they are wrong. They suffer from what economists call **money illusion**, a confusion of real and nominal magnitudes. Here's the source of the illusion: Since real wages are constant, the only reason their nominal wages are rising by 5% a year is the general 5% inflation. If there were no inflation, their nominal wages would not increase at all.

After a time, everyone in the economy would begin to expect that the 5% annual inflation that had occurred in the past would continue in the future. Economists call this **expectations of inflation**. People's expectations of inflation affect all aspects of economic life. For example, in the steady-state economy we just described, automobile producers will expect to increase the price of their products by 5% every year. They will also expect their costs—of labor and steel, for example—to increase by 5% a year. Workers will begin to believe that the 5% increases in their wages will be matched by a 5% increase in the prices of the goods they buy. Continued inflation becomes the normal state of affairs, and people "build it into" their daily decision-making process.

Inflation Expectations and Interest Rates

When the public expects inflation, real and nominal rates of interest will differ because inflation needs to be accounted for in calculating the real return from lending and borrowing. Recall that the nominal interest rate—the rate quoted in the market—is equal to the real rate of interest plus the expected inflation rate. If the real rate of interest is 2% and inflation is 5% a year, the nominal interest rate will be 7%. Although lenders receive 7% a year on their loans, their real return after inflation is just 2%.

In Chapter 29, you saw that in the long run, the *real* rate of interest does not depend on monetary policy because money is neutral; that is, even though the money supply may be higher or lower, the price level will be higher or lower. However, *nominal* rates of interest do depend on monetary policy because monetary policy affects the rate of inflation, which in the long run is determined by the growth of the money supply—that is, whether the Fed expands or contracts it. As Nobel laureate Milton Friedman pointed out, countries with higher money growth typically have higher nominal interest rates than countries with lower money growth rates because they have higher inflation. What this means is that if Country A and Country B have the same real rate of interest, but Country A has a higher inflation rate, it will also have a higher nominal interest rate.

Inflation Expectations and Money Demand

Money demand—the amount of money people want to hold—will also be affected by expectations about inflation. If the public expects 5% inflation a year, then its demand for money will also increase by 5% a year. This is, of course, because people know everything will cost 5% more, so they'll need more money in their pockets to pay for the same goods and services. This is an example of the real-nominal principle:

Money illusion
Confusion of real and nominal magnitudes.

Expectations of inflation
The beliefs held by the public about the likely path of inflation for the future.

REAL-NOMINAL *Principle*

What matters to people is the real value of money or income— its purchasing power—not the face value of money or income.

As long as the Fed allows the supply of money to increase by 5%—the same amount as inflation—the demand for money and its supply will both grow at the same rate. Because money demand and supply are both growing at the same rate, real interest rates and nominal interest rates will not change.

How Changes in the Growth Rate of Money Affect the Steady State

If the growth rate of money changes, however, there will be short-run effects on real interest rates. To continue with our example, suppose the public expects 5% annual inflation and both the money supply and money demand grow at 5% a year. Now suppose the Fed suddenly decreases the annual growth rate of money to 4% while the public continues to expect 5% annual inflation. Because money demand grows at 5% but the money supply grows at only 4%, the growth in the demand for money will exceed the growth in the supply of money. The result will be an increase in both real interest rates and nominal interest rates.

We have seen that higher real rates of interest will reduce investment spending by firms and reduce consumer durable spending by households. With reduced demand for goods and services, real GDP will fall and unemployment will rise. The reduction in the growth rate of the money supply is contractionary. In the long run, however, output will return to full employment through the adjustment process described in Chapter 29. The economy will eventually adjust to the lower rate of money growth, and inflation will eventually fall from 5% to 4% per year to match it. Because money is neutral in the long run, the *real* rate of interest will eventually fall and return to its previous value. In the long run, *nominal* interest rates will be 1% lower since inflation has fallen from 5% to 4% per year, and nominal rates reflect expectations of ongoing inflation.

This basic pattern fits U.S. history in the late 1970s and early 1980s. At that time, the Federal Reserve sharply decreased the growth rate of the money supply, so interest rates rose temporarily. By 1981, interest rates on three-month Treasury bills rose to over 14% from 7% in 1978. The economy went into a severe recession, with unemployment exceeding 10%. By the mid-1980s, however, the economy returned to full employment with lower interest rates and lower inflation rates. By 1986, Treasury bill rates were below 6%.

This is another example in which the long-run effects of policy actions differ from their short-run effects. In the short run, a policy of tight money leads to slower money growth, higher interest rates, and lower output. But in the long run, reduced money growth results in lower interest rates, lower inflation, and no effect on the level of output.

TEST Your Understanding

1. The expected real rate of interest is the nominal interest rate minus the expected inflation rate. True or false? Explain.
2. Explain why, in the long run, an inflation rate of 10% per year will lead to an increase in the demand for money of 10% per year.

Understanding the Expectations Phillips Curve: The Relationship Between Unemployment and Inflation

In the late 1950s, an engineer named A.W. Phillips noticed a negative relationship between the level of inflation and unemployment in British data. Phillips found lower unemployment to be associated with higher inflation: That is, he noticed that the inflation rate rises when economic activity booms and unemployment is low. He also noticed that the inflation rate falls when the economy is in a recession and unemployment is high. This inverse relationship became known as the Phillips curve.

In the early 1960s, Nobel laureates Paul Samuelson and Robert Solow found a similar relationship between unemployment and the level of the inflation rate in the United States. However, these early studies examined periods when there was no significant underlying inflation, and they did not take into account people's expectations of inflation. Once expectations were calculated into the mix in later studies, it became clear that the relationship between inflation and unemployment is more complex. The relationship between unemployment and inflation when there are expectations about inflation is known as the **expectations Phillips curve**.

Expectations Phillips curve

The relationship that describes the links between inflation and unemployment, taking into account expectations of inflation.

The expectations Phillips curve was introduced into the economics profession in the late 1960s by Edmund Phelps of Columbia University and Nobel laureate Milton Friedman, then at the University of Chicago. The expectations Phillips curve included the notion that unemployment varies with *unanticipated inflation*. Friedman argued, for example, that when the inflation rate suddenly increases, it is likely that some of this sudden increase was not fully anticipated. Actual inflation will then exceed expected inflation. Workers will see their nominal wages increase with the inflation, but because they do not fully expect this sudden inflation, they will think that their real wages have increased. With higher perceived real wages being offered, potential workers will be inclined to accept the jobs offered them. As a result, unemployment will fall below the natural rate. That's why we often see an association between increases in the inflation rate and a decrease in the unemployment rate.

After workers recognize that the inflation rate is higher, though, they will incorporate this higher inflation rate into their expectations of inflation. They will no longer confuse the higher nominal wages they are being offered with higher real wages. Unemployment will then return to its natural rate. Thus, there is no permanent relationship between the level of unemployment and the level of inflation.

Similarly, if the inflation rate falls, at least part of this fall may be unexpected. Because inflation is less than expected, workers will believe that their real wages aren't rising as fast as they in fact are rising. With lower perceived real wages being offered, potential workers will be less inclined to accept the jobs offered them. The unemployment rate will increase as a result. However, once they recognize that inflation is lower than they realized, and that the wages being offered them really aren't that low, they'll be more inclined to accept work. Unemployment will then again return to the natural rate. Thus, a decrease in the inflation rate is likely to be associated with temporary increases in unemployment.

Later in this chapter, we will see an example of this relationship between inflation and unemployment in the late 1980s and early 1990s. When there's a "disconnect"

TABLE 30.1

**Expectations and
Business Fluctuations**

	Unemployment	Inflation
Boom	Unemployment below the natural rate	Inflation higher than expected
Recession	Unemployment above the natural rate	Inflation lower than expected

between what people expect and what ultimately occurs, this can adversely affect the economy, as we'll see next. Table 30.1 provides a summary of the key points about the expectations Phillips curve.

Are the Public's Expectations About Inflation Rational?

As we just saw, expectations about inflation affect actual inflation because workers and firms build their inflation forecasts into their wage- and price-setting decisions. Mistakes in predicting inflation therefore have consequences. But *how* do workers and firms form inflation expectations in the first place? And, second, *when* do they form their inflation expectations?

There are two broad-classes of theories of how the public forms its expectations of inflation. Some economists and psychologists, including Nobel laureate Herbert Simon, believe that the public uses simple rules-of-thumb to predict future inflation. A simple rule-of-thumb might be to assume next year's inflation will be the same as this year's inflation. According to this view, it is unreasonable to expect too much sophistication from the public because of the complexity of the economy and forecasting difficulties.

In the 1970s, a group of economists led by Nobel laureate Robert E. Lucas, Jr., from the University of Chicago developed an alternative view, called the theory of **rational expectations**. The rational expectations theory portrayed workers and firms as much more sophisticated, basing their expectations on all the information available to them. According to the theory, the public, on average, anticipates the future correctly. Although the public may make mistakes in specific instances, on average the public's expectations are rational or correct.

Rational expectations
The economic theory that analyzes how people form expectations in such a manner that, on average, they forecast the future correctly.

The two approaches—rules-of-thumb versus rational expectations—tend to deliver similar predictions when the economy is very stable and there are no major policy changes. However, when there are major policy changes—for example, when new policies are introduced to fight inflation or reduce federal deficits—the two approaches predict different outcomes. The rational expectations theory predicts the public will anticipate the consequences of these policies and change its expectations about inflation accordingly; the rule-of-thumb theory says it won't. Which view is correct? The truth lies somewhere in the middle. The public, particularly sophisticated firms, does appear to take advantage of available information. On the other hand, there is evidence that a considerable amount of inertia and nonrationality enters into the public's decision-making process, too. And sometimes, the public may be rational about smaller things but miss the big picture. For example, during the stock market boom in the late 1990s, investors may have had an accurate assessment of *which* tech stocks were relatively the most promising but failed to recognize that *all* tech stocks were overvalued.

The other major issue is *when* are inflation expectations formed? As we discussed in Chapter 23, both workers and firms often make explicit long-term contracts or enter into implicit long-term agreements. With long-term contracts, workers and firms must make forecasts far into the future. For example, if a union is setting wages for three years, it will need to forecast inflation three years into the future and set current and future wages today based on that forecast. This is clearly very difficult, so it is understandable how mistakes can occur when decisions must be made far in advance. Indeed, workers and firms can be quite "rational" but still make mistakes when predicting inflation simply because of the long time frames involved. Wage contracts that were set in the early 1980s, for example, would have "rationally" anticipated continued high inflation, although changes in monetary policy brought inflation down below what was predicted.

U.S. Inflation and Unemployment in the 1980s

We can use the expectations Phillips curve to help understand the patterns of inflation and unemployment that occurred in the 1980s. For the sake of this discussion, we will assume that workers and firms follow relatively simple rules-of-thumb and that sudden increases in inflation are partly unanticipated and thus accompanied by lower unemployment. Conversely, sudden decreases in inflation are accompanied by temporarily higher unemployment.

When President Jimmy Carter took office at the beginning of 1977, the inflation rate was approximately 6.5% per year and unemployment exceeded 7% of the labor force. By 1980, inflation had risen to 9.4%. There were two reasons for this increase. One: Utilizing fiscal and monetary policy, the Carter administration had steadily reduced unemployment to under 6% by 1979. Because the natural rate of unemployment was close to 6% of the labor force at that time, this led to an increase in the annual inflation rate. Two: There was an oil shock in 1979, which also contributed to higher inflation.

Fears of even higher inflation led President Carter to appoint a well-known inflation fighter, Paul Volcker, as the chairman of the Federal Reserve. Volcker immediately began to institute a tight money policy, and interest rates rose sharply by 1980. When President Ronald Reagan took office, he supported Volcker's policy. Eventually, high real-interest rates took their toll, and unemployment rose to over 10% by 1983. As actual unemployment exceeded the natural rate of unemployment, the inflation rate fell, just as was predicted by the expectations Phillips curve. By 1986, the inflation rate fell to approximately 2.7% per year with unemployment at 7% of the labor force. The severe recession had done its job in reducing the inflation rate.

However, as we can see in Figure 30.1, after 1986 the unemployment rate began to fall again, from about 7% percent to a little over 6% in 1987. Notice that as actual unemployment fell below the natural rate (which, at that time, was about 6.5%), inflation began to rise, increasing from about 2.75% to 3%. By 1989, as unemployment continued to fall, annual inflation had risen to 4.5%, and the Fed then raised interest rates to combat it. This reduced output and increased unemployment to over 7%. Notice that by 1992, inflation had fallen dramatically, as unemployment exceeded the natural rate.

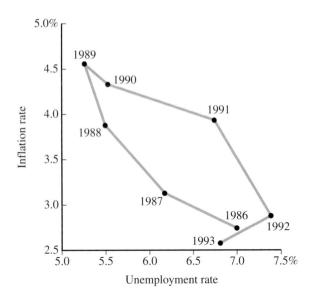

FIGURE 30.1

The Dynamics of Inflation and Unemployment, 1986–1993

Inflation rose and the unemployment rate fell below the natural rate, and inflation later fell as unemployment exceeded the natural rate.

Source: Economic Report of the President (Washington DC: U.S. Government Printing Office, yearly).

President George H.W. Bush suffered the consequences of this inflation-fighting episode. By the time he took office in 1989, actual unemployment was below the natural rate of unemployment, inflation had been rising, and this is when the Fed started slowing down the economy. The rate of inflation was eventually reduced, but the recovery back to full employment in 1992–1993 came too late in Bush's term to be fully appreciated by the voters, and he lost his bid for reelection.

The public's belief that the economy was not performing well cost George H. W. Bush his bid for re-election.

Shifts in the Natural Rate of Unemployment in the 1990s

Up to this point, we have assumed that the natural rate of unemployment is a constant—say, for example, 5% of the labor force. If actual unemployment falls below this constant rate (the economy is hot, in other words), inflation will tend to increase. Similarly, if the actual unemployment exceeds 5% (the economy is sluggish), inflation will fall.

But the natural rate of unemployment can shift over time. At the beginning of the 1980s in the United States, most economists believed that the natural rate of unemployment was between 6% or 7%. By the late 1990s, many economists had begun to believe that the natural rate of unemployment had fallen to about 5%. What factors can shift the natural rate of unemployment? Economists have identified a number of them:

▶ *Demographics.* The composition of the workforce can change, decreasing the natural rate. For example, we know teenagers have higher unemployment rates than adults. If changes in population lead to a lower percentage of teenagers in the labor force, we would expect the natural rate of unemployment to decrease. A change in demographics appears to have been what caused the natural rate of unemployment to decline in the United States in the 1990s.

▶ *Institutional changes.* Changes in laws, regulations, and economic institutions can influence the natural rate of unemployment. Suppose the government shortens the length of time unemployed workers can collect benefits. We would then expect the unemployed to return to work more rapidly and the natural rate of unemployment to fall. Some economists have argued that the rise of temporary employment agencies in the United States during the 1990s made the labor market more efficient. Workers were matched more quickly with jobs, and this contributed to the decline of the natural rate. In Europe, a very different set of institutional factors had the opposite result: Generous benefits for the unemployed increased the time they spent unemployed. Restrictions on employers making it difficult to fire workers led to employers hiring fewer of them in the first place. Both these factors raised the natural rate of employment.

▶ *The state of the economy.* Some economists believe the economic performance of the economy itself may influence the natural rate of unemployment. Suppose the economy goes into a long recession. During that time, many young people may not be able to find jobs and fail to develop a strong work ethic. Other workers may lose some of their skills during a prolonged period of unemployment. Both factors could lead to longer-term unemployment and an increase in the natural rate of unemployment.

▶ *Changes in growth of labor productivity.* If the growth rate in labor productivity falls, wages must also rise more slowly because they are tied to productivity increases in the long run. However, if workers don't realize this, they might continue to push for higher nominal wage increases and be less inclined to accept lower nominal wages. This will increase the natural rate of employment. Similarly, if productivity growth is higher than anticipated, wages will rise more quickly because firms will be willing to pay more to retain their workers and recruit new ones. As a result of this unexpected productivity growth, workers may not be as aggressive in asking for additional nominal wage increases, because they are pleased with what they are already getting. They will be more inclined to accept these wages, and this will effectively lower the natural rate of unemployment. Some economists believe that this in fact happened in the late 1990s when productivity growth soared and the natural rate of unemployment temporarily

fell. Actual unemployment fell to near 4% without any visible signs of increasing inflation. Of course, once workers in the economy understand that a shift in productivity
growth has occurred, the natural rate will return to its original value, closer to, say, 5%.

Typically, macroeconomists look at a country's labor market as a whole and do not
distinguish between unemployment in different sectors of the economy. But as "A
Closer Look: The Natural Rate and Regional Differences in Unemployment" suggests,
it might be fruitful to do so.

TEST Your Understanding

3. **If inflation increases faster than expected, will the actual unemployment rate be above
   or below the natural rate of unemployment?**
4. **"Rational expectations are equivalent to expectations based on rules-of-thumb." True
   or false?**
5. **Will an increase in the fraction of young people in the labor force tend to raise or lower
   the natural rate of unemployment?**

A CLOSER LOOK

The Natural Rate and Regional Differences in Unemployment

At any point in time, some regions of a country may experience difficulties while others prosper.

For example, high oil prices will simultaneously benefit oil producers in Texas but hurt businesses and consumers in northern states like Vermont that rely heavily on natural gas for heating. Likewise, recessions can affect different parts of the country in different ways.

Does this matter when it comes to understanding the behavior of inflation and unemployment? It does, because low unemployment and high unemployment have somewhat different effects on wages. When unemployment is low, firms compete for workers and bid up wages sharply. However, when unemployment is high, it is more difficult for firms to cut wages because workers tend to resist wage cuts. What this means is that even if the total unemployment rate in the country appears to be at the natural rate of unemployment, there could still be upward inflation pressure if wages increase faster in the low-unemployment regions than they fall in the high-unemploy-

ment regions. As a consequence, the greater the differences in unemployment across regions, the higher the natural rate of unemployment will be in the country as a whole.

In 2004, two economists working at the Federal Reserve Bank of St. Louis studied how regional differences in unemployment have varied over time. These economists found that variations were relatively high during the 1980s but fell sharply in the 1990s. This had two implications. First, it meant that the U.S. labor market operated more like a truly national than a regional market in the 1990s. Second, their work strongly suggested that the natural rate of unemployment fell in the 1990s. Based on their analysis, these economists estimated that the effect was quite large and that the natural rate fell by about two percentage points—just because differences in unemployment from state to state were smaller.

Source: Howard Wall and Gylfi Zoëga, "U.S. Regional Business Cycles and the Natural Rate of Unemployment," Federal Reserve Bank of St. Louis Review, vol. 86, no. 1, January/February 2004, pp. 23–31.

How the Credibility of a Nation's Central Bank Affects Inflation

Why are the heads of central banks (such as the chair of the Federal Reserve Board of Governors) typically very conservative and constantly warning about the dangers of inflation? The basic reason is that these monetary policymakers can influence expectations of inflation, and expectations of inflation will influence actual behavior. For example, when workers anticipate inflation, they will push for higher nominal wages. If policymakers are not careful in the way they respond to this, they can actually make it difficult for a society to fight inflation.

Consider an example. A large union is negotiating wages for workers in the auto and steel industries. If the union negotiates a very high nominal wage, other unions will follow, negotiating for and winning higher wages. Prices will inevitably rise as a result, and the Fed will begin to see higher inflation emerge. Suppose the Fed has been keeping the money supply constant. What are its options?

We depict the Fed's dilemma in Figure 30.2. By setting a higher nominal wage, the union shifts the aggregate supply curve from AS_0 to AS_1. The Fed then has a choice:

▶ Keep the money supply and aggregate demand at AD_0. The economy will initially fall into a recession.
▶ Increase the money supply and raise aggregate demand from AD_0 to AD_1. This will keep the economy at full employment but lead to higher prices.

The actions of the union will depend on what its leaders expect the Fed to do. On the one hand, if they believe that the Fed will not increase aggregate demand, their actions will trigger a recession. Union leaders know this and might be reluctant to

FIGURE 30.2

Choices for the Fed: Recession or Inflation
If workers push up their nominal wages, the aggregate supply curve will shift from AS_0 to AS_1. If the Fed keeps aggregate demand constant at AD_0, a recession will occur at point a, and the economy will eventually return to full employment at point e. If the Fed increases aggregate demand, the economy remains at full employment at f but with a higher price level.

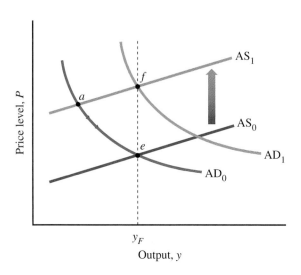

negotiate a high wage because of it. If they don't negotiate an increase in nominal wages, the economy will remain at full employment and there will be no increase in prices. On the other hand, if union leaders believe that the Fed will increase aggregate demand, they have nothing to lose and will push for higher nominal wages. The result will be higher prices in the economy.

As this example illustrates, expectations about the Fed's determination to fight inflation will affect behavior in the private sector. If the Fed is credible or believable in its desire to fight inflation, it can deter the private sector from taking aggressive actions that drive up prices. This is the reason the heads of central banks are conservative, preferring to risk increasing unemployment rather than risk an increase in inflation. For example, having a conservative chair of the Fed, someone who strongly detests inflation, sends a signal to everyone in the economy that the Fed will be unlikely to increase the money supply, regardless of what actions are taken in the private sector.

New Zealand took a different approach to ensure the credibility of its central bank. Since 1989, the central bank has been operating under a law that specifies that its only goal is to attempt to maintain stable prices, which, in practice, requires it to keep inflation between 0% and 2% a year. This policy sharply limits the central bank's ability to stabilize real GDP, but it does signal to the private sector that the central bank will not be increasing the money supply, regardless of the actions taken by wage setters or unions.

Our example suggests that with a credible central bank, a country can have lower inflation without experiencing extra unemployment. Some political scientists and economists have suggested that central banks that have true independence from the rest of the government, and are therefore less subject to political influence, will be more credible in their commitment to fighting inflation.

There is evidence to support this conjecture. Figure 30.3 plots an index of independence against average inflation rates from 1955 to 1988 for 16 countries. The

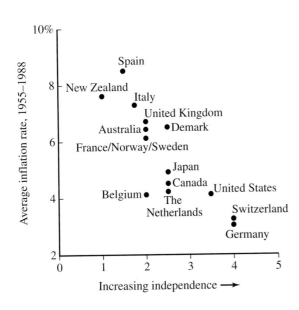

FIGURE 30.3

How Central Bank Independence Affects Inflation

Central banks that are more independent have, on average, lower inflation rates.

A CLOSER LOOK

Inflation Expectations and the Bank of England

On May 6, 1997, the Chancellor of Exchequer in Great Britain, Gordon Brown, announced a major change in monetary policy. From that time forward, the Bank of England would be more independent of the government. Although the government would still retain the authority to set the overall goals for policy, the Bank of England would be free to pursue its policy goals without direct political control.

Mark Spiegel, an economist with the Federal Reserve Bank of San Francisco, studied how the British bond market reacted to the policy change. Spiegel did this by comparing the interest-rate changes on two types of long-term bonds: bonds that are automatically adjusted (or indexed) for inflation and bonds that are not. The difference between the two interest rates primarily reflects expectations of inflation. Thus, if the gap narrowed following the policy announcement, this would be evidence that the new policy reduced expectations of inflation. If it did not, the announced policy would have had no effect on inflation expectations.

After the announcement, the gap narrowed. Based on this evidence, he concluded that the announcement did, indeed, cause expectations about inflation to fall by about half a percentage point.

Source: "British Central Bank Independence and Inflation Expectations," *Federal Reserve of San Francisco Economic Letter*, November 28, 1997.

points appear to lie along a downward-sloping line, meaning that more independence is associated with lower inflation. Germany and Switzerland, the countries that had the most-independent central banks during that time period, had the lowest inflation rates. Another piece of evidence is provided by the changes in the United Kingdom, as "A Closer Look: Inflation Expectations and the Bank of England" explains.

As our discussion illustrates, how a central bank influences expectations is important for understanding the behavior of prices and output in an economy. So is understanding how the private sector forms its inflation expectations in the first place. The theory of rational expectations that we discussed earlier has been used extensively to explain the credibility of central banks. In our example, the theory of rational expectations implies that the union will, on average, anticipate whether or not the Fed will expand the money supply in the face of wage increases. A credible Fed will tend to deter wage increases by not expanding it. Many economists believed that Fed Chairman Alan Greenspan was very credible in his determination to fight inflation. This in itself helped reduce inflation during the 1990s. People expected Greenspan would refuse to set out the "punchbowl" of money, and they were right.

Inflation and the Velocity of Money

Countries sometimes experience stunning inflation rates. For example, in 15 months from August 1922 to November 1923, the price level in Germany rose by a factor of 10 billion! To explain these extremely high inflation rates and their relationship to money growth, we now introduce a concept that is closely related to money demand: the **velocity of money**.

The velocity of money is defined as the ratio of nominal GDP to the money supply:

$$\text{velocity of money} = \text{nominal GDP/money supply}$$

Velocity of money
Nominal GDP divided by the money supply. It is also the rate at which money turns over during the year.

One useful way to think of velocity is that it is the number of times that money must change hands, or turn over, in economic transactions during a given year for an economy to reach its GDP level. To understand this, consider a simple example. Suppose that nominal GDP is $5 trillion per year and the money supply is $1 trillion. The velocity of money in this economy will then be as follows:

$$\text{velocity} = \$5 \text{ trillion per year/\$1 trillion} = 5 \text{ per year}$$

In this economy, the $1 trillion money supply has to change hands, or turn over, 5 times a year to purchase the $5 trillion of nominal GDP. If the money supply turns over 5 times in one year, this means that people are holding each dollar of money for 365 days/5, or 73 days a year. If velocity is very high, people, on average, turn over money very quickly and do not hold it for a very long time. If velocity is low, people turn over money slowly and hold onto it longer.

To further understand the role of money and velocity, let's rewrite the definition of velocity as

$$\text{money supply} \times \text{velocity} = \text{nominal GDP}$$

or

$$M \times V = P \times y$$

where M is the money supply, V is the velocity of money, P is a price index for GDP, and y is real GDP. This equation is known as the equation of exchange, or the **quantity equation**. On the right side, $P \times y$ is nominal GDP. It is the product of the price index and real GDP. It also represents total nominal spending. On the left side, the money supply, M, is multiplied by V, the velocity, or turnover rate, of money.

Quantity equation
The equation that links money, velocity, prices and real output. In symbols, we have $M \times V = P \times y$.

As you can see, the quantity equation links the money supply and velocity to nominal GDP. If velocity is predictable, we can use the quantity equation and the supply of money to predict nominal GDP. But it's not quite that easy; the velocity of money does vary over time. For example, in the United States between 1959 and 2003, the velocity of M2 (the measure of the money supply that includes currency, demand deposits, saving accounts, and deposits in money market mutual funds) varied between 1.4 and 2.0. In other words, the total amount of M2 held by the public turned over between 1.4 and 2.0 times a year for the U.S. economy to reach nominal GDP.

The basic quantity equation can be used to derive a closely related formula for understanding inflation in the long run:

$$\text{growth rate of money} + \text{growth rate of velocity}$$
$$= \text{growth rate of prices} + \text{growth rate of real output}$$

Growth version of the quantity equation

An equation that links the growth rates of money, velocity, prices, and real output.

We will call this the **growth version of the quantity equation**. Here is how to use this formula: Suppose that money growth is 10% a year, the growth of real output is 3% a year, and velocity has zero growth (it is constant). Then the rate of growth of prices—the inflation rate, in other words—is

$$10\% + 0\% = \text{growth rate of prices} + 3\%$$
$$7\% = \text{growth rate of prices (inflation)}$$

Inflation will be 7% a year. The formula allows for real economic growth and for growth in velocity. For example, if velocity grew during this period at the rate of 1% a year instead of 0, the annual inflation rate will be 8% $(10 + 1 - 3)$. This formula is used by economists to provide quick estimates of the inflation rate.

As we've learned, there is a definite link between increases in the growth of money and the rate of inflation. Inflation was lowest in the 1950s, when money growth was lowest. It was also highest in the 1970s, when money growth was highest. The link is not perfect because real GDP and velocity grew at different rates during these two decades. However, years of economic research have revealed that sustained increases in money growth will, indeed, lead to inflation.

The links between money growth and inflation are particularly dramatic when money growth is extremely high. But what leads countries to vast increases in their money supply? We'll explore that next.

TEST Your Understanding

6. Complete this statement with "real" or "nominal": The velocity of money is equal to _____ GDP divided by the money supply.
7. If the growth of the money supply is 6% a year, velocity decreases by 1%, and there is no growth in real GDP, what is the inflation rate?

Hyperinflation

Hyperinflation

An inflation rate exceeding 50% per month.

The inflation rates observed in the United States in the last 40 years are insignificant compared to some of the inflation rates around the world throughout history. Economists call very high inflation rates—over 50% per month, which is approximately 13,000% per year—**hyperinflation**. One of the first hyperinflation studies was

TABLE 30.2

Hyperinflations and Velocity

Country	Dates	Monthly Rate of Inflation	Monthly Rate of Money Growth	Approximate Increase in Velocity
Greece	November 1943 to November 1944	365%	220%	14.00
Hungary	August 1945 to July 1946	19,800	12,200	333.00
Russia	December 1921 to January 1924	57	49	3.70

Source: Adapted from Phillip Cagan, "The Monetary Dynamics of Hyperinflation," in *Studies in the Quantity Theory of Money*, edited by Milton Friedman (Chicago: University of Chicago Press, 1956), p. 26.

conducted by Phillip Cagan of Columbia University in the 1950s. Table 30.2 presents selected data from his study.

Greece, Hungary, and Russia are three countries that have experienced hyperinflation. According to the data in Table 30.2, for a period of one year, Greece had a monthly inflation rate of 365%. A monthly inflation rate of 365% means the price level rises by a factor of 4.65 each month. (If the price level rises by 4.65, its percent increase is $(4.65 - 1)/1 = 3.65$, or 365%.) To get a sense of what this means, suppose that we had inflation of this magnitude in the United States. At the beginning of the month, $1 could buy a large order of French fries. Because prices are rising by a factor of 4.65 each month, by the end of the month it would take $4.65 to buy the same order of French fries, and $1 by the end of the month would be worth only $1/4.65 = 0.215$, or 21.5 cents. After two months, a dollar would be worth only $(0.215) \times (0.215) = 0.046$ of its original value, or 4.6 cents. Suppose this continues month after month. After one year, a dollar bill would be worth only 1 millionth of 1 cent! In hyperinflations, money doesn't hold its value very long.

In Hungary after World War II, prices rose by 19,800% each month. The hyperinflation in Russia in the early 1920s seems moderate by comparison: Prices there rose by only 57% per month. However, hyperinflations have also occurred in recent times. The chapter-opening story highlights Russia in the 1990s. Table 30.3 presents data on three hyperinflations during the 1980s—in Bolivia, Argentina, and Nicaragua, all averaging about 100% per month.

TABLE 30.3

Hyperinflations in the 1980s

Country	Year	Rate of Inflation		Monthly Money Growth Rate
		Yearly	Monthly	
Bolivia	1985	1,152,200%	118%	91%
Argentina	1989	302,200	95	93
Nicaragua	1988	975,500	115	66

Source: International Financial Statistics Yearbook, 1992 (Washington, DC: International Monetary Fund).

During Germany's hyperinflation in the 1920s, it was cheaper to start a fire with currency than it was to purchase wood for kindling.

On the basis of the quantity theory, we suspect that these hyperinflations must have all been caused by money growth. We can see this in the data. For example, in Greece, the monthly inflation of 365% was accompanied by 220% money growth. In Hungary, the monthly inflation of 19,800% was caused by 12,200% money growth.

The value of money deteriorates sharply during hyperinflations and no longer serves as a good store of value. In these extreme circumstances, we would expect that people wouldn't want to hold money very long but would immediately try to spend it. In other words, we would expect the velocity of money to increase sharply during hyperinflations. This is precisely what happens. The last column of Table 30.2 shows how velocity increases during hyperinflations. In the hyperinflation in Greece, velocity increased by a factor of 14. In the hyperinflation in Hungary, velocity increased by over 333 times.

During hyperinflations, money doesn't facilitate exchange well. Because prices are changing so fast and unpredictably, there is typically massive confusion about the true value of commodities. Different stores may be raising prices at different rates, so the same commodities may sell for radically different prices. People spend all of their time hunting for bargains and the lowest prices, a process that becomes very costly in human terms. It also means they have less time to produce goods and services. No country can easily live very long with a hyperinflation. The government must take swift measures to end it before it completely destroys the economy.

How Budget Deficits Lead to Hyperinflation

If the cause of hyperinflations is excessive money growth, why do governments allow the money supply to grow so fast, risking economic catastrophe? The answer lies in understanding how some governments finance their deficits—the gap between government spending and revenues.

A government deficit must be covered in some way. If a government wants to spend $1,000 but is collecting only $800 in taxes, where can it get the needed $200? One option is to borrow the $200 by selling government bonds—IOUs—to the public. In the future, the government will have to repay the $200 in bonds plus the interest the public earns on them. Another alternative is to print $200 of new money. All governments have the ability to run the printing presses and come up with $200 in new currency. The revenue raised from money creation is called **seignorage**. In principle, governments can do a combination of both as long as the deficit is covered.

Seignorage
Revenue raised through money creation.

government deficit = new borrowing from the public + new money created

Now we are in a position to understand how hyperinflations originate. Consider Hungary after World War II. Its economy was destroyed by the war, and its citizens were demanding government services. The government had a limited ability to collect taxes because of the poor state of the economy, but it gave in to the demands from its citizens for spending at levels that far exceeded what it could collect. The result was a large deficit. Then the government faced a problem: How would this large deficit be financed? No individuals or governments wanted to buy bonds or IOUs from Hungary (lend it money) because the country's economy was in such bad shape the prospects for repayment in the near future were grim. Unable to borrow, Hungary resorted to printing money at a massive rate. The result was hyperinflation.

To end hyperinflation, governments must eliminate their budget deficits by either increasing taxes, cutting spending, or both. This, of course, will cause some economic pain. There is, however, no other remedy. Once the deficit has been cut and the government stops printing money, the hyperinflation will end. Without money growth to feed it, hyperinflation will quickly die of starvation.

Economists who emphasize the role that the supply of money plays in determining nominal income and inflation are called **monetarists**. The most famous monetarist is Friedman, who studied complex versions of the quantity equation and explored the role of money in all aspects of economic life. Friedman had many influential students, such as Philip Cagan, who is best known for his work on hyperinflations. They, along with other monetarist economists, pioneered research on the link between money, nominal income, and inflation. During the 1960s, little attention was paid to the role of money in determining aggregate demand. The work of Friedman and other monetarists was extremely influential in changing opinions of economic thinkers. Moreover, they were also insistent that, in the long run, inflation was a monetary problem. Today, most economists agree with the monetarists that, in the long run, inflation is caused by growth in the money supply.

Monetarists
Economists who emphasize the role of money in determining nominal income and inflation.

Economic Experiment

Money Illusion

Economists say that people suffer from money illusion if their behavior is influenced by nominal changes that are also not real changes. Consider the following scenarios and be prepared to discuss them in class.

a. Erin bought an antique clock for $100. Two years later, Betsy bought an identical clock for $121. Meanwhile, there had been inflation each year of

10%. Both Erin and Betsy sold their clocks to other collectors. Erin sold hers for $130; Betsy sold hers for $133. Who profited more from their transactions?

b. Bob and Pete are classic comic book traders. A year ago, Bob and Pete each bought the same comic book for $10. Bob sold his a couple of days later for $20. Pete waited a year and sold his for $21. If inflation last year were 6%, who made the better deal? ●

USING THE TOOLS

1. Inflation: A Recipe for Japan?

In the late 1990s, Japan's economy was still in a prolonged slump. Nominal interest rates were approximately zero, which many economists believed limited the scope for monetary policy. Professor Paul Krugman of Princeton University disagreed. He argued that Japan's central bank should increase the money supply rapidly with the intention of causing inflation. Moreover, it should credibly promise to continue this inflation policy into the future. The result, he predicted, would be increased investment and higher GDP growth.

Krugman's recommendation was based on the distinction between real and nominal interest rates. Can you explain the logic of his recommendation?

2. Public Pronouncements and Fed Officials

When Alan Blinder, a Princeton University professor of economics, was appointed vice-chair of the Federal Reserve in 1994, he gave a speech to a group of central bankers and monetary policy

specialists. In that speech, he repeated one of the lessons in this chapter: In the long run, the rate of inflation is independent of unemployment and depends only on money growth; in the short run, lower unemployment can raise the inflation rate. Blinder's speech caused an uproar in the financial press. He was attacked by some commentators as not being sufficiently vigilant against inflation. Use the idea of credibility to explain why an apparently innocent speech would cause such an uproar in the financial community.

3. Pay Incentives for Fed Officials?

In the private sector, the pay of executives is typically tied to the performance of their company. Could this work in the public sector as well? Suppose that the pay for the chairman of the Federal Reserve were tied to the price of long-term bonds. That is, if bond prices rose, the chairman received a bonus, but if they fell, the chairman's salary would decrease. Would this provide a credible incentive for the chairman to keep inflation low? (*Hint:* Think of the links between inflation, interest rates, and bond prices.) Do you see any disadvantages to this proposal?

4. Targeting the Natural Rate?

Since the natural rate of unemployment is the economists' notion of what constitutes "full employment," it might seem logical for the Fed to use monetary policy to move unemployment toward its natural rate. However, many economists believe such a policy would be unwise because the natural rate may shift over time and policymakers may misjudge the correct rate.

What would happen if the Fed targeted a 5% unemployment rate but the true natural rate were 6%?

SUMMARY

In this chapter, we explored the role expectations of inflation play in the economy and how societies deal with inflation. Interest rates, as well as changes in wages and prices, both reflect expectations of inflation. These expectations depend on the past history of inflation and on expectations about central bank behavior. To reduce inflation, policymakers must increase actual unemployment above the natural rate of unemployment. We also looked at the ultimate causes of hyperinflations. Here are the key points to remember from this chapter:

1　In the long run, higher money growth leads to higher inflation and higher nominal interest rates.

2　A decrease in the growth rate of money will initially lead to higher real-interest rates and higher nominal-interest rates. In the long run, real rates return to their original level; nominal rates are permanently lower because of reduced inflation.

3　The rate of inflation increases when actual unemployment falls below the natural rate of unemployment; the rate of inflation decreases when actual unemployment exceeds the natural rate of unemployment. Economists explain this relationship using the expectations Phillips curve.

4　How the public forms expectations of inflation and the time frame in which it must form them are important factors in understanding the behavior of inflation and unemployment.

5　Monetary policymakers need to be cautious about the statements and pronouncements they make because what they say can influence inflation expectations. Conservative central bankers can dampen expectations of inflation.

6　The quantity equation and the growth version of the quantity equation show the relationship between money, velocity, and nominal income.

7　Governments sometimes print new money to finance large portions of their budget deficits. When they do, the result is rapid inflation. Stopping a hyperinflation requires closing the government deficit and ending money creation.

KEY TERMS

expectations of inflation, 688
expectations Phillips curve, 690
growth version of the quantity
　equation, 700
hyperinflation, 700

monetarists, 703
money illusion, 688
nominal wages, 687
quantity equation, 699

rational expectations, 691
real wages, 687
seignorage, 703
velocity of money, 699

PROBLEMS AND DISCUSSION QUESTIONS

1 Interpret the following statement: "High interest rates are the evidence of loose monetary policy, not tight monetary policy."

2 If a business borrows funds at 10% per year, the business has a 40% tax rate, and the annual inflation rate is 5%, what are the real after-tax costs of funds to the business?

3 Are workers or firms more likely to have more accurate information about the future course of inflation?

4 Some economists argue that the natural rate of unemployment did not really decrease in the United States in the late 1990s, but there were temporary factors that kept the inflation from rising. How would you go about determining whether the natural rate of unemployment decreased in the late 1990s in the United States?

5 If the government increases the rate at which it injects money into the economy, individuals and firms will hold onto money for shorter periods. Can you explain this?

6 If the growth rate of money is 10% per year, annual inflation is 7%, and the growth rate of velocity is 1% per year, what is the growth rate of real output?

7 Some economists argue that foreign aid can reduce both the likelihood and the severity of hyperinflations. Explain this argument.

8 How could we determine if individuals use rules of-thumb to estimate inflation?

9 What are some of the most important factors that have affected the natural rate of unemployment in the United States over the last 30 years?

10 Explain why credibility in fighting inflation is very important for central banks.

11 Web Exercise. In the 1990s, the U.S. Treasury introduced bonds that were indexed to inflation. Go to the Website for the Bureau of the Public Debt (*http://www.publicdebt.treas.gov/sec/seciis.htm*) and read about these bonds. Search the Web (or other sources) and compare the interest rates on 30-year Treasury bonds that are indexed for inflation with those that are not. What factors can explain the difference in interest rates?

12 Web Exercise. Since teenagers and younger workers tend to have higher unemployment rates than older workers, some economists have argued that changes in the age composition of the labor force can partly explain shifts in the natural rate. Using the Website for the Bureau of Labor Statistics (*http://www.bls.gov*), find information on the age composition of the labor force today and compare it to 10 years ago.

MODEL ANSWERS TO QUESTIONS

Chapter-Opening Questions

1 Countries with lower rates of money growth will have lower inflation rates than countries with higher money growth. Nominal interest rates (which reflect inflation) will also be lower.

2 In the long run, actual unemployment returns to the natural rate of unemployment and inflation is largely determined by money growth. Therefore, lower unemployment will lead to higher inflation

but actual unemployment will return to the natural rate of unemployment.

3 It is prudent to have conservative heads of central banks because the private sector will then be less tempted to aggressively raise wages and prices.

4 When inflation is high, money loses value quickly, so people do not hold onto money very long.

5 Budget deficits must be financed by either issuing debt or creating money. When deficits are very large, it is difficult to issue debt, so money is created, causing massive inflation.

Test Your Understanding

1 True, that is the definition.
2 Prices will rise by 10% a year and therefore so will money demand.

3 Below.
4 False, rational expectations take into account all the available information.
5 Raise.
6 Nominal.
7 5%

Current Issues in Macroeconomic Policy

conomists are often cautious and try to warn policymakers that carrying out effective economic policy is difficult. But in the realm of politics, decisions must ultimately be made. As we learned in Chapter 1, at one point, U.S. President Harry S. Truman had had enough of his cautious economists: "All my economists say, '. . . . on the hand. . . . . on the other hand,' " bemoaned Truman. "Give me a one-handed economist!"

Decisions about government spending, taxes, deficits, interest rates, and exchange rates may seem very abstract, but they seriously impact our lives. Poor economic policies can lead to the virtual collapse of countries. Policy-making therefore requires prudence. Of course, it is always very easy to criticize politicians in power when something goes wrong. In another famous quote, Truman recognized that decision-making is not easy. Before air-conditioning was commonplace, he was known to have remarked, "If you can't stand the heat, get out of the kitchen."

As a student and citizen you are inevitably drawn into economic debates. In most cases, the debates are complex. They are a mixture of facts, theories, and opinions. Value judgments play a large role in economic debates. Your views on the proper role of tax policy, for example, will depend on whether you believe that low-income earners should receive a higher share of national income. Your views on the size of government will depend on whether you believe individuals or the government should play a larger role in economic affairs.

In previous chapters, you learned the basic vocabulary of economics and studied different theories of the economy. Now you are ready to examine some of the key policy issues in macroeconomics. In this chapter, we will focus on three macroeconomics issues that are the subject of much debate. After reading this chapter, you should have an informed opinion on these three issues:

1 Should the government balance its budget?
2 Should the Federal Reserve just target inflation and not worry about output and unemployment?
3 Should people be taxed on what they earn or on what they spend?

Unlike the chapter-opening questions in other chapters, there are no simple answers to these questions.

Should We Balance the Federal Budget?

Before we begin to consider the answers to that question, let's review some terms from Chapter 24: The purchase of goods and services by the government and the transfer payments (Social Security, welfare, and so on) it makes to its citizens are the **government's expenditures**. A **surplus** occurs when the government's revenues exceed its expenditures. The government runs a **deficit** when it spends more than it receives in revenues from either taxes or fees. The **government debt** is the *total* of all of its yearly deficits. For example, if a government initially had a debt of $100 billion and then ran deficits of $20 billion the next year, $30 billion the year after that, and $50 billion during the third year, its total debt at the end of the third year would be $200 billion (the initial $100 billion debt plus the successive yearly deficits of $20 billion, $30 billion, and $50 billion). If a government ran a surplus, it would decrease its total debt. For example, suppose the debt were $100 billion and the government ran a surplus of $10 billion. With the surplus of $10 billion, the government would buy back $10 billion of debt from the private sector, thereby reducing the remaining debt to $90 billion.

In our discussion in this chapter, we will be focusing on the debt held by the public, not the total federal debt, which includes debt held by other governmental agencies. Sometimes popular accounts in the press or on the Web highlight the total federal

Government expenditure
Spending on goods and services plus transfer payments.

Surplus
The excess of total revenues over total expenditures.

Deficit
The excess of total expenditures over total revenues.

Government debt
The total of all past government deficits.

debt. However, the debt held by the public is the best measure to assess the burden that the federal debt can have on the economy.

The Budget in Recent Decades

The fiscal picture for the United States has changed substantially over the last 25 years. Beginning in the 1980s and through most of the 1990s, the federal budget ran large deficits—"deficits as far as the eye can see," as David Stockman, the director of the Office of Management and Budget in President Reagan's administration, put it. What Stockman could not see at that point, however, was what would occur in the late 1990s. In fiscal year 1998 (during President Clinton's administration), the federal government ran a budget surplus of $69 billion—its first surplus in 30 years. It continued to run surpluses for the next three fiscal years as well.

The surplus emerged for two key reasons. First, economic growth was very rapid and tax revenues—including tax revenues from the sales of stock and bonds—grew more quickly than anticipated. Second, there were also federal budget rules in place that limited total spending.

When President George W. Bush took office in January 2001, the large surplus led him to propose that substantial tax cuts be made. Bush and Congress then passed a 10-year tax cut amounting to $1.35 billion over the course of the decade. Although the tax cuts were large, the Congressional Budget Office (CBO) estimated at that time that the federal government would nonetheless continue to run surpluses through 2010.

The CBO noted that, as a result of these federal government surpluses, the outstanding stock of federal debt held by the public would be reduced. Since GDP would be growing over this period, the stock of debt relative to GDP, which is the standard way to measure the effect of debt in an economy, would also decline. The CBO estimated that in 2011, the ratio of debt to GDP would fall despite Bush's tax cuts. Figure 31.1 depicts the debt-to-GDP ratio from 1791 to 2003. As you can see, except for the period in the 1980s, the ratio rises sharply during wars and falls during peacetime. With neither a war nor a recession looming on the horizon in early 2001, the CBO predicted the GDP–debt ratio would be relatively low by the end of the decade.

Unfortunately, a series of events intervened to bring deficits back into the picture. The collapse of the stock market and the recession that began in 2001 after Bush's tax cuts were passed sharply reduced tax revenues. Additional tax cuts subsequently passed to stimulate the economy added to the deficit. The terrorist attacks that year also led to higher spending, on items like homeland security and financing the wars that were launched in Afghanistan and Iraq. As a result, in 2004, the CBO forecasted that the debt-to-GDP ratio would increase by 2011, not decrease as it predicted earlier. The federal government ran a budget deficit of over $400 billion in fiscal year 2004, a far cry from surpluses just several years earlier.

The Budget and Social Security

Federal budget figures include revenue and expenditure from the Social Security system. Over the next decade, the Social Security portion of the budget is expected to run a surplus because of the huge number of baby boomers currently paying taxes into the

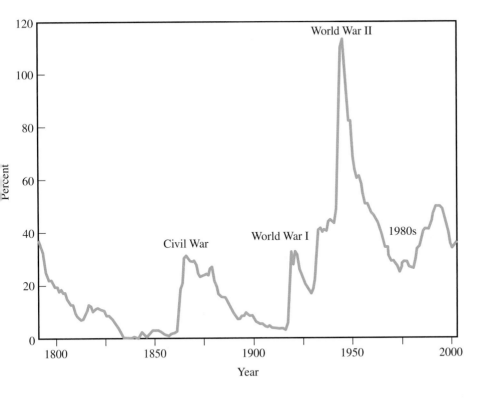

FIGURE 31.1

Debt as a Percent of GDP, 1791–2003
The nation's debt to GDP ratio tends to rise sharply during wars because more spending is needed to finance them. However, the ratio also can rise during peacetime, as it did during the Reagan presidency in the 1980s.

Sources: Congressional Budget Office, "The Long-Term Budget Outlook," December 2003, and updates.

ystem. That won't last forever, though. Some economists argue that Social Security unds should not be included in federal budget figures because the money will be needed to make future Social Security payments to these baby boomers. Over the longer horizon, the surpluses in the Social Security account will disappear and turn to deficits. As our society grows older, spending on both Social Security and Medicare will ncrease. It's those increasing expenditures that are causing the CBO to predict emerging federal deficits and sharp increases in the debt-to-GDP ratio to levels comparable o World War II, unless taxes are raised and/or spending is cut significantly.

As we have seen, federal budgets are heavily affected by a wide range of factors, ncluding wars, demographic pressures, recessions, as well as the choices made by our politicians on spending and taxes. But what principles should guide our policymakers? should they cut spending and raise taxes to reduce the national debt over time? Or does the level of the national debt really matter? Let's take a look at the debates over the national debt.

The Debates

1. Do Deficits Lead to Inflation?

If a government is spending $2,000 but is collecting only $1,600 in taxes, where does it get the $400 needed to fill the gap? One option would be to borrow the $400 from the public in return for government bonds (in effect, IOUs). In the future, the government would have to pay back the $400 plus any interest on the bonds. Another way to cover the gap is simply to print $400 worth of new money. In principle, governments could use a mix of borrowing money and printing money, as long as the total covers its deficits:

$$\text{government deficit} = \text{new borrowing from the public} + \text{new money created}$$

In the United States, the Treasury Department issues government bonds to finance the deficit. The Federal Reserve has the option of buying existing government bonds, including those newly issued by the Treasury Department. If the Federal Reserve does purchase the government's bonds, the purchase creates money by taking debt out of the hands of the public in exchange for money. Economists call the purchase by a central bank of newly created government debt **monetizing the deficit**. If governments finance deficits by creating new money, the result will be inflation. In the United States, we finance only a very small portion of our deficits by creating money. For example, between 1992 and 1993, the Federal Reserve purchased only $15 billion in government bonds of approximately $270 billion issued by the Treasury during that period. The remainder, about $255 billion in bonds, were sold to the public.

Monetizing the deficit

Purchases by a central bank of newly issued government bonds.

If a country has no options other than creating money to finance its deficits—in other words, if the public is unwilling to buy its bonds, as was the case with Hungary following World War II—those deficits will inevitably cause inflation. As we discussed in Chapter 30, hyperinflations occur when economies run large deficits and monetize them. Germany and Russia after World War I, Bolivia and Argentina in the 1980s, and Russia in the 1990s are just some of the countries that, in addition to Hungary, endured massive inflations because they monetized their deficits. However, large, stable countries like the United Kingdom, the United States, and Japan don't monetize much of their debt because they are able to borrow from the public. In these countries, deficits do not lead inevitably to inflation.

2. Is Government Debt a Burden on Future Generations?

The national debt (another commonly used term for total government debt) can impose two different burdens on society, both of which fall on the shoulders of future generations. First, a large debt can reduce the amount of capital in the economy and thereby reduce future income and real wages for its citizens. Here's how.

The savings of individuals and institutions flow into capital formation and increase an economy's capital stock. For example, when savers purchase new stocks and bonds, the companies issuing them use the proceeds to invest in plants and equipment.

When the government runs a deficit and increases its national debt, it also finances its spending by selling bonds to these same savers, who might hold both types of assets in, say, their retirement portfolios. Further, let's say that the total amount that the public can save is fixed at $1,000. If the government needs to finance a $200 deficit, and does so by selling new bonds, that means that only $800 in savings is available to invest in private companies. The selling of $200 in government bonds to finance the deficit therefore "crowds out" $200 that could have been raised by private companies.

The result of government deficits is that less savings are available to firms for investment. As we discussed in earlier chapters, reduced saving will ultimately reduce the stock of private capital and the building of new factories and the purchasing of equipment to expand production and raise GDP. As a result, there will be less capital deepening. With lower capital per worker, real incomes and real wages will be lower than they otherwise might have been. Governments can spend the proceeds of bor-owing on investments such as productive infrastructure—in this case, there will not e the adverse effects on future real wages and incomes. With productive investment, overnment deficits will not be a burden on society.

Second, a large national debt will mean that higher taxes will be imposed on future enerations to pay the interest that accumulates on the debt. Just like your college oans, the bill eventually comes due—even for the national debt.

Sometimes you hear that these interest payments are not a real burden because we owe the national debt to ourselves." This is a misleading argument for several reaons. First, we don't owe the interest payments only to ourselves. In 2003, approximately 37% of U.S. public debt was held by foreigners, the largest share in 40 years. econd, a high proportion of the debt is held by older, wealthy individuals or by institutions, but the taxes levied to service it will be paid by everyone in the United States.

Some economists do not believe that government deficits, resulting in government lebt, impose a burden on a society. These economists believe in **Ricardian equivalence**, he proposition that it does not matter whether government expenditure is financed by axes or financed by issuing debt. To understand the case for Ricardian equivalence, onsider this example. A government initially has a balanced budget. It then cuts taxes nd issues new debt to finance the deficit left by the reduction in taxes. Everyone understands that the government will have to raise taxes in the future to service the lebt, so everyone increases savings to pay for the taxes that will be increased in the uture. If saving rises sufficiently, the public—everyone—will be able to purchase the new debt without reducing the funds they invest in the private sector. Since net investment doesn't decline, there will be no debt burden.

As you can see, Ricardian equivalence requires that savings by the private sector ncrease when the deficit increases. Do savers behave this way? It is actually difficult to orovide a definite answer because many other factors must be taken into account in any empirical studies of saving. It appears, however, that during the early 1980s, savings decreased somewhat when government deficits increased. This is precisely opposite to what Ricardian equivalence predicts. As long as Ricardian equivalence does not fully nold true, it's reasonable to assume the government debt imposes a burden on society.

Nonetheless, many economists believe that using the deficit as the sole measure of a society's future burdens doesn't tell the whole story. These economists believe we should look at broader measures. "A Closer Look: Measuring Fiscal Imbalances" describes this new approach.

Ricardian equivalence
The proposition that it does not matter whether government expenditure is financed by taxes or by debt.

3. How Do Deficits Affect the Size of Government?

Nobel laureate James Buchanan has argued that people are less aware of government deficits than the taxes they're forced to pay. Therefore, financing government expenditures through deficits, rather than through higher taxes, will inevitably lead to higher government spending and bigger government. Although this argument may seem plausible, there are two problems related to it. First, in recent U.S. history, spending by state and local governments has grown much faster than federal spending. However, state and local governments face many more restrictions when it comes to borrowing money than the federal government faces. For example, many states require legislators to run a balanced budget. Deficit spending isn't allowed. Second, if this were true, why did the federal government run surpluses in the late 1990s if politicians trying to get reelected prefer higher government spending and deficits to higher taxes and surpluses?

A CLOSER LOOK

Measuring Fiscal Imbalances

Even though federal budget-deficit projections have increased in recent years, they still don't accurately portray the long-run fiscal problems facing the United States. As the population ages, life expectancies increase, and health care costs continue to grow, expenditures on Social Security and Medicare are expected to increase significantly, too. Although payroll taxes today exceed expenditures, in the not-too-distant future, these taxes will fall far short of anticipated expenditures. Over time, there will be an escalating gap between revenues and expenditures, which would have to be met by outright borrowing.

How can we measure what the gap will be? Economists Jagadeesh Gokhale of the Cato Institute and Kent Smetters of the University of Pennsylvania have developed a more comprehensive measure of a nation's indebtedness. The method includes estimating the present value of the gap between the government's revenues and expenditures and adding it to the current national debt.

This new, total measure, which Gokhale and Smetters call the "fiscal imbalance," was calculated in 2003 to be approximately $44 trillion, or four times GDP. This is a huge number. Even during World War II, government debt was only 1.2 times GDP. In the long run, a fiscal imbalance of this size is not sustainable—no one will lend the U.S. government that amount of money. To eliminate these imbalances will require dramatic increases in taxes or reduced expenditures. To maintain the current level of benefits, workers and firms would have to pay nearly 30% in payroll taxes—about double what they pay today. Or, income taxes would also have to nearly double. Alternatively, benefits programs could be scaled back.

Gokhale and Smetters estimate that about 80% of the fiscal imbalance will stem from Medicare—rising health care costs for the elderly. What these numbers suggest is that our current health care system for retirees will need to undergo fundamental reform to make it more sustainable. Otherwise, the United States will need to radically increase taxes to meet the shortfall.

Based on: Jagadeesh Gokhale and Kent Smetters, "Piling Up Future Debts," National Center for Policy Analysis, Brief Analysis, No. 453, September 2003.

More recent thinking suggests that deficits can be used strategically to actually reduce the growth of government. During the 1980s, for example, the government ran large deficits caused by a combination of a deep recession and major tax cuts. The deficits subsequently made it difficult for politicians to propose new spending programs. Proponents of smaller government, therefore, may wish to cut taxes to reduce surpluses or increase deficits in order to make it more difficult for other politicians to increase government spending. These deficit proponents want to create deficits to prevent "putting sand in Congress's sandbox." Some politicians supported President Bush's tax cut in 2001, which reduced the surplus over a 10-year period, precisely for this reason.

Can Deficits Be Good for an Economy?

Recall from the fiscal policy chapter that during a downturn running a deficit helps stimulate private-sector spending. Consequently, the government may deliberately run one to pull the economy out of a recession. The deficit the government creates puts additional income into the hands of the public. With more money, people don't have to drastically cut their consumption spending. Because total spending in the economy does not fall as much, the severity of the recession is lessened.

Deficits automatically emerge during recessions, which also stabilizes the economy. Recall how automatic stabilizers work. As incomes fall during a recession, so do tax payments. Moreover, transfer payments such as welfare and food stamps rise. Because government spending increases while tax revenues fall, the deficit must, of course, rise. However, this may be what it takes to steer the economy back to full employment.

The existence of automatic stabilizers and the use of expansionary fiscal policy during recessions suggest that we should not worry about short-run government deficits. Over short time periods, deficits can help the economy to cope with shocks, such as oil price increases or a collapse in the stock market. They give the government some room to maneuver out of a recession. Most economists believe automatic stabilizers reduced economic fluctuations during the twentieth century.

Deficits can also play a role in tax smoothing. Suppose there is a large, temporary increase in government spending, as might occur during a war. The government could either finance the war by running a deficit and issuing debt or by increasing tax rates to keep the budget in balance. Professor Robert Barro of Harvard University has argued that it is more efficient to keep tax rates relatively constant than to raise them sharply and then lower them later. Temporarily raising tax rates to very high levels could cause distortions in economic behavior that we would like to avoid. Thus, by running deficits and only gradually raising taxes later to service the debt, we avoid creating excess distortions in the economy.

5. Would a Balanced-Budget Amendment Really Work?

For many years, there were strong efforts to enact a constitutional amendment to balance the federal budget. As recently as 1995, Congress came very close to passing a balanced-budget amendment, sending it back to the states for ratification. It passed in the House of Representatives but failed by a single vote in the Senate. How would a balanced-budget amendment actually work?

Many different budgetary constitutional amendments have been proposed. They all require that after a phase-in period, Congress propose in each fiscal year a budget in which total revenues (excluding borrowing) cover total expenditures. The amendments also have various escape clauses—for example, to allow borrowing during wartime. Some amendments also allow Congress to suspend the requirement to balance the budget for other reasons, such as during a recession when deficits naturally emerge. Finally, some versions of the amendment would limit the rate of spending increases to the rate at which GDP is growing.

Proponents of the balanced-budget amendment say that it will finally exert discipline on the federal government, preventing large deficits in peacetime, such as those that occurred in the 1980s. With a balanced budget we could be sure to avoid the effects of deficits: reduced capital formation and shifting tax burdens onto future generations.

Congress continually debates the appropriate size and composition of the nations's budget.

Critics of a balanced-budget amendment point to many different problems, such as the following:

▶ A balanced budget may not allow enough flexibility, or room, for the government to effectively deal with recessions. Under some versions of the amendment, unless three-fifths of Congress votes to suspend requirements, the government would have to cut expenditures or raise taxes during a recession. This would make the recession worse and limit the ability of the government to use fiscal policy to stabilize the economy.
▶ The Constitution is not the right mechanism to try to enforce complicated budget rules. As various interested parties challenge the actions of Congress, the courts would become heavily involved in federal budget matters.
▶ Congress could devise special budgets to get around the requirement, for example, by taking some types of spending "off budget," which means simply not counting it as part of the official budget.
▶ Congress could also find nonbudgetary ways to carry out the policies that it desires. For example, it could issue more regulations or impose mandates or requirements on businesses or other governments to carry out its will. These regulations or mandates could be even more costly to the economy than added deficits.

TEST Your Understanding

1. If a government runs a surplus, will it increase or decrease outstanding debt?
2. Proponents of Ricardian equivalence are primarily concerned about deficits crowding out the stock of capital. True or false? Explain.
3. Explain how deficits can lead to inflation.

Should the Fed Target Inflation?

Some Background

In Chapter 20, we examined some of the costs of inflation, including the following:

- Menu costs—the costs firms incur to change their posted prices.
- Shoe-leather costs—the costs individuals and firms pay for the time and resources they spend trying to reduce their holdings of money.
- Distortions in our tax and banking systems because inflation isn't yet factored into them.
- Arbitrary redistributions of money between debtors and creditors from unanticipated inflation.

In the early years of the first decade of 2000, the rate of inflation had fallen to roughly between 1% and 2%. Some economists thought the time was right for the Fed to concentrate on simply keeping the inflation rate low and stable. In other words, they thought that the Fed should use monetary policy to "target" an appropriate inflation rate and make its primary objective keeping inflation in check.

In recent years, various inflation "targeting" methods have been adopted in a number of developed countries, including Canada, the United Kingdom, New Zealand, Sweden, Australia, and Spain. In addition, many developing countries have found that inflation targeting increased the autonomy of their central banks, helping them fight inflation.

The Debates

1. Should the Fed Only Focus on Inflation?

Proponents of inflation targeting argue that the Fed should have only one primary goal: controlling inflation. We have learned that in the long run, monetary policy can influence only the level of prices, not the level of employment. They argue that having the Fed worry about other factors—unemployment or the exchange rate—will distract the Fed from its mission. Preoccupation with other goals can easily lead the Fed astray and lead to long-run inflationary pressures building in the economy. Moreover, if the Fed were committed to the single goal of controlling inflation, its credibility would be enhanced. As we have seen, if the Fed is credible, the private sector will become more responsive to changes in monetary policy. For example, long-term interest rates will become more responsive to changes in short-term rates if the public understands what the Fed's motives are and what it's doing. And credible policies may actually decrease the need for active monetary policies. Having a single goal would also help to keep the Fed free from political pressures. Such political pressures might include attempts by one political party or the other to stimulate the economy or give financial markets a temporary boost before an election.

Other proponents of inflation targeting hold a somewhat less rigid view. Although these proponents believe fighting inflation should be the primary objective of the Fed, or a central bank, they believe an inflation-targeting regime could be designed to give the central bank some flexibility. For example, the central bank could be required to target a broader range of inflation—say, between 1% and 3%—and meet the target several years in the future. Under either of these alternatives, central banks would have some room to meet employment or other policy objectives besides just inflation. In practice, many countries do allow some "wiggle room" in their inflation targeting regimens by using broad inflation bands or distant targets.

However, even this is too much for many other economists who strongly object to having the Fed concentrate solely on controlling inflation. In the United States, the president and the Congress are frequently incapable of quickly reaching a consensus when a fiscal policy is immediately needed to stave off or end a recession. Of course, automatic fiscal stabilizers exist, but they are often not sufficient to cushion the economy when a shock hits. Practically speaking, only monetary policy is available to stabilize output and prevent deep recessions from emerging. If monetary policy is geared solely toward controlling inflation, as inflation-targeting proponents would like, and fiscal policies are difficult for Congress and the president to pass, that leaves the government no other tools to fight a recession.

Another issue relates to the level for an inflation target. Suppose there were general agreement that the ultimate goal should be total price stability—that is, zero inflation. There would still be legitimate questions about what constitutes "stable" prices. It is very difficult to measure changes in prices accurately when there is a great deal of technological change occurring in the economy, because technological improvements change the quality of goods so rapidly that government statisticians can't easily catch up with them. If, as many economists believe, our price indexes overstate the true inflation rate, 2% annual inflation may in reality be true price stability.

Another important issue is whether a central bank should worry about asset prices—for example, the price of houses or price of assets held in the stock market—or whether it should just concentrate on the CPI or GDP deflator. Japan clearly suffered from the collapse of overvalued real estate and stock markets in the 1990s. Perhaps, if Japan's central bank had quickly adopted tight monetary policies, it could have prevented the sharp rise in prices of real estate and stocks. Similarly, in the United States, some critics of the Fed believe it should have adopted tighter monetary policies when the stock market soared in the late 1990s. Preventing the market from rising so steeply could have prevented its sharp fall and the 2001 recession that followed.

Some economists like the idea of the Fed having to meet targets, but they have suggested alternatives to inflation targeting. One alternative would be for the Fed to target the growth rate in nominal GDP instead of inflation. Since the growth rate in nominal GDP reflects both the growth in real GDP as well as the growth in prices (inflation), such a target would address both concerns—how fast the economy should grow and what the appropriate price level in it should be.

Critics of stabilization policy of course believe that not using monetary policy to try to stabilize the economy would actually improve our economic performance. In their view, attempts to stabilize the economy have done more harm than good over the years by making fluctuations worse. In previous chapters, we discussed the difficulties in conducting stabilization policy. These include lags, uncertainties about the strength and timing of policies, and difficulties in estimating the natural rate of unemployment. If you believe these difficulties are insurmountable, you will likely think the Fed should target just inflation. If you think they can be overcome, you will likely believe the Fed should be allowed to stabilize output and employment too.

2. Who Would Set the Inflation Target If There Were One?

Even if the United States decided to adopt inflation targeting as a policy, several important questions would remain. Perhaps the most important is: Who would set the targets?

In the United Kingdom, which adopted targeting in 1992, it is ultimately the elected government that decides on the inflation target for the central bank. These elected officials typically specify a range for the inflation rate that the bank must meet. The central bank is heavily involved in the discussions and has an opportunity to present its views to the public through its publications and published minutes of its meetings. But ultimately, it is the elected government that makes the final decision.

In other countries, the central bank has even more influence in setting the inflation target. In New Zealand, for example, the central bank has the responsibility of "achieving and maintaining stability in the general level of prices" without any competing goals, such as stabilizing employment or output. The law also requires the head of the central bank and the finance minister to negotiate inflation goals and make them public.

What would be an appropriate arrangement for the United States? Under current law, the Fed chairman reports regularly to Congress, but the Fed has considerable power to use monetary policy to stabilize output as well as to fight inflation as it pleases. Would our Congress and president be willing to cede power to the Fed and allow it to focus only on fighting inflation? And, if they did, would Congress or the president want to determine the target range for inflation and instruct the Fed how quickly to meet these targets?

As you can see, changing our current system would involve major decisions about who has authority and control over our economic system. Currently, the Fed has considerable power and autonomy. Although inflation targeting might make the Fed more independent, another phenomenon could occur, too: Congress and the president might end up with more power over monetary policy. And that might lead to more inflation, not less.

 **TEST Your Understanding**

4. How can there be "wiggle room" in a system of inflation targeting?
5. What is a possible alternative to targeting just the inflation rate?
6. Suppose your goal was total price stability—zero inflation. Even in this case, why might targeting a higher level of inflation be appropriate?

Should We Tax Consumption Rather than Income?

Some Background

As we discussed in earlier chapters, the United States is a country with a low savings rate. This hurts our long-run growth prospects because our investment spending is determined by our own savings and savings from abroad. Many factors—not purely

Should taxes be based on consumption?

economic ones—contribute to our low saving rate. For example, colleges generally give less financial aid to students whose families have saved for their education. Many of our welfare programs cut the benefits of families who have saved in the past and still have some funds left in their accounts. The U.S. tax system also discourages savings. Here's how.

In the United States, you must pay taxes on both the wages you earn and the earnings you make on your savings. Suppose that you earn $100 at your job and you have a tax rate of 20%. That means you keep $80 after taxes. Now suppose that you save $50 of that money and invest it at 10%. At the end of one year, you will have earned an additional $5 on the $50 you saved (10% × $50), but you will get to keep only $4 of it because the government will take $1 in taxes (20% × $5). So, you will have to pay the government $21 in total: $20 on the $100 you earned in wages, plus $1 on the $5 you earned on your savings. If you did not save at all, you would pay only $20 in taxes, not $21.

Not all tax systems work this way. Tax systems that are based on consumption do not penalize individuals who save. Sales taxes in the United States and value-added taxes abroad are familiar examples of **consumption taxes**. It is also possible to create a consumption tax from an income tax by not taxing the earnings on savings—just as we do with tax-exempt bonds issued by state and municipal governments. Or as an alternative, the government could allow savings to be deducted from gross income before the calculation for total taxes owed is made. The key feature of consumption taxation is that you do not face any additional taxes if you decide to save more of your income.

Consumption taxes

Taxes based on the consumption, not the income, of individuals.

There are, however, ways in the United States to save money and still curb your axes. In addition to buying tax-exempt bonds, you can invest in an IRA (individual etirement account) or 401K, 403B, and Keogh plans, which are also types of retirement accounts. The money in pension funds is treated similarly. It isn't taxed until the person who contributed it retires and withdraws it. During retirement, most people earn less money than when they were working, so the tax rate they pay on the money they withdraw from these accounts is lower. Also, the money accumulates more quickly because it grows tax-free while it's in these accounts. In practice, the U.S. tax system is a hybrid system: halfway between an income tax and a consumption tax.

The Debates

Proponents claim that taxes based on consumption will increase total savings and may even be more equitable. Let's explore these claims.

. Will Consumption Taxes Lead to More Savings?

There is no question that taxing consumption instead of savings creates an incentive to save. However, there's no guarantee the incentive will actually result in more money saved in the economy. Suppose the tax burden is shifted to consumption by reducing the tax rate on savings. People will want to take advantage of this incentive and reduce their consumption and increase their saving. On the other hand, people will also want to spend more, too, because with the tax cut, they are wealthier.

Although there has been much research done on how a consumption tax would affect savings, the results are far from conclusive. It is true that individuals will allocate their savings to tax-favored investments over investments that are not favored. For example, they will put money into their IRAs. What is not clear is whether the funds they will put there are literally new savings—meaning reduced consumption—or merely transfers from other accounts, such as conventional savings accounts, which do not have the same tax advantages. Untangling these effects is a difficult issue, and it remains an active area of ongoing research.

The tax system imposed on corporations in the United States also creates disincentives to save and invest. Suppose you purchase a share of stock in a corporation. When the corporation earns a profit, it pays taxes on the profit at the corporate tax rate. When the corporation pays you a dividend on the stock out of the profits it earns, you must pay taxes on the dividend income that you receive. Corporate income is taxed twice, in other words—first when it is earned by the corporation and again when it is paid out to shareholders.

Some economists have argued that the corporate taxes lead to less efficient investment because they result in capital flowing into other sectors of the economy (into real estate, for example) that do not suffer from double taxation. For this reason, in 2003 Congress passed a bill introduced by President Bush that lowered—but did not eliminate—taxes on corporate dividends.

. Are Consumption Taxes Fair?

The basic idea behind a consumption tax seems fair. Individuals should be taxed on what they take away from the economy's total production—that is, what they consume—not on what they actually produce. If an individual produces a lot but does not consume the proceeds from what was produced, and instead plows it back into the economy for invest ment, that individual is contributing to the growth of total output and should b rewarded, not punished. Individual A earns $50 and consumes it all; individual B earn $100 but consumes only $40. Who should pay more?

In practice, moving to a consumption tax system could have a major impact o the distribution of income in the economy. Suppose we simply exempted the return from savings from the income tax. This would clearly favor wealthy and high-incom individuals who save the most and earn a lot of income in interest, dividends, rent and capital gains. Table 31.1 shows the capital gains earned by people in variou income classes from 1979 to 1988. **Capital gains** are the profits investors earn whe they sell stocks, bonds, real estate, or other assets. As you can see, taxpayers wit annual incomes exceeding $200,000 earned over half of the economy's capital gain over this period. Obviously, capital assets are highly concentrated among the wealth

If capital gains and other types of capital income were not taxed, total tax revenu would fall, and the government would have to raise tax rates on everyone to maintai the same level of spending. Excluding capital income from taxation does have it costs. Certain types of consumption taxes, however, would not necessarily cause shar changes in relative tax burdens. For example, the "flat tax" designed by Robert E. Ha of Stanford University and Alvin Rabushka of the Hoover Institute brings the per sonal income tax and corporate income tax into a single, unified tax system. The fla tax would allow corporations to deduct investment spending made, for example, o new plants and equipment from the firm's income before the tax on it is calculated Since the tax would allow a deduction for investment spending (spending that ulti mately must be financed by saving), it can essentially be viewed as a type of consump tion tax. Now suppose the corporation makes an extraordinary return on its invest ment. The extraordinary return would be taxed in full. Owners of the corporatio thus may earn extraordinary gains, but if they do, they will pay taxes on these gains.

Some economists today believe it is important we continue to ensure that hig income individuals pay a significant share of total taxes. In the last several decades, th distribution of income has become more unequal, as superstar athletes, famous actor and musicians, CEOs, and successful entrepreneurs and investors have all earned larg fortunes. The tax system is one way we have to at least partially reduce inequalities i

Capital gains

Profits investors earn when they sell stocks, bonds, real estate, or other assets.

TABLE 31.1

Share of Capital Gains by Income

Income Class	Share of Capital Gains
$10,000–20,000	2.6%
$20,000–30,000	2.9
$30,000–40,000	4.4
$40,000–50,000	3.4
$50,000–75,000	9.0
$75,000–100,000	8.5
$100,000–200,000	15.7
$200,000 and over	56.8

Source: Congressional Budget Office, *Perspective on the Ownership of Capital Assets and the Realization of Capital Gains*, May 1997. (Based on a 10-year average from 1979 to 1988. Excludes category reporting negative income.)

come. Critics of consumption taxes worry that moving our tax system in that direction
will take away this important tool for social equality. However, other economists believe
that high-income individuals already shoulder a very high share of the total tax burden
and that we need to focus on designing an efficient system to promote economic growth.

TEST Your Understanding

7. Give an example of savings completely free of tax that you can make.
8. Why wouldn't switching to a consumption tax necessarily increase total savings?
9. Explain why the money earned from stock dividends is essentially taxed twice.

USING THE TOOLS

In this chapter, we explored several policy issues
using a variety of different tools. Take this
opportunity to do your own economic analysis.

1. Applications

1. **Debt and Deficits in Belgium**
   Here are some data for Belgium in 1989:

   GDP: 6160 billion Belgian francs
   Debt: 6500 billion Belgian francs
   Deficit: 380 billion Belgian francs
   Interest rate on bonds: 8.5%

   Use these data to answer the following
   questions:
   a. What are the deficit/GDP ratio and
      debt/GDP ratio? How do these ratios
      compare to the same ratios in the United
      States today? To what period in U.S.
      history does the debt/GDP ratio in
      Belgium correspond?
   b. Approximately how much of
      the budget in Belgium is devoted to
      interest payments on its debt? If
      Belgium could wipe out its debt
      overnight, what would happen to its
      current budget deficit?

2. **Targeting the Price Level with
   Supply Shocks**
   Suppose the Fed had brought
   the inflation rate down to zero in
   order to stabilize the price
   level. An adverse supply
   shock (like an increase in the
   world price of oil) now hits the
   economy.
   a. Using the aggregate demand-and-supply
      model, show how targeting the price level
      would make the fall in output from the
      shock greater as compared to no policy
      at all.
   b. Some proponents of price level or
      inflation targeting recommend that the
      Fed target "core inflation" based on a
      price index that excludes supply shocks.
      What is their rationale?

3. **IRAs and a Zero Tax Rate**
   With an IRA, you get to deduct the amount
   you contribute from your current taxable
   income, invest the funds free from tax, but
   then pay taxes on the full amount you
   withdraw when you retire. Suppose your tax
   rate is 50% and you initially deposit $2,000 in
   an IRA. The proceeds double in seven years to

$4,000. You then retire and pay taxes on the $4,000 at your 50% rate.

a. Taking into account your tax deduction for the IRA, how much did your investment in the IRA really cost you? What is your return after seven years?

b. Explain why this is the same outcome you would have had if you were free from all taxes (were taxed at a rate of zero), you invested $1,000 for seven years, and doubled your initial investment.

SUMMARY

In this chapter, we explored three topics that are the center of macroeconomic policy debates today. Here are the key points to remember:

1 A deficit is the difference between the government's current expenditures and revenue. The government debt is the sum of all past yearly deficits.

2 Deficits can be financed through either borrowing or money creation. Money creation leads to inflation.

3 Deficits can be good for the country. Automatic stabilizers and expansionary fiscal policy both work through the creation of deficits.

4 The national debt involves two burdens: The national debt can reduce the amount of capital in an economy, leading to lower levels of income; it

can also result in higher taxes that future generations will have to pay.

5 A number of developed countries have recently changed their monetary policy to emphasize targeting the inflation rate or a range for the inflation rate.

6 While targeting inflation can increase the credibility of a central bank, it does limit the tools left for active stabilization policy.

7 A consumption tax would increase the incentive for private savings. However, it is not clear that total savings would necessarily increase, and there would be concerns about the fairness of this form of taxation.

KEY TERMS

PROBLEMS AND DISCUSSION QUESTIONS

1 A country has outstanding debt of $10 billion. The interest rate on the debt is 10% per year. Expenditures (other than interest payments) are $1 billion and taxes are $1 billion. What is the debt at the end of next year?

2 In the previous example, suppose that the inflation rate was 5% per year. By how much did the real burden of the debt increase?

3 Why are government deficits more serious in countries with limited abilities to borrow from the private sector?

4 How is a decrease in the age at which workers are eligible for Social Security similar to an increase in the government deficit?

5 In what ways could a balanced-budget requirement limit the ability of the government to conduct fiscal policy? Do you think this is a serious loss?

6 With near-term surpluses and very large long-term deficits, one economist argued that "tax smoothing" required increases in current taxes, which would mean increasing current surpluses even further. Another economist, fearful of the consequences in Congress of budget surpluses, advocated cutting taxes to reduce the surplus. Explain the logic of both positions.

7 An economist suggests that what matters for financial markets is a stable inflation rate, not a zero inflation rate. As long as inflation is stable, all individuals can take this into account in their actions. What are the costs associated with a stable 2% inflation rate? Do you believe that it is easier or more difficult to stabilize inflation at 2% rather than at zero?

8 Some economists believe that the Federal Reserve should follow strict rules for the conduct of monetary policy. These rules would require the Fed to make adjustments to interest rates based on information that is fully available to the public, information such as the current unemployment rate and the current inflation rate. What do you see as the pros and cons of such an approach?

9 Suppose the government launches a new program that allows individuals to place funds of up to $2,000 in a tax-free account. Do you believe that this will have a significant effect on national savings?

10 Evaluate this quote: "Since high-income individuals save more, any tax policies that favor savings will also help the wealthy at the expense of the poor."

11 Web Exercise. The Website for the Congressional Budget Office (*http://www.cbo.gov*) contains its projections for future budget surpluses and deficits as well as options for increasing the surplus. Using this site, find some options you think are desirable that would have a significant effect on increasing the budget surplus.

12 Web Exercise. Have you ever thought that it would be easy to cut government spending or raise taxes to improve the surplus? Now is your chance to find out. Play the National Budget Simulation game at *http://www.nathannewman.org/nbs/*. What changes can you make to really improve the deficit without disrupting the functions of government?

MODEL ANSWERS TO QUESTIONS

Test Your Understanding

1 Decrease.

2 False, they believe deficits do not matter.

3 They can lead to inflation if the Fed monetizes the deficits.

4 The targets can be broad or far into the future.

5 Nominal income is an alternative target that takes into account both real growth and inflation.

6 Because of difficulties in measuring prices precisely and an upward bias in price indices.

7 An IRA is an example.

8 Although there is an increased incentive to save, there is also a wealth effect and people may want to spend more.

9 It is taxed at the corporate level first, then at the individual level.

11

The International Economy

International Trade and Public Pol

At a 2004 press conference, the chairman of the Council of Economic Advisers, Gregory Mankiw, was asked about the fact that many U.S. companies are "outsourcing" jobs—that is, sending jobs Americans used to do to workers abroad to perform. Mankiw responded by saying, "Outsourcing is a growing phenomenon, but it's something we should realize is probably a plus for the economy in the long run." His comments immediately set off a political firestorm. Even the Speaker of the House said of Mankiw: "His theory fails a basic test of real economics."

Does it? As economists have pointed out, outsourcing jobs is part and parcel of specialization, comparative advantage, and free trade. When *New York Times* columnist Thomas Friedman was visiting India to report on the growth of firms there providing services to U.S. companies, he noted that while some skilled tasks like computer programming and cartoon animation were outsourced to India, other tasks formerly done in India were actually being outsourced to the United States. For example, when one animation company wanted to produce an animated epic about the Indian god Krishna, they "outsourced" the script to an Emmy Award-winning writer in the United States. Sometimes the process of trade takes unexpected twists.

Source: Thomas L. Friedman, "What Goes Around . . . ," *New York Times*, February 26, 2004.

s the world economy grows, our policies toward international trade become ever more important. Many people view trade as a "zero-sum game." They believe that if one country gains from international trade, another must lose. Based on this belief, they advocate restricting trade with other countries. Indeed, the United States does restrict trade to protect American jobs in many sectors, like those in the apparel and steel industries. One lesson from this chapter is that free trade could, in principle, make everyone better off. The challenge for policymakers is to develop a set of principles that accomplish this goal—or come as close as possible to accomplishing it.

In this chapter, we discuss the benefits of international trade and the effects of policies that restrict it. Here are some of the practical questions that we will answer:

1 What are the trade-offs associated with free trade? Who wins? Who loses?
2 Why is a tariff (a tax on an imported good) superior to an import quota?
3 Why might the export price of a product be less than its domestic price?
4 Do trade laws inhibit environmental protection?
5 Does trade increase income inequality?

Benefits from Specialization and Trade

What if you lived in a nation that could produce everything it consumed and didn't depend on any other country for its economic livelihood? If you were put in charge of your nation, would you pursue such a policy of national self-sufficiency? Although self-sufficiency might sound appealing, it would actually be better for your country to specialize in the production of some products and then trade some of them to other countries. You saw in Chapter 3 that specialization and exchange can make both parties better off. In this chapter, we use a simple example to explain the benefits of specialization and international trade between two nations.

Let's say there are two nations; each produces computer chips and shirts, and each nation consumes computer chips and shirts. Table 32.1 shows the daily output of the two goods for the two nations, Shirtland and Chipland. In a single day, Shirtland can produce a maximum of either 108 shirts or 36 computer chips, while Chipland can produce a maximum of either 120 shirts or 120 computer chips. The last two rows of the table show the opportunity costs of the two goods. Recall the principle of opportunity cost

Principle OF OPPORTUNITY COST

The opportunity cost of something is what you sacrifice to get it.

	Shirtland	Chipland
Shirts produced per day	108	120
Chips produced per day	36	120
Opportunity cost of shirts	1/3 chip	1 chip
Opportunity cost of chips	3 shirts	1 shirt

In Chipland, there is a one-for-one trade-off of shirts and chips: The opportunity cost of one shirt is one chip, and the opportunity cost of one chip is one shirt. In Shirtland, people can produce three times as many shirts as chips in a given amount of time: The opportunity cost of one chip is three shirts; conversely, the opportunity cost of one shirt is one-third of a chip.

Production Possibilities Curve

Let's start by seeing what happens if each of these nations is self-sufficient. Each nation can use its resources (labor, land, buildings, machinery, equipment) to produce its own shirts and its own chips. The **production possibilities curve** shows all the feasible combinations of the two goods, assuming that the nation's resources are fully employed. This curve, which we discussed in an earlier chapter, provides a sort of menu of production options. To keep things simple, we assume that the curve is a straight line, indicating a constant trade-off between the two goods. As shown by Shirtland's production possibilities curve in Figure 32.1, the following combinations of chips and shirts are possible:

Production possibilities curve

A curve showing the combinations of two goods that can be produced by an economy, assuming that all resources are fully employed.

1 *All shirts and no chips:* point *r*. If Shirtland uses all its resources to produce shirts, it will produce 108 shirts per day.
2 *All chips and no shirts:* point *t*. If Shirtland uses all its resources to produce chips, it will produce 36 chips per day.
3 *Equal division of resources:* point *h*. Shirtland could divide its resources between shirts and chips to produce daily 54 shirts and 18 chips.

All the other points on the line connecting points *r* and *t* are also feasible. One option is point *s*, with 28 chips and 24 shirts. The steepness of the curve's slope—3.0—shows the opportunity cost of computer chips: one chip per three shirts. Figure 32.1 also shows the production possibilities curve for Chipland. Chipland can produce daily 120 shirts and no chips (point *b*), 120 chips and no shirts (point *d*), or any combination of chips and shirts between these two points. In Chipland, the trade-off is one shirt per computer chip: The opportunity cost of a chip is one shirt, so the slope of the production possibilities curve is 1.0.

Each nation could decide to be self-sufficient, picking a point on its production possibilities curve and producing everything it wants to consume. For example, Shirtland could pick point *s*, producing daily 28 chips and 24 shirts, and Chipland

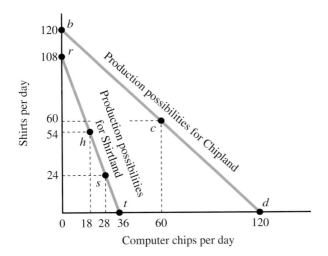

FIGURE 32.1

Production Possibilities Curve
The production possibilities curve shows the combinations of two goods that can be produced with a nation's resources. For Chipland, there is a one-for-one trade-off between the two goods. For Shirtland, the trade-off is three shirts for every computer chip. In the absence of trade, Shirtland can pick point *s* (28 chips and 24 shirts), and Chipland can pick point *c* (60 chips and 60 shirts).

Shirtland Possibilites

Point	Shirts	Chips
r	108	0
h	54	18
s	24	28
t	0	36

Chipland Possibilities

Point	Shirts	Chips
b	120	0
c	60	60
d	0	120

could pick point *c*, producing daily 60 chips and 60 shirts. In the language of international trade, this is a case of **autarky**, or self-sufficiency (in Greek, *aut* means "self" and *arke* means "to suffice").

Autarky
A situation in which each country is self-sufficient, so there is no trade.

Comparative Advantage and the Terms of Trade

Would the two nations be better off if each nation specialized in the production of one good and traded with the other nation? To decide which nation should produce a particular good, we need to look at each good and figure out which nation has the lower opportunity cost of producing it. As you saw in Chapter 3, the nation with the lower opportunity cost has a **comparative advantage** in producing that good. As we emphasized in Chapter 3, it is comparative advantage that matters for trade—not **absolute advantage**, the ability of a nation to produce a particular good at a lower absolute cost than that of another nation. Let's see how it works.

Comparative advantage
The ability of one person or nation to produce a good at an opportunity cost that is lower than the opportunity cost of another person or nation.

1 *Chips produced in Chipland.* The opportunity cost of one chip is one shirt in Chipland, and the opportunity cost of one chip is three shirts in Shirtland. Chipland has a comparative advantage in the production of chips. Because Chipland sacrifices fewer shirts to produce one chip, Chipland should produce chips.

Absolute advantage
The ability of one person or nation to produce a good at a lower absolute cost than another person or nation.

2 *Shirts produced in Shirtland.* The opportunity cost of one shirt is one chip i Chipland, and the opportunity cost of one shirt is 1/3 of a chip in Shirtland. Whe it comes to producing shirts, Shirtland has a comparative advantage because it sac rifices fewer chips to produce one shirt. Shirtland should therefore produce shirts

Trade will make it possible for people in each specialized nation to consume bot goods. At what rate will the two nations exchange shirts and chips? To determine th **terms of trade**, let's look at how much Shirtland is willing to pay to get one chip an how much Chipland is willing to accept to give up one chip.

1 To get one chip, Shirtland is willing to pay up to three shirts. That's how man shirts it would sacrifice if it produced its own chip. For example, if the nation agree to exchange two shirts per chip, Shirtland could rearrange its production producing one less chip but three more shirts. After exchanging two of the newl produced shirts for one chip, Shirtland will have the same number of chips bu one additional shirt.

2 To give up one chip, Chipland is willing to accept any amount greater than on shirt. For example, if the nations agree to exchange two shirts per chip, Chiplan could rearrange its production, producing one more chip and one less shirt. Afte it exchanges the newly produced chip for two shirts, Chipland will have the sam number of chips but one additional shirt.

There's an opportunity for mutually beneficial trade to take place between the two countries because the willingness to pay—three shirts by Shirtland—exceeds the will ingness to accept—one shirt by Chipland. It's possible for Shirtland and Chipland t split the difference between the willingness to pay and the willingness to accept exchanging two shirts per chip. This will actually make both countries better off i terms of the total amount of goods they can consume. We'll see why next.

The Consumption Possibilities Curve

A nation that decides to specialize and trade is no longer limited to the options show by its own production possibilities curve. The **consumption possibilities curve** shows the combinations of two goods (computer chips and shirts in our example) tha a nation can consume when it specializes in one good and trades with another nation

Figure 32.2 shows the consumption possibilities curve for our two nations, assum ing that they exchange two shirts per chip.

▶ In Panel A, Chipland specializes in chip production, the good for which it has comparative advantage. It produces 120 chips and no shirts (point *d*). Given th terms of trade, Chipland can exchange 40 of its 120 chips for 80 shirts, leading t point *x*. At point *x*, Chipland can consume 80 chips and 80 shirts.

▶ In Panel B, Shirtland specializes in shirts production. It produces 108 shirts and n chips (point *r*). Given the terms of trade, it can exchange 80 shirts of its 108 shirt for 40 chips, leading to point *y* on its consumption possibilities curve. Shirtland ca consume 28 shirts and 40 ships.

Terms of trade

The rate at which two goods will be exchanged.

Consumption possibilities curve

A curve showing the combinations of two goods that can be consumed when a nation specializes in a particular good and trades with another nation.

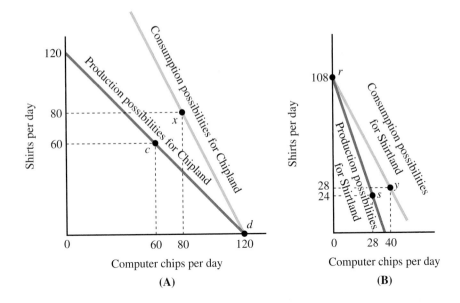

FIGURE 32.2

Consumption Possibilities Curve
The consumption possibilities curve shows the combinations of computer chips and shirts that can be consumed if each country specializes and trades. In Panel A, Chipland produces 120 chips and trades 40 of these chips to Shirtland for 80 shirts. In Panel B, Shirtland produces 108 shirts and trades 80 of these shirts to Chipland for 40 chips. The trade allows each nation to consume more.

How do the outcomes with specialization and trade compare to the autarky outcomes? Chipland moves from point *c* (autarky) to point *x*, so trade increases the consumption of each good by 20 units. Shirtland moves from point *s* to point *y*, so this nation consumes 12 additional chips and 4 additional shirts.

In Figure 32.2, each consumption possibilities curve lies above the nation's production possibilities curves, meaning that each nation has more options about how much to consume under specialization and trade. In most cases, a nation picks a point on the consumption possibilities curve that provides more of each good. Of course, this is a very simple example. In the actual world market, there are many countries producing and trading many goods. The marketplace determines what the terms of those trades will be depending upon supply, demand, and pricing.

The Employment Effects of Free Trade

You've now seen that trade allows each nation to consume more of each good. But we haven't yet discussed the effects of trade on employment. Under free trade, each nation will begin to specialize in a single good, causing considerable changes in the country's employment in different industries. In Chipland, the chip industry doubles in size—output increases from 60 to 120 chips per day—while the shirt industry disappears. Workers and other resources will leave the shirt industry and move to the chip industry. In Shirtland, the flow is in the opposite direction: Workers and other resources move from the chip industry to the shirt industry.

Is free trade good for everyone? Switching from self-sufficiency to specialization and trade increases consumption in both nations, so on average, people in each nation benefit from free trade. But some people in both nations will be harmed by free trade. In Chipland, for example, people in the shirt industry will lose their jobs when the shirt industry disappears. Some workers can easily move into the expanding computer-chip industry; for these workers, free trade is likely to be beneficial. However, other shirt workers will be unable to make the move to the chip industry; they will be forced to accept lower-paying jobs or face unemployment. Free trade is likely to make these displaced workers worse off.

There is a saying, "Where you stand on an issue depends on where you sit." In our example, a worker sitting at a sewing machine in Chipland is likely to oppose free trade because that worker is likely to lose a job. A worker sitting at a workstation in a computer-chip fabrication facility is likely to support free trade because the resulting increase in computer-chip exports will generate more employment opportunities in that industry.

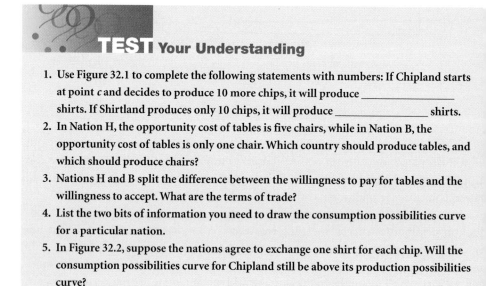

TEST Your Understanding

1. Use Figure 32.1 to complete the following statements with numbers: If Chipland starts at point *c* and decides to produce 10 more chips, it will produce _____ shirts. If Shirtland produces only 10 chips, it will produce _____ shirts.
2. In Nation H, the opportunity cost of tables is five chairs, while in Nation B, the opportunity cost of tables is only one chair. Which country should produce tables, and which should produce chairs?
3. Nations H and B split the difference between the willingness to pay for tables and the willingness to accept. What are the terms of trade?
4. List the two bits of information you need to draw the consumption possibilities curve for a particular nation.
5. In Figure 32.2, suppose the nations agree to exchange one shirt for each chip. Will the consumption possibilities curve for Chipland still be above its production possibilities curve?

Protectionist Policies

Now that you know the basic rationale for specialization and trade, we can explore the effects of public policies that restrict it. All the restrictions we explore limit the gains from specialization and trade. We will consider four common import-restriction policies: an outright ban on imports, an import quota, voluntary export restraints, and a tariff.

Import Ban

To show how an import ban affects the market, let's start with an unrestricted market—no import ban. Figure 32.3 shows the market for shirts in Chipland, a nation with a comparative advantage in producing computer chips, not shirts. The domestic supply curve shows the quantity of shirts supplied by firms in Chipland. Looking at point *m*, we see that Chipland firms will not supply any shirts unless the price is at least

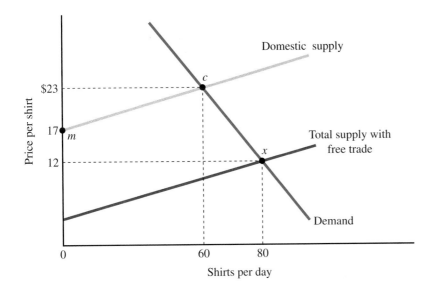

FIGURE 32.3

Effects of an Import Ban
In the free-trade equilibrium, demand intersects the total supply curve at point *x*, with a price of $12 and a quantity of 80 shirts. If shirt imports are banned, the equilibrium is shown by the intersection of the demand curve and the domestic supply curve (point *c*). The price increases to $23.

$17 per shirt. The total supply curve for shirts, which shows the quantity supplied by both domestic firms and foreign firms (in Shirtland), lies to the right of the domestic supply curve. At each price, the total supply of shirts exceeds the domestic supply because foreign firms supply shirts too. Point *x* shows the free-trade equilibrium: The demand curve from domestic residents intersects the total supply curve at a price of $12 per shirt and a quantity of 80 shirts. Because this price is below the minimum price for domestic firms, domestic firms produce no shirts, and all the shirts in Chipland are imported from Shirtland.

What will happen if Chipland bans imported shirts? Foreign suppliers will disappear from the shirt market, so the total supply of shirts will be the domestic supply. In Figure 32.3, point *c* shows the equilibrium when Chipland bans imported shirts: The domestic demand curve intersects the domestic supply curve at a price of $23 per shirt and a quantity of 60 shirts. In other words, the decrease in supply resulting from the import ban increases the price consumers have to pay for shirts and decreases the quantity available for them to buy.

Quotas and Voluntary Export Restraints

An alternative to an import ban is an import quota—a limit on the amount of a good that can be imported. An import quota is a restrictive policy that falls between free trade and an outright ban: Imports are cut but not eliminated. For example, if a quota were put on shirts, the price consumers would have to pay would fall somewhere between the price they would pay with free trade ($12 per shirt, as in our example) and the price they would pay if imported shirts were banned ($23 per shirt). Where exactly the price would fall would depend on how high or low the quotas are.

Import quotas are illegal under international trading rules. To get around these rules, an exporting country will sometimes agree to a **voluntary export restraint (VER)**. A VER is similar to an import ban. When an exporting nation adopts a VER, it

Voluntary export restraint (VER)

A scheme under which an exporting country voluntarily decreases its exports.

OneKey
OneKey is
all you need

Import quota

A limit on the amount of a good that can be imported.

Import licenses

Rights, issued by a government, to import goods.

cuts its exports to avoid having to face even more restrictive trade policies importing countries might be tempted to impose on them. Although VERs are legal under world trading rules, they violate the spirit of international free-trade agreements. In any case quotas and VERs have the same effect. Like a quota, a VER increases the price of the restricted good, making it more feasible for domestic firms to participate in the market.

Figure 32.4 shows the effect of an **import quota** or VER. Starting from the free trade equilibrium at point *x*, an import quota will shift the total supply curve to the left: At each price there will be a smaller quantity of shirts supplied because foreign suppliers aren't allowed to supply as many. The total supply curve when there is an import quota or VER will lie between the domestic supply curve and the total supply curve under free trade. The equilibrium under an import quota or VER occurs at point *q*, where the demand curve intersects the total supply curve under an import limitation. The $20 price per shirt with the import quota exceeds the $17 minimum price of domestic firms, so domestic firms supply 22 shirts (point *e*). Under a free-trade policy they would have supplied no shirts.

A quota or a VER produces winners and losers. The winners include foreign and domestic shirt producers. In our example, foreign firms can sell shirts at a price of $20 instead of $12 each, and the price is high enough for domestic firms to participate in the market. This generates benefits for the firms and their workers. The losers are consumers, who pay a higher price for shirts. In some cases, the government issues **import licenses** to some citizens, who can then buy shirts from foreign firms at a low price such as $12, and sell the shirts at the higher domestic price, $20. Since import licenses provide profits to the holder, they are often awarded to politically powerful firms or individuals; moreover, since they are so valuable, there is the risk that government officials may be paid bribes for the licenses.

We know that consumers pay higher prices for goods that are subject to protectionist policies, but how much more? Here is one example. In the United States, voluntary export restraints on Japanese automobiles in 1984 increased the price of a Japanese car by about $1,300 and the price of a domestic car by about $660.[1]

FIGURE 32.4

Market Effects of a Quota, a VER, or a Tariff

An import quota shifts the supply curve to the left. The market moves upward along the demand curve to point *q*, which is between point *x* (free trade) and *c* (an import ban). We can reach the same point with a tariff that shifts the total supply curve to the same position.

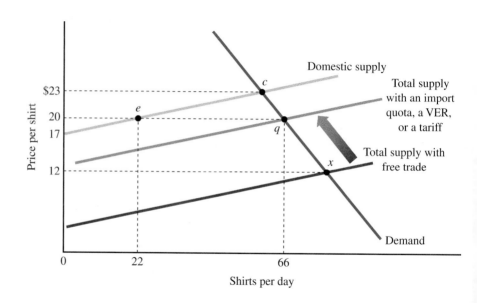

Tariffs

An alternative to a quota or a VER is an import **tariff**, which is a tax on an imported good. Tariffs have the same effect as quotas and VERs. We know from our earlier discussions that a tax shifts the supply curve to the left and increases the equilibrium price. In Figure 32.4, suppose the tariff shifts the total supply curve with free trade so that it intersects the domestic demand curve at point *q*. In other words, we reach the same point we reached with the quota: Consumers pay the same $20 price per shirt, and domestic firms produce the same quantity: 22 shirts.

There is one fundamental difference between a quota and a tariff. An import quota allows importers to buy shirts from foreign suppliers at a low price—say, $12 per shirt—and sell them for $20 each, the artificially high price. In other words, importers make money from the quota. Under a tariff, the government gets the money, collecting $8 per shirt from foreign suppliers. Citizens in Chipland will prefer the tariff to the quota because the government can use the revenue from the tariff to cut other taxes or expand public programs.

In the real world, tariffs can have major effects. One trade expert estimated that cutting industrial tariffs by 50% would increase the output of the world's economy by $270 billion per year. Similar easing of restrictions on agricultural products would cut the world's food bill by $100 billion.[2]

> **Tariff**
> A tax on an imported good.

Responses to Protectionist Policies

A restriction on imports is likely to lead to further restrictions on trade. For example, if Chipland bans shirt imports, the shirt industry in Shirtland might retaliate by banning computer chips from Chipland. A trade war of this sort could escalate to the point where the two nations return to self-sufficiency. If this happens, the two countries

At times countries will try to restrict imports through tariffs, quotas, or voluntary export restraints. Automobile imports have been subject to voluntary export restraints.

would be forced to scale back their consumption. We can see that by looking back at Figure 32.2: Chipland will move from point *x* to point *c*, and Shirtland will move from point *y* to point *s*. This sort of retaliatory response is common. Because it is, we know that protecting one industry in a nation is likely to harm that nation's other exports. Chipland's shirt industry, if protected from imports, may grow, but it will be at the expense of its computer-chip industry.

There are many examples of import restrictions that have led to retaliatory policies and substantially lessened trade. The most famous was the Smoot–Hawley tariff of 1930. When the United States increased its average tariff on imports to 59%, its trading partners retaliated with higher tariffs on U.S. products. The resulting trade war reduced international trade and deepened the worldwide depression of the 1930s.

The threat of retaliatory policies may persuade a nation to loosen its protectionist policies. For example, in 1995, the United States announced that it would impose 100% tariffs on Japanese luxury cars if Japan didn't ease its restrictions on imported auto parts. Just hours before the tariffs were to take effect, the two nations reached an agreement that was expected to increase the sales of U.S. auto parts to Japanese firms. In 2002, President Bush imposed tariffs on steel. However, when faced with the threat of retaliatory policies in Europe, he ended the sanctions in 2003.

Import restrictions also create an incentive to smuggle goods. The restrictions create a gap between the cost of purchasing the restricted goods abroad and the price goods can be sold for in the protected economy, so there is a profit to be made.

TEST Your Understanding

6. Complete the following statement: If a country bans the importation of a particular good, the market equilibrium is shown by the intersection of the _____ curve and the _____ curve.
7. Complete the statement with "above" or "below." The equilibrium price under an import quota is _____ the price that occurs with an import ban and _____ the price that occurs with free trade.
8. From the perspective of consumers, which is better, a tariff or a quota?
9. In Figure 32.4, what fraction of the shirt market is supplied by domestic firms under a quota system?

Rationales for Protectionist Policies

Why would a government impose protectionist policies like an import ban, quota, VER, or tariff? There are three possible reasons:

1 To shield workers from foreign competition
2 To nurture infant industries until they mature
3 To help domestic firms establish monopolies in world markets

To Shield Workers from Foreign Competition

One of the most basic arguments for protectionism is that it shields workers in industries that would be hurt by trade. Suppose that relative to the United States, nations in the Far East have a comparative advantage in producing textiles. If the United States were to reduce existing tariffs on textiles, domestic manufacturers could not compete. They would have to close their factories and lay off workers. In an ideal world, the laid-off workers would take new jobs in other sectors of the economy. In practice, this is difficult. Many workers don't immediately have the skills to go to work in other sectors, and obtaining these skills takes time. Moreover, the textile industry is heavily concentrated in the southeastern part of the United States. Politicians from that region will try to keep tariffs in place to prevent the temporary unemployment and changes in employment patterns in their areas—they have an incentive to protect their own constituents, even though it may cause major economic losses for the economy. The result of this protection will be less-efficient production, higher prices, and lower consumption for the United States. How much does it cost to protect a job? "A Closer Look: The Cost of Protecting Jobs" presents some recent evidence.

To Nurture Infant Industries

During World War II, the United States built hundreds of boats, called Liberty ships, for the Navy. As more and more of these ships were built, each required fewer hours to complete because workers acquired knowledge during the production process and got better at it. Engineers and economists call this phenomenon **learning by doing**. To

Learning by doing
Knowledge gained during production that increases productivity.

A CLOSER LOOK

The Cost of Protecting Jobs

The Federal Reserve Bank of Dallas recently examined the cost the United States paid to protect jobs in 20 different industries. Below are the top five industries in terms of costs per job saved:

Protected Industry	Jobs Saved	Annual Cost per Job Saved
Benzenoid chemicals	216	$1,376,436
Luggage	226	1,285,078
Softwood lumber	605	1,044,271
Sugar	2,261	826,104
Polyethylene resins	298	812,928

The annual costs of saving a job in these industries is staggering—in three of these cases it is over a million dollars a year! In other industries, the costs per job may be a bit lower, but the total cost to the economy is much higher because the number of jobs saved is much greater. In textiles and apparels, the annual cost per job is "only" $199,241, but the total cost of protecting this industry is $33.6 billion a year.

Source: Federal Reserve Bank of Dallas, *Annual Report 2002*, p. 19.

Protection for Candle Makers

In response to the spread of protectionism, the French economist Frédéric Bastiat (1801–1851) wrote the following fictitious petition, in which French candle makers asked for protection from "unfair" competition:

We are suffering from the intolerable competition of a foreign rival, placed, it would seem, in a condition so far superior to ours for the production of light, that he absolutely inundates our national market at a price fabulously reduced. The moment he shows himself, our trade leaves us—all of our customers apply to him; and a branch of native industry, having countless ramifications, is all at once rendered completely stagnant. This rival . . . is none other than the sun.

What we pray for is, that it may please you to pass a law ordering the shutting up of all windows, sky-lights, dormer windows, curtains, blinds, bull's eyes; in a word all openings, holes, chinks, clefts, and fissures, by or through which the light of the sun has been in use to enter houses, to the prejudice of the meritorious manufactures with which we . . . have accommodated our country—a country which, in gratitude, ought not to abandon us now.

Does it not argue to the greatest inconsistency to check as you do the importation of coal, iron, cheese, and goods of foreign manufacture, merely because . . . their price approaches zero, while at the same time you freely admit, and without limitation, the light of the sun, whose price is during the whole day at zero?

Source: Frédéric Bastiat, *Economics Sophisms* (Edinburgh: Oliver & Boyd, 1873), pp. 49–53.

learn a new game, such as Ping-Pong, you learn by doing. At first, you may find it difficult to play, but your skills improve as you go along.

Tariffs and other protectionist policies are often defended on the grounds that they protect new or **infant industries** that are in the early stages of learning by doing. A tariff shields a young industry from the competition of its more mature rivals. After the infant industry "grows up," the tariff can eventually be eliminated because the industry is able to compete. In practice, infant industries rarely become competitive with their foreign rivals. During the 1950s and 1960s, many Latin American countries used tariffs and other policies to protect their young manufacturing industries from foreign competition. Unfortunately, the domestic industries never became as efficient as foreign suppliers, and the Latin American countries that tried this policy suffered. Another problem with protecting an infant industry is that once an industry is given tariff protection, it is difficult to take it away. For an interesting discussion of the merits of protecting an industry from "unfair" competition, read "A Closer Look: Protection for Candle Makers."

Infant industries

Industries that are at an early stage of development.

To Help Domestic Firms Establish Monopolies in World Markets

If the production of a particular good requires extremely large economies of scale, the world market will support only a few, or perhaps just one, firm. In this case, a nation might be tempted to adopt policies to ensure a company within its borders will end up eing the world monopolist. Suppose the commercial aircraft industry can support only one large firm; if two firms enter the industry, both will lose money. A nation ould agree to provide financial support to a domestic firm to guarantee that the firm will make a profit. With such a guarantee, the domestic firm will enter the industry. Knowing this, a foreign firm will be reluctant to enter, so the domestic firm will capture the monopoly profit. The country the successful firm is located in will benefit rom higher production and more jobs for its citizens.

One famous example of this is the case of Airbus, an airplane manufacturing consortium in Europe. Several European countries provided large subsidies for the firms producing the Airbus brand of planes. These subsidies allowed the firms associated with Airbus to underprice some of their rivals in the United States, and at least one U.S. manufacturer of commercial airplanes was forced out of business.

What could go wrong with these monopoly-creation policies? If both nations subsidize their domestic firms, both firms will enter the market and lose money. The taxpayers in both countries will then have to pay for the subsidies. And there is the possibility a nation may pick the wrong industry to subsidize. Together, the British and French subsidized an airplane known as the Concorde, which flew at supersonic speeds, rapidly shuttling passengers between Europe and the United States. Although the Concorde captured the market, the market was not worth capturing. The venture lost money because the Concorde was very costly to develop and fly and few people were willing to pay a large premium for supersonic travel. The Concorde stopped flying in 2003.

TEST Your Understanding

10. Comment on the following statement: If we eliminated our textile tariffs, the dislocated workers could easily switch to other jobs.
11. Explain the infant-industry argument.
12. List the two problems associated with subsidizing an industry in the hope of establishing a worldwide monopoly.

A Brief History of International Tariff and Trade Agreements

Since 1980, the average U.S. tariff has been about 5% of the value of imported goods, a rate that is close to the average tariffs in Japan and most European nations but very low by historical standards. As we noted earlier, when the Smoot–Hawley tariffs were implemented in the 1930s, the average U.S. tariff was a whopping 59% of a product's price. Tariffs are lower today because several international agreements subsequently reduced them.

The first major trade agreement following World War II was the **General Agreement on Tariffs and Trade (GATT)**. This agreement was initiated in 1947 by the United States and 23 other nations and now has over 146 member nations. There

General Agreement on Tariffs and Trade (GATT)

An international agreement that has lowered trade barriers between the United States and other nations.

World Trade Organization (WTO)

An organization that oversees GATT and other international trade agreements.

have been nine rounds of GATT negotiations over tariffs and trade regulations resulting in progressively lower tariffs for the member nations. The last completed set of negotiations, the Uruguay round (1994), decreased tariffs by about one-third of the previous level. In 1995, the **World Trade Organization (WTO)** was formed to enforce GATT and other international trade agreements. Under GATT's "most favored nation" provision, a country that reduces tariffs for one nation must do so for all members of GATT. This provision helps reduce tariffs throughout the world.

A new round of trade negotiations began in Doha, Qatar in 2001. In these negotiations, the member countries set an ambitious agenda, including cutting the protections for agricultural and service products. The Qatar round focused on giving a large share of the benefits gained from trade liberalization to developing countries, who felt that they did not gain as much in the previous round compared to the developed countries.

In addition to the large group of nations involved in the WTO, other nations have formed trade associations to lower trade barriers and promote international trade. Here are some of the most well-known agreements:

▶ The North American Free Trade Agreement (NAFTA) took effect in 1994 and will be implemented over a 15-year period. The agreement will eventually eliminate all tariffs and other trade barriers between Canada, Mexico, and the United States.
▶ The European Union (EU) was designed to remove all trade barriers within Europe and create a single market. Initially, the EU consisted of just six countries: Belgium, Germany, France, Italy, Luxembourg, and the Netherlands. Denmark, Ireland, and the United Kingdom joined in 1973; Greece in 1981; Spain and Portugal in 1986; and Austria, Finland, and Sweden in 1995. In 2004, the biggest ever enlargement took place with 10 new countries joining the EU.
▶ The leaders of 18 Asian nations have formed an organization called Asian Pacific Economic Cooperation (APEC). In 1994, APEC signed a nonbinding agreement to reduce trade barriers among these nations.

Some economists are concerned that these regional trade agreements may stand in the way of broader international trade agreements under GATT. Although regional agreements may lead to reduced tariffs for neighboring, or member, countries, they do little to promote efficiency across the globe. For example, a Belgian firm may find it easier to sell goods into France than a firm from South America that has a lower cost of production.

Recent Policy Debates and Trade Agreements

We're now ready to discuss three recent policy debates concerning international trade:

1 Are foreign producers dumping their products?
2 Do trade laws inhibit environmental protection?
3 Does trade cause income inequality?

Are Foreign Producers Dumping Their Products?

Although tariff rates have been reduced in recent years, a number of controversies surrounding free trade remain. One of these controversies relates to **dumping**. A firm is dumping when the price it charges in a foreign market is either lower than the price it charges in its home market or lower than its production cost. Dumping is illegal under international trade agreements; hundreds of cases of alleged dumping are presented to WTO authorities each year. Here are some recent cases in which the WTO concluded that dumping had occurred: Hong Kong VCRs sold in Europe; Chinese bicycles sold in the United States; Asian TV sets sold in Europe; steel from Brazil, India, Japan, and Spain sold in the United States; U.S. beef sold in Mexico; and Chinese computer disks sold in Japan and the United States. Under the current provisions of the WTO, a nation can impose antidumping duties on products that are being dumped within its borders.

Why would a firm dump—charge a low price in the foreign market? The first reason is price discrimination. **Price discrimination** occurs when a firm charges a different price to different customers buying the same product. If a firm has a monopoly in its home market but faces strong competition in a foreign market, it will naturally charge a higher price in the home market. What the firm is doing is using its monopoly power to charge higher prices to consumers at home and charge lower prices to consumers abroad where it faces competition. This strategy maximizes its profits.

To illustrate how international price discrimination works, let's look at the case of Korean VCRs.[3] In the 1980s there were only three firms, all Korean, selling VCRs in Korea, but there were dozens of firms selling VCRs in Europe. The lack of competition in Korea generated very high prices for Korean consumers: They paid much more than European consumers paid for identical Korean VCRs and VCRs produced by firms in other countries. Essentially, Korean firms used their market power to discriminate against consumers in their own country. When international trade authorities concluded these companies were, indeed, dumping VCRs in Europe, the Korean firms responded by cutting prices in their home market. However, they didn't increase their prices in Europe— much to the delight of European consumers and the dismay of European producers, who had sought relief from the dumping in the first place.

This brings up a second reason for dumping: **predatory pricing**—cutting prices in an attempt to drive rival firms out of business. The predatory firm sets its price below its production cost. The price is low enough that both the predator and its prey (a firm in the foreign market) lose money. After the prey goes out of business, the predator increases its price to earn a monopoly profit.

Although the rationale for antidumping laws is to prevent predatory pricing, it is difficult to determine whether low prices are the result of this or price discrimination. Many economists are skeptical about how frequently predatory pricing actually occurs versus price discrimination; they suspect that many nations use their antidumping laws as protectionist policies in disguise. Because WTO rules limit tariffs and quotas, some nations may be tempted to substitute antidumping duties for these protectionist policies.

Until the 1990s, antidumping cases were brought almost exclusively by Australia, New Zealand, Europe, Canada, and the United States. However, starting in the 1990s,

Dumping
A situation in which the price a firm charges in a foreign market is lower than either the price it charges in its home market or the production cost.

Price discrimination
The process under which a firm divides consumers into two or more groups and picks a different price for each group.

Predatory pricing
A pricing scheme under which a firm decreases its price to drive a rival out of business, and increases the price when the other firm disappears.

the number of antidumping cases alleged by developing countries began to rise. Today, approximately half of the cases are brought by developing countries. Professor Thomas Prusa of Rutgers University has studied antidumping and found that it is a potent weapon for protecting domestic industries. If an antidumping case is settled and a tariff is imposed as a result, imports typically fall by 50% to 70% during the first three years of the protection period. Even if a country loses a claim, imports still fall by 15% to 20%.[4]

Do Trade Laws Inhibit Environmental Protection?

In recent trade negotiations, a new player—environmental groups—appeared on the scene. Starting in the early 1990s, environmentalists began to question whether policies that liberalized trade could harm the environment. They were concerned whether increased trade would lead to world-wide environmental degradation. An important issue that attracted their attention was the killing of dolphins by tuna fishers.

Anyone who catches tuna with a large net will also catch the dolphins that swim with the tuna, and most of the dolphins will die. In 1972, the United States outlawed the use of tuna nets by U.S. ships. However, ships from other nations, including Mexico, were still catching tuna with nets and selling that tuna in the United States. The United States responded with a boycott of Mexican tuna caught with nets. The Mexican government complained to an international trade authority that the tuna boycott was an unfair trade barrier. The trade authority agreed with Mexico and forced the United States to remove the boycott.

Under current WTO rules, a country can adopt any environmental standard it chooses, as long as it does not discriminate against foreign producers. For example, the United States can limit the exhaust emissions of all cars that operate in the United States. As long as emissions rules apply equally to all cars, domestic and imports, the rules are legal according to the WTO. An international panel upheld U.S. fuel efficiency rules for automobiles on this principle.

The tuna boycott was a violation of WTO rules because killing dolphins does not harm the U.S. environment directly. For the same reason, the United States cannot ban imported goods produced by factories that generate air or water pollution in other countries. It is easy to understand why WTO rules do not allow countries to restrict trade on the basis of the methods that are used to produce goods and services. Countries differ in the value they place on the environment. For example, a poor nation may be willing to tolerate more pollution if it means attaining a higher standard of living for its citizens.

If trade restrictions cannot be used to protect the dolphins and deal with other global environmental problems, what else can we do? International agreements have been used for a variety of different environmental goals, from limiting the harvest of whales to reducing the chemicals that deplete the ozone layer. These agreements are difficult to reach, however, so some nations will be tempted to use trade restrictions to pursue environmental goals. If they do, they will encounter resistance because WTO rules mean that a nation can pursue its environmental goals only within its own borders.

The ban by the European Union of hormone-treated beef is one example of how environmental and health concerns can affect international trade.

Trade disputes about environmental issues are part of a larger phenomenon that occurs when trade issues and national regulations collide. At one time, most trade disputes were simply matters of protecting domestic industries from foreign competition. Agriculture, textile, and steel industries around the world frequently benefited from various forms of protection. But in recent years, a new breed of trade disputes has erupted revolving around social problems and the role of government regulation should play in solving them.

The European Union, for example, has banned imports of hormone-treated beef. The United States and Canada successfully challenged this ban with the WTO. They argued that there was no scientific evidence that concluded hormone-treated beef adversely affected human health. The European Union refused to rescind the ban and, as a consequence, the United States and Canada were permitted to impose tariffs on a wide range of European products that affected many of its industries.

The European Union's ban on hormone-treated beef was intended to protect European farmers from imports, but it also reflected the nervousness of Europeans about technology. After all, Europe banned all hormone-treated beef, not just imported beef. Shouldn't a country have a right to pursue this policy, even if it is not based on the best science of the day? Although the costs of the policy are straightforward in terms of higher beef prices, the benefits, in terms of potential safety and peace of mind, are much more difficult to assess. Similar issues will arise as genetically modified crops become more commonplace. As a world trading community, we will have to decide at what point we allow national policy concerns to override principles of free trade.

Does Trade Cause Inequality?

Inequality in wages has been growing in the United States since 1973. The wages of skilled workers have risen faster than the wages of unskilled workers. World trade has also boomed since 1973. Could there be a connection between the two?

Trade theory suggests a link between increased trade and increased wage inequality. Here is how they might be linked. Suppose the United States produces two types of goods: one using skilled labor (say, airplanes) and one using unskilled labor (say, textiles). The United States is likely to have a comparative advantage in products that use skilled labor, and developing countries are likely to have a comparative advantage in products that use unskilled labor. An increase in world trade will increase both exports and imports. An increase in U.S. exports means we'll need to produce more goods requiring skilled labor, so the domestic demand for skilled labor will increase and so will the wages of these workers. At the same time, an increase in U.S. imports means that we'll be buying more goods produced by unskilled laborers abroad, so the demand for unskilled workers here will decrease, and these people's wages will fall. As a result, the gap between the wages of the two types of workers in the United States will increase.

Economists have tried to determine how much trade has contributed to growing wage inequality in the United States. As usual, there are other factors that make such a determination difficult. It is difficult, for example, to distinguish between the effects of trade and the effects of technical progress. Technical change, such as the rapid introduction and use of computers, will also tend to increase the demand for skilled workers and decrease the demand for unskilled workers. Economists have noted, however, that the exports of goods using skilled labor and the imports of goods using unskilled labor have both increased, just as the theory predicts. Nonetheless, at least some of the increased wage inequality is caused by international trade.

One response to this undesirable side effect of trade is to use trade restrictions to protect industries that use unskilled workers. Another approach is to make the transition to an economy with more skilled than unskilled jobs less traumatic. In the long run, of course, workers will move to industries that require skilled labor, and they will eventually earn higher wages. However, in the short run the government could facilitate the transition by providing assistance for their education and training.

Why Do People Protest Against Free Trade?

We have seen that there are important policy issues surrounding trade. Under current international trade rules, a country cannot dictate the terms under which another country actually produces the goods and services that it sells—even if it harms the environment. It is also possible that free trade can contribute to inequality within the United States. But do these reasons explain the passion we sometimes see in protests against free trade, such as the riots in 1999 in Seattle at a WTO meeting or the protestors dressed in death masks gathering at world trade meetings?

Possibly, but it is more likely that the protestors are driven by something more basic. As we have seen in this chapter, trade and specialization provide important

In recent years, the World Trade Organization has generated considerable political controversy in the United States and abroad.

opportunities to raise living standards throughout the globe. But they also mean that individuals and nations surrender some of their independence and sovereignty. By not producing precisely what we consume, we become dependent on others to trade. By cooperating with other nations, we need to develop agreed-upon rules that, at times, limit our own actions.

The protestors may simply not understand the principles of trade, but they also may be subconsciously reacting against a perceived loss in independence and control. But in today's world, "no man is an island." Nations have become increasingly dependent on one another. Multinational corporations are the ultimate symbol of this interdependence, producing and distributing goods on a global scale. As symbols, companies like McDonald's or Nike can come under attack by the protestors. The benefits of trade, however, are so vast that countries will need to find ways to address issues of sovereignty and control while retaining an open and prosperous trading system.

TEST Your Understanding

13. What is dumping?
14. What restrictions do WTO rules place on a nation's environmental policies?
15. Consider a nation having a comparative advantage in the production of goods using unskilled labor. What types of workers will benefit from increased trade, and what types of workers will lose?

Economic Experiment

Protectionist Policies

Recall the market equilibrium experiment from Chapter 4. We can modify the experiment to show the effects of protectionist policies on equilibrium prices and quantities. On the supply side of the market, there are domestic apple producers and foreign apple pro-ducers; the domestic producers have higher unit costs. After several trading periods without any government intervention, you can change the rules as follows:

a. Apple imports are banned: Foreign producers can-not participate in the market.

b. There is a tariff (a tax on imports) of $5 per bushel. ●

USING THE TOOLS

In this chapter, we've discussed the trade-offs associated with protectionist policies and have used supply and demand curves to show the market effects of protectionist policies. Here are some opportunities to do your own economic analysis.

1. Incentives for Smuggling

If a country bans imports, smugglers may try to penetrate its markets. Suppose Chipland bans shirt imports, causing some importers to bribe customs officials, who "look the other way" as smugglers bring shirts into the country. Your job is to combat shirt smuggling. Use the information in Figure 32.3 in this chapter to answer the following questions:

a. Suppose importers can sell their shirts on the world market at a price of $12 per shirt. How much is an importer willing to pay to get customs officials to look the other way?

b. What sort of change in trade policy would make your job easier?

2. Trade in Genetically Modified Crops

Suppose the residents of a country become fearful of using genetically modified crops in their food supply. Consider the following two possible scenarios:

a. Aware of consumer sentiment, the largest supermarket chains in the country vow they will not purchase food products that use genetically modified crops.

b. The government, aware of voter sentiment during an election year, bans the import of the food products that use genetically modified crops.

In both cases, no genetically modified crops enter the country. Do either of these cases run afoul of WTO policies?

3. Ban on Shoe Imports

Consider a country that initially consumes 100 pairs of shoes per hour, all of which are imported. The price of shoes is $40 per pair before the ban. Depict graphically the market effects of the ban.

4. Tariffs on Steel Imports

When the United States placed a tariff on steel imports in 2002, foreign producers naturally complained. But there were also complaints from U.S. firms operating in other industries. Why would other types of firms strongly object to the tariffs on U.S. steel imports?

SUMMARY

In this chapter, we discussed the benefits of specialization and trade, and we explored the trade-offs associated with protectionist policies. There is a basic conflict between consumers, who prefer free trade because free trade decreases prices, and workers in the protected industries, who want to keep their jobs. Here are the main points of the chapter:

1 If one country has a comparative advantage vis-à-vis another country in producing a particular good (a lower opportunity cost), specialization and trade will benefit both countries.

2 An import ban or an import quota increases prices, protecting domestic industries, but domestic consumers pay the price.

3 Because the victims of protectionist policies often retaliate, the protection of a domestic industry can harm an exporting industry.

4 A tariff (tax on imports) generates revenue for the government, whereas an import quota—a limit on imports—generates revenue for foreigners or importers.

5 In principle, the laws against dumping are designed to prevent predatory pricing. In practice, predatory pricing laws are often used to shield domestic industries from competition and allegations of it are hard to prove.

6 Under WTO rules, each country may pursue its environmental goals only within its own borders.

7 International trade has contributed to the widening gap between the wages of low-skilled and high-skilled labor.

KEY TERMS

absolute advantage, 731
autarky, 731
comparative advantage, 731
consumption possibilities curve, 732
dumping, 743
General Agreement on Tariffs and
    Trade (GATT), 741

import licenses, 736
import quota, 736
infant industries, 740
learning by doing, 739
predatory pricing, 743
price discrimination, 743
production possibilities curve, 730

tariff, 737
terms of trade, 732
voluntary export restraint (VER),
    735
World Trade Organization (WTO),
    742

PROBLEMS AND DISCUSSION QUESTIONS

1 In one minute, Country B can produce either 1,000 TVs and no computers or 500 computers and no TVs. Similarly, in one minute, Country C can produce either 2,400 TVs or 600 computers.

a. Compute the opportunity costs of TVs and computers for each country. Which country has a comparative advantage in producing TVs? In producing computers?

b. Draw the production possibilities curves for the two countries.

2 In Country U, the opportunity cost of a computer is 10 pairs of shoes. In Country C, the opportunity cost of a computer is 100 pairs of shoes.

a. Suppose the two countries split the difference between the willingness to pay for computers and the willingness to accept computers. Compute the terms of trade, that is, the rate at which the two countries will exchange computers and shoes.

b. Suppose the two countries exchange one computer for the number of shoes dictated by the terms of trade you computed in part (a). Compute the net benefit from trade for each country.

3 In Figure 32.2, suppose the two countries trade 35 computer chips for 70 shirts. For each country, compute the amounts of chips and shirts consumed.

4 Consider two countries, Tableland and Chairland, each capable of producing tables and chairs. Chairland can produce the following combinations of chairs and tables:

▶ All chairs and no tables: 36 chairs per day
▶ All tables and no chairs: 18 tables per day

Tableland can produce the following combinations of chairs and tables:

▶ All chairs and no tables: 40 chairs per day
▶ All tables and no chairs: 40 tables per day

In each country, there is a fixed trade-off of tables for chairs.

a. Draw the two production possibilities curves, with chairs on the vertical axis and tables on the horizontal axis.

b. Suppose that each country is initially self-sufficient and divides its resources equally between the two goods. How much does each country produce and consume?

c. Which country has a comparative advantage in producing tables? Which has a comparative advantage in producing chairs?

d. If the two countries split the difference between the buyer's willingness to pay for chairs and the seller's willingness to accept, in terms of chairs per table, what are the terms of trade?

e. Draw the consumption possibilities curves.

f. Suppose each country specializes in the good for which it has a comparative advantage, and they exchange 14 tables for some quantity of chairs. Compute the consumption bundles—bundles mean the consumption of tables and chairs—for each country.

5 A common approach to restrict automobile imports is to use voluntary export restraints. Evaluate the wisdom of this approach and propose an alternative policy.

6 Evaluate this comment: "If a country bans imports, smuggling is inevitable. We should welcome smuggling because it improves consumer welfare."

7 The European Union is committed to eliminating most of the trade barriers among its member nations. What types of people will benefit? Which types will lose?

8 What is the cost to consumers for each sugar industry job protected by import restrictions? In your opinion, is protecting these jobs worthwhile at this cost? If not, how much should we as a society be willing to pay for each job that is protected?

9 Suppose the president of a nation proposes it switch from a system of import quotas to a system of tariffs, with the idea that the switch will not affect the quantity of goods imported. Who will be in favor of the switch? Who will oppose it? Would you expect the proponents and the opponents to have the same political influence on the president?

10 Suppose residents of one nation are very fearful of biotechnology and they pass a law prohibiting the sale of all genetically altered foods in their country. Another nation, which produces these foods, claims that this law is an unfair trade barrier. In your view, should the first nation be allowed to prevent these imports, even if there is no scientific basis for its claim?

11 Web Exercise. Go to the Website for the World Trade Organization (*http://www.wto.org*) and explore some of the ongoing trade disputes. Pick one or two of these disputes and find additional background information, such as newspaper stories, on the Web. Use this information to understand the nature of the controversy.

12 Web Exercise. Go to the Website for the U.S. Trade Representative (*http://www.ustr.gov*), which is an office within the executive branch of the government. From the Website, what are some of the key trade issues for the U.S. government today?

MODEL ANSWERS TO QUESTIONS

Chapter-Opening Questions

1 The winners are the domestic nation's consumers, who pay lower prices, and the domestic nation's workers in export industries. The losers are people in the domestic nation who lose their jobs as imports replace domestically produced goods.

2 A tariff generates revenue for the government; a quota generates profits for importers.

3 First, if a firm has a monopoly in its home market but faces strong competition in a foreign market, the firm will naturally charge a higher price in the home market (it will price discriminate). Second, a firm may be engaging in predatory pricing—the practice of cutting prices in an attempt to drive rivals out of business.

4 Under current WTO rules, a country cannot adopt any environmental standard that discriminates against foreign producers. For example, the United States cannot impose an import ban on goods that are produced in polluting factories in other nations. This rule means that global environmental issues must be resolved with international agreements, not trade restrictions.

5 Although trade increases income inequality, it is unclear just how much of the recent increase in inequality can be attributed to the expansion of trade.

Test Your Understanding

1 50, 78 (108 − 30).

2 Nation B should produce tables, and Nation H should produce chairs.

3 Three chairs per table: Nation H is willing to pay five chairs, and Nation B is willing to accept one chair.

4 We need to know the maximum output of the good for which the nation has a comparative advantage and the terms of trade.

5 No. The consumption curve will be the same as the production curve.

6 Demand, domestic supply.

7 Below, above.

8 If a quota and a tariff led to the same price for a good, consumers would be indifferent between them. However, as citizens, they should prefer the tariff since the revenue generated goes to the government, which can use it to fund public programs or reduce taxes.

9 Domestic firms supply 22 units, which is one-third of the total equilibrium quantity supplied by the market (66).

10 This is false. Some workers do not have the skills to immediately go to work in other sectors, and it takes time to obtain new skills.

11 It takes some time for a new industry to learn by doing, so it may be sensible to protect a young industry when it is vulnerable to competition from foreign firms. However, in practice this does not work very well.

12 If two nations subsidize firms in the same industry, each nation could lose money. In addition, a nation might pick the wrong industry to subsidize.

13 A foreign firm is dumping when it sells a product in another country at a price below the price it charges in its own market or below its cost. It is difficult to determine whether dumping is occurring, and many countries used dumping laws under the guise of protectionism.

14 A nation's environmental laws must not discriminate against imported goods. The laws must apply equally to imports and domestic goods.

15 The wage of unskilled labor will increase; the wage of skilled labor will decrease.

NOTES

1. *A Review of Recent Developments in the U.S. Automobile Industry Including an Assessment of the Japanese Voluntary Restraint Agreements* (Washington, DC: U.S. International Trade Commission, February 1985).

2. Gary C. Hufbauer, "The Benefits of Open Markets and the Costs of Trade Protection and Economic Sanction," ACCF Center for Policy Research, http://www.accf.org/Hufbauer1297.htm

3. Taeho Bark, "The Korean Consumer Electronics Industry: Reaction to Antidumping Actions," Chapter 7 in *Antidumping: How It Works and Who Gets Hurt*, edited by J. Michael Finger (Ann Arbor, MI: University of Michigan Press, 1993).

4. Virgina Postrel, "Curb Demonstrates Faults of Courting Special Interests," *New York Times*, June 14, 2001, p. C1.

The World of International Finance

oday, the world currency markets are always open. When foreign exchange traders in New York City are sound asleep at 3:00 A.M., their counterparts in London are already on their phones and computers at 8:00 A.M. In Tokyo, it's 6:00 P.M., and the day is just ending. By the time Tokyo traders return home after their long commutes, the New York traders are back at work. The currency markets keep working even when mere human beings rest.

On any given day, trillions of dollars of value are exchanged in these markets. The fortunes of industries and sometimes countries are determined by the ups and downs of currencies. Do these markets work efficiently and effectively?

Glossary

Absolute advantage The ability of one person or nation to produce a good at a lower absolute cost than another person or nation.

Accelerator theory The theory of investment that says current investment spending depends positively on the expected future growth of real GDP.

Accounting profit Total revenue minus explicit costs.

Adverse-selection problem A situation in which the uninformed side of the market must choose from an undesirable or adverse selection of goods.

Aggregate demand curve The relationship between the level of prices and the quantity of real GDP demanded.

Aggregate supply curve The relationship between the level of prices and the quantity of output supplied.

Anticipated inflation Inflation that is expected.

Appreciation of a currency An increase in the value of a currency.

Assets The uses of the funds of a bank, including loans and reserves.

Asymmetric information A situation in which one side of the market—either buyers or sellers—has better information about the product than the other.

Autarky A situation in which each country is self-sufficient, so there is no trade.

Automatic stabilizers Taxes and transfer payments that stabilize GDP without requiring policymakers to take explicit action.

Autonomous consumption spending The part of consumption that does not depend on income.

Autonomous consumption The part of consumption that does not depend on income.

Average fixed cost (AFC) Fixed cost divided by the quantity produced.

Average variable cost (AVC) Total variable cost divided by the quantity produced.

Average-cost pricing policy A regulatory policy under which the government picks the point on the demand curve at which price equals average cost.

Balance of payments deficit Under a fixed exchange rate system, a situation in which the supply of a country's currency exceeds the demand for the currency at the current exchange rate.

Balance of payments surplus Under a fixed exchange rate system, a situation in which the demand for a coun-

try's currency exceeds the supply of the currency at the current exchange rate.

Balance sheet An account for a bank that shows the sources of its funds (liabilities) as well as the uses for the funds (assets).

Bank run Panicky investors trying to withdraw their funds from a bank they believe may fail.

Barter Trading goods directly for goods.

Board of Governors of the Federal Reserve The seven-person governing body of the Federal Reserve system in Washington, DC.

Break-even price The price at which the economic profit is zero; price equals average total cost.

Budget deficit The difference between spending and revenues for a government.

Budget line The line connecting all the combinations of two goods that exhaust a consumer's budget.

Budget set A set of points that includes all the combinations of goods that a consumer can afford, given the consumer's income and the prices of the goods.

Budget surplus The difference between revenues and spending for a government—the opposite of a budget deficit.

Capital account The value of capital transfers and transactions in non-produced, non-financial assets in the international accounts.

Capital deepening Increases in the stock of capital per worker.

Capital gains Profits investors earn when they sell stocks, bonds, real estate, or other assets.

Carbon tax A tax based on a fuel's carbon content.

Cartel A group of firms that collude explicitly, coordinating their pricing decisions.

Central bank A banker's bank; an official bank that controls the supply of money in a country.

Centrally planned economy An economy in which a government bureaucracy decides how much of each good to produce, how to produce the goods, and who gets them.

Ceteris paribus The Latin expression meaning other variables being held fixed.

Chain index A method for calculating changes in prices that uses base years from neighboring years.

Change in demand A change in the amount of a good demanded resulting from a change in something other than the price of the good; represented graphically by a shift of the demand curve.

Change in quantity demanded A change in the quantity consumers are willing to buy when the price changes; represented graphically by movement along the demand curve.

Change in quantity supplied A change in the quantity firms are willing to sell when the price changes; represented graphically by movement along the supply curve.

Change in supply A change in the amount of a good supplied resulting from a change in something other than the price of the good; represented graphically by a shift of the supply curve.

Classical model Models that assume wages and prices adjust freely to changes in demand and supply.

Closed economy An economy without international trade.

Collective bargaining Negotiations between a union and a firm over wages, working conditions, and job security.

Command-and-control policy A policy under which the government commands each firm to produce no more than a certain volume of pollution and specifies the pollution-control technology used.

Commodity money A monetary system in which the actual money is a commodity, such as gold or silver.

Comparative advantage The ability of one person or nation to produce a good at a lower opportunity cost than another person or nation.

Complements Two goods related in such a way that a decrease in the price of one good increases the demand for the other good.

Concentration ratio A measure of the degree of concentration in a market; the four-firm concentration ratio is the percentage of the market output produced by the four largest firms.

Constant-cost industry An industry in which the average cost of production is constant; the long-run supply curve is horizontal.

Consumer price index (CPI) A price index that measures the cost of a fixed basket of goods chosen to represent the consumption pattern of individuals.

Consumer surplus The difference between a consumer's willingness to pay for a product and the price that he or she pays for the product.

Consumption expenditures Purchases of newly produced goods and services by households

Consumption function The relationship between the level of income and consumption spending.

Consumption possibilities curve A curve showing the combinations of two goods that can be consumed when a nation specializes in a particular good and trades with another nation.

Consumption taxes Taxes based on the consumption, not the income, of individuals.

Contestable market A market in which the costs of entering and leaving are low, so the firms that are already in the market are constantly threatened by the entry of new firms.

Contractionary policy Government policy actions that lead to decreases in output.

Convergence The process by which poorer countries "catch up" with richer countries in terms of real GDP per capita.

Corporate bond A bond sold by a corporation to the public in order to borrow money.

Corporate tax A tax levied on the earnings of a corporation.

Cost-of-living adjustments (COLAs) Automatic increases in wages or other payments that are tied to a price index.

Craft union A labor organization that includes workers from a particular occupation, for example, plumbers, bakers, or electricians.

Creative destruction The process by which competition for monopoly profits leads to technological progress.

Cross elasticity of demand A measure of the responsiveness of the quantity demanded to changes in the price of a related good; computed by dividing the percentage change in the quantity demanded of one good (X) by the percentage change in the price of another good (Y).

Crowded out The reduction in a component of GDP that results when government spending is increased or taxes are decreased.

Crowding in The increase of investment (or other component of GDP) in the long run caused by a decrease in government spending.

Crowding out The reduction in investment (or other component of GDP) in the long run caused by an increase in government spending.

Crowding out The reduction in investment (or other component of GDP) in the long run caused by an increase in government spending.

Current account The sum of net exports (exports minus imports) plus income received from investments abroad plus net transfers from abroad.

Custom duties Taxes levied on goods imported to the United States

Cyclical unemployment The component of unemployment that accompanies fluctuations in real GDP.

Deadweight loss from monopoly A measure of the inefficiency from monopoly; with a constant-cost industry, equal to the difference between the consumer-surplus loss from monopoly pricing and the monopoly's profit.

Deadweight loss from taxation The difference between the total burden of a tax and the amount of revenue collected by the government.

Deadweight loss The decrease in the total surplus of the market.

Deficit The excess of total expenditures over total revenues.

Deflation Negative inflation or falling prices.

Demand schedule A table of numbers that shows the relationship between price and quantity demanded, *ceteris paribus.*

Deposit insurance Federal government insurance on deposits in banks and savings and loans.

Depreciation of a currency A decrease in the value of a currency.

Depreciation The wear and tear of capital as it is used in production.

Depression The common name for a severe recession.

Devaluation A decrease in the exchange rate to which a currency is pegged in a fixed rate system.

Diminishing returns As one input increases while the other inputs are held fixed, output increases at a decreasing rate.

Discount rate The interest rate at which banks can borrow from the Fed.

Discouraged workers Workers who left the labor force because they could not find jobs.

Discretionary spending The spending programs that Congress authorizes on an annual basis.

Diseconomies of scale A situation in which an increase in the quantity produced increases the long-run average cost of production.

Dominant strategy An action that is the best choice for a player, no matter what an opponent does.

Double coincidence of wants The problem in a system of barter that one person may not have what the other desires.

Dumping A situation in which the price a firm charges in a foreign market is lower than either the price it charges in its home market or the production cost.

Duopolists' dilemma A situation in which both firms in a market would be better off if both chose the high price but each chooses the low price.

Duopoly A market with two firms.

Durable goods Goods that last for a long period of time, such as household appliances.

Econometric models Mathematical computer-based models that economists build to capture the actual dynamics of the economy.

Economic cost The opportunity cost of production, including both explicit and implicit costs.

Economic fluctuation Movements of GDP above or below normal trends.

Economic growth Sustained increases in the real production of an economy over a period of time.

Economic profit Total revenue minus total economic cost.

Economics The study of choice when there is scarcity, that is, a situation in which resources are limited and can be used in different ways.

Economies of scale A situation in which an increase in the quantity produced decreases the long-run average cost of production.

Elastic demand The price elasticity of demand is greater than 1.

Employed People who have jobs.

Entitlement and mandatory spending Spending that Congress has authorized by prior law.

Equilibrium output The level of GDP at which the demand for output equals the amount that is produced.

Equimarginal rule Pick the combination of two things that equalizes the marginal benefit per dollar spent.

Estate and gift taxes Taxes levied on the estates and gifts of individuals.

Euro The common currency in Europe.

Excess burden of a tax Another name for deadweight loss.

Excess demand A situation in which, at the prevailing price, consumers are willing to buy more than producers are willing to sell.

Excess reserves Any additional reserves that a bank holds above required reserves.

Excess supply A situation in which, at the prevailing price, producers are willing to sell more than consumers are willing to buy.

Exchange rate The rate at which currencies trade for one another in the market.

Expansion The period after a trough in the business cycle during which the economy recovers.

Expansionary policies Government policy actions that lead to increases in output.

Expectations of inflation The beliefs held by the public about the likely path of inflation for the future.

Expectations Phillips curve The relationship that describes the links between inflation and unemployment, taking into account expectations of inflation.

Expected real interest rate The nominal interest rate minus the expected inflation rate.

Experience rating A situation in which each firm pays a different price for medical insurance, depending on the past medical bills of its employees.

Explicit cost The firm's actual cash payments for its inputs.

Exports Goods produced in the home country (for example, the United States) and sold in another country.

External cost of production A cost incurred by people outside the firm.

Factor markets The markets in which labor and capital are traded.

Factors of production The inputs used to produce goods and services.

Featherbedding Work rules that increase the amount of labor required to produce a given quantity of output.

Federal excise taxes Taxes levied directly on the sale of selected products by the federal government.

Federal funds market The market in which banks borrow and lend reserves to and from one another.

Federal funds rate The interest rate on reserves that banks lend each other.

Federal Open Market Committee (FOMC) The group that decides on monetary policy; it consists of the 7 members of the Board of Governors plus 5 of 12 regional bank presidents on a rotating basis.

Federal Reserve Banks One of 12 regional banks that are an official part of the Federal Reserve System.

Fiat money A monetary system in which money has no intrinsic backing.

Financial account The value of a country's sales less purchases of assets. A sale of a domestic asset is a surplus item on the financial account, while a purchase of a foreign asset is a deficit item on the financial account.

Financial intermediaries Organizations that receive funds from savers and channel them to investors.

Firm's short-run supply curve A curve showing the relationship between the price of a product and the quantity of output supplied by a firm in the short run.

Firm-specific demand curve A curve showing the relationship between the price charged by a specific firm and the quantity that can be sold by that firm.

Fiscal policy Changes in taxes and spending that affect the level of GDP.

Fiscal year The calendar on which the federal government conducts its business, which runs from October 1 to September 30.

Fixed cost (FC) Cost that does not depend on the quantity produced.

Fixed exchange rates A system in which governments peg exchange rates.

Flexible exchange rates A currency system in which exchange rates are determined by free markets.

Foreign exchange market intervention The purchase or sale of currencies by governments to influence the market exchange rate.

Free-rider problem A problem that occurs when people try to benefit from a public good without paying for it.

Frictional unemployment The part of unemployment associated with the normal workings of the economy, such as searching for jobs.

Full employment The level of employment that occurs when the unemployment rate is at the natural rate.

Full-employment output The level of output that results when the economy is producing at full employment.

Game theory A framework to explore the actions and reactions of interdependent decision-makers.

Game tree A graphical representation of the consequences of different strategies.

GDP deflator An index that measures how the price of goods included in GDP changes over time.

General Agreement on Tariffs and Trade (GATT) An international agreement that has lowered trade barriers between the United States and other nations.

Gold standard A monetary system in which gold backs up paper money

Government debt The total of all past government deficits.

Government expenditure Spending on goods and services plus transfer payments.

Government purchases Purchases of newly produced goods and services by all levels of government.

Grim-trigger strategy A strategy where a firm responds to underpricing by choosing a price so low that each firm makes zero economic profit.

Gross domestic product (GDP) The total market value of all the final goods and services produced within an economy in a given year.

Gross investment Actual investment purchases.

Gross national product (GNP) GDP plus net income earned abroad.

Growth accounting A method to determine the contribution to economic growth from increased capital, labor, and technological progress.

Growth rate The percentage rate of change of a variable.

Growth version of the quantity equation An equation that links the growth rates of money, velocity, prices, and real output.

Guaranteed price-matching strategy A strategy where a firm guarantees it will match a lower price by a competitor; also known as a "meet-the-competition" policy.

Human capital The knowledge and skills acquired by a worker through education and experience and used to produce goods and services.

Hyperinflation An inflation rate exceeding 50% per month.

Illiquid Not easily transferable to money.

Implicit cost The opportunity cost of nonpurchased inputs.

Import licenses Rights, issued by a government, to import goods.

Import quota A limit on the amount of a good that can be imported.

Imports A good produced in a foreign country and purchased by residents of the home country (for example, the United States).

Income effect for leisure demand The change in leisure time resulting from a change in real income caused by a change in the wage.

Income effect The change in consumption resulting from a change in purchasing power caused by a price change. As income rises, a worker may choose to work fewer hours and enjoy more leisure.

Income elasticity of demand A measure of the responsiveness of the quantity demanded to changes in consumer income; computed by dividing the percentage change in the quantity demanded by the percentage change in income.

Increasing-cost industry An industry in which the average cost of production increases as the total output of the industry increases; the long-run supply curve is positively sloped.

Indifference curve A curve showing the different combinations of two goods that generate the same level of utility or satisfaction.

Indifference map A set of indifference curves, each with a different utility level.

Indirect taxes Sales and excise taxes.

Individual demand curve A curve that shows the relationship between price and quantity demanded by an individual consumer, *ceteris paribus.*

Individual income taxes Taxes levied on the income earned by individuals.

Individual supply curve A curve showing the relationship between price and quantity supplied by a single firm, *ceteris paribus.*

Individuals working part-time for economic reasons Individuals who would like to work full time but are forced to take part-time jobs.

Indivisible input An input that cannot be scaled down to produce a smaller quantity of output.

Industrial union A labor organization that includes all types of workers from a single industry, for example, steelworkers or autoworkers.

Inelastic demand The price elasticity of demand is less than 1.

Infant industries Industries that are at an early stage of development.

Inferior good A good for which an increase in income decreases demand.

inflation rate The percentage rate of change in the price level.

Inflation Sustained increases in prices.

Input-substitution effect The change in the quantity of labor demanded resulting from an increase in the price of labor relative to the price of other inputs.

Inside lags Lags in implementing policy.

Intermediate goods Goods used in the production process that are not final goods or services.

Inventory cycle The process by which an increase in demand would lead firms to produce more for their inventories, thereby increasing demand further.

Kinked demand curve model A model under which firms in an oligopoly match price reductions by other firms but do not match price increases by other firms.

Labor force participation rate The fraction of the population over 16 years of age that is in the labor force.

Labor force The employed plus the unemployed.

Labor Human effort, including both physical and mental effort, used to produce goods and services.

Labor productivity Output produced per hour of work.

Labor union An organized group of workers. Unions try to increase job security, improve working conditions, and increase wages and fringe benefits for their members.

Laffer curve A relationship between tax rates and tax revenues that illustrates that high tax rates do not always lead to high tax revenues if they discourage economic activity.

Law of demand The higher the price, the smaller the quantity demanded, *ceteris paribus*.

Law of one price The theory that goods easily tradeable across countries, should sell at the same price, expressed in a common currency.

Learning by doing Knowledge gained during production that increases productivity.

Learning effect The increase in a person's wage resulting from the learning of skills required for certain occupations.

Lender of last resort A central bank is the lender of last resort, the last place, all others having failed, from which banks in emergency situations can obtain loans.

Liabilities The sources of funds for a bank, including deposits of a financial intermediary.

Limit pricing A scheme under which a monopolist accepts a price below the normal monopoly price to deter other firms from entering the market.

Liquid Easily convertible to money on short notice.

Liquidity demand for money The demand for money that represents the needs and desires individuals or firms can fill on short notice without incurring excessive costs.

Liquidity trap A situation in which interest rates are so low, they can no longer fall.

Long-run aggregate supply curve A vertical aggregate supply curve. It reflects the idea that in the long run, output is determined solely by the factors of production.

Long-run average cost of production (LAC) Long-run total cost divided by the quantity of output produced.

Long-run demand curve for labor A curve showing the relationship between the wage and the quantity of labor demanded over the long run, when the number of firms in the market can change and firms can modify their production facilities.

Long-run marginal cost (LMC) The change in long-run cost from producing one more unit of output.

Long-run market supply curve A curve showing the relationship between the market price and quantity supplied in the long run.

Long-run neutrality of money An increase in the supply of money has no effect on real interest rates, investment, or output in the long run.

Long-run total cost (LTC) The total cost of production in the long run when a firm is perfectly flexible in its choice of all inputs and can choose a production facility of any size.

M1 The sum of currency in the hands of the public, demand deposits, other checkable deposits, and travelers' checks.

M2 M1 plus other assets, including deposits in savings and loans and money market mutual funds.

Macroeconomics The branch of economics that looks at a nation's economy as a whole.

Marginal benefit The extra benefit resulting from a small increase in some activity.

Marginal change A small, one-unit change in value.

Marginal cost The additional cost resulting from a small increase in some activity.

Marginal labor cost The increase in total labor cost resulting from one more unit of labor.

Marginal product of labor The change in output from one additional unit of labor

Marginal propensity to consume (MPC) The fraction of additional income that is spent.

marginal propensity to import The fraction of additional income that is spent on imports.

Marginal rate of substitution (MRS) The rate at which a consumer is willing to trade or substitute one good for another.

Marginal revenue The change in total revenue that results from selling one more unit of output.

Marginally attached workers Individuals who have worked in the past but stopped working for a variety of reasons.

Marginal-revenue product of labor (MRP) The extra revenue generated from one more unit of labor; MRP is equal to the price of output times the marginal product of labor.

Market An arrangement that allows people to exchange things.

Market demand curve A curve showing the relationship between price and quantity demanded, *ceteris paribus*.

Market economy An economy in which people exchange things, trading what they have for what they want.

Market equilibrium A situation in which the quantity of a product demanded equals the quantity supplied, so there is no pressure to change the price.

Market failure A situation in which a market fails to be efficient because of external benefits, external costs, imperfect information, or imperfect competition.

Market power The ability to affect the price of a product

Market supply curve A curve showing the relationship between price and quantity supplied, *ceteris paribus.*

Market supply curve for labor A curve showing the relationship between the wage and the quantity of labor supplied.

Marketable pollution permits A system under which the government picks a target pollution level for a particular area, issues just enough pollution permits to meet the pollution target, and allows firms to buy and sell the permits; also known as a cap-and-trade system.

Means-tested Based on the income of individuals or families.

Median-voter rule A rule suggesting that the choices made by government will reflect the preferences of the median voter.

Medicaid A federal government health program for the poor.

Medicare A federal government health program for the elderly.

Medium of exchange The property of money that exchanges are made through the use of money.

Menu costs Costs of inflation that arise from actually changing prices.

Merger A process in which two or more firms combine their operations.

Microeconomics The study of the choices made by households, firms, and government and of how these choices affect the markets for goods and services.

Midpoint method A method of computing a percentage change by dividing the change in the variable by the average value of the variable, or the midpoint between the old value and the new one.

Minimum efficient scale The output at which the long-run average-cost curve becomes horizontal.

Mixed market A market in which products of different qualities are sold for the same price.

Monetarists Economists who emphasize the role of money in determining nominal income and inflation.

Monetary policy The range of actions taken by the Federal Reserve to influence the level of GDP or the rate of inflation.

Monetizing the deficit Purchases by a central bank of newly issued government bonds.

Money Anything that is regularly used in exchange.

Money illusion Confusion of real and nominal magnitudes.

Money market The market for money in which the amount supplied and the amount demanded meet to determine the nominal interest.

Money multiplier An initial deposit leads to a multiple expansion of deposits. In the simplified case increase in deposits = (initial deposit) x (1/reserve ratio).

Monopolistic competition A market served by many firms selling slightly different products.

Monopoly A market in which a single firm serves the entire market.

Monopsony A market in which there is a single buyer of an input.

Moral hazard Insurance encourages risky behavior.

Multilateral real exchange rate An index of the real exchange rate with a country's trading partners.

Multiplier The ratio of the total shift in aggregate demand to the initial shift in aggregate demand.

Multiplier-accelerator model A model in which a downturn in real GDP leads to a sharp fall in investment, which triggers further reductions in GDP through the multiplier.

Nash equilibrium An outcome of a game in which each player is doing the best he or she can, given the action of the other players.

National income Net national product less indirect taxes.

Natural monopoly A market in which the economies of scale are so large that only a single large firm can survive.

Natural rate of unemployment The level of unemployment at which there is no cyclical unemployment.

Negative relationship A relationship in which an increase in the value of one variable decreases the value of another variable.

Neoclassical theory of investment A theory of investment that says both real interest rates and taxes are important determinants of investment.

Net exports Exports minus imports.

Net international investment position Domestic holdings of foreign assets minus foreign holdings of domestic assets.

Net investment Gross investment minus depreciation.

Net national product (NNP) GNP less depreciation.

New growth theory Modern theories of growth that try to explain the origins of technological progress.

Nominal GDP The value of GDP in current dollars

Nominal interest rates Interest rates quoted in the market.

Nominal value The face value of an amount of money.

Nominal wages Wages expressed in current dollars.

Nondurable goods Goods that last for short periods of time, such as food.

Normal good A good for which an increase in income increases demand.

Normative economics Analysis that answers the question "What ought to be?"

Oligopoly A market served by a few firms.

Open economy An economy with international trade.

Open market purchase The Fed's purchase of government bonds, which increases the money supply.

Open market sale The Fed's sales of government bonds to the public, which decreases the money supply.

Opportunity cost What you sacrifice to get something.

Output effect The change in the quantity of labor demanded resulting from a change in the quantity of output produced.

Outside lags The time it takes for policies to work.

Owners' equity The funds provided to a bank by its owners.

Patent The exclusive right to sell a particular good for some period of time.

Paying efficiency wages The practice of a firm paying a higher wage to increase the average productivity of its workforce.

Peak The time at which a recession begins.

Perfectly competitive market A market with a very large number of firms, each of which produces the same standardized product in amounts so small that no individual firm can affect the market price.

Perfectly competitive market A market with hundreds or thousands of sellers and buyers of a standardized good. Each buyer and seller takes the market price as given. Firms can easily enter or exit the market.

Perfectly elastic demand The price elasticity of demand is infinite.

Perfectly elastic supply The price elasticity of supply is infinite.

Perfectly inelastic demand The price elasticity of demand equals 0.

Perfectly inelastic supply The price elasticity of supply equals 0.

Permanent income Income (including transfer payments) received by households.

Personal disposable income Personal income after taxes.

Personal income An estimate of a household's long-run average level of income.

Planned expenditures Another term for total demand for goods and services.

Political business cycle The effects on the economy of using monetary or fiscal policy to stimulate the economy before an election to improve reelection prospects.

Pollution offset A credit received for supporting a project that either reduces the pollution emissions of another firm or organization or results in the absorption of pollutants; also known as a reduction credit.

Pollution tax A tax or charge equal to the external cost per unit of waste.

Positive economics Analysis that answers the questions, "What is?" or "What will be?"

Positive relationship A relationship in which an increase in the value of one variable increases the value of another variable.

Predatory pricing A pricing scheme under which a firm decreases its price to drive a rival out of business and increases the price when the other firm disappears.

Present value The maximum amount a person is willing to pay today to receive a payment in the future.

Price discrimination The process under which a firm divides consumers into two or more groups and picks a different price for each group.

Price elasticity of demand A measure of the responsiveness of the quantity demanded to changes in price; computed by dividing the percentage change in quantity demanded by the percentage change in price.

Price elasticity of supply A measure of the responsiveness of the quantity supplied to changes in price; computed by dividing the percentage change in quantity supplied by the percentage change in price.

Price fixing An arrangement in which two firms coordinate their pricing decisions.

Price leadership An implicit agreement under which firms in a market choose a price leader, observe that firm's price, and match it.

Price ratio The ratio of the price of one good to the price of a second good; the market trade-off.

Price-change formula A formula that shows the percentage change in equilibrium price resulting from a change in demand or supply, given values for the price elasticity of supply and the price elasticity of demand.

Private cost of production The production cost borne by a firm, which typically includes the costs of labor, capital, and materials.

Private good A good that is consumed by a single person or household.

Private investment expenditures Purchases of newly produced goods and services by firms.

Procyclical Moving in same direction as real GDP.

Producer surplus The difference between the price a producer receives for a product and the producer's willingness to accept for the product.

Product differentiation A strategy monopolistic firms use to distinguish their products from competitors'.

Product markets The markets in which goods and services are traded.

Production function The relationship between the level of output and the factors of production.

Production possibilities curve A curve showing the combinations of two goods that can be produced by an economy, assuming that all resources are fully employed.

Production possibilities curve A curve that shows the possible combinations of products that an economy can produce, given that its productive resources are fully employed and efficiently used.

Public choice economics A field of economics that explores how governments actually operate.

Public good A good that is available for everyone to consume, regardless of who pays and who doesn't.

Purchasing power parity Theory of exchange rates, stating that the exchange rate between two currencies is determined by the price levels in the two countries.

Q-theory of investment The theory of investment that links investment spending to stock prices.

Quantity demanded The amount of a product consumers are willing to buy.

Quantity equation The equation that links money, velocity, prices and real output. In symbols, we have $M \times V = P \times y$.

Quantity supplied The amount of a product firms are willing to sell.

Rational expectations The economic theory that analyzes how people form expectations in such a manner that, on average, they forecast the future correctly.

Real business cycle theory The economic theory that emphasizes how shocks to technology can cause fluctuations in economic activity.

Real exchange rate The market exchange rate adjusted for prices.

Real GDP A measure of GDP that controls for changes in prices.

Real GDP per capita Gross domestic product per person adjusted for changes in prices. It is the usual measure of living standards across time and between countries.

Real interest rate The nominal interest rate minus the inflation rate.

Real value The value of an amount of money in terms of what it can buy.

Real wage The wage paid to workers adjusted for changes in prices.

Real wages Nominal or dollar wages adjusted for changes in purchasing power.

Recession Commonly defined as six consecutive months of negative economic growth.

Rent seeking The process of using governments to obtain economic profit.

Required reserves The fraction of banks' deposits that banks are legally required to hold in their vaults or as deposits at the Fed.

Reserve ratio The ratio of reserves to deposits.

Reserves The fraction of banks' deposits set aside in either vault cash or as deposits at the Federal Reserve.

Retained earnings Corporate earnings that are not paid out as dividends.

Revaluation An increase in the exchange rate in a fixed exchange system.

Ricardian equivalence The proposition that it does not matter whether government expenditure is financed by taxes or by debt.

Right-to-work laws Laws that prohibit union shops, where union membership is required as a condition of employment

Rule of 70 A rule of thumb that says that output will double in 70/x years where x is the percentage rate of growth.

Saving Total income minus consumption.

Savings function The relationship between the level of income and the level of savings.

Scarcity A situation in which resources are limited in quantity and can be used in different ways.

Seasonal unemployment The component of unemployment attributed to seasonal factors.

Seignorage Revenue raised through money creation.

Sequential decision-making game A game in which one player makes a choice before the other.

Services Reflect work done in which people play a prominent role in delivery, ranging from haircutting to health care.

Shoe-leather costs Costs of inflation that arise from trying to reduce holdings of cash.

Short run in macroeconomics The period of time that prices do not change very much.

Short-run aggregate supply curve A relatively flat horizontal supply curve. It reflects the idea that prices do not change very much in the short run and that firms adjust production to meet demand

Short-run aggregate supply curve A relatively flat horizontal supply curve. It reflects the idea that prices do not change very much in the short run and that firms adjust production to meet demand.

Short-run average total cost (ATC) Short-run total cost divided by the quantity of output; equal to AFC plus AVC.

Short-run demand curve for labor A curve showing the relationship between the wage and the quantity of labor demanded over the short run, the period when the firm cannot change its production facility.

Short-run marginal cost (MC) The change in short-run total cost resulting from producing one more unit of the good.

Short-run market supply curve A curve showing the relationship between price and the quantity supplied in the short run.

Short-run total cost (TC) The total cost of production in the short run, when one or more inputs (for example, the production facility) is fixed; equal to fixed cost plus variable cost.

Shut-down price The price at which the firm is indifferent between operating and shutting down; equal to the minimum average variable cost.

Signaling effect The increase in a person's wage resulting from the signal of productivity provided by completing college.

Simultaneous decision-making game A game in which each player makes a choice without the other person knowing what that choice is.

Slope of a curve The change in the variable on the vertical axis resulting from a one-unit increase in the variable on the horizontal axis.

Social cost of production Private cost plus external cost.

Social insurance taxes Taxes levied on earnings to pay for Social Security and Medicare.

Social Security A federal government program to provide retirement support and a host of other benefits.

Speculative demand for money The demand for money that reflects holding money over short periods is less risky than holding stocks or bonds.

Stabilization policies Policy actions taken to bring the economy closer to full employment or potential output.

Stagflation A decrease in real output with increasing prices.

Stock of capital The total of all the machines, equipment, and buildings in the entire economy.

Store of value The property of money that it preserves value until it is used in an exchange.

Structural unemployment The component of unemployment reflecting a mismatch of skills and jobs.

Substitutes Two goods that are related in such a way that an increase in the price of one good increases the demand for the other good.

Substitution effect An increase in the wage will raise the opportunity cost of leisure and lead to an increase in hours worked.

Substitution effect for leisure demand The change in leisure time resulting from a change in the wage (the price of leisure) relative to the price of other goods.

Substitution effect The change in consumption resulting from a change in the price of one good relative to the price of another good.

Sunk cost A cost a firm has already paid or has agreed to pay some time in the future.

Supply schedule A table of numbers that shows the relationship between price and quantity supplied, *ceteris paribus*.

Supply shocks External events that shift the aggregate supply curve.

Supply-side economics A school of thought that emphasizes the role that taxes play in the supply of output in the economy.

Surplus The excess of total revenues over total expenditures.

Tariff A tax on an imported good.

Technological progress An increase in output without increasing inputs.

Terms of trade The rate at which two goods will be exchanged.

Thin market A market in which some high-quality goods are sold but fewer than would be sold in a market with perfect information.

Tie-in-sales A business practice under which a consumer of one product is required to purchase another product.

Tit-for-tat A strategy where one firm chooses whatever price the other firm chose in the preceding period.

Total product curve A curve showing the relationship between the quantity of labor and the quantity of output produced.

Total revenue The money the firm gets by selling its product; equal to the price times the quantity sold.

Total surplus The sum of consumer surplus and producer surplus.

Trade deficit The excess of imports over exports.

Trade surplus The excess of exports over imports.

Transactions demand for money The demand for money based on the desire to facilitate transactions.

Transfer payments Payments to individuals from governments that do not correspond to the production of goods and services.

Trough The time at which output stops falling in a recession.

Trust An arrangement under which the owners of several companies transfer their decision-making powers to a small group of trustees, who then make decisions for all the firms.

Unanticipated inflation Inflation that is not expected.

Unemployed People who are looking for work but do not have jobs.

Unemployment insurance Payments received from the government upon becoming unemployed.

Unemployment rate The fraction of the labor force that is unemployed.

Uniform abatement policy A policy under which each polluter is required to reduce pollution by the same amount.

Unit of account The property of money that prices are quoted in terms of money.

Unitary elastic The price elasticity of demand equals 1.

Utility The satisfaction experienced from consuming a product.

Utility-maximizing rule Pick the affordable combination that makes the marginal rate of substitution equal to the price ratio.

Value added The sum of all the income (wages, interest, profits, rent) generated by an organization.

Variable A measure of something that can take on different values.

Variable cost (VC) Cost that varies as the firm changes its output.

Velocity of money Nominal GDP divided by the money supply. It is also the rate at which money turns over during the year.

Voluntary export restraint (VER) A scheme under which an exporting country voluntarily decreases its exports.

Wage–price spiral Changes in wages and prices causing more changes in wages and prices.

Wealth effect The increase in spending that occurs because the real value of money increases when the price level falls.

Willingness to accept The minimum amount a producer is willing to accept as payment for a product; equal to the marginal cost of production.

Willingness to pay The maximum amount a consumer is willing to pay for a product.

Withholding Taxes collected directly from the paychecks of workers.

World Trade Organization (WTO) An organization that oversees GATT and other international trade agreements.

Photo Credits

Chapter 1: Page 1, Bob Krist/Bob Krist Photography; page 2, Kathy Collins/Getty Images, Inc., Taxi; page 3, Bob Krist/Bob Krist Photography; page 4 Main Space Science Systems/NASA/AFP /Getty Images, Inc., Agence France Presse; page 9 (left), Reproduced by permission of the Master and Fellows of St. John's College, Cambridge; page 9 (right), Cydney Conger/Corbis/Bettmann; page 11, Cralle, Gary/Getty Images Inc., Image Bank

Chapter 2: Page 26, Owaki-Kulla/Corbis/Bettmann; page 27, Bob Krist/Bob Krist Photography; page 30 (left), Jacques M. Chenet/ Corbis/Bettman; page 30 (right), Picture Arts/ Corbis Royalty Free; page 31, AP Wide World Photos

Chapter 3: Page 44, AP Wide World Photos; page 45, Bob Krist/Bob Krist Photography; page 51, PRNewsFoto/Walt Disney Television Animation; page 53, Hulton-Deutsch Collection/Corbis/Bettmann; page 54, Hulton-Deutsch Collection/Corbis/Bettmann

Chapter 4: Page 60, Owen Franken/Corbis/Bettmann; page 61, Bob Krist/Bob Krist Photography; page 72 (left), AP Wide World Photos; page 72 (right), David Buffington/Getty Images, Inc., Photodisc; page 79, Glen Allison/Getty Images, Inc., Photodisc

Chapter 5: Page 93, Bryan F. Peterson/Corbis/Bettmann; page 94, Jonathan Novrok/PhotoEdit; page 95, © Bryan F. Peterson/Corbis; page 100, Spencer Grant/PhotoEdit; page 104, Les Stone/Corbis/Sygma; page 108, Keith Brofsky/Getty Images, Inc., Photodisc

Chapter 6: Page 120, AP Wide World Photos; page 121, © Bryan F. Peterson / Corbis; page 132, Nick Koudis/Getty Images, Photodisc; page 134, Leland Bobbe/Corbis/Bettmann

Chapter 7: Page 138, Bruce Burkhardt/Corbis/Bettmann; page 139, © Bryan F. Peterson/Corbis; page 146, Shepard Sherbell/Corbis/Bettmann; page 151, AP Wide World Photos; page 163, Jacques Denzer Parker/Index Stock Imagery, Inc.

Chapter 8: Page 169, Greg Nikas/Corbis/Bettmann; page 170, Michael Newman/PhotoEdit; page 171, © Greg Nikas/Corbis; page 178, These materials have been reproduced with the permission of eBay Inc. © eBay Inc. All rights reserved; page 181, Bryan Yablonsky/Duomo Photography Incorporated; page 187, Spencer Grant/PhotoEdit

Chapter 9: Page 194, Michael Busselle/Corbis; page 195, © Greg Nikas/Corbis; page 196 Phil Borden/PhotoEdit; page 203, Mike Greenlar/The Image Works; page 208, Martin Barraud/Getty Images Inc., Stone Allstock; page 211, AP Wide World Photos

Chapter 10: Page 218, Dr. Seth Shostak/Photo Researchers, Inc.; page 219, © Greg Nikas/Corbis; page 225, Peter Weimann/Peter Arnold, Inc.

Chapter 11: Page 233, ™ & © Boeing. Used under license. Image © Boeing Management Co. All rights reserved; page; page 234, Myrleen/PhotoEdit; page 235, ™ & © Boeing. Used under license. Image © Boeing Management Co. All rights reserved; page 244, Zigy Kaluzny/Getty Images Inc., Stone Allstock; page 248, Billy E. Barnes/PhotoEdit; page 249 Marilyn Kazmers-SharkSong/Dembinsky Photo Associates; page 251, California Department of Water Resources

Chapter 12: Page 260, Spencer Grant/PhotoEdit; page 261, ™ & © Boeing. Used under license. Image © Boeing Management Co. All rights reserved; page 270, Chip Henderson/Chip Henderson Photography; page 275, AP Wide World Photos

Chapter 13: Page 288, David Young Wolff/PhotoEdit; page 289, ™ & © Boeing. Used under license. Image © Boeing Management Co. All rights reserved; page 299, Paul Conklin/PhotoEdit; page 302, Jim Karageorge/Getty Images, Inc., Taxi; page 306, Michael Newman/PhotoEdit

Chapter 14: Page 312, Michael Newman/PhotoEdit; page 317, Jackson Vereen/Foodpix/Getty Images, Inc.

Chapter 15: Page 326, Stockbyte; page 327, ™ & © Boeing. Used under license. Image © Boeing Management Co. All rights reserved; page 333, Michael P. Godomski/Photo Researchers, Inc.; page 346, Bill Aron/PhotoEdit; page 347, Advertisement courtesy of Pen World® International magazine and World Publications, Inc.; page 351, Courtesy of Martha Nash Legg

Chapter 16: Page 356, David Young-Wolff/PhotoEdit; page 357, ™ & © Boeing. Used under license. Image © Boeing Management Co. All rights reserved; page 361, Brant Ward/The San Francisco Chronicle/Corbis/SABA Press Photos, Inc.; page 362, Collection of The New York Historical Society, negative #71880; page 372, AP Wide World Photos

Chapter 17: Page 377, Jeff Sherman/Getty Images, Inc., Taxi; page 378, Jon Feingersh/Corbis/Bettmann; page 379, Jeff Sherman/Getty Images, Inc.–Taxi; page 387, Ariel Skelley/Corbis/Bettmann; Catherine Karnow/ Corbis/Bettmann page 390, © Catherine Karnow/Corbis;

Chapter 18: Page 404, Ford Motor Company; page 405, Jeff Sherman/Getty Images, Inc.–Taxi; page 407, Getty Images Inc., Hulton Archive Photos

Chapter 19: Page 419, Matthew Borkoski/Index Stock Imagery, Inc.; page 420, EyeWire Collection/Getty Images, Photodisc; page 421, Matthew Borkoski/Index Stock Imagery, Inc.; page 424 (left), Michael S. Yamashita/Corbis/Bettmann; page 424 (right), William Taufic/Corbis/Bettmann; page 438 (left), Hulton-Deutsch Collection/Corbis/Bettmann; page 438 (right), Getty Images Inc., Image Bank; page 440, www.comstock.com

Chapter 20: Page 444, www.comstock.com; page 445, Mathew Borkowski/Index Stock Imagery, Inc.; page 446, © Ariel Skelley/Corbis; page 451, Reprinted with permission of Monster; page 455 (left & right), Courtesy of Ford Motor Company

Chapter 21: Page 467, Lauren Goodsmith/The Image Works; page 468, Jochen Tack/Peter Arnold, Inc.; page 469, Lauren

Answers to Odd-Numbered Problems and Discussion Questions

Chapter 1

1. Truman's sign indicated that the ultimate responsibility for making decisions rested with him: He could not "pass the buck" onto someone else. An economist who provided advice on the trade-offs from a particular policy would help Truman make his decision.
3. What is the extra cost from one more advertisement? How much extra revenue would the firm earn by running one more advertisement?

APPENDIX TO CHAPTER 1

1. a. See Figure S.1.
   b. The slope is $5.
   c. The monthly bill will increase by $15.
3. 10%, –2%, 6%.
5. The number of burglaries will decrease by 4.

Chapter 2

1. a. The opportunity cost of the loan to the friend is the interest the person could have earned if the $100 were in a bank account instead.
   b. The opportunity cost of the logs is the amount of money the firm could get by selling the logs on the log market today.
   c. The opportunity cost of the land is the value of land in its next-best alternative, for example, a classroom building, a library, or a student center.
3. The economic cost is $285,000, the sum of $50,000 for the opportunity cost of Jack's time, $10,000 for the opportunity cost of the building, $75,000 for workers, and $150,000 for supplies.

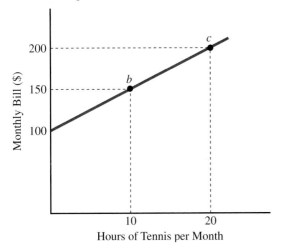

FIGURE S.1 Relationship Between Hours of Tennis and the Monthly Tennis Club Bill

5. You could compute the marginal cost of a unit and then compute the marginal benefits (in terms of lives saved or medical expenses avoided) for different quantities of units. To satisfy the marginal principle, the city should buy another unit as long as the marginal benefit exceeds the marginal cost.
7. No. Eventually, we expect output to increase at a decreasing rate (diminishing returns) as more and more workers share the machine.

Chapter 3

1. As shown in the following table, both can be made better off from specialization and exchange.

	Abe		Bea		Total	
	Paintings per week	Pizzas per week	Paintings per week	Pizzas per week	Paintings per week	Pizzas per week
Abe and Bea are self-sufficient.	6	24	2	5	8	29
Abe and Bea specialize.	0	36	12	0	12	36
After specializing, Abe and Bea exchange 1 pizza per painting.	0 + 6 = **6** (Abe gets 6 paintings)	36 – 6 = **30** (Abe gives up 6 pizzas)	12 – 6 = **6** (Bea gives up 6 paintings)	0 + 6 = **6** (Bea gets 6 pizzas)	12	36
Gain from specialization and exchange.	0	6	4	1	4	7

3. a. The total score is maximized by having Lucy in the graduate course (score = 60) and Buster in the undergraduate course (score = 24).
   b. Lucy has an absolute advantage in both courses and a comparative advantage in the graduate course: She is three times as productive in the graduate course, but only twice as productive in the undergraduate course.

Chapter 4

1. a. w, $150,200 per day.
   b. demand, increase.
   c. supply, decrease.
3. a. The cost of producing computers will decrease, so the production of computers will be more profitable and firms will supply more of them. The supply curve will shift to the right, decreasing the equilibrium price.
   b. The tax increases the production cost, shifting the supply curve to the left and increasing the equilibrium price.
5. Education at private and at public schools are substitutes, so the tuition hike will shift the demand for private education to the right, increasing the equilibrium price and quantity.

7. If price and quantity both increase, we know from Table 4.5 that demand has increased. We shift the demand curve to the right, increasing the price and quantity.
9. The supply curve for shirts shifts to the left, increasing the equilibrium price and decreasing the equilibrium quantity.

Chapter 5

1. The price elasticity is 1.30 = the percentage change in quantity (13%) divided by the percentage change in price (10%). Demand is elastic.
3. Each brand has many substitute goods (all the other brands), so the demand for a specific brand will be more elastic than the demand for running shoes in general.
5. Inelastic: An increase in price increases total revenue, whereas a decrease in price decreases total revenue.
7. Use the elasticity formula: The 10% increase in the price of beer will decrease the quantity of beer consumed by 13%, decreasing the highway death rate by the same percentage. Therefore, the number of highway deaths will decrease by 13 (13% of 100).
9. a. The predicted change in quantity is 20% = 4 (the elasticity) times the 5% price change. The quantity sold drops from 100 million gallons to 80 million gallons, so the tax will generate $8 million.
   b. The national elasticity is larger, so the analysts would understate the reduction in quantity demanded and thus overestimate the revenue generated by the tax. Specifically, they will predict a quantity of 95 million gallons instead of 80 million gallons and revenue of $9.5 million instead of $8 million. Because it is relatively easy to buy gasoline in a nearby city, the demand for gasoline will be relatively elastic at the city level

Chapter 6

1. a. The *MRS* (5 rides for one video game) exceeds the price ratio (2 riders per video game).
   b. At point *d* (3 rides and 24 video games), the MRS equals the price ratio.
3. The *MRS* is less than the price ratio, so you should consume fewer CDs and more movies. For the graph, place CDs on the horizontal axis and movies on the vertical axis. The slope of the budget line is 3 movies per CD. At the initial point, the slope of the indifference curve is 1 movie per CD. The indifference curve is flatter than the budget line, so you should move up the budget line to a higher indifference curve (fewer CDs and more movies).
5. a. Suppose he achieves the same utility level in weeks one and two. If he consumes fewer CDs and more arcade games in week two, he will be further up his indifference curve, with a higher *MRS*.
   b. He will be better off because balanced consumption is preferred to extremes. Draw a line between the two points on his indifference curve. The midpoint is the average consumption, and it will lie on a higher (more northeasterly) indifference curve.

7. Applying the equimarginal rule, utility is the miles driven on a tank of fuel, and marginal utility is the miles per gallon of fuel (mpg). The rule suggests that to maximize utility, a driver should equate the mpg of gasohol divided by the price of gasohol to the mpg of gasoline divided by the price of gasoline. If the consumer picks one fuel or the other, she or he should pick the fuel that has the higher mpg divided by price. For example, suppose the price of gasohol is $1 per gallon and the price of gasoline is $1.25. If gasohol has a mpg of 18 and gasoline has a mpg of 25, gasoline is a better buy: It provides 20 miles per dollar, compared to 18 miles per dollar for gasohol. Although gasoline is more expensive, its higher mpg more than offsets the higher price per gallon. The rule suggested in the quote is misguided because it doesn't take into account differences in mpg.

Chapter 7

1. We assume that buyers and sellers have enough information to make informed choices and that there are no external benefits and no external costs. The assumption of informed choices is likely to be violated in the case of used cars: Buyers don't know the quality of the car. The assumption of no external benefits is likely to be violated for national defense, space exploration, public radio, and education. The assumption of no external costs is likely to be violated for goods that generate pollution such as paper, transportation (auto and bus), and electricity.
3. a. *A + B + C*
   b. *D + E + F*
   c. *A + B + C + D + E + F*
   d. *A + B + D*
   e. *F*
   f. *A + B + D + F*
   g. *A*
   h. *B + D + F*
   i. *A + B + D + F*
5. The supply of clothing to an individual city is much more elastic than the supply of housing, so price controls would decrease the quantity of clothing supplied by a larger amount. In addition, everyone would have to wait in line to get clothing. In contrast, people who occupy rent-controlled apartments don't have to find a new apartment every week, so they avoid most of the queuing and search costs and provide political support for rent control.
7. In the market equilibrium, there are 100 taxis and the price of taxi service is $3, which is just high enough to cover the cost of providing taxi service. If the government issues more than 100 medallions, no one will use the extra medallions, and the medallion policy will have no effect on the market: The price of taxi service will be $3, and the price of a medallion will be zero.
9. For parts (a) and (b), as in the case of taxi medallions, the quantity restrictions will increase the equilibrium price and decrease the equilibrium quantity. For part (c), the import restrictions shift the market supply curve to the left, increasing the equilibrium price and decreasing the equilibrium quantity.

11. a. No. Part of the tax will be shifted backward onto input suppliers, including laborers who work in auto factories and dealerships.

   b. The price elasticity of demand for automobiles and the responsiveness of input suppliers to changes in input prices.

13. The tax increases the equilibrium price to $56 and decreases the equilibrium quantity to 80 rooms. Consumers pay $6 more per room, and suppliers receive a net price of $46 = $56 − $10 tax.

15. The quantity of grooming services hasn't changed, so the demand for services must have decreased, pulling down the price of pet services and thus decreasing the profits of license holders.

Chapter 8

1. Suppose Groucho wants to join a social club to associate with people who are richer than he is, and he assumes that other people join clubs for the same reasons. A club will invite him to join only if he would increase the average income of the club. In other words, Groucho will be invited to join only groups in which most people are poorer than he is, clubs with an adverse selection of people. The same reasoning applies if Groucho wants to associate with people who are wittier than he is, and he assumes that other people feel the same way. A club that asks him to join will have an average wit level that is less than his, so he will be forced to interact with dimwits.

3. Suppose you're willing to pay the average value of the two types of cameras ($60) for a 50% chance of getting a plum. If you expect a greater than 50% chance of getting a plum, it will be wise to buy a used camera. Given the adverse-selection problem, your chance of getting a plum is likely to be less than 50%.

5. The detector eliminates the imperfect information problem, so the two types of used cars will be sold in separate markets, with one price for lemons ($2,000 in our example) and another price for plums ($4,000). There is no adverse selection because each buyer knows exactly what type of car he or she will get.

7. Like the lie detector, the genetic tests eliminate the adverse-selection problem, this time for insurance companies. The insurance companies will charge higher prices to those who are likely to contract the diseases and lower prices to those who are not. This may strike many people as unfair.

9. If Ira doesn't have fire insurance, he will spend money on the prevention program because the benefit is the avoidance of an expected loss of $10,000 (a 10% chance of losing $100,000), which exceeds the $5,000 cost. If he has an insurance policy covering 80% of the loss, the benefit is the avoidance of an expected loss of $2,000 (a 10% chance of losing $80,000). The benefit is less than the $5,000 cost, so he won't spend money on the program. Ira will be indifferent with a coverage rate of 50%. In this case, the benefit is the avoidance of an expected loss of $5,000 (a 10% chance of losing $50,000), which is equal to the cost.

FIGURE S.2 **Pollution Tax Makes the Equilibrium Quantity of a Polluting Good Zero**

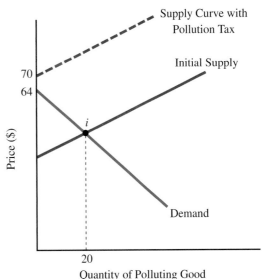

Chapter 9

1. See Figure S.2. The demand curve intersects the supply curve at 20 units per day. The pollution tax shifts the supply curve upward and to the left by such a large amount that the supply curve lies entirely above the demand curve. For this to occur, the spillover cost from the pollutant must be very high, the cost of abatement must be very high, and the demand for goods must be relatively low.

3. a. The production cost per ton with zero pollution is $62.

   b. The marginal cost associated with going from 1 gallon to 0 gallons is $12. For firms to make this choice, the marginal benefit of abatement (the tax savings) must be at least $12.

5. We could adjust other taxes to mitigate any undesirable effects on the poor. For example, we could decrease the sales tax rate or adjust the income tax rates.

7. The high-cost firm would save $6,100 by getting a fourth permit, and the low-cost firm would bear an additional abatement cost of $5,500 by giving up one of its permits. Splitting the difference, the market price would be $5,800.

9. If the oldest firms have the highest cost-abatement technology, they will hold on to their permits rather than selling them. Trading could be encouraged by giving some permits to newer firms, ones with low-cost abatement technology. Those firms will sell some of the permits if the selling price of permits exceeds the extra abatement cost they incur.

Chapter 10

1. a. No. The cost of $120 exceeds the willingness to pay of each citizen, so no one will provide the display.

   b. No. With a cost of $40 per citizen, the cost exceeds the willingness to pay of two of three citizens (Marian and Sam).

c. The total cost ($120) is three-fourths the total willingness to pay ($160 = $100 + $30 + $20). If each citizen paid three-fourths of his or her willingness to pay, the display could be provided and each would be better off.

3. The free-rider problem disappears because if any person does not contribute, the public good won't be provided. This money-back guarantee makes it more likely that everyone will contribute and get 30¢ at the end of the experiment.

5. a. The benefit is $8,000 (80,000 citizens times $0.10 per person), which exceeds the cost of $5,000. Since the benefit exceeds the cost, the provision of the additional litter is socially efficient.

b. No. The benefit to the rancher ($0.10) is less than the cost ($5,000).

c. The citizens could contribute to a wolf-preservation fund to provide the rancher with enough money to offset the cost of a litter of wolves. For example, if each citizen contributed $0.07 (70% of his or her benefit), they could raise a total of $5,600. By paying this amount to the landowner who hosts the wolf litter, the rancher would be better off by $600, and each of the citizens would be better off by $0.03.

7. a. The median voter now has a desired budget of $6 billion, so each candidate will propose a budget very close to $6 billion.

b. The answer will not change because the median voter is still the person with the $6 billion budget.

Chapter 11

1. The average cost is $15 for 40 shirts, $9 for 100 shirts, $7 for 200 shirts, and $6 for 400 shirts.

3.

Labor	Output	Marginal Product
0	0	
1	5	5
2	11	6
3	15	4
4	18	3
5	19	1

5. There are no diminishing returns, so marginal cost is constant.

7. The $12,500 figure includes some of the fixed cost of production (design and tooling costs), so it is an average cost, not a marginal cost.

9. As shown in Figure 11.7, the average cost for the large generator is $4.60 (point b), compared to an average cost of $5.00 for the small generator (point c).

11. a. False. The principle of diminishing returns is applicable to the short-run cost curves, not the long-run curves.

b. True. Diminishing returns imply increasing short-run marginal cost.

c. False. Diminishing returns imply increasing short-run marginal cost but do not imply increasing short-run average cost. If the output is small enough, the spreading of fixed costs will generate a negatively sloped short-run average-cost curve even if there are diminishing returns.

d. False. The first sentence implies that the short-run average-cost curve is positively sloped. This means that the short-run marginal cost exceeds the short-run average cost.

Chapter 12

1.

Tables per hour	Total cost	Marginal cost
3	120	—
4	155	35
5	200	45
6	270	70

3. At the current output level, the firm is violating the marginal principle, so it is not doing the best it can. Marginal revenue (the price of $22) is less than the marginal cost ($45); to maximize profit, the firm should produce less output. It is possible that with lower output, total revenue could exceed total cost, and the firm would be profitable. Alternatively, total revenue could be less than total cost, but total revenue could exceed variable cost, so it would be sensible to continue operating.

5. The manager is bluffing. His total revenue ($35,000) exceeds the variable cost ($30,000 for the farm workers). The $20,000 paid for seed and fertilizer was incurred months ago, and it is a sunk cost that will be ignored in the decision about whether to harvest the crop. Because his total revenue exceeds his variable cost, the farmer will harvest the crop even if the workers don't accept a wage cut.

7. We cannot draw a supply curve or complete the price elasticity of supply because we cannot be certain that the other variables that affect the supply of gasoline (the price of inputs, technology) did not change over this period.

9.

Number of firms	Industry output	Total cost for typical firm	Average cost per lamp
40	400	$300	$30
80	800	$360	$36
120	1,200	$420	$42

We have 3 points on the long-run supply curve: At a price of $30, the quantity is 400 lamps; at a price of $36, the quantity is 800 lamps; at a price of $42, the quantity is 1,200 lamps.

11. Because the industry uses such tiny amounts of the relevant inputs, the prices of these inputs won't change as the industry grows. Therefore, the average cost per haircut does not depend on the quantity of haircuts. The long-run supply curve is horizontal, for example, at a constant cost of $10 per haircut.

Chapter 13

1. To maximize profit, the restaurant will pick the quantity at which marginal revenue equals marginal cost. Using the

marginal-revenue formula, we can compute the marginal revenue at each price and quantity:

Price	$10	$9	$8	$7
Quantity	30	40	50	60
Marginal revenue	$7	$5	$3	$1

Marginal revenue equals marginal cost at a price of $8 and a quantity of 50 meals.

3. On average, the payback per dollar spent on these lottery games is about 50¢. In other words, for every $100 spent by players, the state pays $50 in prizes. The commercial gambling games have much higher paybacks: The payback per dollar is 81¢ for horse racing and 89¢ for slot machines. The lottery games have lower paybacks because each state has a monopoly on lottery games: The state outlaws commercial lotteries. If the state allowed other organizations to offer lottery games, the competition between commercial and state lottery games would increase the payback from lottery games.

5. The artificial barrier to entry will generate higher prices and a smaller quantity demanded. If we eliminated the barriers, there would be more teams, and ticket prices would fall, increasing total attendance.

7. Monopoly power increases prices in the game of Monopoly, consistent with the conclusions in this chapter. In monopoly, prices increase with monopoly power despite the fact that the quantity provided on the market does not decrease. In contrast, in the normal analysis of monopoly, price increases because the quantity drops, and the market moves up the market demand curve.

9. The consumer advocate is assuming that the demand for the drug is perfectly inelastic, so an increase in price does not have any effect on the quantity demanded. This is unrealistic and is inconsistent with the law of demand.

11. The marginal revenue for business travelers is $MR = \$300 - 2.0 \times 120 = \$60$, which is less than the marginal cost, so the airline should increase the price for business travelers. The marginal revenue for tourists is $MR = \$300 - 1.0 \times 80 = \$220$, which is greater than the marginal cost, so the airline should decrease the price for tourists.

13. This price-discrimination scheme is based on the notion that bargain hunters are early birds. The large discounts for early fabric purchases attract consumers who would otherwise not buy fabric at the regular price.

Chapter 14

1. The following table shows price and average cost for different numbers of arcades. Price exceeds average cost for the first four arcades, so the equilibrium number of arcades is 4.

Number of arcades	1	2	3	4	5
Price	$0.50	$0.48	$0.46	$0.44	$0.42
Average cost	$0.34	$0.37	$0.40	$0.43	$0.46

3. There are two logical errors in the expert's statement. First, the entry of firms will decrease the market price, and the market will move downward along the market demand curve. Therefore, the total quantity of pizzas demanded will exceed 3,000 (the quantity associated with the monopoly price). Second, as shown in all the examples in this chapter, we expect the typical firm to operate along the negatively sloped portion of its average-cost curve, not the horizontal portion. In other words, we expect each firm to produce fewer than 1,000 pizzas per day. These two observations suggest that there will be more than three pizzerias. For example, if the decrease in price increases the quantity demanded to 4,000 and each store produces only 800 pizzas per day, there will be five pizzerias (4,000 divided by 800).

5. A firm that cuts three lawns will have a total cost of $30 ($18 in fixed cost + $12 in variable cost (3 lawns times $4 per lawn), or an average cost of $10 per lawn. In equilibrium, the price will be equal to average cost, which happens with a quantity of 60 lawns. Dividing the 60 lawns cut by 3 lawns per firm, there will be 20 firms in equilibrium.

7. The city must have issued a sufficiently large number of licenses that entry continued to the point where economic profit reached zero. In graphical terms, the demand curve facing the typical firm is tangent to the negatively sloped average-cost curve: Average cost equals price, so economic profit is zero and no one is willing to pay anything for a license.

Chapter 15

1. See Figure S.3. The profit per firm under the duopoly outcome is $500 (a profit of $5 per passenger times 100 passengers). The profit per firm under the cartel is $750 (a profit of $10 per passenger times 75 passengers). Each firm will pick the low price. The path of the game is X to Z to rectangle 4.

3. One reason for low prices at these sales is that there is no punishment for underpricing the other firm. Any prior arrangement for cartel pricing would evaporate when one firm knows that it will soon go out of business.

FIGURE S.3 **Game Tree for Airporter Price-Fixing Game**

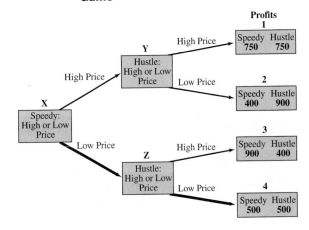

5. If both firms pick the high price, each will get a profit of $360. If both pick the low price, each will get a profit of $250. For each firm, picking the low price is the dominant strategy.

   If firms pick prices each day, Bizarre weighs the benefit of undercutting ($140 on the day of undercutting) against the cost (the difference between the high-price profit, $360, and the low-price profit, $250, times the number of days remaining after the undercutting). On the first day, the cost is $220, which exceeds the benefit of $140. Assuming that Bizarre is not savvy enough to think about the end game (the last day), she will not undercut Weird.

7. The longer the time both firms will be in the market, the greater the opportunity for punishing a firm that undercuts, so the more likely price fixing will work. Longtime is more likely to have price fixing that keeps prices high.

9.

	Neither Advertises		Both Advertise		Only A Advertises	
	A	B	A	B	A	B
Net revenue from sales ($ million)	5	5	12	12	17	1
Cost of advertising ($ million)	0	0	10	10	10	0
Profit ($ million)	5	5	2	2	7	1

The outcome is that although both would be better off if neither advertises, both will advertise—the advertisers' dilemma. From the industry perspective, the benefit of a pair of advertising campaigns is $14 million, compared to a cost of $20 million.

Chapter 16

1. An increase in demand shifts the demand curve to the right, and the new demand curve will intersect the negatively sloped long-run average-cost curve at a larger quantity and a lower average cost (price). The exploitation of scale economies will cause the regulated price to drop. In contrast, in a competitive market, an increase in demand increases the equilibrium price if the supply curve is positively sloped.

3. Consumer surplus decreases by $700. For the 150 that are units sold at the higher price, consumers lose an amount equal to the change in price ($4) times the quantity consumed (150), or $600. In addition, the price hike reduces the quantity consumed, and the loss of consumer surplus for the 151st through the 200th units is equal to the change in price ($4) times the change in quantity (50 units) times 1/2, or an additional $100. The total profit of the firms increases from $200 ($1 per unit times 200 units sold) to $750 ($5 per unit times 150 units). The increase in profit ($550) is less than

the loss of consumer surplus ($700), so the net loss for society is $150.

5. Giving the gates to Gotcha will allow the airline to maintain its monopoly power and continue to charge higher prices than would occur if there was competition.

Chapter 17

1. The payroll tax shifts the supply curve to the left: At every price, a smaller quantity is supplied. The leftward shift of the supply curve increases the equilibrium wage to a wage above $10.

3. Some people will work fewer hours, so they will pay less in taxes: They pay a lower rate on fewer hours. Other people will work the same number of hours and pay less in taxes too: They pay a lower rate on the same number of hours. Even a person who works more hours could pay less in taxes: If the increase in hours is small relative to the decrease in the hourly tax rate, the tax bill (hours times the tax rate) will actually decrease. The only people who will pay more in taxes are the workers who increase their hours by an amount that is large relative to the decrease in the hourly rate.

5. a. The supply of teachers is large relative to demand, so wages are relatively low. This could result from the psychological rewards from teaching, the work hours, or the free summer time.

   b. This is effectively a minimum wage for teachers, and it has the same effect as a minimum wage for any occupation: The increase in the wage will decrease the quantity demanded, so some teachers will lose their jobs.

7. Let's assume that the program is paid for by government, not coal companies. The program will increase the supply of coal workers, shifting the supply curve to the right. The equilibrium wage will decrease.

9. Like a minimum wage, a comparable-worth policy that increases wages in some occupations will decrease the quantity of labor demanded, so fewer workers will be hired. In addition, higher wages lead to higher production costs and output prices, so consumers will be harmed. An alternative policy is to break down the barriers that have discouraged women from choosing certain occupations.

Chapter 18

1. The demand is elastic, so a decrease in price will generate a large change in quantity demanded, and total income (wage times number of workers) will increase. To maximize total income, the union should cut wages.

3. a. For the first 4 workers, the marginal revenue product (MRP) exceeds the marginal labor cost (MLC), so the firm should hire 4 workers.

   b. The competitive outcome is the quantity at which the wage equals the MRP. This happens with wage = $10 and a quantity of 6 workers. A minimum wage of $10 would generate this outcome.

Chapter 19

1. If we are interested in the increase in the production of goods and services, we should be interested in the growth of real GDP. If we also care about the increase in prices, we should be interested in the growth of nominal GDP.
3. We calculate the value of the goods produced in 2007 using the prices in 2006 and 2007. For 2006, the value of production is $24,000. For 2007, the value of production is $26,200. The value of production (attributable all to price changes) rose by 9.2%. If the price index for 2006 was 100, the price index for 2007 would be 1.092.
5. No, because you need to compare the price index in one year to a value in another year.
7. Refrigerators are an example of a good that depreciates. If a refrigerator costs $2,000, lasts for 10 years, and depreciates evenly over 10 years, the yearly depreciation would be $200.
9. Deterioration in air quality should be subtracted from NNP to arrive at national income. Improvements to air quality should be added.
11. If the Department of Commerce used a base year in which computer prices were high, it would overstate the growth of real GDP and understate the growth of overall prices.

Chapter 20

1. The labor force is 6 million (employed plus unemployed); the labor force participation rate is 60% (labor force divided by population 16 years and older); the unemployment rate is 8.3% (unemployed divided by labor force).
3. This belief is based on the idea that with high unemployment rates, there are likely to be discouraged workers.
5. There will always be frictional and structural unemployment.
7. The inflation rate is 9.1% [(60 − 55)/55].
9. The conventional unemployment rate is 7.4% (8 million/108 million). An alternative measure would add the discouraged workers to total unemployment. This would also increase the labor force by the same amount. The alternative unemployment measure would be 10.7% (12 million/112 million).
11. It would reduce the costs of changing prices and thereby reduce menu costs.

Chapter 21

1. The economists believe that high payroll taxes are the cause of high unemployment and slow employment growth.
3. With a reduction of the supply in young workers, overall wages would rise for union members.
5. Towns near the border with Mexico have more migration and hence a larger supply of labor. The result is lower wages.
7. The graph would show the demand curve for labor shifting to the right as technology improves in the economy. According to this theory, real wages therefore rise during booms and fall during recessions.
9. Today, many more women work full-time and provide support for their families. The labor supply for these women is not likely to be very sensitive to changes in wages and thus is more likely to look like that of men.

11. With limited opportunities for domestic investment, savings will flow abroad. This is accomplished through a trade surplus.

Chapter 22

1. It will double in 23.3 years (70/3) and increase by a factor of 4 in 46.6 years.
3. No, growth does not necessarily lead to inequality.
5. We measure it through growth accounting. We ask how much growth can be explained by increases in labor and capital. The remainder is attributed to technological progress.
7. Public investment increases by 5% (one-half of 10%). Private savings and investment fall by 2% (20% of 10%). Thus, total investment (public and private) increases.
9. Although income may have been increasing during this period, the fall in height suggests that basic nutrition and overall welfare may have been decreasing. This perhaps could be accounted for by rapid increases in the population of cities and the stresses of urban life in this period.

Chapter 23

1. A lower price level will increase spending through the wealth effect, the interest rate effect, and the effects of foreign trade.
3. An increase in the marginal propensity to consume means that a higher fraction of income will be re-spent in each of the spending rounds.
5. Rents on apartments are sticky with month-long or year-long leases. They are sticky because it is costly to move and change apartments.
7. As the classical aggregate supply curve moved to the right, prices would fall.
9. When aggregate demand fails, the aggregate demand curve shifts to the left, and prices and output fall. In the long run, the Keynesian aggregate supply curve falls to restore the economy to full employment.

Chapter 24

1. Policymakers need to know the value of the multiplier to gauge the size of the proper dose of fiscal stimulus or contraction.
3. States with more generous unemployment insurance will pay out more funds to unemployed workers during downturns. This will enable those workers to avoid cutting their spending as much as they would have to in the absence of the unemployment insurance.
5. The inside lags of fiscal policy arise because there are typically sharp differences of opinion within Congress and between the Congress and the president on the proper levels and structures of spending and taxation.
7. Deficits are primarily a problem when they persist when the economy is at full employment.
9. College students typically would spend their rebate, since they perceive their incomes will be higher in the future but they cannot borrow against this future income. A middle-aged man might be more likely to save some of the rebate for retirement.

Chapter 25

1. a. 800
   b. 2
   c. $S = 0.5y - 200$
   d. 200
3. The multiplier is 2.04. Therefore, investment spending needs to rise by 73.5.
5. No. Raising tax rates will also lower GDP.
7. a. GDP will rise.
   b. No. Inventories could rise because demand falls short of the expectations of producers.
9. GDP will fall because of the balanced-budget multiplier.
11. A number of factors contribute to a more stable economy today. Automatic stabilizers are more important today than in the past. The private sector now knows that the government will play an active role in stabilizing the economy, which makes private-sector behavior more stable. Finally, new inventory management practices may have played a role in stabilizing the economy.

Chapter 26

1. Plant and equipment spending are governed in part by expectations of changes in GDP, which can be volatile. Housing will depend on interest rates. Inventories will be volatile because they depend on changes in demand over very short periods of time.
3. The statement is true because, with a zero rate of interest and thus no opportunity cost for invested funds, the savings in gas would ultimately pay for the costs of leveling the mountain.
5. At an 8% interest rate, the present value of the payout is worth about $9.82 million. At a 5% interest rate, the present value of the payout increases to $12.46 million.
7. Yes, because the real rate of interest in this case is −1%.
9. The individual reduces risk through diversification.
11. The depositors will no longer have an incentive to monitor the investment practices of banks and the banks can take more risks.

Chapter 27

1. They are accepted in exchange.
3. M2 stays the same but M1 falls.
5. They were not fully equivalent to money because they were accepted in exchange only by large banks and credit unions and not, for example, by stores or by individuals.
7. Credit cards are not part of the money supply because they simply represent loan transactions. Debit cards are used to transfer funds from existing deposit accounts to a purchaser.
9. Multiple expansion of deposits occurs because recipients of loans deposit funds into another bank and that bank is only required to keep a fraction of the new deposits as required reserves.

Chapter 28

1. You may have an opportunity to buy a rare CD at a music store and need cash on hand. You could not buy the CD with a bond.
3. You would want to sell bonds because bond prices would fall as interest rates rose.
5. The money supply increases any time the Fed makes a purchase.
7. Trade is more important for the economy of the Netherlands than for that of the United States. Therefore, monetary policy would have more of an effect through exchange rates in the Netherlands.
9. The outside lags in monetary policy tend to be long because monetary policy must work through changing investment spending. Firms may be reluctant to make major changes in their investment plans in the face of relatively small changes in interest rates.

Chapter 29

1. They worried that unemployment had fallen below the natural rate.
3. Interest rates rise because of an increase in money demand during an economic expansion. Investment first rises because of the accelerator effect at the beginning of an expansion and falls, for the same reason, as the GDP slows down at the end of the expansion.
5. Money is neutral in the long run.
7. Tax cuts will lead to higher consumer spending. This crowds out investment in the long run through higher interest rates.
9. It is costly to guard and store large sums of money. However, interest rates are unlikely to fall too far below 0%—perhaps only a few tenths of 1%.

Chapter 30

1. High interest rates in the long run result from high inflation rates. High inflation rates occur only when there is rapid growth in the money supply.
3. Typically, firms have better access to information than workers.
5. If the government increases the money supply at a faster rate, inflation will rise. The rise in inflation will raise interest rates and the cost of holding money. Therefore, people will hold money for shorter periods of time.
7. With increased foreign aid, the government has less need to print money to finance a deficit.
9. Key factors that economists believe have affected the natural rate include: changes in the demographic composition of the labor force, institutional changes, changes in the state of the economy (whether it is hot or cold), and changes in the growth rate of productivity.

Chapter 31

1. The interest on the debt is $1 billion. The budget deficit (spending + interest − taxes) is $1 billion. Therefore, the debt at the end of the year is $11 billion.

3. They are more likely to need to print money, which causes rapid inflation.
5. It could induce a government to take contractionary actions during economic downturns. This could be serious if there are not sufficient escape mechanisms.
7. With a stable 2% inflation rate and full institutional adjustment, there are both menu costs and shoe-leather costs. It may be more difficult to maintain a commitment to a 2% inflation rate than to zero inflation or price stability.
9. It depends on whether individuals really increase their savings (by cutting consumption) or just shift existing funds into the tax-free accounts.

Chapter 32

1. a. In Country B, the opportunity cost of 1 computer is 2 TVs, and the opportunity cost of 1 TV is 1/2 of a computer. In Country C, the opportunity cost of 1 computer is 4 TVs, and the opportunity cost of 1 TV is 1/4 of a computer. Country B has the comparative advantage of producing computers, and Country C the comparative advantage of producing TVs.
   b. The production possibility curves are straight lines for both countries, the slope being the opportunity costs and the intercepts being the maximum level of production of each good.
3. Chipland produces 120 chips and exchanges them for 70 shirts, ending up with 85 chips and 70 shirts. Shirtland produces 108 shirts and exchanges 70 of them for 35 chips, ending up with 35 chips and 35 shirts.
5. If the VERs were replaced with a tariff, the government would collect revenue. Under VERs, the importers earn large profits.

7. Consumers will benefit because prices will decrease. As each nation shifts its production to the goods for which it has a comparative advantage, workers in expanding industries will benefit, while workers in other industries will lose. The challenge for policymakers is to facilitate this transition.
9. Taxpayers will favor the shift because they will earn revenue. The firms importing goods will lobby against this because they will lose the profits they earn from the quotas. Firms may be more effective in lobbying than taxpayers because the losses are concentrated among a few firms, but the benefits are spread widely across taxpayers.

Chapter 33

1. a. The yen will appreciate.
   b. The pound will depreciate.
   c. The pound will appreciate.
3. The real exchange rate for the South American country would rise against the dollar because the percentage increase in the prices of its goods was less than the percentage depreciation of its exchange rate.
5. −$25 billion.
7. This will lead to investors wishing to sell the currency and a depreciation of the exchange rate.
9. With a fixed exchange rate, the increase in Mexican prices (at a faster rate than U.S. prices increased) led to a rise in the cost of Mexican goods relative to U.S. goods, or an appreciation in Mexico's real exchange rate.
11. Countries are often reluctant to depreciate their currencies because it will lead to a rise in the price of imported goods and also hurt their ability to borrow money over the long run.

Index